Translating *Nephesh* in the Psalms into Chinese

An Exercise in Intergenerational, Literary Bible Translation

Hui Er Yu

MONOGRAPHS

© 2018 Hui Er Yu

Published 2018 by Langham Monographs
An imprint of Langham Publishing

Langham Partnership
PO Box 296, Carlisle, Cumbria CA3 9WZ, UK
www.langham.org

ISBNs:
978-1-78368-469-4 Print
978-1-78368-470-0 ePub
978-1-78368-471-7 Mobi
978-1-78368-472-4 PDF

Hui Er Yu has asserted her right under the Copyright, Designs and Patents Act, 1988 to be identified as the Author of this work.

All rights reserved. No part of this publication may be reproduced, stored in a retrieval system or transmitted, in any form or by any means, electronic, mechanical, photocopying, recording or otherwise, without the prior written permission of the publisher or the Copyright Licensing Agency.

All Scripture quotations, unless otherwise indicated, are taken from the Holy Bible, New International Version®, NIV®. Copyright ©1973, 1978, 1984, 2011 by Biblica, Inc.™ Used by permission of Zondervan.

British Library Cataloguing-in-Publication Data
A catalogue record for this book is available from the British Library

ISBN: 978-1-78368-469-4

Cover & Book Design: projectluz.com

Langham Partnership actively supports theological dialogue and an author's right to publish but does not necessarily endorse the views and opinions set forth here or in works referenced within this publication, nor can we guarantee technical and grammatical correctness. Langham Partnership does not accept any responsibility or liability to persons or property as a consequence of the reading, use or interpretation of its published content.

Hui Er Yu's research provides a contextualized theory of Bible translation for the Chinese-speaking world and demonstrates how to apply this theory, which is based on Ernst Wendland's Literary Functional Equivalence (LiFE) model, in translating biblical poetry. The research provides an updated mapping of the possible meanings of the Hebrew word נֶפֶשׁ, a key anthropological term in the ancient Semitic world and in the Old Testament. This exploration is valuable for linguistics, for Bible translation and for contemporary theological anthropology, especially in Chinese Christianity where the misunderstanding of this term is deeply entrenched. The most remarkable aspect of Dr Yu's research is that she pioneered the inclusion of children and youth in an intergenerational Bible translation team. This not only challenges the traditional understanding of the role of children in Christian ministry but practically shows how to optimize and integrate their contribution in the very sophisticated enterprise of Bible translation.

Johannes Malherbe, PhD
Head of Academics, Postgraduate School,
South African Theological Seminary, Sandton, South Africa

The principles and procedures that undergird the new field of intergenerational ministry are fresh and appealing. This work will be of benefit, especially to those who are interested in interdisciplinary study, as it yields proper biblical insights into anthropology and places considerable worth on the task of accurate Bible translation and rigorous textual analysis. For that we can be grateful to its author.

Dennis Ngien, PhD
Professor of Systematic Theology,
Tyndale University College and Seminary, Toronto
Research Professor, Wycliffe College, University of Toronto, Canada

It is a great pleasure to endorse the work of a person who is very gifted with biblical languages and research. The interpretation and translation of the Hebrew noun "nephesh" has been an issue among various Chinese versions. Thus, the Chinese church has been deeply influenced by the popular "trichotomy" of Watchman Nee. Dr Yu's work opens a new door for Chinese Bible translation by clarifying the various concepts of the word "nephesh." She also provides concrete suggestions for some biblical passages and with the help of her work, we may expect progress for the Chinese translations of the Bible.

Kyungrae Kim, PhD
Vice President and Academic Dean,
Faith Bible Seminary, Flushing, New York, USA

Describing the history of the approach to Bible translation in general and specifically the history of Chinese Bible translation, Hui Er Yu applies insights from the various disciplines to reach conclusions that highlight important ways in which the insights can be applied to provide accurate and effective translations of the Bible. She is to be particularly commended for bringing children into the conversation about Bible translation.

Véroni Krüger, PhD
Founder-President, The Word for the World Bible Translators

Contents

Foreword ix

Preface xiii

Acknowledgements xv

Abstract xvii

List of Abbreviations xix

Chapter 1 1
   Introduction
     1.1 The Gap 1
     1.2 Bridging the Gap 9
     1.3 Objectives of the Study 9
     1.4 Outline 10
     1.5 Hypothesis 11
     1.6 Key Terms 12
         1.6.1 First Language and Mother Tongue 12
         1.6.2 Common Language 12
     1.7 Delimitations 13
         1.7.1 The Selected Passages for Translating 13
         1.7.2 The History of Bible Translation 14
         1.7.3 The Theory of Translation 14
         1.7.4 The Enterprise of Bible Translation 15
         1.7.5 Bible Versions 15
     1.8 Presuppositions 15
         1.8.1 The Nature of the Scriptures 15
         1.8.2 The Issue of Formal and Dynamic/Functional
             Translation 16
         1.8.3 Gospel, Language and Culture 16
     1.9 Potential Value 17

Chapter 2 19
   A Literary Approach to Bible Translation
     2.1. Introduction 19
     2.2. The History and Major Issues of Bible Translation 20
         2.2.1. Introduction 20
         2.2.2. Early Bible Translation and Related Issues 20

    2.2.3 A Brief History and Major Issues of Chinese Bible
          Translation 39
    2.2.4 Conclusion 59
  2.3 The Development of Translation Studies..60
    2.3.1. Introduction 60
    2.3.2 The Development of the Field of Translation 62
    2.3.3 LiFE: A Literary Functional-Equivalence Model...............77
  2.4 Conclusion 97

Chapter 3 99
Children as Crucial Members of an Intergenerational
Bible Translation Team

  3.1 Introduction 99
  3.2 An Overview of Childhood Studies..100
    3.2.1 Introduction 100
    3.2.2 Key Concepts in Childhood Studies 101
    3.2.3 The Birth of Childhood Studies 106
    3.2.4 The Development of Childhood Studies
          in Christianity...108
  3.3 Insights from Childhood Studies for the Present Research..........112
    3.3.1 Introduction 112
    3.3.2 Children Are Integral to the Church..................................113
    3.3.3 Children Need the Whole Bible..133
    3.3.4 Children Can Contribute to the Enterprise of Bible
          Translation..140
    3.3.5 Conclusion 143
  3.4 Intentional Intergenerational Ministry 143
    3.4.1 Introduction 143
    3.4.2 The Term IIM..144
    3.4.3 The Foundations of IIM 145
    3.4.4 The Practices of IIM 166
    3.4.5 The Outcomes of IIM..171
  3.5 Conclusion 172

Chapter 4 175
The Possible Meanings of the Hebrew Word נֶפֶשׁ *in the OT and Its*
Translation in Chinese

  4.1 Introduction 175
  4.2 A Brief Literature Review of the Hebrew Word נֶפֶשׁ..................178
    4.2.1 Introduction 178
    4.2.2 Etymological Issues...179

4.2.3 A Brief Survey of the Etymological Study on נֶפֶשׁ 181
4.2.4 נֶפֶשׁ in the Hebrew OT...182
4.2.5 נֶפֶשׁ and Its Greek Equivalent ψυχή in the LXX
and the NT..195
4.2.6 Conclusion 205
4.3 The Interpretations of נֶפֶשׁ in Chinese Bible Versions 206
4.3.1 Introduction 206
4.3.2 The Interpretations of נֶפֶשׁ in RCUV 206
4.3.3 Conclusion 212
4.4 The Divergence in the Interpretations of נֶפֶשׁ 213
4.4.1 Introduction 213
4.4.2 The Divergence in the Interpretations of נֶפֶשׁ among
Prominent Chinese and English Bible Versions 213
4.4.3 Conclusion 217
4.5 The Controversy over Watchman Nee's Trichotomy 218
4.5.1 Introduction 218
4.5.2 Nee's Argument on the Translations of נֶפֶשׁ/ψυχή
and רוּחַ/πνεῦμα 219
4.5.3 An Overview of Nee's Teaching on Man as
Tripartite Being..221
4.5.4 The Controversy Caused by Nee's Tripartite
Theological Anthropology 224
4.5.5 A Way to Reduce the Controversy 226
4.5.6 Conclusion 227
4.6 A Call for Reconsidering
the Translation of נֶפֶשׁ..227

Chapter 5.. 231
*Translating נֶפֶשׁ in the Psalms into Chinese: An Exercise in
Intergenerational, Literary Bible Translation*
5.1 Introduction 231
5.2 The Training Course for the Intergenerational Bible
Translation Team..234
5.3 The Exercise in Intergenerational, Literary Bible Translation 236
5.3.1 Psalm 35 236
5.3.2 Psalm 63...269
5.3.3 Psalm 107...286
5.4 Further Discussions/Observations...303
5.4.1 The Appropriate Translation of נֶפֶשׁ in the
Three Selected Psalms..303

  5.4.2 The Critical Issue Regarding the Chinese
    Translations of נֶפֶשׁ 308
  5.4.3 The Version Readable for All Generations by the IBTT
    through LiFE 309
 5.5 Conclusion 311

Chapter 6 313
Conclusion – Findings and Implications
 6.1 Introduction 313
 6.2 Summary of Research Findings Regarding נֶפֶשׁ 314
 6.3 Summary of the Foundations for Intergenerational
   Participation in Bible Translation 319
 6.4 Feedback, Comments, and Reflections Regarding
   Intergenerational, Literary Bible Translation 321
  6.4.1 The Feedback from the Participants 321
  6.4.2 The Comments of OT Scholars 328
  6.4.3 The Reflection on Wendland's LiFE................................332
  6.4.4 Some General Observations Regarding
    Bible Translation 337
 6.5 Future Perspectives..338
  6.5.1 Expanding the Horizon 338
  6.5.2 Training Church Leaders...339
  6.5.3 Training Congregations...339
  6.5.4 Launching the Intergenerational Bible Translation 339
 6.6 Final Comments 340

Appendix A 343
The IBTT's Suggestions on the Translation of נֶפֶשׁ

Appendix B 351
The Feedback from the Participants of the IBTT

Bibliography... 371

List of Chinese Dictionaries Used 405

Subject Index 407

Author Index.. 411

Scripture Index... 415

Foreword

It gives me great pleasure to write a few words in commendation of a book that arises from an exceptional dissertation that I recently examined. This multifaceted study by Dr Yu is an excellent, indeed ground-breaking, example of evangelical scholarship being rigorously applied to the original text of Scripture, with significant potential also for widespread contemporary application within the global Chinese Christian church.

I might briefly summarize the scholarly contribution of this outstanding monograph regarding the following aspects of current biblical studies and intercultural communication, with special reference to Scripture translation:

a) It features the application of a distinctive "literary-structural" methodology to the analysis and translation of three complete Psalms (35, 63, 107), including two rather lengthy ones, from biblical Hebrew into Chinese. This discourse-oriented approach offers many fresh insights regarding the sense and significance of these original prayer-praise texts. Furthermore, the author's expertly employed ten-step methodology becomes a valuable model for others who may wish to analyse other instances of biblical poetry in a similarly meticulous, procedure-based, and goal-oriented manner.

b) More specifically, this richly documented book successfully undertakes a comprehensive, lexicographical analysis of the semantically complex term נֶפֶשׁ "breath, life, living thing, person, self" in the Old Testament and the partially corresponding term ψυχή in the Septuagint and New Testament. In the process, four languages are involved – those of the original Hebrew and Greek texts, the bridge-language of English, as well as twentieth-century and current Chinese. This is a most detailed, contextually based comparative examination that other biblical scholars will do well to evaluate and reflect upon in future studies of this important, though frequently misunderstood scriptural concept – also on the local Chinese theological scene with particular reference to the "Watchman Nee controversy" regarding the interpretation of נֶפֶשׁ.

c) Along the way, Dr Yu presents a helpful overview of the important history of Bible translation and its specific historical application within the Chinese Christian setting (in itself of vital contemporary relevance) – again with special reference to the negative influence of Watchman Nee's misleading trichotomous interpretation upon the translation of Chinese Bibles over the years and right up to the present day.

d) In terms of practical theology, this book offers a lucid exposition of the relatively new concept "intergenerational" ministry in Christian congregational life, with an innovative, potentially influential application to modern Bible translation practice. Although I have been personally involved in this field as a consultant for many years, I must admit that I had not thought of – let alone tried – this significant extension in practice to the engagement of smaller children in our worldwide educational and communicative enterprise.

e) This is not simply an idealized vision or ivory-tower proposal either. Dr Yu also complements her precise description of a most helpful methodology with concrete instructions regarding actually "how to do it" – that is, how to effectively organize and manage an intergenerational Bible translation project within the local Christian congregation. Though necessarily limited in scope, her experiment will undoubtedly serve also in this respect as a helpful model, including her suggestions for reviewing/testing the product through documented personal interviews and revising initial translation draft versions in keeping with the project's designated communicative purpose.

This clearly written and systematically argued example of scholarly research and writing has great interdisciplinary relevance for all those working in a

Chinese-speaking context as well as in many other areas of Christian cross-cultural communication and ministry. *Translating Nephesh in the Psalms into Chinese* therefore stands out as yet another most interesting and informative addition to the growing number of the scholarly studies in the prestigious Langham Monographs series.

Prof Ernst R. Wendland
Centre for Bible Interpretation and Translation
Department of Ancient Studies, Stellenbosch University, South Africa

Preface

This work is a revised version of the author's dissertation where several disciplines are integrated, including Old Testament studies, translation studies, childhood studies, and intergenerational ministry. Due to the limitation of space, the majority of addenda are not included, such as the ten-step exegetical analyses to achieve a literary translation. The full, original dissertation is available at South African Theological Seminary.

Acknowledgements

I would first like to express my most profound gratitude to my thesis adviser Dr Johannes Malherbe, the Head of Postgraduate School at South Africa Theological Seminary. He guided me on this very interesting and exciting journey of thesis writing, which integrated several disciplines I am very interested in. He also allowed the thesis to be my work, but steered me in the right direction and offered constructive criticism when needed. What is noteworthy is that this research made my dream come true earlier (i.e. teaching children and teenagers biblical Hebrew).

A very special note of appreciation goes to the faithful readers of the manuscript. They are Dr Kyungrae Kim of Faith Bible Seminary in NY, who ignited my fire for studying biblical languages and acted as a translation consultant of this research, and Dr Dennis Ngien of Tyndale University College & Seminary in Toronto, who mentored me and provided profound theological reflections. Their unfailing encouragement and company helped me complete the research smoothly.

I am greatly indebted to Mujen Home Educators Association in Taiwan for supporting the exercise in the intergenerational Bible translation. My sincere thanks are extended to Huì Yuán Xióng, a coworker of Mujen who recruited the translation team, and to all the participants: Nǎi Wǎi Lǚ, Jùn Qíng Yáng, Wén Qí Chén, Bǐng Jūn Huáng, Yì Chén, Zǐ Xīn Gāo, Yìng Xuān Lǚ, Nǎi Yuán Lǚ, Mǎn Zhēn Huáng, Shū Rén Lóng, Xiàn Píng Gān, and Huì Rú Huáng. Their active participation encouraged me to bring this study to completion.

Special thanks are extended to Chinese OT scholars who made critical comments on the translations produced by the intergenerational Bible translation team. They are Dr Paul Theophilus of Alliance Bible School of Central and South America in Panama, Dr Grace Ko of Canadian Chinese School of Theology in Toronto, and Dr Daisy Tsai of Logos Evangelical Seminary.

I am particularly grateful to the support from my home church, North York Christian Community Church in Toronto, especially from Senior Pastor Dominic Tse who agreed to the adjustment of my role in children's ministry so that I could pursue my studies; from Rev Sunny Wong who shared the responsibility of leadership with me; and from Pastor So Ying Chu who is my faithful prayer partner. I am also grateful to Jolin Kan and Emma Liang who proofread the manuscript, and to Jiā Yíng Zhāng who helped me perceive more about what is understandable for grade 1 students before the formal translation exercise.

Last but not least, my deepest gratitude and debt go to my husband Chih Cheng Chen and my two sweet sons, Joshua and Shawn. The former allowed me to focus on the PhD study; the latter not only shared the chores, but also translated the Chinese feedback of the participants into English. They especially, have brought me many smiles over the course of my study. They are truly God's gifts and blessings to me.

Abstract

The Hebrew anthropological term נֶפֶשׁ occurs 754 times in the Old Testament and has traditionally been rendered as "soul." Parkhurst already challenged this understanding in 1778, Briggs in 1897 and many others since then. Yet, despite being a poor translation, it remained popular and provided a basis for Christian views regarding the constituent parts of human beings, e.g. dichotomy in the West and trichotomy in the Chinese faith community. The latter mainly resulted from Watchman Nee's literal translation approach and his insistence that the only appropriate translation of נֶפֶשׁ is "魂 hún (soul)." As the most influential theologian in the Chinese Christian evangelical world of the twentieth century, Nee's tripartite anthropology strengthened Chinese Christians' negative attitude towards physical aspects of life in this world and caused controversy among contemporary Chinese theologians.

Another critical issue with contemporary Chinese Bible translation is the absence of using a rigorous, systematic translation theory based upon translation studies in Chinese Bible translation projects. This is surprising in view of the renaissance of translation studies in China since the late 1970s. A final critical issue is that there is no Chinese Bible that is accessible for children and rendered directly from the original languages.

After exploring theories from various fields such as translation studies, childhood studies, and intergenerational ministry, the researcher decided to adapt and apply Wendland's LiFE approach to Bible translation. She also opted to pioneer the use of an intergenerational Bible translation team (IBTT) to produce a comprehensible Chinese Bible version for readers of all ages, including children. The IBTT comprised twelve members – four children, four teenagers, and four adults, with ages ranging from seven to fifty-one years. After receiving a basic training, the IBTT's main tasks were to assess the accuracy of the translations of נֶפֶשׁ and to produce a more artistic and readable Bible version for all generations through the application of the LiFE approach.

The project not only reached the preceding two goals effectively, but had many additional benefits to the participants, such as gaining a deeper understanding of the Bible, increasing their knowledge of biblical Hebrew, recognizing and supporting the important task of Bible translation, and building closer relationships with each other. It is hoped that this project will inspire Bible societies to produce Bibles *for* and *by* people of different ages, including children and teenagers, building greater unity within the church and fostering a deeper understanding of God's Word.

List of Abbreviations[1]

1. Bible Translations

Chinese Bible Versions

CUV	和合本 [Chinese Union Version]
RCUV	和合本修訂版 [Revised Chinese Union Version]
CNV	聖經新譯本 [Chinese New Version]
LZZ	呂振中譯本 [Lu Zhen Zhong Bible Translation]
TCVRE	現代中文譯本修訂版 [Today's Chinese Version: Revised Edition]
CCB	當代譯本修訂版 [Chinese Contemporary Bible]
CNET	新英語譯本聖經中譯本 [Chinese New English Translation]
DCT	新譯簡明聖經 [The Holy Bible: A Dynamic Chinese Translation]
CNLT	新普及譯本 [Chinese New Living Translation]
CCV	新漢語譯本 [Contemporary Chinese Version]
CSB	中文標準譯本 [Chinese Standard Bible]
WCB	環球聖經譯本 [Worldwide Chinese Bible]

English Bible Versions

NIrV   New International Reader's Version

---

1 Except for the abbreviations listed here, the rest of the abbreviations in this study follow those in *The SBL Handbook of Style*. See Billie Jean Collins et al., eds., *The SBL Handbook of Style: For Biblical Studies and Related Disciplines*, 2nd ed. (Atlanta, GA: SBL, 2014).

LEB	Lexham English Bible

2. General Abbreviations

1cs/p	first person, common, singular/plural
2ms/p	second person, masculine, singular/plural
2fs/p	second person, feminine, singular/plural
3ms/p	third person, masculine, singular/plural
3fs/p	third person, feminine, singular/plural
BFBS	British and Foreign Bible Society
cent.	century
HDC	漢語大詞典 [Hanyu Da Cidian (Chinese Dictionary)]
IBTT	Intergenerational Bible Translation Team
IBTTV	Intergenerational Bible Translation Team Version
IIM	Intentional Intergenerational Ministry
LiFE	Literary Functional Equivalence
MCD	現代漢語詞典 [Modern Chinese Dictionary]
SL	source language
TL	target language

CHAPTER 1

Introduction

1.1 The Gap

The Hebrew anthropological term נֶפֶשׁ occurs 754 times in the Old Testament (OT) and has traditionally been rendered as "soul."[1] Very early on, this is questioned by Parkhurst and Briggs. The former asserts that no passage in the OT indicates that נֶפֶשׁ has the meaning "soul."[2] The latter contends that "soul in English usage at the present time conveys usually a very different meaning from נֶפֶשׁ in Hebrew."[3] The same position is held today by many biblists. For example, Brueggemann also argues that it is "unfortunate that . . . נֶפֶשׁ is commonly rendered 'soul.'"[4]

Such stereotypical rendering as soul has led to stimulating Christians, influenced by Greek philosophy, to advocate the formulation of the constituent parts of human beings, e.g. dichotomy. This results in controversy on the issue of Hebraic conception of human beings for centuries.[5] Murphy laments, "most of the dualism that has appeared to be biblical teaching has

---

1. For example, in KJV, the majority of נֶפֶשׁ is rendered as "soul" (475 out of 754 occurrences).

2. John Parkhurst, "נפש," *An Hebrew and English Lexicon, without Points* (London: printed for B. Law, no. 13, Ave-Maria-Lane, in Ludgate-Street; and W. Faden, the Corner of St Martin's Lane, Charing-Cross, MDCCLXXVIII, 1778), 408.

3. Charles A. Briggs, "The Use of נפש in the Old Testament," *Journal of Biblical Literature* 16, no. 1/2 (1897): 30.

4. Walter Brueggemann, *Theology of the Old Testament: Testimony, Dispute, Advocacy* (Minneapolis, MN: Fortress Press, 1997), 453.

5. Nancey Murphy, *Bodies and Souls, or Spirited Bodies?* (Cambridge, UK; New York: Cambridge University Press, 2006), 17.

been a result of *poor* translation" (italics added).⁶ Nida (see §2.3.2.2.2.3) further points out that viewing נֶפֶשׁ as soul is to neglect the literary or situational context. This not only causes incorrect interpretation and misunderstanding, but also diminishes the word's wealth of referents (e.g. breath, life, living thing, person, self).⁷

This issue has impacted the Chinese Christian community in many ways. Watchman Nee (1903–1972), arguably the most influential theologian in the Chinese Christian evangelical world of the twentieth century,⁸ misunderstood the principle of literal translation and thus insisted that the only appropriate translation of נֶפֶשׁ is "魂 *hún* (soul)."⁹ This interpretation was incorporated in his views of trichotomy which directly or indirectly influenced 70 percent of Chinese Christians.¹⁰ As a result, Nee's tripartite anthropology not only stimulates Chinese Christians' negative attitude towards the physical part of life in this world, but also causes high controversy among contemporary Chinese theologians.¹¹

Although criticized by Nee,¹² the Chinese Union Version's translations of נֶפֶשׁ as "靈魂 *líng hún* (spirit-soul)" or "靈 *líng* (spirit)" play a crucial role in reinforcing Chinese believers' acceptance of Nee's tripartite anthropology since it is the most popular, authoritative and influential Bible version in contemporary Chinese Christian communities.¹³ If נֶפֶשׁ as "靈魂 *líng hún*

---

6. Murphy, *Bodies and Souls*, 36.

7. Eugene A. Nida, *God's Word in Man's Language* (New York: Harper & Brothers, 1952), 65–66.

8. Qìng Bào Zēng 曾慶豹, "無所憑依、無因而起: 倪柝聲的神學人類學及其文化底蘊" [The theological anthropology of Watchman Nee: In the context of Taoist tradition], 漢語基督教學術論評 [Sino-Christian studies] 12 (2011): 161.

9. Watchman Nee, 屬靈人 [The spiritual man] (Hong Kong: Christian Press, 2006 [1928]), 47–48.

10. Jǐn Lún Lǐ 李錦綸, "對中國教會人觀的系統性反省" [Reflection on the anthropology of the China church], 中國與福音學刊 [China and the Gospel journal] 3, no. 1 (2003): 143.

11. Zēng 曾, "倪柝聲的神學人類學" [The theological anthropology of Watchman Nee]," 160, 162.

12. Nee, 屬靈人 [The spiritual man], 28–29.

13. Róu Yù Zhuāng 莊柔玉, "《和合本》在中文聖經多元系統中的位置—前景與挑戰" [The position of the Chinese Union version in the Chinese Bible polysystem: Prospective and challenge], 中國神學研究院期刊 [China Graduate School of Theology Journal] 49 (2010): 41.

(spirit-soul)" or "靈 *líng* (spirit)"[14] is problematic, its translation as "心 *xīn* (heart)"[15] calls for reconsideration as well. This is because in Chinese understanding, the implication of the trichotomy of "靈, 魂, 體 *líng, hún, tǐ* (spirit, soul, body)" is almost synonymous to that of the trichotomy of "靈, 心, 身 *líng, xīn, shēn* (spirit, heart, body)."[16] The latter is even more prevailing and common in Chinese thinking.[17]

The aforementioned issues in both Chinese and Western Christian communities result from the misinterpretation and mistranslation of נֶפֶשׁ. Therefore, it is necessary to determine its correct meanings. However, the word נֶפֶשׁ is not easy to define, as Jacob notes.[18] Making the task of determining its meaning even harder is the influence from etymological considerations, which put some senses to the polysemous word נֶפֶשׁ, such as neck/throat, and sustenance, etc.[19] In the past decades, Christian scholars have identified this as the fallacy of etymology for a word with high occurrences.[20]

Unfortunately, prominent Chinese and English Bible versions and dictionaries seem to have been influenced by etymological studies. For example, נֶפֶשׁ as neck/throat is found in Psalm 69:1 (e.g. LZZ, TCVRE, CNET, NIV 2011, ESV, NRSV). Another example of the influence is probably demonstrated by the divergence in the meaning of נֶפֶשׁ between TDOT

---

14. In the *Chinese Union Version* (CUV), נֶפֶשׁ as "靈魂 *líng hún* (spirit-soul)" occurs twenty-three times; as "靈 *líng* (spirit)" four times. See Xiào Bǎi Ráo 饒孝柏, 屬靈人的再思 [Rethinking on "the spiritual person"] (Taipei: Campus Evangelical Fellowship Press, 2010), 240.

15. In CUV, נֶפֶשׁ as "心 *xīn* (heart)" occurs about 180 times. See Ráo 饒, 屬靈人的再思 [Rethinking on "the spiritual person"], 240.

16. The common word order of "靈, 心, 身 *líng, xīn, shēn* (spirit, heart, body)" is "身, 心, 靈 *shēn, xīn, líng* (body, heart, spirit)." Such change is to make the comparison between this trichotomy and that of "靈, 魂, 體 *líng, hún, tǐ* (spirit, soul, body)" more easily.

17. Zēng 曾, "倪柝聲的神學人類學" [The theological anthropology of Watchman Nee], 164.

18. Edmund Jacob, "The Anthropology of the Old Testament," in *Theological Dictionary of the New Testament*, vol. 9, eds. Gerhard Kittel and Gerhard Friedrich, trans. Geoffrey W. Bromiley (Grand Rapids, MI: Eerdmans, 1974), 617.

19. Hayim Tawil, "נפש," in *An Akkadian Lexical Companion for Biblical Hebrew: Etymological-Semantic and Idiomatic Equivalents with Supplement on Biblical Aramaic* (Jersey City, NJ: KTAV, 2009), 244–246.

20. James Barr, *The Semantics of Biblical Language* (Eugene, OR: Wipf and Stock, 1961), Ch. 6; Moisés Silva, *Biblical Words and Their Meaning: An Introduction to Lexical Semantics*, rev. and exp. ed. (Grand Rapids, MI: Zondervan, 1994), Ch. 1; D. A. Carson, *Exegetical Fallacies*, 2nd ed. (Grand Rapids, MI: Baker Books, 1996), 28–33.

and DCH. TDOT has only six different lexical meanings, which include throat/gullet.[21] DCH has twelve meanings, which include palate/throat/gullet, neck, sustenance, perfume, and sepulcher/funerary monument, etc.[22] The divergence in the two dictionaries is probably influenced by the extent to which etymology is applied. Another possible reason for the divergence is the fact that lexicographers derive their meanings from various existing sources, for example, those collected in grammar books and translations.[23] The different senses of נֶפֶשׁ in Psalm 23:3 in the preceding dictionaries may be such a case. TDOT takes its meaning as a "whole person";[24] while DCH views it as belonging to the category of "soul, heart, mind."[25] This brings out another issue, that is, the divergence in the translations of נֶפֶשׁ in different Bible versions,[26] which confirms Jacob's observation that the term נֶפֶשׁ is "as hard to define as it is to translate."[27]

The preceding discussion shows that it is necessary to determine the semantic range of נֶפֶשׁ and reconsider its translations in the OT since erroneous translation leads one to misinterpret and misunderstand God's Word. It also underlines the importance of the translators' accurate understanding of translation theory and the text to avoid exegetical fallacies such as those made by Nee. Thus, it is essential to explore translation studies, which developed into an independent discipline in 1970s,[28] and choose a translation theory and method for the present translation exercise even if this study does not undertake a complete translation. This is in accordance with the argument in Péng's "Contemplating the Future of Chinese Bible Translation: A Functionalist Approach," where he shows the importance of informing the

---

21. H. Seebass, "נפש," in *Theological Dictionary of the Old Testament*, vol. 9, eds. G. Johannes Botterweck, Helmer Ringgren, and Heinz-Josef Fabry, trans. John T. Willis, David E. Green, and Douglas W. Stott, (Sheffield: Sheffield Academic Press, 1998), 497–517.

22. David J. A. Clines, ed., "נפש," *The Dictionary of Classical Hebrew*, vol. 5 (Sheffield: Sheffield Academic, 2001), 724–734.

23. Silva, *Biblical Words and Their Meaning*, 137.

24. Seebass, "נפש," 510.

25. Clines, "נפש," 725.

26. For example, in Gen 35:18, נֶפֶשׁ is rendered differently in Chinese and English versions, such as "氣 *qì* (breath)" in RCUV, CNV, LZZ, TCVRE, CNET, NIV 2011, "靈魂 *líng hún* (spirit-soul)" in CUV, CCV, NASB 1995, ESV, NRSV, or "life" in LEB.

27. Jacob, "Anthropology of the Old Testament," 617.

28. Mary Snell-Hornby, *The Turns of Translation Studies: New Paradigms or Shifting Viewpoints?* (Amsterdam; Philadelphia: John Benjamins, 2006), 40–41. Used by permission.

audience of the approach employed in Bible translation.²⁹ Péng's argument indirectly reflects a critical issue with contemporary Chinese Bible translation (i.e. the absence of using a rigorous, systematic translation theory and method based upon translation studies in Chinese Bible translation projects). This is surprising in view of the renaissance of translation studies in China since the late 1970s.³⁰ For example, the Contemporary Chinese Version (NT) of 2010 lists three translation principles and five translation steps in its preface, which do not provide a specific, systematic approach from the perspective of translation studies.

Another critical issue with contemporary Chinese Bible translation is that no Chinese Bible is accessible for children and rendered directly from the original languages. As a homeschooling mother of two sons and children's worker within evangelical churches for about fifteen years, the present author has observed that children usually have difficulty in understanding the translations of the most popular Bible version (i.e. the Chinese Union Version [CUV] published in 1919). As to other easier versions, the Today's Chinese Version: Revised Edition (TCVRE), directly translated from the original languages, targets readers in the junior high school reading level. The Chinese Contemporary Bible (CCB) is also translated from the original languages and is designed for a general audience with a seventh-grade education or above. The Chinese New Living Translation (CNLT) is a paraphrased version, whose translation is mainly based on New Living Translation (NLT 1971). The Holy Bible: A Dynamic Chinese Translation (DCT) is based on the New International Version and the New American Standard Bible, whose target audience is young and older readers. Though the latter two versions might be easier than TCVRE and CCB, they are not translated according to the original texts and are not widely accepted by Chinese Christians due to the popularity of CUV. This means there is space for further development regarding a Chinese Bible version that is readable for and accepted by children.

---

29. Guó Wěi Péng 彭國瑋, "Contemplating the Future of Chinese Bible Translation: A Functionalist Approach," *The Bible Translator* 63, no. 1 (2012): 14.

30. Edwin Gentzler, "A Global View of Translation Studies: Towards an Interdisciplinary Field," in *Translation, Globalisation, and Localisation: A Chinese Perspective*, eds. Wang Ning and Sun Yifeng (Clevedon, UK; Buffalo, NY: Multilingual Matters, 2008), 117.

In this regard, some might argue that children need a Bible in their language. However, when English Bible versions suitable for children whose first language is English, such as the NIrV and the Easy-to-Read-Version, are analyzed, they demonstrate the use of wider vocabularies and more complex sentence structures than those in Wycliffe Associates' EasyEnglish, a version for those who are "from a wide diversity of cultures and who speak a wide range of mother tongues."[31] These findings indirectly support the present researcher's argument that for children as first-language speakers, a "general" Bible version is suitable and acceptable.[32] Children's competence with first language will be further explored later.

In contemporary Bible translation, teamwork,[33] and the integration of the theories of various disciplines are indispensable.[34] Drawing upon this, the researcher explores theories from different fields, including translation studies, childhood studies, and intergenerational ministry, and finds it important to bring together and train an intergenerational Bible translation team to produce a comprehensible Chinese Bible version for readers of all ages, including children. This is briefly discussed as follows.

First, in the West, due to the dysfunction of family and the indifference of society in the postmodern era, an intentional intergenerational ministry (IIM) is encouraged in neighborhoods, communities, corporations, organizations, and churches.[35] For Gambone, IIM possesses the potential to "start a movement to bring Christ's intergenerational message of unconditional love to an aging society suffering from generational isolation, separation

---

31. R. G. Betts, "Wycliffe Associates EasyEnglish: Challenges in Cross-Cultural Communication," 2003, http://www.mt-archive.info/CLT-2003-Betts.pdf.

32. Johannes S. Malherbe, "Big Words and Little Ears: Bible Translation and Children in Africa," The Bible Interpretation and Translation in Africa Conference, Pietermaritzburg, South Africa: University of KwaZulu-Natal, 2005, 14.

33. Harriet Hill et al., *Bible Translation Basics: Communicating Scripture in a Relevant Way* (Dallas, TX: SIL International, 2011), 268; Ernst R. Wendland, *Translating the Literature of Scripture: A Literary-Rhetorical Approach to Bible Translation* (Dallas, TX: SIL International, 2004), 371; Mildred L. Larson, *Meaning-Based Translation: A Guide to Cross-Language Equivalence*, 2nd ed. (Lanham; New York; Oxford: University Press of America, 1998), 513.

34. Andy Cheung, "A History of Twentieth Century Translation Theory and Its Application for Bible Translation," *Journal of Translation* 9, no. 1 (2013): 13.

35. James V. Gambone, *All Are Welcome: A Primer for Intentional Intergenerational Ministry and Dialogue* (Crystal Bay, MN: Elder Eye Press, 1998), v.

and neglect."³⁶ This is also a critical issue for the contemporary Chinese community in mainland China in that it is experiencing an aging society resulting from the one-child policy³⁷ and suffering from generational separation caused by urbanization and modernization.³⁸

Although IIM is still viewed "as something outside of the core mission of the congregation,"³⁹ some churches are focusing on this ministry.⁴⁰ The present author has already put it into practice for more than a decade in the settings of home education and children's ministry at church. The author witnesses the practicability of different generations serving, studying, and playing together and sees how the interaction of various generations is advantageous to all. Therefore, structuring and facilitating an intergenerational team to participate in Bible translation is a feasible exercise. This could be regarded as a good example of IIM that involves different generations, including children who have been marginalized by modern churches.⁴¹

Second, the enterprise of Bible translation is often accomplished by a translation committee consisting of middle-aged biblical scholars and experts whose speech becomes more conservative, as showed by community studies of variation, that "increasing age corresponds with increasing conservatism in speech."⁴² Social dialect research also indicates that vernacular speech is ". . . high in childhood and adolescence, and then steadily reduce[s] as

---

36. Gambone, *All Are Welcome*, vii.

37. Yà Fú Hé 何亞福, "'一胎化'政策的由來及影響" [The origin and influence of the "one-child policy"], 2014, http://blog.boxun.com/hero/wiyouzhiguang/73_1.shtml; Tabitha Michelle Powell, "The Negative Impact of the One Child Policy on the Chinese Society as It Relates to the Parental Support of the Aging Population," Master's thesis (Georgetown University, 2012), iii.

38. Powell, "Negative Impact," 39.

39. Gambone, *All Are Welcome*, vi.

40. Christine M. Ross, "A Qualitative Study Exploring Characteristics of Churches Committed to Intergenerational Ministry," PhD diss., Saint Louis University, 2006.

41. A. L. Allen, "Children as Disciples, Not Simply Discipled: Reconsidering the Role of Children in the Christian Church," 2014, 9, http://www.inter-disciplinary.net/probing-the-boundaries/wp-content/uploads/2014/05/allenchildpaper.pdf. Allen, in "Children as Disciples," laments that "children face the marginalization and oppression of a modern church that does not take them seriously as co-participants in its ministry"; see also Judith Sadler, "Learning Together: All-Age Learning in the Church," in *Learning in the Way: Research and Reflection on Adult Christian Education*, ed. Jeff Astley (Herefordshire, UK: Gracewing, 2000), 120.

42. Penelope Eckert, "Age as a Sociolinguistic Variable," in *The Handbook of Sociolinguistics*, ed. Florian Coulmas (Oxford, UK: Blackwell, 1997), 152.

people approach middle age when societal pressures to conform are greatest. Vernacular usage gradually increases again in old age as social pressures reduce."[43] Therefore, to produce a new translation that may be effective and accepted by all age groups, including children, it seems essential to involve children, adolescents, even senior adults in the process of Bible translation.

As to the question of whether children are competent to participate in the process of Bible translation, Mishler asserts that "first-grade children and adults do not differ significantly in the length of their utterances including their questions . . . first-grade children have the ability to vary speech style, and to use features of adult conversation."[44] Kornei Chukovsky comes to the same conclusion based on his research among Russian-speaking children.[45] He fully agrees with A. N. Gvozdev who states:

> At [the age of eight] the child has already mastered to such a degree the entire complicated grammatical system, including the finest points of esoteric syntactic and morphological sequences in the Russian language, as well as the solid and correct usage of many single exceptions, that the Russian language, thus mastered, becomes indeed his own.[46]

Therefore, children might not be fully competent in writing their language but they can still be competent in spoken language. This is sufficient for them to join in the discussion of Bible translation. And their participation, in turn, can help produce a general Bible version suitable for both young and adult readers.

Wendland notes that a translation project involving as many readers as possible in areas such as contextualization and consultation may produce

---

43. Janet Holmes, *An Introduction to Sociolinguistics*, 2nd ed. (Harlow: Person, 2001), 168.

44. Quoted in Janet K. Black, "Assessing Kindergarten Children's Communicative Competence," in *Language, Children and Society: The Effect of Social Factors on Children Learning to Communicate*, eds. Olga K. Garnica and Martha L. King, International Series in Psychobiology and Learning (Oxford, UK: Pergamon Press, 1979), 39.

45. Kornei Chukovsky, *From Two to Five*, 2nd ed., ed. and trans. Miriam Morton (Berkeley; Los Angeles; London: University of California Press, 1971), 7.

46. Quoted in Chukovsky, *From Two to Five*, 10.

a version that is more acceptable.[47] This pioneering argument encourages the researcher to suggest that children should be involved not only in the operations of contextualization and consultation, but also in the latter part of composing a provisional translation in the production of readable Bible versions for young readers. This is because they can help suggest or determine words, phrases, or sentences that are understandable to them.

1.2 Bridging the Gap

Given the preceding issues, the researcher proposes that convening and training an intergenerational translation team to participate in Bible translation is a promising exercise, through which the problematic translations of נֶפֶשׁ in the Chinese OT will be addressed. Furthermore, the team will contribute to produce a Chinese Bible version readable for readers of all ages, including children.

1.3 Objectives of the Study

The main objective of the present research is to explore the most appropriate way to render the Hebrew word נֶפֶשׁ in the Psalms in contemporary Chinese. What follows are the five subsidiary objectives:

First, the researcher explores Chinese Bible translation history, which is connected to the early development of Bible translation history as a whole.

Second, the researcher explores translation theory and then selects an approach for the present translation enterprise.

Third, the researcher explores the contribution that young Bible readers can make to the translation process.

Fourth, the researcher studies the possible meanings of the Hebrew word נֶפֶשׁ and how they are applied, especially in Chinese versions.

Fifth, the researcher explores the translation process as an intergenerational Bible translation team attempts to render the Hebrew word נֶפֶשׁ in the Psalms into contemporary Chinese and to produce a translation readable for all generations.

---

47. Ernst R. Wendland, *LiFE-Style Translating*, 2nd ed. (Dallas, TX: SIL International, 2011), 407.

1.4 Outline

This book is divided into six chapters.

Chapter 1: Introduction

Chapter 1 first describes the problem for the present research and suggests a way to solve the problem. Then, the research objectives are presented, followed by the outline of the study, the hypothesis, the definitions, the delimitations, the presuppositions and the value of such a study.

Chapter 2: A Literary Approach to Bible Translation

Chapter 2 comprises two major sections. The first section begins by tackling the history and major issues of Chinese Bible translation, which are divided into two parts: (1) early Bible translation and related issues, and (2) the history and major issues of Chinese Bible translation.

The second section provides a critical descriptive overview of the development of translation studies. This is demonstrated by Lefevere and Bassnett's three models before the twentieth century, followed by Snell-Hornby's observation on the development of translation studies from the twentieth century onwards. This section concludes with the selection of Wendland's Literary Functional Equivalence (LiFE) as the theory and method for the present translation task.

Chapter 3: Children as Crucial Members of an Intergenerational Bible Translation Team

Chapter 3 begins with the premise that children are important members of God's people, a fact which is substantiated by the significance and nature of children and childhood in the Bible and recent theological reflection. Then this chapter explores the idea, practice, and outcome of intergenerational ministry, in which the children as important members of God's people can be nurtured by older Christians and can make meaningful contributions to most, if not all, the functions of the church. This chapter ends with the proposition that intergenerational participation, including children, in Bible translation is a feasible approach in producing a readable Bible version for readers of all ages, including children.

Chapter 4: The Possible Meanings of the Hebrew Word נֶפֶשׁ in the OT and Its Translation in Chinese

Chapter 4 first provides a literature review of the Hebrew word נֶפֶשׁ. Second, it examines the use of נֶפֶשׁ in the OT and the use of its NT counterpart ψυχή to determine its semantic range. Third, a survey is made of how this word has been translated in Chinese and English Bible versions, followed by the discussion of the influence of Watchman Nee. This chapter ends with an argument for the necessity of reconsidering the translations of נֶפֶשׁ.

Chapter 5: Translating נֶפֶשׁ in the Psalms into Chinese: An Exercise in Intergenerational, Literary Bible Translation

Chapter 5 first provides the motivation for the selection of members of the translation team and the summary of the training course for the team. Then it presents a description of the translation process itself. Here, the team attempts to translate Psalms 35, 63 and 107[48] through Wendland's approach to produce a literary version. Next, the translation results are delineated, analyzed and compared to the existing Bible versions.

Chapter 6: Conclusion – Findings and Implications

Chapter 6 begins with a summary of research findings. In this part, the findings in the three selected psalms are applied to the use of נֶפֶשׁ in the rest of the Psalms, and in the OT as a whole. This is followed by a summary of the foundations for intergenerational participation in Bible translation. Then this chapter presents the feedback from the participants, the comments of OT scholars on the three newly translated psalms, and the researcher's reflections regarding the intergenerational Bible translation through the LiFE approach. Next, recommendations for further study are provided. This chapter concludes with the researcher's final comments.

1.5 Hypothesis

The present author hypothesizes that the participation of an intergenerational team in the process of Bible translation can not only facilitate the findings of the appropriate translations of נֶפֶשׁ in Chinese Bible, but also

---

48. For the reason behind the selection of the three psalms, see §1.7.1.

will help produce new translations acceptable for readers of all ages, including children.

The author also assumes that the intergenerational Bible translation team structured for this research is a good example of intergenerational ministry.

1.6 Key Terms

The following technical terms in the present research require clear definition.

1.6.1 First Language and Mother Tongue

First language and mother tongue are used as synonyms in this research, which mean the language(s) a person has learned from birth or within the critical period, or the language(s) a person speaks best.[49]

1.6.2 Common Language

In his *Bible Translation for Popular Use*, Wonderly makes a clear distinction between *common language* and *popular language*,[50] which blurs in the mind of most people, even Bible translators.[51] Wonderly defines common language as

> part of the total resources of a given language common to the usage of both educated and uneducated. Common language avoids on the one hand the literary embellishments that are beyond the reach of the uneducated classes, and on the other hand the elaborations of slang and other nonstandard forms that are unacceptable (and in part unintelligible) to the educated.[52]

In a highly literate country, there are critical diversities in the speech of different social classes, based on socioeconomic and educational levels, occupational specializations, etc.[53] In such situations, *common language* translation is required to produce a Bible version for popular use.

---

49. Nikolay Slavkov, "What Is Your 'First' Language in Bilingual Canada? A Study of Language Background Profiling at Publicly Funded Elementary Schools across Three Provinces," *International Journal of Bilingual Education and Bilingualism* (2015): 2–3.

50. William L. Wonderly, *Bible Translations for Popular Use* (London: United Bible Societies, 1968), 3.

51. Philip C. Stine, *Let the Words Be Written: The Lasting Influence of Eugene A. Nida* (Atlanta: SBL, 2004), 84.

52. Wonderly, *Bible Translations*, 3.

53. Wonderly, 3.

In contrast, in a country where the language spoken by a people shows "little specialization along social, occupational, and literary lines," the differences in the speech of various social classes are usually not profound.[54] In such a country, the majority of a language's speakers "share the same cultural heritage, talk about the same things, and associate with one another without sharply defined social barriers."[55] In this case, a Bible version for popular use calls for translating in *popular language*, that is, "the contemporary language in a form that is shared by the entire population that speaks it."[56]

The present study will employ the *common language* translation because it is suitable for highly literate, linguistically diversified Chinese communities.

1.7 Delimitations

In an attempt to narrow the scope of this study and make clear which aspects will be included, several delimitations have been identified.

1.7.1 The Selected Passages for Translating

Since space does not permit a comprehensive examination of all the 754 occurrences of נֶפֶשׁ in the Hebrew OT, this study will focus on three selected psalms (i.e. Pss 35, 63, 107). The selection is motivated by the following considerations:

First, Psalms is the book with the highest occurrences of the Hebrew word נֶפֶשׁ in the OT (144 times).

Second, the songs of petition, thanksgiving, and praise are the dominant genres in the Psalms. For Gunkel, there are five basic psalm types: individual lament, community lament, thanksgiving, praise, and royal psalms.[57] However, Waltke and Yu rather see "three basic types: petition, thanksgiving, and praise."[58] Moreover, though Wendland also suggests that there are five major literary genres in the Psalms (songs of petition, thanksgiving, praise,

---

54. Wonderly, 3.
55. Wonderly, 3.
56. Wonderly, 3.
57. Hermann Gunkel, *The Psalms: A Form-Critical Introduction*, trans. Thomas M. Horner, Biblical Series 19 (Philadelphia: Fortress, 1967).
58. Bruce K. Waltke and Charles Yu, *An Old Testament Theology: An Exegetical, Canonical, and Thematic Approach* (Grand Rapids, MI: Zondervan, 2007), 875.

instruction and profession of trust), he notes that most of psalms fall into the first three categories.[59] In brief, the songs of petition, thanksgiving, and praise can be viewed as the most representative genres in the Psalms. Thus, in this study one psalm from each of the last three genre types with the most frequent use of נֶפֶשׁ will be selected.

Finally, psalms with four or more occurrences of נֶפֶשׁ are: Psalms 35 (eight times), 42 (six times), 63 (four times), 86 (four times), 107 (five times), 119 (eight times), 143 (five times). Gleaned from Wendland[60] with slight adjustments, the psalms with the most frequent occurrence of נֶפֶשׁ by genre are:

> Petition: Psalms 35 (eight times), 42 (six times), 86 (four times), 143 (five times)
>
> Praise: Psalm 63[61] (four times)
>
> Thanksgiving: Psalm 107 (five times)
>
> Instruction: Psalm 119 (eight times)

Thus, Psalms 35, 63, 107 have been chosen as representative examples because they fall into the three main genres in the Psalms: petition, praise, and thanksgiving.

1.7.2 The History of Bible Translation

After a brief exploration of the early history of Bible translation, this research will give particular attention to the history and major issues of Chinese Bible translation.

1.7.3 The Theory of Translation

This research will mainly focus on Bible translation theory, though secular translation theory will be mentioned when needed.

---

59. Ernst R. Wendland, *Analyzing the Psalms: with Exercises for Bible Students and Translators*, 2nd ed. (Dallas, TX: SIL International, 2002), 32–33.

60. Wendland, *Analyzing the Psalms*, 60.

61. Though Wendland classifies Psalm 63 as a song of profession of trust, the re-evaluation of this classification is encouraged by him. See Wendland, *Analyzing the Psalms*, 60. Since Psalms 63 refers to God's works in general, rather than "a specific act of deliverance in answer to a petition" as in the songs of thanksgiving, and exalts God for his חֶסֶד, it could be viewed as a song of praise according to Waltke and Yu, *An Old Testament Theology*, 881.

1.7.4 The Enterprise of Bible Translation

According to Wendland, there are "three essential operations involved in the production of a Bible translation – composition, contextualization, and consultation."[62] The current exercise mainly concentrates on the first critical operation (i.e. composition).

1.7.5 Bible Versions

The translation of the present work is based on the *Biblia Hebraica Stuttgartensia*, but the verse numbers throughout the whole study follow those of the Chinese Union Version (CUV). In some cases, such as quotations, the verse number is directly followed by a number with a square bracket, which indicates the verse number in the Masoretic Text (MT).

All English verses in this study are from the New International Version (NIV 2011), unless indicated otherwise.

When analyzing the translation results in chapter 5 and chapter 6, the work refers mainly to well-known Chinese Bible versions, including the Chinese Union Version (CUV) and its revised version (RCUV), the Chinese New Version (CNV), Lu Zhen Zhong Bible Translation (LZZ), the Today's Chinese Version (revised edition, TCVRE), the Chinese Contemporary Bible (CCB), the Chinese New English Translation Bible (CNET), and The Holy Bible: A Dynamic Chinese Translation (DCT).

1.8 Presuppositions

Presuppositions that have a profound effect on one's thought and writing while tackling such research should be recognized and stated "up front"[63] as follows:

1.8.1 The Nature of the Scriptures

The present researcher assumes that the authors of the Bible employ normal human language to communicate God's message in their particular social, cultural and historical contexts.[64] This challenges the views of many

---

62. Wendland, *LiFE-Style Translating*, 406.

63. Kevin Smith, *Academic Writing and Theological Research: A Guide for Students* (Johannesburg, South Africa: South African Theological Seminary Press, 2008), 146.

64. Stine, *Let the Words Be Written*, 60.

conservative Bible translators that "not only were the thoughts of the Bible inspired by God through the Holy Spirit, but also the words [and forms] themselves."[65] Conservative Bible translators overemphasize the divine character of the Bible and minimize the character of it as human literature.[66] However, as Arichea maintains, only when Bible translators regard the Scripture as normal human composition does the task of translation become possible.[67]

1.8.2 The Issue of Formal and Dynamic/Functional Translation

Ellington points out that all Bible translators might move back and forth along a continuum between the extremes of absolute *foreignization* (formal equivalence) and absolute *domestication* (dynamic or functional equivalence) as circumstances, languages, and audiences require.[68] Indeed, the degree of foreignization or domestication in Bible translation will largely depend on the *purpose* (goal or *Skopos*) of the translation. For example, the translations in an interlinear or scholarly edition, such as William Propp's commentary on Exodus 1–18, are highly and intentionally foreignized. Nonetheless, a version that is translated to meet the needs of readers of all ages, including children, should be domesticated to a great degree. Because this study focuses on children's understanding of Scripture, the latter approach is adopted.

1.8.3 Gospel, Language and Culture

In its worldwide expansion, Christianity took up various languages and cultures as an instrument to mediate gospel.[69] Sanneh asserts:

> If Pentecost was the monument to the salvific potential of mother tongues, then St Paul was the preeminent person who

---

65. Stine, 59.

66. Daniel C. Arichea, "Theology and Translation: The Implications of Certain Theological Issues to the Translation Task," in *Bible Translation and the Spread of the Church: The Last 200 Years*, ed. Philip C. Stine (Leiden; New York: Brill, 1990), 50.

67. Archiea, "Theology and Translation," 50.

68. John Ellington, "Schleiermacher Was Wrong: The False Dilemma of Foreignization and Domestication," *The Bible Translator* 54, no. 3 (2003): 315.

69. Lamin Sanneh, "Gospel and Culture: Ramifying Effects of Scriptural Translation," in *Bible Translation and the Spread of the Church: The Last 200 Years*, ed. Philip C. Stine (Leiden; New York: Brill, 1990), 13–18.

carved his name on that monument . . . Paul's view is that God does not absolutize any culture, whatever the esteem of that culture. Furthermore, Paul believed that all cultures have cast upon them the breath of God's favor, thus cleansing them of all stigma of inferiority and untouchability.[70]

Thus, before a loving and gracious God, all languages and cultures are equal, having the potential of serving as an effective instrument to mediate the message of the one true God.

1.9 Potential Value

The present work will contribute to the scholarship of the subject matter in several ways:

First, Chinese biblical scholars still rely heavily on traditional, incorrect western interpretations of the Hebrew word נֶפֶשׁ. Through proper exegetical approaches and close textual examination, this study may provide contextually appropriate translations of נֶפֶשׁ so that God's Word can be correctly rendered.

Second, Chinese children need a Bible translation which they can understand and use. CUV (the most popular, influential version) is difficult for children. CNLT and DCT (the easiest versions) are not translated from original texts; they are both translated from adults' perspective. This research includes children in the process of Bible translation, assuming that the resultant translation may also be accessible to and appropriate for young readers.

Third, the intergenerational Bible translation team can serve as a good example of how intergenerational ministry is carried out, thus facilitating its development in the ministry of the church. In other words, if children can contribute to the arduous enterprise of Bible translation, it is possible for them to participate in and contribute to ordinary church ministries as well.

---

70. Sanneh, "Gospel and Culture," 14–15.

CHAPTER 2

A Literary Approach to Bible Translation

2.1. Introduction

Bible translation enables the communication of God's word to the world by means of transferring "the meaning of a biblical text from its source language to some other receptor language."[1] In both Bible and secular translation for over two millennia, "[t]he dichotomy of literal-versus-free translation has been present and dominant from the earliest discussion of translation principles."[2] Thanks to the development of translation studies, contemporary translators can freely choose the approach they desire: either one that is more literal or freer according to the purpose of a translation project.[3] Today all translators are encouraged to consider interdisciplinary and intercultural dimensions.[4]

To better understand Bible translation and then choose a translation theory and method, this chapter first presents a brief history of Bible translation, along with its major issues, and next explores the development of

---

1. Glen G. Scorgie, "Introduction and Overview," in *The Challenge of Bible Translation: Communicating God's Word to the World*, eds. Glen G. Scorgie, Mark L. Strauss, and Steven M. Voth (Grand Rapids, MI: Zondervan, 2003), 20.

2. Philip A. Noss, "A History of Bible Translation: Introduction and Overview," in *A History of Bible Translation*, ed. Philip A. Noss (Rome: Edizioni di storia e letteratura, 2007), 13; see also Susan Bassnett, *Translation* (London: Routledge, 2014), 5–6.

3. Péng 彭, "Contemplating the Future of Chinese Bible Translation," 14.

4. Cheung, "Twentieth Century Translation," 13.

translation studies, ending with a choice of a literary model as the translation approach for the present study.

2.2. The History and Major Issues of Bible Translation

2.2.1. Introduction

This study mainly focuses on the history of Chinese Bible translation, which can be traced back to the seventh century CE. However, it is helpful to give a glimpse of the early development of Bible translation history as a whole here, and then connect it with the Chinese Bible translation history. Accordingly, this section consists of two parts. The first part presents the early development of Bible translation history. The second part is related to the brief history and major issues of Chinese Bible translation.

2.2.2. Early Bible Translation and Related Issues

The story of the tower of Babel episode (Gen 11), showing how God divided the world into a variety of tongues, caused translation to be a necessary task.[5] The first *oral* Bible translation enterprise was reported in Nehemiah 8:7–8, where the majority of the Jews just returning from the exile in Babylon (ca. 532 BC) had lost the facility of employing their own language and spoke in Aramaic, "the lingua franca of the Babylonian Empire."[6] This necessitated the translation and explanation of the Hebrew Scriptures in Aramaic in the temple and the synagogues.

According to Jinbachian, the history of Bible translation in the West can be divided into four periods: the first period from 532 BC to 700 CE; the second covering the period of the Arab Islamic empire from 700 CE to 1500 CE; the third including Renaissance and Reformation period (the sixteenth to eighteenth centuries); and the fourth relating to the modern era, covering the nineteenth century up to the present.[7] Here only the first period needs

---

5. Jewish Publication Society, "A Short History of Bible Translations," in *The Jewish Bible*, JPS Guide (Philadelphia, PA: Jewish Publication Society, 2008), 33.

6. Manuel Jinbachian, "Introduction: The Septuagint to the Vernaculars," in *A History of Bible Translation*, ed. Philip A. Noss (Rome: Edizioni de storia e letteratura, 2007), 35.

7. Jinbachian, "Introduction," 29.

to be explored because it corresponds with the time frame that this study refers to (i.e. the period before the first Bible translation into Chinese in the seventh century CE).

In this period, the ancient Bible versions can be grouped into two categories: "ancient versions of the OT made for the use of Jews" and "ancient versions intended chiefly for Christians."[8] Due to space limitations, the Septuagint will receive more attention because it is the first and the most important Bible translation.

2.2.2.1. Ancient Versions of the OT for the Jews

The Septuagint and the Jewish Targumim are translations for and by the Jews. Both are *primary* translations (i.e. translated directly from the original text).[9]

2.2.2.1.1 The Septuagint

2.2.2.1.1.1 The origin of the Septuagint

The name Septuagint (LXX) is a designation originating from the legendary tradition that seventy (-two) translators produced the Greek translation of the Hebrew Scripture.[10] The English word "Septuagint" derives from Latin *Septuaginta*, "seventy," a shortened form of the title *Interpretatio Septuaginta Virorum*, "The Translation of the Seventy Men."[11] In the most ancient Greek manuscripts of the OT, this version is delineated as the version "according to the LXX" (κατὰ τοὺς ἑβδομήκοντα).[12]

This Greek OT version is not only the first and the most important Bible translation,[13] but also "the first example of the translation of the complete

---

8. Bruce M. Metzger, *The Bible in Translation: Ancient and English Versions* (Grand Rapids, MI: Baker Academic, 2001), 13, 25.

9. Jinbachian, "Introduction," 30.

10. Ellis R. Brotzman, *Old Testament Textual Criticism: A Practical Introduction* (Grand Rapids, MI: Baker Books, 1994), 73.

11. Karen H. Jobes and Moisés Silva, *Invitation to the Septuagint* (Grand Rapids, MI: Baker Academic, 2000), 32.

12. H. B. Swete, *An Introduction to the Old Testament in Greek* (Cambridge: Cambridge University Press, 1914), 10–11.

13. Bleddyn J. Roberts, "The Manuscripts, Text and Versions," in *The Cambridge History of the Bible, Vol. 2: The West from the Fathers to the Reformation*, ed. G. W. H. Lampe, electronic ed. (New York: Cambridge University Press, 2004 [1969]), 14.

corpus of sacred, legal, historical and poetic literature of one people, in a language of the Semitic cultural world, to the language of classical Greek culture."[14] Moreover, from an ethnic perspective, Sebastian Broke comments that the LXX is "the first translation of the religious books of an oriental ethnic group into Greek."[15] This helps explain why this version has been considered the most important translation ever made.[16]

While tradition holds that seventy-two Jewish elders (six from each tribe) translated the Bible in seventy-two days,[17] this translation of the Torah was rather translated by five different translators[18] from "the Alexandrian diaspora for whom Greek was the language of everyday life."[19] In other words, the origin of the Greek Torah probably arose within the Alexandrian Jewish

---

14. Julio Trebolle Barrera, *The Jewish Bible and the Christian Bible: An Introduction to the History of the Bible*, trans. Wilfred G. E. Watson (Grand Rapids, MI: Eerdmans, 1998), 301.

15. Quoted in Benjamin G. Wright III, "The Jewish Scriptures in Greek: The Septuagint in the Context of Ancient Translation Activity," in *Biblical Translation in Context*, ed. Frederick W. Knobloch (Bethesda, MD: University Press of Maryland, 2002), 3; see also Isaac L. Seeligmann, "Problems and Perspectives in Modern Septuagint Research," *Textus* 15 (1990): 169.

16. Elias J. Bickerman, *The Jews in the Greek Age* (Cambridge, MA: Harvard University Press, 1988), 101; Abraham Wasserstein and David Wasserstein, *The Legend of the Septuagint: From Classical Antiquity to Today* (Cambridge: Cambridge University Press, 2006), 1.

17. The LXX's oldest witness, the famous Letter of Aristeas, relates the tradition that during the reign of Ptolemy II Philadelphus (282–246 BC) seventy-two Jewish elders were summoned from Palestine to Alexandria for the task of translating the law of Moses into Greek in seventy-two days. See R. H. Charles, ed., *The Letter of Aristeas* (Oxford: Clarendon, 1913), http://www.ccel.org/c/charles/otpseudepig/aristeas.htm. The majority of the details in the letter were unquestionably fictional except for the dating (ca. 275 BC), the parties involved (the Jews), the location (Alexandria) and the initial scope (the Torah). See Leonard Greenspoon, "Septuagint," in *The New Interpreter's Dictionary of the Bible*, vol. 5, ed. Katharine D. Sakenfeld (Nashville, TN: Abingdon, 2009), 171. Some historical factors in the letter are disputable. Cf. Emanuel Tov, *Textual Criticism of the Hebrew Bible*, 3rd rev. and exp. ed. (Minneapolis: Fortress, 2012), 129–131; Harry Sysling, "Translation Techniques in the Ancient Bible Translations: Septuagint and Targum," in *A History of Bible Translation*, ed. Philip A. Noss (Roma: Edizioni di storia e letteratura, 2007), 281; Jennifer M. Dines, *The Septuagint* (London: T & T Clark, 2004), 28–33; Wasserstein and Wasserstein, *Legend of the Septuagint*, 25–26; Martin Hengel, *The Septuagint as Christian Scripture: Its Prehistory and the Problem of Its Canon*, trans. Mark E. Biddle (Grand Rapids, MI: Baker Academic, 2004), 25; Jobes and Silva, *Invitation to the Septuagint*, 33–37; Ernst Würthwein, *The Text of the An Introduction to the Biblia Hebraica*, trans. Erroll F. Rhodes, 2nd rev. ed. (Grand Rapids, MI: Eerdmans, 1995), 52–53; Brotzman, *Old Testament Textual Criticism*, 73; Sidney Jellicoe, *The Septuagint and Modern Study* (Oxford: Clarendon, 1968), 55–56.

18. Hayeon Kim, "Multiple Authorship of the Septuagint Pentateuch," *Bulletin of Judaeo-Greek Studies* 40 (2007): 2–3.

19. Würthwein, *Text of the Old Testament*, 52.

community itself, whose members were no longer familiar with Hebrew and, thus, in need of such a translation[20] for liturgical and educational purposes.[21]

2.2.2.1.1.2 *The development*

The LXX received a great welcome from Greek-speaking Jews. For example, in his *Life of Moses* II, Philo considered "these translators not mere interpreters but hierophants and prophets to whom it had been granted in their honest and guileless minds to go along with the most pure spirit of Moses."[22] Put differently, for Philo, the LXX was inspired by God just as the original Hebrew.[23] He also reported that when an annual "solemn assembly [was] held and a festival [was] celebrated in the island of Pharos, . . . those admirable, and incomparable, and most desirable laws [the LXX] were made known to all people," including the Jews.[24] Before 70 CE, the LXX was "used on an equal footing with the Hebrew text."[25]

In the first century CE, this tradition was expanded to embrace all the biblical books translated by different individuals in various places such as Alexandria and Palestine.[26] After 70 CE, the call for revisions or new translations was intensified in Jewish communities because of the necessity to correct the older and freer Greek translations and due to the resistance of the "Christianization" of the LXX.[27] In other words, the fact that the Christians made the LXX their own and employed it in disputes with the Jews led to the Jews' rejection of that version and the replacement of it with recensions or new translations that were "faithful to the proto-masoretic Hebrew text, declared the official text at the beginning of the 2nd century CE."[28]

---

20. Würthwein, 52.

21. Metzger, *Bible in Translation*, 13.

22. Judaeus Philo, *The Works of Philo: Complete and Unabridged*, trans. and updated by C. D. Yonge (Peabody, MA: Hendrickson, 1995), 494.

23. The belief that this Greek translation had been divinely inspired paved the way for several church fathers, e.g. St Irenaeus and St Augustine, to assert that the LXX was more precise in presenting God's Word than the Hebrew Bible. See Metzger, *Bible in Translation*, 18; Frederick C. Grant, *Translating the Bible* (Greenwich, CT: Seabury, 1961), 22.

24. Philo, *Works of Philo*, 494.

25. Barrera, *Jewish Bible and the Christian Bible*, 124.

26. Tov, *Textual Criticism*, 128–129.

27. Tov, 141; Hengel, *Septuagint as Christian Scripture*, 43.

28. Barrera, *Jewish Bible and the Christian Bible*, 309, 312–313.

A typical example of the disputes between Jews and Christians was regarding the rendering of Isaiah 7:14, where the LXX translated עַלְמָה as παρθένος "virgin" rather than νεᾶνις "a young woman, girl, maiden." This translation enabled the Christians to interpret Isaiah 7:14 as "a prophecy of the virgin birth of Christ," stimulating the *dialogue* between Justin and the Jew Trypho.[29] For Justin, Isaiah 7:14 contained a true prophecy of the virginal birth of Christ. But Trypho argued that the meaning of עַלְמָה was not "virgin" but "young woman" and that the Isaiah message only referred to King Hezekiah.[30] The Jews' rejection of this translation by the LXX was reflected in the well-known Jewish recensions produced by Theodotion and Aquila, and the Jewish-Christian Symmachus in the second century who deliberately translated the word as νεᾶνις to correct the misunderstanding of this passage.[31]

These Jewish recensions described above belonged to the pre-Hexaplaric revisions,[32] which were followed by the Hexapla, and post-Hexaplaric revisions. Due to its "paramount importance for the textual history of the LXX,"[33] Origen's Hexapla, whose primary aim was to secure a revised Septuagint text,[34] "occupied a central position in the classification of the revisions."[35]

The Hexapla, the great critical work of Origen made up of about 6,500 pages, produced in the middle of the third century CE in Caesarea, was set out in six parallel columns. The first provides the Hebrew proto-Masoretic text; the second is a transliteration in Greek script; the third is the version of Aquila; the fourth is the translation of Symmachus; the fifth is the revised and annotated version of the Septuagint text; and the sixth is the version

---

29. Hengel, *Septuagint as Christian Scripture*, 30; Barrera, *Jewish Bible and the Christian Bible*, 313, 511.

30. Justin Martyr, "Dialogue of Justin, Philosopher and Martyr with Trypho, a Jew," in *The Ante-Nicene Fathers: The Apostolic Fathers with Justin Martyr and Irenaeus*, vol. 1, eds. A. Roberts, J. Donaldson, and A. C. Coxe (Buffalo, NY: Christian Literature Company, 1885), 231–232.

31. Wordnik, "*Neanis*," 2014, http://www.wordnik.com/words/neanis.

32. After the second century, the Greek translation of the Bible, for Jews, "gradually became less and less important." In contrast, the legend of this tradition "grew and developed a great deal" among Christians. See Wasserstein and Wasserstein, *Legend of the Septuagint*, 95.

33. Tov, *Textual Criticism*, 142.

34. P. R. Ackroyd and C. F. Evans, eds., *The Cambridge History of the Bible*, vol. 1 (New York: Cambridge University Press, 2004), 458.

35. Tov, *Textual Criticism*, 142.

of Theodotion.[36] As to the post-Hexaplaric revisions, the most crucial one was that of Lucian of Antioch (Syria), who was martyred in ca. 312 CE.[37]

Finally, this tradition not only encompassed all of the books of the typical Hebrew canon, but also consisted of the material that is nowadays classified as deuterocanonical,[38] some of which were originally composed in Greek.[39]

2.2.2.1.1.3 The term Septuagint
This tradition's long and complicated history caused the name Septuagint to be used indistinctly both in antiquity and today. According to Greenspoon, there are several different uses for the term Septuagint in antiquity:

> [T]he earliest Greek translation of the Pentateuch . . . the earliest Greek translation of the entire OT, the fifth column of Origen's Hexapla . . . any authoritative Greek text recognized as scriptural (but not viewed as part of the NT), and the entire Greek tradition (including revisions, recensions, various fresh translation, etc.)[40]

Calling for the precise use of the term, modern "scholars usually distinguish between the collection of sacred Greek writings named the 'Septuagint' and the reconstructed original translation, called the Old Greek (OG) translation."[41]

2.2.2.1.1.4 The canon of the LXX
The issue of canonicity is important in the history of early Bible translation. Indeed, the three earliest extant codices for the LXX, *Vaticanus* (fourth century CE), *Sinaiticus* (fourth century CE) and *Alexandrinus* (fifth century

---

36. Gerard J. Norton, "Jews, Greeks and the Hexapla of Origen," in *The Aramaic Bible: Targums in Their Historical Context*, eds. D. R. G. Beattie and M. J. McNamara, Journal for the Study of the Old Testament Supplement Series 166 (Sheffield: JSOT, 1994), 419; Grant, *Translating the Bible*, 25.

37. Tov, *Textual Criticism*, 146; Grant, *Translating the Bible*, 26.

38. The deuterocanonical contains 1 Esdras, 2 Esdras, Psalm 151, the Wisdom of Solomon, Ecclesiasticus (Ben Sirah), the additions to Esther (some of which are original Semitic compositions; others of which are original Greek ones), Judith, Tobit, Baruch, the Letter of Jeremiah, and the additions to Daniel. See Greenspoon, "Septuagint," 175.

39. Tov, *Textual Criticism*, 129; Greenspoon, "Septuagint," 174–175.

40. Greenspoon, "Septuagint," 174–175; cf. Jobes and Silva, *Invitation to the Septuagint*, 30–33.

41. Tov, *Textual Criticism*, 129; cf. Jobes and Silva, *Invitation to the Septuagint*, 32.

CE), differ from each other in the number of books forming it, their order, contents and wording.[42] Not following typical Hebrew canon, they all include some of the apocryphal books.[43] In Philo's time, however, there was no evidence that apocryphal books were included in the Hebrew canon.[44]

2.2.2.1.1.5 Translation techniques in the LXX

Tov points out that in Ptolemaic Egypt two types of translation approaches were known. The literal approach was typical for commercial and judicial documents, while the meaning-based approach was used for literary documents.[45] When the LXX is analyzed book by book, Tov finds a wide range among translation of the books, from the very literal to the more meaning-based.[46] The literal approach was used in the translation of Judges, Psalms, Ecclesiastes, Lamentations, Ezra-Nehemiah and Chronicles. The meaning-based approach was used in the translation of Job, Proverbs, Isaiah, Daniel and Esther. The remaining books range between the two extremes.[47]

Nowadays, LXX specialists generally believe that each book or block of material must be studied on its own to ascertain which translation techniques are employed.[48] Therefore, one must be cautious about making sweeping generalizations about translation choices made in the book as a whole, for example, "positing a strong anti-anthropomorphic tendency throughout the LXX or an equally widespread promotion of certain messianic ideas."[49] As far as the former issue is concerned, the LXX translators, in many cases, literally reproduced the Hebrew anthropomorphic expressions of God. For

---

42. Greenspoon, "Septuagint," 174–175.

43. Paul D. Wegner, *The Journey from Texts to Translations: The Origin and Development of the Bible* (Grand Rapids, MI: Baker Books, 1999), 50.

44. R. T. Beckwith, *The Old Testament Canon of the New Testament Church and Its Background in Early Judaism* (Grand Rapids, MI: Eerdmans, 1985), 385–386.

45. Emanuel Tov, "The Septuagint," in *Mikra: Text, Translation, Reading and Interpretation of the Hebrew Bible in Ancient Judaism and Early Christianity*, eds. Martin Jan Mulder and Harry Sysling (Peabody, MA: Hendrickson, 2004 [1988]), 169. For further exploration about translation theory and techniques in antiquity, see Staffan Olofsson, *The LXX Version: A Guide to the Translation Technique of the Septuagint*, Coniectanea Biblica, Old Testament Series 30 (Stockholm: Almquist & Wiksell International, 1990), 5–10.

46. For further discussion regarding the translation technique of the Septuagint, see Sysling, "Translation Techniques," 281–292; Olofsson, *LXX Version*.

47. Tov, "Septuagint," 172–173.

48. Barrera, *Jewish Bible and the Christian Bible*, 318.

49. Greenspoon, "Septuagint," 173–174.

instance, "the פֶּה of the Lord" (Jer 9:11) is translated literally as "the mouth (στόμα) of the Lord,"[50] and "the light of your פָּנֶה" (Ps 4:7) as "the light of your face (πρόσωπον)."[51] But in other cases, translators deliberately avoided the anthropomorphisms. For example, in Numbers 12:8, the translators substituted "He [Moses] sees the *form* of the LORD" for "He sees the *glory* of the Lord." In Exodus 4:24, "the LORD met him [Moses]" was replaced by "the *angel of the* Lord met him."[52]

2.2.2.1.1.6 The importance of the LXX

The LXX is of great significance in biblical studies because its text differs profoundly from the other textual witnesses (e.g. the Masoretic Text, the Targumim, the Qumran Text). It is also crucial "as a reflection of early biblical exegesis, Jewish-Greek culture, and the Greek language," and as an understanding of "early Christianity since much of the vocabulary and some religious ideas of the NT are based on it."[53] Moreover, it serves "as the basis for virtually all the oriental translations and indeed for the Latin translation too."[54]

2.2.2.1.2 The Targumim

Targum תַּרְגּוּם is both an Aramaic and Hebrew word, meaning "translation." It is often used in its Hebrew plural form (i.e. Targumim תַּרְגּוּמִים).[55] In rabbinic literature, the Targum is employed "almost exclusively for the translation of the Bible . . . into Aramaic" even though sometimes for translations into Greek.[56]

---

50. Bernard M. Zlotowitz, *The Septuagint Translation of the Hebrew Terms in Relation to God in the Book of Jeremiah* (New York: KTAV, 1981), 13.

51. Arthur Soffer, "The Treatment of Anthropomorhisms and Anthropopathisms in the Septuagint," in *Studies in the Septuagint: Origins, Recensions, and Interpretations: Selected Essays, with a Prolegomenon by Sidney Jellicoe*, ed. Harry M. Orlinsky (New York: KTAV, 1974), 86.

52. Sysling, "Translation Techniques," 291.

53. Tov, *Textual Criticism*, 128.

54. Wasserstein and Wasserstein, *Legend of the Septuagint*, 96.

55. Paul V. M. Flesher and Bruce D. Chilton, *The Targums: A Critical Introduction* (Waco, TX: Baylor University Press, 2011), 7.

56. Alberdina Houtman and Harry Sysling, *Alternative Targum Traditions: The Use of Variant Readings for the Study in Origin and History of Targum Jonathan*, Studies in the Aramaic Interpretation of Scripture 9 (Leiden; Boston: Brill, 2009), 9, 16.

2.2.2.1.2.1 The origin of the Targumim

As mentioned above, Nehemiah 8:7–8 gives an account of the first *oral* practice of Bible translation (into Aramaic) in ca. 532 BC, earlier than the initial production of the LXX in ca. 275 BC. Although in postexilic Judaism Hebrew was "still understood and used in intellectual circles, especially among theologians," the knowledge of it began to wane.[57] This was because Aramaic as the language of the Upper Euphrates region became the official written language during the periods of the Neo-Babylonian (627–538 BC) and Persian empires (538–331 BC) and therefore replaced Hebrew as the dominant language of the Jewish people.[58]

The *oral* rendering of the Hebrew Scriptures, starting from Ezra's time in the postexilic community, lasted for some four centuries. They were then put into writing between the second century BC and the fifth century CE.[59] It is worth noting that the written form of the Aramaic translation was prohibited in rabbinic era (ca. from first to fifth centuries)[60] because the Hebrew Scriptures, for rabbis, should be credited with greater respect and honor than a translation.

Accordingly, in synagogal worship, after the sacred Hebrew Scriptures were read, a simultaneous interpreter with softer voice would explain the meaning in Aramaic *from memory*. Some synagogues might have observed the rabbinic teaching, but many did not, partly because of the difficulty of interpretation in Aramaic from memory. This difficulty necessitated the written form of the Targumim,[61] which "also served a purpose in private devotional study and in the school system."[62]

2.2.2.1.2.2 The Targum texts and translation techniques

A series of Targumim, each one with its own history, is known today and can be classified according to their dialects.

---

57. Würthwein, *Text of the Old Testament*, 79.
58. David G. Burke, "The First Versions: The Septuagint, the Targums, and the Latin," in *A History of Bible Translation*, ed. Philip A. Noss (Roma: Edizioni di storia e letteratura, 2007), 75.
59. Burke, "First Versions," 35.
60. Beckwith, *Old Testament Canon*, 26.
61. Flesher and Chilton, *Targums*, 5–6.
62. Houtman and Sysling, *Alternative Targum Traditions*, 10.

The first Aramaic dialect, Jewish Literary Aramaic, is a dialect employed around Judea from ca. 200 BC to ca. 200 CE. Targum Onqelos to the Pentateuch and Targum Jonathan to the Prophets were written in Jewish Literary Aramaic. Both of them were credited with an official status and found favor in Babylonia even though they were composed in Judea.[63] Targum Onqelos, the oldest and the most authoritative Targum, represented a rather literal translation of the Hebrew text except the poetical section containing many exegetical elements.[64] Targum Jonathan, in general, resembled Onqelos in style, language, and approach, although it contained more additional materials than Onqelos.[65]

The second Aramaic dialect used in translation is Jewish Palestinian Aramaic, also called Galilean Aramaic, which began to appear in the late second or early third CE. Jewish Palestinian Aramaic was employed to compose the Palestinian Targumim for the Pentateuch, including (1) Targum Neofiti, a nearly complete rendering of the entire Pentateuch, (2) the Fragment-Targumim containing renderings of merely 850 isolated verses, phrases, or words, and (3) the fragmentary remains of approximately thirty-eight Palestinian Targumim discovered in the Cairo Geniza.[66] These Targumim combined literal translations of the Hebrew text with a considerable amount of additional interpretative, sometimes even highly creative, material (plus, paraphrases, glosses).[67]

The third dialect used in translation is Late Jewish Literary Aramaic, which, based on Jewish Literary Aramaic and Jewish Palestinian Aramaic, absorbed lexical items from Syriac and Babylonian Aramaic. This dialect was used to compose Targum Pseudo-Jonathan for the Pentateuch and the Targumim for most of the books of the Writings later in, or sometimes

---

63. Flesher and Chilton, *Targums*, 9.

64. Tov, *Textual Criticism*, 149; Stephen A. Kaufman, "Targums," in *The New Interpreter's Dictionary of the Bible*, vol. 5, ed. Katharine D. Sakenfeld (Nashville, TN: Abingdon, 2009), 471.

65. Tov, *Textual Criticism*, 150; Brotzman, *Old Testament Textual Criticism*, 70.

66. Flesher and Chilton, *Targums*, 10; Metzger, *Bible in Translation*, 21; Brotzman, *Old Testament Textual Criticism*, 7; Sysling, "Translation Techniques," 293.

67. Flesher and Chilton, *Targums*, 10; Cécile Dogniez, "Some Similarities between the Septugint and the Targum of Zechariah," in *Translating a Translation: The LXX and Its Modern Translations in the Context of Early Judaism*, ed. H. Ausloos et al., Bibliotheca Ephemeridum Theologicarum Lovaniensium 213 (Leuven ; Dudley, MA: Peeters, 2008), 91.

even after, the rabbinic period. Pseudo-Jonathan originated its translation from Targum Onqelos though it looked more like one of the Palestinian Targumim. The incorporation of more than fifteen hundred of its own additions into the rendering made Pseudo-Jonathan quite a different document. As to the Targumim for the various books of the Writings, it is worth noting that they were composed individually, and, thus, were not regarded as a group like the Pentateuchal or Prophetic Targumim.[68] Each translation had its own unique characteristics. For instance, the Targum to the Psalms combined strict literalism with extreme paraphrase. The Targumim to the five Megilloth are extremely paraphrastic.[69]

The Targum of Proverbs was the only one that did not fit any one of the three dialects. Based on the Peshiṭta version of Proverbs, it is written "in a dialect that mixes Syriac and Jewish Palestinian Aramaic."[70]

The preceding statements regarding translation techniques are only general descriptions. Like the LXX, the translation methods used in individual Targumim call for scrutinies, such as the avoidance of anthropomorphism[71] and the converse translation, giving a sense opposite to the plain meaning of Scripture.[72]

2.2.2.1.2.3 *The importance of the Targumim*

The value of the Targumim consists in their contribution to Aramaic, Jewish exegetical traditions (i.e. halakhic and haggadic),[73] and textual criticism.[74]

---

68. Flesher and Chilton, *Targums*, 10–11.
69. Brotzman, *Old Testament Textual Criticism*, 72.
70. Flesher and Chilton, *Targums*, 11.
71. Kaufman, "Targums," 472; Sysling, "Translation Techniques," 299; Philip S. Alexander, "Jewish Aramaic Translations of Hebrew Scriptures," in *Mikra: Text, Translation, Reading and Interpretation of the Hebrew Bible in Ancient Judaism and Early Christianity*, eds. Martin Jan Mulder and Harry Sysling (Peabody, MA: Hendrickson, 2004 [1988]), 226.
72. Sysling, "Translation Techniques," 301; Alexander, "Jewish Aramaic Translations," 228; Michael L. Klein, "Converse Translation: A Targumic Technique," *Biblica* 57, no. 4 (1976): 515–537.
73. Barrera, *Jewish Bible and the Christian Bible*, 330.
74. Tov, *Textual Criticism*, 149.

2.2.2.2 Ancient Versions Intended Chiefly for Christians

Ancient versions intended chiefly for Christians can be grouped into two categories: early Eastern versions of the Bible and early Western versions of the Bible.[75]

2.2.2.2.1 Early Eastern versions of the Bible

The main early Eastern Bible versions produced before the seventh century CE can be divided into three categories:[76]

- The primary translations rendered directly from the original text: such as the Syriac Peshiṭta and the Coptic New Testament.
- The secondary translations rendered from the primary translations, mainly from the LXX: such as the Armenian, Coptic (both Sahidic and Bohairic OTs), Syro-Hexapla (a Syriac version), and Ethiopic (Ge'ez).
- The tertiary translations translated from secondary translations: such as the Georgian.

Space constraints do not allow comprehensive examinations of the translations above. Therefore, the present study will briefly explore the primary translation that is the most important and authorized by the church of the East (i.e. the Syriac Peshiṭta).[77]

2.2.2.2.1.1 The Syriac Peshiṭta

Syriac was an Aramaic dialect that was similar to Hebrew[78] spoken in Edessa and north-Western Mesopotamia. Especially, it was "very close to the Aramaic used in Palestine at the time of Jesus and the Apostles."[79] The word Peshiṭta (ܦܫܝܛܬܐ) often bears the adjectival meaning "straight, simple, obvious," deriving from the feminine form of the passive participle of the

---

75. Wegner, *Journey from Texts to Translations*, 244, 252.
76. Jinbachian, "Introduction," 30; Metzger, *Bible in Translation*, 13–50; Wegner, *Journey from Texts to Translations*, 244–252.
77. Metzger, *Bible in Translation*, 25; George M. Lamsa, *The Holy Bible from Ancient Eastern Manuscripts: Containing the Old and New Testaments Translated from the Peshitta, the Authorized Bible of the Church of the East* (Philadelphia: A. J. Holman, 1957).
78. Metzger, *Bible in Translation*, 26.
79. Jinbachian, "Introduction," 36.

verb *pešaṭ*, "to stretch out, to extend."[80] The Syriac church employed "the Peshiṭta" (i.e. "the simple or plain [version]") to indicate the version of the OT in common use, but the exact meaning of this name remains uncertain.[81] As the Latin Vulgate in the West, the Peshiṭta found favor in the East.[82]

(1) The origin of the Syriac Peshiṭta

The designation "Peshiṭta" was found for the first time in the *Hexameron* of Moses bar Kefa (died 903 CE), who, referring to Jacob of Edessa's reports (ca. 700 CE), asserted that the Old Testament Peshiṭta originated in the time of Abgar (ca. second century), a believing king of Edessa who sent men to Jerusalem and to the region of Palestine for translating the Hebrew OT into Syriac.[83] However, in the absence of external confirmation, some modern scholars remain unconvinced of the origin and early history of the Old Testament Peshiṭta.[84]

Nevertheless, after further investigation made on the basis of its text, Weitzman points out that the Old Testament Peshiṭta was most likely produced by non-rabbinic Jewish translators (rather than Christian ones) in Edessa (instead of Adiabene). These translators were among a small Jewish community estranged from the rabbinic majority and eventually embracing Christianity.[85] As to the date of translation, Joosten, in line with Weitzman, insists that the earliest composition of the Old Testament Peshiṭta

---

80. Peter B. Dirksen, "The Old Testament Peshiṭta," in *Mikra: Text, Translation, Reading, and Interpretation of the Hebrew Bible in Ancient Judaism and Early Christianity*, eds. M. J. Mulder and H. Sysling (Peabody, MA: Hendrickson, 2004), 256; M. P. Weitzman, *The Syriac Version of the Old Testament: An Introduction* (Cambridge, UK; New York: Cambridge University Press, 1999), 2–3.

81. Würthwein, *Text of the Old Testament*, 85; see also Dirksen, "Old Testament Peshiṭta," 256.

82. C. S. C. Williams, "The History of the Text and Canon of the New Testament to Jerome," in *The Cambridge History of the Bible, Vol. 2: The West from the Fathers to the Reformation*, ed. G. W. H. Lampe (New York: Cambridge University Press, 2004), 36–37; Metzger, *Bible in Translation*, 25.

83. Dirksen, "Old Testament Peshiṭta," 255–256; Weitzman, *Syriac Version*, 248.

84. Dirksen, "Old Testament Peshiṭta," 255–256; Roberts, "Old Testament," 25; Metzger, *Bible in Translation*, 26; Robert F. Shedinger, "Did Tatian Use the Old Testament Peshitta? A Response to Jan Joosten," *Novum Testamentum* 41, no. 3 (1999): 278; Brotzman, *Old Testament Textual Criticism*, 81.

85. Weitzman, *Syriac Version*, 244–247.

(Pentateuch) was no later than 150 CE.[86] This is because the Old Testament Peshiṭta was one of the sources for Tatian's Diatessaron composed in ca. 170 CE,[87] which was the earliest known harmony of the four Gospels.[88] As to the date of the last books (i.e. Chronicles and Ezra-Nehemiah), Weitzman suggests that they were rendered in ca. 200 CE.[89]

(2) Translation techniques in the Syriac Peshiṭta

For early revisers of the Old Testament Peshiṭta, the text before them called for an update of the language to make it more accessible. The revisers' move of the Old Testament Peshiṭta away from the Hebrew original led to "a fuller and more idiomatic text."[90] The early revision operated "within the closed field of the Peshiṭta text, without reference to any outside authority."[91] In the fifth century, the breakup of the Syriac-speaking church into mutually hostile sects probably terminated the further revision of the Old Testament Peshiṭta. This seems to explain why the schisms were not reflected in an obvious textual division between East, the Nestorians, and West, the Jacobites.[92]

By the seventh century, the literal translation approach became dominant, which, "together with increased regard for the accuracy of LXX, led Paul of Tella in 615–17 CE to make the Syrohexapla, a literal Syriac translation of the fifth column of Origen's Hexapla."[93] However, the Old Testament Peshiṭta was not supplanted by this version, nor by Jacob of Edessa's version done in ca. 705 CE, which was a combination of the plain wording of the

---

86. Jan Joosten, "The Old Testament Quotations in the Old Syriac and Peshitta Gospels: A Contribution to the Study of the Diatessaron," *Textus*, no. 15 (1990): 74–76; Jan Joosten, "Tatian's Diatessaron and the OT Peshitta," *Journal of Biblical Literature* 120, no. 3 (2001): 509; Jan Joosten, "The Old Testament in the New: The Syriac Versions of the New Testament as a Witness to the Text of the OT Peshitta," in *The Peshitta: Its Uses in Literature and Liturgy: Papers Read at the Third Peshitta Symposium*, ed. B. ter Haar Romeny (Leiden; Boston: Brill, 2006), 102–103; Weitzman, *Syriac Version*, 258; see also Janet M. Magiera, *Aramaic Peshitta New Testament Translation: With Explanatory Footnotes Marking Variant Readings, Customs, and Figures of Speech* (San Diego: Light of the Word Ministry, 2006), 8.

87. Joosten's argument has been fiercely challenged by Shedinger (1999) in his *Did Tatian Use the Old Testament Peshitta? A Response to Jan Joosten*.

88. Wegner, *Journey from Texts to Translations*, 245.

89. Weitzman, *Syriac Version*, 258.

90. Weitzman, 300–301.

91. Weitzman, 300–301.

92. Weitzman, 300–301.

93. Weitzman, 62.

Old Testament Peshiṭta and the accurate wording of the Syrohexapla. In the ninth century, the Old Testament Peshiṭta developed into a *textus receptus* (standard text) accepted by both the East and West Syriac-speaking church.[94]

The diversity of translators is manifested in the variety of the style and quality of the translations. For example, while the Pentateuch and the Song of Songs are very literal, the Psalms and Minor Prophets are free translations. Ruth is a paraphrastic rendering. Moreover, the inclusion of non-Hebraic books of the Apocrypha in the Old Testament Peshiṭta manuscripts demonstrates the influence of the LXX.[95]

As for the New Testament Peshiṭta, it was "the result of a revision of the old Syriac version with the text adapted to the Greek text known in Antioch"[96] at the beginning of the fifth century.[97] This revision preserved a myriad of elements of the Old Syriac, but also repaired certain omissions and refined sentences without impairing its faithfulness to the Greek.[98] The New Testament Peshiṭta, lacking 2 Peter, 2 and 3 John, Jude, and Revelation, became the authoritative biblical text of the Syriac-speaking church.[99]

(3) The importance of the Syriac Peshiṭta

The Old Testament Peshiṭta is "the earliest translation of the whole [OT] canon into another Semitic language. It is thus potentially an important witness to the biblical text."[100] The Syriac Peshiṭta is the basis of translations in other languages, such as the Sogdian and some of the Arabic versions.[101]

---

94. Weitzman, 303.

95. Metzger, *Bible in Translation*, 27.

96. Barrera, *Jewish Bible and the Christian Bible*, 360; see also Andreas Juckel, "Research on the Old Syriac Heritage of the Peshitta Gospels. A Collation of MS Bibl. Nationale Syr. 30 (Paris)," *Hugoye: Journal of Syriac Studies* 12, no. 1 (2009): 114.

97. Metzger, *Bible in Translation*, 28.

98. Barrera, *Jewish Bible and the Christian Bible*, 360; Williams, "History of the Text," 36.

99. P. J. Williams, "Versions, Ancient," in *The New Interpreter's Dictionary of the Bible*, vol. 5, ed. Katharine D. Sakenfeld (Nashville, TN: Abingdon, 2007), 733; Metzger, *Bible in Translation*, 28.

100. Weitzman, *Syriac Version*, 2; see also Dirksen, "Old Testament Peshiṭta," 258–259; Wegner, *Journey from Texts to Translations*, 246.

101. Metzger, *Bible in Translation*, 29.

Moreover, through Syriac language and literature Greek culture passed to the East and later to the Islamic world.[102]

2.2.2.2.2 Early Western versions of the Bible

The main early Western Bible versions produced before the seventh century CE include the *Vetus Latina* (the Old Latin), the Latin Vulgate, and the Gothic. Among them only the Latin Vulgate is a primary translation,[103] which will be discussed below.

2.2.2.2.2.1 The Latin Vulgate

The Vulgate, produced by Jerome (ca. 342–420) (see §2.3.2.1), a biblical translator and exegete with linguistic and philological competence,[104] served as a sacred text in the Western church for more than a thousand years, "extending the influence of the Latin language through time and over geographical realms further than the Roman Empire had ever reached."[105] According to Metzger, it is almost impossible to calculate the impact of the Vulgate which penetrated into all areas of Western culture.[106] The Vulgate, meaning "the most common text," was a term never used for the title of the Latin translation by Jerome himself, but started to appear in the sixteenth century.[107]

Jerome also made great contributions to Bible translation, such as his letter to Pammachius, "The best kind of translator," composed in Bethlehem in 395, becoming "the founding document of Christian translation theory."[108]

---

102. Barrera, *Jewish Bible and the Christian Bible*, 358.
103. Jinbachian, "Introduction," 30; Wegner, *Journey from Texts to Translations*, 252–258.
104. Andrew Cain and Josef Lössl, "Introduction," in *Jerome of Stridon: His Life, Writings and Legacy*, eds. Andrew Cain and Josef Lössl (Farnham; Burlington, VT: Ashgate, 2009), 4.
105. Noss, "History of Bible Translation," 16.
106. Metzger, *Bible in Translation*, 29.
107. Burke, "First Versions," 84; Michelle P. Brown, "Spreading the Word," in *In the Beginning: Bibles before the Year 1000*, ed. Michelle P. Brown (Washington, DC: Freer Gallery of Art & Arthur M. Sackler Gallery, Smithsonian Institution, 2006), 56.
108. Douglas Robinson, *Western Translation Theory: From Herodotus to Nietzsche* (Manchester, UK: St Jerome, 1997), 23.

(1) The origin of the Latin Vulgate

Because of the increasing number of Latin-speaking Christians, there was a growing variety of Old Latin translations from the Greek.[109] The Old Latin versions were carried out by "various people, at various times and in various places, with various degrees of success."[110] Pope Damasus in 383 entrusted Jerome with the task of producing a uniform and dependable Latin translation.[111]

(2) The development

Jerome first revised the Old Latin Gospels in light of the Greek New Testament, and these appeared in 383 CE.[112] Due to the reverence for the Old Latin, he tended to retain its wording when the distinction in meaning between Old Latin and Greek was negligible.[113] Jerome also kept the order of Gospels found in the Old Latin (i.e. Matthew, John, Luke and Mark), and paid particular attention to certain passages because of their eminence in the liturgy.[114]

Apart from the revision of the Gospels, Jerome also translated the OT books from the Hebrew text, the version of Tobit and Judith. But the remaining of the NT and deuterocanonical books were probably translated by his follower Rufinus the Syrian.[115] Unfortunately, Jerome's project, which was finished by ca. 405 CE, employing the Hebrew to revise translations based on the Greek OT, was viewed as controversial. This explains why the reception of the OT revision made by Jerome was slower than that of the NT.[116]

One of the most notable opponents of Jerome's OT translation was Augustine, who thought that "this move to the Hebrew text away from the

---

109. C. Brown Tkacz, "Labor Tam Utilis: The Creation of the Vulgate," *Vigiliae Christianae* 50, no. 1 (1996): 45.

110. Bruce M. Metzger, *The Early Versions of the New Testament: Their Origin, Transmission, and Limitations* (Oxford: Clarendon, 1977), 330.

111. Williams, "Versions, Ancient," 733; Metzger, *Bible in Translation*, 32; Wegner, *Journey from Texts to Translations*, 254.

112. Williams, "Versions, Ancient," 733; cf. Tkacz, "Labor Tam Utilis," 48.

113. Metzger, *Bible in Translation*, 33; Tkacz, "Labor Tam Utilis," 48.

114. Barrera, *Jewish Bible and the Christian Bible*, 355; Tkacz, "Labor Tam Utilis," 48.

115. Burke, "First Versions," 85; Metzger, *Bible in Translation*, 33; Barrera, *Jewish Bible and the Christian Bible*, 355.

116. Williams, "Versions, Ancient," 733.

Septuagint would prove treacherous in that it would undermine the authority of the Greek text."[117] But Jerome himself maintained that "recourse to the Hebrew text was the way to solve differences between translations."[118] He further pointed out that Christians were supposed to consult the Hebrew OT because Jesus and the Apostles quoted and alluded to the Old Testament supposedly according to the Hebrew.[119]

By the eighth or ninth century the Old Latin was replaced by Jerome's Latin version, which eventually reached its climax when the Council of Trent proclaimed the Vulgate as the authentic and authoritative Bible of the Roman Catholic Church on 8 April 1546.[120]

(3) Translation techniques in the Latin Vulgate

In his own writing, including his letters, his prefaces[121] and prologues to his translations of biblical books, Jerome demonstrated his serious respect for literary dimensions of the Scriptures.[122] He not only analyzed the styles, meters, and formats of the Scriptures, but also directly and indirectly compared the biblical books to classical literature. These comparisons, demonstrating Jerome's thoughts and comments, were discussed in his biblical prefaces and prologues, which have proved very valuable to later scholars.[123]

While translating Scripture,[124] Jerome believed "the very order of the words of Scripture is a mystery" transcending human knowledge; therefore,

---

117. Augustine cited in Burke, "First Versions," 87–88; see also Benjamin Kedar, "The Latin Translations," in *Mikra: Text, Translation, Reading and Interpretation of the Hebrew Bible in Ancient Judaism and Early Christianity*, eds. Martin J. Mulder and Harry Sysling (Peabody, MA: Hendrickson, 2004 [1988]), 320; Metzger, *Bible in Translation*, 34; Wegner, *Journey from Texts to Translations*, 255; Barrera, *Jewish Bible and the Christian Bible*, 356.

118. Jerome cited in John Cameron, "The Rabbinic Vulgate?," in *Jerome of Stridon: His Life, Writings and Legacy*, eds. Andrew Cain and Josef Lössl (Farnham; Burlington, VT: Ashgate, 2009), 124.

119. Jerome cited in Cameron, "Rabbinic Vulgate?," 124.

120. Burke, "First Versions," 88; Brown, "Spreading the Word," 56; Wegner, *Journey from Texts to Translations*, 255.

121. The first introduction of full prefaces into the Bible, a practice borrowed from classical literature, made Jerome a unique translator in ancient Bible translation history. See Tkacz, "Labor Tam Utilis," 43.

122. Tkacz, 43.

123. Tkac, "Labor Tam Utilis," 43"; Burke, "First Versions," 88.

124. Apart from Bible translation, Jerome was in line with Cicero and Horace (see §2.3.2.1) who both in theory and practice clung to the rhetorical method of translating for sense, not word for word. See Charles L. Stinger, *Humanism and the Church Fathers:*

a translator "must preserve the order so as not to endanger the profundity of the text."[125] However, Jerome, in practice, failed to follow this dictum rigorously in order to make figures of speech intelligible. For example, the Prophets and Psalms are more literal, but the books of Joshua, Judges, Ruth, and Esther are freer.[126]

(4) The importance of the Latin Vulgate

The Vulgate was used as the dominant Bible text throughout the Western church for nearly one thousand years and profoundly influenced the various Reformation-era vernacular translations in Europe,[127] such as Wycliffe's English translation (fourteenth century), followed by the first printed Bible in German (1466), Italian (1471), Catalán (1478), Czech (1488), and French (1530).[128] It was also viewed as "a great and definitely a most influential literary accomplishment" and was the focus of theological debates and scholarly studies.[129] Significantly, Jerome's vision to work from the Hebrew directly enabled the Hebraic spirit to continue to influence subsequent human affairs as Kedar writes, "Israelite and Jewish emotion and thought from earliest beginnings on down to the times of Jesus, were passed on unto the new centres of civilization and their letters. Dozen[s] of fundamental concepts and a thousand phrases were transferred from Hebrew into Latin, and then from Latin into modern tongues."[130]

After this short overview of the history of Bible translation before the seventh century, it is now time to switch the historical stage to Cháng ān in China, where the first Chinese Bible (partial) was produced in the seventh century.

Ambrogio Traversari (1386-1439) and Christian Antiquity in the Italian Renaissance (Albany: State University of New York Press, 1977), 101.

125. Stinger, *Humanism*, 101.
126. Burke, "First Versions," 88.
127. Burke, 89; Kedar, "Latin Translations," 335; Metzger, *Bible in Translation*, 35; Wegner, *Journey from Texts to Translations*, 254.
128. Metzger, *Bible in Translation*, 35.
129. Kedar, "Latin Translations," 335.
130. Kedar, 335.

2.2.3 A Brief History and Major Issues of Chinese Bible Translation

2.2.3.1 Introduction

While there are some Chinese Bible translations written in dialects or produced for tribes,[131] this study will mainly investigate Chinese Bible versions using formal written language. The only exception is Mandarin, a dialect of Běi jīng, which became the official written and spoken language of China in 1932, known as modern standard Chinese.[132]

The history of Chinese Bible translation can be divided into four periods: (1) the starting period (from Táng Dynasty to 1807), (2) the expansion period (1807–1854), (3) the popularizing period (1854–1919), and (4) the enculturating period (1919–present).[133]

2.2.3.2 The Starting Period (from the Táng Dynasty to 1807)

The enterprise of translating the Bible into Chinese in this period was conducted by individual Nestorians and Catholic missionaries. The large-scale practice of Bible translation had not yet been launched.[134]

---

131. Róu Yù Zhuāng 莊柔玉, 基督教聖經中文譯本權威現象研究 [A study of the phenomenon of authoritativeness in the Chinese translations of the Protestant Bible], 譯經叢書 [Monograph series on Bible translation 1] (Hong Kong: International Bible Society, 2000), 14; A. J. Garnier 賈立言, "漢文聖經本小史" [Chinese versions of the Bible], in 新約聖經流傳史略—附漢文聖經本小史(賈立言 著) [The New Testament and its transmission: With an essay on the Chinese versions of the Bible by Garnier], ed. George Milligan (Hong Kong: Shí zhēn Publishing House, 1999 [1934]), 137–146; Marshall Broomhall, *The Bible in China* (London; Toronto: China Inland Mission, 1934), 98–124.

132. "Modern Standard Chinese," 2014, http://zh.wikipedia.org/wiki/现代標準漢語. Before 1932, the official spoken language used by each dynasty was mainly influenced by the location of the capital. See, "The Official Spoken Language in Ancient China," 2017, http://mypage.direct.ca/w/wfung/heshantongyi/Chinese%20Antiquity%20Language/Chinese%20Antiquity%20Language.html. A fully developed Chinese written system can be traced back to the Shang dynasty (14th to 11th BC). Due to the few examples of writing that precede the fourteenth century, it is hard to reconstruct the process of how it reached its mature stage. See Jerry Norman, "The Beginnings of Chinese Writing," in *Classical Chinese Literature: An Anthology of Translations*, eds. John Minford and Joseph S. M. Lau (New York: Columbia University Press; Hong Kong: Chinese University Press, 2000), 6–7. A general designation for the formal written language before 1932 is "classical Chinese" (文言文 *wén yán wén*), which can be classified into three separate categories according to Milne: the high, middle, and low styles (see §2.2.3.3.1). These styles were used in the composition of early versions of the Chinese Bible (for more details, see the discussions below).

133. Zhuāng 莊, 基督教聖經中文譯本權威現象研究 [A study of the phenomenon of authoritativeness in the Chinese translations of the Protestant Bible], 16–17.

134. Zhuāng 莊, 16.

2.2.3.2.1 Nestorian Bible translation activities

As noted above, the schisms in the fifth century caused the Syriac-speaking church to split into two hostile groups – the Nestorians (East Syriac) who were later condemned as heretics by the Council of Ephesus in 431,[135] and the Jacobites (West Syriac). The former appeared to have taken the gospel as far as China.

大秦景教流行中國碑 *dà qín jǐng jiāo liú háng zhōng guó bēi* (The Nestorian Stele)[136] was the earliest evidence of the coming of Christianity to China, and of Bible translation into Chinese in the seventh century. A nine-foot-high marble Stele was erected in Cháng ān (now Xī ān) in 781[137] to commemorate the propagation of gospel during the Táng Dynasty (618–910 CE).[138] 1,780 Chinese characters and some Syriac letters were inscribed on it, composed in classical Chinese (文言文 *wén yán wén*)[139] by a Nestorian monk named Adam (also known as 景淨 Jǐng Jìng) to describe the history of Nestorian Christianity from its beginnings in China. Adam reported the arrival of a delegation of Nestorians led by their bishop Alopen in Cháng ān in 635 with 530 scriptures in Syriac and icons of Christ, Mary, and the saints.[140]

---

135. Toshikazu S. Foley, *Biblical Translation in Chinese and Greek: Verbal Aspect in Theory and Practice* (Leiden; Boston: Brill, 2009), 6.

136. 大秦景教流行中國碑 *dà qín jǐng jiāo liú uan zhōng guó bēi* literally means "Memorial of the Propagation in China of the Luminous Religion from Dà-qín" (Dà-qín probably refers to Syria or Persia, or even the Roman empire), whose different English titles include: the Nestorian Monument, Nestorian Stone, and Nestorian Inscription. See Daniel H. Bays, *A New History of Christianity in China*, Blackwell Guides to Global Christianity (Chichester; Malden, MA: Wiley-Blackwell, 2012), 7; Foley, *Biblical Translation*, 6.

137. It was around 1623 CE when the Nestorian Stele was unearthed in the neighborhood of Xī ān. See Bays, *New History of Christianity*, 7; Bì Chǔ Zhào 趙壁礎, 重譯景教碑 [Re-translating the Nestorian Stele], 中華民族探源叢書: 景教歷史系列 [The history of the Luminous Religion 1] (Austin, TX: Bì Chǔ Bookstore, 2006), 3–10.

138. During the Táng Dynasty, the Chinese people were unified politically and linguistically. The official spoken language of the Táng Dynasty was 河洛話 *hé luò huà*. See "The Official Spoken Language in Ancient China." The formal written language was classical Chinese (文言文 *wén yán wén*).

139. For the researcher, the classical Chinese used in the Stele might be identified as the high style in terms of Milne's scheme, which is remarkably concise (see §2.2.3.3.1).

140. Bays, *New History of Christianity*, 7–9; Foley, *Biblical Translation*, 6; Jìng Mín Fù 傅敬民, 聖經漢譯的文化資本解讀 [The cultural and capital interpretation of translating the Bible into Chinese] (Shàng Hǎi: Fù Dàn University Publisher, 2009), 82–83; Shù Lín Tán 譚樹林, 馬禮遜與中西文化交流 [Robert Morrison and Sino-Western cultural communication] (Hangzhou: Chinese Academy of Fine Arts Press, 2003), 99; Zhuāng 莊, 基督教聖經中文譯本權威現象研究 [A study of the phenomenon of authoritativeness in

The delegation was "formally greeted and escorted in a dignified procession to the emperor."[141]

As to the time of translating the Bible into Chinese, after examining critical evidence, such as the original text of the Nestorian Stele[142] and the list of biblical books discovered at Dūn huáng Stone Cave in Shā zhōu in 1908,[143] Foley asserts that "early Nestorian missionaries probably had begun translating at least parts of the Bible into Chinese almost immediately upon their arrival in the mid-seventh century."[144] Nowadays, these renderings are known as 景教文典 *Jǐng jiào Classics*.[145]

In order to produce translations accepted by the Chinese, Nestorian missionaries contextualized the Christian message in the formal Chinese

---

the Chinese translations of the Protestant Bible], 9–10; Wéi Běn Zhào 趙維本, 譯經溯源: 現代五大中文聖經翻譯史 [Tracing Bible translation: A history of the translation of five modern Chinese versions of the Bible] (Hong Kong: China Graduate School of Theology, 1993), 8; Broomhall, *Bible in China*, 16–17.

141. Bays, *New History of Christianity*, 9; see the Stele, "賓迎入內 *bīn yíng rù nèi*."

142. The Nestorian Stele reported the actual translation activities: "翻經建寺、存歿舟航 *fān jīng jiàn sì, cún mò zhōu uan* (The Scriptures were translated, and churches were built, so that the living and the dead would be saved; translation mine)." See Shàng Yǔ Chén 陳上宇, "《大秦景教流行中國碑》—碑文：譯文、原文、英文" [The Nestorian Stele-inscription: Modern Chinese translation, original text, English translation], 2011, http://blog.sina.com.cn/s/blog_621e6d160102dukl.html; Zhào 趙, 重譯景教碑 [Re-translating the Nestorian Stele], 52.

143. There were only a few preserved biblical texts from the Táng Dynasty, but the Chinese translated titles of canonical books discovered at Dūn huáng Stone Cave proved the practice of Bible translation at the time. The titles of books include 渾元經 *Hún uan jīng* (Genesis), 牟世法王經 *Móu shì fǎ wáng jīng* (the book of Moses), 刪河律經 *Shān hé lǜ jīng* (Zechariah), 寶路法王經 *Bǎo lù fǎ wáng jīng* (Epistle(s) of St Paul), and 啟真經 *Qǐ zhēn jīng* (Revelation). See Foley, *Biblical Translation*, 7; Zhào 趙, 譯經溯源 [Tracing Bible translation], 9–10; Wéi Fán Wāng 汪維藩, "聖經譯本在中國" [The Chinese versions of the Bible], *Studies in World Religions* 49, no. 1 (1992): 71–84.

144. Foley, *Biblical Translation*, 6–9; see also Fù 傅, 聖經漢譯的文化資本解讀 [The cultural and capital interpretation of translating the Bible into Chinese], 83–84; Zhào 趙, 譯經溯源 [Tracing Bible translation], 9–10.

145. The existing 景教文典 *Jǐng jiào Classics (or Nestorian Classics)* includes four passages extracting from the Bible: 序聽迷詩所經 *Xù tīng mí shī suǒ jīng*, 一神論 *Yī shén lùn* of the early Táng Dynasty, 宣元至本經 *Xuān uan zhì běn jīng*, and 至玄安樂經 *Zhì xuán ān lè jīng* of the middle/late Táng Dynasty. See Dōng Shēng Rèn 任東升, 聖經漢譯文化研究 [Study on the translation of Bible translation into Chinese] (Hú běi: Hú běi education press, 2007), 162; Shào Jūn Wēng 翁紹軍, 漢語景教文典詮釋 [Sino-Nestorian document: Commentary and exegesis], 歷代基督教思想學術文庫 [Chinese academic library of Christian thought in history 102] (Hong Kong: Institute of Sino-Christian Studies, 1995), 9; Qián Zhī Zhǔ 朱謙之, 中國景教 [The Luminous religion in China] (Běi jīng, China: Dōng-fāng Publishing House, 1993), 112.

language (i.e. classical Chinese). They not only used concepts from indigenous dominant philosophical-religious traditions in China, such as Confucianism and Taoism, but also adopted terms from Buddhism, a foreign religion introduced to China in the early first century CE.[146]

In spite of Nestorian missionaries' zeal to evangelize the Chinese through enculturation, there were no Christians left in China in the tenth century.[147] Though scholars have not reached a consensus yet in terms of the causes of the decline and disappearance of Táng Christianity, there are two factors worthy of particular attention: Táng wǔ zōng's destroying Buddha event and the enculturation of the gospel. The former was related to a decree from the throne in 845, cracking down on foreign religions, especially Buddhism.[148] It is worth noting that near the end of the edict the emperor added, "余僧及尼並大秦穆護，祆僧皆勒歸俗 *yú sēng jí ní bìng dà qín mù hù, yāo sēng jiē lè guī sú*,"[149] referring to the Nestorians (大秦 Dà qín) and believers of other foreign religions who were compelled to return to lay life. This was disastrous for the Nestorians. Many think the Nestorians made the situation worse, by attempting to enculturate the gospel through borrowing of terms from Buddhism and Daoism. This supposedly led to "Christianity's loss of doctrinal integrity and its fading from the scene."[150]

---

146. Foley, *Biblical Translation*, 9–10; Fù 傅, 聖經漢譯的文化資本解讀 [The cultural and capital interpretation of translating the Bible into Chinese], 89–96; Yàn Qín Zhāng 張艷琴, "析漢語景教經典的改寫譯經思想" [Analyzing the thought of rewriting and translation of Chinese Nestorian classics], *Journal of Ji-Nan University (Philosophy and Social Sciences)* 28, no. 6 (2006): 144.

147. Bays, *New History of Christianity*, 10; Fù 傅, 聖經漢譯的文化資本解讀 [The cultural and capital interpretation of translating the Bible into Chinese], 85; Broomhall, *Bible in China*, 25.

148. Bays, *New History of Christianity*, 10; Sēn Fù Yáng 楊森富, 中國基督教史 [History of Christianity in China], 4th ed. (Taipei: Taiwan shāng wù yìn shū guǎn, 1984), 167.

149. Guāng Sī-Mǎ 司馬光, 資治通鑑 [History as a mirror], vol. 248, 1071–1086, http://www.angelibrary.com/oldies/zztj/248.htm.

150. Bays, *New History of Christianity*, 10–11; see also Fù 傅, 聖經漢譯的文化資本解讀 [The cultural and capital interpretation of translating the Bible into Chinese], 85; Zhāng 張, "析漢語景教經典的改寫譯經思想" [Analyzing the thought of rewriting and translation of Chinese Nestorian classics], 145.

2.2.3.2.2 Catholic Bible translation activities

Catholic missionaries did not arrive in China until three centuries later when they resumed the task of translating Bible into Chinese.[151] In 1294, the Franciscan monk Giovanni da Montecorvino (1247–1328) reached Cambaluc (now Běi jīng) with Latin and Greek versions of the Bible, and later he translated the NT and Psalms into Mongolian, the official language of the Yuán Dynasty.[152]

In 1582, during the reign of Míng Dynasty (1368–1644), Father Matteo Ricci (1552–1610) and his fellow Jesuits first came to Macao, and the following year moved to mainland China.[153] They were involved in translating the Ten Commandments into Chinese.[154] Matteo Ricci also translated various works into Chinese in the hope that the translations would enhance evangelization efforts.[155] By 1637, with the Jesuit's efforts, more than 340 treatises in Chinese upon religion, philosophy, and other subjects were printed.[156]

About 1700, Jean Basset (1662–1707), belonging to Missions Étrangères,[157] translated the Gospels, Acts, Pauline Epistles, and parts of Hebrews from

---

151. Foley, *Biblical Translation*, 16; Fù 傅, 聖經漢譯的文化資本解讀 [The cultural and capital interpretation of translating the Bible into Chinese], 99; Broomhall, *Bible in China*, 25.

152. Foley, *Biblical Translation*, 16; Fù 傅, 聖經漢譯的文化資本解讀 [The cultural and capital interpretation of translating the Bible into Chinese], 99; Marián Gálik, *Influence, Translation, and Parallels: Selected Studies on the Bible in China* (Sankt Augustin, Germany: Monumenta Serica Institute, 2004), 81; Zhào 趙, 譯經溯源 [Tracing Bible translation], 11; Broomhall, *Bible in China*, 31.

153. Michela Fontana, *Matteo Ricci: A Jesuit in the Ming Court* (Lanham; Boulder; New York; Toronto; Plymouth, UK: Rowman & Littlefield, 2011), 33; Fù 傅, 聖經漢譯的文化資本解讀 [The cultural and capital interpretation of translating the Bible into Chinese], 105; Zhào 趙, 譯經溯源 [Tracing Bible translation], 12.

154. Garnier, "漢文聖經本小史" [Chinese versions of the Bible], 95; Guāng Luó 羅光, 利瑪竇傳 [The biography of Matteo Ricci] (Tái zhōng:Guāng Qǐ Publishing House, 1960), 168.

155. Eva Hung, "Translation in China: An Analytical Survey," in *Asian Translation Traditions*, eds. Eva Hung and Judy Wakabayashi (Manchester, UK; Northampton, MA: St Jerome, 2005), 92; Jacques Gernet, 中國與基督教 [China and Christianity] (Shanghai: Shanghai Classics, 2003), 8, 16; Henry Bernard, 天主教十六世紀在華傳教誌 [The Catholic Mission records of 16th century in China], trans. Xùn Huá Xiāo 蕭濬華 (Taipei: Taiwan shāng wù yìn shū guǎn, 1964), 262.

156. Broomhall, *Bible in China*, 35.

157. Jost Oliver Zetzsche, *The Bible in China: The History of the Union Version or the Culmination of Protestant Missionary Bible Translation in China*, Monumenta Serica Monograph Series 45 (Sankt Augustin, German: Monumenta Serica Institute, 1999), 28–29.

the Vulgate into Chinese.¹⁵⁸ A number of Basset's manuscripts survived and, in1739, were discovered in Guǎng dōng. Then, they were sent to Sir Hans Sloane of the Royal Society in London who in turn donated them to British Museum.¹⁵⁹ Thus, Basset's manuscripts, known as the Sloane Manuscript #3599, were later made available to pioneer Protestant translators, such as Robert Morrison and John Marshman.¹⁶⁰

Great strides in early Chinese Bible translation were made by Louis de Poirot, a Jesuit (1735–1813) who reached China in 1770¹⁶¹ and, by 1790, had translated almost the whole Bible from the Vulgate into colloquial Chinese, whose title was 古新聖經 Gǔ xīn shèng jīng.¹⁶² In the preface to his translation, de Poirot insisted on literal translation. He wrote: "那翻譯的名士 . . . 守全按著聖經的本文本意，不圖悅人聽 . . . 。 *nà fān yì de míng shì . . . shǒu quán àn zhe shèng jīng de běn wén běn yì, bù tú yuè rén tīng . . .* (The famous translators . . . translate rigorously according to the original meaning of the text of the Bible; they intend not to please the reader. . .)" (translated by the author).¹⁶³

Despite the long history of Catholic missionaries' activities in China, Bible translation was, for a long time, a private matter and not intended for public dissemination.¹⁶⁴ This perhaps explains why their influence on modern Bible translators is less than that of the Protestants. Some of the significant influences by early Catholic translators include the rendering of

---

158. Yáng 楊, 中國基督教史 [History of Christianity in China], 364; Hubert W. Spillett, *A Catalogue of Scriptures in the Languages of China and the Republic of China* (London: British and Foreign Bible Society, 1975), xi.

159. Tán 譚, 馬禮遜與中西文化交流 [Robert Morrison and Sino-Western cultural communication], 101; Mù Shì Xǔ 許牧世, "中文聖經翻譯簡史" [A brief history of Chinese Bible translation], *Jīng Fēng* 69 (1982): 36. Some of Basset's MSS are held at Hong Kong University (Fung Ping Shan Library) and a copy of the MSS is held in the library of the Studium Biblicum Franciscanum, Hong Kong.

160. Zhào 趙, 譯經溯源 [Tracing Bible translation], 18; A. C. Moule, "A Manuscript Chinese Version of the NT (British Museum, Sloane 3599)," *Journal of the Royal Asiatic Society* 85, no. 1 (1949): 23.

161. Zhào 趙, 譯經溯源 [Tracing Bible translation], 14.

162. Zetzsche, *Bible in China*, 27; Moule, "Manuscript Chinese," 33.

163. Tán 譚, 馬禮遜與中西文化交流 [Robert Morrison and Sino-Western cultural communication], 102.

164. Thor Strandenaes, *Principles of Chinese Bible Translation: As Expressed in Five Selected Versions of the New Testament and Exemplified by Mt 5 :1–12 and Col 1* (Uppsala, Sweden: Almqvist & Wiksell International, 1987), 20.

religious terminology into Chinese, e.g. "傳道 *chuán dào* (evangelism or preach the Word)," and the transliteration of biblical names, e.g. "耶穌 *Yē sū* (Jesus)."¹⁶⁵

It is worth noting that the first complete Catholic Bible in Chinese was not produced until 1968 when Allegra and his committee published their translation at Studium Biblicum Franciscanum.¹⁶⁶ This 150-year gap in activity since Louis de Poirot was "filled by the new vigorous forces of Protestant missionaries."¹⁶⁷

2.2.3.3 The Expansion Period (1807–1854)

Early Catholic Bible translation activities (late thirteenth–eighteenth century) were succeeded by efforts made by the Protestants during the expansion period, from the time of R. Morrison's arrival in China in 1807 to the publication of Delegates' version in 1854.¹⁶⁸

The most important achievement in this period was the production of the first-ever complete Bible in classical Chinese (深文理譯本 High *wén lǐ* versions) made almost simultaneously by Morrison and Milne in Guǎngdōng (1823), entitled 神天聖書 *Shén tiān shèng shū* (the Holy Bible),¹⁶⁹ and by Marshman and Lassar in India (1822).¹⁷⁰ These were followed by other High *wén lǐ* versions, such as those by Gützlaff and the Delegate.

---

165. Foley, *Biblical Translation*, 17; Matteo Ricci, 天主實義 (下卷) [The true meaning of the Lord of Heaven, vol. 2] (Taipei: Institute for National Defense and Security Research and Zhōng huá dà diǎn biān yìn huì, 1967 [1603]), 69–70.

166. Arnulf Camps, "Father Gabriele M. Allegra, O.F.M. (1907–1976) and the Studium Biblicum Franciscanum: The First Complete Chinese Catholic Translation of the Bible," in *Bible in Modern China: The Literary and Intellectual Impact*, eds. Irene Eber, Sze-kar Wan, and Knut Walf (Sankt Augustin: Institute Monumenta Serica, 1999), 68–69.

167. Foley, *Biblical Translation*, 18.

168. Zhuāng 莊, 基督教聖經中文譯本權威現象研究 [A study of the phenomenon of authoritativeness in the Chinese translations of the Protestant Bible], 16.

169. Morrison's 神天聖書 *Shén tiān shèng shū* (the Holy Bible) was recognized as the first complete Chinese Bible even though Marshman/Lassar's version was published one year earlier. This is because the translation activities of the former took place in China, but that of the latter in India. See Jīn Huá Mài 麥金華, 大英聖書公會與官話《和合本》聖經翻譯 [The British and Foreign Bible Society and the translation of the Mandarin Chinese Union version] (Hong Kong: Christian Study Center on Chinese Religion and Culture, 2010), 22.

170. Péng 彭, "Contemplating the Future of Chinese Bible Translation," 4; Zhào 趙, 譯經溯源 [Tracing Bible translation], 167; Broomhall, *Bible in China*, 50.

2.2.3.3.1 Morrison/Milne's version

Robert Morrison (1782–1834) of the London Missionary Society arrived in Guǎng dōng in 1807. A critical issue in Bible translation confronted by Morrison from the very beginning was the choice of appropriate Chinese style in translation. After examining Chinese literature, Morrison's colleague Milne identified three different styles in Chinese:[171] (1) a high style which is remarkably concise, such as the classical works 四書 *Sì shū (Four Books)* and 五經 *Wǔ jīng (Five Classics)*, (2) a middle style which is found in historical novels, such as 三國演義 *Sān guó yǎn yì (History of Three Kingdoms)*, a work much admired in China, and (3) a low style which is colloquial, such as the imperial text 聖諭 *Shèng yù (Imperial Edict)* and works of lighter fiction.[172]

Hoping to reach a wider readership, Morrison adopted the middle style, while at the same time avoiding colloquial coarseness.[173] However, in practice, he did not follow this middle style rigorously in translating the NT. This could be demonstrated by the fact that Basset's version, which was in a lower form of classical Chinese, was employed extensively by Morrison.[174] His NT was done in 1813, and with the cooperation of Milne, the OT was produced in 1819. Both were published together in Malacca, Malaysia in 1823, entitled 神天聖書 Shén tiān shèng shū (the Holy Bible).[175]

---

171. Milne's identification of the various styles of Chinese had great influence on Western missionaries for the remainder of the nineteenth century, even if their conclusions on what style to adopt naturally differed. See Zetzsche, *Bible in China*, 35.

172. William Milne, 新教在華傳教前十年回顧 [A retrospect of the first ten years of the Protestant mission to China] (Zhèng zhōu, China: Elephant Publishing House, 2008 [1820]), 89.

173. Zetzsche, *Bible in China*, 34.

174. Uchida Keiichi 內田慶市, "馬禮遜參照的漢譯聖書: 新發現的白日昇譯新約聖經稿本" [The Chinese Bible used by Robert Morrison: A newly discovered manuscript of the New Testament translated by Jean Basset], in 自上帝說漢語以來：《和合本》聖經九十年 [Ever since God speaks Chinese: The 90th anniversary of the Chinese Union Version Bible], eds. Pǐn Rán Xiè 謝品然 and Qìng Bǎo Zéng 曾慶豹, Bible Translation and Hermeneutics Series (Hong Kong: Center for Advanced Biblical Studies and Application, 2010), 55ff; Zetzsche, *Bible in China*, 35–36. Basset's version was copied out by Robert Morrison and his Chinese friend named Sān Dé Róng 容三德 in 1805. See Tán, *Robert Morrison and Sino-Western Cultural Communication*, 101, 106; Moule, "Manuscript Chinese," 23; Marshall Broomhall, *Robert Morrison: A Master-Builder*, Modern Series of Missionary Biographies (New York: George H. Doran Co., 1924), 118.

175. Foley, *Biblical Translation*, 18–19; Zetzsche, *Bible in China*, 42–43; Garnier, " 漢文聖經本小史" [Chinese versions of the Bible], 104–105; Zhào 趙, 譯經溯源 [Tracing Bible translation], 17.

In an important letter written on 25 November 1819, Morrison expressed his thoughts about translation as follows: "The duty of a translator of any book is two-fold; first, to comprehend accurately the sense, and to feel the spirit of the original work; and secondly, to express in his version faithfully, perspicuously, and idiomatically (and, if he can attain it, elegantly), the sense and spirit of the original."[176] For Morrison, the first criterion was more important than the second because of his insistence on faithfulness to the original text.[177]

2.2.3.3.2 Marshman/Lassar's version

The English Baptist Joshua Marshman (1768–1837) came to China in 1799 and worked on Bible translation in Serampore, India, in response to a Congregational minister William Moseley's circular that urged "the establishment of a Society for the translation of the Holy Scriptures into the languages of the most populous Oriental nations."[178] Another significant figure in this work was Joannes Lassar, a young American born and raised in Macao, a professor of Chinese with the special duty of translating the Bible into Chinese. He moved to Serampore in 1807 or 1808 where the translation work was conducted.[179]

While working on this version, Marshman viewed himself as the actual translator. Nonetheless, a comprehensive evaluation of the role that Lassar played in translating demonstrates that the latter was the dominant translator, with Marshman playing a role as "the inspiring factor."[180] The proofreading of the work involved several different people, including Lassar himself, Marshman's oldest son John Clark Marshman (1794–1877), at least two Chinese, and Marshman himself who edited the renderings by consulting

---

176. Eliza Armstrong Morrison, 馬禮遜回憶錄(全集): 他的生平與事工 [Memoirs of the life and labors of Robert Morrison, D. D.], trans. Zhào Míng Dèng 鄧肇明 (Hong Kong: Chinese Christian Literature Council, 2008 [1839]), 285.

177. Tán 譚, 馬禮遜與中西文化交流 [Robert Morrison and Sino-Western cultural communication], 110; Zhào 趙, 譯經溯源 [Tracing Bible translation], 17; Broomhall, *Robert Morrison*, 122.

178. Zhào 趙, 譯經溯源 [Tracing Bible translation], 17; Broomhall, *Bible in China*, 50.

179. Zetzsche, *Bible in China*, 45–46.

180. Zetzsche, 47.

the Greek NT and the Vulgate.[181] Due to the similarity of the wording in Morrison's and Marshman's translations, some scholars speculate that Marshman also referred to Basset's manuscripts.[182] In 1822, this Chinese Bible was printed in Serampore.[183]

2.2.3.3.3 The revision of Morrison/Milne's version and Gützlaff's NT

In 1836, the Qīng Dynasty prohibited the public distribution of Christian literature, which, however, did not discourage an enthusiastic new generation of Bible translators from their work. When missionaries to China increased in number, the call for the improvement of previous translations became stronger.[184]

First, the task of revising Morrison's 神天聖書 Shén tiān shèng shū (the Holy Bible) fell to a committee consisting of K. F. A. Gützlaff (1803–1851, Netherlands Missionary Society), W. H. Medhurst (1796–1857, London Missionary Society), and E. C. Bridgman (1801–1861, American Board of Commissioners for Foreign Missions), with the assistance of Morrison's son, J. R. Morrison (1814–1843). The NT with Medhurst's final editing was published in 1837, entitled 新遺詔書 Xīn yí zhào shū (New Testament). The OT was printed in 1840.[185]

Unfortunately, Medhurst's new translation was rejected by the British and Foreign Bible Society (BFBS) because of his principles of translation. According to Medhurst, a translation should not only be subject to strict fidelity to the source language, but should also take the target language and the cultural situation of the reader into consideration.[186] BFBS's rejection was not surprising because at that time "there was only one authorized

---

181. Zetzsche, *Bible in China*, 47; Zhì Yí Chéng 誠質怡, "聖經之中文譯本" [The Chinese translation of the Bible], in 聖經漢譯論文集 [Essays on Chinese Bible translation], ed. Bǎo Luó Jiǎ 賈保羅 (Hong Kong: Christian Fǔ qiáo Publishing House, 1965), 5.

182. Zhì Gāng Lǐ 李志剛, 基督教早期在華傳教史 [A history of early Christian missions in China] (Taipei: Taiwan shāng wù yìn shū guǎn, 1985), 162.

183. Zetzsche, *Bible in China*, 47–48; Zhào 趙, 譯經溯源 [Tracing Bible translation], 18.

184. Zetzsche, 59–60; Zhào 趙, 18.

185. Foley, *Biblical Translation in Chinese and Greek*, 19; Zhào 趙, 譯經溯源 [Tracing Bible translation], 18–19.

186. Zetzsche, *Bible in China*, 74.

English version and a strong belief in a literally unchangeable word of God in the Bible."[187]

Then, in 1840, Gützlaff revised Medhurst's NT renderings, entitled 救世主耶穌新遺詔書 Jiù shì zhǔ Yē sū xīn yí zhào shū (The Savior Jesus: The New Testament) (translated by the author). This revision did not find favor with the missionary community, but it was adopted and printed by the Tài píng rebels.[188]

2.2.3.3.4 Delegates' version (DV)

Thanks to the Treaty of Nán jīng and the British Annexation of Hong Kong in 1842 after the Opium War, the Protestant mission in China saw an abrupt change. The Treaty of Nán jīng provided protection for missionaries in the second half of the nineteenth century. Hong Kong, which was ceded to Great Britain by the Qing dynasty, became a new rally-center.[189] In 1843, fifteen missionaries from British and America gathered together in Hong Kong "to inaugurate a new version of the Scriptures which should be 'better adapted for general circulation than any hitherto published.'"[190]

Though the translators failed to come to a consensus regarding translation principles, style and the question of key terms,[191] leading to the division of the committee, the 委辦譯本 Wěi bàn yì běn (Delegates' Version) (DV) was

---

187. Zetzsche, 74.

188. Zetzsche, 72; Zhào 趙, 譯經溯源 [Tracing Bible translation], 19–20; Broomhall, *Bible in China*, 72. 洪秀全 Xiù Quán Hóng (1813–1864), the founder of the Tài píng rebellion against the imperial power in hopes of reformations in religion, morality, society and economy, became a Christian and claimed in 1837 that he was the "messiah" to establish a Christian kingdom in China. This rebellion lasted for fifteen years, wasting the richest provinces of China and costing the lives of some fifteen millions of people. See En Shèng Zhǎn 詹恩勝, "評介夏著－天國的隕落: 太平天國宗教再研究" [The review of a book 'Heaven's fall: The further study of Taiping heavenly kingdom's religion' by Xia Chun Tao], *Zhōng Zhèng History Journal* 13 (2010): 169; P. Richard Bohr, "Jesus, Christianity, and Rebellion in China: The Evangelical Roots of the Taiping Heavenly Kingdom," in *The Chinese Face of Jesus Christ*, ed. Roman Malek, Monumenta Serica Monograph Series 50 (Sankt Augustin, Germany: Jointly published by Institut Monumenta Serica and China-Zentrum, 2002), 645–652.

189. Foley, *Biblical Translation*, 21; Fù 傅, 聖經漢譯的文化資本解讀 [The cultural and capital interpretation of translating the Bible into Chinese], 121. As noted above, the activities of missionaries at that time were limited to Guǎng dōng, Macao, and countries in Southeast Asia, such as India and Malaysia.

190. Broomhall, *Bible in China*, 62.

191. Such as "God" and "baptize."

nevertheless finished in 1854[192] and became the most frequently printed and broadly circulated Chinese version in the nineteenth century.[193]

2.2.3.4 *The Popularizing Period (1854–1919)*

The preceding Protestant versions were all composed in High wén lǐ style (or middle style according to Milne's categories, see §2.2.3.3.1) and thus were only accessible to a minority of the educated class. But the versions of this period were aimed at the Chinese majority and thus translated in an easier style. This attempt was made possible when extraordinary changes occurred in China. The following are two examples of changes that paved the way for the popularization of the Chinese Bible.

On the one hand, the call for religious, moral, social and economic reformations from the Tài píng rebels and China's failure in anti-invasion wars since the nineteenth century gradually shook Chinese traditional thoughts and concepts, leading to a number of reformations in China, such as the promotion of 白話文 *Bái huà wén* as a literary style in The May 4th New Culture Movement.[194] In response to this trend, the Protestant missionaries started to employ easier written language in translating (i.e. Mandarin,[195] and Easy wén lǐ [a lower form of classical Chinese according to Milne's categories, see §2.2.3.3.1]).[196]

On the other hand, following the Treaty of Nán jīng (1842) noted above, the Treaty of Tiān jīn (1858) and the Convention of Běi jīng (1860) again provided a beneficial environment that enabled missionaries to enter Tiān jīn

---

192. Zetzsche, *Bible in China*, 186; Garnier, "漢文聖經本小史" [Chinese versions of the Bible], 108–111.

193. Strandenaes, *Principles of Chinese Bible Translation*, 14.

194. The May 4th New Cultural Movement in the early twentieth century is "The Renaissance in China," aiming to criticize and innovate national culture. One of the greatest contributions in this movement is 胡適 Shì Hú's promotion of 白話文 *Bái huà wén*, a literary style that uses common expressions and vocabulary. See Shù Yú Chén 陳漱渝, "五四新文化運動和五四文學革命" [The May 4th New Cultural Movement and the May 4th Literary Revolution], *Journal of Jiāngsū Administration Institute* 50, no. 2 (2010): 130, 132,136.

195. Mandarin, a dialect of Běi jīng (see §2.2.3.1), has long been spoken by the officials in the law courts. With provincial variations, it is the speech of the vast majority of the Chinese people. 胡適 Shì Hú points out that Mandarin extends over nine-tenths of Chinese territory. See Broomhall, *Bible in China*, 79.

196. Zhuāng 莊, 基督教聖經中文譯本權威現象研究 [A study of the phenomenon of authoritativeness in the Chinese translations of the Protestant Bible], 16–17; Zhào 趙, 譯經溯源 [Tracing Bible translation], 22.

and Běi jīng, as well as the interior of China. This allowed them to better appreciate the potential of using Mandarin in Bible translation. Realizing using Mandarin in Bible translation would benefit the illiterate majority, especially when the Bible was read aloud, both the British and American translators participated wholeheartedly in translating the Bible into Mandarin.[197]

In sum, in response to the profound changes in China due to the internal trouble and outside aggression, and with the attempt to meet the need of various readership, Protestant missionaries tried to produce Chinese versions in easier styles (i.e. Mandarin and Easy wén lǐ, in addition to the existing High wén lǐ), so that the gospel could reach a much wider audience.

2.2.3.4.1 Two early important versions in Mandarin
Two early important versions in Mandarin during this period were the Běi jīng version of the NT, as well as Shereschewsky's Mandarin OT.[198]

2.2.3.4.1.1 The Běi jīng version of the NT
Even though the earliest effort to produce a NT Mandarin version was made by Medhurst and Stronach in Shàng hǎi in 1854,[199] the Běi jīng version, produced by Burdon, Schereschewsky, Blodget, Edkins, and Martin in 1872, was viewed as the first major attempt to put the NT into Mandarin.[200] It was compared by some to the Authorized Version in English,[201] but was reproached for being too classical and not consistent enough.[202] It was also criticized for using paraphrases rather than direct translations. For example, ὁ θεὸς τοῦ αἰῶνος "god of this world" in 2 Corinthians 4:4 was translated with the Buddhist term "魔王 *mó wáng* (king of demons)."[203]

---

197. Zetzsche, *Bible in China*, 139–141.

198. Péng 彭, "Contemplating the Future of Chinese Bible Translation," 7; Garnier, "漢文聖經本小史" [Chinese versions of the Bible], 128–131; Zhào 趙, 譯經溯源 [Tracing Bible translation], 24–25.

199. Mù Shì Xǔ 許牧世, 經與釋經 [The Bible and hermeneutics] (Hong Kong: Chinese Christian Literature Council, 1983), 137.

200. Zetzsche, *Bible in China*, 145–150.

201. J. Lees, "Letter to a Friend on Wen-Li v. Vernacular," *The Chinese Recorder and Missionary Journal* 23 (1892): 180.

202. C. C. Baldwin, "Notes on the Revision of the Mandarin New Testament," *The Chinese Recorder and Missionary Journal*, no. 38 (1907): 26, 92.

203. G. E. Moule, "Mr. John's Version: Or Another?" *The Chinese Recorder and Missionary Journal* 16 (1885): 379–380.

2.2.3.4.1.2 Shereschewsky's Mandarin OT

Born as a Jew, and having attended rabbinical schools until the age of nineteen, Shereschewsky, with an idiomatic command of spoken Mandarin, was entrusted with continuing the translation of the OT single-handedly. His first draft was done in 1873. The final revision was finished by Shereschewsky himself and probably to some degree by Blodget, and published in 1874/1875. In 1878, for the first time, Shereschewsky's OT appeared with the Běi jīng NT in one volume, "published as a combined effort by the ABS[204] and BFBS."[205] However, the style of these two renderings did not harmonize perfectly. Shereschewsky's OT was done in a higher style of Mandarin than the Běi jīng version. However, "the publication was almost unanimously highly praised and welcomed."[206]

Indeed, in the history of Chinese Bible translation, Shereschewsky is truly well known and respected. This was because of "his uncommon abilities and remarkable achievement." He persevered in the translation and revision of the Chinese Bible for thirty-two years, more than anyone else in the course of Chinese Bible translation, despite being completely paralyzed from a sunstroke in 1881 and suffering from the disease for the rest of his life.[207]

2.2.3.4.2 The first Easy wén lǐ version

Though the Mandarin versions were popular and used in the north of China, they were not widely understood by the people in the south, where numerous dialects exist with significant differences among them. Thus missionaries started to seek another form of language that would be between the classical style (深文理 High wén lǐ) of the DV and Mandarin. This issue was discussed for the first time in 1877, and Griffith John was the first to publish a translation of the NT in a lower form of classical Chinese (淺文理 Easy wén lǐ) in 1885.[208] Even if the definition of Easy wén lǐ led to controversy

---

204. The American Bible Society.
205. Zetzsche, *Bible in China*, 151–153; Zhào 趙, 譯經溯源 [Tracing Bible translation], 25.
206. Zetzsche, 153; Zhào 趙, 23.
207. Zetzsche, 153–154.
208. Zetzsche, 161; Xǔ 許, "中文聖經翻譯簡史" [A brief history of Chinese Bible translation], 31; Garnier, "漢文聖經本小史" [Chinese versions of the Bible], 120.

among missionaries,[209] the aim of using the lower form was apparent (i.e. to produce a version composed in a literary form or style that would be accepted by both the elite and the majority of non-elite Chinese).[210] With this readership in mind, John, in his "leading rules for translation," proposed principles allowing for non-literal renderings, even though he knew this approach would draw criticism. He argued that a literal version "would be of no value to either the heathen or the Christian. To the one it would be a mere laughing stock, and to the other a serious stumbling-stone."[211]

2.2.3.4.3 Other Easy wén lǐ and Mandarin versions

From the 1860s to the 1880s, Easy wén lǐ style and Mandarin were the two most popular (and even competing) translations in Chinese. After completing the translation of the Mandarin Běi jīng version, a number of its translators continued to produce Easy wén lǐ versions, such as Burden and Blodget's Easy wén lǐ NT (1884) and Schereschewsky's Easy wén lǐ translation (1899, 1906, 1910). The latter was the most popular version before the publication of the Union version in 1919.[212] John's Mandarin NT based on his Easy wén lǐ version was published in 1889 as well.[213] Such an atmosphere of rivalry caused unease among the young Chinese churches. This catalyzed the 1890 Conference to discuss the direction of a union version.[214]

2.2.3.4.4 Union version (UV)

Desiring a Chinese translation whose status would be similar to that of the English Authorized and Revised Version, the great Missionary Conference, held in Shàng hǎi in 1890, decided to produce "One Bible in Three Versions" (i.e. Union versions in High wén lǐ, Easy wén lǐ, and Mandarin), all based

---

209. 淺文理 Easy wén lǐ is a form close to Milne's third category, see §2.2.3.3.1

210. Zetzsche, *Bible in China*, 162.

211. Griffith John, "Leading Rules for Translation," *The Chinese Recorder and Missionary Journal* 16 (1885): 381–382.

212. Zetzsche, *Bible in China*, 174–183; Xǔ 許, 經與釋經 [The Bible and hermeneutics], 136.

213. Zetzsche, 170–174; Xǔ 許, "中文聖經翻譯簡史" [A brief history of Chinese Bible translation], 32.

214. Mài 麥, 大英聖書公會與官話《和合本》聖經翻譯 [The British and Foreign Bible Society and the translation of the Mandarin Chinese Union version], 30; Zhào 趙, 譯經溯源 [Tracing Bible translation], 32–33.

on the English Revised Version.[215] There were eighteen translation principles adopted for all three versions of the UV, in the hope that the new versions would maintain the strengths of earlier versions, such as consistency, naturalness of the Chinese, and readability, at the same time seeking a more literal approach.[216] If needed, explanatory readings, maps, chapter and sectional headings could be added.[217] "Thus after many long and weary years, this much-to-be-desired arrangement was made."[218]

But the reality was, as the saying goes, "easier said than done," as one of the translators observed, "It's a long road from Genesis to Revelation."[219] Indeed, the road was long enough for radical alterations to occur in the history of the nation. Since the Conference of 1890, Broomhall reported, "Vast and revolutionary forces had been at work, and the very language had changed. A flood of newspapers and periodicals, together with a new system of education, had so simplified style that three versions were now unnecessary."[220]

Consequently, the General Conference of 1907 decided to combine the two classical projects and leave only one coexisting with the Mandarin project.[221] After twenty-seven years of hard efforts, both the wén lǐ UV and the Mandarin UV were published in 1919.[222] The latter was widely accepted and became the most popular and authoritative Bible ever published in the Chinese language, and "its lasting influence upon Chinese Christians could, to some degree, be comparable to that of the King James Version on English-speaking Christians."[223]

---

215. Broomhall, *Bible in China*, 87–89.

216. Zetzsche, *Bible in China*, 225–226; Zhào 趙, 譯經溯源 [Tracing Bible translation], 37.

217. Broomhall, *Bible in China*, 89.

218. Broomhall, 89.

219. Broomhall, 89.

220. Broomhall, 90.

221. Broomhall, 90.

222. Zhào 趙, 譯經溯源 [Tracing Bible translation], 34–37.

223. Foley, *Biblical Translation*, 28–29; see also Zhuāng 莊, 基督教聖經中文譯本權威現象研究 [A study of the phenomenon of authoritativeness in the Chinese translations of the Protestant Bible], 19; Zhào 趙, 譯經溯源 [Tracing Bible translation], 36.

2.2.3.5 The Enculturating Period (1919–present)

The Mandarin UV of 1919 (known as the Chinese Union Version nowadays) marked the most significant and final contribution of missionaries to Chinese Bible translation. From then on, Chinese Christians were expected to carry out responsibilities of translating the Bible into Chinese.[224]

2.2.3.5.1 The early mother tongue Chinese Bible translator

Before the first-ever whole Chinese Bible produced by mother tongue speakers 呂振中 Lǚ, Zhèn Zhōng, there were some early mother tongue translators worthy of notice.

2.2.3.5.1.1 Mark and Luke by 馮亞生 Féng, Yǎ Shēng

The earliest mother tongue Chinese Bible translation was attributed to 馮亞生 Féng, Yǎ Shēng (1792–1829) and 馮亞學 Féng, Yǎ Xué who left China for Europe in 1816. They went to Berlin in 1823 and were to be the first Chinese living in Germany. Later, they were employed by the Prussian king Friedrich Wilhelm III and sent to Halle, where they taught Chinese. In 1828, Féng, Yǎ Shēng as a Christian translated Luther's *Smaller Catechism* as well as Mark and Luke from Luther's Bible into Chinese.[225]

2.2.3.5.1.2 Matthew and Mark by 何進善 Hé, Jìn Shàn

The first rendering of a biblical book to be published by a Chinese was credited to 何進善 Hé, Jìn Shàn (1817–1871), who "became a Christian in 1838 and was taken on as a student of English, Greek, and Hebrew by the LMS missionary James Legge" (1815–1897). More than a decade later, Matthew (1854) and Mark (1856), which "were translated and furnished with commentaries by Hé and revised by Legge, were published in Hong Kong."[226]

---

224. Zhuāng 莊, 基督教聖經中文譯本權威現象研究 [A study of the phenomenon of authoritativeness in the Chinese translations of the Protestant Bible], 17. Before the enculturating period, Chinese people mainly served as Chinese teachers, assistants and partners in the task of Bible translation. See Rèn 任, 聖經漢譯文化研究 [Study on the translation of Bible translation into Chinese], 214–224.

225. Foley, *Biblical Translation*, 29; Zetzsche, *Bible in China*, 125.

226. Rèn 任, 聖經漢譯文化研究 [Study on the translation of Bible translation into Chinese], 224; Zetzsche, *Bible in China*, 127–128.

2.2.3.5.1.3 Mark 1–4 by 嚴復 Yán, Fù

嚴復 Yán, Fù (1853–1921) was the most influential translator of English works on political economy and ethics into Chinese, which had become the standard texts on the subject.[227] In the preface to his own translation of T. H. Huxley's *Evolution and Ethics* entitled 天演論 Tiān-yǎn lùn (1898), Yán proposed three translation principles – fidelity (信 *xìn*), fluency (達 *dá*) and elegance (雅 *yǎ*).[228] These were broadly recognized as "the fundamental tenets of twentieth-century Chinese translation theory"[229] by both biblical and secular Chinese translators.[230]

Yán was commissioned and supported by the BFBS to produce a Chinese Bible version in the hope that it would eventually become a great classic in Chinese literature.[231] Regrettably, without knowledge of biblical languages, Yán only translated the first four chapters of Mark, based on the English Revised Version, entitled 馬可所傳福音: 第一章至第四章 Mǎ Kě suǒ chuán fú yīn: dì yī zhāng zhì dì sì zhāng (Mark 1–4 in wén lǐ Chinese).[232] However, Yán's version appeared to pave the way for translating the Bible into Chinese as a literary work.[233]

2.2.3.5.1.4 The New Testament by 朱寶惠 Zhū, Bǎo Huì

朱寶惠 Zhū, Bǎo Huì (1889–1970) learned Greek at Nán jīng Theological Seminary and was the main Chinese assistant to the American Southern Presbyterian missionary Absalom Sydenstricker (1852–1931) in his translation of the NT into Mandarin in 1929.[234] Due to Sydenstricker's sudden

---

227. Foley, *Biblical Translation*, 30; Zetzsche, *Bible in China*, 129.

228. Another rendering for Yán, Fù's three translation principles is "faithfulness (信 *xìn*), comprehensibility (達 *dá*) and elegance (雅 *yǎ*)." See Elsie Chan, "Translation Principles and the Translator's Agenda: A Systemic Approach to Yan, Fu," in *Crosscultural Transgressions: Research Models in Translation Studies II: Historical and Ideological Issues*, ed. Theo Hermans (Manchester, UK: St Jerome, 2002), 62.

229. Dé Hóng Leo Chén 陳德鴻, *20 世紀中國翻譯理論: 風氣、問題與爭辯* [Twentieth-century Chinese translation theory: Modes, issues and debates] (Amsterdam; Philadelphia: J. Benjamins, 2004), 4.

230. Zetzsche, *Bible in China*, 129.

231. Zetzsche. 129.

232. Foley, *Biblical Translation*, 30.

233. Rèn 任, 聖經漢譯文化研究 [Study on the translation of Bible translation into Chinese], 226.

234. Bǎo Huì Zhū 朱寶惠, 重譯新約全書 [The New Testament translated from the original] (Nán Jīng, China: xīn yì shèng jīng liú tōng chù, 1936), preface.

death in 1930, Zhū took over the translation task and published his translation of the NT in 1936,[235] with the financial support from Sydenstricker's daughter Pearl S. Buck (1892–1973), an American author and Nobel Prize-winner.[236] Zhū's version, known as 重譯新約全書 Zhòng yì xīn yuē quán shū (The New Testament Translated from the Original), was appreciated for its fidelity to the Greek original text, and, thus, was recently reprinted in 1993 and 2007 in Hong Kong.[237]

2.2.3.5.2 The complete Chinese Bible by 呂振中 Lǚ, Zhèn Zhōng
Among other mother tongue translators, Zhū, Bǎo Huì was the first to accomplish the work of translating the NT into Chinese independently. Another great stride was made by 呂振中 Lǚ, Zhèn Zhōng (1898–1988). Despite political and social instability in China from the 1920s to 1970s,[238] Lǚ was the first and the only mother tongue translator to produce a complete Chinese Bible independently in the history of Chinese Bible translation.[239]

Lǚ taught Greek in Yān jīng University. In 1940, based on the Greek version compiled by Alexander Souter from Oxford University, Lǚ launched his translation. This version, entitled 呂譯新約初稿 Lǚ yì xīn yuē chū gǎo (The First Draft of the NT by Lǚ) (translated by the author), was published in 1946 with five hundred copies for the reference of NT scholars only. At the same year, Lǚ left China for America and Britain to further study Greek and Hebrew.[240]

After thirty years' effort, Lǚ's whole Chinese Bible was published in 1970, claiming to maintain the consistency with the meaning and the structure

---

235. Rèn 任, 聖經漢譯文化研究 [Study on the translation of Bible translation into Chinese], 229.
236. Foley, *Biblical Translation*, 31.
237. Foley, 31.
238. Qí Duàn 段琦, 中國基督教本色化史稿 [The history of enculturation of Chinese Christianity] (Taipei: Christian Cosmic Light Holistic Care Organization, 2005), Ch. 9–12.
239. Rèn 任, 聖經漢譯文化研究 [Study on the translation of Bible translation into Chinese], 235.
240. Rèn, 235–236.

of the original texts.²⁴¹ His literal translation stood the test of time and was reprinted in Hong Kong in 2004.²⁴²

2.2.3.5.3 Versions after the 1970s

Since the 1970s, a number of newer versions of the Chinese Bible by mother tongue translators have been produced with the financial sponsorship by the Bible society.²⁴³ Following are the important works used in Chinese faith communities.

Two new versions produced in the 1970s, which were criticized for heavily relying on English versions as a textual basis, were 現代中文譯本 Xiàn dài zhōng wén yì běn (Today's Chinese Version) (TCV, 1979) from Today's English Version of 1976 and 當代聖經譯本 Dāng dài shèng jīng yì běn (Chinese Living Bible) (CLB, 1979) from the Living Bible of 1971.²⁴⁴

In the 1990s, based on original languages, 聖經新譯本 Shèng jīng xīn yì běn (Chinese Bible New Version) (CNV) was published in 1992. And a second Catholic Chinese Bible, 天主教牧靈聖經 Tiān zhǔ jiāo mù líng shèng jīng (Chinese Pastoral Bible) (CPB) was printed in 1999. TCV of 1979 was revised in 1997, known as 現代中文譯本修訂版 Xiàn dài zhōng wén yì běn xiū dìng bǎn (Today's Chinese Version: Revised Edition) (TCVRE).

Two revisions were completed in 2010, including 和合本修訂版 Hé hé běn xiū dìng bǎn (Revised Chinese Union Version) (RCUV) and 當代譯本修訂版 Dāng dài yì běn xiū dìng bǎn (Chinese Contemporary Bible) (CCB). Besides, three new NT versions based on the original text appeared (i.e. 新漢語譯本 [新約] Xīn hàn yǔ yì bě [xīn yuē] [Contemporary Chinese Version] [NT] in 2010, 中文標準譯本 [新約] Zhōng wén biāo zhǔn yì běn [xīn yuē] [Chinese Standard Bible] (NT) in 2011, and 環球聖經譯本 [新約] Huán qiú shèng jīng yì běn [xīn yuē] (Worldwide Bible Version) (NT) in 2015). The translation of the OT in the last three Chinese Bible translation projects is currently underway.

---

241. Lǚ's NT is based on the 17th edition of the Nestle-Aland Greek text; OT on the MT, the Septuagint, and the Vulgate. See Rèn, 236.

242. Cái Wàng Xiào 蔡王肖才望, "呂振中《新譯新約全書》譯本考察" [An exploration of the literal translation of the New Testament by Lǚ Zhèn-Zhōng], *Journal of Shǎnxī Agriculture University (Social Science Edition)* 12, no. 2 (2013): 110; Foley, *Biblical Translation*, 32.

243. Foley, *Biblical Translation*, 32.

244. Foley, 32.

Over the past two decades, the majority of Chinese Bible translations were carried out by various translation committees with the emphasis on being "忠於原文 zhōng yú yuán wén (faithful to the original languages)."[245] The exception includes 新譯簡明聖經 Xīn yì jiǎn míng shèng jīng (The Holy Bible: A Dynamic Chinese Translation) (DCT), which is mainly based on NIV and NASB; 新英語譯本聖經中譯本 Xīn yīng yǔ yì běn shèng jīng zhōng yì běn (Chinese New English Translation Bible) (CNET), which is based on NET; 新普及譯本 Xīn pǔ jí yì běn (Chinese New Living Translation) (CNLT), which is based on NLT.

Finally, there is an interesting phenomenon in the enculturation period. That is, though the task of the Chinese Bible translation was taken over by mother tongue translators, the Mandarin UV (i.e. CUV) produced by missionaries in 1919 continues to be the most popular and authoritative Chinese Bible version up to date.[246]

2.2.4 Conclusion

The first half of chapter 2 begins with the history of Bible translation before the seventh century, followed by that of Chinese Bible translation from the seventh century onwards. From this chronological survey of Bible translation, one finds that the practice of Bible translation has been long established without a systematic, rigorous translation theory (only with simple translation principles), and that the issue of literal versus non-literal (or free/idiomatic/dynamic) has long existed in the history of both Western and Chinese Bible translation.

Regarding Chinese Bible translation, since Morrison's 神天聖書 Shén tiān shèng shū (The Holy Bible) in 1823, missionaries from various Bible societies have followed their own translation principles when translating the Bible into Chinese,[247] which have been adopted and expanded by Chinese translators. For example, three translation principles and five translation steps are listed in the preface of the Contemporary Chinese Version (NT) in

---

245. Péng 彭, "Contemplating the Future of Chinese Bible Translation," 11.

246. Zhuāng 莊, "《和合本》在中文聖經多元系統中的位置—前景與挑戰" [The position of the Chinese Union version in the Chinese Bible polysystem: Prospective and challenge], 41; Zhuāng 莊, 基督教聖經中文譯本權威現象研究 [A study of the phenomenon of authoritativeness in the Chinese translations of the Protestant Bible], 17.

247. Zhào 趙, 譯經溯源 [Tracing Bible translation], 32.

2010. This seems to note a critical issue[248] with contemporary Chinese Bible translation, namely, conducting the practice of Bible translation without a rigorous, systematic translation theory even though the field of translation has developed into an academic discipline in the second half of the twentieth century. For this reason, this study will explore the discipline of translation studies in attempt to find a proper theory and method for the exercise of translating the three selected psalms into Chinese (the Hebrew word נֶפֶשׁ will receive particular attention).

2.3 The Development of Translation Studies

2.3.1. Introduction

As noted earlier, 嚴復 Yán, Fù's three translation principles (fidelity, fluency, and elegance) enunciated in 1898 have achieved canonical status in the twentieth century for both biblical and secular Chinese translators.[249] However, his triad now seems to be "condemned as paradoxical if not contradictory" from the perspective of contemporary translation theory.[250] Such reflection on translation issues can perhaps be traced back to the latter part of the 1970s when China opened to the outside world and "started an ambitious programme of cultural reform"[251] after the political and social instability in China from the 1920s to 1970s (see §2.2.3.5.2).

Since the late 1970s, translation has been undergoing a renaissance in China.[252] Gentzler points out that "in addition to the boom in translation practice, and increasing research on the histories of translation in China, there is also a very strong movement in theory, both cultural theory and translation theory."[253] Regarding the latter, Chén vividly describes Chinese translation scholars' paradoxical attitude toward the West as follows:

---

248. In his "Contemplating the Future of Chinese Bible Translation," 15, Péng points out the importance of informing the audience of the method and theory employed in Bible translation.

249. Chén 陳, 20 世紀中國翻譯理論 [Twentieth-century Chinese translation theory], 4; Zetzsche, Bible in China, 129.

250. Chan, "Translation Principles," 61.

251. Gentzler, "Global View of Translation Studies," 117.

252. Gentzler, 117.

253. Gentzler, 121. Cf. Holmes's "map" of translation studies in §2.3.2.2.3.1.

Much of the current evaluation of Chinese translation theory has tended toward one of two extremes: either it has been valorized as belonging to a distinctive, separate tradition, so that any attempt to seek Western equivalents can only be futile, or it has been denigrated as lacking in analytical depth and philosophical insight as compared with Western translation theory.[254]

Wáng and Sūn also observe that "some Chinese translation scholars, motivated by ideology, are adamantly opposed to translation theories developed in the West, insisting that they are of no use or relevance to translation practice in China."[255] This contradicts Wáng and Sūn's perspective who assert:

> [I]n recent years, modern scholarship demands a certain global perspective that precludes a gross overemphasis on the so-called uniqueness or authenticity residing in the Chinese language and culture, which serves as a neat excuse for refusing to integrate translation studies with the rest of the world, especially the Western world.[256]

In line with Wáng and Sūn, the second half of chapter 2 first explores the development of translation studies,[257] and then selects an appropriate translation paradigm as an approach through which the intergenerational Bible translation exercise in this study will be conducted.

---

254. Chén 陳, *20 世紀中國翻譯理論* [Twentieth-century Chinese translation theory], 3.

255. Níng Wáng and Yi Feng Sūn, "Introduction," in *Translation, Globalisation and Localisation: A Chinese Perspective*, eds. Níng Wáng and Yi Feng Sūn (Clevedon, UK; Buffalo, NY: Multilingual Matters, 2008), 5.

256. Wang and Sūn, "Introduction," 4–5. Jin's translation of *Ulysses* into Chinese is a good example of applying a western approach in Chinese translation. His other book *Literary Translation: Quest for Artistic Integrity* of 2003 is viewed as "valuable to translators of literature between almost any pair of languages, not just Chinese and English." See William McNaughton, "Introduction," in *Literary Translation: Quest for Artistic Integrity*, by Di Jin (Manchester, UK; Northampton, MA: St Jerome, 2003), xiii. Thus, it is unnecessary for Chinese translators to confine themselves to the so-called unique or authentic Chinese translation theory.

257. It is unsuitable to define this relatively new discipline of translation studies here because of its continuing development in the past decades. As Gentzler, in "Global View of Translation Studies," 112, suggests, "only by viewing translations from a global perspective and by being open to interdisciplinary approaches might translation studies scholars arrive at a more comprehensive definition of translations."

2.3.2 The Development of the Field of Translation

In the twentieth century, translation theory underwent considerable evolution, especially in the second half of the century.[258] The sheer quantity of publications in this field makes it impossible to cover everything here. However, in this section, the basic contours of the development of translation theory will be briefly outlined, including Lefevere and Bassnett's three models[259] before the twentieth century and Snell-Hornby's observation on the development in translation studies[260] from the twentieth century onwards.

2.3.2.1 Lefevere and Bassnett's Three Models

For Bassnett, the distinction between word-for-word (literal) and sense-for-sense (idiomatic/dynamic) translation "is still as powerful today as it was 2000 years ago."[261] Indeed, the shifts between these two opposite approaches dominated the translation field over the past 2000 years, of which Lefevere and Bassnett's three models provide a brief illustration.

The first model Lefevere and Bassnett suggest is the Jerome Model. This model, named after Jerome (ca. 347–ca. 420 CE) who translated the Bible into Latin (the Vulgate), establishes "the acknowledged and unacknowledged standards of much of translation in the West until about two hundred years ago."[262] In central position in this model is a rigid concept of equivalence in transposing the Bible into another language. Stated slightly differently, the Bible, as a sacred text, "must be translated with the utmost fidelity."[263]

Such faithfulness and equivalency are secured by using good dictionaries, which implies that those who can employ a dictionary should be of the capacity to translate. Thus, word-for-word substitution, with the minimum of the adjustments in the syntax of the target language, could produce an

---

258. Cheung, "Twentieth Century Translation," 1.
259. André Lefevere and Susan Bassnett, "Introduction: Where Are We in Translation Studies?," in *Constructing Cultures: Essays on Literary Translation*, eds. Susan Bassnett and André Lefevere (Clevedon; Philadelphia: Multilingual Matters, 1998), 1–10.
260. Snell-Hornby, *Turns of Translation Studies*.
261. Bassnett, *Translation*, 5–6.
262. Lefevere and Bassnett, "Introduction," 2.
263. Lefevere and Bassnett, 2. Apart from Bible translation, Jerome insists on sense-for-sense translation. In his Epistle 57.6, Jerome writes: "From my youth up I have always aimed at rendering sense not words . . . A literal translation from one language to another obscures the sense." See Stine, *Let the Words Be Written*, 158 n. 4.

accurate and equivalent Bible translation. Lefevere and Bassnett comment that "to be able to elevate faithfulness to this central position, to the exclusion of many other factors, the Jerome model ha[s] to reduce thinking about translation to the linguistic level only."[264]

The second model suggested by Lefevere and Bassnett is the Horace model, a model associated with the name of the Roman poet Horace (65 BC–8 BC). This "historically predates the Jerome model, but has been overshadowed by it for about fourteen centuries."[265] The Horace model calls for translators to be faithful to their customers, rather than to a source text.[266] The responsibility of the translators is to fulfill the expectations of their clients. That is, the negotiation between the clients or patrons and the languages involved is indispensable, which "militates heavily against the kind of faithfulness[267] traditionally associated with equivalence."[268]

The Schleiermacher Model (see §2.3.2.2.1.3) is Lefevere and Bassnett's third model, named after the German philosopher and theologian Friedrich Schleiermacher (1768–1834).[269] In his famous lecture entitled "On the different ways of translation," Schleiermacher demanded that the translation should sound and read like a foreign text (i.e. the translator needs to preserve the alterity of the source text and denies the privileged position of the receiving language or culture). He opposed the approach through which the translation reads and sounds as if it is originally composed in the TL.[270]

From the three models presented above, one observes not only that the pendulum of translation theory has swung back and forth between the opposite ends of word-for-word (the first and third models) and sense-for-sense

---

264. Lefevere and Bassnett, "Introduction," 2.

265. Lefevere and Bassnett, 3.

266. This is the approach adopted by modern "*Skopos* Theory" and its practice, e.g. Christiane Nord, *Translating as a Purposeful Activity: Functionalist Approaches Explained* (Manchester: St Jerome, 1997).

267. This is not necessarily the case. In his *Translating as a Purposeful Activity*, 127–128, Nord proposes a function-plus-loyalty model, which is "an answer to those critics who argue that the functional approach leaves translators free to do whatever they like with any source text, or worse, what their clients like. The loyalty principle takes account of the legitimate interests of the three parties involved" (i.e. initiators, target receivers, and original authors).

268. Lefevere and Bassnett, "Introduction," 3.

269. Lefevere and Bassnett, 7.

270. Lefevere and Bassnett, 8.

(the second model) translation, but also that translating should take language and culture into consideration (i.e. the TL community's needs and desires).

2.3.2.2 Snell-Hornby's Turns of Translation Studies

In her book, *The Turns of Translation Studies: New Paradigms or Shifting Viewpoints*, Snell-Hornby notes that "there is a broad consensus that many basic insights and concepts in Translation Studies today go back to the German Romantic Age, which forms our historical starting point."[271] She sees the development of translation studies as divided into several distinct parts: the precursors, the pioneers, the pragmatic turn in the 1970s, the cultural turn of the 1980s, the interdiscipline in the 1990s, and finally at the turn of the millennium. This scheme provides a clear yet brief outline for the exploration of the development of translation studies.

2.3.2.2.1 The precursors

Snell-Hornby argues that the discipline of translation studies can be traced back to the prominent precursors, such as Goethe, Humboldt, and Schleiermacher in the German Romantic period of the late eighteenth and early nineteenth centuries, and later to Benjamin and Rosenzweig in the early twentieth century.[272] In what follows, their critical thinking related to this field is summarized.

2.3.2.2.1.1 Johann Wolfgang von Goethe (1749–1832)

In 1819, in his *West-Ostlicher Diwan*, Goethe presented a tripartite model, the "epochs" of translation.[273]

The first is the prosaic epoch, domesticating translations and acquainting the audience with foreign culture on the audience's own terms. Luther's Bible translation is an example of this approach.[274]

The second is the parodistic epoch, in which the translators merely intend to "appropriate foreign content and to reproduce it in his own sense, even though he tries to transport himself into foreign situations."[275]

---

271. Snell-Hornby, *Turns of Translation Studies*, 3.
272. Snell-Hornby, 3.
273. André Lefevere, *Translating Literature: The German Tradition from Luther to Rosenzweig* (Assen: Van Gorcum, 1977), 35–37.
274. Lefevere, *Translating Literature*, 35.
275. Lefevere, 36.

The third epoch is "to be called the highest and the final one," aiming to "make the original identical with the translation."²⁷⁶ The translators attaching themselves "closely to his original more or less abandons the originality of his nation, and so a third comes into existence, and the taste of the multitude must first be shaped towards it."²⁷⁷ This is in accordance with Schleiermacher's ideal, later to be taken up by Walter Benjamin.²⁷⁸

2.3.2.2.1.2 Wilhelm von Humboldt (1767–1835)
In the introduction to his translation of Aeschylus' *Agamemnon* (1816), Humboldt maintains that a translator should strive to avoid "obscurity and un-Germanness," aim at clarity and fidelity to the text as a whole, and emphasize "the necessity for empathy between the translator and the author."²⁷⁹ Concerning a translator's role, he notes:

> A translation cannot and should not be a commentary. It should not contain obscurities originating in vacillating use of language and clumsy construction; but where the original only hints, without clearly expressing, where it allows itself metaphors whose meaning is hard to grasp, where it leaves out mediating ideas, there the translator would go wrong if he were to introduce, of his own accord, a clarity which disfigures the character of the text.²⁸⁰

2.3.2.2.1.3 Friedrich Daniel Ernst Schleiermacher (1768–1834)
In his famous lecture, "On the different ways of translation," delivered in 1813, Schleiermacher identified two basic translation approaches: "Either the translator leaves the author in peace, as much as possible, and moves the reader towards him; or he leaves the reader in peace, as much as possible, and moves the author towards him."²⁸¹ It is worth noting that Schleiermacher himself did not coin precise terms to refer to these two methods, which are

---

276. Lefevere, 36.
277. Lefevere, 36.
278. Snell-Hornby, *Turns of Translation Studies*, 12.
279. Quoted in Lefevere, *Translating Literature*, 40, 43.
280. Quoted in Lefevere, 43.
281. Quoted in Lefevere, 74.

today recognized as *foreignization* and *domestication*.²⁸² As noted in Lefevere and Bassnett's third model, Schleiermacher recommended producing translations that tend towards a foreign likeness.

Schleiermacher also made another striking distinction between "genuine translation" and "mere interpreting." "Genuine translation" refers to *paraphrase* employed in scholarly and scientific texts and *imitation* applying to literary works of art. "Mere interpreting" is used in both oral and written translation of normal business texts.²⁸³

In sum, today's scholars consider German theorists of the early nineteenth century to be important precursors of modern translation studies, even for the English-speaking community.²⁸⁴

However, after the Romantic Age, "the German tradition stagnated and was subject to some intense internal criticism."²⁸⁵ For example, Jakob Grimm (1785–1863) lashed out at strict translations because they "pedantically strain themselves to weave a copy of the dress, and fall short of the source text whose form and content naturally and spontaneously agree."²⁸⁶ In addition, when German nationalism became more aggressive, translation was seen as "conquest" (Nietzsche, 1844–1900), "hence anticipating the arguments of postcolonial translation critics over a hundred years afterwards."²⁸⁷ These explain why Venuti (2000), in *The Translation Studies Reader*, leaves a long gap after Schleiermacher and Humboldt and begins with Walter Benjamin's essay "The Task of the Translator."²⁸⁸

2.3.2.2.1.4 Walter Benjamin (1892–1940)
Walter Benjamin was the most important scholar in German translation theory of the early twentieth century. His essay, "The Task of the Translator," was published in 1923, against the historical background of the Depression

---

282. Snell-Hornby, *Turns of Translation Studies*, 8–9.
283. Snell-Hornby, 7.
284. Snell-Hornby, 16.
285. Snell-Honrby, 16.
286. Quoted in Lefevere, *Translating Literature*, 95.
287. Snell-Hornby, *Turns of Translation Studies*, 17.
288. Snell-Hornby, 16.

and the ensuing rise of Nazi dictatorship, leading to Benjamin's suicide in 1940.[289]

Contrary to such monumental crises were Benjamin's mystical thoughts on translation as part of the "afterlife" which assures the survival of the foreign text through transformation.[290] Benjamin expressed the features of an ideal translation as follows:

> Real translation is transparent, it does not hide the original; it does not steal its light, but allows the pure language, as if reinforced through its own medium, to fall on the original work with greater fulness. This lies above all in the power of literalness in the translation of syntax, and even this points to the word, not the sentence, as the translator's original element.[291]

In line with Schleiermacher and Goethe's "third epoch" of translation, Benjamin argued that a translation should be a radical form of literalism.[292]

2.3.2.2.1.5 Franz Rosenzweig (1886–1929)

In contrast with Benjamin, Rosenzweig, a Jewish theologian working on a new German translation of the Hebrew OT, in his 1926 essay "The Scriptures and Luther," describes "all speech as translation."[293] He stresses that "literary translation is absolutely essential as an antidote against the aggressive, imperialist nationalism."[294]

Rosenzweig firmly advocates compromise and thus criticizes Schleiermacher's dichotomy and his tendency to distort "a very complex and entangled and never antithetically separated reality."[295] He suggests viewing Schleiermacher's maxim, not as "either/or," but as a means of disentangling that intricate reality, leading to the critical question: "at which points in the work is the reader moved and at which points the original [moved]."[296]

---

289. Snell-Hornby, 17–18.
290. Snell-Hornby, 18.
291. Quoted in Lefevere, *Translating Literature*, 102.
292. See Snell-Hornby, *Turns of Translation Studies*, 18.
293. Quoted in Snell-Hornby, 18.
294. Quoted in Lefevere, *Translating Literature*, 94.
295. Quoted in Lefevere, 111.
296. Quoted in Lefevere, 111.

Rosenzweig's comments indicate that translation theory has "moved from the concept of two extremes to a complex terrain in-between."[297]

2.3.2.2.2 The pioneers

After the precursors[298] came the pioneers, people such as Jakobson, Levý, and Nida who were active after the Second World War, proposing their theories against the backdrop of two critical academic trends. The first was translation viewed as a subdivision of linguistics, leading to debates among "distinguished scholars from a variety of traditions in linguistics and other neighbouring disciplines."[299] The other was a call for making translation theory as scientific as possible due to an increasing concern with accuracy.[300] Such environments paved the way for developing translation into a new discipline.

2.3.2.2.2.1 Roman Jakobson (1896–1982)

In his 1959 essay "On Linguistic Aspects of Translation," Jakobson proposes a triadic system of translation as follows:

> We distinguish three ways of interpreting a verbal sign: it may be translated into other signs of the same language, into another language, or into another, nonverbal system of symbols. These three kinds of translation are to be differently labelled:
>
> - Intralingual translation or *rewording* is an interpretation of verbal signs by means of other signs of the same language.

---

297. Snell-Hornby, *Turns of Translation Studies*, 19.

298. Apart from German theorists, there were two eminent figures from other traditional translation theories: the French translator Etienne Dolet (1509–1546) and the Scottish lawyer and scholar Alexander Fraser Tytler (1748–1813). In his "Essay on the Principles of Translation" of 1791, Tytler proposed translation principles which remain emphasized in translator training nowadays: "the need for mastery of both source and target language, for understanding the author's sense and meaning, and for translating in an appropriate and idiomatic style with all the ease of the original composition." See Snell-Hornby, *Turns of Translation Studies*, 19.

299. Snell-Hornby, *Turns of Translation Studies*, 20.

300. Kevin Windle and Anthony Pym, "European Thinking on Secular Translation," in *The Oxford Handbook of Translation Studies*, eds. Kirsten Malmkjaer and Kevin Windle, Electronic ed. (Oxford; New York: Oxford University Press, 2012), §1.8.

- Interlingual translation or *translation proper* is an interpretation of verbal signs by means of some other language.
- Intersemiotic translation or *transmutation* is an interpretation of verbal signs by means of signs of nonverbal sign systems.[301]

The crucial contribution of Jakobson's triad to translation studies is that he went "beyond language in the verbal sense and [did] not look merely across languages."[302] His essay also stimulated fierce debates concerning "meaning" and "equivalence." The latter caused many further attempts to define "the nature of equivalence" over the following twenty years.[303]

2.3.2.2.2.2 Jiří Levý (1926–1967)

Levý was a literary historian and translator, whose main work, *The Art of Translation*, published in 1963, was a book on literary translation.

According to Levý, literary translation is "a form of art in its own right, and has a position somewhere between creative and 'reproductive' art . . . The translated work is an artistic reproduction, the translation process is one of artistic creativity."[304] Based on these innovative ideas, Levý developed two sorts of translation norms: one is the "reproductive" norm, requiring fidelity as based on proper understanding of the text; the other is the "artistic" norm, requiring the fulfillment of aesthetic criteria.[305] Fidelity and artistic style are by no means mutually exclusive. Translation norms, for him, are "not static and absolute but always depend on their historical context."[306]

In his 1967 essay, "Translation as a Decision Process," Levý maintained that from a *teleological*[307] perspective, "translation is a process of

---

301. Roman Jakobson, "On Linguistic Aspects of Translation," in *The Translation Studies Reader*, ed. Lawrence Venuti (London: Routledge, 2000 [1959]), 114.
302. Snell-Hornby, *Turns of Translation Studies*, 21.
303. Jeremy Munday, *Introducing Translation Studies: Theories and Applications* (New York: Routledge, 2012), 58.
304. Quoted in Snell-Hornby, *Turns of Translation Studies*, 22.
305. See Snell-Hornby, 22.
306. Quoted in Snell-Hornby, 22.
307. The word "teleology" derives from the Greek τέλος (*telos*, root: τελε-, "end, purpose") and -λογία (*logia*, "a branch of learning"), coined in 1728 by the German philosopher Christian von Wolff in his work *Philosophia rationalis, sive logica*. See, "Teleology,"

communication: the objective of translating is to impart the knowledge of the original to the foreign reader."³⁰⁸ From the pragmatic perspective, Levý continued, translating is viewed as a decision-making process, "a series of a certain number of consecutive situations – moves, as in a game – situations imposing on the translator the necessity of choosing among a certain (and very often exactly definable) number of alternatives."³⁰⁹

2.3.2.2.2.3 Eugene Nida (1914–2011)
Nida is recognized as the most influential theorist in the twentieth-century Bible translation, whose thoughts also had a significant impact on secular theorists³¹⁰ and thus will be considered in more detail here.

Though often criticized,³¹¹ Nida's dynamic equivalence model has been and remains widely used. In the 1960s, continually focusing on real and practical translation issues and intending to equip translators in extraordinarily different cultures, Nida accomplished what few of his predecessors attempted. That is, he produced "a systematic analytical procedure for translators working with all kinds of texts"; he "factored into the translation equation the receivers of the [target text] and their cultural expectations."³¹²

Gleaned from his abundant practical work on Bible translation from the 1940s onwards, Nida developed and presented his theory in two major works: *Toward a Science of Translating*³¹³ and the co-authored *The Theory*

---

accessed 10 July 2016, https://en.wikipedia.org/wiki/Teleology#Etymology. With the term *teleological*, Levý was already anticipating the *skopos* theory. See Erich Prunč, *Einführung in Die Translationswissenschaft* [Introduction to translation science] (Graz: Institut für Translationswissenschaft, 2001), 219.

308. Jiří Levý, "Translation as a Decision Process," in *The Translation Studies Reader*, ed. Lawrence Venuti (London: Routledge, 2000 [1967]), 148.

309. Levý, "Translation as a Decision," 148.

310. Stephen Pattemore, "Framing Nida: The Relevance of Translation Theory in the United Bible Societies," in *A History of Bible Translation*, ed. Philip A. Noss (Roma: Edizioni di storia e letteratura, 2007), 220; Susan Bassnett, *Translation Studies* (London; New York: Routledge, 2005), 3–4.

311. Eberhard Werner, "The Mandate for Bible Translation: Models of Communication and Translation in Theory and Practice in Regard to the Science of Bible Translation," 2013, 200, accessed 25 January 2014, http://www.sil.org/resources/archives/51438.

312. Munday, *Introducing Translation Studies*, 69.

313. Eugene A. Nida, *Toward a Science of Translating: With Special Reference to Principles and Procedures Involved in Bible Translating* (Leiden: Brill, 1964).

and Practice of Translation.[314] The title of the first book, Munday points out, demonstrates Nida's intention to "move Bible translation into a more scientific era" by integrating works in linguistics.[315] He further comments:

> [Nida's] more systematic approach borrows theoretical concepts and terminology both from semantics and pragmatics and from Noam Chomsky's work on syntactic structure which formed the theory of a universal generative-transformational grammar (Chomsky 1957, 1965).[316]

The key features of Chomsky's generative-transformational model can be summarized as follows:

- Phrase-structure rules generate an underlying or **deep structure** which is
- transformed by transformational rules relating one underlying structure to another (e.g. active to passive), to produce
- a final **surface structure**, which itself is subject to phonological and morphemic rules.

  . . . The most basic of such structures are **kernel sentences**, which are simple, active, declarative sentences that require the minimum of transformation (e.g. *the wolf attacked the deer*).[317]

Chomsky's model motivated Nida and Taber to develop their three-stage system of translation (analysis → transfer → restructuring) as follows:

- Analysis, in which the surface structure (i.e. the message as given in language A) is analyzed in terms of (a) the grammatical relationships and (b) the meanings of the words and combinations of words,
- transfer, in which the analyzed material is transferred in the mind of the translator from language A to language B, and

---

314. Eugene A. Nida and Charles Taber, *The Theory and Practice of Translation* (Leiden: Brill, 1969).
315. Munday, *Introducing Translation Studies*, 61.
316. Munday, 61.
317. Munday, 61–62.

- restructuring, in which the transferred material is restructured in order to make the final message fully acceptable in the receptor language.[318]

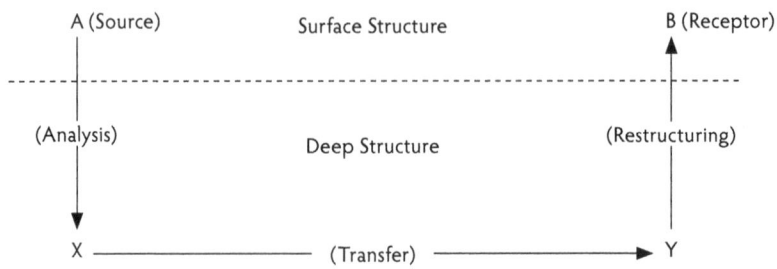

Nida's three-stage system of translation[319]

While analyzing individual words, borrowing from semantic and pragmatic theories, Nida argued that a word gets meaning according to its context and generates different responses through its culture.[320] He identified three kinds of meaning: linguistic, referential and emotive (connotative) meaning.

Linguistic meaning derives from the relationship between different linguistic structures. For instance, the following expressions with the possessive pronoun *his* bear different meanings: *his car* means "he possesses a car"; *his mistake* means "he performs a mistake"; *his humility* equals "humility is the quality of him."[321]

Referential meaning is the denotative "dictionary meaning." For example, *daughter* denotes female child.[322]

Emotive meaning is the associations a word generates. Almost the only way to analyze emotive meaning is using "contexts, either cultural or

---

318. Nida and Taber, *Theory and Practice*, 33.
319. Nida and Taber, *Theory and Practice*, 33; Cheung, "Twentieth Century Translation," 6.
320. Nida, *Toward a Science of Translating*, 33ff.
321. Nida, 57–60.
322. Nida, 70, 85.

linguistic."³²³ For example, in the sentence, "Don't worry about that, son," the term "*son* is a term of endearment or may in some contexts be patronizing."³²⁴

Besides, the technical terms "formal equivalence" and "dynamic equivalence" are substituted for the terms "literal" and "free," used in the age-old translation debates. Nida defined them as follows:

> Formal equivalence focuses attention on the message itself, in both form and content. In such a translation one is concerned . . . that the message in the receptor language should match as closely as possible the different elements in the source language . . . A translation of dynamic equivalence aims at complete naturalness of expression, and tries to relate the receptor to modes of behavior relevant within the context of his own culture.³²⁵

2.3.2.2.3 The pragmatic turn of the 1970s

The 1950s and 1960s could be viewed as the linguistic era,³²⁶ within which the pioneers just mentioned developed their translation theories more or less related to linguistics. But since the 1970s, translation theorists began to strive for the emancipation of translation studies from linguistics, which is the so-called "pragmatic turn."³²⁷ Snell-Hornby points out: "The pragmatic turn in linguistics as reflected in the speech-act theory, the rise of text-linguistics, the functional approach to language with the inclusion of its social and communicative aspects, clearly indicated the general trends of the 1970s."³²⁸

The trends, on the one hand, broadened the perspectives within linguistics, leading to "the reorientation from the isolated concept of the linguistic sign and the abstract concept of the language system . . . to a holistic notion of the text as part of the world around."³²⁹ On the other hand, the trends broke down barriers between the separate disciplines, leading to

---

323. Nida, 71.
324. Munday, *Introducing Translation Studies*, 65.
325. Nida, *Toward a Science of Translating*, 159.
326. Cheung, "Twentieth Century Translation," 1.
327. Snell-Hornby, *Turns of Translation Studies*, 35.
328. Snell-Hornby, 40.
329. Snell-Hornby, 40.

"an invaluable process of cross-fertilization, whereby the study of language was enriched by insights from anthropology, philosophy, sociology, and psychology."[330]

2.3.2.2.3.1 James Holmes (1924–1986)
At that time, a great stride to further reinforce the domain of translation studies as a distinct discipline was made by Holmes's seminal paper, "The Name and Nature of Translation Studies" (1972), where the term "translation studies" was first coined.[331] For Holmes, terms such as "art," "craft" or the "principle" used in this discipline, were too vague, and the more "learned" terms, such as "translatology," too abstract. The term "science" was also rejected by Holmes because it is "usually limited to the exact or natural sciences and implicitly excludes literary studies and the arts subjects in general."[332]

Holmes mapped out structures for the new discipline as having three branches: theory, descriptive studies (pure areas) and practice (applied translation studies).[333] He maintained that the three branches should mutually inform each other, noting: "Translation theory, for instance, cannot do without the solid, specific data yielded by research in descriptive and applied Translation Studies, while on the other hand one cannot even begin to work in one of the other two fields without having at least an intuitive theoretical hypothesis as one's starting point."[334]

Significantly, Holmes's theory presents an overall framework, covering the whole spectrum of translation studies. His framework was later put forward by the leading Israeli translation scholar Gideon Toury as in the following figure:

---

330. Snell-Hornby, 40.
331. Snell-Hornby, 40–41.
332. James Holmes, "The Name and Nature of Translation Studies," in *The Translation Studies Reader*, ed. Lawrence Venuti (New York; London: Routledge, 2004 [1972]), 182.
333. Holmes, "Name and Nature," 184, 189.
334. Holmes, 190.

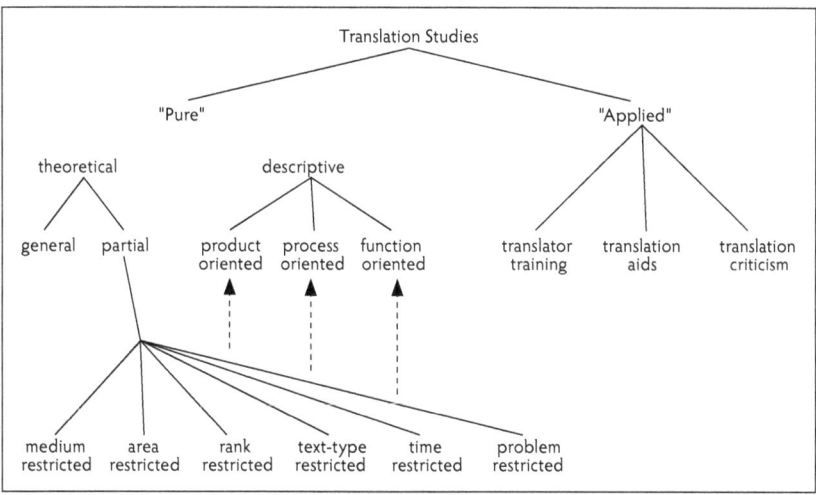

Holmes's "Map" of Translation Studies [335]

During the 1980s and 1990s, translation studies in Europe developed principally "down the middle branch of Holmes's model, that of descriptive studies,"[336] while the theory and practice branches grew rapidly in the United States.[337]

2.3.2.2.4 The cultural turn of the 1980s

The "pragmatic turn" of the 1970s, Snell-Hornby points out, laid the foundation for translation studies to be an independent discipline; the "cultural turn" of the 1980s subsequently established the basic profile of translation studies.[338]

The "cultural turn"[339] refers to "an attempt at moving the study of translation from a more formalist approach to one that laid emphasis on extra-textual factors related to cultural context, history and convention."[340] As

---

335. Toury, *Descriptive Translation Studies – And Beyond* (Amsterdam; Philadelphia: John Benjamins, 1995), 10.
336. Gentzler, "Global View of Translation Studies," 113.
337. Gentzler, 115.
338. Snell-Hornby, *Turns of Translation Studies*, 40.
339. In 1990, Bassnet and Lefevere co-published *Translation, History and Culture* (London: Routledge), formally putting forward the idea of cultural turn in translation.
340. Giuseppe Palumbo, *Key Terms in Translation Studies* (London; New York: Continuum, 2009), 30.

Hermans comments: "Translation used to be regarded primarily in terms of relations between texts, or between language systems. Today it is increasingly seen as a complex transaction taking place in a communicative, sociocultural context. This requires that we bring the translator as a social being fully into the picture."[341]

2.3.2.2.5 The interdiscipline in the 1990s

During the 1990s, there were two crucial turns within translation studies. The first was a methodical one originating from the necessity of more empirical studies in the field of translation and interpreting. This led to the investigation of new areas, principally in interpreting studies (e.g. court interpreting, sign language), "but also in cognitive domains concerning the translation process."[342] The second turn resulted from globalization and great strides in technology,[343] leading to fundamental changes in the work of the translator.[344]

Some critical issues discussed in this decade included translation studies as an interdiscipline, postcolonial translation and gender-based translation studies. Undoubtedly, the 1990s was "a time of consolidation in the new discipline of translation studies."[345]

2.3.2.2.6 At the turn of the millennium

At the beginning of the new millennium, the discipline of translation studies is viewed with "high optimism and great expectations."[346] Nowadays, translation studies, incorporating a wide range of research, is regarded as "interdisciplinary and intercultural, borrowing heavily from such areas as linguistics, literature studies, cultural studies, postcolonial studies, anthropology, psychology, and political science."[347]

---

341. T. Hermans, "Norms and the Determination of Translation: A Theoretical Framework," in *Translation, Power, Subversion*, eds. Román Álvarez and M. Carmen-África Vidal (Clevedon; Philadelphia: Multilingual Matters, 1996), 26.

342. Snell-Hornby, *Turns of Translation Studies*, 4.

343. For example, electronic translation aids like *Paratext* (UBS) and *Translator's Workplace* (SIL).

344. Snell-Hornby, *Turns of Translation Studies*, 4.

345. Snell-Hornby, 3, 149.

346. Snell-Hornby, 150.

347. Cheung, "Twentieth Century Translation" 13.

Cheung suggests that Bible translators should "seek to understand the practice of Bible translation from the wider perspective of translation studies, thereby incorporating ideas from secular researchers."[348] This is precisely what Wendland has done in his LiFE model.

2.3.3 LiFE: A Literary Functional-Equivalence Model

2.3.3.1 Introduction

As already noted, Nida's approach was widely accepted, but often criticized.

His *Toward a Science of Translating* (TASOT)[349] of 1964 was accredited as the "'Bible' not just for Bible translation but for translation theory in general."[350] The co-authored *The Theory and Practice of Translation* (TAPOT) was "the logical outgrowth of the previous book,"[351] which in turn became "the key reference point for Bible translators."[352] Then, the work *From One Language to Another* (FOLTA) by de Waard and Nida[353] could be read as a good commentary to TAPOT.[354] It was in FOLTA where de Waard and Nida replaced the terminology "dynamic equivalence" used in TASOT and TAPOT with "functional equivalence" due to the misunderstanding caused by the former.[355] This substitution was done without intention to suggest anything essentially different between the terminologies.[356]

---

348. Cheung, 13.

349. Since the abbreviations for Nida's books occur only here, they won't be listed in the abbreviation section of this thesis.

350. Edwin Gentzler, *Contemporary Translation Theories* (London: Routledge, 1993), 44; see also Stine, *Let the Words Be Written*, 5.

351. Nida and Taber, *Theory and Practice*, vii.

352. Aloo Osotsi Mojola and Ernst Wendland, "Scripture Translation in the Era of Translation Studies," in *Bible Translation: Frames of Reference*, ed. Timothy Wilt (Manchester, UK: St Jerome, 2003), 1.

353. Jan de Waard and Eugene A. Nida, *From One Language to Another: Functional Equivalence in Bible Translating* (Nashville, TN: Nelson, 1986).

354. Pattemore, "Framing Nida," 224.

355. de Waard and Nida, *From One Language to Another*, vii–viii.

356. But one can find that there is a much greater concern for the literary-structural features of the SL in FOLTA, which requires a correspondingly broader range of rhetorical functions for adequately expressing the intended meaning in the TL. See de Waard and Nida, *From One Language to Another*, 119–120.

From the beginning, Nida's approach was accepted rapidly in the Bible translation community.[357] The same principles, in essence, were adopted by Bible translation scholars, such as Beekman and Callow,[358] Larson,[359] and Barnwell.[360] By 1985, Nida's theory had come into its own.[361]

However, since the 1990s, criticism of Nida's approach has increased greatly.[362] Through the lens of translation studies nowadays, Mojola and Wendland comment: "Nida may be considered a trail-blazer for this discipline, in view of his intellectual rigour, his work in a wide variety of cultures, and his multidisciplinary approach to translation. But the trail has become a highway, and Bible translators have much to learn from others traveling on it."[363]

Mojola and Wendland also observe that works composed from a dynamic or functional-equivalence perspective often neglect the "issues related to the translation of the Bible as *literature*,"[364] which is of growing interest to Bible translators.[365] They thus adopt contemporary translation approaches that are particularly related to secular literature[366] in the hope that these theo-

---

357. P. Kirk, "Holy Communicative? Current Approaches to Bible Translation," in *Translation and Religion: Holy Untranslatable?*, ed. Lynne Long (Clevedon, UK: Multilingual Matters, 2005), 91; Pattemore, "Framing Nida," 223.

358. John Beekman and J. Callow, *Translating the Word of God: With Scripture and Topical Indexes* (Grand Rapids, MI: Zondervan, 1974).

359. Mildred L. Larson, *Meaning-Based Translation: A Guide to Cross-Language Equivalence* (Lanham, MD: University Press of America, 1984).

360. Kirk, "Holy Communicative?," 91. See, Katharine Barnwell, *Bible Translation: An Introductory Course in Translation Principles*, 3rd rev. ed. (Dallas, TX: Summer Institute of Linguistics, 1986); Katharine Barnwell, *Teacher's Manual to Accompany Bible Translation: An Introductory Course in Translation Principles*, 3rd ed. (Dallas, TX: Summer Institute of Linguistics, 1987).

361. D. A. Carson, "The Limits of Dynamic Equivalence in Bible Translation," *Evangelical Review of Theology* 9, no. 3 (1985): 200.

362. Kirk, "Holy Communicative?," 91.

363. Mojola and Wendland, "Scripture Translation in the Era of Translation Studies," 10.

364. Wendland points out that de Waard and Nida did refer to the significance of analyzing the literary features of biblical texts, but they paid little attention to "the study of discourse genres or larger text structures or to how literary features can be handled in translation." See Ernst R. Wendland, "A Literary Approach to Biblical Text Analysis and Translation," in *Bible Translation: Frames of Reference*, ed. Timothy Wilt (Manchester, UK; Northampton, MA: St Jerome, 2003), 180.

365. Mojola and Wendland, "Scripture Translation in the Era of Translation Studies," 13.

366. These contemporary translation methods include functionalist approach, descriptive approach, text-linguistic approach, postcolonial approaches, literalist approach,

ries could help "better understand the age-old task of Bible translation."[367] After such investigations, Wendland proposes literary functional-equivalence translation[368] which "does not really represent a new translation method," but a mixed model that places pedagogical methods at the very center.[369]

To better understand Wendland's literary functional-equivalence translation, three critical terms in the title of his model call for discussion (i.e. literature, functional equivalence, and translation).

2.3.3.2 The Bible as Literature

In line with a myriad of biblical scholars,[370] Wendland maintains that the Bible is well-crafted literature,[371] consisting of various genres and their associated stylistic features.[372] He quotes Linton to substantiate this perspective: "the Bible is literature, the kind of writing that attends to beauty, power, and memorability as well as to exposition. It is like a rich chord compared to a single note."[373]

Wendland points out that the analysis and interpretation of the Bible through a *literary* approach are not new. This approach has already been

---

interpretive approach, comparative approach, professional approaches, relevance theory approach, and foreignization v. domestication. See Mojola and Wendland, "Scripture Translation in the Era of Translation Studies," 13–25; Wendland, *Translating the Literature of Scripture*, 47–80.

367. Mojola and Wendland, "Scripture Translation," 13.
368. Wendland, *LiFE-Style Translating*, 110.
369. Werner, "Mandate for Bible Translation," 230.
370. In his "A Literary Approach to Biblical Text Analysis and Translation," 179 n. 2, Wendland lists a number of scholars who view the Bible as literature, such as Dorsey (1999), Harvey (1998), Wilson (1997), Breck (1994), Berlin (1994), McCann (1993), Powell (1990), and Alter (1985).
371. The argument that the Bible is literature was challenged by Mazor who asserts that "the Bible cannot be considered a literary work but a collection of books with a defined pragmatic goal," which seeks to "educate, teach, preach, and impart knowledge, values, and religious instruction." See Yair Mazor, *Who Wrought the Bible?: Unveiling the Bible's Aesthetic Secrets* (Madison, WI: University of Wisconsin Press, 2009), 21–22.
372. Wendland, "A Literary Approach to Biblical Text Analysis and Translation," 179; Wendland, *LiFE-Style Translating*, 109.
373. Calvin D. Linton, "The Importance of Literary Style in Bible Translation Today," in *The NIV: The Making of a Contemporary Translation*, ed. Kenneth L. Barker (Grand Rapids, MI: Academie Books, 1986), 16; quoted in Wendland, "A Literary Approach to Biblical Text Analysis and Translation," 179.

practiced by renowned theologians in the past, such as Augustine, Jerome, and Martin Luther. He quotes Augustine:[374]

> I could . . . show those men who cry out their own form of language as superior to that of our authors [of Scripture] . . . that all those powers [i.e. rhetoric] and beauties [i.e. artistry] of eloquence which they make their boast, are to be found in the sacred writings which God in his goodness has provided to mould our characters, and to guide us from this world of wickedness to the blessed world above.[375]

For Wendland, the term "literature" is well defined in *Webster's New World College Dictionary*:[376]

a) All writings in prose or verse, especially those of an imaginative or critical character, without regard to their excellence; often distinguished from scientific writing, news reporting, etc.

b) All of such writings considered as having permanent value, excellence of form, great emotional effect, etc.

c) All the writings of a particular time, country, region, etc., specifically those regarded as having lasting value because of their beauty, imagination, etc.[377]

The defining aspects above, Wendland notes, are significant and mutually related. He also points out that sense (b) implicitly refers to "the three basic dimensions of all texts" – content ("having permanent value"), form ("excellence of form"), and function ("great emotional effect"). The latter two textual qualities (i.e. form and function) are "more of a challenge to translators than is content,"[378] and thus will be further discussed when ex-

---

374. Wendland, *Translating the Literature of Scripture*, 37.

375. Augustine of Hippo, "On Christian Doctrine," in *Nicene and Post-Nicene Fathers: St Augustin's City of God and Christian Doctrine*, vol. 2, ed. P. Schaff, trans. J. F. Shaw (Buffalo, NY: Christian Literature Company, 1887), 577.

376. Wendland, *LiFE-Style Translating*, 62–63.

377. Victoria Neufeldt, ed., "Literature," *Webster's New World College Dictionary* (New York: Macmillan, 1996), 789.

378. Wendland, *LiFE-Style Translating*, 63. Wendland asserts, "The content that Bible translators have to deal with in most situations is relatively fixed, other than for certain text-critical issues and matters of interpretation." See Wendland, 63.

ploring the analysis and translation of biblical poetry below (see §2.3.3.7.1 and §2.3.3.7.2).

2.3.3.3 The Concept of Functional Equivalence

Wendland states that de Waard and Nida's functional equivalence does mention a literary-rhetorical approach[379] to Bible translation, but "the bigger picture is for the most part missing."[380] He criticizes[381] that in de Waard and Nida's approach, "translators are not given much guidance as to how the complete texts of different literary genres may be meaningfully analyzed as wholes, either in terms of the SL text or their own language."[382]

Recognizing the limitation of de Waard and Nida's approach, Wendland says that his notion of functional equivalence mainly borrows from three useful approaches to communication theory and translation: *Skopos* theory, relevance theory, and cognitive poetics.[383]

2.3.3.3.1 Skopos theory

Skopos theory, pioneered by K. Reiss and H. Vermeer in the early 1980s, and further developed by C. Nord in the late 1990s,[384] is "an explicit goal-oriented, process-directed, project-based approach to translation theory and practice."[385] This theory regards "function" as a prominent aspect in translation:

> Each text is produced for a given purpose and should serve this purpose. The *Skopos* rule thus reads as follows: translate/interpret/speak/write in a way that enables your text/translation to function in the situation in which it is used and with

---

379. de Waard and Nida, *From One Language to Another*, 112–119.
380. Wendland, *Translating the Literature of Scripture*, 46.
381. Despite Wendland's criticism of de Waard and Nida's approach, Werner argues that Wendland's holistic paradigm "remains bound by the restrictions of dynamic equivalence." See Werner, "Mandate for Bible Translation," 232.
382. Wendland, *Translating the Literature of Scripture*, 46.
383. Wendland, *LiFE-Style Translating*, 95–97.
384. Wendland, *Translating the Literature of Scripture*, 50.
385. Wendland, *LiFE-Style Translating*, 95 n. 1.

the people who want to use it and precisely in the way they want it to function.³⁸⁶

Skopos theory, known as "a fully functional approach," emphasizes the communicative "purpose (normally referred to only in the singular) that a particular translation is designed to perform for its primary target audience within a given sociocultural setting."³⁸⁷ In other words, "in *Skopostheorie* the particular goal of the text within the *TL* settings will largely determine the manner and style of translating in accordance with the governing framework for the translation project as a whole."³⁸⁸

This differs considerably from the focus of the functions in de Waard and Nida's functional equivalence. The goal of the latter is to "seek to employ a functionally equivalent set of forms which in so far as possible will match the meaning [i.e. functions] of the original source-language text."³⁸⁹ Thus, in translating through de Waard and Nida's approach, it is the principal communication functions (plural!) of the SL text that need to be determined and then reproduced in the TL text.³⁹⁰

These two functionalist perspectives, Wendland points out, are not mutually exclusive. He suggests that "both viewpoints are needed so that the author-intended aims of the Scriptures, as well as the needs, desires and expectations of a contemporary audience are respected and ultimately satisfied, to the degree possible, during the translation process."³⁹¹

It is noteworthy that recognizing the inevitable loss of message resulting from translating, Wendland concedes that a choice of which aspects of message need to be conveyed must always be made. This calls for thorough discussion and then is to be "spelled out within the project *Brief* and its *Skopos*."³⁹²

---

386. H. Vermeer (1989), quoted in Christiane Nord, *Translating as a Purposeful Activity: Functionalist Approaches Explained* (Manchester: St Jerome, 1997), 29.
387. Wendland, *Translating the Literature of Scripture*, 50–51.
388. Wendland, 51.
389. de Waard and Nida, *From One Language to Another*, 36.
390. Wendland, *Translating the Literature of Scripture*, 51.
391. Wendland, *LiFE-Style Translating*, 96.
392. Wendland, 96.

2.3.3.3.2 Relevance theory

Relevance Theory (RT), proposed by Gutt,[393] is "a cognitive, inferential approach to text processing, communication, and translation."[394] The former (cognitive) refers to "cognitive environment," which views the concept of "context"[395] as one's psychological state of mind, rather than a tangible or physical one. The latter (inferential) means that the communication between people depends "not only on verbal texts and their contexts, but also on [the] assumed shared knowledge and crucial features of the context (the social and situational environment)."[396] In RT, discourse is viewed as *optimally relevant* (or fully acceptable) if it affords "adequate contextual effects" for the audience, yet "without requiring unnecessary processing effort."[397]

Applying RT to his LiFE model, Wendland writes that "our aim, under most circumstances, is to communicate in a way that is able to achieve greater *efficiency* in terms of lower mental effort and *effectiveness*, or greater personal benefit for the envisaged audience."[398]

Thus, for Wendland, serious translators need to deliver significant messages in a way that is easiest for the audience to comprehend, "yet also with an appreciable amount of rhetorical impact and esthetic appeal, resulting in a significant number of cognitive, emotive, or volitional effects within a particular setting."[399]

---

393. Ernst-August Gutt, *Relevance Theory: A Guide to Successful Communication in Translation* (Dallas, TX: Summer Institute of Linguistics, 1992).

394. Wendland, *LiFE-Style Translating*, 95 n. 1.

395. Wendland elucidates that context in terms of "cognitive environment" is "an all-encompassing rational construct, composed of a vast array of personal beliefs and assumptions about the world, including specific elements of a person's knowledge, associations, and inferences (propositional, or logical, as well as empirical)." See Ernst R. Wendland, *Contextual Frames of Reference in Translation: A Coursebook for Bible Translators and Teachers* (Manchester, UK; Kinderhook, NY: St Jerome, 2008), 28.

396. Wendland, *LiFE-Style Translating*, 96.

397. Gutt, *Relevance Theory*, 24–25.

398. Wendland, *LiFE-Style Translating*, 96.

399. Wendland, 96.

2.3.3.3.3 Cognitive poetics

Cognitive poetics is "a specific application of cognitive linguistics to the study of literary texts (poetics)."[400] Wendland writes of Stockwell's formulation[401] as follows: Cognitive poetics "stresses the perceptual notion of figure and ground; the close interconnection of experience, cognition, meaning, and language; the importance of 'readerly' interpretation (how readers/hearers perceive and understand verbal texts); and the primary mental strategies that all people employ when they interpret any text."[402]

From the aspect of cognitive poetics, translation may be viewed as the textual "mapping of different knowledge domains guided by the principle of analogy."[403]

2.3.3.4 What Is Translation?

Wendland argues that *meaningful* translation (contrary to *mechanical* translation) as a "creative, yet controlled, compositional activity" is an extraordinary "specialized, complex, and varied type of verbal communication."[404] It is related to "an interpersonal, transformative *sharing* of the same text between two different systems of language, thought, and culture."[405] With these in mind, Wendland first provides a simple definition of translation: Translation is "the practice of intercultural and interlingual communication. It is an intricate, at times artful, process of semiotic textual exchange, or verbal 'transubstantiation' (trans-FORM-ation)."[406]

Thus, translation involves two basic procedures: *re-conceptualization* and *re-composition*.

Wendland elaborates *re-conceptualization* as:

> The intercultural re-ideation of a given SL text, which is a meaningful and purposeful selection, arrangement, and

---

400. Wendland, 95 n. 1.
401. Peter Stockwell, *Cognitive Poetics: An Introduction* (London: Routledge, 2002).
402. Wendland, *LiFE-Style Translating*, 95 n. 1.
403. Kristin de Troyer, "'And God Was Created...': on Translating Hebrew into Greek," in *The Bible through Metaphor and Translation: A Cognitive Semantic Perspective*, ed. Kurt Feyaerts, Religions and Discourse 15 (Oxford; New York: Lang, 2003), 210.
404. Wendland, *LiFE-Style Translating*, 102.
405. Wendland, 102.
406. Wendland, 102.

differentiation of signs, whether oral or written, as it is conceptually transferred from one worldview domain and value system to another... The first procedure requires the cognitive processing and conversion of all the deep-level semantic and pragmatic features of the original text in terms of the target language and cultural setting.[407]

The second procedure *re-composition* refers to:

> The semantically accurate, formally appropriate, and pragmatically acceptable interlingual re-signification of the original text in a specific TL, along with any essential paratextual or extra-textual bridge and background material needed to facilitate comprehension... [T]he second [procedure]... deals with the more overt surface-level semantic, structural, and stylistic aspects of verbal composition..., [and then creates] a linguistic representation in the TL.[408]

Significantly, several crucial factors are influencing the definition and evaluation of translation as "the multilingual, intersemiotic, cross-cultural process of textual, as well as cognitive, transformation," among which are:

- the **model** of translation that one adopts (whether source-text oriented or target-text oriented, . . . cognitive-poetic, or relevance based);
- the **motive**, or purpose (*Skopos*), of the translation in relation to a designated target audience in one or more preferred settings of use;
- the **manner** in which the re-composition process is carried out (e.g. literal versus idiomatic), including one's view or opinion of the original text.[409]

Given the complicated issues related to translation, Wendland goes on to propose a more precise definition of translation:

---

407. Wendland, 102.
408. Wendland, 102.
409. Wendland, 102.

> Translation is the conceptually mediated re-composition of one contextually framed text within a different communication setting in the most relevant, functionally equivalent manner possible; that is, stylistically marked, more or less, in keeping with the designated job commission agreed upon for the TL project concerned.[410]

After examining the critical issues regarding literature, functional equivalence, and translation, Wendland proceeds to define his literary functional-equivalence approach to translation.

2.3.3.5 Defining a Literary Functional-Equivalence (LiFE) Translation

Wendland's LiFE model intends to produce a version "that is more *literary* in nature rather than less."[411] A well-trained and competent translation team should be capable of making such a version manifesting "artistic qualities on all strata of linguistic structure in the TL." Wendland further explains:

> [A LiFE version] is normally composed within the framework of a TL genre that is a functional equivalent of the primary SL discourse being rendered, but having its own distinctive stylistic features that operate as a formal "package" to convey the principle communicative purpose(s) of the original text.[412]

Wendland also emphasizes that different degrees and levels of literary application are possible, depending on the main communicative goal and the real circumstances, such as human, financial, and technical issues. These are considered during the project-planning stage, and then incorporated into the project *Skopos* and formulated in an explicit *Brief*. For Wendland, "[e]ven a little bit of LiFE can mean a lot to any translation."[413] However, it is worth noting that for a translation to qualify as a literary one, "*at least one prominent element of stylistic form* in the translated text needs to be artfully modified in

---

410. Wendland, 104; Wendland, *Translating the Literature of Scripture*, 85.
411. Wendland, *LiFE-Style Translating*, 108–109.
412. Wendland, 108–109. Wendland, in *LiFE-Style Translating*, 111, notes that if there is no TL correspondent available, translators need to invent "their own hybrid genre," based on the proper speech styles that exist in the vernacular.
413. Wendland, 109–110.

a systematic, consistent manner and for a definite rhetorical purpose."[414] Finally, Wendland's LiFE "is not a 'one-way-only' method; rather it offers a broad continuum of possibilities," which is schematized below:[415]

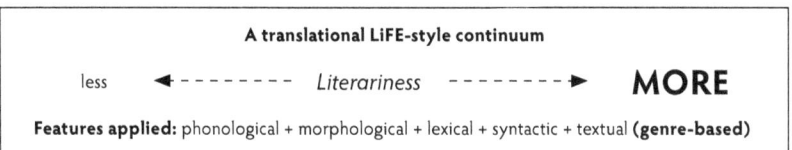

2.3.3.6 Preparing for a Poetic LiFE Translation

Besides the common word-by-word, verse-by-verse exegetical-hermeneutical analysis, LiFE pays particular attention to two distinct general operations, which enable translators to "more completely and accurately determine the non-referential dimensions of meaning":[416]

- **Artistic text analysis**, which stresses "the formal, esthetic, and iconic" dimensions[417] of verbal discourse, focusing on "the poetic and expressive functions of communication."[418]
- **Rhetorical text analysis**, which emphasizes "the functional, dynamic element[419] of verbal discourse," focusing on "the affective and imperative functions of communication."[420]

Thus, LiFE intends "to stimulate emotive *solidarity* and communicative *power* within the audience." Meanwhile, there is a special concern for the *appeal*[421]

---

414. Wendland, 109–110.
415. Wendland, 125.
416. Wendland, 123.
417. For example, beautiful, euphonious, memorable, sensually appealing. See Wendland, *LiFE-Style Translating*, 123.
418. Wendland, 123.
419. For example, powerful, persuasive, influential, purposefully effective. See Wendland, 123.
420. Wendland, 123.
421. "Appeal" is related to the concern of "what makes the text esthetically attractive – capturing the eyes and ears of the audience and facilitating the other communicative aims that the author sought to achieve in and through his[/her] text." See Wendland, *LiFE-Style Translating*, 123.

and *potency* (power and persuasiveness)[422] of both the SL and TL texts.[423]

What follows is Wendland's concise description of the key point of his LiFE model:

> [In the LiFE model, a] literary method of analysis is needed to fully investigate the compositional aspects of biblical discourse since such an approach pays special attention to a text's macro- and microstructure, its stylistic distinctives, its functional dimension, as well as the emotive and connotative aspects of the discourse. By this means, then, the necessary foundation is also laid for effecting a corresponding communication of the literature of Scripture in another language, literary tradition, and cultural setting.[424]

2.3.3.7 Analyzing and Translating Biblical Poetry

As mentioned earlier, there are three basic dimensions of all texts – content, form, and function. The latter two, Wendland stresses, are more challenging for translators, and need further elucidation. Since this study will conduct the translating of biblical poetry through Wendland's approach, these two challenging dimensions (form and function) will be further elaborated.

2.3.3.7.1 The major stylistic forms of Hebrew poetry

This section refers to the major stylistic forms of Hebrew poetry,[425] including parallel phrasing, sound effects, figurative language, condensed expression, emphatic devices, shifting patterns, poetic structures,[426] all of which must be examined in initial stages before translation.

2.3.3.7.1.1 Parallel phrasing

Parallelism as probably the most significant feature of Hebrew poetry is manifested in the composition of a discourse "in the form of paired,

---

422. "Potency" refers to the concern of "what it is that compels listeners to feel experientially the Bible's impact, emotions, attitudes, moods, exhortations, and admonitions (under the operation of the Holy Spirit)." See Wendalnd, *LiFE-Style Translating*, 123.

423. Wendland, 123.

424. Wendland, 123.

425. Wendland, 185.

426. Wendland, 186–220.

comparatively short, rhythmic lines called cola," a plural form of "colon." These lines, together called bicolon, correspond to each other semantically, and often formally as well (e.g. "similar length, vocabulary, sounds, word forms or word order, and grammatical constructions").[427]

The lines in a bicolon are "designated as A or B (plus C or D in the case of a less common third or fourth line)." According to Wendland's model, there are four main ways that line B functions as a complement to line A: similarity, contrast, cause-effect, or addition.[428]

2.3.3.7.1.2 Sound effects

The composition of Hebrew poetry is intended to "be recited aloud and usually in public." Accordingly, different sound techniques are employed to enhance the articulation of the spoken aspects of the text and thereby also increase its memorability.[429]

The following are three prominent sound effects:

> **Rhythm**, which is demonstrated by "the regular recurrence of some perceptible, often predictable pattern of sound, though the pattern may be modified at any time to create some added impact."[430]
>
> **Assonance/consonance** (also called alliteration), the former of which is clusters of repeated vowels, and the latter of which is clusters of repeated consonants.[431]
>
> **Puns** (a form of word play), which is related to "two words with similar sounds but different meanings."[432]

2.3.3.7.1.3 Figurative language

Figures of speech enable competent poets to employ vivid imagery and colorful language, appealing to "the imagination for a specific communication

---

427. Wendland, 186.
428. Wendland, 186.
429. Wendland, 188.
430. Wendland, 189.
431. Wendland, *Analyzing the Psalms*, 171.
432. Wendland, *LiFE-Style Translating*, 191.

purpose."[433] This literary technique "creates a little break or shift in the flow of discourse that causes the reader or hearer to pause and take notice."[434] The following are three common pairs of figures (paired due to the similarity between them) in Hebrew poetry:[435]

Simile and metaphor

- **Simile**. A simile occurs as a comparison between a topic (T) and its image (I) is unambiguous. The ground of comparison (G) "may be stated or left unexpressed, but there is always an overt *marker* (M), such as 'like' or 'as,' to indicate the non-literal nature of the expression." For example, "They (T) are *like* (M) a lion (I), eager to tear (G)" (Ps 17:12).[436]
- **Metaphor**. In a metaphor, a topic is more immediately associated with an image to impress the audience more forcefully. There is no explicit marker (e.g. "like" or "as") to indicate a comparison. In the Psalms, the ground of comparison in most metaphors is implicitly stated in the text, thus calling for careful examination in the nearby context and further study on "the relevant historical, cultural, biological, and geographical setting as well as the religious practices of ancient Israel."[437] Occasionally, the topic of a metaphor is even left implicit and only the image is present.[438]

Metonym and synecdoche

- **Metonym** refers to "the *substitution* of the name or designation of one thing for that of another closely associated with it."[439]
- **Synecdoche** denotes that "a *part* of something is used to refer to the *whole* (or vice versa), or a *particular* is used to refer to the *general* (or vice versa)."[440]

---

433. Wendland, 191.
434. Wendland, *Analyzing the Psalms*, 139.
435. Wendland, *LiFE-Style Translating*, 192.
436. Wendland, *Analyzing the Psalms*, 140.
437. Wendland, 142.
438. Wendland, 143.
439. Wendland, 147.
440. Wendland, 148.

Personification and anthropomorphism
- **Personification** demonstrates that "an inanimate or lifeless thing or abstraction is represented as if it were a human being, a living person."[441]
- **Anthropomorphism** involves that "God, or some other spirit being who is not a human, is spoken of as though he had a human body."[442]

2.3.3.7.1.4 Condensed expression
While composing poetry, poets employ every word purposefully and often deliberately leave out certain expected words or concepts, driving the audience to determine from the context due to the implicit expression. Such a condensed expression "is what gives poetry its typical rhythmic form and evocative content."[443] There are three common kinds of condensation in Hebrew poetry: verb gapping,[444] pronominal reference,[445] and allusion.[446]

2.3.3.7.1.5 Emphatic devices
Emphatic forms are used to reinforce "the rhetorical effect of the other more characteristically poetic features, such as parallelism."[447] They also serve to indicate "boundaries and thematic peaks in the discourse arrangement of both poetry and poetic prose."[448]

Along with parallel expression, emphatic techniques also include:

Intensifiers, which are common single words in Hebrew, such as כִּי "surely," הִנֵּה "see," אַשְׁרֵי "blessed," etc.[449]

---

441. Wendland, 150.

442. Wendland, 152.

443. Wendland, *LiFE-Style Translating*, 193.

444. For example, in Isa 3:25, the verb "fall" in the first colon also applies to the second colon: "Your men will fall by the sword, your warriors in battle." See Wendland, 193.

445. For example, the pronoun "it" in Isa 7:7b is a condensed expression: "It will not take place, it will not happen." See Wendland, 194.

446. Wendland, 193–194. Wendland, in *LiFE-Style Translating*, 194, notes that the figurative allusion in Ps 51:7a is an instance of a condensed expression: "Cleanse me with hyssop, and I will be clean." What lies behind the condensed expression (allusion) calls for further exploration.

447. Wendland, 194.

448. Wendland, 194.

449. Wendland, 195.

Exclamations, which are terse, intensified utterances, serving to emotively amplify a particular dimension of the prophet's message.[450]

Rhetorical questions, which are question forms without expecting an answer and are "a forceful expression of the speaker's attitude, opinion, and emotions with regard to a particular issue."[451]

Hyperbole, which is an explicit exaggeration, serving to stress and amplify a certain perspective or strong opinion.[452]

Irony and sarcasm, the former of which serves to deliver an indirect complaint or criticism and the latter is "a more intense and forceful type of irony," being used to "ridicule, reprove, rebuke, warn, condemn, or verbally injure the addressee."[453]

2.3.3.7.1.6 Shifting patterns
When intending to highlight a specific dimension of content or creating some particular artistic or emotive effect, a poet sometimes uses "a deliberate departure from the norms of discourse," or what Wendland calls shifting patterns.[454] What follows are four types of shift:

Pronouns. In a pronominal shift, the pronouns change, but the personal referent remains the same.[455]

Word order. The reasons for moving certain syntactic elements around within the short poetic clause (colon) include euphony (a pleasing sound), a flowing rhythm, or the creation of topical or constituent focus.[456]

Insertion. Insertion (hyperbaton) "is patterned according to the formula A-X-B, where A-B is a standard grammatical

---

450. Wendland, 195.
451. Wendland, 196.
452. Wendland, 197.
453. Wendland, 197–198.
454. Wendland, 198.
455. Wendland, 198.
456. Wendland, 200.

construction that has an unexpected, seemingly misplaced or added element, X, inserted within it."⁴⁵⁷ The insertion, for the sake of special effect, may be a single word, a phrase, or an entire clause (colon).⁴⁵⁸

Style. In terms of the shift of style, the Hebrew poets may creatively utilize their "literary skills, [their] personal style, to inject some formal and/or semantic surprise into the text."⁴⁵⁹ Usually, this is done by means of "a pronounced modification in the current referential content, an ordinary linguistic construction, the prevailing connotative tone, or the general communicative purpose."⁴⁶⁰

2.3.3.7.1.7 Poetic structures

In Hebrew poetry, the lines (cola) and couplets (bicola) are combined to form larger units with a single major topic. Such segments may be called "*stanzas* if they are similar in size and structure, or *strophes* if they are not."⁴⁶¹ The latter is "more common in the Hebrew corpus of lyrical, elegiac, and prophetic books" than the former.⁴⁶² As to where a larger unit begins and ends (especially where it begins), the analyst needs to locate definite linguistic and literary *markers*. An abundance of markers will "also serve to mark peaks within a section, especially in the middle or at its ending; this possibility needs to be investigated as well."⁴⁶³

Before delving into different markers, five main kinds of boundary-making recursion need to be sketched out: *inclusio* [a-X-a'], *exclusio* [X-a, Z, a'-Y], *anaphora* [a-X, a'-Y], *epiphora* [X-a, Y-a'], *anadiplosis* [X-a, a'-Y] "(a/a'=the reiterated material; X=the same discourse unit; Y=a different discourse unit; and Z=a third discourse unit)."⁴⁶⁴

---

457. Wendland, 200.
458. Wendland, 201.
459. Wendland, 201.
460. Wendland, 201.
461. Wendland, 206.
462. Wendland, 206.
463. Wendland, 207.
464. Wendland, 207.

Markers of aperture (a new beginning)

- **Recursion** is the most crucial marker of text divisions, including exact lexical repetition (the most diagnostic), close similarity (or strong contrast), corresponding structures, and common themes or motifs.

    A beginning of a unit may be indicated by the opening segment of a structure pattern of *anaphora* [a-X, a'-Y], *inclusio* [a-X-a'], *exclusio* [X-a, Z, a'-Y], and *anadiplosis* [X-a, a'-Y].[465]

- **Formulas** (conventional literary expressions) often occur in the Hebrew prophets.[466] They are announcements of messages from Yahweh and can be employed as emphasis ("intensifiers") in poetic discourse, functioning obviously to open a unit.[467]

- **Shifts** in textural content, form, or function serve as the beginning of a new unit of poetry. The following are various kinds of shifts:

    > [S]hifts include an overtly marked change in the speaker, addressee(s), setting (time, place), dramatic circumstances, interpersonal relationships, tone or atmosphere, point of view or perspective, topic under discussion, literary genre, main event sequence, or principal character.[468]

- **Intensifiers**, "while not diagnostic in and of themselves," are common at the beginning of a new poetic unit to reinforce one of the other three markers of aperture already present. What follows is a list of literary forms used as intensifiers:

    > [Literary forms as intensifiers comprise] vocatives (especially divine names and praise epithets), imperatives, rhetorical or leading questions, exclamations, graphic figurative language, contrastive imagery, asyndeton (i.e.

---

465. Wendland, 207.
466. For example, Hosea 1:1; 2:16, 21; Amos 3:1, 11, 12, 13. See Wendland, 209.
467. Wendland, 209.
468. Wendland, 209.

the absence of any conjunction or transitional expression), and utterances that express irony or hyperbole.[469]

Markers of closure (a point of conclusion)
The markers of closure are more ambiguous as compared to those of aperture. However, if the markers of aperture are not strong, the analyst needs to examine the preceding verse in the discourse to find whether there are any prominent signs of a closure or not. If there are, then a structural boundary between the two verses could be posited more confidently. There are three prominent indicators of closure:

- **Recursion**: The various kinds of literary indicators of closure are closely related to that of aperture. What follows may be a useful summary:

    Aperture is marked by *anaphora* [a-X, a'-Y], closure by *epiphora* [X-a, Y-a'], and both aperture and closure by *inclusio* [a-X-a'], *exclusio* [X-a, Z, a'-Y], and *anadiplosis* [X-a, a'-Y].[470]

- **Formulas** that indicate closure consist of prophetic speech expressions, for instance, נְאֻם־יְהוָה "oracle of Yahweh" (Hos 11:11), and אָמַר יְהוָה "says Yahweh" (Amos 5:17).[471]

- **Intensifiers** are related to emphatic utterance that either summarizes, underscores, or concludes the argument that has been well developed in the previous discourse. This category includes direct speech, exclamation, prediction, condensed utterance, graphic imagery, and key thematic or theological assertion.[472]

Markers of cohesion (bonds of connection)
Different connections that make the inner parts of a segment cohesive should substantiate the outer boundaries of a poetic text indicated by markers of aperture and closure. The main cohesion-producing devices of Hebrew poetry

---

469. Wendland, 209.
470. Wendland, 209.
471. Wendland, 209.
472. Wendland, 210.

are refrain (a repeated colon/bicolon), overlap, chiasmus, and acrostic,[473] the last two of which are delineated as follows:

- **Chiasmus**: A-B=B'-A' as the basic structure of a chiasmus may be extended as A-B-C…X…C'-B'-A' (termed as "palistrophe, introversion," or "reverse parallel structure"). In the latter case, X represents additional, optional structural elements. "The core of a chiasmus often presents information of special thematic importance and/or pragmatic import."[474]
- **Acrostic**: An acrostic is a highly formalized type of poetry in which the initial letters of successive lines (cola) or strophes/stanzas observe a traditional downward sequence of the twenty-two letters of the Hebrew alphabet.[475]

2.3.3.7.2 The major functions of Hebrew poetry

The selection and arrangement of literary forms are to enhance the performance of primary aims of communication. The following is a list of functions carried out by the expert use of poetic forms either in the original biblical text or modern translations:

- To broadly organize and arrange (i.e. give definition and coherence to the thematic structure of) a given poetic text
- To spotlight within the text a set of selected theological truths, religious instructions, and moral imperatives
- To forcefully impress upon listeners
- To express with greater or lesser degrees of intensification the author/speaker's emotions, moods, and attitudes, and to *evoke* corresponding feelings within the audience
- To render the translation more memorable, hence also more memorizable and transmittable
- To engage God's people psychologically and spiritually more fully in a meaningful worship experience, especially via the familiar phatic (ritual) forms of liturgical language[476]

---

473. Wendland, 210–214.
474. Wendland, 212.
475. Wendland, 213.
476. Wendland, 220–221.

2.3.3.8 A Methodology for Literary-Poetic Text Analysis

In his *LiFE-Style Translating*, Wendland proposes a ten-step exegetical methodology to achieve a poetic LiFE translation.[477] He notes that "various modifications could be made to the ten steps in terms of composition and order of arrangement, and perhaps several steps could be combined into one."[478] His ten-step exegetical methodology is listed as follows:

Step 1: Study the context
Step 2: Specify the literary genre
Step 3: Find the points of major disjunction
Step 4: Plot the patterns of formal and conceptual repetition
Step 5: Discover and evaluate the artistic and rhetorical features
Step 6: Do a complete discourse analysis
Step 7: Investigate the referential framework
Step 8: Connect the cross-textual correspondences
Step 9: Determine the functional and emotive dynamics
Step 10: Coordinate form-functional matches

Finally, for Wendland, a vital part of the translation enterprise is to "attempt (at least) to reproduce in the TL a similar level of specific as well as general communicative significance as found in the SL text."[479] In a LiFE translation, this could be done (1) by fully investigating a source text's macro- and microstructure, its stylistic distinctives, its functional dimension, and the emotive and connotative aspects of the discourse, etc.; (2) by choosing from "the total inventory of vernacular linguistic and literary resources" those most closely corresponding to the artistic qualities on various levels of linguistic structure in the SL.[480]

2.4 Conclusion

Thanks to the rapid development of translation studies in the past century, contemporary Chinese Bible translators should no longer be confused by 嚴復 Yán, Fù's triad (fidelity, fluency, and elegance) or subject to the dichotomy

---

477. Wendland, 126–148.
478. Wendland, 126.
479. Wendland, 221.
480. Wendland, 221.

of literal-versus-free translation. They can choose any appropriate approach with peace of mind, depending on the *Skopos* of a translation project.

As noted in the first half of this chapter (the history of Chinese Bible translation), a weakness of contemporary Chinese Bible translation is that of conducting the practice of Bible translation without using rigorous, systematic translation methods or theories. In line with Péng, the present researcher insists that it is essential to inform the audience of the translation approach used in a Bible version.[481] Because the Bible is literature, it is appropriate to adopt Wendland's LiFE as the translation theory and method for the present study. Since LiFE is a relatively new approach, it is necessary to convene and train a Bible translation team.

Currently, there are no Chinese Bible versions easily understood by children that are based on the original text. Thus, this study aims to produce Bible translations with artistic qualities that speak to them. Can children themselves as Bible readers contribute to such a translation task? Can they be important members of a translation team? What kind of Bible version is suitable for them? To such issues this study now turns.

---

481. Péng 彭, "Contemplating the Future of Chinese Bible Translation," 15.

CHAPTER 3

Children as Crucial Members of an Intergenerational Bible Translation Team

3.1 Introduction

Should young children be exposed to the Bible? Some may argue that they are so innocent that the dark stories in the Bible are inappropriate for them. However, this has been questioned by a majority of contemporary thinkers who study children's spirituality and its relationship to Christian theology.[1] This simplistic, one-dimensional view of children is one of the reasons that led to the development and publication of what came to be called children's Bibles,[2] in which the Bible canon and the gospel are profoundly distorted.[3] Different kinds of such narrow views toward children can be found both in society and the church. In today's consumer culture, children are regarded "as being commodities, consumers, or even economic burdens."[4] In the church, children are viewed as sinful, developing creatures in need of instruction

---

1. Rebecca Nye, *Children's Spirituality: What It Is and Why It Matters*, 3rd impression (London: Church House, 2013), 80.

2. For more discussions on children's Bibles and their negative impact, see Malherbe, "Big Words and Little Ears," §4.1.

3. Gretchen Wolff Pritchard, *Offering the Gospel to Children* (Cambridge, MA: Cowley, 1992), 42. For further discussions, see §§3.3.3.2–3.3.3.3.

4. Marcia J. Bunge, "Historical Perspectives on Children in the Church: Resources for Spiritual Formation and a Theology of Childhood Today," in *Children's Spirituality: Christian Perspectives, Research, and Applications*, ed. Donald Ratcliff et al. (Eugene, OR: Cascade, 2004), 44.

and guidance.⁵ This is reflected in children's low priority while the church develops its ministry.⁶ Allen laments that "children face the marginalization and oppression of a modern church that does not take them seriously as co-participants in its ministry."⁷

Childhood studies in Christianity has challenged today's church to take children seriously. The church needs to consider sincerely how to involve the marginalized and oppressed children in the Christian community and ministry. And intergenerational ministry is a promising approach.

Chapter 3 begins with an overview of childhood studies, followed by applying the findings from childhood studies in Christianity to argue that: children are integral to the church; children need the whole Bible; children can contribute to the enterprise of Bible translation. The second half of this chapter focuses on intergenerational ministry, delving into its background, definition, foundations, principles, practices, and outcomes. This chapter concludes by proposing the idea of an intergenerational Bible translation team.

3.2 An Overview of Childhood Studies

3.2.1 Introduction

Children and childhood are now popular issues in a wide range of academic disciplines. The rapidly increasing area of childhood studies⁸ "offers the potential for interdisciplinary research that can contribute to an emergent paradigm wherein new ways of looking at children can be researched and theorized."⁹

---

5. Marcia J. Bunge, "A More Vibrant Theology of Children," in *Christian Reflection: A Series in Faith and Ethics*, 13, 2003, accessed 6 June 2014, http://www.baylor.edu/ifl/christianreflection/ChildrenarticleBunge.pdf.

6. Wess Stafford, *Too Small to Ignore: Why the Least of These Matters Most* (Colorado Springs, CO: WaterBrook, 2007), 8.

7. Allen, "Children as Disciples, Not Simply Discipled," 9.

8. Since childhood studies is largely "Western" in origin, this research mainly explores its development in the West. Special attention is paid to its development in Christianity. Chinese theologians pay little attention to this new discipline. Hope this research can be translated into Chinese to bridge the gap.

9. Mary Jane Kehily, "Understanding Childhood: An Introduction to Some Key Themes and Issues," in *An Introduction to Childhood Studies*, ed. Mary Jane Kehily (Maidenhead, UK;

Rather than an exhaustive examination, this section briefly explores the field of childhood studies from both conceptual and historical dimensions. Accordingly, key concepts in this area are first explored, followed by a short history of childhood studies with a focus on its development in Christianity.

3.2.2 Key Concepts in Childhood Studies

What is childhood studies? For Kehily, the answer is neither simple nor straightforward because various disciplines "have developed different ways of approaching the study of children, using different research methods driven by a far from coherent set of research questions."[10] Therefore, the present study intends not to offer an unambiguous definition of childhood studies, but to provide two critical concepts in this regard: (1) Children as social agents; (2) The distinctions between the three concepts – childhood, children, and child.[11]

3.2.2.1 Children as Social Agents

Children as social agents[12] is "the most important claim of the new childhood studies literature in the social sciences,"[13] which is one of the disciplines (or methods) that delve into this field.

Children as social agents means that "children not only have minds of their own but also have values, aspirations, and societies of their own."[14] Thus, both "listening to children's voice" and "hearing clearly what they have to say" are indispensable to childhood studies.[15] Children can not only help

---

New York: Open University Press, 2009), 1.

10. Kehily, "Understanding Childhood," 1.

11. Allison James, "Understanding Childhood from an Interdisciplinary Perspective: Problems and Potentials," in *Rethinking Childhood*, eds. Peter B. Pufall and Richard P. Unsworth (New Brunswick, NJ: Rutgers University Press, 2004), 32–36.

12. Drawing upon the UN Convention of 1989 and earlier international agreements in 1924 and 1959, Wall maintains that the language of children's rights (children as agents) should be balanced with the languages of adult responsibility. That is, "children are not just little adult agents deserving the same rights as all but are also profoundly vulnerable, relational, conditioned, and in need of special care from others." See John Wall, "Childhood Studies, Hermeneutics, and Theological Ethics," *The Journal of Religion* 86, no. 4 (2006): 541–542.

13. Wall, "Childhood Studies," 538.

14. Peter B. Pufall and Richard P. Unsworth, "Preface," in *Rethinking Childhood*, eds. Peter B. Pufall and Richard P. Unsworth (New Brunswick, NJ: Rutgers University Press, 2004), xi.

15. James, "Understanding Childhood," 35.

"shape [adult] ideas of childhood and [adult] expectations of what children can or cannot do," but also contribute to define issues regarding themselves from "their own experiences and perceptions."[16] For example, based on "a national survey of a representative sample of over 11,000 young people aged between 14 and 16 years,"[17] Asbridge points out:

> Looking at childhood through the eyes of a child we see a model of the child as a complete person ("self"), although still learning and growing. They see themselves as active participants in relationships with adults (as well as their peers) in a variety of environments. They have a sense of self, values and an understanding of their relationship to the environment and others that is not necessarily dependent upon the instruction, interpretation or mediation of adults.[18]

The significance of children or young people's role in childhood studies is vividly portrayed by Woodhead's metaphor, "Childhood studies can be represented as the hub of a wheel that is held in place by the tension of multiple radiating spokes of enquiry.[19] Children and young people are the hub, reflecting the core interest in their experiences, status, rights and well-being."[20]

3.2.2.2 The Distinctions between the Three Concepts – Childhood, Children, and Child

In childhood studies, it is crucial to critically employ the three terms – childhood, children, and child.[21] Unfortunately, their definitions or interpretations differ among scholars.

---

16. James, "Understanding Childhood," 36.

17. This survey was conducted by the Children's Society as one part of the Good Childhood Inquiry in the UK. See Nigel Asbridge, "What Is a Child?," in *Through the Eyes of a Child: New Insights in Theology from a Child's Perspective*, eds. Anne Richards and Peter Privett (London: Church House, 2009), 17.

18. Asbridge, "What Is a Child," 17–18.

19. The "multiple radiating spokes of enquiry" means that childhood studies has an interdisciplinary focus for critical analysis, research, and debate. See Martin Woodhead, "Childhood Studies: Past, Present and Future," in *An Introduction to Childhood Studies*, ed. Mary Jane Kehily, 2nd ed. (Maidenhead, UK; New York: Open University Press, 2009), 31.

20. Woodhead, "Childhood Studies," 31.

21. James, "Understanding Childhood," 32.

Oxford dictionary defines the term childhood as: "The state of being a child; the stage of life or period during which one is a child; the time from birth to puberty."[22] LeVine is slightly more specific: The conception of childhood varies "in form and content across culturally differing populations and historical periods, but in all there is recognition of childhood as a distinct period of life with age-related properties, norms, and expectations."[23]

These definitions differ significantly from that of Montgomery who claims: "The idea that childhood is a specific stage of life, separated from adulthood, does not hold true in many places, where there are many stages of social immaturity that last well beyond puberty and even marriage."[24]

In line with Montgomery, Shweder contends that "the reality of childhood . . . goes far beyond the universal recognition of phases of life prior to adulthood."[25] He further notes: "Childhood assumes different forms here and there, now and then; and from a comparative perspective, one more properly speaks of *childhoods*, in the plural, than of *childhood*, in the singular."[26]

The preceding differing interpretations on the word childhood are an instance that signifies the struggles with the definitions of the terms childhood, children, and child. As Bluebond-Langner and Korbin observe: "As we study children and childhoods, we need to confront the messiness and untidiness of social reality, not reduce it. Similarly, we need to continue to problematize the nature and development of the individual . . . we are still struggling with definitions of the terms child, youth, and childhood."[27]

---

22. J. Simpson, ed., "Childhood," *Oxford Dictionary*, accessed 22 July 2016, http://www.oed.com.myaccess.library.utoronto.ca/view/Entry/31631?redirectedFrom=childhood#eid.

23. Robert A. LeVine, "Child: Historical and Cultural Perspectives," in *The Child: An Encyclopedic Companion*, ed. Richard A. Shweder (Chicago; London: University of Chicago Press, 2009), 139.

24. Heather Montgomery, *An Introduction to Childhood: An Anthropological Perspective of Children's Lives* (Malden, MA: Wiley-Blackwell, 2009), 54.

25. Richard A. Shweder, "Introduction," in *The Child: An Encyclopedic Companion*, ed. Richard A. Shweder (Chicago; London: University of Chicago Press, 2009), xxviii.

26. Shweder, "Introduction," xxx.

27. Myra Bluebond-Langner and Jill E. Korbin, "Challenges and Opportunities in the Anthropology of Childhoods: An Introduction to 'Children, Childhoods, and Childhood Studies,'" *American Anthropologist* 109, no. 2 (2007): 245. For Galbraith, it is not childhood that needs to be defined, since that is the natural state. Rather, there is a struggle to define adulthood: "What is really called into question by childhood studies, what is raised to visibility that was previously taken for granted as given, is the meaning of *adulthood* in relation to

Archard contends that such struggles might be reduced if the "boundaries are set, [the] dimensions ordered and [the] divisions managed" while defining or conceptualizing the terms.[28] This is exactly what James attempts in her formulations on the distinctions between the three concepts – childhood, children, and child in childhood studies. Her formulations are pertinent to the present study and thus are explored at length below.

James maintains that "a focus on age" is essential to childhood studies, and adds that "a theoretical focus on *age* allows us to explore, analytically, how *childhood* comes to be constituted for *children* in the social world and, therefore, how we might properly grasp a *child's* perspective on the social world that takes this cultural shaping of *children's* experiences into account" (emphases added).[29]

James further argues that "formulations and nomenclature" are of significance.[30] Uncritical use of the terms – *childhood*, *children*, and *child* – fails to grasp the core values of childhood studies. For instance, *the child* is a common usage to indicate a whole category of people (i.e. *children*). This, however, "not only dismisses the individuality of children but also, by collectivizing children, reduces their significance as social actors."[31] James uses the following example to emphasize her concern: the term "the disabled" employed to delineate disabled people is criticized because of its assumption that "their disabled bodies define their personhood."[32] Therefore, James argues "against the uncritical use of an age-based term, the child, to confer identities on children."[33] She points out that once a child's age is held in abeyance, a child's individual qualities and varying competence in different

---

childhood. The crisis of legitimacy in all areas of authority in the last half of the 20th century is particularly urgent with respect to the category *adults*. In fact, it may be that it is only by consciously reentering a childhood perspective on adulthood that we can find our way through some of the most difficult moral and intellectual challenges of our era." See Mary Galbraith, "Hear My Cry: A Manifesto for an Emancipatory Childhood Studies Approach to Children's Literature," *The Lion and the Unicorn* 25, no. 2 (2001): 190.

28. David Archard, *Children: Rights and Childhood* (London: Taylor & Francis e-Library, 2005), 27, accessed 25 June 2014, http://books.scholarsportal.info/viewdoc.html?id=10684.

29. James, "Understanding Childhood," 32.

30. James, 33.

31. James, 33.

32. James, 33.

33. James, 33.

social context manifest. For example, for children involved in the fishing industry in Norway, "their age-based child status was temporarily suspended and their skill was judged in accordance with the task at hand."[34] That means, the age-based term, *the child*, fails to convey the whole spectrum of children's qualities and competence that are beyond their age. What follows is James's clarification of the terms.

Of the three terms, *childhood* is the only one "that embraces the temporality of the developmental aspects of children's lives."[35] The concept of childhood, generally, serves "as an analytical term to mark out a particular space in the life course, the temporal space that follows infancy[36] and precedes adulthood."[37] After defining the term *childhood*, James relates it to the term *children* which "is the classificatory label given to the category of people who inhabit that temporal space or time of life called childhood."[38] Thus, like the term *childhood*, *children* becomes an analytic term. It is employed to include "a collection of individuals who can be structurally grouped together by virtue of their sharing a set of assumed characteristics."[39] The characteristics can be identified as biological (e.g. being sexually immature), developmental (e.g. having limited cognitive competence), social (e.g. street children), or cultural (e.g. children's literature), etc.[40]

The term *child*, for James, should be predicated of "the individual social actor" standing before us. Thus, the term *child* is "primarily descriptive rather than analytic (unlike childhood or children)" even though it indeed points out "a young person's position in the life course and his or her potential membership in the category *children*."[41] Then, James stresses that to grasp a child's perspective on the social world, which is core to childhood studies, one needs to recognize a critical point that "our day-to-day encounters with

---

34. A. Solberg, *Negotiating Childhood: Empirical Investigations and Textual Representations of Children's Work and Everyday Lives* (Stockholm: Nordic Institute for Studies in Urban and Regional Planning, 1994), quoted in James, "Understanding Childhood," 35.
35. James "Understanding Childhood," 33.
36. In the present study, infancy is viewed as a part of childhood.
37. James, "Understanding Childhood," 34.
38. James, 34.
39. James, 34.
40. James, 34.
41. James, 34.

the individual child are necessarily informed by our understanding of the analytical concepts of childhood and children, but they are not – or should not be – dependent on them."[42]

Based on the preceding "dialectical relationship between child and children,"[43] one discerns that a child is advanced or backward for his/her age by comparing his/her competence with one's common understanding of the competence of other children at the same age. However, the age-based model of children's competence fails to take their sociocultural experience into consideration. James argues that bracketing off age from judging a child's competence can facilitate adult understanding of a child from different kinds of dimensions, such as skill, efficiency, communication of ideas, as exemplified by children's participation in the fishing industry in Norway. James then cites Alderson who comments in relation to children's consent to surgery: "Competence is more influenced by the social context and the child's experience than by innate ability. [To respect children means we must not] think in sharp dichotomies of wise adult/immature child, infallible doctor/ignorant patient, but to see wisdom and uncertainty shared among people of varying ages and experience."[44]

For James, "holding age in abeyance" is a critical way to help adults "in not just listening to children's voices but also hearing clearly what they have to say." This is the core value of childhood studies.[45] (This argument is of particular importance when referring to children as sources of revelation of insights and representatives of Jesus in §3.3.2.6.)

After exploring the conceptual dimension of childhood studies, this study now turns to its historical level.

3.2.3 The Birth of Childhood Studies

Although the term "childhood studies" is fairly new, the interdisciplinary field of study that it denotes can be traced back to the late nineteenth-century

---

42. James, 34.
43. James, 34.
44. Priscilla Alderson, *Children's Consent to Surgery* (Milton Keynes, UK: Open University Press, 1993), 158, cited in James, "Understanding Childhood," 35.
45. James, "Understanding Childhood," 32, 35.

scholarship. As early as 1895, James Sully's[46] *Studies of Childhood* was published, "a book with a very modern sounding title."[47] During the early twentieth century, the psychology of child development[48] was recognized as "the dominant paradigm for studying children as well as for professional practice in care and education."[49] However, the academic spark on the topic of childhood was not ignited until the publishing of *Centuries of Childhood*, the first general historical study of childhood by the French historian Philippe Ariès.[50] His argument that "childhood did not exist" in medieval society[51] has stimulated much debate,[52] sparking "serious scholarly attention" on childhood studies since the 1970s.[53]

In the last two decades, childhood studies, much of which was "conducted on the analogy of women's studies[54] and African-American studies,"[55] became firmly established "as a recognized area of academic research bridging several disciplines."[56] Theories from sociology, anthropology, developmen-

---

46. Sully is profoundly influenced by Darwin's *Biographical Sketch of an Infant* in 1877. See Woodhead, "Childhood Studies," 18.

47. Woodhead, "Childhood Studies," 18.

48. In terms of the psychology of child development, Piaget's stage theory was the most influential in the Western world. See David Elkind and John H. Flavell, eds., *Studies in Cognitive Development: Essays in Honor of Jean Piaget* (London; New York: Oxford University Press, 1969).

49. Woodhead, "Childhood Studies," 18.

50. Archard, *Children*, 15.

51. Philippe Ariès, *Centuries of Childhood: A Social History of Family Life*, trans. Robert Baldick (New York: Vintage Books, 1962), 128.

52. Hugh Cunningham, *Children and Childhood in Western Society Since 1500*, 2nd ed. (Harlow, UK; New York: Pearson Longman, 2005), 4; James, "Understanding Childhood," 27. An example of such debate is from Naomi Steinberg, *The World of the Child in the Hebrew Bible* (Sheffield, UK: Sheffield Phoenix, 2013), 122. After examining the Hebrew Bible, he concludes: "I have found in the biblical text evidence to argue against Ariès . . . that ancient Israel recognized childhood as a stage of life separate from adulthood." Though Ariès's argument of the modern "invention" of childhood is criticized, his work has been accepted as extraordinarily crucial and authoritative in the field of social science until now. See Cunningham, *Children and Childhood*, 7; Archard, *Children*, 15.

53. Steinberg, *World of the Child*, 6.

54. The development of childhood studies paralleled that of women's studies in the 1970s. This was recognized by anthropologist Theodore Schwartz, "The Acquisition of Culture," *Ethos* 9 (1981): 10, 16.

55. Wall, "Childhood Studies," 524–525.

56. Bonnie J. Miller-McLemore, "Childhood Studies and Pastoral Counseling," *Sacred Spaces: The E-Journal of the American Association of Pastoral Counselors* 6 (2014): 7; see also Kehily, "Understanding Childhood," 1.

tal psychology, biology, history, educational theory, literature, philosophy, cultural studies, law, etc., have given an adequate account of childhood as a helpful[57] category.[58] Nonetheless, it was not until the last decade that childhood studies "earned a place in the study of religion," including Christianity.[59]

3.2.4 The Development of Childhood Studies in Christianity

Though, as mentioned above, childhood studies was burgeoning in many disciplines and thus providing abundant resources for religious reflection, Christianity was slow to join this field. What follows are some observations on this phenomenon:

- Children-related issues are considered by some to be "beneath the work of serious scholars or theologians and suitable only for practitioners or educators."[60]
- Some view children "as a less than respectable subject matter."[61] For example, the evaluation of childhood studies by the American Academy of Religion signifies that "studying children means lowering one's academic standards and promoting parochial agendas."[62] Such a view "captures the general anxiety and prejudice that surrounds the topic of children in religious studies."[63]
- Theologians are prone to "engage issues of children, if they do so at all, around specific and isolated questions such as abortion, health insurance, and spiritual formation."[64]

---

57. Childhood studies has also impacted public policy, such as the formation and interpretation of the 1989 United Nations Convention on the Rights of the Child. See Wall, "Childhood Studies," 525.

58. Miller-McLemore, "Childhood Studies and Pastoral Counseling," 7; Wall, "Childhood Studies," 524–525; Archard, *Children*, 30.

59. Miller-McLemore, "Childhood Studies and Pastoral Counseling," 7.

60. Marcia J. Bunge, "The Child, Religion, and the Academy: Developing Robust Theological and Religious Understandings of Children and Childhood," *The Journal of Religion* 86, no. 4 (2006): 552.

61. Miller-McLemore, "Childhood Studies and Pastoral Counseling," 8.

62. Miller-McLemore, 8.

63. Miller-McLemore, 8.

64. Wall, "Childhood Studies," 528.

Nevertheless, this situation began to change at the turn of the twenty-first century due to the magnitude of production devoted to this field. This is well elaborated by the articles composed by Bunge,[65] Wall,[66] and Miller-McLemore.[67] The first two provide "a goldmine of bibliographical resources with extensive footnotes listing representative publications"[68] from different perspectives. The third serves as an update and supplement to the first two.

In her article, Bunge separates the "emerging scholarship on children and childhood in religious studies and theology" into several categories:[69]

- works from religious educators who *reconsider* basic assumptions about faith formation and religious education, resulting from the awakening that "previous theories often excluded not only insights from child development but also sound theological understandings of children themselves";[70]
- publications from scholars in the fields of pastoral care and practical theology;
- works on spiritual formation at home;
- works by educators and psychologists who delve into "the complexities of child and adolescent spirituality";
- works by social scientists who propose "provocative methodological questions about how to study or even define children's spirituality";
- writings from practitioners who compose their works by "intentionally integrating social-scientific and religious insights" for the sake of children at risk worldwide;
- articles in theological and biblical journals, which comprise the works from "scholars in theology, ethics, biblical studies, historical theology, history, cultural studies, and comparative religions."[71]

---

65. Bunge, "Child, Religion, and the Academy."
66. Wall, "Childhood Studies."
67. Miller-McLemore, "Childhood Studies and Pastoral Counseling."
68. Miller-McLemore, 17.
69. Bunge, "Child, Religion, and the Academy," 555. In her footnotes, Bunge provides exhaustive lists of the publications for each category.
70. Bunge, "Child, Religion, and the Academy," 555.
71. Bunge, 556–558.

Apart from the publications noted above, Bunge also mentions dissertations, projects, conferences, and institutes focusing on this subject. Then, she pays particular attention to significant works composed by historians, biblical and theological scholars.[72] These contribute to the formulation of Christian *theologies of childhood*, followed by the construct of *child theologies*.[73]

Differing from Bunge's categories, Wall creates typologies from methodological perspectives, which also gives a glimpse of the early development of childhood studies in Christianity. He first divides this discipline into four typologies: developmental-psychological, family-psychological, politico-sociological, and family-sociological approaches, to which he adds an emerging approach: theological ethics of childhood.[74]

Given the incredible amount of literature that has appeared after Bunge's and Wall's articles, Miller-McLemore updates these publications, including studies concerning interreligious exploration, multiple explorations of children's spirituality, and tools for research on children and religion,[75] but deploring the disregard for children in the domain of religion and abuse.[76]

---

72. Bunge, 557–573.

73. Christian scholars have not reached a consensus about the usage of these terminologies. For example, in her "Biblical and Theological Perspectives on Children, Parents, and 'Best Practices' for Faith Formation: Resources for Child, Youth, and Family Ministry Today," *Dialog* 47, no. 4 (2008): 350, Bunge defines that theologies of childhood "aim to provide theological understandings of children and childhood and our obligations to children themselves;" whereas child theologies are to "reexamine not only conceptions of children and obligations to them but also fundamental doctrines and practices of the church." Though Bunge tries to distinguish "child theologies" from "theologies of childhood," Miller-McLemore, in "Childhood Studies and Pastoral Counseling," 22, notes that her arguments are not clear enough. Differing from Bunge, Jerome W. Berryman, in *Godly Play: An Imaginative Approach to Religious Education* (Minneapolis, MN: Augsburg Press, 1991), 158, suggests that "the theology of childhood is about children and adults discovering that child." For more discussions on child theologies, see Haddon Willmer and Keith J. White, *Entry Point: Towards Child Theology with Matthew 18* (London, UK: WTL, 2013); Keith J. White, "Insights into Child Theology through the Life and Work of Pandita Ramabai," 2006, 1–11, accessed 1 June 2014, http://www.childtheology.org/wp-content/uploads/2013/02/OCMS-31.10.06.pdf.

74. Wall, "Childhood Studies," 525. Wall's footnotes provide exhaustive lists of the representative publications for each typology.

75. Miller-McLemore, "Childhood Studies and Pastoral Counseling," 23–24.

76. Miller-McLemore, 24. Gleaned from Robert A. Orsi's article, "A Crisis about the Theology of Children," *Harvard Divinity School Bulletin* (2002): 27–29, Miller-McLemore, in "Childhood Studies and Pastoral Counseling," 24, asserts that "unfortunately, disregard for children as a subject of study and religious tolerance for [the] abuse go hand in hand."

Through the three articles' comprehensive explorations of the literature of childhood studies, one finds that this field involves a myriad of different disciplines that it is hard to provide a universal definition for the new discipline **childhood studies**. It is also difficult to offer a universal formulation on the nature of childhood and children.

A more pertinent formulation[77] for this study is from Bunge who contends that there are at least six critical and "almost paradoxical perspectives"[78]

---

77. The following are some other examples of the formulation on the nature of children and childhood from different disciplines. For example, as discussed above, children as social agents is an idea from the perspective of social sciences. From the field of anthropology, some societies view children as incompetent or subordinate; others regard them as equals. Children are also an economic investment, a means of forming families and giving status. See Heather Montgomery, *Introduction to Childhood*, 56–68. Among the religious and philosophical thinkers of the late twentieth and early twenty-first century, there are different views towards children. One is that of a bottom-up approach, arguing that children are "agents and constructors of their own worlds, participants in larger social meaning, uniquely gifted by God, and bearers of full human rights." See John Wall, "Child: Religious and Philosophical Perspectives," in *The Child: An Encyclopedic Companion*, ed. Richard A. Shweder (Chicago; London: University of Chicago Press, 2009), 147.

78. In her article of 2003 and subsequent publications, Bunge continually reiterates six paradoxical perspectives on children and childhood in Christianity: "More Vibrant Theology of Children"; "Rediscovering the Dignity and Complexity of Children: Resources from the Christian Tradition," *Sewanee Theological Review* 48, no. 1 (2004): 51–63; "Historical Perspectives on Children in the Church"; "Child, Religion, and the Academy"; "The Dignity and Complexity of Children: Constructing Christian Theologies of Childhood," in *Nurturing Child and Adolescent Spirituality : Perspectives from the World's Religious Traditions*, ed. Karen Marie Yust et al. (Lanham, MD ; Toronto: Rowman & Littlefield, 2006), 53–68; "Beyond Children as Agents or Victims: Reexamining Children's Paradoxical Strengths and Vulnerabilities with Resources from Christian Theologies of Childhood and Child Theologies," in *The Given Child: The Religions' Contribution to Children's Citizenship*, eds. Trygve Wyller and Usha S. Nayar (Göttingen: Vandenhoeck & Ruprecht, 2007), 27–50; "Biblical and Theological Perspectives on Children," 348–360; "Historical Perspectives on Children in the Church," in *Toddling to the Kingdom: Child Theology at Work in the Church*, ed. John Collier (London, UK: Child Theology Movement, 2009), 98–113; "Biblical and Theological Perspectives and Best Practices for Faith Formation," in *Understanding Children's Spirituality: Theology, Research, and Practice*, ed. Kevin E. Lawson, Kindle ed. (Eugene, OR: Cascade, 2012), 3–25; "Christian Understandings of Children: Central Biblical Themes and Resources," in *Children, Adults, and Shared Responsibilities: Jewish, Christian, and Muslim Perspectives*, ed. Marcia J. Bunge (Cambridge, UK: Cambridge University Press, 2012), 59–78. The paradoxical views toward children are also recognized by John T. Carroll who, in "Children in the Bible," *Interpretation* 55, no. 2 (2001): 121, argues that "[t]he Christian scriptures, like Christian tradition generally and much of contemporary culture, express deep ambivalence about children." See also Archard, *Children*, 29, 37; Peter B. Pufall and Richard P. Unsworth, "Introduction: The Imperative and the Process for Rethinking Childhood," in *Rethinking Childhood*, eds. Peter B. Pufall and Richard P. Unsworth (New Brunswick, NJ: Rutgers University Press, 2004), 1.

on the nature of children and childhood based on the Bible and Christian tradition,[79] which are:

> [Children] as gifts of God and signs of God's blessing, though they are sinful and selfish; as developing creatures in need of instruction and guidance, yet as fully human and made in the image of God; and as models of faith, sources of revelation, and representatives of Jesus, though they be orphans, neighbors, and strangers who need to be treated with justice and integrity.[80]

Such preliminary understandings on the nature of children and childhood are extremely valuable because "the field of systematic theology in the 20th century has been largely silent on the question of children."[81] This is also because the church's theology concerning children shapes the practices and ministries toward them.[82]

What follows are further insights from childhood studies that are pertinent to the present study, especially in biblical and theological domains.[83]

3.3 Insights from Childhood Studies for the Present Research

3.3.1 Introduction

Insights from childhood studies help elucidate and confirm the following claims related to the present research: (1) children are integral to the

---

79. Bunge, "Child, Religion, and the Academy," 562–568.
80. Bunge, "A More Vibrant Theology of Children," 13.
81. Dawn DeVries, "Toward a Theology of Childhood," *Interpretation* 55, no. 2 (2001): 162; see also Donald Ratcliff, "The Spirit of Children Past: A Century of Children's Spirituality Research," *Christian Education Journal* 4, no. 2 (2007): 232. Generally speaking, children are a neglected subject in Christian theology's related disciplines, such as biblical studies, systematics, ethics, pastoral or liturgical theology. This is made evident by the fact that almost every dictionary or standard textbook in these disciplines contains no whole article devoted to topics on any child, children, or childhood; even "passing references to children in relation to other topics are also strangely infrequent." See Stephen Burns, *Worship in Context: Liturgical Theology, Children and the City* (Peterborough, UK: Epworth, 2006), 99.
82. Scottie May et al., *Children Matter: Celebrating Their Place in the Church, Family, and Community* (Grand Rapids, MI: Eerdmans, 2005), 52.
83. Theologians mentioned below may have paradoxical views toward children. This study intends not to delve into individual theologian's full concepts on childhood and children, but to use their arguments that are related to the present purpose.

church;[84] (2) children need the whole Bible; (3) children can contribute to the enterprise of Bible translation.

3.3.2 Children Are Integral to the Church

3.3.2.1 Introduction

As mentioned earlier, children are often marginalized "in churches as much as in society as a whole."[85] In discussing children's sufferings from poverty, Couture laments that "the church and the theological school are poor to the extent that they are tenuously connected to the children."[86] However, the findings from childhood studies in Christianity in the past decade make it possible to transform the church's attitude toward children and childhood (from indifference to respect and care) and engagement in the fuller development of theology and ministry. Results of these studies can spur the church to embrace children as they are willing to accept the following truths: (1) childhood's eternal significance; (2) children as holy gifts and blessings; (3) children as fully human and young fellow disciples; (4) children's vulnerability; (5) children's voice necessary to be heard and respected; (6) Children as spiritual models.

3.3.2.2 Childhood's Eternal Significance

In terms of human lifespan, modern thinkers tend to utilize physical or biological categories to view life as a sum total of a series of phases. When one phase is exhausted, it leads on to the next; then the very meaning of the preceding phase is to disappear into the next. According to this conceptual framework, childhood is merely a progression into the future that lies ahead. Once this future arrives, childhood itself disappears. In other words, childhood is less important than adulthood. This understanding of childhood prevails among Christians because they "lay special emphasis on the merely subordinate role of childhood."[87]

---

84. This point is explored at length because of its significance for intergenerational ministry in the second half of this chapter.

85. Judith Sadler, "Learning Together," 120.

86. Pamela D. Couture, *Seeing Children, Seeing God: A Practical Theology of Children and Poverty* (Nashville, TN: Abingdon Press, 2000), 47.

87. Karl Rahner, *Further Theology of the Spiritual Life 2*, trans. David Bourke, Theological Investigations 8 (New York: Seabury, 1977), 34.

In his essay entitled "Ideas for a Theology of Childhood," Rahner[88] criticizes the tendency to view human life as a progression of phases. For him, childhood is not a stage to be superseded. The idea of "the unsurpassable value of childhood" is based on his conception of eternity as a gathering up of all time. A human being as a subject is at all stages capable of grasping him/herself as a whole.[89]

According to the Christian view, Rahner argues, the totality of one's existence is "saved and redeemed in its complete and consummated state."[90] Thus, eternity is not the ultimate stage toward which one advances in time, but "the enduring validity of [one's] existence before God as lived in freedom." Put differently, eternity is a gathering up of "the totality of one's life as freely lived." Thus, the temporal mode of existence is not to be left behind, "but by compressing it, so to say, and bringing it with [one] in its totality into [one's] eternity . . . [One's] future is the making present of [one's] own past as freely lived."[91]

For Rahner, understanding the relationship between human existence and eternal life is true for all phases of human life, including childhood which "most of all suffers from the impression that it is a mere provisional conditioning for the shaping of adult life in its fulness."[92] Rahner emphasizes that childhood is not limited to a stage to be put behind us as quickly as possible, but an "abiding reality." That means, childhood endures as "that which is coming to meet us as an intrinsic element in the single and enduring completeness of the time of our existence considered as a unity" (i.e. the eternity of human beings as saved and redeemed).[93] Or put simply, childhood is a part of human "eschatological future."[94] Accordingly, human

---

88. Mercer notes that Rahner, unlike myriads of theologians of his time and prior eras who merely refer to children while discussing other theological issues, devotes this whole essay to children, mainly focusing on the nature of childhood. See Joyce Ann Mercer, *Welcoming Children: A Practical Theology of Childhood* (St Louis, MO: Chalice Press, 2005), 150.

89. Rahner, *Further Theology*, 33–35. This is similar to say that life is now: the past leads up to today, and today is the introduction to what follows.

90. Rahner, *Further Theology*, 35.

91. Rahner, 35.

92. Rahner, 35.

93. Rahner, 36.

94. Mercer, *Welcoming Children*, 150; see also Mary Ann Hinsdale, "'Infinite Openness to the Infinite': Karl Rahner's Contribution to Modern Catholic Thought on the Child,"

beings "do not move away from childhood in any definitive sense, but rather move towards the eternity of this childhood, to its definitive and enduring validity in God's sight."[95] Rahner concludes: "The values of imperishability and eternity are attached to childhood . . . It must be the case that childhood is valuable in itself, that it is to be discovered anew in the ineffable future which is coming to meet us."[96]

In view of childhood's eternal significance, Christians should commit themselves to recognize, cherish, and appreciate the presence of children in the church.

3.3.2.3 Children as Holy Gifts and Blessings

Many passages in the Bible portray children as gifts[97] of God or signs of God's blessing. For example, in Genesis 1:28, human reproduction is "an order of creation under God's special blessing."[98] God's unique blessing is given to Rebekah before her departure to marry Isaac: "Our sister, may you increase to thousands upon thousands" (Gen 24:60). Apparently, mothers with many children are viewed as blessed.[99] Children as gifts and blessings are also reflected in Jacob's response to Esau's question of "who are these with you?" by saying, "They are the children God has graciously given your servant" (Gen 33:5).[100] Leah, Jacob's first wife, views her sixth son Zebulun as

---

in *The Child in Christian Thought*, ed. Marcia J. Bunge (Grand Rapids, MI: Eerdmans, 2001), 423.

95. Rahner, *Further Theology*, 36.

96. Rahner, 37.

97. Though Shier-Jones suggests avoiding the association of children with gifts, implying that they are possessed by someone, this study, in line with Bunge and other Christian scholars (e.g. Miller-McLemore), refers to children as gifts from God. Cf. Angela Shier-Jones, "The Never-Land of Religion and the Lost Childhood of the Children of God," in *Children of God: Towards a Theology of Childhood*, ed. Angela Shier-Jones (Peterborough: Epworth, 2007), 200; Bunge, "Biblical and Theological Perspectives," 9; Bonnie J. Miller-McLemore, *Let the Children Come: Reimagining Childhood from a Christian Perspective* (San Francisco, CA: Jossey-Bass, 2003), 83.

98. Hans-Ruedi Weber, *Jesus and the Children: Biblical Resources for Study and Preaching* (Atlanta: John Knox, 1979), 8; see also Victor P. Hamilton, *The Book of Genesis: Chapters 1–17*, NICOT (Grand Rapids, MI: Eerdmans, 1990), 139.

99. Weber, *Jesus and the Children*, 8; Terence E. Fretheim, "'God Was with the Boy' (Genesis 21:20): Children in the Book of Genesis," in *The Child in the Bible*, eds., Marcia J. Bunge, Terence E. Fretheim, and Beverly Roberts Gaventa (Grand Rapids, MI: Eerdmans, 2008), 7.

100. May et al., *Children Matter*, 27.

a precious gift presented by God (Gen 30:20).[101] On this verse, John Calvin makes a comment that the birth of offspring serves to conciliate spouses and increases their love for each other.[102]

God's promise to and covenant with Abraham also shows that children are God's gifts and a sign of his blessings. God promises to bless Abraham and make of him "a great nation" by granting him innumerable descendants (Gen 12:2; 13:16; 15:5).[103] And the promised child Isaac, who is a proof of divine favor,[104] is a crucial part of God's covenant with Abraham (Gen 12, 17).[105]

Children as divine blessings from generation to generation are often mentioned by the patriarch. For instance, Jacob blesses his grandsons in Genesis 48:15–16 by saying, "May the God . . . bless these boys . . . and may they increase greatly on the earth"; he also blesses his son in Genesis 49. Undoubtedly, children are "the fulfillment of God's promises to [the] families, and they in turn carry on [the] promises of life and blessing into successive generations."[106]

In Psalm 127:3, children "are a 'heritage' from the Lord and a 'reward,'"[107] on which John Calvin comments, "Children are not the fruit of chance, but . . . God, as it seems good to Him, distributes to every man His share of them."[108] Psalm 128:1, 3–4 says that those who fear the Lord will be blessed with their wife and children. Proverbs 17:6 says, "Children's children are a crown to the aged."[109]

---

101. Bunge, "Historical Perspectives on Children in the Church," 45; Roy B. Zuck, *Precious in His Sight: Childhood and Children in the Bible* (Grand Rapids, MI: Baker Books, 1996), 49.

102. John Calvin, *Commentaries on the Book of Moses Called Genesis*, vol. 2, trans. John King (Grand Rapids, MI: Eerdmans, 1948), 147–148.

103. Judith M. Gundry-Volf, "'To Such as These Belongs the Reign of God': Jesus and the Children," *Theology Today* 56, no. 4 (2000): 470.

104. Cornelia B. Horn and John W. Martens, *"Let the Little Children Come to Me:" Childhood and Children in Early Christianity* (Washington, DC: Catholic University of America Press, 2009), 43.

105. Timothy A. Sisemore, "Theological Perspectives on Children in the Church: Reformed and Presbyterian," in *Nurturing Children's Spirituality: Christian Perspectives and Best Practices*, ed. Holly Catterton Allen (Eugene, OR: Cascade, 2008), 95.

106. Fretheim, "God Was with the Boy," 7.

107. Bunge, "Historical Perspectives on Children in the Church," 45.

108. John Calvin, *Commentaries*, vol. 6 (Grand Rapids, MI: Eerdmans, 1984), 111.

109. May et al., *Children Matter*, 28.

Aside from the Scripture, theologians today and in the past also describe children as God's gifts and blessings. Clement of Alexandria maintains that children represent a blessing to their parents: "[T]he loss of children is . . . among the chiefest evils; the possession of children is consequently a good thing."[110] Johannes Amos Comenius considers children more precious than gifts of gold, silver, pearls, and gems.[111] For Berryman, children are God's free gifts because of their wonder, playfulness, and creativity.[112] Miller-McLemore writes: "Children can evoke new energy even as they demand energy, sometimes sparking fresh engagement, enhanced creativity, and even religious awe before life itself."[113]

It is worth noting that children are not only blessings to the family, but also blessings to the community, the nation, and even the whole world. For example, the boy Samuel (1 Sam 3:20) becomes a trustworthy prophet. The baby Moses (Exod 2) will deliver the Israelites from the oppression of the Egyptians.[114] Most notably, the messianic child, baby Jesus, will fulfill the redemptive reign of peace. Based on Isaiah 9:6; Matthew 18:3, 5; Mark 10:14, Moltmann asserts that the messianic child is "a metaphor of . . . hope,"[115] and then he expands his proposition by contending that children are metaphors of hope. He writes: "With every child, a new life begins, original, unique, incomparable . . . It is these differences that we need to respect if we want to love life and allow an open future . . . With every beginning of a new life, the hope for the reign of peace and justice is given a new chance."[116]

---

110. Clement of Alexandria, *Stromateis, Book 2 Ch. 23: On Marriage*, accessed 10 September 2014, http://www.earlychristianwritings.com/text/clement-stromata-book2.html.

111. Johannes Amos Comenius, *The School of Infancy*, 1631, ch. 1, accessed 14 July 2016, http://www.christianitytoday.com/history/issues/issue-13/from-archives-school-of-infancy.html.

112. Jerome W. Berryman, *Children and the Theologians: Clearing the Way for Grace* (Harrisburg, PA: Morehouse, 2009), 41.

113. Miller-McLemore, *Let the Children Come*, 150.

114. Kristin Herzog, *Children and Our Global Future: Theological and Social Challenges* (Cleveland, OH: Pilgrim Press, 2005), 22.

115. Jürgen Moltmann, "Child and Childhood as Metaphors of Hope," *Theology Today* 56, no. 4 (2000): 592.

116. Moltman, "Child and Childhood," 603; see also Herbert Anderson and Susan B. W. Johnson, *Regarding Children: A New Respect for Childhood and Families* (Louisville, KY: Westminster John Knox, 1994), 20, 29.

Following Moltmann's thought, Herzog, in her *Children and Our Global Future*, adds that "with every adult who in the midst of our technologically and scientifically managed world 'becomes like a child,' eternal life breaks into the universe."[117] Anderson and Johnson go further to point out that "[r]egarding children with respect and recognizing the childhood in us all is not only essential for vital human community, it is fundamental for our salvation. If childness dies, we will never see God."[118]

Schleiermacher sees children as wonderful blessings to the community of faith: they instill fresh and cheerful spirit into adults;[119] their dependence on adults enables them to grow in sanctification; their simplicity draws adults back into the most basic of human relationship; their flexibility and forgiveness encourage adults to receive the gift of reconciliation that Christ grants them.[120]

Mercer, after examining children in the Gospel of Mark, proposes a "liberatory theology of childhood," arguing that "children and childhood are gifts from God not because they are carefree, but because God has a purpose for children. God gives children to the church and the world so that God may be known."[121] Children as "gifts embodying divine love and reconciliation" are participants "in a contentious life of resisting injustice and sin."[122] Besides, based on 1 Peter 4:7–11 and Ephesians 4:11–16, Bunge

---

117. Herzog, *Children and Our Global Future*, 18.

118. Anderson and Johnson, *Regarding Children*, 22.

119. Barnabas also makes a connection between renewal and children: "[H]aving renewed us by the remission of our sins, [the Lord] hath made us after another pattern, [it is His purpose] that we should possess the soul of children, inasmuch as He has created us anew by His Spirit." See Barnabas, "The Epistle of Barnabas," in *The Ante-Nicene Fathers, Vol. 1: The Apostolic Fathers with Justin Martyr and Irenaeus*, eds. A. Roberts, J. Donaldson, and A. C. Coxe (Buffalo, NY: Christian Literature Company, 1885), 140.

120. Friedrich Schleiermacher, *The Christian Household: A Sermonic Treatise*, trans. Dietrich Seidel and Terrence N. Tice, Schleiermacher Studies and Translations 3 (Lewiston, NY: Edwin Mellen, 1991), 46–48, 52. DeVries notes that though viewing highly of children, Schleiermacher is by no means to romanticize them. Instead, he advocates not letting children develop "naturally" because they are "born with as much potential for sin as for salvation." See Dawn DeVries, "'Be Converted and Become as Little Children': Friedrich Schleiermacher on the Religious Significance of Childhood," in *The Child in Christian Thought*, ed. Marcia J. Bunge (Grand Rapids, MI: Eerdmans, 2001), 340–341.

121. Mercer, *Welcoming Children*, 66.

122. Mercer, 66.

and Willmer assert that children are not "just gifts *of* God but also gifted *by* God . . . [who] is working in, for and through children."[123]

In sum, children are holy gifts and blessings. The church that embraces and welcomes them will be blessed.

3.3.2.4 Children as Fully Human and Young Fellow Disciples

Children made in the image of God (*imago Dei*) are whole and complete human beings.[124] They are little brothers and sisters by faith in Christ and children of God.[125]

The implicit evidence for the claim that children are fully human is Genesis 1:27, "God created mankind in his own image, in the image of God he created them." It implies that "children, like adults, possess the fullness of humanity and are fully human" from the beginning of their life.[126]

The equality of children and adults is affirmed by Cyprian of Carthage: "[A]ll men are like and equal, since they have once been made by God; and our age may have a difference in the increase of our bodies, according to the world, but not according to God . . . since He shows Himself a Father to all with well-weighed equality for the attainment of heavenly grace."[127] Children and adults are of equal value. Both groups are viewed as full human beings created by God, who stand on the same level and enjoy the benefits of salvation.[128] "[A]ge makes no difference at all in the equality of the divine grace," writes Wright.[129]

---

123. Marcia J. Bunge and Haddon Willmer, "How Does History Help Us?," in *Toddling to the Kingdom: Child Theology at Work in the Church*, ed. John Collier (London, UK: Child Theology Movement Ltd., 2009), 117.

124. Bunge, "Biblical and Theological Perspectives," 9.

125. Mercer, *Welcoming Children*, 157.

126. Bunge, "Biblical and Theological Perspectives," 9; see also W. Sibley Towner, "Children and the Image of God," in *The Child in the Bible*, eds. Marcia J. Bunge, Terence E. Fretheim, and Beverly Roberts Gaventa (Grand Rapids, MI: Eerdmans, 2008), 321.

127. Cyprian of Carthage, "The Epistles of Cyprian: Epistle 58: To Fidus, on the Baptism of Infants," in *The Ante-Nicene Fathers, Vol. 5: Fathers of the Third Century: Hippolytus, Cyprian, Novatian*, eds. A. Roberts, J. Donaldson, and A. C. Coxe (Buffalo, NY: Christian Literature Company, 1886), 354.

128. O. M. Bakke, *When Children Became People: The Birth of Childhood in Early Christianity*, trans. Brian McNeil (Minneapolis, MN: Fortress, 2005), 71–72.

129. David F. Wright, "How Controversial Was the Development of Infant Baptism in the Early Church?," in *Church, Word, and Spirit: Historical and Theological Essays in Honor of Geoffrey W. Bromiley*, eds. James E. Bradley and Richard A. Muller (Grand Rapids,

Gregory of Nyssa, in his "On Infants' Early Deaths," also notes that God who creates all human beings in his own image is deeply concerned about the salvation of infants as well as adults.[130] That means, in God's eyes, infants are essentially equal in value to adults even if Gregory does not address this issue unambiguously.[131]

In his "Ideas for a Theology of Childhood," Rahner argues that the child is a human being from the very beginning of a lifetime: "[T]he child is already the man, that right from the beginning he is already in possession of that value and those depths which are implied in the name of man. It is not simply that he gradually grows into a man. He is a man."[132]

Children with God's image are not only whole and complete human beings who need protection and reverence, but also young disciples who can fully participate in Christ's church.[133] After examining Mark's narrative, Mercer asserts that "children are disciples – in fact, they are model discipleship where others fail . . . In Mark, God gives the gift of children so that the church will know how to live out its vocation as disciples."[134] Thus, the church should not simply view children as needing to be educated for future participation; it has to take them seriously "as already being disciples who contribute to the mission and work of the body of Christ."[135]

In line with Mercer, Allen sees "children as disciples, not simply discipled."[136] Based on Luke 18:15–17, she maintains that Luke makes clear that children are valued in the kingdom of God. Jesus's deeding the kingdom itself to children strongly proves that they have "something unique and concrete to offer in their discipleship."[137] So, children are not merely

---

MI: Eerdmans, 1987), 51–52; see also James M. M. Francis, *Adults as Children: Images of Childhood in the Ancient World and the New Testament* (Bern: Lang, 2006), 147.

130. Gregory of Nyssa, "On Infants' Early Deaths," in *The Nicene and Post-Nicene Fathers, Vol. 5: Gregory of Nyssa*, eds. P. Schaff and H. Wace (New York: Christian Literature Company, 1893), 375–378.

131. Bakke, *When Children Became People*, 77.

132. Rahner, *Further Theology*, 37.

133. Allen, "Children as Disciples," 1.

134. Mercer, *Welcoming Children*, 67. For further discussions, see Francis, *Adults as Children*, ch. 4.

135. Mercer, *Welcoming Children*, 67.

136. Allen, "Children as Disciples," 1.

137. Allen, 11–12.

passive recipients of blessings from Jesus; they are active participants. This is substantiated by their being among Jesus's followers.[138] As White, a leader in the emerging Child Theology Movement, puts it, "babies, children and young people, are chosen by God to be partners[139] in His mission."[140]

In addition, for Allen, Jesus's teaching in this same pericope not only promotes the equality, dignity, and respect among all human beings, but also reverses the structure of the household: "the heads of households must themselves *depend upon* the young and the possession-less for their welcome into the Kingdom."[141] With this in mind, Allen goes on to examine both Luke's gospel account and Acts and concludes that *inter*-dependencies are "inherent in the Christian communities" and that adults and children need each other: "We need one another . . . young and old, Christian disciples need one another and are *dependent* one on the other, for the true *community* and *kinship* characteristic of discipleship at its core."[142] Thus, adults as senior disciples rely on the example of children for their entrance into God's kingdom; on the other hand, children as young disciples need adults' protecting, nurturing, and passing on the faith to them.[143]

In brief, children and adults, both created in God's image and as whole and complete human beings and disciples, need to "journey together in commitment to one another led by God."[144] Then, "beautiful, enriching

---

138. Allen, 12.

139. Having children as partners, adults can see that they are always children to God, chosen in their weakness. To choose the weak things of this world is God's nature; thus no one can boast. See Keith J. White, "The Child in the Midst of the Biblical Witeness," in *Toddling to the Kingdom: Child Theology at Work in the Church*, ed. John Collier (London, UK: Child Theology Movement Ltd., 2009), 157.

140. White, "Insights into Child Theology," 4.

141. Allen, "Children as Disciples," 12. White, in his "Child in the Midst," 158, also points out that unless adults "hold on to the child in the midst . . . [they] lose a vital sign of the Kingdom of God."

142. Allen, "Children as Disciples," 13.

143. Bunge, "Biblical and Theological Perspectives," 10.

144. Catherine Stonehouse, *Joining Children on the Spiritual Journey: Nurturing a Life of Faith* (Grand Rapids, MI: Baker Books, 1998), 195.

spiritual formation occurs for all."[145] So there is a call for the church to put children in its midst, or even at its heart, just as Jesus does concretely.[146]

3.3.2.5 Children's Vulnerability

Although children are fully human from the very beginning of a lifetime, they are also needy and vulnerable. They are "orphans, neighbors, victims, and strangers in need of compassion and justice."[147]

The Bible describes many ways in which children suffer and are victims:[148] poverty, slavery,[149] war,[150] hunger and/or famine,[151] political conflict,[152] violence,[153] illness and health concerns,[154] and suffering due to the depravity of people[155] around them.[156]

Many passages in the Bible report God's care for vulnerable children. In the OT, God commands the Israelites "to live as a covenant people by caring for the widow, orphan, and stranger,"[157] the most vulnerable people

---

145. Stonehouse, *Joining Children*, 195. Miller-McLemore, in *Let the Children Come*, 169, goes further to note that "disregard for children in general amounts to a spiritual crisis on the part of adults."

146. White, "Insights into Child Theology," 4; Herzog, *Children and Our Global Future*, 122.

147. Bunge, "Biblical and Theological Perspectives," 9.

148. Ma. Marilou Ibita and Reimund Bieringer, "(Stifled) Voices of the Future: Learning about Children in the Bible," in *Children's Voices: Children's Perspectives in Ethics, Theology and Religious Education*, eds. Annemie Dillen and Didier Pollefeyt (Leuven: Peeters, 2010), 92–102.

149. For example, Neh 5:1–5; 2 Kgs 4:1; Matt 18:23–25.

150. For example, Lam 1:4–5; Esth 3:13.

151. For example, Lam 1:11; 4:3–4, 8–10; 5:1–10; Ezek 5:12.

152. For example, 2 Kgs 11:2; Exod 2:1–10; Matt 2:16–23.

153. For example, Gen 19:8; Judg 19:24; 2 Sam 13:11–21.

154. For example, 1 Kgs 17:17–24; 2 Sam 4:4; Mark 5:21–24, 35–43; Luke 7:11–15.

155. For example, Judg 11:20–30; Gen 21:9–20.

156. David Deeks and Angela Shier-Jones, "Moulding and Shaping: Education," in *Children of God: Towards a Theology of Childhood*, ed. Angela Shier-Jones (Peterborough: Epworth, 2007), 69.

157. David H. Jensen, *Graced Vulnerability: A Theology of Childhood* (Cleveland: Pilgrim Press, 2005), 17. Brueggemann maintains that "*human obligation* is rooted in a sense of *divine commitment* to the most vulnerable in society." After examining the OT through the lens of children, he concludes that the enactment of a compassionate, justice-seeking human ethic must include the following elements: "nurture for our own children and defense of other vulnerable children." See Walter Brueggemann, "Vulnerable Children, Divine Passion, and Human Obligation," in *The Child in the Bible*, eds. Marcia J. Bunge, Terence E. Fretheim, and Beverly Roberts Gaventa (Grand Rapids, MI: Eerdmans, 2008), 399, 420.

in society (Exod 22:22–24; Deut 10:17–18; 14:28–29).[158] In the NT, Jesus inaugurates his ministry with "its own preference for the vulnerable . . . On many occasions, he heals children" (Mark 5:35–43; 7:24–30; 9:14–29; John 4:46–54).[159]

There are many examples of Christians today and in the past who have taken the situation of poor children seriously. For example, in the very early Christian era, the church became "a literal 'sanctuary' for children" because adults often abandoned their children at its door.[160] In the late Middle Ages, Christians established hospitals to accept orphaned children in the hope of reducing infanticide.[161] In the sixteenth century, Martin Luther and Philipp Melanchthon effected "positive policies and reforms in Germany for universal education that included girls and the poor."[162] In the eighteenth century, Francke and John Wesley founded orphanages and schools for children. Nowadays, faith-based organizations are established to help children at risk.[163]

The vulnerability of children is perhaps most visible in infancy. Jensen, in his *Graced Vulnerability*, asserts that infants' wails of hunger and cries to be held are "actually the marks of relationship and dependence of life in God's world. Infants cry not out of selfishness, but to speak of a profound need for another."[164] Infants need the protection and sustenance of a caregiver, without which they cannot survive.[165] Moreover, they rely on "emotional and unconscious loving nurture for the development of the brain and mental

---

158. Bunge, "Biblical and Theological Perspectives," 9.
159. Jensen, *Graced Vulnerability*, 22–23.
160. Couture, *Seeing Children, Seeing God*, 48.
161. Couture, 48–49.
162. Bunge, "Historical Perspectives on Children in the Church," 50.
163. Bunge, "Biblical and Theological Perspectives," 10.
164. Jensen, *Graced Vulnerability*, 49. Augustine of Hippo, in his *Confessions*, trans. with an introduction by R. S. Pine-Coffin (Harmondsworth, Middlesex: Penguin Books, 1961), 27–28, views an infant's cry as a manifestation of sin: "It can hardly be right for a child, even at that age, to cry for everything . . . I have myself seen jealousy in a baby and know what it means. He was not old enough to talk, but whenever he saw his foster-brother at the breast, he would grow pale with envy." As mentioned in §3.1, regarding children as sinful is one of the narrow views towards children in the church.
165. Jensen, *Graced Vulnerability*, 49.

health."[166] In other words, the vulnerability is "a fact of the God-given relatedness into which all persons are born."[167]

Unfortunately, such human relatedness is prone to rupture and destruction as human beings use others "as objects for [their] own self-aggrandizement."[168] Nowadays, children suffer from a number of "plagues:" poverty – "material poverty and the poverty of tenuous connections,"[169] famine, disease, war, hard labor, "the predations of the sex trade, the marching 'success' of the global economy."[170] Jensen notes it is not enough to describe the vulnerability of childhood; it is necessary to appeal to "an ethic of care for children."[171]

In *Seeing Children, Seeing God*, Couture maintains that "caring *with* vulnerable children is a means of grace, a vehicle through which God makes God's self known to us and to them" (emphasis added).[172] Jensen notes Couture's language: "In caring 'with' the vulnerable children in our midst, [Couture] avoids the trap of paternalism: the privileged adult who knows best and thus bestows grace on the impoverished child. In [her] account, the dynamic of care is reciprocal: the adult who cares is also enriched and nurtured by the child."[173]

Couture also argues that relationships with the most vulnerable children "involve works of mercy and works of piety – traditionally called the means

---

166. Vivienne Mountain, "Four Links between Child Theology and Children's Spirituality," *International Journal of Children's Spirituality* 16, no. 3 (2011): 264. Mountain, in "Four Links Between Child Theology," 264, asserts that loving human relationships are indispensable for children to thrive, which is increasingly evident from neuroscience, attachment research, and interpersonal neurobiology.

167. Jensen, *Graced Vulnerability*, 49; see also Anderson and Johnson, *Regarding Children*, 25.

168. Jensen, *Graced Vulnerability*, 49.

169. Couture, *Seeing Children, Seeing God*, 14. A study shows that a lack of relationship with extended families and communities is the main reason for producing a virtual epidemic of emotional and behavioral problems. See The Commission on Children at Risk, "Hardwired to Connect: The New Scientific Case for Authoritative Communities," in *Authoritative Communities: The Scientific Case for Nurturing the Whole Child*, ed. Kathleen Kovner Kline (New York: Springer Verlag, 2008), 3.

170. Jensen, *Graced Vulnerability*, 36, 49.

171. Jensen, 50. For full discussions regarding the ethic of care for children, see, for example, John Wall, *Ethics in Light of Childhood* (Washington, DC: Georgetown University Press, 2010); Kathleen Marshall and Paul Parvis, *Honouring Children: The Human Rights of the Child in Christian Perspective* (Edinburgh: Saint Andrew Press, 2004).

172. Couture, *Seeing Children, Seeing God*, 13.

173. Jensen, *Graced Vulnerability*, 50.

of grace – that, when kept in right relation with one another, give deep meaning to the love of neighbor and the love of God."[174] Through such practices, "*the church can genuinely transform itself and influence society and culture* . . . [then] our children will be well cared for."[175]

In a word, the church should be a place where vulnerable children are protected and cared for; their basic needs are met; justice for them is advocated. Indeed, the church should be the "sanctuary" for vulnerable children, as Jensen,[176] and Anderson and Johnson suggest.[177]

3.3.2.6 Children's Voice Necessary to Be Heard and Respected

The church needs to listen to and learn from children because they are sources of revelation of insights and representatives of Jesus.[178]

The Bible qualifies children as sources of revelation of insights. For example, in the days that "the word of the Lord was rare" and "there were not many visions" (1 Sam 3:1), the boy Samuel saw God's vision and mediated God's message to Eli (1 Sam 3).[179] In Psalm 8:2, David proclaimed: "Out of the mouth of babies and infants, you have established strength because of your foes, to still the enemy and the avenger" (ESV 2001). In his commentary of 1557, Calvin renders Psalm 8 as a defense of God's providence and verse 2 as declaring: " . . . the providence of God, in order to make itself known to mankind, does not wait till men arrive at the age of maturity, but even from the very dawn of infancy shines forth so brightly as is sufficient to confute all the ungodly."[180]

For Calvin, children, "no less than adults, are recipients of and manifest God's fatherly goodness";[181] more than this, "the tongues of infants, although they do not as yet speak, are ready and eloquent enough to . . . celebrate the

---

174. Couture, *Seeing Children, Seeing God*, 15.
175. Couture, 15.
176. Jensen, *Graced Vulnerability*, 111–115.
177. Anderson and Johnson, *Regarding Children*, ch. 6.
178. Cf. Bunge, "Biblical and Theological Perspectives," 11.
179. Bunge, 11.
180. John Calvin, *Commentary on the Book of Psalms*, vol. 1, trans. James Anderson (Grand Rapids, MI: Eerdmans, 1949), 95.
181. Barbara Pitkin, "Psalm 8:1–2," *Interpretation* 55, no. 2 (2001): 179.

praise of God."[182] In his reading on the latter part of verse 2, Calvin notes that the psalmist (David) "imposes upon the infants the office of defending the glory of God . . . [who] needs not strong military forces to destroy the ungodly; instead of these, the mouths of children are sufficient for his purpose."[183] In line with Calvin's interpretation of babies and infants in Psalm 8:2, Spurgeon points out that the name of God is made perfect by both the songs of angels in the heaven above and the praise of little children before his enemies on earth:

> [W]hile here below, the lisping utterances of babes are the manifestations of his strength in little ones. How often will children tell us of a God when we have forgotten! How doth their simple prattle refute those learned fools who deny the being of God! Many men have been made to hold their tongues, while sucklings have borne witness to the glory of the God of heaven . . . Did not the children cry "Hosannah!" in the temple, when proud Pharisees were silent and contemptuous?[184]

Wilhelm Rudolph, also focusing on real young children and what comes out of their mouths, interprets Psalm 8:2 in a modern context: "the cries of children, from the delivery room to the school-yard, are profound signs of life and the power of life and testify to God's creative power against all who deny it."[185] In a word, God uses young children to reveal himself to the world.

Another pericope describing children as sources of revelation of insights is Matthew 21:14–16, where children's true insight about Jesus is recognized by Jesus himself. This is demonstrated by his citation of Psalm 8:2 to rebuke the chief priests and scribes' objection to the children's acclamation in the temple: "Hosanna to the Son of David," identifying Jesus as the expected Messiah.[186] Jesus's affirmation of the children's praise is "an affirmation that children who 'know nothing' can also 'know divine secrets' and believe in

---

182. Calvin, *Book of Psalms*, 96.
183. Calvin, 97.
184. Charles H. Spurgeon, *The Treasury of David: An Expository and Devotional Commentary on the Psalms* (Grand Rapids, MI: Baker Books, 1983), 90.
185. Quoted in Pitkin, "Psalm 8:1–2," 178.
186. Gundry-Volf, "Such as These," 478.

him."[187] This incident exhibits the mystery[188] that the truth is hidden from the learned and wise, but revealed to the children (Matt 11:25).[189]

As noted above, Couture argues that God reveals himself through the practices of caring *with* vulnerable children.[190] Miller-McLemore adds that God presents "in the faces of vulnerable children helped in times of need."[191] Mercer, based on Mark's gospel, asserts that "practices with children as the ones reckoned least in status, power, and importance" are pivotal to understand and enact "right relationships in God's newly inaugurated reign."[192]

Children are not only sources of revelation of insights, but also representatives of Jesus.[193] Jesus says, "Whoever welcomes one of these little children in my name welcomes me; and whoever welcomes me does not welcome me but the one who sent me" (Mark 9:37; see also Matt 18:5; Luke 9:48). Moltmann points out: "By way of these identifications, Jesus declares children his representatives in society: Just as the God of his messianic mission is in him, so Christ is present in every child. Thus, whoever takes in a child, takes in Christ."[194]

Gundry-Volf further notes that because of their weakness and vulnerability, children thus represent Jesus "as a humble, suffering figure" who denied himself,[195] "radically symbolized by the cross."[196] "Welcoming the child signifies receiving Jesus and affirming his divinely given mission as the

---

187. Gundry-Volf, 479.
188. Rahner, in *Further Theology*, 42, notes that childhood is a mystery.
189. W. A. Strange, *Children in the Early Church: Children in the Ancient World, the New Testament and the Early Church* (Carlisle, UK: Paternoster, 1996), 56.
190. Couture, *Seeing Children, Seeing God*, 13.
191. Miller-McLemore, *Let the Children Come*, 149.
192. Mercer, *Welcoming Children*, 66.
193. Bunge, "Biblical and Theological Perspectives," 10; White, "Child in the Midst," 159; John T. Carroll, "'What Then Will This Child Become?': Perspectives on Children in the Gospel of Luke," in *The Child in the Bible*, eds. Marcia J. Bunge, Terence E. Fretheim, and Beverly Roberts Gaventa (Grand Rapids, MI: Eerdmans, 2008), 189; Herzog, *Children and Our Global Future*, 13; Judith M. Gundry-Volf, "The Least and the Greatest: Children in the New Testament," in *The Child in Christian Thought*, ed. Marcia J. Bunge (Grand Rapids, MI: Eerdmans, 2001), 45; Robin Maas, "Christ as the Logos of Childhood: Reflections on the Meaning and Mission of the Child," *Theology Today* 56, no. 4 (2000): 458; Moltmann, "Child and Childhood," 599; Couture, *Seeing Children, Seeing God*, 13.
194. Moltmann, "Child and Childhood," 599.
195. Gundry-Volf, "Least and the Greatest," 45.
196. Willmer and White, *Entry Point*, 16, 125.

suffering Son of Man."[197] Like Jesus himself, children are emissaries of God the Father, "a revelation of what life in the kingdom, our omega, is meant to be – not a means but an end."[198]

To sum up, children are sources of revelation of insights, as well as representatives of Jesus. Adults should respect them, protect them, listen to their voices, and honor their questions and insights.[199]

3.3.2.7 Children as Spiritual Models

The Bible shows that children are spiritual models;[200] they can have meaningful relationship with God.[201] For example, God spoke to Samuel when he was a child (1 Sam 3:1–14). During the sad days when the calves of Bethel and the images of Baal were set up everywhere, Obadiah affirmed "I your servant have worshiped the Lord since my youth" (1 Kgs 18:12). God was with Jeremiah when he was only a boy (Jer 1:6 NRSV). As a newborn baby, the Lord's hand was with John the Baptist (Luke 1:66). From a very young age, Timothy knew the Holy Scriptures (2 Tim 3:15).

Children as spiritual models is also affirmed by Jesus who exhorts his followers to change and become like little children so that they can enter the kingdom of heaven (Matt 18:3). According to the immediate context (i.e. Matt 18:5), Willmer and White argue that the way to help adults become

---

197. Gundry-Volf, "Least and the Greatest," 45.

198. Maas, "Christ as the Logos," 458.

199. Bunge, "Biblical and Theological Perspectives," 12.

200. Although children like adults are sinners, they demonstrate some spiritual maturity, such as humility (Matt 18:4). The argument of children as spiritual models is also supported by the outcomes of IIM, which indicate that adults derived "spiritual insights from children in the areas of trust, forgiveness, honesty, love, and fear." See Allen and Ross, *Intergenerational Christian Formation: Bringing the Whole Church Together in Ministry, Community and Worship* (Downers Grove, IL: IVP Academic, 2012), 173. Taken from Intergenerational Christian Formation by Holly Catterton Allen and Christine Lawton Ross. Copyright © 2012 by Holly Catterton Allen and Christine Lawton Ross. Used by permission of InterVarsity Press, PO Box 1400, Downers Grove, IL 60515, USA. www.ivpress.com. Permission granted for all following references to this title.

201. The basic statement of this section follows that of Bunge ("Historical Perspectives on Children in the Church," 49), which is under her heading "models of faith," a phrase the researcher chose not to use. This is because the Bible clearly shows that children are ideal models in some aspects, and can have meaningful relationship with God, but there is little support for the idea that they are models of "faith." Matthew 18:1–5 is sometimes given as evidence of this view, but this is challenged on the grounds that it is the "humility" of one child that is held as a model.

like the little children is to receive them. Adults "as children of the heavenly Father" are to understand themselves "with the help of the child in the midst."[202] Cavalletti suggests that becoming like little children is Jesus's call for adults "to a lifelong journey of growth and transformation – of continually turning and changing and becoming always more like them."[203] In other words, one who begins as a child undergoes "the wonderful adventure of remaining a child forever, becoming a child to an ever-increasing extent, making [one's] childhood of God real and effective" in one's own childhood, for this is the task of one's maturity.[204]

In both Matthew 18:1–5 and Luke 18:15–17, Jesus spurs his followers to possess "childlike" qualities, such as humility,[205] "a key constituent" of becoming like little children.[206] In Mark 10:13–16, Jesus indicates that entering the kingdom of God "as a child" involves a twofold childlike status: complete dependence on God, and a corresponding quality – trust.[207]

Apart from humility, dependence, and trust noted above, the following children's qualities can also enrich the moral and spiritual lives of adults. Clement of Alexandria, in his *Paed.*, states that Jesus's teaching on children concentrates on children's simplicity, which is to serve an example for adults.[208] Children are "gentle, and therefore more tender, delicate, and simple, guileless, and destitute of hypocrisy, straightforward and upright in

---

202. Willmer and White, *Entry Point*, 121–122.

203. Sofia Cavalletti, *The Religious Potential of the Child: Experiencing Scripture and Liturgy with Young Children*, trans. Patricia M. Coulter and Julie M. Coulter (Chicago, IL: Liturgy Training Publications, 1992), 14.

204. Rahner, *Further Theology*, 50.

205. James L. Bailey, "Experiencing the Kingdom as a Little Child: A Rereading of Mark 10:13–16," *Word & World* 15, no. 1 (1995): 64; Keith J. White, "'He Placed a Little Child in the Midst': Jesus, the Kingdom, and Children," in *The Child in the Bible*, eds. Marcia J. Bunge, Terence E. Fretheim, and Beverly Roberts Gaventa (Grand Rapids, MI: Eerdmans, 2008), 371; Gundry-Volf, "Such as These," 475; Robert H. Stein, *Luke*, The New American Commentary 24 (Nashville, TN: Broadman & Holman, 1992), 454. Reaped from Bakke, *When Children Became People*, ch. 2, Willmer and White, in *Entry Point*, 127, point out that the child in Matt 18:4 signifies humility "because in the culture which Jesus shared with his disciples it was accepted as normal that the child was lowly, a servant, near the margins."

206. Willmer and White, *Entry Point*, 122.

207. Gundry-Volf, "Such as These," 474.

208. Clement of Alexandria, "Paedagogus," in *The Ante-Nicene Fathers, Vol. 2: Fathers of the Second Century: Hermas, Tatian, Athenagoras, Theophilus, and Clement of Alexandria (Entire)*, eds. A. Roberts, J. Donaldson, and A. C. Coxe (Buffalo, NY: Christian Literature Company, 1885), 212.

mind."[209] They are able to lay aside "the cares of this life, and depend on the Father alone."[210]

Origen, Clement's pupil, in his *Comm. Matt.*, adopts and develops his mentor's ideal image of childhood, explaining that the basic characteristic of childhood is its lack of sexual desire. Another quality associated with children is their indifference toward status and wealth, things that adults think "to be good, but are not."[211] These are marks of childlike simplicity that Jesus exhorts his disciples to imitate.[212]

The shepherd of Hermas, a literary work of the second century, also associates children with simplicity and innocence. The author, in Herm. Mand. 2 (27), writes that "[God] said to me, 'Be simple and guileless, and you will be as the children who know not the wickedness that ruins the life of men.'"[213] Moreover, the author, in Herm. Sim. 9.28 (105), presents his vision of an ideal church where its members behave as innocent babes: "[W]ithout doing evil . . . all infants are honourable before God . . . Blessed, then, are ye who put away wickedness from yourselves, and put on innocence. As the first of all will you live unto God."[214]

Irenaeus, in his *Epid.*, emits a similar idea: "Adam and Eve were naked and were not ashamed, for their thoughts were innocent and childlike."[215] Tertullian, in his homily *Bapt.* chapter 18, refers to childhood as "the innocent period of life."[216] He, in treatise *Mon.* chapter 8, further notes that

---

209. Clement, "Paedagogus," 214.

210. Celement, 213.

211. Origen, "Commentary on the Gospel of Matthew," in *The Ante-Nicene Fathers*, vol. 9, ed. A. Menzies, trans. J. Patrick (New York: Christian Literature Company, 1897), 484.

212. Wall, *Ethics in Light of Childhood*, 21.

213. A. Roberts, J. Donaldson, and A. C. Coxe, eds., "Pastor of Hermas," in *The Ante-Nicene Fathers, Vol. 2: Fathers of the Second Century: Hermas, Tatian, Athenagoras, Theophilus, and Clement of Alexandria* (Entire) (Buffalo, NY: Christian Literature Company, 1885), 20.

214. Roberst, Sonaldson, and Coxe, "Pastor of Hermas," 53.

215. Irenaeus, *Proof of the Apostolic Preaching*, trans. and annotated by Joseph P. Smith, Ancient Christian Writers: The Works of the Fathers in Translation 16 (Westminster, MD: Newman Press, 1952), 56.

216. Tertullian, "On Baptism," in *The Ante-Nicene Fathers, Vol. 3: Latin Christianity: Its Founder, Tertullian*, eds. A. Roberts, J. Donaldson, and A. C. Coxe (Buffalo, NY: Christian Literature Company, 1885), 678.

children's lack of sexual desire is a manifestation of innocence.[217] Cyprian, in his response to Fidus on the baptism of infants, asserts that recently born infants have not sinned on their own account (i.e. they are innocent).[218] Briefly, these ante-Nicene fathers[219] congruously regard children as models for adult emulation because of their innocence.[220]

Chrysostom, the founder of Eastern Orthodox Christianity, in his *Hom. Matt.*, views young children as simplistic, free of passion, indifferent toward status, wealth, and poverty, and thus uncorrupted by worldly values,[221] noting:

> [T]o be lowly, and to trample under foot worldly pride [like the little children] . . . Let us also then, if we would be inheritors of the Heavens, possess ourselves of this virtue with much diligence. For this is the limit of true wisdom; to be simple with understanding; this is angelic life; yes, for the soul of a little child is pure from all the passions . . . The young child is not grieved at what we are grieved, as at loss of money and such things as that, and he does not rejoice again at what we rejoice, namely, at these temporal things.[222]

For Chrysostom, children are ideal models for adults to follow.

In his homily on Mark 10:13–16 (1834), Schleiermacher puts an emphasis on children's openness and capacity to be at the moment. He asserts that being with God in Christ in the present, without worrying about past

---

217. Tertullian, "On Monogamy," in *The Ante-Nicene Fathers, Vol. 4: Fathers of the Third Century: Tertullian, Part Fourth; Minucius Felix; Commodian; Origen, Parts First and Second*, eds., A. Roberts, J. Donaldson, and A. C. Coxe (Buffalo, NY: Christian Literature Company, 1885), 65.

218. Cyprian of Carthage, "Epistles of Cyprian," 354.

219. In general, the ante-Nicene fathers more often affirm children as paradigms for adults. See Bakke, *When Children Became People*, 57–72. However, they also recognize their original sin as later promulgated by Augustine. See Jonathan Hill, *The History of Christian Thought* (Oxford, UK: Lion, 2003), 85–86.

220. Wall, *Ethics in Light of Childhood*, 21.

221. Though similar to Clement and Origen's arguments, Chrysostom does not focus on sexuality. He also denies original sin. See John Chrysostom, *Baptismal Instructions*, trans. annotated by Paul W. Harkins, Ancient Christian Writers: The Works of the Fathers in Translation 31 (Westminster, MD: Newman Press, 1963), 57.

222. Chrysostom, *Homily on Matthew*, accessed 1 July 2014, http://www.newadvent.org/fathers/200162.htm.

or future, is God's promise of eternal life. Christ provides the opportunity to be in the eternal now, and children find it easier than the typical adult to be entirely absorbed by the communion with God in the present.[223] Thus, the adult must retrieve "this childlike perception, as if by conversion."[224]

Like Schleiermacher, Rahner refers to children's openness, but from a different perspective. For Rahner, children are ideal models[225] because of their "infinite openness." On the basis of this infinite openness, adults "become what they are – precisely children." He explains that to attain the mature childhood of adults is to "bravely and trustfully" maintain the childlike infinite openness in all circumstances, despite that "the experiences of life . . . seem to invite us to close ourselves." Putting such childlike openness into practice in an actual manner is essential for developing an authentic religious existence. It is worth noting that this infinite openness is made possible by God and "upheld by his act of self-bestowal" (i.e. by "the grace of divine sonship in the Son").[226]

In brief, children are spiritual models and have meaningful relationship with God. Adults should "recognize that [children] can positively influence the community and moral and spiritual lives of adults."[227]

---

223. Schleiermacher in DeVries, "Be Converted and Become as Little Children," 339; DeVries, "Toward a Theology of Childhood," 166.

224. DeVries, "Be Converted and Become as Little Children," 339.

225. On the one hand, Rahner, in *Further Theology*, 41, affirms the idealistic dimension of childhood; on the other hand, he, based on Paul's teachings and Matthew 11:16, recognizes the reality of children being immature and weak. Hinsdale, in "Infinite Openness to the Infinite," 424, states that although Rahner believes original sin, his view is "considerably more optimistic than that of Augustine, the Reformers or even the Council of Trent." Indeed, Rahner, in *Further Theology*, 39, argues that though children are born into "a history of guilt, of gracelessness," they and their "origins are indeed encompassed by the love of God through the pledge of that grace which, in God's will to save all mankind, comes in all cases and to every man from God in Christ Jesus."

226. Rahner, *Further Theology*, 43, 48–49.

227. Bunge, "Biblical and Theological Perspectives," 12. Paul Welter, in *Learning from Children* (Wheaton, IL: Tyndale House, 1984), 165, contends that adults need to spend time with children because they can teach adults faith, hope, love, the healing process, and growth as a way of life. He notes that "each member of [the church] is encouraged to get down on eye level with at least one child every Sunday morning."

3.3.2.8 Conclusion

Children matter.[228] Therefore, the church needs to cherish the presence of children in it because of childhood's eternal significance. The church should welcome children, acknowledging them as God's gifts and blessings. The church needs to respect children because they are whole and complete human beings and young fellow disciples. It must become a sanctuary where vulnerable children are embraced and cared for. It needs to take children seriously and listen to their voice carefully because they are sources of revelation of insights, and representatives of Jesus. It should recognize that children can enrich the moral and spiritual lives of adults because of their ideal qualities and meaningful relationship with God.

God calls the church to put children at its heart while developing various ministries, and one promising approach is intergenerational ministry, which will be examined at length in §3.4. Now, this study turns to discuss two more issues regarding children: children need the whole Bible, and children can contribute to the enterprise of Bible translation.

3.3.3 Children Need the Whole Bible

This section begins with the general argument that children, at different ages, need to hear and understand God's Word. Then, the weaknesses of popular children's Bibles are explored, followed by a discussion on children's need for the whole Bible.

3.3.3.1 Children's Need for Hearing and Understanding God's Word

The Bible explicitly indicates that children need to hear and understand God's Word. Before his word was put into writing, God chose Abraham "so that he will direct his children and his household after him to keep the way of the Lord by doing what is right and just" (Gen 18:19). In Exodus 10:2; 13:8, 14, "[p]arents were commanded to tell their children about the miraculous exodus from Egypt."[229] In Deuteronomy 4:9; 6:7, 20; 11:19, parents were instructed to teach their children God's commandments. Then, Moses wrote down the commandments and exhorted the Israelites to read

---

228. May et al., *Children Matter*.
229. Malherbe, "Big Words and Little Ears," 6.

the law every seven years before the whole assembly – men, women, children, and the foreigners. Thus, "they can listen and learn to fear the Lord . . . and follow carefully all the words of this law" (Deut 31:9–12). Similar assemblies involving men, women, and children are attested in Joshua 8:35 and Nehemiah 8:2.[230]

A favored theme of the wisdom literature[231] in the OT is instruction, the aim of which is the reverence of God as manifested in the Tora.[232] This is an essential attitude before God which needs to be inculcated in the heart of children. For example, the psalmist of Psalm 34 summons, "Come, my children, listen to me; I will teach you the fear of the Lord" (v. 11). The psalmist of Psalm 119 echoes, "How can a young person stay on the path of purity? By living according to [God's] word." In the book of Proverbs, a key component "is the instruction from father to son and this quite often involves obedience or the keeping of commands."[233] Moreover, with poetic language, the prophet Joel (1:3) commanded the elders to recount the word of God to future generations.[234]

In the NT, there are passages confirming that "in biblical times it was seen as very important for children to hear and understand the reading of the Bible."[235] For example, Luke (2:46–47) reported that the twelve-year-old boy Jesus was able to listen to the teachers at the temple and ask them questions, which amazed those around him at his understanding and answers. In Acts 22:3, the Apostle Paul introduces himself as "thoroughly trained in the law of our ancestors." 2 Timothy 3:15 says that Timothy had learned the Holy Scriptures from his early youth.[236]

Apart from biblical commands, some traditions or testimonies illustrate children's need of hearing and understanding the word of God. This is first

---

230. Malherbe, 6.
231. The wisdom literature in the OT "comprises principally the books of Job, Proverbs, and Ecclesiastes, and may also be found in portions of the psalms and prophets . . . [Its] starting point, as for all wisdom, is the reverence of God." See Peter C. Craigie, "Wisdom, Wisdom Literature," ed. W. A. Elwell et al., *Baker Encyclopedia of the Bible* (Grand Rapids, MI: Baker Book House, 1988), 2149–2150.
232. Weber, *Jesus and the Children*, 10.
233. Malherbe, "Big Words and Little Ears," 6.
234. Malherbe, 6.
235. Malherbe, 6.
236. Malherbe, 6.

demonstrated by classical Judaism. Weber points out: "The Jewish rabbis, in the time of Jesus and the centuries thereafter, continued to emphasize this all important relationship between the children and the Torah. The schools were totally devoted to the reading, memorizing and understanding of the one and only text book – the Hebrew Bible."[237]

Neuwirth also notes that Jewish children, when beginning to speak, are already exposed to informal learning of the Torah. From the age of five, they need to study the Torah formally.[238]

In the Christian community, missionaries' focus on teaching children the Bible is part of the reason for the increase in the total number of Christians in Africa from eight million (or 10 percent) in 1900 to 351 million (or 48.4 percent) in 2000.[239] Another example comes from an everyday Christian mother, Carrie Ward, who journeyed through the Bible with her three small children together – one chapter a day. In her *Together: Growing Appetites for God*, she writes:

> I am thankful for the way God made [children's] minds like little sponges, soaking up details that I sometimes overlook . . . I have watched my children remember, and help each other remember, passages in remarkable detail. As our reading continued, God also answered my prayer that they would understand. I praise God for the way I have witnessed his word being implanted in the minds of my children.[240]

With Augustine, Ward asserts with confidence, "'When we read Scripture, God speaks to us' . . . you're never too old and, as our story will tell, never too young to hear God speak."[241]

In brief, children need to hear and understand God's Word. This is not only an injunction of the Bible itself, but is also substantiated by different traditions and testimonies. Finally, as earlier arguments indicate, children

---

237. Weber, *Jesus and the Children*, 11.
238. Rav Yehoshua Y. Neuwirth, *The Halachoth of Educating Children* (Jerusalem: Feldheim, 1999), 3–19, 45–47.
239. Patrick Johnstone and Jason Mandryk, *Operation World*, 6th ed. (Carlisle, UK: Paternoster, 2001), 21.
240. Carrie Ward, *Together: Growing Appetites for God* (Chicago, IL: Moody, 2012), 27.
241. Ward, *Together*, 18.

are full human beings and part of the church; as such, they also need all of God's revelation (i.e. the *whole* Bible).

3.3.3.2 The Weakness of Children's Bibles

Bible formats for children, according to Malherbe, can be grouped into five categories: "children's Bibles, Bibles for children,[242] Bibles in easy English,[243] multimedia presentations and general Bibles that make provision for children."[244] As space is limited here, only the first and last categories, which are more pertinent to the present study, will be explored. As general Bibles will be discussed in §3.3.4, children's Bibles are the focal point here.

Children's Bibles[245] belong to "the literary genre of children's literature"[246] and are very popular in the Christian community. The majority of children's Bibles employing a highly simplified language consist of *selected* and/or *retold narratives* with pictures and introductory material (italics added).[247]

One of the most important early children's Bibles was "Passional," produced by Luther and included in the final section of his prayer book in 1529. Luther's Passional text comprised fifty small pages with illustrations on each page. It contained mainly the traditional passion story, but also other stories and quotations from the Bible.[248] Two decades later, Luther's Passional faded from memory and was replaced by Hartman Beyer's collection of Bible stories (1555), which were initially intended for adults, but soon came to be read by children.[249] In the eighteenth century, under the influence of Enlightenment pedagogical imperatives, Johann Hubner

---

242. Such as The Living Bible, the New Century Version, and the Contemporary English Version. The translators of these versions view children as a separate social group with unique needs, experiences, views, questions and even their own "language." This approach may be designated as "'generationalist' because of its focus on the age stratification of society." See Malherbe, "Big Words and Little Ears," 10.

243. Such as the Good News Translation, which is intended for English as second-language speakers.

244. Malherbe, "Big Words and Little Ears," 8.

245. For Bottigheimer, children's Bibles are also known as Bible story collections. See Ruth B. Bottigheimer, *The Bible for Children: From the Age of Gutenberg to the Present* (New Haven, CT: Yale University Press, 1996), xiv.

246. Ruth B. Bottigheimer, "Bible Reading, 'Bibles' and the Bible for Children in Early Modern Germany," *Past and Present* 139 (1993): 68 n. 7.

247. Pritchard, *Offering the Gospel to Children*, 41.

248. Bottigheimer, "Bible Reading," 69.

249. Bottigheimer, 73.

removed Bible stories that he felt were inappropriate for children,[250] such as Amnon's incest with Tamar and David's adultery with Bathsheba.[251] Ever since the end of the nineteenth century, children's Bibles have flourished.[252] The popularity of children's Bibles might result from those notions emerging from the Enlightenment ("away from negative exempla and toward positive behavioral examples"),[253] or from the choice of simplified language for children promoted in the twentieth century,[254] etc.

Despite the popularity, the preceding aspects strongly influenced the content, form, and style of children's Bibles and led to negative consequences. For instance, Bible stories mix "sacred text with secular values" due to "their authors' effort to use the Bible to shape a meaningful present."[255] Another consequence is that the gospel might be distorted because of the proclamation of the kiddie gospel, an easy Good News – a simple blessing, rather than "a sacrament of life out of death."[256]

Therefore, Pritchard, in her *Offering the Gospel to Children*, makes a loud appeal: "There is a crying need for a [whole] Bible for young readers that will open a door for them into the church's own story . . . and [they] in turn may be able to 'tell those who come after.'"[257] In their book, *The Bible: A Child's Playground*, Gobbel and Gobbel assert that "it is not sufficient that [children] . . . hear stories based on some biblical passage or character. Children must have direct access to the biblical content itself."[258] This is the focal point of the next section.

---

250. Bottigheimer, in "Bible Reading," 76, argues that Hubner's editing was "not in a theological context, but in social and pedagogical terms that reflected secular values but conflicted with scriptural sources."

251. Bottigheimer, 75–76. The desexualization of children's Bibles "coincided with eighteenth-century emphasis on sexual innocence among the young." See Bottigheimer, *Bible for Children*, 137–138.

252. Penny Schine Gold, *Making the Bible Modern: Children's Bibles and Jewish Education in Twentieth-Century America* (Ithaca: Cornell University Press, 2004), 189.

253. Bottigheimer, *Bible for Children*, 218.

254. Gold, *Making the Bible Modern*, 119.

255. Bottigheimer, *Bible for Children*, 218.

256. Pritchard, *Offering the Gospel to Children*, 32, 39.

257. Pritchard, 46.

258. A. Roger Gobbel and Gertrude G. Gobbel, *The Bible: A Child's Playground* (Philadelphia, PA: Fortress, 1986), 34. As noted in §3.3.3.1, Jewish children are already exposed to informal learning of the Torah while beginning to speak. The researcher suggests

3.3.3.3 Children's Need for the Whole Bible

While some assert that children should be shielded from the more negative parts of the Bible, many, including the present researcher, believe children need the whole Bible, comprising both dark and light content. This viewpoint is supported by the following reasons: (1) the scriptural call to tell the whole story; (2) children's need for diverse language to express their religious experiences; (3) children's need for the whole gospel connected with the whole Bible.

3.3.3.3.1 The scriptural call to tell the whole story

In their interpretation of Psalm 78:1–8, May et al., argue that this pericope "instructs that the whole story be told." Apart from acknowledging God's power and saving acts, "the dark or unpleasant stories" need to be told to children, "so that they might learn from the mistakes of their ancestors."[259] The book of Deuteronomy has abundant similar instructions to tell the complete story, e.g. Deuteronomy 6:20–22.[260] Moreover, 2 Timothy 3:16 states, "All Scripture is God-breathed and is useful for teaching, rebuking, correcting and training in righteousness." Like young Timothy, what children need while being "equipped for every good work" (2 Tim 3:15, 17) is the entire God-breathed Scripture. Finally, Jesus warned against omitting anything from the Torah (Matt 5:18).

3.3.3.3.2 Children's need for diverse language to express their religious experiences

Berryman maintains that children, at different ages, need darker language to express their complex experiences and sense of life. For example, his experience with sick and dying children for more than a decade convinces him that "young children know a lot about death and have religious experiences."[261] He describes that children in the Texas Medical Center "helped one another prepare for death when parents and other significant adults were not able to help them . . . At times the children even parented their parents as the

---

that children at the same age can hear the *whole* Bible with the help of parents or caregivers who read God's Word to them.

259. May et al., *Children Matter*, 178–179.
260. May et al., 179–180.
261. Berryman, *Godly Play*, 143, 154.

end came near."²⁶² Therefore, there is no need to keep children from darker stories in the Bible because of their innocence.²⁶³ After all, innocence, as noted above, is but one dimension of children's qualities. It should not be taken alone, or taken to extremes.

3.3.3.3.3 Children's need for the whole gospel connected with the whole Bible

As indicated earlier, often children's Bibles only share small pieces of the story that are considered appropriate for them, such as Jesus as teacher and healer, rather than offering the whole story in its original and unedited form. Pritchard laments that such a "kiddie gospel" is "a gospel that hides the bitter realities and glorious promises of Scripture." This can result in a distortion of children's devotional lives.²⁶⁴

Pritchard affirms that the whole²⁶⁵ gospel cannot be separated from the OT, whose heart is "a continuing pattern of exile and return, of loss, hope, and restoration,²⁶⁶ of new life out of renunciation and death."²⁶⁷ This pattern emerges not only from narrative, "but from prophecy, psalm, and hymns; from vision and exhortation; from parable, image, and metaphor."²⁶⁸ Unfortunately, many children's Bibles contain only narrative. This not only extremely distorts the OT canon, but also dismisses the significant passages which link the Old Testament to the New. Worst of all, many children's Bibles fail to present the whole picture of God's plan of salvation.²⁶⁹

Pritchard insists that children can grasp the whole gospel:

> Children know that our life on earth is itself the story of exile and loss . . . They know that their greatest need is to find their way home to where they will be welcomed, loved, and fed, and

---

262. Berryman, 143.
263. Nye, *Children's Spirituality*, 80.
264. Pritchard, *Offering the Gospel to Children*, 5, 42.
265. "Whole" is a key term in the Lausanne movement: "the whole church taking the whole gospel to the whole world." See Lausanne Theology Working Group, "The Whole Church Taking the Whole Gospel to the Whole World," 2010, accessed 17 July 2016, https://www.lausanne.org/content/twg-three-wholes.
266. The instigator of this cycle is God's grace, responded to by persistent sin.
267. Pritchard, *Offering the Gospel to Children*, 41–43.
268. Pritchard, 41–43.
269. Pritchard, 41–43.

to come of age, inherit the kingdom, receive the crown of life, and know that all tears are forever dried and all that was lost has been found.[270]

This beautiful picture as recorded in and promised through the whole Bible is not found in many, if not the majority of, children's Bibles.

To sum up this section, offering the whole Bible to children is necessary so that they can access the whole gospel. They need "dark language" to address Christian and even life experiences. Perhaps most important, the Scriptures themselves give the command to share Scriptures with children.

3.3.4 Children Can Contribute to the Enterprise of Bible Translation

As noted above, the findings from childhood studies show it is necessary and advantageous for children to be involved in the church. Intentional intergenerational ministry (IIM) provides a promising approach to make this happen. If this is the case, what type of Bible is needed when developing IIM in the church? One of the best possibilities is versions comprehensible for general readers, including children, which is one of the five Bible formats for children proposed by Malherbe (§3.3.3.2). Such versions were already in view by early theologians like Erasmus[271] and Luther. Both of these scholars promoted Scriptures in mother tongue, which could be read and understood by common people. Luther himself made clear, noting that for the German readership in the sixteenth century,

> [w]e do not have to inquire of the literal Latin, how we are to speak German, as these asses do. Rather we must inquire about

---

270. Pritchard, 44.

271. In the preface to the first edition of his Greek New Testament (1516), Erasmus notes: "I vehemently dissent from those who would not have private persons read the Holy Scriptures nor have them translated into the vulgar tongues . . . I should like all women to read the Gospel and the Epistles of Paul." See James White, "Erasmus of Rotterdam: His New Testament and Its Importance," accessed 17 July 2016, http://vintage.aomin.org/erasmus.html#1-20. In the preface to the third edition of the foregoing work (1522), Erasmus further elucidated this thought: "Like St Jerome I think it a great triumph and glory to the cross if [the word of God] is celebrated by the tongues of all men; if the farmer at the plow sings some of the mystic Psalms, and the weaver sitting at the shuttle often refreshes himself with something from the Gospel. Let the pilot at the rudder hum over a sacred tune, and the matron sitting with gossip or friend at the colander recite something from it." See White, "Erasmus of Rotterdam: His New Testament and Its Importance."

this of the mother in the home, *the children on the street*, the common man in the marketplace. We must be guided by their language, the way they speak, and do our translating accordingly. That way they will understand it and recognize that we are speaking German to them (italics added).[272]

Thus, an ideal Bible version in Luther's mind seems to be one rendered in common language spoken by ordinary people, including children.

But far too often, the task of Bible translation is conducted by middle-aged professionals whose speech has become conservative, as pointed out by Eckert: "increasing age corresponds with increasing conservatism in speech."[273] Social dialect research confirms this point of view: "[Vernacular speech is] . . . high in childhood and adolescence, and then steadily reduce[s] as people approach middle age when societal pressures to conform are greatest. Vernacular usage gradually increases again in old age as social pressures reduce."[274] Thus, it seems ideal for children, adolescents, even senior adults to participate in a normal Bible translation team to produce a new translation that may be effective and accepted by a wide gamut of readers.

The idea that children can assist with Bible translation may be new and unexpected. Yet, Talay-Ongan points out that "by five years of age, the child's language sounds quite like that of mature language-users."[275] Mishler concludes from his research that "first-grade children and adults do not differ significantly in the length of their utterances including their questions . . . first-grade children have the ability to vary speech style, and to use features of adult conversation."[276] Similarly, research among Russian-speaking children confirms this point of view, as A. N. Gvozdev argues:

> At [the age of eight] the child has already mastered to such a degree the entire complicated grammatical system, including

---

272. Martin Luther, "On Translation: An Open Letter," in *Word and Sacrament I*, eds. E. T. Bachmann and H. T. Lehmann, Luther's Works 35 (Philadelphia, PA: Fortress, 1960 [1530]), 189.

273. Eckert, "Age as a Sociolinguistic Variable," 152.

274. Holmes, *Introduction to Sociolinguistics*, 168.

275. Ayshe Talay-Ongan, *Typical and Atypical Development in Early Childhood: The Fundamentals* (New York: Teachers College Press, 1998), 173.

276. Quoted in Black, "Assessing Kindergarten," 39.

the finest points of esoteric syntactic and morphological sequences in the Russian language, as well as the solid and correct usage of many single exceptions, that the Russian language, thus mastered, becomes indeed his own.²⁷⁷

If children are competent in speaking their mother tongue at a very early age, it is certainly possible for them to participate in the discussion surrounding a Bible translation, leading to a quality translation for readers of all ages. What follows is an example of children's participation in the enterprise of Bible translation from the history of Chinese Bible translation.

As noted in §2.2.3.3.2, Joshua Marshman (1768–1837) came to China in 1799 and began Bible translation into Chinese in 1807–1808. In his letter (1813) to the BFBS, he mentions that there were seven different reviewers to edit the drafts produced by himself and Johannes Lassar. Of the reviewers, one was Marshman's son, John Clark Marshman (1794–1877),²⁷⁸ a boy of no more than thirteen or fourteen years old.

Coming back to Wendland's LiFE model, he notes three equally critical operations "involved in the production of a Bible translation – composition, contextualization, and consultation." The latter two rely heavily on the participation of a target audience, which makes participants feel that they are "a valued part of the project. As a result, they will be more likely to welcome and use the version as it gradually becomes available to them over the years."²⁷⁹ Thus, children as Bible readers should participate in the operations of contextualization and consultation according to Wendland's suggestion. This stimulates the researcher to propose that children's involvement in the latter part of the operation of composition is necessary in terms of producing an easier Bible version for young readers. The main reason is that children as social agents (§3.2.2.1) can help suggest or determine which words, phrases, and sentences are understandable to them. Finally, children are sources of revelation of insights (§3.3.2.6); their participation in the present translation task might provide some insights for this study.

---

277. Quoted in Chukovsky, *From Two to Five*, 10.
278. Zetzsche, *Bible in China*, 46–47.
279. Wendland, *LiFE-Style Translating*, 406–407.

3.3.5 Conclusion

The findings from childhood studies challenge conventional, popular Christian views regarding children. Through the preceding survey, this study argues that children not only need the whole Bible, but furthermore can and should participate in the task of Bible translation. Childhood studies within and even outside the Christian realm provides further understanding on the nature of childhood and children, which should spur the church to take children seriously and to involve them as active participants in the faith community. One promising approach is intentional intergenerational ministry, to which this study now turns.

3.4 Intentional Intergenerational Ministry

3.4.1 Introduction

In the West, intentional intergenerational[280] ministry (IIM) is a movement carried out in churches, neighborhoods, communities, corporations, and organizations which addresses problems of dysfunctional families and the indifference of society in the postmodern era.[281] Its goal is to "start a movement to bring Christ's intergenerational message of unconditional love to an aging society suffering from generational isolation, separation and neglect."[282] This is also a crucial issue in mainland China caused by one-child policy, urbanization and modernization,[283] as noted in §1.1.

In a society defined by isolation and age segregation, IIM is understood "as something outside of the core mission of the congregation."[284] However,

---

280. In terms of intergenerationality, there are three popular terms which tend to be used interchangeably: intergenerational, cross-generational, and multi-generational. For Chechowich, the first two are preferable because "multi-generational does not necessarily mean the generations are interacting." See Faye E. Chechowich, "Intergenerational Ministry: A Review of Selected Publications since 2001," *Christian Education Journal*, Series 3, vol. 9, no. 1 (2012): 182. The present study adopts the term "intergenerational."

281. Gambone, *All Are Welcome*, v.

282. Gambone, vii.

283. Powell, "Negative Impact," iii, 39.

284. Gambone, *All Are Welcome*, vi; see also James V. Gambone, *Together for Tomorrow: Building Community Through Intergenerational Dialogue* (Crystal Bay, MN: Elder Eye, 1997), 17.

a growing number of churches is committing themselves to it[285] and reaping the benefits.[286] Therefore, structuring and facilitating an intergenerational team to participate in Bible translation should be an exercise worth trying.

The next part of chapter 3 examines the terminology concerning IIM, followed by investigating the foundations of IIM from biblical, theoretical, theological, and social-scientific perspectives. Then, the practices and outcomes of IIM are explored. This chapter ends with the conclusion that an intergenerational Bible translation team is not only feasible and valuable, but also beneficial for participants of all ages.

3.4.2 The Term IIM

The word *inter* indicates the concept of connecting or between, and thus *intergenerational*[287] implies dialogue and activity among persons of "two or

---

285. Jim Merhaut, "Outcomes and Practices of Intergenerational Faith Formation," in *Generations Together: Caring, Praying, Learning, Celebrating, & Serving Faithfully*, eds. Kathie Amidei, Jim Merhaut, and John Roberto, Kindle edition (Naugatuck, CT: Lifelong Faith Publications, 2014), ch. 4; Brenda Snailum, "Implementing Intergenerational Youth Ministry within Existing Evangelical Church Congregations," *Christian Education Journal* 9, no. 1 (2012): 165; Christine M. Ross, "Characteristics of Churches."

286. John Roberto, "Our Future Is Intergenerational," *Christian Education Journal*, Series 3, vol. 9, no. 1 (2012): 106.

287. Though sometimes employed descriptively in religious literature, the term *intergenerational* was not a prominent term until Whites' *Intergenerational Religious Education* of 1988 was published. See Holly Catterton Allen and Christine Lawton Ross, *Intergenerational Christian Formation*, 64. After White, the term *intergenerational* is also used by several Christian scholars. For example, intergenerational Christian education (Prest, *From One Generation to Another* [Capetown: Training for Leadership, 1993]; Harkness "Intergenerational and Homogeneous-Age Education: Mutually Exclusive Strategies for Faith Communities," *Religious Education* 95, no. 1 [2000]: 51–63), intentional intergenerational ministry (Gambone, *All Are Welcome*), intergenerational faith formation (Martinerau, Weber and Kehrwald, *Intergenerational Faith Formation: All Ages Learning Together* [New London, CT: Twenty-Third Publications, 2008]; Roberto, "Our Fututre in Intergenerational"), and intergenerational Christian formation (Allen and Ross, *Intergenerational Christian Formation*). Besides, some ideas, though they are not expressed in "intergenerational" terms, offer similar concepts for intergenerationality. For example, community of believers (C. Ellis Nelson, *Where Faith Begins* [Atlanta: John Knox, 1967]), enculturation (John H. Westerhoff, *Will Our Children Have Faith?*, rev. and exp. ed. [Harrisburg, PA: Morehouse, 2000]), interplay across the generations (Gabriel Moran, *Interplay: A Theology of Religion and Education* [Winona, MN: Saint Mary's Press, 1981]), church as an ecology of faith nurture (James W. Fowler, *Weaving the New Creation: Stages of Faith and the Public Curch* [San Francisco, CA: HarperSanFrancisco, 1991]), and strong-group entity (Jospeh H. Hellerman, *When the Church Was a Family: Recapturing Jesus' Vision for Authentic Christian Community* [Nashville, TN: B & H Academic, 2009]). For fuller discussions, see Allen and Ross, *Intergenerational Christian Formation*, 65–73. Allen and Ross, in *Intergenerational Christian Formation*, 74, point out that though varying in wording, all the preceding phrases emphasize "the

more different age groups,"[288] which "enables people of differing generations to be more connected with one another."[289] The phrase *intentional intergenerational ministry* was coined by James Gambone and refers to a form of ministry in which "the entire church makes a commitment to involve as many generations in as many parts of church as possible."[290] This approach can be seen as a foundation of a Christian's faith journey and be regarded as part of the core mission of a congregation.[291]

3.4.3 The Foundations of IIM

This study explores the foundations of IIM from biblical, theoretical, theological, and social-scientific perspectives.

3.4.3.1 Biblical Support

Much of Scripture justifies an intergenerational approach. In what follows, some of those passages are discussed and grouped into several categories: God's plan for the generations, intergenerational gatherings, generations passing on the faith, a covenant community as an all-age community, and the intergenerational body of Christ.

3.4.3.1.1 God's plan for the generations

Isaiah 41:4 says, "Who has done this and carried it through, calling forth the generations from the beginning? I, the Lord – with the first of them and with the last – I am he." This verse demonstrates "the fact that the generations are foundationally significant in the plan of God."[292] Psalm 33:11 also describes the generations created by God as the vehicle to reveal and manifest plans that are in his heart: God has established his throne on the earth (Lam 5:19); his kingdom, dominion (Dan 4:3), and renown (Exod 3:15; Ps 102:12) endure; his love (Exod 20:6), mercy (Luke 1:48), faithfulness

---

importance of fostering intentionally cross-generational opportunities for the purpose of nurturing Christian learning, growth and formation."

288. James W. White, *Intergenerational Religious Education: Models, Theory and Prescription for Interage Life and Learning in the Faith Community* (Birmingham: Religious Education Press, 1988), 18.

289. Ross, "Characteristics of Churches," 9.

290. Gambone, *All Are Welcome*, vi.

291. Gambone, vi, 2.

292. Daphne Kirk, *Reconnecting the Generations: Empowering God's People, Young and Old, to Live, Worship and Serve Together* (Suffolk, UK: Kevin Mayhew Ltd, 2001), 7.

(Ps 119:90), righteousness, and salvation (Isa 51:8) continue throughout human time.[293] Before Jesus came, the Jews were called upon to share with each generation. The plan of God's salvation culminated when Jesus entered the sequence of generations. Then, "each generation is responsible for passing on the good news of redemption to their generation and the generations coming after them."[294]

3.4.3.1.2 Intergenerational gatherings

In the religion of Israel, people of all ages are not just included;[295] they are "assimilated or incorporated with a deep sense of belonging into the body or the family of God's covenant people."[296] This is best illustrated by the instructions on feasts and celebrations. For example, before his death, Moses gives instructions for one of the festivals, the Feast of Booths:

> Assemble the people – men, women and children, and the foreigners residing in your towns – so they can listen and learn to fear the Lord your God and follow carefully all the words of this law. Their children, who do not know this law, must hear it and learn to fear the Lord your God as long as you live in the land you are crossing the Jordan to possess (Deut 31:12–13).[297]

Through the festivals, the Israelites are reminded of who they are, who God is, and what God has done for them. When young people dance, sing, eat, listen to the stories and ask questions, they come to know their identity.[298] Such knowing implies more than intellectual information, but rather knowing by experiencing.[299]

---

293. Kirk, *Reconnecting the Generations*, 9.
294. Kirk, 8–10.
295. John S. Pridmore, *The New Testament Theology of Childhood* (Hobart, Australia: Ron Buckland, 1977), 28–29.
296. Eddie Prest, *From One Generation*, 25.
297. Allen and Ross, *Intergenerational Christian Formation*, 80.
298. Allen and Ross, 80.
299. Terence E. Fretheim, "יָדַע (Yādaʻ)," in *New International Dictionary of Old Testament Theology and Exegesis*, vol. 2, ed. Willem A. VanGemeren (Grand Rapids, MI: Zondervan, 1997), 410.

In addition to festivals, 2 Chronicles 20 says that men, women, and children gathered in God's presence before marching to the battleground, praising him.

All the generations of the Israelites also gather for important events. For instance, after the Israelites return from captivity to Jerusalem,

> Ezra the priest brought the Law before the assembly, which was made up of men and women and all who were able to understand. He read it aloud from daybreak till noon as he faced the square before the Water Gate in the presence of the men, women and others who could understand. And all the people listened attentively to the Book of the Law. (Neh 8:2–3)

Then, in the dedication of the wall of Jerusalem, the Israelites offer great sacrifices, and there is great joy from God among the people, including women and children (Neh 12:27–43).[300]

Much influenced by its OT origins, the faith community in the NT times maintains the intergenerational entity, with persons of all ages viewed as integral parts of a whole.[301] For example, "the most vivid depiction of a cross-generational event anywhere in the Gospels" is found in Luke 2:41–47, where Jesus listens to the elders and asks them questions.[302] The Gospels report that Jesus welcomes the children.[303] In 1 Peter 5:1–5, Peter exhorts the elders and the youth to clothe themselves with humility toward one another.[304] Based on Colossians 3:20 and Ephesians 6:1–3, Banks infers that

---

300. Allen and Ross, *Intergenerational Christian Formation*, 79.

301. Allan G. Harkness, "Intergenerationality: Biblical and Theological Foundations," *Christian Education Journal*, Series 3, vol. 9, no. 1 (2012): 127; Allan G. Harkness, "Intergenerational Education for an Intergenerational Church?," *Religious Education* 93, no. 4 (1998): 436; Roberto, "Our Future Is Intergenerational," 106.

302. James Frazier, "All Generations of Saints at Worship," in *Across the Generations: Incorporating All Ages in Ministry: The Why and How*, ed. Vicky Goplin et al. (Minneapolis, MN: Augsburg Fortress, 2001), 57.

303. Darwin Glassford, "Fostering an Intergenerational Culture," in *The Church of All Ages: Generations Worshiping Together*, ed. Howard Vanderwell (Herndon, VA: Alban Institute, 2008), 72; Francis, *Adults as Children*, 147.

304. Gunnar Mägi, "Intergenerational Church: A Philosophy of Ministry and an Educational Curriculum for a Cross-Generational Community of Faith" (University of Tartu, 2004), 44.

not only adults, but also children are regularly present in the house church, participating in the Lord's Supper and the Passover Feast, etc.[305]

3.4.3.1.3 Generations passing on the faith

Faith is passed on through generations. As Brueggemann notes: "In the world of the Bible, the family (or clan or tribe) provides individuals with deep roots into the past, bold visions for the future, a sense of purpose, and a set of priorities for the present."[306]

Psalm 89:1 declares, "I will sing of the Lord's great love forever; with my mouth I will make your faithfulness known through all generations," indicating that God's people "continue through the generations because each age tells the next."[307] Psalm 145:4 proclaims, "One generation commends your works to another; they tell of your mighty acts." Allen and Ross interpret this verse to mean that every generation is responsible for sharing God's mighty deeds with other generations "so that all can worship and praise God together."[308] McIntosh also notes that "each generation has an evangelistic mandate to communicate the good news to all generations."[309] Drawing from Deuteronomy 6:6–9, Allen and Ross argue that although the significance of "generational transmission for spiritual formation" has been often perceived as speaking exclusively to parents, this passage conveys "the communal sense that faith in God is to be modeled and taught in the home as well as among the faith community, across the generations."[310]

In Matthew 28:19, Jesus says, "go and make disciples of all nations." Through discipleship – an intergenerational imperative[311] – each generation can form the next generation. The interaction between generations "in

---

305. Robert J. Banks, *Paul's Idea of Community: The Early House Churches in Their Cultural Setting*, rev. ed. (Grand Rapids, MI: Baker Academic, 1995), 82.

306. Quoted in Roland D. Martinson and Diane E. Shallue, "Foundations for Cross-Generational Ministry," in *Across the Generations: Incorporating All Ages in Ministry: The Why and How*, ed. Vicky Goplin et al. (Minneapolis, MN: Augsburg Fortress, 2001), 5.

307. Howard Vanderwell, "Biblical Values to Shape the Congregation," in *The Church of All Ages: Generations Worshiping Together*, ed. Howard Vanderwell (Herndon, VA: The Alban Institute, 2008), 28.

308. Allen and Ross, *Intergenerational Christian Formation*, 80.

309. Gary L. McIntosh, *One Church, Four Generations: Understanding and Reaching All Ages in Your Church* (Grand Rapids, MI: Baker Books, 2002), 198.

310. Allen and Ross, *Intergenerational Christian Formation*, 81.

311. Harkness, "Intergenerationality," 123.

reminding each other of the truth of the gospel and the acts of God is an indispensable element of the continuation" of the faith community.[312]

3.4.3.1.4 A covenant community as an all-age community

The term of "covenant," White notes, implies "connectedness among generations."[313] In Genesis 17:7, God makes a covenant with Abraham, saying, "I will establish my covenant as an everlasting covenant between me and you and your descendants after you for the generations to come, to be your God and the God of your descendants after you." Accordingly, Mounstephen and Martin propose that God's covenant community is an all-age community. One significant pericope in this regard is found in Joel 2:28: "I will pour out my Spirit on all people. Your sons and daughters will prophesy, your old men will dream dreams, your young men will see visions."[314] Again, people of all ages made in the image of God are included in the covenant community.[315]

The imagery of the covenant community is reinforced in the NT. Many passages describe that all ages are present in spiritual settings or house churches, etc. For example, when Jesus responds to his disciples' question about the greatest in the kingdom of heaven, children are there and viewed as ideal models in Jesus's teaching concerning life in God's kingdom community (Matt 18:1–6; 19:13–14).[316] In the early house church, all generations gather together, praying together (Acts 12:12),[317] breaking bread together, ministering to one another (Acts 2:46–47; 4:32–35),[318] and getting baptized together (Acts 16:15, 33).[319]

---

312. Vanderwell, "Biblical Values," 27.

313. White, *Intergenerational Religious Education*, 70.

314. Philip Mounstephen and Kelly Martin, *Body Beautiful?: Recapturing a Vision for All-Age Church* (Cambridge, UK: Grove Books, 2004), 6–7; see also Peter Menconi, *The Intergenerational Church: Understanding Congregations from WWII to WWW.com* (Littleton, CO: Sage, 2010), 6.

315. Mounstephen and Martin, *Body Beautiful?*, 7.

316 Harkness, "Intergenerationality," 123; Allen and Ross, *Intergenerational Christian Formation*, 83.

317. Floyd V. Filson, "The Significance of the Early House Churches," *Journal of Biblical Literature* 58, no. 2 (1939): 106.

318. Allen and Ross, *Intergenerational Christian Formation*, 83.

319. Mounstephen and Martin, *Body Beautiful?*, 8; Vanderwell, "Biblical Values," 23.

Paul's teaching in Ephesians 5:21 ("Submit to one another out of reverence for Christ") takes on an intergenerational dimension and gives new insight into the covenant community: "[D]istinctions of age, sex, and social standing are secondary to one's membership in the faith community and the associated mutual interdependence implied by that membership."[320]

3.4.3.1.5 The intergenerational body of Christ

While discussing a church's objectives, Lewis and Demarest, based on Acts 2:42, argue that a church should "stimulate enriching fellowship" among the membership and "encourage mutual caring among all its members intergenerationally, irrespective of gender, marital status, and socioeconomic standing."[321] Their interpretation can be summarized as: "*all* are the body of Christ."[322]

In 1 Corinthians 12:27, Paul refers to the church as the body of Christ: "[Y]ou are the body of Christ, and each one of you is a part of it." This metaphor indirectly portrays that each person is crucial to the church. Once "one person is absent, neglected, or marginalized, the body suffers."[323] In Ephesians 4:15–16, Paul further emphasizes the body of Christ metaphor and portrays Christ as the head of the body: "[S]peaking the truth in love, we will grow to become in every respect the mature body of him who is the head, that is, Christ. From him the whole body, joined and held together by every supporting ligament, grows and builds itself up in love, as each part does its work." Put simply, the body of Christ metaphor encourages all members of the church to live a life of "selflessness that will promote spiritual maturity."[324]

In sum, numerous biblical passages show the significance of intergenerationality and the interactions between generations, which lay the primary foundations for IIM.

---

320. Harkness, "Intergenerationality," 124–125.
321. Gordon R. Lewis and Bruce A. Demarest, *Integrative Theology*, vol. 3 (Grand Rapids, MI: Zondervan, 1994), 275.
322. Allen and Ross, *Intergenerational Christian Formation*, 84.
323. Glassford, "Fostering an Intergenerational Culture," 79.
324. Glassford, 79.

3.4.3.2 Theoretical Support

Although the preceding section lays out strong biblical foundations of IIM, there is a need to find connections between God's directives and current theory. In the following section, some theoretical perspectives are examined to provide significant insight into IIM, including developmental theory, sociocultural learning theory, social learning theory, and situated learning theory.

3.4.3.2.1 Insight from developmental theory

Though developmental theories have been useful in understanding processes of individual developmental growth, they have a downside. DeVries notes that "developmental theories tend to distance adults from children" by means of conveying the notion that "earlier phases of development are taken as relatively less valuable than later phases."[325] This is problematic according to the findings presented earlier, for example, Rahner's views on the unsurpassable value of childhood. However, there is another aspect of this field that "has been somewhat neglected," but can offer profound insight to IIM: the emphasis on "the influence and importance of social interaction."[326] This is a theme found in theories of some prominent developmentalists, such as Piaget, Erikson, Kohlberg, and Fowler.

3.4.3.2.1.1 Jean Piaget

Piaget, widely known as a cognitive psychologist, delineates four phases of cognitive development: the *sensorimotor* stage (birth to age two), characterized by organized motor response by infants; the *preoperational* stage (ages two to seven) at which children operate more by intuitive thought than by logic; the *concrete operational* stage (ages seven to eleven) at which the young thinker has a concrete understanding of reality; and the *formal operational* stage (from age eleven on), characterized by abstract conceptualization, symbolic representation, and historical perspective-taking.[327]

---

325. DeVries, "Toward a Theology of Childhood," 163.
326. Allen and Ross, *Intergenerational Christian Formation*, 87.
327. Jean Piaget, *Six Psychological Studies*, trans. Anita Tenzer (New York: Random House, 1967), 8–70; see also Jean Piaget and Bärbel Inhelder, *The Psychology of the Child*, trans. Helen Weaver (New York: Basic Books, 1969).

In Piaget's thinking, except for age and genetic unfolding, five factors influence the movement from one stage to the next: maturation, experience, social transmission, equilibration and contradictions.[328] Except for maturation, the other four factors generally happen in social settings. Thus, social interaction plays an essential role in cognitive development.[329]

3.4.3.2.1.2 Erik Erikson

Though known as an ego psychologist and a Piagetian cognitivist,[330] Erikson's most significant contribution is in the area of social psychology.[331] In his work, *Childhood and Society*, Erikson identifies eight ages (stages or phases) of humans and delineates them as psychosocial conflicts or crises:[332] basic trust vs. basic mistrust (age one), autonomy vs. shame and doubt (ages two to three), initiative vs. guilt (ages four to six), industry and inferiority (ages seven to eleven), identity vs. role confusion (ages twelve to twenty), intimacy vs. isolation (ages twenty-one to thirty-two), generativity vs. stagnation (ages thirty-three to fifty-five), ego integrity vs. despair (age fifty-five on).[333] These developmental tasks are learned through social interaction.[334]

More pertinent to this study, Erikson's work pays particular attention to the interaction of generations. For example, he writes of the interaction between children and parents: "the family brings up a baby by being brought up by him" or her.[335]

---

328. Herbert P. Ginsburg and Sylvia Opper, *Piaget's Theory of Intellectual Development* (Englewood Cliffs, NJ: Prentice-Hall, 1988), 213–229.

329. Allen and Ross, *Intergenerational Christian Formation*, 88.

330. Allen and Ross, 88.

331. White, *Intergenerational Religious Education*, 94.

332. Though describing his developmental stages as psychosocial conflicts or crises, Erikson does not "consider all development a series of conflicts or crises," but claims that "psychosocial development proceeds by critical steps – 'critical' being a characteristic of turning points, of moments of decision between progress and regression, integration and retardation." See Erik H. Erikson, *Childhood and Society*, 2nd ed. (New York: Norton, 1963), 270–271.

333. Erikson, *Childhood and Society*, ch. 7.

334. Erikson, 270.

335. Erikson, 69.

3.4.3.2.1.3 Lawrence Kohlberg

Kohlberg has been called "a most creative contributor to contemporary thinking about moral development."[336] The following is his formulation of "levels and stages of development" (each level consists of two stages): At the *preconventional* level, moral value resides in external factors. That means, children (ages four to ten) obey rules to avoid punishment (stage one), or obey rules to obtain rewards and get favors (stage two). At the *conventional* level, moral value resides in performing good or right roles. Some adolescents and most adults conform to stereotypical images and avoid disapproval of others (stage three), or avoid censure and resultant guilt (stage four). As to the highest, *postconventional* level that only some adults attain, moral value resides in conformity with standards, rights, and obligations. Those who reach this level conform to standards agreed upon by the whole society (stage five), or adhere to right as defined by conscience in accord with self-chosen ethical principles (stage six).[337]

Kohlberg's scheme makes clear that a process of moral development requires interaction between the organism and the social environment.[338] Put simply, a critical element in moral development is to interact with other people.

3.4.3.2.1.4 James Fowler

In formulating a Christian-oriented theory of child development, Fowler has woven strands of Piaget, Erikson, and Kohlberg to construct a theory of faith development.[339] His faith stages comprise primal faith (infancy), intuitive-projective faith (early childhood), mythic-literal faith (middle childhood and beyond), synthetic-conventional faith (adolescence and beyond), individuative-reflective faith (young adulthood and beyond), conjunctive faith (early midlife and beyond), and universalizing faith (midlife and

---

336. White, *Intergenerational Religious Education*, 109.

337. Lawrence Kohlberg, *Collected Papers on Moral Development and Moral Education* (Cambridge, MA: Harvard University Laboratory for Human Development, 1973), 72–73; Lawrence Kohlberg, *Essays on Moral Development (Vol. 2): The Psychology of Moral Development* (San Francisco, CA: Harper & Row, 1984), 44.

338. Kohlberg, *Essays on Moral Development*, 58; Lawrence Kohlberg, "Development as the Aim of Education," *Harvard Educational Review* 42, no. 4 (1972): 457.

339. White, *Intergenerational Religious Education*, 115.

beyond).³⁴⁰ Community, for him, plays a critical role in faith development: "faith development occurs as a person wrestles with the giveness and crises of his/her life, and draws adaptively upon the models of meaning provided by a nurturing community (or communities) in construing a world which is given coherence by his/her centering trusts and loyalties."³⁴¹

In order to formulate the dynamics of faith-building, Fowler draws a triadic figure that he calls "the dynamic triad of faith," which includes self, others and a shared center(s) of value and power.³⁴² Concerning this "triadic" he explains: "faith involves a relationship in which we as selves are related to others in mutual ties of trust and loyalty, of reliance and care; but that dyad is grounded in our common relatedness to a third member, a center of value and power that bears the weight of ultimacy for us."³⁴³ Obviously, for Fowler, social interaction is essential in the process of faith development.

In sum, although these developmental theories have some drawbacks as noted above, their emphasis on the influence and significance of social interaction, especially Erikson's stress on socialization across the generations, contributes to the construct of intergenerationality.

3.4.3.2.2 Insight from sociocultural learning theory

The sociocultural learning theory is a broad learning macrotheory that can explain "why intergenerational settings might be especially conducive places for learning, growing and being formed spiritually."³⁴⁴ This theory puts "a stronger emphasis on the social interaction of the learning environment . . .

---

340. James W. Fowler, *Faithful Change: The Personal and Public Challenges of Postmodern Life* (Nashville, TN: Abingdon Press, 1996), 57–67; James W. Fowler, *Weaving the New Creation: Stages of Faith and the Public Church* (San Francisco, CA: HarperSanFrancisco, 1991), 191–195.

341. James W. Fowler, "Faith Development Theory and the Aims of Religious Socialization," paper read at a special meeting of the Religious Education Association, Oct 24–26 1975, Milwaukee, WI, 16.

342. Fowler, *Faithful Change*, 21; James W. Fowler, *Stages of Faith: The Psychology of Human Development and the Quest for Meaning* (San Francisco, CA: Harper & Row, 1981), 17, 91.

343. Fowler, *Faithful Change*, 21.

344. Holly Catterton Allen, "Bringing the Generations Together: Support from Learning Theory," *Christian Education Journal*, Series 3, vol. 2, no. 2 (2005): 323; see also Holly Catterton Allen, "Nurturing Children's Spirituality in Intergenerational Christian Settings," in *Children's Spirituality: Christian Perspectives, Research, and Applications*, ed., Donald Ratcliff et al. (Eugene, OR: Cascade, 2004), 271.

and promotes the idea that *the social setting itself* is crucial to the learning process."[345] Lev Vygotsky is the best-known psychologist in this field.[346]

Vygotsky (1896–1934) contends that psychological processes as higher mental functions "have their source not in biological structures or the learning of the isolated individual but in historically developed socio-cultural experience."[347] For Vygotsky, the higher mental functions as "social"[348] bear two senses: "First, like other aspects of culture, their development is part of the development of the socio-cultural system and their existence is dependent on transmission from one generation to the next through learning. Second, they are nothing other than the organization and means of *actual social behavior* that has been taken over by the individual and internalized."[349]

Furthermore, Vygotsky proposes three zones of development:
- Zone of Actual Development where the leaner actually is developmental
- Zone of Potential Development where the learner potentially should be
- Zone of Proximal Development where the amount of assistance is required for a learner to move from the Zone of Actual Development and the Zone of Potential Development.[350]

It is the Zone of Proximal Development (ZPD) that intersects with intergenerational theory.[351] The ZPD is "the phase in development in which the [learner] has only partially mastered a task but can participate in its execution with the assistance and supervision of an adult or more capable peer."[352]

---

345. Allen and Ross, *Intergenerational Christian Formation*, 99.

346. Allen and Ross, 99.

347. Robert W. Rieber and Aaron S. Carton, eds., *The Collected Works of L. S. Vygotsky, Vol. 1: Problems of General Psychology*, trans. and with an introduction by Norris Minick (New York: Plenum, 1987), 19, 21.

348. Vygotsky notes that "Any higher mental function was external [and] social before it was internal . . . It appears first between people as an intermental category, and then within the child as an intramental category." Quoted in Rieber and Carton, *Collected Works*, 21.

349. Quoted in Rieber and Carton, *Collected Works,* 21.

350. Quoted in James Riley Estep Jr., "Spiritual Formation as Social: Toward a Vygotskyan Developmental Perspective," *Religious Education* 97, no. 2 (2002): 152.

351. Allen and Ross, *Intergenerational Christian Formation*, 102.

352. James V. Wertsch and Barbara Rogoff, "Editors' Notes," in *Children's Learning in the "Zone of Proximal Development,"* eds. Barbara Rogoff and James V. Wertsch (San Francisco, CA: Jossey-Bass, 1984), 1.

Allen and Ross apply the notion of the ZPD to IIM, arguing that human beings learn to be members of their community through their active participation in that community, learning from more experienced members.[353] They further note that: "Intergenerational Christian settings are authentic, complex, *formative* environments, made up of individuals at various stages in their faith journeys, teaching some and learning from others as they participate in their community of believers."[354]

3.4.3.2.3 Insight from social learning theory

Social learning theory also provides crucial insight for IIM. Here particular attention is paid to the works of Mead and Bandura.

3.4.3.2.3.1 Margaret Mead

Mead, a social scientist, is best known for her cultural anthropological work.[355] In her last book, *Culture and Commitment*, she identifies three different cultures:

Postfigurative cultures are "those in which 'change is so slow and imperceptible' that the future is a repeat of the past, such as primitive societies. In such cultures, grandparents play important roles in conveying traditions and values; children's 'sense of identity and destiny' is unchallengeable."[356]

Cofigurative cultures are those in which "the present is the guide to future expectations."[357] In this kind of cultures, "the prevailing model for members of the society is the behavior of their contemporaries" and thus it is "natural" for the behavior of the young to differ from that of their parents and grandparents.[358]

Prefigurative cultures are ones in which "the elders have to learn from the children about experiences which they have never had."[359] Mead states

---

353. Ideally, this begins with their own family.
354. Allen and Ross, *Intergenerational Christian Formation*, 102.
355. Allen and Ross, 91.
356. Margaret Mead, *Culture and Commitment: The New Relationships between the Generations in the 1970s*, rev. and updated (New York: Columbia University Press, 1978), 13–14.
357. Mead, *Culture and Commitment*, 13.
358. Mead, 39.
359. Mead, 13.

that the cultures influenced by technology after World War II belong to this category.³⁶⁰ She explains:

> Today, nowhere in the world are there elders who know what the children know, no matter how remote and simple the societies are in which the children live. In the past there were always some elders who knew more than any children in terms of their experience of having grown up within a cultural system. Today there are none.³⁶¹

In *prefigurative* cultures, relations between generations deteriorate sharply, and family and society are endangered.³⁶² Mead is right to argue that "the continuity of all cultures depends on the living presence of at least three generations," and that "the hope of an endangered but potentially self-healing world" is to demand that "everyone listen and be listened to."³⁶³ Mead's work speaks directly to intergenerational issues.³⁶⁴

3.4.3.2.3.2 Albert Bandura

Where traditional psychological theories emphasize learning from *direct* experience, Bandura asserts that human beings have "an advanced cognitive capacity for *observational* learning that enables them to shape and structure their lives through the power of *modeling*" (italics added).³⁶⁵ Observational learning through social modeling is not "simple response mimicry," it is a "higher level of learning and serves much broader generative functions."³⁶⁶ He maintains: "In abstract observational learning, observers extract the principles or standards embodied in the thinking and actions exhibited by others. Once they acquire the principles, they can use them to generate new instances of the behavior that go beyond what they have seen, read, or heard."³⁶⁷

---

360. Mead, 64.
361. Mead, 75.
362. Mead, 119.
363. Mead, 14, 157.
364. Allen and Ross, *Intergenerational Christian Formation*, 92.
365. Albert Bandura, "On the Psychosocial Impact and Mechanisms of Spiritual Modeling," *International Journal for the Psychology of Religion* 13, no. 3 (2003): 167.
366. Bandura, "On the Psychological Impact," 169.
367. Bandura, 169.

Then, Bandura applies his theory to the spiritual domain, focusing on "the influential role of modeling in transmitting values, spiritual belief systems, and spiritual lifestyle practices."[368] He emphasizes the significance of linking spiritual beliefs to spiritual practices because religiosity is not merely "an intrapsychic self-engagement with a Supreme Being," but an embracing of human beings. Abstract doctrines alone are difficult to grasp if there are no concrete exemplars of these doctrines for believers to follow. Fortunately, congregations provide multiple models of believers who live up to their doctrinal beliefs.[369]

Applying Bandura's principle to IIM, Allen and Ross argue that "intergenerational Christian settings provide spiritual models up and down the age spectrum for believers to *observe* and emulate on their own formative spiritual journeys."[370]

3.4.3.2.4 Insight from situated learning theory

Jean Lave and Etienne Wenger coined the term "situated learning" and "communities of practice"[371] while researching several apprenticeships,[372] such as midwives, tailors, and meat cutters. Such learning "involves the construction of identities": Situated "learning involves the whole person; it implies not only a relation to specific activities, but a relation to social communities – it implies becoming a full participant, a member . . . a different person with respect to the possibilities enabled by these systems of relations."[373] In other words, through ongoing participation in communities of practice along with

---

368. Bandura, 171.

369. Bandura, 170–171.

370. Allen and Ross, *Intergenerational Christian Formation*, 94.

371. Communities of practice are "groups of people who share a concern or a passion for something they do and learn how to do it better as they interact regularly." See Etienne Wenger, "Communities of Practice," accessed 10 October 2016, https://www.learning-theories.com/communities-of-practice-lave-and-wenger.html.

372. The Bible reports many examples of apprenticeships. For example, Elijah and Elisha, Eli and Samuel, Mary and Elizabeth, Jesus and the disciples, Peter and John, Paul and Timothy, Titus, and others. See Patty Meyers, *Live, Learn, Pass It On: The Practical Benefits of Generations Growing Together in Faith* (Nashville, TN: Discipleship Resources, 2006), 64–68.

373. Jean Lave and Etienne Wenger, *Situated Learning: Legitimate Peripheral Participation* (Cambridge, UK; New York: Cambridge University Press, 1991), 53.

more experienced members, apprentices come to *identify* with the particular community (i.e. they *become* midwives, tailors, or meat cutters).[374]

Associating situated learning theory with IIM, Allen and Ross claim: "Intergenerational faith settings provide situative learning opportunities that forge persons who identify with the Christian community of practice . . . [B]elievers are formed spiritually while participating authentically and relationally with practicing Christians further along on the journey. Intergenerational events, activities and experiences provide continual opportunities *for all ages* to be learning with those just ahead of them."[375]

In short, building on biblical foundations, the insights from developmental theory, sociocultural learning theory, social learning theory, and situated learning theory further substantiate the significance of IIM. Now is the time to investigate the theological foundations of IIM.

3.4.3.3 Theological Support

As mentioned above, the social setting itself is essential to the learning process. This section delves into the theological understanding of faith communities "as authentic, complex, spiritually formative environments where believers learn Christian concepts, experience them and negotiate their meaning as they are being formed spiritually."[376] This is evident in two prominent theological formulations: the community of God and community as family and body.

3.4.3.3.1 The community of God

God exists in community.[377] God is the embodiment and creator of community.[378] Community is made clear in the very beginning of the Bible: "In the beginning God created the heavens and the earth. Now the earth was formless and empty, darkness was over the surface of the deep, and the

---

374. Allen and Ross, *Intergenerational Christian Formation*, 103.
375. Allen and Ross, 103.
376. Allen and Ross, 110.
377. Stanley J. Grenz, *Theology for the Community of God* (Grand Rapids, MI: Eerdmans, 2000).
378. Robert J. Banks, "The Biblical Approach to Community," *Christian Education Journal* 13, no. 3 (1993): 19.

Spirit of God was hovering over the waters . . . Then God said, 'Let us make mankind in our image, in our likeness'" (Gen 1:1–2, 26).

Grenz asserts that community is "God's purpose for creation . . . Just as the triune God is the eternal fellowship of the trinitarian members, so also God's purpose for creation is that the world participates in community."[379] Similarly, Gruenler notes that one of the most remarkable characteristics of the triune God is that "he speaks, converses, and is eminently social."[380] The triune God "is social and that creation, insofar as it images God, is also social in nature."[381] Prest expresses this fact by noting that humans are to be "social beings – an extension of God's image on earth."[382]

The notion of the social trinity is that God is "a communion[383] of three Persons" – Father, Son, and Holy Spirit – who "exist in mutual relations with one another. Each is distinct from the others, but each is what it is in relation to the others."[384] As Gregory of Nyssa asserts, the three persons are "divided without separation and united without confusion."[385] Gregory of Nanzianzus depicts the mystery of triune life[386] by employing the image of the dance (*perichoresis*),[387] rendered by Latin authors as *circuminsessio*. The dance metaphor suggests "moving around, making room, relating to one another without losing identity."[388] For Volf, *perichoresis* is related to "the reciprocal interiority of the trinitarian persons. In every divine person as a subject, the other persons also indwell; all mutually permeate one another,

---

379. Grenz, *Theology for the Community of God*, 112.

380. Royce G. Gruenler, "John 17:20–26," *Interpretation* 43, no. 2 (1989): 178.

381. Gruenler, "John 17:20–26," 183.

382. Prest, *From One Generation*, 8.

383. "Being as communion" is a phrase used to refer to God and popularized by the Orthodox theologian John Zizioulas through his book of 1985, *Being as Communion: Studies in Personhood and the Church*. See Harkness, "Intergenerationality," 126.

384. Clark H. Pinnock, *Flame of Love: A Theology of the Holy Spirit* (Downers Grove, IL: InterVarsity Press, 1996), 30.

385. Quoted in Cornelius Plantinga, Jr., "Gregory of Nyssa and the Social Analogy of the Trinity," *The Thomist* 50 (1986): 330.

386. For more about the mystery of the Trinity, see Donald G. Bloesch, *God, the Almighty: Power, Wisdom, Holiness, Love* (Downers Grove, IL: InterVarsity Press, 1995), ch. 7.

387. *Perichoresis* literally means "mutual indwelling or, better, mutual interpenetration" and refers to "the understanding of both the Trinity and Christology." See S. M. Smith, "Perichoresis," in *Evangelical Dictionary of Theology*, ed. Walter A. Elwell (Grand Rapids, MI: Baker Academic, 2001), 906.

388. Pinnock, *Flame of Love*, 31.

though in so doing they do not cease to be distinct persons."[389] Karl Barth also writes of the inner relation between the persons of the Godhead, "The divine modes of being mutually condition and permeate one another so completely that one is always in the other two."[390]

The Trinity as a divine reality comprising three persons in relationship can be perceived from another aspect. God is the Father in relationship to the Son; God is the Son in relationship to the Father. "Father and Son are what they are because of the other one."[391] The Holy Spirit as the third person in the Trinity is to be "the bond between the Father and the Son, insofar as He is the Love . . . [F]rom the very fact that the Father and the Son mutually love one another, it follows that their mutual love, which is the Holy Spirit, must proceed from them both."[392] This is the so-called *filioque* (and the Son) doctrine – the Western formulation of "the divine mystery that the Holy Spirit proceeds from the Father 'and the Son.'"[393]

Perceived "as persons in a full sense of 'person,'[394] i.e., as distinct centers of love, will, knowledge,"[395] Father, Son, and Holy Spirit interweave "their distinctive patterns of personhood within an essential unity," and exhibit "a characteristic attitude of love and interpersonal communion as servants of one another, always glorifying and deferring to one another."[396] As Allen and Ross contend, the relationship among the triune God is "to be reflected

---

389. Miroslav Volf, *After Our Likeness: The Church as the Image of the Trinity* (Grand Rapids, MI: Eerdmans, 1998), 209.

390. Karl Barth, *Church Dogmatics: The Doctrine of the Word of God*, vol. 1.1 § 8–12, eds. Geoffrey W. Bromiley and Thomas Forsyth Torrance (London; New York: T & T Clark, 2009), 370.

391. Pinnock, *Flame of Love*, 30–31.

392. Thomas Aquinas, *New English Translation of St Thomas Aquinas's Summa Theologiae*, trans. Alfred J. Freddoso, 289, accessed 25 October 2014, http://www3.nd.edu/~afreddos/summa-translation/Part%201/st1-ques37.pdf.

393. Dennis Ngien, *Apologetic for Filioque in Medieval Theology* (Milton Keynes, UK: Paternoster, 2005), ix; see also G. W. Bromiley, "Filioque," in *Evangelical Dictionary of Theology*, ed. Walter A Elwell (Grand Rapids, MI: Baker Academic, 2001), 452.

394. Greshem points out that "the relation between human and divine persons is not univocal but analogical." See John L. Gresham, "The Social Model of the Trinity and Its Critics," *Scottish Journal of Theology* 46 (1993): 342. See also Pinnock, *Flame of Love*, 30.

395. Plantinga, Jr., "Gregory of Nyssa," 325.

396. Gruenler, "John 17:20–26," 178.

among the body of Christ in similar attitudes of love, connectedness, honor, and deference."[397]

In sum, in the community of God consisting of three persons, "true individuality is not separateness or egocentricity but faithful inter-relatedness in oneness."[398] Humans are created "to indwell each other in the same way that the Father, Son and Holy Spirit mutually indwell each other in a *trinitarian fellowship*."[399] Human beings of all ages as an extension of God's image on earth are called to "live in relationships with a deep sense of togetherness and belonging"[400] – to "participate together as a community of love."[401] This is what Jesus prays for the unity of the faith community in John 17:22–23: "I have given them the glory that you gave me, that they may be one as we are one – I in them and you in me – so that they may be brought to complete unity. Then the world will know that you sent me and have loved them even as you have loved me."

3.4.3.3.2 Community as family and body

Banks observes that two basic images used in the NT for the faith community are the family and the body; the former, for Banks, is the most important metaphorical usage of all.[402] The NT delineates church members as the family of God; the head of the family is God the Father. Drawing from Galatians 4:6, Banks suggests that "'God has sent the Spirit of his Son into our hearts' so that, along with Jesus, we are able to address God in the most intimate terms as 'Abba! Father!'"[403] Christians are not only children of God but also parents and children or brothers and sisters in Christ. For example, Paul views Onesimus as his child (Phlm 10). In Colossians 4:9, Paul also regards Onesimus as the faithful and dear brother. Moreover, Paul treats Apphia (Phlm 2) and Phoebe (Rom 16:1) as his sisters and Rufus's

---

397. Allen and Ross, *Intergenerational Christian Formation*, 111.
398. Gruenler, "John 17:20–26," 183.
399. Jack O. Balswick, Pamela Ebstyne King, and Kevin S. Reimer, *The Reciprocating Self: Human Development in Theological Perspective* (Downers Grove, IL: InterVarsity Press, 2005), 288.
400. Prest, *From One Generation*, 8.
401. Balswick et al., *Reciprocating Self*, 290.
402. Banks, *Paul's Idea of Community*, 49.
403. Banks, 49.

mother as his mother (Rom 16:13).[404] All members of the divine family, as they have opportunities, are to "work for the good of all" (Gal 6:10 NRSV).[405]

The same perspective of viewing community as family is also found in Jesus's teaching. On being told that his mother and brothers have arrived, Jesus says, "Who are my mother and my brothers?" Then, he looks at those around him and says, "Here are my mother and my brothers! Whoever does God's will is my brother and sister and mother" (Mark 3:33–35). Balswick et al., note that "Jesus radically redefine[s] the meaning of family. The church needs to be a community characterized by family-type relationships."[406] Similarly, Hellerman reads the so-called anti-family[407] passages (e.g. Mark 3:31–35; Matt 10:34–38; Luke 14:25–27) in the Gospels as pointing to: "Jesus radically challenge[s] His disciples to disavow primary loyalty to their natural families in order to join the new surrogate family of siblings He was establishing – the family of God."[408] Barton notes: "The kingdom of heaven, the fatherhood of God and belonging to the 'spiritual' family over which Jesus is the 'lord' and 'householder' are what is of supreme importance: and every earthly and mundane tie is subordinate to that new, eschatological reality."[409]

Another basic metaphor in the NT to represent the Christian community is the body. As noted earlier, Paul describes Christian members as parts of the human body and Christ as the head of the body. In 1 Corinthians 12:21–23, he further encourages all Christians to honor and value each church member by saying:

> The eye cannot say to the hand, "I don't need you!" And the head cannot say to the feet, "I don't need you!" On the contrary, those parts of the body that seem to be weaker are

---

404. Banks, 51.

405. Banks, 50.

406. Balswick et al., *Reciprocating Self*, 294; see also Stephen C. Barton, "Living as Families in the Light of the New Testament," *Interpretation* 52, no. 2 (1998): 137–139.

407. Barton rejects the argument that Mark and Matthew's gospels are anti-family. He maintains that "the thrust of the gospel is better described as being suprafamilial." See Stephen C. Barton, *Discipleship and Family Ties in Mark and Matthew* (Cambridge; New York: Cambridge University Press, 1994), 122, 217.

408. Joseph H. Hellerman, *When the Church Was a Family*, 64.

409. Barton, *Discipleship and Family*, 218.

indispensable, and the parts that we think are less honorable we treat with special honor. And the parts that are unpresentable are treated with special modesty.

Furthermore, the picture of church as family or body is vividly portrayed by Paul's "one another" passages, where each church member is to

> be kind to one another; honor one another; live in harmony with one another; instruct one another; wait for one another; serve one another; carry each other's burdens; encourage one another and build each other up; live in peace with one another; bear with one another in love; submit to one another.[410]

Allen and Ross contend that when children, new believers, and seasoned saints take part in such a Christian community as family and body, they can *learn* Christian concepts together, "*experience* them and *socially negotiate* their meaning; they are being formed spiritually into the image of Christ."[411]

This section concludes with the Greek term *koinōnia*, whose basic meaning is "participation." It is often translated as "fellowship" or "communion."[412] It is utilized to "refer both to Christians' participation in the life of God and to the communal life it creates."[413]

Allen and Ross associate *koinōnia* with situative-sociocultural theory mentioned above, arguing that *koinōnia* is a term that accords with "the situative-sociocultural perspective, that is, the idea that growing-becoming-being formed is intrinsically embedded in the social community."[414]

3.4.3.4 Social-Scientific Support

In 2003, the Commission on Children at Risk published a report entitled "Hardwired to Connect: The New Scientific Case for Authoritative

---

410. For example, Rom 12; 15; 1 Cor 11; Gal 5–6; 1 Thess 5; Eph 4–5. See Allen and Ross, *Intergenerational Christian Formation*, 115.

411. Allen and Ross, 115.

412. J. R. McRay, "*Koinōnia*," in *Evangelical Dictionary of Theology*, ed. Walter A. Elwell (Grand Rapids, MI: Baker Academic, 2001), 445.

413. Joseph A. Komonchak, Mary Collins, and Dermot A. Lane, eds., "*Koinōnia*," in *The New Dictionary of Theology* (Wilmington, DE: Michael Glazier, 1987), 557.

414. Allen and Ross, *Intergenerational Christian Formation*, 115.

Communities."[415] According to the report, large numbers of American children suffer from mental illness, emotional distress and behavioral problems,[416] which in many cases come about from the fact that children's basic needs for connectedness are not satisfied. Scientific evidence in this report indicates that children are "hardwired to connect" to others, to "moral meaning and to the possibility of the transcendent. Meeting these basic needs for connectedness is essential to health and to human flourishing."[417]

These findings led the commission to offer a definitive recommendation: "We believe that building and strengthening *authoritative communities* is likely to be our society's best strategy for ameliorating the current crisis of childhood and improving the lives of US children and adolescents" (emphasis added).[418] The report describes main characteristics of an authoritative community as follows:

- *It is a social institution that includes children and youth.*
- It treats children as ends in themselves.
- *It is warm and nurturing.*
- It establishes clear limits and expectations.
- *The core of its work is performed largely by nonspecialists.*
- *It is multigenerational.*
- *It has a long-term focus.*
- *It reflects and transmits a shared understanding of what it means to be a good person.*
- It encourages spiritual and religious development.
- *It is philosophically oriented to the equal dignity of all persons and to the principle of love of neighbor.*[419]

The italicized characteristics of an authoritative community, Allen and Ross note, are similar to that of *intergenerational* faith communities (i.e. churches).[420]

---

415. "Hardwired to Connect" is a report from the Commission on Children at Risk, co-sponsored by the YMCA of the USA, Dartmouth Medical School, and Institute for American Values.

416. The Commission on Children at Risk, "Hardwired to Connect," 3.

417. The Commission on Children at Risk, 26.

418. The Commission on Children at Risk, 26.

419. The Commission on Children at Risk, 26. Italics in the original.

420. Allen and Ross, *Intergenerational Christian Formation*, 128.

3.4.3.5 Conclusion

Biblical, theological, theoretical, and social-scientific support lays a solid foundation for IIM. This provides a strong rationale for implementing IIM in the church even though age- or stage-specific gatherings also significantly influence faith formation.[421] In what follows, the study explores the practices and outcomes of IIM.

3.4.4 The Practices of IIM

Intergenerational ideas[422] and practices[423] have been proposed in the past three decades. For reasons of space, this section focuses on the most critical issue and practice pertinent to the present study: creating a culture of intergenerationality and developing intergenerational learning.

3.4.4.1 Creating a Culture of Intergenerationality

Roberto asserts that in societies and congregations that are characterized by "age segregation, in which adults and children have minimal contact or common activities, there are many forces that make the *(re)*establishment of IIM *countercultural*" (italics added).[424] Thus, the most urgent task for implementing IIM in the church is to "establish intergenerational community as

---

421. Roberto, "Our Future Is Intergenerational," 110; Allen and Ross, *Intergenerational Christian Formation*, 46.

422. For a comprehensive list of ideas of IIM, see Allen and Ross, *Intergenerational Christian Formation*, Appendix A; see also Jim Merhaut and John Roberto, "A Congregational Toolkit for Becoming Intentionally Intergenerational," in *Generations Together: Caring, Praying, Learning, Celebrating, & Serving Faithfully*, eds. Kathie Amidei, Jim Merhaut, and John Roberto, Kindle ed. (Naugatuck, CT: Lifelong Faith Publications, 2014), ch. 5; Roberto, "Our Future Is Intergenerational," 112–117; J Gardner, *Mend the Gap: Can the Church Reconnect the Generations?* (Nottingham, UK: InterVarsity Press, 2008), ch. 9; Mägi, "Intergenerational Church," 103; Gambone, *All Are Welcome*, 78–84, etc.

423. White, in *Intergenerational Religious Education*, 33, suggests six basic models: intergenerational worship, worship-education program, family group, weekly class, workshop or event and all-congregation camp. Other practices include: intergenerational mission trip, in Roberto, "Our Future Is Intergenerational," 116; fellowship, in Holly Catterton Allen, "Bringing the Generations Back Together: Introduction to Intergenerationality," *Christian Education Journal* 9, no. 1 (2012): 102; mentoring, in Meyers, *Live, Learn, Pass It On*, ch. 4; retreat, in Margie Fiedler, "Across the Generations in Retreat and Camping Ministry," in *Across the Generations: Incorporating All Ages in Ministry: The Why and How*, ed. Vicky Goplin et al. (Minneapolis: Augsburg Fortress, 2001), 96; service and outreach, in Menconi, *The Intergenerational Church*, 205, etc.

424. Roberto, "Our Future Is Intergenerational," 109.

a core value"[425] (i.e. to create and foster a culture of intergenerationality).[426] The experts in Snailum's study make the same suggestion: "Transitioning from a predominantly age-stratified ministry mindset to an intergenerational culture requires a paradigmatic shift in philosophy and core values, and efforts to create intergenerational community need to be an integral part of the whole church's vision, mission, and purpose."[427]

In other words, IIM should not be perceived as a new *model* for ministry, but rather a new *mindset*.[428] This must be cultivated both on leadership and congregational levels.[429]

3.4.4.1.1 Leadership level

Leadership plays a key role in making IIM successful.[430] Allen and Ross note that for the church to move toward IIM, the whole ministry team, particularly the senior pastor, needs to embrace this vision, and then pass it on to lay leaders. This requires the involvement of leaders' head, heart, and hands over a period of several months. The following is Allen and Ross's head-heart-hands approach:[431]

Head (informational/cognitive). Once leaders affirm the need for IIM, they have to acquire a deeper, more informed understanding of it: exploring, for example, biblical, theological, theoretical, and sociological foundations of IIM, and discussing the strengths of both age segregation and intergenerationality.[432]

Heart (spiritual/affective). "Only when the heart is captured will real change be possible."[433] The following are basic guidelines for engaging the heart, suggested by Allen and Ross: First, reinforce "a big-picture discussion" on the fundamental goals of IIM, followed by the question of how

---

425. Snailum, "Implementing Intergenerational Youth Ministry," 168.
426. Allen and Ross, *Intergenerational Christian Formation*, ch. 13; Glassford, "Fostering an Intergenerational Culture," 71–93.
427. Snailum, "Implementing Intergenerational Youth Ministry," 168.
428. Snailum, 168.
429. Allen and Ross, *Intergenerational Christian Formation*, 180, 184.
430. Snailum, "Implementing Intergenerational Youth Ministry," 169.
431. Allen and Ross, *Intergenerational Christian Formation*, 180–181.
432. Allen and Ross, 181.
433. Allen and Ross, 182.

various ministries in the church meet those goals. Next, ask participants to reflect on the foundations of IIM, and spur them to think how a more intergenerational approach might enhance reaching their goals. Then, lead a discussion that contrasts and compares the spiritual needs of all age groups. Finally, continually ask God to open the hearts for IIM.[434]

Hand (experiential/behavioral). "[N]ew experiences can light the fire for change."[435] An excellent experiential introduction to intergenerationality is to plan a retreat for the ministry staff and lay leaders, including all family members of all ages. During the retreat, the facilitators need to remind participants of the goals of IIM frequently.[436]

3.4.4.1.2 Congregational level

Allen and Ross state that once leaders have grasped "the essence and the significance of cultivating a more[437] age-integrated community," they have to "winningly" invite the congregations to join the journey of IIM.[438] For the church as a whole to embrace IIM, all congregations, children through seniors, need to "join the leaders on their head-heart-hands journey into a commitment to bringing the generations together."[439]

Intergenerational experts in Snailum's study agree that there are three major barriers or hindrances to implementing IIM in the church:

- Failure to transition to an intergenerational paradigm
- Lack of understanding the basis and need for intergenerational ministry

---

434. Allen and Ross, 182, 184.

435. Allen and Ross, 184.

436. Allen and Ross, 184. Ideas and resources for intergenerational retreat, see Allen and Ross, Appendix A and B.

437. Here "more" does not mean to substitute all age-specific ministries for IIM. As Snailum's panel of intergenerational experts suggests, churches interested in IIM need to "keep intergenerational values in balance with age-specific ministry." See Snailum, "Implementing Intergenerational Youth Ministry," 168.

438. Allen and Ross, *Intergenerational Christian Formation*, 184–185.

439. Allen and Ross, 185.

- Self-centeredness is the enemy[440] of intergenerational community[441]

Thus, creating a culture of intergenerationality[442] is crucial at the very outset of implementing IIM in the faith community.

3.4.4.2 Developing Intergenerational Learning

Intergenerational learning, Roberto maintains, is "a way to educate the whole community, bringing all ages and generations together to learn *with* and *from* each other" (emphasis added).[443] It puts together "learning, building community, sharing faith, praying, celebrating, and practicing faith. The key point is that everyone is learning together."[444]

A basic intergenerational learning format proposed by Martineau, Weber, and Kehrwald, employed by over fifteen-thousand parishes of the Catholic Church[445] and hundreds of churches across the United States,[446] is structured as follows:[447]

Program overview and opening prayer. An overview of the program could be posted on flip chart sheets, PowerPoint slides, or small pocket-sized pieces of paper for individual participants.

All-age learning experience. This offers learners with "a common experience to engage them in the topic of the session." Methods serving this purpose could be drama, simulations, games, storytelling, etc.

---

440. Group-centeredness is another enemy of IIM in that people prefer to interact and dialogue with members of their own age and social group (e.g. adults, even more specifically, men and women's Bible studies).

441. Snailum, "Implementing Intergenerational Youth Ministry," 168.

442. Besides Allen and Ross, other intergenerational scholars also emphasize the importance of creating a culture of IIM. For example, Gambone offers ten useful suggestions: start using the word "intergenerational," think in terms of five generations, act for future generations, understand that "intergenerational" means more than just a program, make everyone in your community generationally accountable, interact personally with all generations, be passionate, seek out criticism, celebrate Intergenerational Week in your church and be involved for the "long haul" (a long-term commitment). See Gambone, *All Are Welcome*, 98–102.

443. Roberto, "Our Future Is Intergenerational," 113.

444. Roberto, 113.

445. Allen and Ross, *Intergenerational Christian Formation*, 211.

446. Roberto, "Our Future Is Intergenerational," 114.

447. Martineau et al., *Intergenerational Faith Formation*, 73–78.

In-depth learning experience. This generally contains three primary learning formats: *whole group*, *age group*, and *learning activity centers*, which are selected according to audience, facilitation, physical space, and topic.

- The *whole group* format offers a series of facilitated learning activities for all learners gathering in one large space at the same time.
- The *age group* format offers parallel, age-appropriate learning for three or more groups at the same time. Although age groups are segregated, each focuses on the same topic through the use of learning activities best suited for their learning abilities.
- The *learning activity center* format offers structured intergenerational and age-specific learning activities at various stations or centers in a common area.

Sharing learning reflections and applications. Participants share what they have learned with each other and prepare for applying their learning to daily life, utilizing resources and activities offered in print or online.

Closing prayer service.[448]

Allen and Ross also provide several recommendations that are helpful in putting intergenerational learning into practice:[449]

- Offer the intergenerational learning setting as an option. That is, have other good learning options available for those who do not wish to join.
- Suggest an age limit for more complex material.
- Limit the study to six to ten weeks with a finite topic.
- Enlist the most creative and experienced adults, youth and children's teachers to collaborate in constructing the teaching/learning materials.[450]

---

448. For full instructions on this basic intergenerational learning format, see Martineau et al.'s book *Intergenerational faith formation*, ch. 5. For more on intergenerational learning, see John Roberto, *Becoming a Church of Lifelong Learners: The Generations of Faith Sourcebook* (New London, CT: Twenty-Third Publications, 2006).

449. Allen and Ross, *Intergenerational Christian Formation*, 209.

450. Koehler suggests that the best way to produce intergenerational curriculum is to "take a unit for younger learners and adapt it upward . . . It is easier to add information, concepts, and activities for adults than it is to adjust adult-oriented material to children"

- Recruit and train a team of enthusiastic teachers (including those who constructed the materials).

In terms of constructing creative, effective intergenerational teaching/learning materials, a sound pedagogical approach is essential. This includes the utilization of all the senses: seeing, hearing, touching, tasting, and smelling; the consideration of various learning styles: collaborative, analytical, commonsense, and dynamic;[451] the respect for multiple intelligences:[452] linguistic, logical-mathematical, musical, bodily-kinesthetic, spatial, interpersonal, intrapersonal, and naturalist intelligence.[453]

Undoubtedly, when convening and training an intergenerational group as the Bible translation team, the most urgent tasks for the present author as the facilitator are to cultivate the concepts of intergenerationality and to develop the intergenerational learning experiences among the participants.

3.4.5 The Outcomes of IIM

Drawing from critical evaluative research on intergenerationality, Allen and Ross conclude that "intergenerational experiences in faith-based settings

---

because "adults can learn more from an approach for children than children can learn from an adult-oriented approach." See George E. Koehler, *Learning Together: A Guide for Intergenerational Education in the Church* (Nashville, TN: Discipleship Resources, 1977), 61, 55.

451. Allen and Ross, in *Intergenerational Christian Formation*, 207, note that it is "established that when teaching children, one should utilize all the senses . . . as well as a variety of learning styles . . . When all generations are present, *all* benefit when those teaching keep these pedagogical principles in mind."

452. Martineau et al., in *Intergenerational Faith Formation*, 48, assert that "the intelligences are not divided by age or developmental stage, but are rather based on innate capacities that cross generations." For full discussions on the theory of multiple intelligences, see Howard Gardner, *Multiple Intelligences: New Horizons in Theory and Practice*, completely rev. and updated (New York: Basic Books, 2006).

453. Martineau et al., *Intergenerational Faith Formation*, 48–49. People with naturalist intelligence "are keenly aware of how to distinguish the diverse plants, animals, mountains, or cloud configurations in their ecological niche." See Gardner, *Multiple Intelligences*, 19.

nurture spiritual growth and development."[454] They group the benefits and outcomes[455] of these researches into several categories:[456]

General findings. The studies show that most participants "enjoy age-inclusive settings – they like interrelating with each other."

For children. After regularly participating in intergenerational small groups, children talked about prayer "more frequently and more relationally than did children who were not involved in intergenerational settings." After taking part in a full year's Family-Centered Intergenerational Religious Education, families and children mentioned God and read the Bible more. Through intentional intergenerational activities, children and youth had access to role models and opportunities to find mentors with a mature faith. Finally, children learned content while they were involved in intergenerational Christian educational experiences.

For adults. The studies prove that adults participating in intergenerational Christian educational experiences learned content. (This is contrary to opponents' assumption that the intergenerational learning material would be too elementary for adults to get new content.) Moreover, adults derived spiritual insights from children, such as trust, forgiveness, honesty, love, and fear.

For congregations. Church attendance increased across summer-long intergenerational programs. The leaders of the churches implementing IIM reported a stronger sense of unity. Church leaders "perceived the generations were no longer afraid of one another."[457]

3.5 Conclusion

The biblical, theological, theoretical and social-scientific foundations of IIM, the positive outcomes of its practices, as well as the findings from childhood studies and translation studies examined in the first part of this

---

454. Allen and Ross, *Intergenerational Christian Formation*, 172.

455. Another recent result is from Merhaut whose survey of leaders in congregations engaged in intergenerational faith formation indicates five important outcomes: strong families, a greater sense of community, increased adult faith formation, a safe learning environment, and motivated learners. See Merhaut, "Outcomes and Practices," ch. 4.

456. Allen and Ross, *Intergenerational Christian Formation*, 172–173.

457. Allen and Ross, 172–173.

chapter provide strong support for the possible advantages of incorporating an intergenerational approach in Bible translation, especially including children. Put differently, children and people of different generations could be crucial members of a Bible translation team.

Since the Hebrew word נֶפֶשׁ will be the test case in the exercise of intergenerational Bible translation in chapter 5, chapter 4 will first explore its possible meanings and how they are applied in Chinese Bible versions.

CHAPTER 4

The Possible Meanings of the Hebrew Word נֶפֶשׁ in the OT and Its Translation in Chinese

4.1 Introduction

In what precedes, it has been suggested that an intergenerational, literary approach to Bible translation should be feasible in the context of the Chinese community. In this chapter, one Hebrew key term from the OT (נֶפֶשׁ) is identified as a problem area in previous Chinese translations, and whose incorrect rendering has even given birth to a particular exegesis and theology. In next chapter, this issue will serve as an example at the center of an experiment concerning an intergenerational, literary approach to Bible translation.

Chinese biblical scholars have not yet given much attention to the Hebrew word נֶפֶשׁ. They rely heavily on the works of the West, which are valuable resources but sometimes fail to agree with each other. In the example of the lexical meaning of Hebrew נֶפֶשׁ, DCH regards the sense of נֶפֶשׁ in Psalm 23:3 as belonging to the category of "soul, heart, mind,"[1] which contradicts its rendering as a "whole person" in TDOT.[2]

---

1. Clines, "נפש," 725.
2. Seebass, "נפש," 510.

In fact, the DCH offers twelve[3] different kinds of lexical meanings of נֶפֶשׁ; the TDOT only six meanings.[4]

Such differences may result from the fact that lexicographers get their meanings from different existing sources, such as those found in grammar books and various translations.[5] This implies that lexical meaning is profoundly affected by the lexicographers' choice of references (e.g. different versions of translations) and that correct translations are essential for compiling lexicons. Furthermore, the accuracy of translation is indispensable for correct interpretation of the Bible. For example, the translations of the Hebrew anthropological term נֶפֶשׁ, rendered stereotypically as ψυχή in the LXX and later into English as "soul," have been motivating Christians, influenced by Greek philosophy, to develop a dichotomous conception of the human constitution. This has led to the centuries-old controversy concerning the Hebraic conception of the person.[6] Murphy points out that "most of the dualism that has appeared to be biblical teaching has been a result of *poor translation*" (italics added).[7]

Chinese Christian scholars are not exempted from this kind of controversy. For example, Watchman Nee (1903–1972), the most influential figure in the Chinese Christian community of the twenieth century,[8] misconstrues the principle of literal translation and thus maintains that נֶפֶשׁ as "魂 *hún* (soul)"[9] is the only appropriate rendering. This is one of the reasons that lead to his teaching on tripartite anthropology,[10] which is a dominant perspective

---

3. The meanings of נֶפֶשׁ in DCH are: (1) palate, throat, gullet, (2) neck, (3) appetite, hunger, desire, wish, (4) soul, heart, mind, (5) breath, last breath, soul, (6) life, lives, eternal life, (7) being, creature(s), (8) person, individual, dead body, slave, (9) personal pronoun, reflexive pronoun (oneself), possessive pronoun, (10) sustenance, (11) perfume, and (12) sepulcher, funerary monument. See Clines, "נפשׁ," 724–734.

4. The meanings of נֶפֶשׁ in TDOT are: (1) throat, gullet, (2) desire, (3) vital self, reflexive pronoun, (4) individuated life, (5) living creature, person, and (6) the נֶפֶשׁ of God. See Seebass, "נפשׁ," 497-517.

5. Silva, *Biblical Words and Their Meaning*, 137.

6. Murphy, *Bodies and Souls*, 17.

7. Murphy, 36.

8. Zēng 曾, "倪柝聲的神學人類學" [The theological anthropology of Watchman Nee], 161.

9. In CUV, נֶפֶשׁ is rendered as "靈魂 *líng hún* (spirit-soul)" twenty-three times or "靈 *líng* (spirit)" four times. This is criticized by Nee who argues that "魂 *hún* (soul)" is the only meaning of נֶפֶשׁ. See Nee, 屬靈人 [The spiritual man], 28–29.

10. Nee, 47–48.

very much alive in the church in China today.[11] Nee's theology directly or indirectly influences a good majority of Chinese Christians.[12] In his two critical works, *The Spiritual Man* and *The Release of the Spirit*, Nee asserts that Christians should subjugate the soul and the body so that the spirit can be released. This gives rise to the negative attitude towards this world among Chinese Christians and leads to extensive controversy among contemporary Chinese theologians.[13]

The preceding cases verify Nida's argument: If the Hebrew נֶפֶשׁ is consistently rendered as "soul," it will ignore the literary or situational context. Diminishing the word's wealth of referents (e.g. breath, life, mind, living thing, person, self) leads to inaccurate interpretation and misunderstanding.[14]

Nowadays, the majority of biblical scholars agree that "at least the earlier Hebraic scriptures know nothing of body-soul dualism."[15] This can be traced back to John Laidlaw's proposition that "[t]he antithesis soul and body . . . is absent from the Old Testament."[16] H. Wheeler Robinson also maintains that "the Hebrew conception of personality on its psychological side is distinctly that of a unity, not of a dualistic union of soul (or spirit) and body."[17] Three decades after Robinson's writing, C. Ryder Smith observed that "some recent psychologists seem to teach that the Hebrew was right in emphasizing the

---

11. Tāo Xú 徐弢, "倪柝聲的三元論思想探究" [An inquiry on the trichotomy theory of Watchman Nee], *China Graduate School of Theology Journal* 54 (2013): 39.

12. Jǐn Lún Lǐ 李錦綸, 永活上帝生命主: 獻給中國的教會神學 [The living God as the master of life: Devoted to Chinese church theology] (Taipei: Zhōng-Fú Publishing Ltd. Co., 2004), 309.

13. Zēng 曾, "倪柝聲的神學人類學" [The theological anthropology of Watchman Nee], 160, 162.

14. Nida, *God's Word in Man's Language*, 65–66.

15. Murphy, *Bodies and Souls*, 17. Green notes that biblical studies and neuroscience are two fronts that query the traditional body-soul dualism. The former "almost unanimously supported a unitary account of the human person" since the early twentieth century. The latter, since the 1600s, had evidenced repeatedly "the close mutual interrelations of physical and psychological occurrences, documenting the neural correlates of the various attributes traditionally allocated to the soul." See Joel B. Green, "Soul," in *The New Interpreter's Dictionary of the Bible*, vol. 5, ed. Katharine D. Sakenfeld (Nashville, TN: Abingdon Press, 2009), 359; see also Joel B. Green, *Body, Soul, and Human Life: The Nature of Humanity in the Bible* (Grand Rapids, MI: Baker Academic, 2008), 32–33.

16. John Laidlaw, *The Bible Doctrine of Man: Or, The Anthropology and Psychology of Scripture* (Edinburgh: T & T Clark, 1895), 58.

17. H. Wheeler Robinson, *The Christian Doctrine of Man* (Edinburgh: T & T Clark, 1926), 69.

unity of man."[18] Owen notes that נֶפֶשׁ "has scarcely any of the connotations of the word 'soul' in radical body-soul dualism."[19] In his interpretation of Genesis 2:7, Brueggemann notes that "[t]he articulation of 'breathed on dust' in order to become a 'living being' precludes any dualism."[20] Amos Ḥakham suggests that נֶפֶשׁ "always refers to the body and soul as a single unit," rather than "soul" only.[21]

Given the significance of correct translation, this study aims to find out the contextually appropriate Chinese translations for the Hebrew word נֶפֶשׁ in the three selected psalms. Before the exercise of translating נֶפֶשׁ into Chinese in the next chapter, this chapter first conducts a brief literature review of נֶפֶשׁ to determine its possible meanings. Then, its interpretations in existing Chinese versions are examined, followed by illustrating the divergence in the interpretations of נֶפֶשׁ among prominent Chinese and English versions. Next, the study delves into the influence of Watchman Nee. This chapter ends with a call for reconsidering the translation of נֶפֶשׁ.

4.2 A Brief Literature Review of the Hebrew Word נֶפֶשׁ

4.2.1 Introduction

The word נֶפֶשׁ, occurring 754 times in the MT of the OT, is "as hard to define as it is to translate."[22] For instance, KJV renders it variously as follows: "soul" (475 times); "life" (120 times); "person" (26 times); a reflexive pronoun (20 times); "heart" (16 times); "mind" (15 times); "creature" (10 times); the personal pronoun (9 times); "dead" (5 times); "body, dead body, pleasure" (4 times each); "desire, will" (3 times each) "man, thing, beast,

---

18. C. Ryder Smith, *The Bible Doctrine of Man* (London: Epworth Press, 1951), 3.

19. D. R. G. Owen, *Body and Soul: A Study of the Christian View of Man* (Philadelphia, PA: Westminister, 1956), 167.

20. Brueggemann, *Theology of the Old Testament*, 453; Robert Laurin, "The Concept of Man as a Soul," *The Expository Times* 72, no. 5 (1961): 132; Laidlaw, *Bible Doctrine of Man*, 53.

21. Amos Ḥakham, *The Bible: Psalms with the Jerusalem Commentary*, vol. 1, ed. and trans. Israel V. Berman (Jerusalem: Mosad Harav Kook, 2003), 29; see also Robert A. Di Vito, "Old Testament Anthropology and the Construction of Personal Identity," *The Catholic Biblical Quarterly* 61 (1999): 228.

22. Jacob, "Anthropology of the Old Testament," 617.

appetite, ghost, lust" (2 times each); "breath" (1 time), etc. In fourteen cases, KJV gives no English equivalents for נֶפֶשׁ.²³ Considering the rendering of נֶפֶשׁ as "soul" already in the sixteenth century, Parkhurst notes, "נֶפֶשׁ hath been supposed to signify the *spiritual part* of man, or what we commonly call his *soul*: I must for myself confess, that I can find no passage where it hath *undoubtedly* this meaning."²⁴

Briggs also argues that "soul in English usage at the present time conveys usually a very different meaning from נֶפֶשׁ in Hebrew."²⁵ Brueggemann points out that it is "unfortunate that 'living being' (נֶפֶשׁ) is commonly rendered 'soul.'"²⁶

So, what then does נֶפֶשׁ mean in the OT? The following sections are dedicated to answering this question through (1) the discussion on etymological issues, (2) a brief survey of the etymological study of נֶפֶשׁ, (3) the exploration of נֶפֶשׁ in the Hebrew OT, and (4) נֶפֶשׁ and its Greek equivalent ψυχή in the LXX and the NT.

4.2.2 Etymological Issues

Etymological study has played an important role in the determination of words' meaning in the Hebrew OT, especially when the OT contains no less than 1,300 *hapax legomena* and "about 500 words that occur only twice out of a total vocabulary of about 8,000 words."²⁷ But in the past decades, many have pointed out the dangers of uncritically deriving meaning from etymology.²⁸ As Vendryes notes in his *Language: A Linguistic Introduction to History*:

> Etymology . . . gives a false idea of the nature of a vocabulary for it is concerned only in showing how a vocabulary has been formed. Words are not used according to their historical value.

---

23. A. Murtonen, "The Living Soul: A Study of the Meaning of the Word *Nephesh* in the Old Testament Hebrew Language," *Studia Orientalia* 23, no. 1 (1958): 9–10.

24. Parkhurst, "נפש," 408.

25. Briggs, "The Use of נפש in the Old Testament," 30.

26. Brueggemann, *Theology of the Old Testament*, 453.

27. Silva, *Biblical Words and Their Meaning*, 42; see also Milton Eng, *The Days of Our Years: A Lexical Semantic Study of the Life Cycle in Biblical Israel* (New York: T & T Clark, 2011), 27; Carson, *Exegetical Fallacies*, 33.

28. Barr, *Semantics of Biblical Language*, ch. 6; Silva, *Biblical Words and Their Meaning*, ch. 1; Carson, *Exegetical Fallacies*, 28–33.

> The mind forgets – assuming that it ever knew – the semantic evolutions through which the words have passed. Words always have a *current* value, that is to say, limited to the moment when they are employed, and a *particular* value relative to the momentary use made of them.[29]

Put simply, etymology is not a reliable or an appropriate approach in determining the meaning of a word.[30] This echoes Ferdinand de Saussure's arguments:

> The first thing which strikes one on studying linguistic facts is that the language user is unaware of their succession in time: he is dealing with a state. Hence the linguist who wishes to understand this state must rule out of consideration everything which brought that state about, and pay no attention to diachrony.[31] Only by suppressing the past can he enter into the state of mind of the language user. The intervention of history can only distort his judgment.[32]

Silva points out that "[t]he relative value of [the] use of etymology varies inversely with the quantity of material available for the language."[33] That means, while lacking comparative material, the determination of the meaning of the *hapax legomena* in the OT heavily relies on etymological study

---

29. J. Vendryes, *Language: A Linguistic Introduction to History* (London; New York: Routledge, 2013 [1925]), 176.

30. Carson, *Exegetical Fallacies*, 32. Though etymology is "a clumsy tool" for discerning meaning, Carson, in *Exegetical Fallacies*, 33, suggests that it is critical in the diachronic study of words, in the study of cognate languages, and in the understanding on the meanings of *hapax legomena*, etc.

31. Of de Saussure's influences upon the field of biblical studies, one is that he pioneers "the distinction between 'diachrony' (the history of a term) and 'synchrony' (the current use of a term)." See Grant R. Osborne, *The Hermeneutical Spiral: A Comprehensive Introduction to Biblical Interpretation* (Downers Grove, IL: InterVarsity Press, 2006), 87. For de Saussure, the synchronic viewpoint has the priority to define a word's meaning. See Ferdinand de Saussure, *Course in General Linguistics*, trans. and annotated by Roy Harris (Chicago and La Salle, IL: Open Court, 1986), 90. Full discussions on synchronic and diachronic linguistics, see de Saussure, *Course in General Linguistics*, part II and part III.

32. de Saussure, *Course in General Linguistics*, 81. Osborne, in *The Hermeneutical Spiral*, 87, observes that "Saussure did not deny the validity of etymology together; rather, he restricted it to its proper sphere, the history of words."

33. Silva, *Biblical Words and Their Meaning*, 42.

even if "specification of the meaning of a word on the sole basis of etymology can never be more than an educated guess."[34] Since נֶפֶשׁ occurs 754 times in the MT, etymology has little value for discerning its meanings according to Silva noted above. In brief, the meanings of נֶפֶשׁ gleaned from etymological considerations are nothing but "an educated guess," which call for re-examination.

Silva observes that OT scholars have spent "a remarkable amount of energy searching for cognates and proposing new meanings."[35] Thus, a brief survey of the etymological study on נֶפֶשׁ is helpful for understanding its different translations in various Bible versions and dictionaries.

4.2.3 A Brief Survey of the Etymological Study on נֶפֶשׁ

נֶפֶשׁ has many cognates in the Semitic languages, among which Akkadian, Ugaritic, and Arabic cast most light on Hebrew usage.[36]

The corresponding Akkadian word for נֶפֶשׁ is *napištu*, which means (1) neck, throat, gullet, (2) life, (3) living being, self, (4) person, (5) living, livelihood, subsistence, (6) sustenance,[37] (7) slaves, domestic animals, (8) corpse, (9) breath, (10) any kind of opening, neckerchief, (11) capital case.[38]

---

34. Carson, *Exegetical Fallacies*, 33.

35. Silva, *Biblical Words and Their Meaning*, 43.

36. D. C. Fredericks, "נפשׁ," in *New International Dictionary of Old Testament Theology & Exegesis,* vol. 3, ed. W. VanGemeren (Grand Rapids, MI: Zondervan, 1997), 133.

37. According to his observation on the usage of the Akkadian term *napištu* as sustenance, Victor A. Hurowitz, in "A Forgotten Meaning of *Nepeš* in Isaiah LVIII 10," *Vetus Testamentum* 47, no. 1 (1997): 52, maintains that נֶפֶשׁ in Isa 58:10 has the same sense. However, as discussed above, etymological studies is not an appropriate approach in determining the meaning of a word with many occurrences, such as נֶפֶשׁ.

38. Cf. Tawil, "נפשׁ," 244–246; Jeremy Black, Andrew George, and Nicholas Postgate, eds., "*Napištu(m),*" *A Concise Dictionary of Akkadian* (Wiesbaden, Germany: Otto Harrassowitz, 2000), 239; Ellis Robert Brotzman, "The Plurality of 'Soul' in the Old Testament with Special Attention Given to the Use of *Nepeš*" (doctoral diss., New York University, 1987), 203–206.

In Ugaritic, the word *npš* is cognate to נֶפֶשׁ. It means (1) throat, (2) appetite, (3) person, people (collectively), (4) soul, (5) funerary monument, stela,[39] (6) offering.[40]

The Arabic equivalent for נֶפֶשׁ is *nas*, whose meanings comprise (1) soul, mind, (2) inclination, (3) life, (4) person, self.[41]

This short investigation of cognates of נֶפֶשׁ in the Semitic languages probably provides one of the reasons why נֶפֶשׁ is sometimes rendered so differently in various Bible versions or dictionaries. The composition of the Bible versions and dictionaries is probably influenced by the extent to which etymology is applied. This seems to account for the divergence in the meaning of נֶפֶשׁ between TDOT and DCH (see footnote 3 and 4 of this chapter). For example, TDOT does not include the sense of נֶפֶשׁ as sustenance, perfume, funerary monument; but DCH does.

As mentioned above, while etymological considerations can be of interest, they often represent nothing less than "an educated guess." Thus, a better way to find out what נֶפֶשׁ means in the Hebrew OT is to examine its usage in the Hebrew OT.[42] This semantic approach is the enterprise to which the present study now turns.

4.2.4 נֶפֶשׁ in the Hebrew OT

4.2.4.1 Introduction

The Hebrew word נֶפֶשׁ is a key term in the OT. נֶפֶשׁ is probably "a primitive noun that does not derive from a verbal root."[43] It is feminine; Zimmerli

---

39. נֶפֶשׁ as a funerary monument is not a biblical usage. It seems to originate in some pagan cult and the whole idea is foreign to Judaism. "In post-biblical times it was mentioned only three times in the Mishna." See Wolf Gottlieb, "The Term '*Nepeš*' in the Bible: A Re-Appraisal," *Glasgow University Oriental Society Transactions* 25 (1976): 80.

40. Cyrus H. Gordon, "*Npš*," *Ugaritic Textbook* (Roma: Editrice Pontificio Istituto Biblico, 1998), 446; Brotzman, "Plurality of 'Soul,'" 206–207.

41. Bruce K. Waltke, "נפש," in *Theological Wordbook of the Old Testament*, eds. R. L. Harris, G. L. Archer, Jr., and B. K. Waltke (Chicago, IL: Moody, 1999), 588. Both Ugaritic *npš* and Akkadian *napištu* have the meaning "throat." But this is not the case in Arabic *nas*. See Waltke, "נפש."

42. Stuart Tomas, "נפש and the Doctrine of Men in the OT" (master's thesis, Trinity Evangelical Divinity School, 1986), 3.

43. Seebass, "נפש," 498. The verb נפש is probably a denominative from the substantive; see F. Brown, S. R. Driver, and C. A. Briggs, "נפש," *Enhanced Brown-Driver-Briggs Hebrew and English Lexicon* (Oak Harbor, WA: Logos Research Systems, 2000), 661; Waltke, "נפש,"

regards the masculine plural נְפָשִׁים in Ezekiel 13:20 as an obvious mistake.[44] In the OT text, this word has various meanings, including "breath," "living creature," "person," "life," "appetite," "corpse." Though it can be utilized to refer to animals or God, over seven hundred of its appearances refer to man.[45] As noted above, "soul" is an unfortunate, poor translation of נֶפֶשׁ. Then, what does נֶפֶשׁ mean in the OT?

4.2.4.2 נֶפֶשׁ as Breath

The basic, concrete meaning of נֶפֶשׁ in the OT is probably "breath."[46] While interpreting נֶפֶשׁ, "the Hebraic trait of thinking concretely must be kept foremost in mind."[47] Instead of abstract soul, Wolff notes that נֶפֶשׁ is "designed to be seen together with the whole form of man, and especially with his breath."[48] For example, Genesis 35:18 describes Rachel's physical death right after giving birth to a son with great difficulty as "the going out of the

---

588; Claus Westermann, "נפש," in *Theological Lexicon of the Old Testament*, eds. Ernst Jenni and Claus Westermann, trans. Mark E. Biddle (Peabody, MA: Hendrickson, 1997), 743. It appears only three times in the OT (Exod 23:12; 31:17; 2 Sam 16:14), "significantly always in the reflexive *niphal* with the secondary meaning of 'rest, relaxation'"; see Gottlieb, "The Term '*Nepes*' in the Bible," 71. HALOT has "to breathe freely, to recover"; see L. Koehler, W. Baumgartner, and J. J. Stamm, "נפשׁ," in *The Hebrew and Aramaic Lexicon of the Old Testament*, trans. M. E. J. Richardson (Leiden: Brill, 1994-2000), 711.

44. Walther Zimmerli, *Ezekiel 1: A Commentary on the Book of the Prophet Ezekiel*, eds. Frank Moore Cross, Klaus Baltzer, and Leonard Jay Greenspoon, trans. Ronald E. Clements, Hermeneia (Philadelphia, PA: Fortress, 1979), 289.

45. Tomas, "נפש and the Doctrine of Men in the OT," 1.

46. Waltke, "נפשׁ," 588; Fredericks, "נפשׁ," 133. Some maintain that the concrete meanings of נֶפֶשׁ related to "breath" include "throat" or "neck." See James K. Bruckner, "A Theological Description of Human Wholeness in Deuteronomy 6," *Ex Auditu* 21 (2005): 10; Waltke, "נפשׁ," 588; Seebass, "נפשׁ," 504; Westermann, "נפשׁ," 744; Graham J. Warne, *Hebrew Perspectives on the Human Person in the Hellenistic Era: Philo and Paul* (Lewiston, NY: Mellen Biblical Press, 1995), 62, 72; Ellis R. Brotzman, "Man and the Meaning of נפשׁ," *Bibliotheca Sacra* 145 (1988): 405; Heber Peacock, "Translating the Word for 'Soul' in the OT," *The Bible Translator* 27, no. 2 (1976): 216–217; Hans Walter Wolff, *Anthropology of the Old Testament*, trans. Margaret Kohl (London: SCM, 1974), 11–15; Aubrey R. Johnson, *The Vitality of the Individual in the Thought of Ancient Israel*, 2nd ed. (Cardiff, UK: University of Wales Press, 1964), 4. However, Smith, in *Bible Doctrine of Man*, 8 n. 1, argues that these renderings are based on "rather remote Semitic languages" and demonstrate unnatural translations of נֶפֶשׁ in Isaiah 5:14; Jonah 2:5–7; Ps 69:1; etc. In these texts, as elsewhere, the LXX takes ψυχή; it never translates נֶפֶשׁ as "neck" or "throat." For more discussions on the objection of the translations of נֶפֶשׁ as "neck" or "throat," see Gottlieb, "The Term '*Nepes*' in the Bible," 73; Jacob, "The Anthropology of the Old Testament," 618; Miriam Seligson, *The Meaning of נפש מת in the Old Testament* (Helsinki, Finland: Societas Orientalis Fennica, 1951), 58ff.

47. Warne, *Hebrew Perspectives*, 62.

48. Wolff, *Anthropology of the Old Testament*, 10.

נֶפֶשׁ, that is, the breath."⁴⁹ In 1 Kings 17:21–22, after Elijah's prayer to raise the widow's son, the child's נֶפֶשׁ (i.e. breath) returned upon his inward parts, and he lived.⁵⁰ Brotzman connects these two verses and concludes that "death is described as the 'going out of the breath' while the restoration of life is described as 'the returning of the breath.'"⁵¹ The idea is unambiguously that of "the breath as animating the physical organs of the body."⁵² Conversely, its departure brings death.⁵³

The connection between נֶפֶשׁ and breath is also found in Genesis 2:7, where the Lord breathed (נפח) into Adam's nostrils the breath (נְשָׁמָה) of life;⁵⁴ and he became a living person/being (נֶפֶשׁ חַיָּה).⁵⁵ The association of נְשָׁמָה⁵⁶ with נֶפֶשׁ here demonstrates the human being's unique status. Humanity is "unique and superior to the animal creation in that his existence is the result of a divine animation."⁵⁷ On the contrary, the withdrawal of נְשָׁמָה causes death. At death, the human being taken out of the earth goes back to earth again (Gen 3:19), but the divine breath that animates and preserves a person's body during his/her earthly life "returns to the heavenly regions."⁵⁸ Indeed, everything related to humanity is "earthly and material," even if it

---

49. Brotzman, "The Plurality of 'Soul,'" 146.

50. H. Wheeler Robinson, *The Religious Ideas of the Old Testament* (New York: Charles Scribner's Sons, 1921), 80.

51. Brotzman, "The Plurality of 'Soul,'" 148.

52. Robinson, *Religious Ideas*, 80.

53. Warne, *Hebrew Perspectives*, 63.

54. Based on Job 27:3; 33:4, Laurin, in "The Concept of Man as a Soul," 132, asserts that the breath (נְשָׁמָה) of life here is identical to God's spirit (רוּחַ). For further discussions, see footnote 56 below.

55. Waltke, "נפש," 588.

56. Hamilton, in *The Book of Genesis: Chapters 1–17*, 158–159, states that both נְשָׁמָה (twenty-five times in the OT) and רוּחַ (ca. four hundred times in the OT) mean "breath." The former is applied only to God and to humanity; the latter is applied to God, humanity, animals, and even false gods. The reason why Gen 2:7 uses the less popular נְשָׁמָה for breath is that "it is man, and man alone, who is the recipient of the divine breath." On the contrary, some scholars note that נְשָׁמָה can be ascribed to animals too, such as Seligson, *Meaning of* נפש מת, 73; David Stacey, *The Pauline View of Man: In Relation to Its Judaic and Hellenistic Background* (London: Macmillan; New York: St Martin's, 1956), 90.

57. Warne, *Hebrew Perspectives*, 65.

58. F. C. Porter, "The Pre-Existence of the Soul in the Book of Wisdom and in the Rabbinical Writings," in *Old Testament and Semitic Studies in Memory of William Rainey Harper*, eds. Robert Francis Harper, Francis Brown, and George Foot Moore (Chicago, IL: University of Chicago Press, 1908), 212, 251. Porter, in "Pre-Existence of the Soul," 252, maintains that the divine breath is "individualized . . . when the time comes for [a person]

is created by God himself. And the reality is that humanity's existence as a living person is due to God's "infusion of the breath of life."[59]

The comparison of נֶפֶשׁ and נְשָׁמָה warrants further investigation here. One might say that נֶפֶשׁ is employed "to define the animation of the human as a living person" as explored below; while נְשָׁמָה is employed "to define more precisely a human person's dependency upon God for his or her life."[60] Jacob observes that נֶפֶשׁ always includes נְשָׁמָה but is not limited to it.[61] Finally, a human being does not have נֶפֶשׁ; he is נֶפֶשׁ;[62] whereas, a human being is not נְשָׁמָה, but has it.[63]

Put simply, "breath" is the basic, concrete meaning of נֶפֶשׁ in the OT.

4.2.4.3 נֶפֶשׁ *as Living Creature, Person*

Given the fact that the cessation of breathing means the end of life,[64] נֶפֶשׁ, then, does not designate "an immaterial principle within the human person, which could have its own independent existence apart from the person."[65] Rather, נֶפֶשׁ is "an integral part of the human organism, and [is] perceived as inseparable from the concretely existing human person."[66] Thus, נֶפֶשׁ can be related to "living creature, person"[67] that lives by breathing.[68]

The *locus classicus* of this use of נֶפֶשׁ is probably Genesis 2:7, where the combination of the material (the dust of the ground) and the immaterial (the נְשָׁמָה "breath" of life from God) makes the man become a living נֶפֶשׁ.

---

to be raised from the dead, God will give back the same נְשָׁמָה to the same body, and the same person will live again."

59. Wolff, *Anthropology of the Old Testament*, 60.
60. Warne, *Hebrew Perspectives*, 64; see also Stacey, *Pauline View of Man*, 90.
61. Jacob, "Anthropology of the Old Testament," 618.
62. Wolff, *Anthropology of the Old Testament*, 10.
63. Smith, *Bible Doctrine of Man*, 6.
64. Jacob, "Anthropology of the Old Testament," 618.
65. Warne, *Hebrew Perspectives*, 62.
66. Warne, *Hebrew Perspectives*, 62–63. Delimited by its connection with a body, נֶפֶשׁ is "never used of a disembodied spirit or being after death; the inhabitants of Sheol are never called 'souls.'" See Laurin, "Concept of Man as a Soul," 132.
67. Seebass, "נפש," 515. נֶפֶשׁ as person "gives the term priority in the anthropological vocabulary, for the same cannot be said of either spirit, heart, or flesh." See Jacob, "Anthropology of the Old Testament," 620.
68. Parkhurst, "נפש," 408.

That means, "man is, in his essential nature, a נֶפֶשׁ, a person, an individual."⁶⁹ This gender-inclusive usage is very suitable for legal texts and lists of persons.⁷⁰ Two examples of the former (legal texts) are Leviticus 17:10, where "Every man . . . who eats any blood . . . I will set my face against the נֶפֶשׁ [person] that eats blood," and Leviticus 23:30, where "Every נֶפֶשׁ [person] who does any work on this same day, that נֶפֶשׁ [person] I will destroy from among his people."⁷¹ Examples of the latter (lists of persons) include Exodus 12:4: "according to the number of נְפָשֹׁת [persons]" and Jeremiah 52:29: "in the eighteenth year of Nebuchadnezzar, 832 נֶפֶשׁ [people] from Jerusalem."⁷²

The preceding examples demonstrate that נֶפֶשׁ can be used to designate a single person (Lev 17:10; 23:30), a plural (Exod 12:4),⁷³ or "a collective expression for a whole group of individuals" (Jer 52:29).⁷⁴ One more instance of the collective use of נֶפֶשׁ is found in Genesis 12:5, where the people Abram took with him to Canaan are called הַנֶּפֶשׁ. Wolff observes: "This collective use of נֶפֶשׁ is shown very clearly where numbers are mentioned: the offspring of Leah number 33 נֶפֶשׁ (Gen 46:15), of Zilpah 16 נֶפֶשׁ (v. 18), of Rachel 14 נֶפֶשׁ (v. 22) and of Bilhah 7 נֶפֶשׁ (v. 25); all the offspring of Jacob who came to Egypt were 66 (v. 26) or 70 נֶפֶשׁ (v. 27)."⁷⁵ In a word, נֶפֶשׁ, along with its meaning "breath," means "living creature, person" and can be used as singular, plural, or collective.

4.2.4.4 נֶפֶשׁ *as Vital Self*

After interpreting נֶפֶשׁ as "living creature, person," it is obviously easy for the emphasis to shift to more abstract concepts such as "vital self"⁷⁶ in this section and "life" in the following section. Seebass points out that a crucial

---

69. Brotzman, "Plurality of 'Soul,'" 27.
70. Seebass, "נפש," 515.
71. Wolff, *Anthropology of the Old Testament*, 21.
72. Westermann, "נפש," 755.
73. נֶפֶשׁ in its plural form only occurs fifty-two times in the OT. Ezekiel 13:18–20 comprises a number of the plural forms of נֶפֶשׁ, and in some cases the notion clearly expressed is "persons" or "individuals." See Brotzman, "Man and the Meaning of נפש," 402.
74. Wolff, *Anthropology of the Old Testament*, 21.
75. Wolf, 21.
76. Seebass, "נפש," 510; Gerhard von Rad, *Old Testament Theology*, vol. 1 (Louisville, KY: Westminster John Knox, 2001), 153.

distinction between נֶפֶשׁ as vital self and נֶפֶשׁ as life resides in the fact that נֶפֶשׁ is usually the subject in the former, while it usually is the object in the latter.[77]

Seebass maintains that many texts show that "humans have a relationship with themselves as individuals; this is unmistakably the case when נֶפֶשׁ denotes the vital self."[78] Seebass's argument refers to the pronominal use of נֶפֶשׁ, which is found in both prose and poetry. The regular pronominal use of נֶפֶשׁ in prose is found in Genesis 12:13, where Abram says to Sarai: "Please say that you are my sister so that it may go well with me because of you and my נֶפֶשׁ [i.e. I] may live on account of you."[79] In poetry, נֶפֶשׁ with a personal suffix (e.g. "my נֶפֶשׁ" or "your נֶפֶשׁ") is usually employed to parallel a simple pronoun[80] or that involved in the inflection of the verb, etc.[81] For example, Job 30:25 reads:

> Have I not wept for him who was having a hard time?
> Did not my נֶפֶשׁ grieve for the poor?[82]

Johnson calls this a "*pathetic* periphrasis,"[83] asserting that the use of נֶפֶשׁ "as a substitute for the personal pronoun often betrays a certain intensity of feelings."[84] Johnson further notes in regard to Isaac's blessing of his son in Genesis 27:4, 19, 25, 31: "Thus, when [נֶפֶשׁ] is used of the subject of the action in bestowing a blessing, it appears to spring from and certainly serves to accentuate the view that the speaker needs to put *all his being* into what he says, if he is to make his words effective" (italics added).[85]

Samson's sacrificing himself to destroy his enemies is another example. "The rendering of the English Version (i.e. 'Let me [נַפְשִׁי] die with the Philistines' [Judg 16:30]) is far from doing justice to the emotional content

---

77. Seebass, "נפש," 512; see also Westermann, "נפש," 752.
78. Seebass, "נפש," 510.
79. Brotzman, "Man and the Meaning of נפש," 403.
80. Brotzman, 403.
81. Johnson, *Vitality of the Individual*, 16.
82. Johnson, 16.
83. Johnson, 18; cf. Brotzman, "Man and the Meaning of נפש," 403.
84. Johnson, *Vitality of the Individual*, 18.
85. Johnson, 18.

of the original, and one is forced to admit that the Hebrew really defies anything like a satisfactory translation."[86]

Following Johnson's accent on the intensity of feelings, Goldingay interprets נֶפֶשׁ along with a personal suffix "as a whole being, and specifically a being with longings."[87] Thus, Psalm 63:1 may be rendered as "God, you are my God, I search for you; *my whole being* [נַפְשִׁי] thirsts for you"; verse 5 as "with a rich feast *my whole person* [נַפְשִׁי] is full . . ."; verse 8 as "*My whole person* [נַפְשִׁי] has stuck to you; your right hand has upheld me" (emphases added).[88] Again, the intensity of feelings and emotions can be grasped in the texts where the נֶפֶשׁ is

> the precise subject of the psalms of lamentation: it is frightened (Ps 6:3); it despairs and is disquieted (Pss 42:5f., 11; 43:5); it feels itself weak and despondent (Jonah 2:7); it is exhausted and feels defenseless (Jer 4:31); it is afflicted (Ps 31:7; cf. Gen 42:21) and suffers misery (Isa 53:11). The נֶפֶשׁ is often described as being bitter (מַר), that is to say embittered through childlessness (1 Sam 1:10), troubled because of illness (2 Kgs 4:27), enraged because it has been injured (Judg 18:25; 2 Sam 17:8).[89]

Moreover, נֶפֶשׁ rejoices (Isa 61:10) and loves (Song 1:7).[90] For Seebass, נֶפֶשׁ as vital self "makes expressions denoting repulsion appear even more vivid."[91] For instance, it abhors (Lev 26:11), detests (Num 21:5), and loathes (Job 10:1).

As to the reflexive pronominal use[92] of נֶפֶשׁ, an interesting example is seen in Leviticus 11:43–44, which "deals with ritual uncleanness, and this

---

86. Johnson, 18.

87. John Goldingay, *Psalms*, vol. 2, Baker Commentary on the Old Testament Wisdom and Psalms (Grand Rapids, MI: Baker Academic, 2007), 257.

88. Goldingay, *Psalms*, vol. 2, 254

89. Wolff, *Anthropology of the Old Testament*, 17.

90. Briggs, "Use of נפש in the Old Testament," 27.

91. Seebass, "נפש," 511.

92. Biblical scholars do not reach a consensus in terms of the pronominal use of נֶפֶשׁ. Briggs, in "Use of נפש in the Old Testament," 21–22, notes that there are fifty-three texts where נֶפֶשׁ is used as a reflexive pronoun and seventy texts where נֶפֶשׁ is used as a personal pronoun (i.e. 123 in all). Becker locates a total of 135; quoted in Johnson, *Vitality of the Individual*, 15 n. 3. While Robinson, in *Christian Doctrine of Man*, 16, points out that there

uncleanness is expressed in terms of reflexive action."[93] In Hebrew, reflexive action is expressed either with Hithpael stems וְלֹא תְטַמְּאוּ בָּהֶם "Do not make yourselves unclean by means of them" [v. 43] and הִתְקַדִּשְׁתֶּם "consecrate yourselves" [v. 44]), or with Piel stems plus "your נֶפֶשׁ (plural)" אַל־תְּשַׁקְּצוּ אֶת־נַפְשֹׁתֵיכֶם "Do not defile yourselves" [v. 43] and וְלֹא תְטַמְּאוּ אֶת־נַפְשֹׁתֵיכֶם "Do not make yourselves unclean" [v. 44]).[94]

Briefly, the pronominal use of נֶפֶשׁ both in prose and poetry manifests נֶפֶשׁ as vital self. Indeed, a person does not *have* a vital self but *is* a vital self.[95]

This study now turns to a discussion of נֶפֶשׁ denoting God's vital self.

As has been seen, over 700 out of 745 appearances of נֶפֶשׁ in the OT are related to humanity, that "aspires to life and is therefore living (which also makes [humans] comparable with the animal)."[96] It is rarely used to refer to God. This is because God does not have the bodily, physical appetites and cravings common to human,[97] nor is his life restricted by death.[98] Thus, one can find that substantial strata of the OT avoid referring to the נֶפֶשׁ of God, such as "the older strata of the Pentateuch, up to and including Deuteronomy."[99] Merely twenty-one occurrences can be seen in later language, mainly prophetic and poetic.[100]

In some passages, נֶפֶשׁ is used of God in conveying "forcefully his passionate disinclination or inclination toward someone."[101] More frequently, God's נֶפֶשׁ is employed as the subject of the act to depict God's aversion to

---

are 223 in total, Johnson, in *Vitality of the Individual*, 15 n. 3, comments that there exist difficulties in making a precise analysis on this issue.

93. Brotzman, "Man and the Meaning of נפש," 403.

94. Cf. Steven E. Runge, Joshua R. Westbury, and Kristopher Lyle, eds., *The Lexham Discourse Hebrew Bible*. (Bellingham, WA: Lexham Press, 2014), Lev 11:43–44; Brotzman, "Man and the Meaning of נפש," 403.

95. Cf. Ludwig Köhler, *Old Testament Theology*, trans. A. S. Todd (Philadelphia, PA: Westminster Press, 1957), 142.

96. Wolff, *Anthropology of the Old Testament*, 25.

97. Marter notes that the reason why physical appetites were never attributed to God is that "the pagan neighbors of Israel consistently attributed the grossest bodily appetites to their gods." See E. W. Marter, "The Hebrew Concept of 'Soul' in Pre-Exilic Writings," *Andrews University Seminary Studies* 2 (1964): 104.

98. Waltke, "נפש," 591; Marter, "Hebrew Concept of 'Soul,'" 104.

99. Wolff, *Anthropology of the Old Testament*, 25.

100. Wolff, 25, 232 n. II.6.

101. Waltke, "נפש," 591.

his disobedient people with intensity and passion.[102] For example, Jeremiah 6:8 reads, "be warned, O Jerusalem, lest my [נֶפֶשׁ] be estranged from you"; Jeremiah 5:9, 29; 9:8 report, "should my [נֶפֶשׁ] not take vengeance on such a people?"[103] But as for a positive reading, Westermann notes that "the positive counterpart occurs only rarely with נֶפֶשׁ as the subject."[104] For example, Isaiah 42:1 reads "in whom my [נֶפֶשׁ] is well pleased." Jeremiah 12:7 has "I will give the one I [נַפְשִׁי] love into the hands of her enemies."[105] In other cases, נֶפֶשׁ is used as God's unfettered desire in Job 23:13, or appears merely as a reflexive pronoun, such as Amos 6:8 and Jeremiah 51:14, where God swears by himself.[106] Marter notes: "Doubtless these passages may be considered as examples of anthropomorphism, but if so they emphatically illustrate that in the Hebrew mind the identification of נֶפֶשׁ with the human individual was so complete that the Hebrews could even attribute [נֶפֶשׁ] to God as an individual."[107]

4.2.4.5 נֶפֶשׁ *as Life*

In more than two hundred instances the word נֶפֶשׁ means "life."[108] Seebass points out that "the word denotes not life in general but life instantiated in individuals, animal or human."[109] These uses can be relegated into two categories: נֶפֶשׁ as individual life[110] and נֶפֶשׁ related to blood.[111]

4.2.4.5.1 נֶפֶשׁ *as individual life*

Due to the many appearances of נֶפֶשׁ in this subcategory, grouping its main uses according to certain common features is helpful in understanding its meaning as "life." In such usage, נֶפֶשׁ is usually the object in sentences as

---

102. Westermann, "נפש," 756; cf. Julien Harvey, "Is Biblical Man Still Alive?," *Biblical Theology Bulletin: A Journal of Bible and Theology* 3, no. 2 (1973): 171.
103. Westermann, "נפש," 756.
104. Westermann, 757.
105. Wolff, *Anthropology of the Old Testament*, 25.
106. Wolff, 25; Seebass, "נפש," 516.
107. Marter, "Hebrew Concept of 'Soul,'" 101.
108. Brotzman, "Plurality of 'Soul,'" 45.
109. Seebass, "נפש," 512.
110. Seebass, 512.
111. Brotzman, "The Plurality of 'Soul,'" 45.

noted earlier. First of all, נֶפֶשׁ is related to "threats to life."[112] The first instance is the use of נֶפֶשׁ "life" as the direct object of בקשׁ "seek" (i.e. "seek after someone's life").[113] One of the eighteen texts[114] that represent this usage is Exodus 4:19, where "the LORD said to Moses in Midian, 'Go back to Egypt, for all the men who were seeking your life are dead'" (NASB 1995). Another example is the use of נֶפֶשׁ as the object of לקח "take." Ezekiel 33:6 reads that the sword comes and takes life from them (i.e. the sword kills them);[115] both Elijah (1 Kgs 19:4) and Jonah (Jonah 4:3) request the Lord take their life from them.[116]

Second, נֶפֶשׁ as life occurs in the *talion* formula of "נֶפֶשׁ for נֶפֶשׁ."[117] The earliest version of this use is probably Exodus 21:23,[118] "But if there is serious injury, you are to take life for life [נֶפֶשׁ for נֶפֶשׁ]." Though ransom is permitted in cases of accidental killing of the נֶפֶשׁ, it is unambiguously prohibited in cases of murder (Num 35:31).[119] In Deuteronomy 19:21, the principle of "נֶפֶשׁ for נֶפֶשׁ" applies in cases of false witness as well. Moreover, 1 Kings 19:2 "has Jezebel say that she will make Elijah's life like that of one of the prophets of Baal: life for life."[120] The collocation "נֶפֶשׁ for נֶפֶשׁ" is even employed in the OT once to refer to the life of animals: "Anyone who takes the life of someone's animal must make restituion – life for life" (Lev 24:18).[121]

Third, נֶפֶשׁ is related to risks "in battle or in other, more general, circumstances."[122] An instance of this usage is found in 2 Samuel 23:17 (see also 1 Chr 11:19), where David was unwilling to drink water brought by his followers at the risk of their lives.[123] Similarly, Judges 9:17 reports

---

112. Seebass, "נפשׁ," 513; Westermann, "נפשׁ," 753; Brotzman, "Plurality of 'Soul,'" 45.
113. Seebass, "נפשׁ," 513.
114. Logos Bible Software, Word Study נֶפֶשׁ.
115. Brotzman, "Plurality of 'Soul,'" 48.
116. Brotzman, 48.
117. Waltke, "נפשׁ," 590; Seebass, "נפשׁ," 513; Westermann, "נפשׁ," 753; Brotzman, "Plurality of 'Soul,'" 48–49.
118. Douglas K. Stuart, *Exodus*, vol. 2, The New American Commentary (Nashville: Broadman & Holman, 2006), 492; Seebass, "נפשׁ," 513.
119. Seebass, "נפשׁ," 513.
120. Seebass, 513.
121. Brotzman, "Plurality of 'Soul,'" 50.
122. Brotzman, 61.
123. Seebass, "נפשׁ," 512.

that Gideon cast his נֶפֶשׁ in the battle (i.e. he "exposed his life to the danger of fighting for the sake of Israel.")[124] Even more drastic is the very archaic, poetic composition in Judges 5:18, where Zebulun and Naphtali had fought valiantly and well; the former is especially depicted as people who risked their lives (נֶפֶשׁ) to the point of death.[125]

Fourth, many passages with נֶפֶשׁ have to do with "the deliverance of life."[126] Almost all the verbs within this semantic domain have נֶפֶשׁ as object. For example, with נצל, "and deliver our lives from death" (Josh 2:13; Isa 44:20); with מלט, "if you do not save your life tonight, tomorrow you will be put to death" (1 Sam 19:11); with חלץ, "rescue my life" (Ps 6:5); with ישע, "he will save the lives of the needy" (Ps 72:13).[127] Finally, in Psalm 49:15, the poet is confident that God will פדה "redeem" his life out of the grave.[128]

In sum, נֶפֶשׁ as "life" refers not to life in general, but to life in individuals, with seemingly more emphasis on physical life.

4.2.4.5.2 נֶפֶשׁ *related to blood*

Genesis 9:4, Leviticus 17:11, 14 and Deuteronomy 12:23 are ritual texts which "most clearly illustrate the connection between נֶפֶשׁ and blood."[129] In these texts, "נֶפֶשׁ has nothing whatever to do with a breath-soul or a blood-soul;[130] it simply denotes the vital force."[131] As Seligson notes, it is a common conception that humanity "at an early stage of culture identified blood with the vital force,"[132] as represented in the OT. In the same vein, Johnson views vitality as the defining characteristic of נֶפֶשׁ.[133]

Pedersen goes further to suggest that in the OT each body part, including blood, represents a "principal denomination" of the vital life, or נֶפֶשׁ which

---

124. Brotzman, "Plurality of 'Soul,'" 61–62.
125. Brotzman, 61; Seebass, "נפש," 512.
126. Westermann, "נפש," 752; see also Waltke, "נפש," 590; Seebass, "נפש," 512.
127. Waltke, "נפש," 590.
128. Waltke, 590.
129. Jacob, "Anthropology of the Old Testament," 619.
130. The נֶפֶשׁ as not a breath-soul or a blood-soul means that it is not perceived as a "separate, distinct 'part' of the person." See Warne, *Hebrew Perspectives*, 69.
131. Jacob, "Anthropology of the Old Testament," 619.
132. Seligson, *Meaning of* נפש מת *in the Old Testament*, 28.
133. Johnson, *Vitality of the Individual*, 22.

manifests itself in and through various body organs.[134] For Laurin, this is "simply the principle of synecdoche,"[135] given that נֶפֶשׁ is the individual in his/her totality.[136] Thus, the OT does not understand נֶפֶשׁ as being equated with the blood, but perceives the vital life-force as being manifested through various physical parts, such as blood in this case.[137]

Finally, Jacob's observation on the relation between נֶפֶשׁ, blood and breath is worth noting: "The relation between נֶפֶשׁ and blood is probably along other lines which are independent of the relation between נֶפֶשׁ and breath. Basic to both, however, is the idea of the body as a living organism. When breath and blood leave the body, then every form of life disappears."[138]

4.2.4.6 נֶפֶשׁ as Desire, Appetite

The meaning of נֶפֶשׁ can readily be figuratively extended from the life principle to refer to one's desire or appetite. The physical desire ranges "from the sexual drive of a wild donkey in heat (Jer 2:24), to the physical appetite (Prov 23:2; Eccl 6:7)."[139] Thus, Jeremiah 2:24 reports, "a wild donkey accustomed to the desert, sniffing the wind in her craving בְּאַוַּת נַפְשׁוֹ[140] – in her heat who can restrain her?"

In other cases, נֶפֶשׁ signifies the desire for food: "you may eat grapes according to your appetite [נֶפֶשׁ], until you are satisfied" (Deut 23:24; cf. Ps 78:18).[141] Isaiah 56:11 reads, "They are dogs with mighty appetites [נֶפֶשׁ]; they never have enough."[142] Proverbs 12:10 states that a righteous man is one who knows the נֶפֶשׁ of his beast (i.e. he is "a person who provides for his animal's need for food and drink").[143]

---

134. Johannes Pedersen, *Israel, Its Life and Culture*, vol. 1 (London: Oxford University Press, 1926), 171–176.

135. Cf. Johnson, *Vitality of the Individual*, 37, 69.

136. Laurin, "Concept of Man as a Soul," 132.

137. Warne, *Hebrew Perspectives*, 69–70.

138. Jacob, "Anthropology of the Old Testament," 619.

139. Fredericks, "נפש," 133.

140. Johnson, in *Vitality of the Individual*, 13, asserts that the frequent association of נֶפֶשׁ with אַוָּה can express "a wide range of activity from the simple desire for food . . . to the worshipper's longing for fellowship with God."

141. Waltke, "נפש," 588.

142. Brown et al., "נפש," 660.

143. Brotzman, "Man and the Meaning of נפש," 401.

4.2.4.7 נֶפֶשׁ as Corpse, Body

As has been discussed earlier, נֶפֶשׁ refers to vitality. Thus, נֶפֶשׁ as a deceased or a corpse, for Westermann, is difficult to explain.[144] He argues: "The usage probably derives from the general meaning 'person'; one could regard this designation as a euphemism[145] designed to avoid direct reference to the corpse."[146]

However, for Wolff, the shift of meaning of נֶפֶשׁ from vitality to corpse is understandable.[147] He argues: "The semantic element 'vitality,' which also applies to the animal, has largely contributed to the fact that נֶפֶשׁ can be a term for the person and the enumerable individuals, from which, in extreme cases, the meaning 'corpse' follows."[148]

Commenting on Ezekiel 13:19, Wolff further notes: "Ez. 13:19 distinguishes נְפָשׁוֹת who ought not to die from those who ought not to live . . . This statement suggests a detachment of the concept נֶפֶשׁ from the concept of life; stress lies on the individual being as such. This makes the extreme possibility of speaking of a נֶפֶשׁ מֵת (Num 6:6) comprehensible."[149]

The use of נֶפֶשׁ to denote a corpse only appears in twelve texts[150] in the OT, which is confined to the books of Leviticus, Numbers, and Haggai.[151] These texts are related to "a series of legal ordinances concerned with pollution through contact with a corpse."[152] For example, according to Numbers 6:6, the Nazirite must not go near "a person who has died – a dead individual, a corpse."[153] Here the author of Numbers "is not thinking of a 'dead

---

144. Westermann, "נפש," 756.

145. Westermann, in "נפש," 756, argues that semantic polarization (a feature of the Semitic languages) proposed by Johnson (*Vitality of the Individual*, 22) is not a satisfactory explanation for the usage of נֶפֶשׁ as corpse.

146. Westermann, "נפש," 756.

147. Wolff, *Anthropology of the Old Testament*, 22.

148. Wolff, 25.

149. Wolff, 22.

150. The occurrences are as follows: נֶפֶשׁ or נֶפֶשׁ אָדָם: Lev 19:28; 21:1; 22:4; Num 5:2; 6:11; 9:6, 7,10; 19:13; Hag 2:13; נֶפֶשׁ מֵת: Lev 21:11; Num 6:6. See Brotzman, "Plurality of 'Soul,'" ch. 8.

151. Brotzman, "Plurality of 'Soul,'" 131.

152. Westermann, "נפש," 756.

153. Wolff, *Anthropology of the Old Testament*, 22.

soul,' or of a 'slain life,' but simply of . . . a corpse,"[154] a dead body (נֶפֶשׁ מֵת) (NIV 2011; ESV). In the combination of נֶפֶשׁ מֵת, נֶפֶשׁ is understood as "body." Wolff goes further to accentuate that even without the addition of מֵת, נֶפֶשׁ can still mean the corpse of a human individual in certain cases, such as Numbers 5:2; 6:11.[155]

4.2.4.8 Conclusion

The investigation in this section has shown that נֶפֶשׁ can have the following possible meanings: (1) breath, (2) living creature, person, (3) vital self (pronominal use, the whole being/person), (4) life, (5) desire, appetite, (6) corpse, body.

It has also shown that the meanings of נֶפֶשׁ in the OT are more related to the physical aspects of human beings.[156]

4.2.5 נֶפֶשׁ and Its Greek Equivalent ψυχή in the LXX and the NT

4.2.5.1 Introduction

Among the anthropological terms, ψυχή has been the center of controversies since the beginning of the early church.[157] To make things worse, OT scholars with great unanimity view the rendering of נֶפֶשׁ with ψυχή as "insufficient or even misleading" because it introduces the "Greek doctrine of the soul" or Greek spiritualism or dualism.[158] However, Bratsiotis maintains that there is "an astonishing correspondence" between the Hebrew word נֶפֶשׁ and the Greek word ψυχή if one can commence with the pre-Platonic usage of ψυχή.[159] If this is the case, the semantic range and usage of נֶפֶשׁ in the OT

---

154. Wolff, 22.

155. Wolff, 22.

156. Waltke, "נפש," 591. This is not to say that "the OT presents man as physical only." There are other OT ideas conveying the psychological dimension of humans, such as "the 'spirit' of man," "the heart [לֵבָב] of man," humans in the image of God, and a human's relation to God. See Waltke, 591.

157. Robert Jewett, *Paul's Anthropological Terms: A Study of Their Use in Conflict Settings* (Leiden: Brill, 1971), 334.

158. Westermann, "נפש," 759.

159. Quoted in Westermann, "נפש," 759. Bratsiotis, in Westermann, 759, suggests that "breath" is the basic meaning of ψυχή, which also means: life, person, the seat of desire and emotions, the center of religious expression, etc.

could be further illuminated by its Greek equivalent ψυχή. In what follows, the researcher examines the use of ψυχή in the LXX and the NT respectively.

4.2.5.2 *The Use of* ψυχή *in the LXX*

According to Lys, out of 754 occurrences with נֶפֶשׁ in the OT, 680 are rendered as ψυχή in the LXX. Though the stereotyped rendering of נֶפֶשׁ in the LXX fails to provide a significant clue for the understanding of this term, Lys finds that the more frequent use of the plural in the LXX denotes the tendency to individualize, that can be observed elsewhere in the LXX.[160] He writes: "It is clear from this that the LXX has a tendency to consider the 'soul [נֶפֶשׁ]' in a more individualistic way than does the Hebrew text; the latter was still under the influence of the collective soul; the LXX is more respectful of the reality of each being as an individual person to be distinguished from another."[161]

For Lys, more crucial clues for understanding the various senses of נֶפֶשׁ can be found through the investigation of its translations with something other than ψυχή. He observes the LXX does not utilize any other word with such regularity. The different Greek renderings of נֶפֶשׁ, when explained regarding the context, remain within the range of senses that נֶפֶשׁ has in the OT, with "person" and a pronoun ("self") outnumbering all the other renderings.[162]

It is also important to note that the LXX uses ψυχή sixty-two times for words other than נֶפֶשׁ, such as for בֶּטֶן "belly."[163] For Lys, this interesting phenomenon shows that "the LXX . . . did not understand ψυχή in a Platonic way at all."[164]

Commenting on the preceding investigations, Lys writes:

> [I]t is obvious that where the LXX avoids translating נֶפֶשׁ by ψυχή, it is not in order to reserve ψυχή for a dualistic meaning, since elsewhere ψυχή follows the various Hebrew meanings

---

160. Daniel Lys, "The Israelite Soul According to the LXX," *Vetus Testamentum* 16, no. 2 (1966): 186–187.
161. Lys, "Isralite Soul," 188.
162. Lys, 194–202.
163. Lys, 207–216.
164. Lys, 216.

of נֶפֶשׁ (even when נֶפֶשׁ is absent). The LXX never goes in the direction in which "soul" would be understood as opposite to "body" (as in Platonic dualism).[165]

In sum, the LXX employs ψυχή in much the same way as the Hebrew uses נֶפֶשׁ. The Greek rendering of the Hebrew term appears to "carefully avoid dualism and is an excellent, faithful understanding and interpretation of נֶפֶשׁ."[166]

4.2.5.3 *The Use of* ψυχή *in the NT*

In investigating ψυχή in the NT, the first fact to notice is the surprising infrequency of this term, especially when comparing to other anthropological terms in the NT. For example, in the MT, נֶפֶשׁ (754 times) is roughly twice as common as רוּחַ; but in Paul, the corresponding word ψυχή appears merely thirteen times, while πνεῦμα appears 146 times.[167] Despite his rare use of ψυχή, Paul's anthropology has been misunderstood as dichotomy (body and soul) or trichotomy (body, soul and spirit), which has prevailed in traditional Christian interpretation. However, new criteria for evaluating Paul proposed by Lüdermann in the late nineteenth century became determinative for doing justice to Pauline anthropology.[168] For example, Lüdermann interprets ψυχή as that which "enlivens the outer person," and which is "intimately connected" with the physical dimension of human.[169] He further states: "The word ψυχή always appears . . . in a connexion which shows the human being in a situation of inferiority, and is not to be brought into agreement with the all-embracing and loftier idea of ψυχή found elsewhere in the classical and Hellenistic usage."[170]

---

165. Lys, 227.
166. Lys, 228.
167. W. David Stacey, "St Paul and the 'Soul,'" *The Expository Times* 66 (1955): 274.
168. Warne, *Hebrew Perspectives*, 157.
169. Quoted in Jewett, *Paul's Anthropological Terms*, 336.
170. Quoted in Stacey, *Pauline View of Man*, 125; see also Stacey, "St Paul and the 'Soul,'" 276. In the same vein, Hicks asserts that "what is definitely lacking in the New Testament is any concept of the soul as something to be set over against the body, something superior to it and longing to be free of it, and something that can exist independently of it. Though these concepts would have been well known in New Testament times and were appearing in contemporary Jewish writings including Philo, the New Testament writers clearly rejected them." See Peter Hicks, *The Journey So Far: Philosophy Through the Ages* (Grand Rapids, MI: Zondervan, 2003), 107.

Since Lüdermann, the concept of ψυχή has been understood as similar to the Hebrew term נֶפֶשׁ, and "an interpretation of Pauline anthropology in Hebraic terms has become much more common."[171]

Then, how is the term ψυχή employed by Paul and other NT authors? To this question the present study now turns. Of the 103 occurrences of ψυχή in the NT, none is found in Galatians, Philemon, 2 Thessalonians, the Pastorals, or 2 John. ψυχή is seen relatively frequently in the Synoptics and Acts (fifty-three times). The statistics prove "no particular preference by anyone NT author."[172]

A quick review of the usage of ψυχή in the NT is conducted according to the following groupings: (1) Paul and the deutero-Pauline writings,[173] (2) the Synoptics and Acts, (3) the Johannine corpus, and (4) other writings.[174]

4.2.5.3.1 Ψυχή in Paul and the deutero-Pauline writings

Ψυχή in Paul and the deutero-Pauline writings is rarely used (thirteen times) in comparison with נֶפֶשׁ in the OT as noted above. In the few texts where it occurs, Paul follows "the Hebraic conception of man as an intrinsic unity,[175] with a diversity of aspects."[176] He also perceives ψυχή as "the vitality or

---

171. Warne, *Hebrew Perspectives*, 157–158.

172. A. Sand, "ψυχή," in *Exegetical Dictionary of the New Testament*, vol. 3, eds. Horst R. Balz and Gerhard Schneider (Grand Rapids, MI: Eerdmans, 1990), 501.

173. The reason for reviewing this grouping first is that Paul's anthropology has been misunderstood as dichotomy (body and soul) or trichotomy (body, soul and spirit).

174. Sand, "ψυχή," 500.

175. Jewett, in *Paul's Anthropological Terms*, 449, points out that there are two instances within Pauline corpus "where the basic Judaic uniformity in the use of ψυχή is temporarily broken," for Paul's reformulating the ψυχικός – πνευματικός distinction in 1 Cor 15:44, 46 in order to repair the damage caused by Gnosticism. See also David M. Reis, "Thinking with Soul: *Psychē* and *Psychikos* in the Construction of Early Christian Identities," *Journal of Early Christian Studies* 17, no. 4 (2009): 590–591. Heckel argues that Paul is not teaching a body-soul dualism, but a transformation of the body similar to that of the resurrected Christ. That is, at the final judgment, Christians will receive a "spiritual body." See Theo K. Heckel, "Body and Soul in Saint Paul," in *Psyche and Soma: Physicians and Metaphysicians on the Mind-Body Problem from Antiquity to Enlightenment*, eds. John P. Wright and Paul Potter, reprinted (Oxford: Clarendon Press, 2006), 125. Worth noting is that "as soon as [Paul] has made use of the term as a weapon against its originators, he drops it entirely. ψυχικός never appears again in the Pauline epistles, and its dualistic implications have no influence whatever upon the subsequent use of ψυχή." See Jewett, *Paul's Anthropological Terms*, 449.

176. Stacey, "St Paul and the 'Soul,'" 276.

life-force that makes a living being, or a being living."[177] Thus, ψυχή in Paul means "whole natural life of the person,"[178] "the individual person as subject,"[179] the seat of feelings, thought and will.[180]

1 Thessalonians 5:23 has been used to support the trichotomous view of the human person and needs further investigation. In Christian tradition, Paul's trio πνεῦμα – ψυχή – σῶμα has been understood as the formulation of anthropological trichotomy.[181] Nonetheless, the threefold connection of spirit, soul, and body is "confined to this text alone in Paul and, therefore, cannot provide an adequate basis for a conclusive statement concerning Pauline anthropology."[182] Furthermore, it is the terms ὁλοτελής and ὁλόκληρος that point to the real meaning, instead of the trio πνεῦμα – ψυχή – σῶμα.[183] Stacey argues that Paul is accentuating the whole person to be preserved to the Parousia.[184] Bultmann also suggests that this text "evidently means only that the readers may be kept sound, each in his entirety."[185] Similarly, Jewett states that Paul's insistence in the benediction is to manifest that "God works to sanctify the whole [person]."[186] Sand further notes that: "If one considers the apostle's other anthropological statements, one sees that the three words are used in 1 Thess 5:23 against adversaries who incorrectly see and evaluate human beings dualistically."[187]

Robinson contends that the triad of πνεῦμα, ψυχή and σῶμα is far from a systematic dissection of the different constituents of humanity; "its true

---

177. Gordon Zerbe, "Paul on the Human Being as a 'Psychic Body': Neither Dualist nor Monist," *Direction Journal* 37, no. 2 (2008): 172; see also Rudolf Bultmann, *Theology of the New Testament: With a New Introduction by Robert Morgan*, trans. Kendrick Grobel (Waco, TX: Baylor University Press, 2007), 204; Harvey, "Is Biblical Man Still Alive?," 169.

178. Rom 11:3; 16:4; Phil 2:30; 1 Cor 15:45; 2 Cor 12:15; 1 Thess 2:8.

179. Rom 2:9; 13:1; 2 Cor 1:23.

180. Eph 6:6; Phil 1:27; Col 3:23; 1 Thess 5:23. See Warne, *Hebrew Perspectives*, 158–202; see also Stacey, *Pauline View of Man*, 122–123.

181. Sand, "ψυχή," 502.

182. Warne, *Hebrew Perspectives*, 199.

183. Stacey, *Pauline View of Man*, 123; see also Green, "Soul," 359.

184. Stacey, *Pauline View of Man*, 123.

185. Bultmann, *Theology of the New Testament*, 205.

186. Jewett, *Paul's Anthropological Terms*, 347. The external evaluator of the present dissertation commented that "the trio πνεῦμα – ψυχή – σῶμα used here is simply, but significantly in pragmatic terms, a rhetorical flourish at the conclusion of the epistle."

187. Sand, "ψυχή," 502.

analogy is such an Old Testament sentence as Deut 6:5, where a somewhat similar enumeration emphasizes the totality of the personality."[188] Warne notes that ψυχή in 1 Thessalonians 5:23 is better understood as the seat of feelings, thought and will.[189]

4.2.5.3.2 Ψυχή in the Synoptic Gospels and Acts

In the Synoptic Gospels and Acts, ψυχή (fifty-three occurrences) means earthly, natural physical life,[190] true life (in distinction from purely physical life),[191] the whole being,[192] the seat of emotions and feelings,[193] and human vitality in the widest sense.[194] In this grouping, one problem passage needs to be discussed briefly here.

Matthew 10:28 juxtaposes God, who can destroy both σῶμα and ψυχή, and humans, who can destroy the σῶμα, but not the ψυχή. Jeeves notes that for some, the face value of this pericope could certainly be seen as a proof text to assert the survival of the separate soul at death. As such, the doctrine of the immortal soul seems to be alluded to here.[195] However, "the reference to God's power to destroy the ψυχή and σῶμα in Hades is opposed to the idea of the immortality of the soul."[196] For Schweizer, a human being "can be thought of only as a whole, both ψυχή and σῶμα."[197] Associating this text with Mark 8:35, where true life preserved by God is distinguished from purely physical life, Schweizer further elucidates that the ψυχή, that is, "the true life of man as it is lived before God and in fellowship with God," is not

---

188. Robinson, *Christian Doctrine of Man*, 108.

189. Warne, *Hebrew Perspectives*, 199.

190. For example, Matt 2:20; 6:25; Mark 3:4; 10:45; Luke 12:20; 14:26; Acts 15:26; 20:24.

191. For example, Matt 10:39; 16:25; Mark 8:35–36; Luke 9:24; 17:33.

192. For example, Matt 11:29.

193. For example, Matt 12:18; 26:28; Mark 14:34; Luke 2:35.

194. Cf. Sand, "ψυχή," 502; Eduard Schweizer, "Ψυχή: The New Testament," in *Theological Dictionary of the New Testament*, vol. 9, eds. Gerhard Kittel, Geoffrey W. Bromiley, and G. Friedrich (Grand Rapids, MI: Eerdmans, 1974), 637–647.

195. Malcolm Jeeves, *Human Nature: Reflections on the Integration of Psychology and Christianity* (West Conshohocken, PA: Templeton Foundation, 2006), 104.

196. Schweizer, "Ψυχή," 646; see also John Nolland, *The Gospel of Matthew*, The New International Greek Testament Commentary (Grand Rapids, MI: Eerdmans; Milton Keynes, UK: Paternoster, 2005), 436.

197. Schweizer, "Ψυχή," 646.

influenced by the cessation of physical life.[198] He concludes: "God alone controls the whole man, ψυχή as well as σῶμα . . . man can be presented only as corporeal, but what affects the body does not necessarily affect the man himself, for whom a new body has already been prepared by God."[199]

The body-soul dualism is rejected by Lucan writings as well. Luke 16:22 and 23:43 denote that after death the human being as a whole will either abide in Hades or Paradise. The resurrection appearances of the risen Lord are also delineated with great bodily realism in Luke. In Acts 2:31, Luke avoids referring to the ψυχή not being left in Hades as read in Psalm 16:10, but notes that the σὰρξ of Jesus does not see corruption. All these demonstrate that Luke is unambiguously teaching a bodily resurrection (the continued life of the whole person), rather than the Hellenistic immortality of the soul.[200]

4.2.5.3.3 Ψυχή in the Johannine corpus

Ψυχή occurs twenty times in the Johannine corpus. In most appearances (thirteen times), it means physical life of Jesus,[201] of any other person,[202] or even of creatures in the sea.[203] In other cases, it simply means human being (Rev 18:13), the seat of emotion/thought/will (John 12:27), or appetite/desire (Rev 18:14).

The remaining four occurrences of ψυχή in this grouping are problematic and are therefore briefly explored here. In John 10:24a, the Jews asked Jesus, "ἕως πότε τὴν ψυχὴν ἡμῶν αἴρεις," which is rendered as "How long will you keep us in suspense?" in popular English versions (NIV, NASB, ESV, NRSV, etc.). Michaels notes that although this rendering "makes excellent sense in the context, no such meaning is attested in biblical, classical, or Hellenistic Greek."[204] He examines the context and finds a similar construction in verse

---

198. Schweizer, 643, 646.

199. Schweizer, 646.

200. Schweizer, 646–647; see also Sand, "ψυχή," 502.

201. John 10:11, 15, 17; 1 John 3:16a.

202. John 12:25 (two times); 13:37, 38; 15:13; 1 John 3:16b; Rev 12:11. John 12:25 associates ψυχή with ζωή to avoid "any strict dichotomies between earthly/heavenly, this life/next life." See Jaime Clark-Soles, *Death and the Afterlife in the New Testament* (New York: T & T Clark, 2006), 122.

203. Rev 8:9; 16:3.

204. J. Ramsey Michaels, *The Gospel of John*, The New International Commentary on the New Testament (Grand Rapids, MI; Cambridge: Eerdmans, 2010), 596.

18a (οὐδεὶς αἴρει αὐτὴν ἀπ' ἐμοῦ), where αὐτός is the pronoun for τὴν ψυχὴν μου, meaning that "no one takes it [Jesus's life] from me [Jesus]." Therefore, the appropriate translation of John 10:24a, for Michaels, seems to be: "How long will you take away our life?" or "kill us?"[205] He explains:

> It appears that the language of "killing" or "taking away life" is used here metaphorically, as in our colloquial English expression, "the suspense is killing me" . . . In the wake of the "split" dividing them (v. 19), they [the Jews] are uncertain what to expect, for they are no longer in control. The notion of "killing" or a prolonged death, therefore, is by no means inappropriate as a metaphor for their frustration.[206]

Michaels's argument seems to be reasonable. Ψυχή in John 10:24a means "life," which is consistent with Johannine usage of ψυχή (thirteen out of twenty occurrences as "physical life").

The second problem text is found in 3 John 2, which seems to indicate a distinction between the physical and the spiritual life. Nevertheless, Schweizer suggests that ψυχή is not an antithesis to the bodily dimension here.[207] As noted earlier, ψυχή means the true life before God and in fellowship with God; thus, it might be sound even when one is sick in body. "The hope is that the two [true life and body] will be in harmony, not that they will be separated from one another."[208]

The last two difficult passages are Revelation 6:9 and Revelation 20:4. In both cases, ψυχή is translated "soul" in the majority of popular English versions (NIV, NASB, ESV, NRSV, etc.). Defying the preceding rendering, Schweizer contends that here ψυχή is the person who "survives death prior to his resurrection," who is conscious and corporeal.[209] However, "this inter-

---

205. Michaels, *Gospel of John*, 596; see also Leon Morris, *The Gospel According to John*, The New International Commentary on the New Testament (Grand Rapids, MI: Eerdmans, 1995), 461 n. 71.

206. Michaels, *Gospel of John*, 596.

207. Schweizer, "Ψυχή," 652.

208. Schweizer, 651–652.

209. Schweizer, 654.

mediate state is not a true life; this will come only with the new corporeality at the resurrection."[210]

In Revelation 20:4, ψυχή is the person in "the final state after the first resurrection."[211] Obviously, here ψυχή is not referring to "a purely provisional and definitely non-corporeal state."[212] This is substantiated by "the relation of the word to the relative masculine pronoun, which shows how much it embraces the whole person."[213] Thus, ψυχή is now a word for a person living in eschatological salvation. Again, ψυχή does not convey "any clear distinction between a non-corporeal and a corporeal state."[214]

If Schweizer is right, ψυχή in Revelation 6:9 and Revelation 20:4 refers to the "person" in the intermediate state and in the final state after the first resurrection respectively.

Thus, the meanings of ψυχή (twenty times) in the Johannine corpus consist of physical life (fourteen times), true life (once), human being/person (three times), the seat of emotion/thought/will (once), or appetite/desire (once).

4.2.5.3.4 Ψυχή in other writings of the NT

This section examines statements using ψυχή in other writings of the NT. Ψυχή in Hebrews is largely traditional and refers to the person himself,[215] or to the true and authentic life before God.[216] The problem pericope is Hebrews 4:12, where the word of God can pierce "as far as the division of soul [ψυχή] and spirit [πνεῦμα], of both joints and marrow" (NASB 1995). One may interpret this text as a support for anthropological trichotomy. However, Ellingworth asserts: "It is probably misconceived to seek precise definition in such a poetic passage. The general meaning is clearly that the

---

210. Schweizer, 654.
211. Schweizer, 654.
212. Schweizer, 654.
213. Schweizer, 654.
214. Schweizer, 654.
215. Heb 10:38; 12:3; 13:17. See Sand, "ψυχή," 503.
216. Heb 6:19; 10:39. See Schweizer, "Ψυχή," 650–651.

active power of God's Word reaches into the inmost recesses of human existence."[217]

Besides, as noted already, the majority of occurrences of ψυχή in Hebrews denote "person" or "life." Thus, its rendering as "soul" seems to be inappropriate in this text. This is why Cockerill translates it as "life."[218] In sum, there is no definite trichotomy in view here.[219]

The remaining appearances of ψυχή in James,[220] 1 and 2 Peter,[221] Jude[222] all refer to the whole person or self.

4.2.5.4 Conclusion

After examining the usage of ψυχή in the LXX and the NT, one finds that both utilize ψυχή along with the Hebrew conception of נֶפֶשׁ. The translators of the former interpret נֶפֶשׁ into Greek terms faithfully, and seem to avoid dualism carefully. Surprisingly, compared to the occurrences of the word נֶפֶשׁ in the OT (754 times), NT authors employ ψυχή much less – only 103 times. When ψυχή is used in the NT, its meanings still fall within the semantic range of נֶפֶשׁ of the OT, such as life, which comprises physical life and true life before God and in fellowship with God, individual person, the whole being or self, the seat of emotions, thought and will, appetite/desire, and human vitality in the widest sense.

---

217. Paul Ellingworth, *The Epistle to the Hebrews: A Commentary on the Greek Text*, The New International Greek Testament Commentary (Grand Rapids, MI: Eerdmans; Carlisle: Paternoster, 1993), 263.

218. Gareth Lee Cockerill, *The Epistle to the Hebrews*, The New International Commentary on the New Testament (Grand Rapids, MI; Cambridge, UK: Eerdmans, 2012), 216.

219. Schweizer, "Ψυχή," 651.

220. Jas 1:21 and Jas 5:20 denote the salvation of the whole person. See Peter H. Davids, *The Epistle of James: A Commentary on the Greek Text*, The New International Greek Testament Commentary (Grand Rapids, MI: Eerdmans, 1982), 95.

221. The usage of ψυχή as the whole person or the self "is characteristic of Peter and Luke" (six times in 1 Pet: 1:9, 22; 2:11, 25; 3:20; 4:19, and fifteen times in Acts, e.g. Acts 2:41, 43); see Peter H. Davids, *The First Epistle of Peter*, The New International Commentary on the New Testament (Grand Rapids, MI: Eerdmans, 1990), 60. The two occurrences of ψυχή in 2 Pet 2:8, 14 also mean the person; see Schweizer, "Ψυχή," 653.

222. The only appearance of ψυχή in Jude is in verse 15, which refers to every person (NRSV).

4.2.6 Conclusion

In the past, etymology has been widely used to propose meanings of נֶפֶשׁ in the OT, such as neck, throat, sustenance, and perfume. However, because of its high occurrences in the OT, etymological studies are not an appropriate approach to define its senses. Thus, examining its meaning and usage in the OT itself is indispensable in defining its semantic range. This was the goal of §4.2.4 in this study, and the result demonstrates that the possible meanings of the OT נֶפֶשׁ are (1) breath, (2) living creature, person, (3) vital self (pronominal use, the whole being/person), (4) life, (5) desire, appetite, (6) corpse, body.

Next, this study delved into the usage of ψυχή, the Greek equivalent of נֶפֶשׁ, in the LXX and the NT. The findings derived from such investigations make it obvious that both the LXX and the NT faithfully follow the usage of נֶפֶשׁ in the OT and cast some insights on its usage. For example, the translators of the LXX never translate ψυχή with "throat/neck" (see footnote 46 in this chapter) and avoid bringing about the implication of dualism when interpreting it. Similarly, it was found that the NT writers never use ψυχή[223] to convey the idea of dichotomy or trichotomy. This implies that "soul" is an inappropriate rendering of ψυχή in the NT.

As indicated earlier, poor Bible translations cause misunderstandings of God's Word. In what follows, the researcher investigates the interpretations of נֶפֶשׁ in prominent Chinese Bible versions and points out some problematic passages. Next, particular attention is paid to Watchman Nee, whose trichotomy based on problematic renderings of some biblical anthropological terms (e.g. נֶפֶשׁ/ψυχή as "soul") leads to controversy among contemporary Chinese theologians.

---

223. One development of the meaning of ψυχή in the NT is worthy of notice. That is, it refers to both physical life and true life before God and in fellowship with God. This is slightly different from the usage of the OT נֶפֶשׁ, which is almost related to physical life.

4.3 The Interpretations of נֶפֶשׁ in Chinese Bible Versions

4.3.1 Introduction

The above-mentioned critical findings concerning the semantic range of נֶפֶשׁ undoubtedly draw Chinese Bible translators' attention. For example, CUV, which was published in 1919 and has been the most popular, authoritative and influential Bible version in the contemporary Chinese Christian community,[224] was revised in 2010. This revised version (RCUV) has revised the majority of appearances where נֶפֶשׁ had previously been rendered as "靈魂 *líng hún* (spirit-soul)" or "靈 *líng* (spirit)."

Since the 1970s, some new Chinese Bible translations and revised versions translated by Chinese Christians have been published in modern standard Chinese. However, none of these surpassed the dominant status of CUV as noted above. Thus, this section focuses on the analysis of how נֶפֶשׁ is interpreted in the revised CUV.[225]

4.3.2 The Interpretations of נֶפֶשׁ in RCUV

Due to limitations of space, this section only provides general comments on the interpretation of נֶפֶשׁ in the entire RCUV, rather than providing detail about its interpretation in specific sections of the Hebrew OT, such as the Torah and the Prophets.

4.3.2.1 נֶפֶשׁ *as Life*

The most frequent rendering of נֶפֶשׁ in RCUV is "life." The majority of its occurrences (ca. 230 times) refer to "physical life" (命 *mìng*, 生命 *shēng mìng*, or 性命 *xìng mìng*). For example, in Judges 12:3, Jephthah "拚了命前去攻打亞捫人 *pīn le mìng qián qù gōng dǎ yà mén rén* (Jephthah risked his **life** and crossed over to fight the Ammonites)."[226] Psalm 49:9 reads, "因為贖生命的價值極貴 *yīn wéi shú shēng mìng de jià zhí jí guì* (because the

---

224. Zhuāng 莊, "《和合本》在中文聖經多元系統中的位置—前景與挑戰" [The position of the Chinese Union Version in the Chinese Bible polysystem: prospective and challenge], 41.

225 A complete analysis of the interpretation of נֶפֶשׁ in CUV, see Ráo 饒, 屬靈人的再思 [Rethinking on "the spiritual person."].

226. In this study, the English translations after Chinese are done by the researcher, unless indicated otherwise.

The Possible Meanings of the Hebrew Word נֶפֶשׁ in the OT

ransom for a **life** is costly)." In Genesis 12:13, Abram said to his wife Sarai, "我的**性命**也因你存活 wǒ de xìng mìng yě yīn nǐ cún huó (my **physical life** will be spared because of you)."

In a few cases, נֶפֶשׁ obviously means life in general, e.g. Proverbs 24:14 describes "智慧對你的**生命**正像如此 zhì huì duì nǐ de shēng mìng zhèng xiàng rú cǐ (wisdom for your **life** is like this)."

4.3.2.2 נֶפֶשׁ *as Heart*

Yu notes that heart in present-day Chinese refers to a physical entity, the locus of one's inner self, mental and emotional life.[227] In RCUV, נֶפֶשׁ as heart is never used to denote a physical organ. Based on Yu, the usage of נֶפֶשׁ as heart in RCUV can be divided into two categories: נֶפֶשׁ as the seat of one's inner self and emotions, and נֶפֶשׁ as the seat of one's mental life.

4.3.2.2.1 נֶפֶשׁ as the seat of one's inner self and emotions

In this category, נֶפֶשׁ is rendered as "heart" or phrases directly related to heart, which has the second highest appearance (over 160 times). For instance, Jeremiah 6:8 reads, "免得我心與你生疏 miǎn dé wǒ xīn yǔ nǐ shēng shū (lest my **heart** is alienated from you)." Psalm 63:2 reads, "我的**心靈**渴想你 wǒ de xīn líng kě xiǎng nǐ (my **heart** thirsts for you)." In Exodus 23:9, the Israelites were commanded not to oppress a sojourner, because they knew "寄居者的**心情** jì jū zhě de xīn qíng (the **feelings** of a sojourner)." The majority of the occurrences in this category are found in poetry.

4.3.2.2.2 נֶפֶשׁ as the seat of one's mental life

The mental life of a person includes thought, will, intention, volition, intellect and attention.[228] An important construction in this category is בְּכָל־לֵב וּבְכָל־נֶפֶשׁ, occurring nineteen times in the MT. In eighteen cases, לֵב (or לְבָב) and נֶפֶשׁ occur with personal suffixes except for 2 Kings 23:3. In fifteen texts, this phrase is translated "盡心盡性 jìn xīn jìn xìng[229] (with all heart and all

---

227. Ning Yu, *The Chinese HEART in a Cognitive Perspective: Culture, Body, and Language* (Berlin; New York: Mouton de Gruyter, 2009), viii.

228. Yu, *Chinese HEART*, viii.

229. Deut 4:29; 6:5; 10:12; 11:13; 13:3[4]; 26:16; 30:2, 6, 10; Josh 22:5; 2 Kgs 23:3, 25; 2 Chr 6:38; 15:12; 34:31.

thought)"²³⁰ in RCUV. It is rendered as "盡心盡意 *jìn xīn jìn yì*²³¹ (with all heart and all **mind**)" three times and "一心一意 *yī xīn yī yì*²³² (with one heart and one **mind**)" once.

Other examples are as follows. Genesis 23:8 says, "你們若願意讓我埋葬我的亡妻 *nǐ men ruò yuàn yì ràng wǒ mái zàng wǒ de wáng qī* (If you are **willing** to let me bury my dead wife)." Exodus 15:9 has "滿足我的心願 *mǎn zú wǒ de xīn yuàn* (satisfy **the will of my heart** or satisfy **my will**)." In 1 Chronicles 28:9, David exhorted his son Solomon to "全心樂意地事奉 *quán xīn lè yì dì shì fèng* (wholeheartedly and **willingly** serve)" the God of your father. The usage of נֶפֶשׁ in this category appears about forty-five times.

4.3.2.3 The Pronominal Usage of נֶפֶשׁ

The pronominal usage of נֶפֶשׁ occurs about 115 times in RCUV. נֶפֶשׁ as a personal pronoun (ca. seventy times) is found more frequently in poetry, such as Job 6:11, where נַפְשִׁי rendered as "我 *wǒ* (I)" is parallel to a simple personal pronoun "我 *wǒ* (I),"²³³ and Psalm 25:13, which reads, "他要安然居住 *tā yào ān rán jū zhù* (**he** will dwell at ease)." נֶפֶשׁ as a reflexive pronoun is employed more frequently in prose. For example, Leviticus 20:25 says that let not any unclean creature "使自己成為可憎惡的 *shǐ zì jǐ chéng wéi kě zēng è de* (make **[your]selves** detestable)." In Ezekiel 13:18, the Lord says, will you hunt down the physical lives of my people, but "使自己存活嗎 *shǐ zì jǐ cún huó ma* (keep **[your]selves** alive)."

4.3.2.4 נֶפֶשׁ as Person

Over one hundred times, נֶפֶשׁ is translated as "person" (人 *rén* or 人口 *rén kǒu*). An example in this category is found in Joshua 11:11, where the Israelites "用刀擊殺城中所有的人 *yòng dāo jī shā chéng zhōng suǒ yǒu de*

---

230. The meaning of the term 性 *xìng* in this collocation 盡心盡性 *jìn xīn jìn xìng* is ambiguous. According to HDC, the term 性 *xìng* means "本性 *běn xìng* (human nature)," "生命 *shēng mìng* (life)," or "性情 *xìng qíng* (disposition or temperament)," etc. 性情 *xìng qíng* in HDC is further defined as "思想情感 *sī xiǎng qíng gǎn* (thought/feelings)." Reaped from HDC, the most probable meanings of the term 性 *xìng* in a translator's mind could be "生命 *shēng mìng* (life)" or "思想 *sī xiǎng* (thought)." If the former is the case, then, 盡心盡性 *jìn xīn jìn xìng* means "with all heart and all life;" otherwise, it could mean "with all heart and all thought."

231. 1 Kgs 2:4; 8:48; Jer 32:41

232. Josh 23:14

233. The personal pronoun "I" is the prefixed א in the word אֲיַחֵל.

rén (struck every **person** who was in the city with the sword)." Another example is Ezekiel 27:13, which reports that Javan, Tubal and Meshech "以人口和銅器換你的貨物 yǐ rén kǒu hé tóng qì huàn nǐ de huò wù (exchanged **persons** and vessels of bronze for your merchandise)." In two cases (Num 31:35b, 40b), נֶפֶשׁ is rendered as 口 kǒu, which also means "person" in texts related to population count.

4.3.2.5 נֶפֶשׁ as Living Thing or Creature

There are fourteen texts where נֶפֶשׁ is rendered "living thing or creature." For instance, Genesis 1:21 says that God created "各樣活動的生物 gè yàng huó dòng de shēng wù (every **living creature** that moves)." Leviticus 11:10 mentions "在水裏所有的動物 zài shuǐ lǐ suǒ yǒu de dòng wù (all the **living creatures** that are in the waters)." In one case (Lev 24:18), נֶפֶשׁ refers to "牲畜 shēng chù (livestock)."

4.3.2.6 נֶפֶשׁ as Corpse or Dead Person

The association of נֶפֶשׁ with "corpse" or "dead person" appears in twelve pericopes, which are found in Leviticus (four times), Numbers (seven times), and Haggai (once). In the majority of its appearances, נֶפֶשׁ is translated 屍體 shī tǐ [234] or 死屍 sǐ shī,[235] both of which mean "corpse." There are only two texts (Lev 19:28; 21:1), where נֶפֶשׁ is rendered as "死人 sǐ rén (dead person)."

4.3.2.7 נֶפֶשׁ as Spirit-Soul, Spirit, or Soul

As noted above, the renderings of נֶפֶשׁ as "spirit-soul" or "spirit" were revised in 2010. However, RCUV still retained such translations in six passages, three of which have footnotes to suggest alternative renderings. For example, Genesis 2:7 keeps the original translation made in 1919 (i.e. Adam became "有靈的活人 yǒu líng de huó rén [a living person with **spirit**]"); but its footnote provides an alternative rendering: "有生命的人 yǒu shēng mìng de rén (a person with life)." The footnote in Psalm 16:10 indicates that "我 wǒ (I)" can be substituted for "我的靈魂 wǒ de líng hún (my **spirit-soul**)." The footnote in Psalm 23:3 states that the original rendering "他使我的靈魂甦醒 tā shǐ wǒ de líng hún sū xǐng (he refreshes my **spirit-soul**)" can be replaced by "他使我回轉 tā shǐ wǒ huí zhuǎn (he causes **me** to return)."

---

234. Lev 22:4; Num 5:2; 6:11; 9:6, 7, 10; Hag 2:13.
235. Lev 21:11; Num 6:6; 19:13.

The remaining renderings of נֶפֶשׁ in this grouping are "靈 *líng* (spirit)" in Judges 5:21, "魂 *hún* (soul)" in Isaiah 10:18 and Song of Solomon 5:6.

4.3.2.8 נֶפֶשׁ *as Breath*

In four texts of RCUV, נֶפֶשׁ is rendered as "breath." Genesis 35:18 says that Rachel named her son when she "還有一口氣 *hái yǒu yī kǒu qì* (still had one last **breath**)." The same usage can be found in 2 Samuel 1:9, where Saul was in extreme agony and had only "一口氣 *yī kǒu qì* (one last **breath**)." Again, the reference to human breath is found in Job 11:20, which reports that the hope of the wicked is "氣絕身亡 *qì jué shēn wáng* (the cessation of **breath** and the death of body [i.e. to breathe the last and die])." Finally, נֶפֶשׁ in Job 41:21 is rendered as the "氣 *qì* (breath)" of לִוְיָתָן, a kind of sea creature.

4.3.2.9 נֶפֶשׁ *as Throat*

Only two texts indicate that נֶפֶשׁ means "throat." Jeremiah 4:10 reads, "刀劍已經抵住**喉嚨**了 *dāo jiàn yǐ jīng dǐ zhù hóu lóng le* (the sword has reached the **throat**)." Habakkuk 2:5 reports that an arrogant man "張開**喉嚨**, 好像陰間 *zhāng kāi hóu lóng, hǎo xiàng yīn jiān* (opens his **throat** wide as Sheol)." In its footnote, the translators assume that "張開喉嚨 *zhāng kāi hóu lóng* (opens his **throat**)" can be replaced by "擴充心欲 *kuò chōng xīn yù* (enlarges his **desire of heart**)."

4.3.2.10 נֶפֶשׁ *as Desire or Appetite*

נֶפֶשׁ as sexual "desire" appears once in Jeremiah 2:24, where a wild donkey is described as "慾心發動 *yù xīn fā dòng* (driven by her **heart with sexual desire**)."

נֶפֶשׁ also refers to "appetite" (食慾 *shí yù* or 胃口 *wèi kǒu*) eight times. For example, Isaiah 56:11 has dogs "with mighty appetites" (貪食 *tān shí*). Probably due to idiomatic considerations, נֶפֶשׁ in Isaiah 29:8 and Proverbs 6:30 is translated "飢腸轆轆 *jī cháng lù lù* (very hungry)" and "飢 *jī* (hunger)" respectively.

4.3.2.11 The Other Renderings of נֶפֶשׁ in RCUV

Finally, נֶפֶשׁ has the following meanings: "精神 *jīng shén* (morale)" twice,[236] "精力 *jīng lì* or 力 *lì* (vigour)" twice,[237] "身體 *shēn tǐ* (body)" once,[238] and "香 *xiāng* (perfume)" once.[239]

In over forty passages, RCUV gives no Chinese equivalents for נֶפֶשׁ. There are two main reasons: the context has supposedly already conveyed its meaning, or a synonymous expression is used.

4.3.2.11.1 No Chinese equivalents for נֶפֶשׁ because the context has already conveyed its meaning

An example is found in Leviticus 7:18, which reads "凡吃這祭物**的** *fán chī zhě jì wù de* (**those who** eat of the sacrifice)." A more literal translation of this text should be "凡吃這祭物**的人** *fán chī zhě jì wù de rén* (**the person who** eats of the sacrifice)." In RCUV the last word "人 *rén* (person)" is omitted because "凡 . . . 的 *fán . . . de* (those who)" contains the meaning "person." Another example is 1 Kings 19:4a, saying that Elijah "坐在那裏求死 *zuò zài nà lǐ qiú sǐ* (sat down there and requested that he might die)." In this case, "為他自己 *wéi tā zì jǐ* (for himself)" is left out. The more complete rendering should be that Elijah "坐在那裏**為他自己**求死 *zuò zài nà lǐ wéi tā zì jǐ qiú sǐ* (sat down there and requested **for himself** that he might die)."

4.3.2.11.2 No equivalents for נֶפֶשׁ because a synonymous expression is used

This can be illustrated by 1 Chronicles 11:19a, where three leaders "冒死去打水 *mào sǐ qù dǎ shuǐ* (drew water at the risk of death)" for David. If translated literally, this Chinese text should say that three leaders "冒著生命的危險去打水 *mào zhe shēng mìng de wēi xiǎn qù dǎ shuǐ* (risked their **lives** to draw water)." Here, 冒死 *mào sǐ* and 冒著生命的危險 *mào zhe shēng mìng de wēi xiǎn* are synonymous, meaning "risk one's life."

---

236. Deut 28:65; Ruth 4:15.
237. Num 11:6; Lam 1:16.
238. Lev 26:16.
239. Isa 3:20.

4.3.3 Conclusion

In RCUV, in over one-third of its 754 occurrences, נֶפֶשׁ refers to "physical life" (נֶפֶשׁ as life in general appears rarely). It takes the meaning "heart" in some two hundred contexts. Its pronominal usage occurs about 115 times. Over one hundred appearances are translated as "person." In the remaining texts, נֶפֶשׁ is rendered as "living thing or creature," "corpse," "spirit-soul, soul or spirit," "breath," "throat," "desire or appetite," "energy," "body," "perfume," etc. Apparently, most interpretations of נֶפֶשׁ in RCUV fall within the range related to aspects of the human body.

In §4.2.4.8, drawing on the literature review on נֶפֶשׁ in the Hebrew OT, this study has concluded that its possible meanings are (1) breath, (2) living creature, person, (3) vital self (pronominal use, the whole being/person), (4) life, (5) desire, appetite, (6) corpse, body. These senses of נֶפֶשׁ signify that in the OT the term refers most often to the physical dimensions of humanity, as attested in RCUV.

Nonetheless, one finds several significant differences between the meanings of נֶפֶשׁ in the literature review (LR, see §4.2) and RCUV. First of all, "heart" in RCUV is one of the prominent renderings of נֶפֶשׁ, occurring about two hundred times (ca. fifty appearances in the Psalms); whereas, LR does not include "heart" as a possible meaning. LR ascribes the seat of thought, will, and feelings to "vital self" (pronominal usage of נֶפֶשׁ) or "the whole being/person" as Goldingay suggested, rather than "heart." Second, the semantic range of נֶפֶשׁ in LR is narrower than that in RCUV. Third, LR does not take נֶפֶשׁ as "soul or spirit" into consideration; RCUV has attempted to revise the translations of נֶפֶשׁ as "soul or spirit," but still retains these meanings in six passages. Finally, LR excludes the influence of etymology on the determination of the meaning of נֶפֶשׁ; RCUV seems to remain influenced by etymological considerations. For instance, RCUV renders נֶפֶשׁ as "throat," a meaning based on "rather remote Semitic languages" according to Smith.[240]

The divergence in the meanings of נֶפֶשׁ discussed above is further manifested by the divergence in the interpretations of נֶפֶשׁ among prominent Chinese and English versions. To this enterprise the present study now turns.

---

240. Smith, *Bible Doctrine of Man*, 8 n. 1.

4.4 The Divergence in the Interpretations of נֶפֶשׁ

4.4.1 Introduction

As noted above, Jacob affirms that נֶפֶשׁ is "as hard to define as it is to translate."[241] Thus, it is not surprising to see the divergence in its interpretation and translation.

4.4.2 The Divergence in the Interpretations of נֶפֶשׁ among Prominent Chinese and English Bible Versions

Space does not allow an exhaustive investigation, but a few selected texts illustrate this divergence.

4.4.2.1 נֶפֶשׁ in Genesis 2:7

In Genesis 2:7, God created Adam and he became נֶפֶשׁ חַיָּה, which is rendered as "有靈的活人 yǒu líng de huó rén (a living person with spirit)" (RCUV),[242] "有生命的人 yǒu shēng mìng de rén (a person with life)" (CCV, CCB, TCVRE), "有生命的活人 yǒu shēng mìng de huó rén (a living person with life)" (LZZ, NCV), "活物 wù (a living thing)" (CNET), "a living being" (NIV 2011, NASB 1995, NRSV), or "a living creature" (ESV, LEB). In this case, almost all versions reach a consensus in translating נֶפֶשׁ חַיָּה as a living person, being or creature, or a person with life. RCUV is the exception here, adding the notion of spirit. This does not seem warranted and is problematic, especially because in other occurrences (Gen 1:20, 21, 24, 30; 2:19; 9:10, 12, 15, 16; Lev 11:10, 46; Ezek 47:9) RCUV agrees with the other translations, with נֶפֶשׁ חַיָּה rendered as living beings or creatures.

Note that in 1 Corinthians 15:45 where this verse is quoted, the Greek ψυχὴν ζῶσαν is rendered as "有生命的人 yǒu shēng mìng de rén (a person with life)" (RCUV, CNV, CCV, CCB, TCVRE, DCT), "活的血氣人 huó de xuè qì rén (a living natural person)" (LZZ), "a living being" (NIV 2011, ESV, NRSV), "a living soul" (NASB 1995, LEV). The finding demonstrates

---

241. Jacob, "Anthropology of the Old Testament," 617.

242. The phrase in Gen 2:7 which alludes to the spirit in Adam is not נֶפֶשׁ חַיָּה, but "the breath of life" (נִשְׁמַת חַיִּים) of God. Such an interpretation could be substantiated by Job 32:8, which reads אָכֵן רוּחַ־הִיא בֶאֱנוֹשׁ וְנִשְׁמַת שַׁדַּי תְּבִינֵם (but there is a spirit in man, and the breath of the Almighty gives him understanding); see also Job 4:9; 27:3; 33:4; 34:14.

that prominent Chinese versions do not associate ψυχὴν with "soul" in this text, but with "a person with life" or "a living natural person."

It is worth noting that RCUV has "有靈的活人 yǒu líng de huó rén (a living person with spirit)" in Genesis 2:7, but "有生命的人 yǒu shēng mìng de rén (a person with life)" in 1 Corinthians 15:45. The inconsistency again demonstrates that its rendering of נֶפֶשׁ in Genesis 2:7 is problematic even though the translators added a footnote, indicating that the alternative rendering of נֶפֶשׁ חַיָּה is "有生命的人 yǒu shēng mìng de rén (a person with life)."

4.4.2.2 נֶפֶשׁ in Genesis 35:18

Genesis 35:18 has וַיְהִי בְּצֵאת נַפְשָׁהּ "as her נֶפֶשׁ was going out" (translated by the author), where נֶפֶשׁ is understood as "氣 qì (breath)" (RCUV, CNV, LZZ, TCVRE, CNET, NIV 2011), "靈魂 líng hún (spirit-soul)" (CCV, NASB 1995, ESV, NRSV), or "life" (LEB). The majority of major Chinese versions[243] view נֶפֶשׁ in this passage as "氣 qì (breath)" except for CCV, which has "靈魂 líng hún (soul)." More noteworthy is that while נֶפֶשׁ as breath in RCUV of 2010 is substituted for נֶפֶשׁ as soul in CUV, CCV, a new version published in 2014,[244] still translates נֶפֶשׁ in Genesis 35:18 as "soul," which is a poor translation as indicated above.

4.4.2.3 נֶפֶשׁ in 1 Samuel 18:1

1 Samuel 18:1 states that וְנֶפֶשׁ יְהוֹנָתָן נִקְשְׁרָה בְּנֶפֶשׁ דָּוִד. Here the נֶפֶשׁ of Jonathan and the נֶפֶשׁ of David are rendered as "心 xīn (heart)" (RCUV, CNV, LZZ, CNET),[245] "soul" (NASB 1995, ESV, NRSV, LEB), or "spirit" (NIV 2011). It is interesting that Chinese versions translate נֶפֶשׁ in this text as "heart," while English versions render it as "soul" except NIV 2011 which has "spirit."

---

243. In Gen 35:18, CCB and DCT have no corresponding word for נֶפֶשׁ.

244. At the time of the author's writing, CCV has translated the whole NT and the Pentateuch.

245. CCB translates this text as that Jonathan and David 一見如故 yī jiàn rú gù, meaning that Jonathan and David felt like old friends from their first meeting. TCVRE has "約拿單深深地被大衛所吸引 yuē ná dān shēn shēn dì bèi dà wèi suǒ xī yǐn (Jonathan was attracted by David profoundly)." No equivalents of נֶפֶשׁ can be found in both Chinese versions.

4.4.2.4 נֶפֶשׁ *in 1 Kings 17:21*

1 Kings 17:21 says that תָּשָׁב נָא נֶפֶשׁ־הַיֶּלֶד הַזֶּה עַל־קִרְבּוֹ "let this boy's נֶפֶשׁ return to him!" In this text, נֶפֶשׁ is translated as "生命 *shēng mìng* (life)" (RCUV, CNV, NIV 2011, NASB 1995, ESV, NRSV, LEV),[246] "魂 *hún* (soul)" or "靈魂 *líng hún* (spirit-soul)" (CUV, LZZ, TCVRE), "呼吸 *hū xī* (breath)" (CNET). The comparison shows that prominent English versions all understand נֶפֶשׁ in this text as "life." However, as the aforementioned literature review on נֶפֶשׁ indicates, the appropriate rendering of נֶפֶשׁ in this pericope is "氣息 *qì xī* (breath)" (see § 4.2.4.2).

4.4.2.5 נֶפֶשׁ *in Proverbs 2:10*

Proverbs 2:10 states that knowledge will be pleasant to נַפְשֶׁךָ. RCUV, CNV, LZZ, TCVRE, and CNET translate נַפְשֶׁךָ here as "你 *nǐ* (you)." CUV, CCB, and DCT translate it as "你的靈 *nǐ de líng* (your spirit)," NIV 2011, NASB 1995, ESV, NRSV, and LEV have "your soul." With great unanimity, the prominent English versions understand נֶפֶשׁ in this passage as "soul," which, as noted earlier, Brueggemann regards as an "unfortunate" translation. If so, its Chinese translation as "spirit" seems to be inappropriate as well.

4.4.2.6 נֶפֶשׁ *in Psalm 16:10*

Psalm 16:10 says that לֹא תַעֲזֹב נַפְשִׁי לִשְׁאוֹל "you will not abandon my נֶפֶשׁ to Sheol" (ESV), where נַפְשִׁי is translated as "我的靈魂 *wǒ de líng hún* (my soul)" (RCUV, CNV, CCB, DCT, NASB 1995, ESV, LEB), or "我 *wǒ* (me)" (LZZ, CNET, NIV 2011, NRSV). Acts 2:27 quotes this text as "οὐκ ἐγκαταλείψεις τὴν ψυχήν μου εἰς ᾅδην," where τὴν ψυχήν μου is rendered as "我的靈魂 (my soul)" (RCUV, CNV, LZZ, CCB, DCT, CNET, NASB 1995, ESV, NRSV, LEB), and "我 (me)" (NIV 2011). One can discern that RCUV, CNV, CCB, DCT, NASB 1995, ESV, LEB, and NIV 2011 interpret נַפְשִׁי and its Greek equivalent τὴν ψυχήν μου consistently.[247] The first seven versions have "my soul" and the last version has "me." By contrast, LZZ, CNET and NRSV have "me" for נַפְשִׁי, but "my soul" for τὴν ψυχήν μου.

---

246. CCB translates תָּשָׁב נָא נֶפֶשׁ־הַיֶּלֶד הַזֶּה עַל־קִרְבּוֹ as "求你讓這孩子活過來吧 *qiú nǐ ràng zhè hái zi huó guò lái ba* (Please let the child be alive)." Thus, there is no direct Chinese equivalent for נֶפֶשׁ.

247. Through the comparisons, one can see that the understanding of נֶפֶשׁ in the OT has had certain influence on the translation of the NT.

If the preceding literature review on נֶפֶשׁ in the OT and ψυχή in the NT is right (i.e. they never refer to immortal soul), then the interpretations of נַפְשִׁי and τὴν ψυχήν μου as "my soul" call for reconsideration.

4.4.2.7 נֶפֶשׁ *in Psalm 69:1*

Psalm 69:1 states הוֹשִׁיעֵנִי אֱלֹהִים כִּי בָאוּ מַיִם עַד נָפֶשׁ "Save me, O God, for the waters have come up to נָפֶשׁ," where נָפֶשׁ is viewed as "我 *wǒ* (me)" (RCUV, CNV, CCB, DCT), "我脖子 *wǒ bó zǐ* (my neck)" (LZZ, TCVRE, NIV 2011, ESV, NRSV), "我的咽喉 *wǒ de yān hóu* (my throat)" (CNET), or "my life" (NASB 1995). Obviously, the translators of various versions understand נֶפֶשׁ in this pericope differently. The versions that translate נֶפֶשׁ as "neck" or "throat" are probably influenced by etymological studies on נֶפֶשׁ as noted above.

4.4.2.8 נֶפֶשׁ *in Isaiah 53:11*

Isaiah 53:11 delineates the anguish or suffering of the Messiah's נֶפֶשׁ. RCUV, CCB, and CNET take the meaning "自己 *zì jǐ* (self)." CNV, LZZ, TCVRE, and LEV have "生命 *shēng mìng* (life)," "命 *mìng* (life)," or "一生 *yī shēng* (life)." NIV 2011 has "he," NRSV has "his," and NIV 1984, NASB 1995 and ESV have "soul." Again, the divergence in the rendering of נֶפֶשׁ in this text is obvious.

4.4.2.9 נֶפֶשׁ *in Isaiah 58:10*

Isaiah 58:10 says וְתָפֵק לָרָעֵב נַפְשֶׁךָ וְנֶפֶשׁ נַעֲנָה תַּשְׂבִּיעַ. The second נֶפֶשׁ in this text appears to be easier for the translators. All the important Chinese versions render it as "人 *rén* (person)," NIV 2011 and NRSV have "needs," NASB 1995, ESV, and LEV have "desire" or "appetite." However, the interpretation of the first נֶפֶשׁ is more challenging. RCUV, TCVRE, and CNET have no corresponding Chinese word for it; they respectively translate this text as "向飢餓的人施憐憫 *xiàng jī è de rén shī lián mǐn* (showing mercy to the hungry)," "假如你們給飢餓的人吃 *jiǎ rú nǐ men gěi jī è de rén chī* (if you let the hungry eat)," and "你必要主動的幫助 *nǐ bì yào zhǔ dòng de bāng zhù* (you must take the initiative to help)." LZZ, CCB, and NRSV translate נֶפֶשׁ here as "food," NIV 2011, NASB 1995, and ESV have "yourself" or "yourselves," LEB has "your soul."

Translating נֶפֶשׁ in this passage as "food" seems to be influenced by the meaning of *Akkadian napištu*, which means "sustenance."

4.4.2.10 נֶפֶשׁ *in Ezekiel 7:19*

Ezekiel 7:19 says that "silver and gold will not be able to deliver the Israelites . . . will not satisfy their נֶפֶשׁ or fill their stomachs." נֶפֶשׁ here is rendered as "食慾 *shí yù* (appetite)" (RCUV, NASB 1995), "慾望 *yù wàng* (desire)" (TCVRE), "心 *xīn* (heart)" (CNV, LZZ, CCB, CNET), "hunger" (NIV 2011, ESV, NRSV, LEB).[248] The majority of Chinese versions render נֶפֶשׁ in this verse as "heart" while English versions regard it as "appetite" or "hunger."

4.4.3 Conclusion

The foregoing investigation shows that the divergence in the interpretation of נֶפֶשׁ obviously exists in prominent Chinese and English Bible versions. The differences are illustrated in the following table (the Chinese interpretations are translated into English):

Reference	The text	The different interpretations of נֶפֶשׁ
Gen 2:7	נֶפֶשׁ חַיָּה	a living person with spirit, a person with life, a living person with life, a living thing, a living being, a living creature
Gen 35:18	נַפְשָׁהּ	her breath, her spirit-soul, her soul, her life
1 Sam 18:1	נֶפֶשׁ	heart, soul, spirit
1 Kgs 17:21	נֶפֶשׁ	life, soul, spirit-soul, breath
Prov 2:10	נַפְשְׁךָ	you, your spirit, your soul,
Ps 16:10	נַפְשִׁי	my soul, me
Ps 69:1	נֶפֶשׁ	me, my neck, my throat, my life
Isa 53:11	נַפְשׁוֹ	self, life, he, his, his soul
Isa 58:10	נַפְשְׁךָ	your food, yourself, yourselves, your soul, (no Chinese counterparts)
	נֶפֶשׁ	person, needs, desire, appetite
Ezek 7:19	נַפְשָׁם	appetite, desire, heart, hunger

---

248. LEB's footnote says, "Literally 'selves,' or 'desire.'"

The divergence in the interpretation of נֶפֶשׁ proves Jacob's statement: נֶפֶשׁ is "as hard to define as it is to translate."[249] However, if translators can delve into the study of נֶפֶשׁ in the OT (even its Greek equivalent ψυχή in the LXX and the NT) and exclude the influence of etymological studies because of its high occurrences in the OT, their translations might be more appropriate. This is the goal of the present study.

In conclusion, due to the divergence in the interpretations of נֶפֶשׁ in prominent Chinese and English Bible versions, many texts of the OT where this key term appears call for reconsideration. These occurrences need to be studied in and translated according to context.

In addition to the semantic considerations, which have been discussed in some detail, this study now has to examine the controversy over Watchman Nee's trichotomy.

4.5 The Controversy over Watchman Nee's Trichotomy

4.5.1 Introduction

In the Chinese Christian community, 宋尚節 Shàng Jiē Sòng, 王明道 Míng Dào Wáng, and 倪柝聲 Tuò Shēng Ní (Watchman Nee) are considered the three mighty servants of God who laid the foundation of the Chinese church.[250] Among them, Nee is "the most influential and contributive. His life is inspiring, and his writings are stimulating and very often controversial."[251] Xú points out that Nee's most controversial teaching is his tripartite theological anthropology,[252] in which the rendering of נֶפֶשׁ plays a critical role.

---

249. Jacob, "Anthropology of the Old Testament," 617.

250. Paul Siu, "The Doctrine of Man in the Theology of Watchman Nee," (master's thesis, Bethel Theological Seminary, 1979), 1; cf. Zēng 曾, "倪柝聲的神學人類學" [The theological anthropology of Watchman Nee], 162 n. 3.

251. Siu, "Doctrine of Man," 2.

252. Xú 徐, "倪柝聲的三元論思想探究" [An inquiry on the trichotomy theory of Watchman Nee], 47.

Thus, this section intends to explore (1) Nee's argument on the translations of נֶפֶשׁ/ψυχή and רוּחַ/πνεῦμα, (2) Nee's teaching on man as tripartite being, (3) the controversy caused by Nee's tripartite theological anthropology, and (4) a way to reduce the controversy.

4.5.2 Nee's Argument on the Translations of נֶפֶשׁ/ψυχή and רוּחַ/πνεῦμα

After examining the whole Chinese Bible (CUV) regarding the various translations of רוּחַ/πνεῦμα and נֶפֶשׁ/ψυχή, Nee, in his *The Spiritual Man*,[253] argues that failing to distinguish the rendering of נֶפֶשׁ/ψυχή from that of רוּחַ/πνεῦμα confuses Chinese Christians. The problem, for him, results from the Chinese Bible translators not sticking to the principle of literal translation rigidly.[254] He notes:

> Because the versions of the Bible we ordinarily use do not follow a literal translation of the words [רוּחַ/πνεῦμα] and [נֶפֶשׁ/ψυχή] in a strict way, readers find it difficult to differentiate between the two just by looking at the translated words. In translating the Bible, we should translate these words literally . . . Since God has used two different terms for the spirit and the soul, we should not confuse them.[255]

From Nee's perspective, the literal rendering of רוּחַ/πνεῦμα is "靈 *líng* (spirit)," and that of נֶפֶשׁ/ψυχή is "魂 *hún* (soul)."[256] However, in many cases, both רוּחַ/πνεῦμα and נֶפֶשׁ/ψυχή are translated as "靈魂 *líng hún* (spirit-soul)." Such a rendering increases the difficulty of distinguishing "靈 *líng* (spirit)" from "魂 *hún* (soul)" for readers, which, according to Nee, hinders believers from spiritual growth.[257] Nee contends:

---

253. Zēng 曾, in "倪柝聲的神學人類學" [The theological anthropology of Watchman Nee], 162, points out that *The Spiritual Man* has been the most classic work in the past century. None surpasses its influence on the Chinese church.

254. Nee, 屬靈人 [The spiritual man], 48.

255. Watchman Nee, *The Spiritual Man*, vol. 1 (Anaheim, CA: Living Stream Ministry, 1998), 5.

256. Nee, 屬靈人 [The spiritual man], 25, 28.

257. Nee, 47–48.

[The distinction between "靈 *líng* (spirit)" and "魂 *hún* (soul)" is of] great significance. It has much to do with the spiritual life of the believers. If believers do not know the boundary of their spirits, how can they understand the spiritual life? If they do not understand the spiritual life, how can they grow in their spiritual living? Because believers are either negligent or ignorant of the distinction between the spirit and the soul, they never grow in their spiritual life . . . If we mix up what God has separated, we are bound to suffer loss.[258]

Following Nee's teaching on literal translation, Witness Lee, an important fellow worker of Nee, composed the Recovery Version (NT), where πνεῦμα is translated as "靈 *líng* (spirit)" and ψυχή as "魂 *hún* (soul)" to the greatest extent.[259] Ráo opposes this translation, calling it a "死譯 *sǐ yì* (dead translation)" rather than a "直譯 *zhí yì* (literal translation)."[260] If Lee translated ψυχή as "魂 *hún* (soul)" only, he ignored the word's wealth of referents (see §4.2.5.3). Ironically, even in the Recovery Version (NT) itself, 42 percent of the occurrences of ψυχή are not rendered literally as "魂 *hún* (soul)."[261]

In conclusion, as mentioned earlier, Bible translations affect the accuracy of one's interpretation and understanding of God's Word. If Nee's understanding of literal translation is problematic, then his interpretations of רוּחַ/πνεῦμα and נֶפֶשׁ/ψυχή would be problematic as well. This implies that Nee's tripartite formulations in *The Spiritual Man*, where the preceding original terms play essential roles, are probably inaccurate. The following section is a glimpse into Nee's most controversial teaching: man as tripartite being.[262]

---

258. Nee, 3–4.
259. Ráo 饒, 屬靈人的再思 [Rethinking on "the spiritual person"], 28–29.
260. Ráo, 32.
261. Ráo, 33.
262. Xú 徐, "倪柝聲的三元論思想探究" [An inquiry on the trichotomy theory of Watchman Nee], 47, 49.

4.5.3 An Overview of Nee's Teaching on Man as Tripartite Being

In the very beginning of his most influential work, *The Spiritual Man*,[263] Nee spends over twenty pages to extensively list the various renderings of רוּחַ/πνεῦμα, נֶפֶשׁ/ψυχή, and בָּשָׂר/σάρξ in CUV.[264] He alleges that CUV fails to translate these terms literally and that believers confused by this are prevented from growing in spirituality. With his so-called literal translations of these anthropological terms in mind, and probably influenced by Jessie Penn-Lewis,[265] Nee bases his arguments first on 1 Thessalonians 5:23 and Hebrews 4:12 to elucidate his tripartite theological anthropology (i.e. the constitutional nature of human beings as body, soul, and spirit).[266]

For Nee, traditional Christian body-soul dualism is a belief stemming from the minds of fallen human beings, not from God. He notes that it is undoubtedly correct that the body is the outward shell of human beings, but the Bible never confuses spirit and soul as if the two refer to the same thing. For Nee, not only are spirit and soul different in terms, but also two different substances. Thus, the word of God does not separate human beings into two parts (body and soul), but rather into three: body, soul, and spirit[267] as he affirms while commenting on 1 Thessalonians 5:23:

> Here the apostle mentioned the believers' being sanctified "wholly." This means that the whole being of the believers is to be sanctified. What did he mean when he said that a person is to be sanctified wholly? He meant that a person's spirit, soul,

---

263. Roberts views *The Spiritual Man* as "the single most comprehensive statement" of Nee's doctrine of man, though there are four equally important studies on anthropology by Nee: *The Release of the Spirit, The Normal Christian Life, Spiritual Reality or Obsession, The Latent Power of the Soul*. See Dana Roberts, *Understanding Watchman Nee: The Newest Book on Watchman Nee* (Plainfield, NJ: Logos-Haven Books, 1980), 75.

264. Nee, 屬靈人 [The spiritual man], 25–48. These detailed listings are omitted in the English translation of *The Spiritual Man* (1998).

265. Dongsheng John Wú, "Watchman Nee on Revelation: Gnosticism or Divine Illumination Tradition?," 2013, 2, accessed 12 November 2014, http://www.christiansquare.org:8081/criasia/research/paper/2013-03.pdf; Dongsheng John Wú, *Understanding Watchman Nee: Spirituality, Knowledge, and Formation*, Kindle edition. (Eugene, OR: Wipf & Stock, 2012), ch. 3; Xú 徐, "倪柝聲的三元論思想探究 [An inquiry on the trichotomy theory of Watchman Nee], 44.

266. Nee, 屬靈人 [The spiritual man], 47–48.

267. Nee, 47.

and body are to be preserved complete . . . This verse also tells us clearly that there is a distinction between the spirit and the soul. Otherwise, it would not have said "your spirit *and* soul." Instead, it would have said "your spirit-soul."[268]

For Nee, Hebrews 4:12 is another critical text to substantiate his tripartite concept:

> Just as a priest divided up a whole sacrifice and cut it apart with a knife so that nothing remained hidden, in the same way the Lord Jesus divides those who belong to Him, through the word of God; He pierces and divides every part, whether it be the spiritual, the soulish, or the physical. Since the soul and the spirit can be divided, the two must not be the same thing. Hence, this portion of the Word also considers man to be composed of three elements: the spirit, the soul, and the body.[269]

Pamudji points out that "most trichotomists use 1 Thess 5:23, Heb 4:12 and Gen 2:7 as the central texts to prove their position. Nee is no exception."[270] In his interpretation of Genesis 2:7, Nee argues that the dust of the earth and the breath of God correspond respectively to the body and the spirit of Adam. He views the pre-fallen Adamic nature as the coming together of these two elements (body and spirit), which gives birth to a third element (i.e. the human soul).[271]

Similar to Penn-Lewis, Nee ascribes specific functions for each of these three entities.[272] The body is the "world-consciousness," enabling human beings to communicate with the material world.[273] The soul with its intellect

---

268. Nee, *The Spiritual Man,* vol. 1, 3.

269. Nee, 4–5.

270. P. Pamudji, "Little Flock Trilogy: A Critique of Watchman Nee's Principal Thought on Christ, Man, and the Church" (doctoral diss., Drew University, 1985), 107.

271. Nee, 屬靈人 [The spiritual man], 48–49.

272. Wú, *Understanding Watchman Nee,* ch. 3.

273. Roberts observes that Nee delves into the complexities of the spirit and the soul at length, but does not invest much time in the body. See Dana Roberts, *Secrets of Watchman Nee: His Life, His Teachings, His Influence* (Orlando, FL: Bridge-Logos, 2005), 127. This is, for Chow, because he does not see the latter as important as the former. See Alexander Chow, *Theosis, Sino-Christian Theology and the Second Chinese Enlightenment: Heaven and Humanity in Unity* (New York, NY: Palgrave Macmillan, 2013), 51.

and affections is the "self-consciousness." It belongs to a person's own self and reveals his/her personality. The soul's three natural functions are thinking, willing, and feeling. On the other hand, the spirit is the part with which human beings communicate with God, worship him, serve him, and understand their relationship with him. Thus, it is termed as the part with "God-consciousness." Human beings' spirit has three functions: conscience, intuition, and fellowship. Hence, God dwells in the spirit; the self in the soul; and the senses in the body.[274]

Indeed, Nee sees a hierarchy in these three elements: "Among the three elements of man, the spirit is joined to God and is the highest. The body is in contact with the material world and is the lowest. In-between the two is the soul . . . [which is] the linkage of the other two parts."[275]

Though the body, for Nee, is not comparable in its dignity to the spirit, it is needed and crucial "otherwise, God would not have given man a body."[276] The fact that God the Son became flesh and remains in bodily form forever demonstrates the value and importance of the physical body. Accordingly, Nee contends that full salvation includes the salvation of body, soul, and spirit.[277]

In his other significant work, *The Release of the Spirit*,[278] Nee reminds readers that the ability to employ one's spirit (i.e. inward man)[279] relies on "the two-fold work of God: The breaking of the outward man [soul]. And the dividing of spirit and soul – the separating of [one's] inward man from the outward."[280] Nee connects the breaking of the outward man to the cross.

---

274. Nee, *The Spiritual Man*, vol. 1, 8, 15, 20.

275. Nee, 9.

276. Watchman Nee, *The Spiritual Man*, vol. 3 (Anaheim, CA: Living Stream Ministry, 1998), 659.

277. Nee, *Spiritual Man*, 660; Róng Hóng Lín 林榮洪, 屬靈神學: 倪柝聲思想的研究 [The spiritual theology of Watchman Nee], 3rd ed. (Hong Kong: Chinese Alliance Press, 2003), 72.

278. In the sixty-six volumes of Nee's collected works, *The Spiritual Man* is the only book Nee wrote at the age of twenty-five. See Siu, "Doctrine of Man," 2. The rest of his works are usually "compiled from his sermons and from articles he wrote for newspapers, periodicals, or other special publications." See Wú, *Understanding Watchman Nee*, Introduction.

279. Nee uses the terms "inner man," "outer man," and "outermost man" to denote spirit, soul, and body respectively. See Watchman Nee, *The Release of the Spirit* (Richmond, VA: Christian Fellowship Publishers, 2000 [1955]), 12.

280. Nee, *Release of the Spirit*, 34.

He argues that it is the cross that "reduces the outward man to death. It splits open the human shell," and breaks the outward man – one's opinions, ways, cleverness, self-love, selfish interests, etc. As soon as one's outward man is broken, one's spirit is capable of coming forth readily.[281]

Once the outward man (soul) is broken, one needs to deal with another essential issue. That is, the inward man (spirit) and the outward man are "so intertwined together that what influences the outward also impacts the inward."[282] Nee notes that the only way to divide the inward from the outward is the revelation of the Holy Spirit (Heb 4:12).[283]

4.5.4 The Controversy Caused by Nee's Tripartite Theological Anthropology

As has been seen earlier, Nee's trichotomy is a dominant anthropologic perspective accepted in the contemporary church of China, affecting, by some estimates, up to 70 percent of Chinese Christians.[284] The exploration of Nee's extensive influence is beyond the scope of this research, but the controversy caused by his teaching on trichotomy is worthy of notice. In what follows, the present author will provide some examples of the theological debate from Chinese Christian academia.

In his *The Spiritual Theology of Watchman Nee*, Lín affirms Nee's contribution on the indigenization of Christian theology.[285] But Lín, like many others, rather holds a holistic view of man,[286] maintaining that the distinction between body, soul, and spirit derives from Greek philosophy, rather than from the teaching in the Bible.[287]

Zēng notes that Nee's "biblical psychology" (mortifying the soul and the body, so that the spirit could be released) is a concept "unconsciously"

---

281. Nee, 17–18.
282. Nee, 32.
283. Nee, 34.
284. Lǐ 李, 永活上帝生命主 [The living God as the master of life], 309.
285. Lín 林, 屬靈神學: 倪柝聲思想的研究 [The spiritual theology of Watchman Nee], 278.
286. For more discussions on a holistic view of man, see Lǐ 李, "聖經研究對於整全人觀的提示" [Implications of current biblical research on a holistic view of man], 109–126.
287. Lín 林, 屬靈神學: 倪柝聲思想的研究 [The spiritual theology of Watchman Nee], 280.

influenced by the thought of the Taoist tradition.[288] Such an indigenized theological anthropology, Zēng asserts, explains the reason why Nee's trichotomy is widely accepted in the Chinese church community.[289] Unfortunately, Nee's teaching "has an extensive impact on the Chinese Christians' negative attitude towards this world," such as anti-intellectualism.[290]

Liào suggests that Nee's tripartite anthropology and his doctrine of sanctification may result in believers' uncertainty about their salvation.[291] Moreover, Nee's pessimistic arguments about the world lead to the Chinese church's emphasis on the salvation of human spirit-soul, resulting in the negligence of Christian responsibility in society.[292] Although there is no evidence that Nee's tripartite anthropology derives from Gnosticism of the second and third centuries, the similarity and connection between them are evident.[293]

In a similar vein, Liáng points out that Nee's trichotomous anthropology and its resultant spiritual theology can be termed "Chinese Gnosticism,"[294] indicating that his formulations share much in common with heretical Gnosticism. However, at the end of his article "Watchman Nee on Revelation: Gnosticism or Divine Illumination Tradition?," Wú writes: "[W]e have concluded that the suspicion of Gnostic orientation in Nee's view is in fact not grounded,[295] and that Nee's major theological convictions

---

288. Zēng 曾, "倪柝聲的神學人類學" [The theological anthropology of Watchman Nee,] 160.

289. Zēng, 183.

290. Zēng, 160.

291. Yuán Wēi Liào 廖元威, "倪柝聲三元論人觀" [Watchman Nee's tripartite anthropology], *China and the Gospel Journal* 3, no. 1 (2003): 69.

292. Liao 廖, "倪柝聲三元論人觀" [Watchman Nee's tripartite anthropology], 66.

293. Liào, 64.

294. Jiā Lín Liáng 梁家麟, "華人諾斯底主義的屬靈觀: 倪拓聲 '人的破碎與靈的出來' 研讀" [The spiritual perspective of a Chinese Gnosticism: Studies on Watchman Nee's 'the breaking of the outer man and the release of the spirit'], in 倪拓聲的榮辱升黜 [Watchman Nee: His glory and dishonor] (Hong Kong: Graceful House, 2004), 189, 197; see also Chóng Róng Táng 唐崇榮, 聖靈的引導: 動力的生活 [The guidance of the Holy Spirit: A life full of impetus] (Taipei: Zhōng Fú Publishing, 2004), 65. This accusation may result from Nee's disparagement of the body, which may adversely affect one's concept of the humanity of Christ and the reality or genuineness of his incarnation.

295. Wú quotes Lín's argument (屬靈神學: 倪柝聲思想的研究 [The spiritual theology of Watchman Nee], 71–72) to dismiss the suspicion of Gnostic orientation in Nee's teaching: "While Nee believes that the body is not comparable in its dignity to the spirit, he nonetheless affirms the importance of the body because of the incarnation of Jesus, and

on revelation and illumination have strong parallels with related aspects of the Christian spiritual tradition."[296] Wú, though defending Nee, admits that "there is not enough biblical support for viewing spirit, soul, and body as three different *entities* in the human person."[297]

Yáng notes that Nee's trichotomy not only diminishes the value of all created by God, but also denies the importance of psychology, culture, and art, etc. For Nee, everything developed by the human intellect needs to be rejected, such as science, music, and literature. Human beings should only pursue "spiritual" things. Yet, as Yáng suggests, once "spirituality" is lifted above all else (被架空 *bèi jià kōng*), the "spiritual" life becomes impracticable in daily life.[298]

Indeed, the debate caused by Nee's tripartite theological anthropology is not yet resolved. Certainly, one of the reasons for this is the problematic translations of נֶפֶשׁ/ψυχή in various Chinese versions. Seen through the lens of Bible translation, a reconsideration of these biblical terms may help reduce this controversy.

4.5.5 A Way to Reduce the Controversy

No one can deny Nee is right in emphasizing the importance of correct Bible translation. Regrettably, his understanding of "literal" translation is incorrect, resulting in problematic renderings of God's Word and inaccurate interpretations of it. For example, almost all contemporary prominent Chinese and English versions except RCUV translate נֶפֶשׁ חַיָּה in Genesis 2:7 as "a living person/being/creature/thing," instead of "a living soul." RCUV, which has "靈 *líng* (spirit)" for נֶפֶשׁ, also adds a footnote to suggest an alternative rendering: "a living person (or a person with life)." Obviously, Genesis 2:7 as one of the three central texts for Nee's trichotomy can no longer be used to support his teaching.

---

because during his earthly life Jesus did care about the human body's needs and healings . . . Nee maintains that full salvation includes the salvation of spirit, soul, and body."

296. Wú, "Watchman Nee on Revelation," 21.

297. Wú, 21.

298. Qìng Qiú Yáng 楊慶球, 會遇系統神學 [Encountering systematic theology] (Hong Kong: China Graduate School of Theology, 2001), 75.

Moving beyond the OT texts, rendering ψυχή as "魂 *hún* (soul)" in 1 Thessalonians 5:23 and Hebrews 4:12 is also problematic,[299] considerably weakening Nee's trichotomous teaching based on them. Therefore, one of the promising ways to reduce the controversy caused by Nee is probably to reconsider the translation of נֶפֶשׁ in the OT and that of ψυχή in the NT.

4.5.6 Conclusion

This example concerning Nee demonstrates how important it is to interpret and translate Scripture accurately. To avoid misinterpretations and even false doctrine on theological anthropology, it is crucial to determine the meaning of key anthropological terms like נֶפֶשׁ in the OT and to render them contextually.

4.6 A Call for Reconsidering the Translation of נֶפֶשׁ

The reasons for reconsidering the translation of the Hebrew word נֶפֶשׁ are as follows:

As shown in the various discussions above, נֶפֶשׁ is a key term with many meanings that cannot be rendered by one word such as "soul."

Today, with advances in linguistics and theories of Bible translation, one knows that a word cannot be rendered only by a dictionary reading, or even a word coming from an etymological explanation. Rather, such words must be examined in context; their various meanings determined and then rendered in the TL (this needs a careful investigation of the semantic range of each potential local equivalent). In the process of Bible translation, various critical criteria should be used, e.g. the comparison with ancient translations (i.e. the LXX and Targumim) and other versions as well. However, the most crucial factor for a translator is to examine a word's use and meaning in a given context before searching for a rendering in the TL.

A review of the literature and an examination of a number of various texts (§4.2) have shown that נֶפֶשׁ does have some possible meanings: (1) breath, (2) living creature, person, (3) vital self (pronominal use, the whole being/person), (4) life (especially physical life in Chinese), (5) desire, appetite, (6)

---

299. See §4.2.5.3.1 and §4.2.5.3.4

corpse, body. Such semantic range of נֶפֶשׁ is narrower than that in DCH and RCUV (§4.3), both of which have more than ten possible meanings for נֶפֶשׁ. Thus, it is necessary to reconsider its translation and determine its semantic range in the OT.

In the case of Nee, it is clear that his tripartite theological anthropology was developed by consulting erroneous translations[300] and his misunderstanding as to what constitutes literal translation. These erroneous translations have led to inaccurate interpretations of God's Word and incredible controversy. Clearly, the way to reduce some of the controversy resulting from Nee's trichotomy is to identify the meanings and uses of נֶפֶשׁ in the OT and to ensure they are rendered correctly.

It is surprising to note that although the renderings of נֶפֶשׁ in CUV, the most popular, authoritative and influential Bible version in contemporary Chinese Christian communities, are criticized by Nee, some of CUV's translations of נֶפֶשׁ directly or indirectly reinforce Chinese believers' acceptance of Nee's tripartite anthropology. An example is the translations of נֶפֶשׁ as "靈魂 *líng hún* (spirit-soul)" or "靈 *ling* (spirit)"[301] in CUV (twenty-seven times in total). Among them, twenty-three appearances refer to "靈魂 *líng hún* (spirit-soul)"; four appearances denote "靈 *ling* (spirit)" (e.g. Gen 2:7).[302] According to the present author's observation, for ordinary Chinese believers who only know Nee's trichotomy superficially, but never delve into his teaching, such renderings reinforce his tripartite formulation as biblical truth. Put differently, CUV produces twenty-seven texts which delineate human beings as "靈 *ling* (spirit)" or "靈魂 *líng hún* (spirit-soul)."

As noted above, CUV was revised in 2010, but its revised version (RCUV) still preserves such renderings of נֶפֶשׁ as "靈 *ling* (spirit)," "靈魂 *líng hún* (spirit-soul)," or even "魂 *hún* (soul)" in six texts. The most noteworthy case is Genesis 2:7, where נֶפֶשׁ is still translated as "靈 *ling* (spirit)."

---

300. For example, נֶפֶשׁ as "魂 *hún* (soul)" in Gen 2:7.

301. According to MCD, the semantic ranges of "靈 *ling* (spirit)," "靈魂 *líng hún* (spirit-soul)," or "魂 *hún* (soul)" overlap. The latter two especially can be viewed as synonymous.

302. Ráo 饒, 屬靈人的再思 [Rethinking on "the spiritual person"], 240.

The Possible Meanings of the Hebrew Word נֶפֶשׁ in the OT

As discussed in §1.1, נֶפֶשׁ as "心 *xīn* (heart)" in CUV (ca. 180 times)[303] or RCUV (over 160 times) is perhaps another reason why Nee's trichotomy is so popular among Chinese Christians.

It is worth noting that the book of Psalms has the highest occurrence of נֶפֶשׁ in the OT (144 times), and that about one-third of the cases is translated as "心 *xīn* (heart)." If the translations of נֶפֶשׁ as "靈 *líng* (spirit)," "魂 *hún* (soul)" or "靈魂 *líng hún* (spirit-soul)" need to be revised, its rendering as "心 *xīn* (heart)," then, needs reconsideration as well. This is because one could argue that the trichotomy of "靈, 魂, 體 *líng, hún, tǐ* (spirit, soul, body)" is almost synonymous to that of "靈, 心, 身 *líng, xīn, shēn* (spirit, heart, body)"[304] in Chinese understanding. The latter is prevailing and common in Chinese thinking.[305]

Furthermore, although both נֶפֶשׁ and לֵבָב refer to the seat of thought, will, and feelings, the former puts more emphasis on the vital self, the *intensity* of feelings within the whole person as suggested earlier. Actually, in Chinese, "整個人 *zhěng gè rén* (the whole person)" is a phrase that grasps this Hebrew concept of נֶפֶשׁ better than "心 *xīn* (heart)." For example, Chinese people describe a person who is extremely eager for something as "整個人陷進去 . . . *zhěng gè rén xiàn jìn qù* . . . (The whole person is trapped in . . .)." In this case, "心 *xīn* (heart)" cannot express the intensity of feelings vividly. Similarly, translating נֶפֶשׁ as "心 *xīn* (heart)" in some contexts fails to convey the Hebrew concept faithfully or vividly. In addition, in the construction נֶפֶשׁ בְּכָל־לֵבָב וּבְכָל־נֶפֶשׁ, is never rendered as "心 *xīn* (heart)" in prominent Chinese Bible versions.

Finally, the necessity of reconsidering the renderings of נֶפֶשׁ as "心 *xīn* (heart)," or as "靈 *líng* (spirit)," "魂 *hún* (soul)" or "靈魂 *líng hún* (spirit-soul)" is because none of them convey the nuances of נֶפֶשׁ according to the findings from the preceding literature review and TDOT.

In brief, through the discussions above, one realizes that some problematic Chinese translations of נֶפֶשׁ indeed call for reconsideration. This is

---

303. Ráo, 240.

304. As noted in §1.1, the common word order of "靈, 心, 身 *líng, xīn, shēn* (spirit, heart, body)" is "身, 心, 靈 *shēn, xīn, líng* (body, heart, spirit)."

305. Zēng 曾, "倪柝聲的神學人類學" [The theological anthropology of Watchman Nee], 164.

precisely the task that is conducted in the next chapter through an intergenerational Bible translation team, mainly focusing on the book of Psalms with the highest occurrence of נֶפֶשׁ in the OT.

CHAPTER 5

Translating נֶפֶשׁ in the Psalms into Chinese: An Exercise in Intergenerational, Literary Bible Translation

5.1 Introduction

As discussed in chapter 3, one of the crucial components for churches to effectively develop intentional intergenerational ministry (IIM) is to find a Bible version readable for readers of all ages, including children.

Since the late 1970s, "translation studies" has been undergoing a renaissance in China.[1] However, none of the current Chinese Bible versions is produced through applying a specific, systematic translation theory (§2.2.4). The importance of the enterprise of Bible translation and translators' understanding of translation theory was seen in the discussion of Watchman Nee (§4.5.2). His misunderstanding of the so-called literal translation method led to his misinterpretation of נֶפֶשׁ, upon which his tripartite anthropology is based. Nee's trichotomy is a widely accepted but controversial theological viewpoint; it has led to a very negative attitude towards many elements in this world (§4.5.4). Regretfully, the translations of נֶפֶשׁ in CUV, the most popular and authoritative Chinese Bible version in the contemporary Chinese Christian community, seem to make Nee's teaching more acceptable. Thus, it is necessary to reconsider its Chinese translations through

---

1. Gentzler, "A Global View of Translation Studies," 117.

a specific, systematic translation approach (see §4.6 for more reasons for the reconsideration).

In order to carry out this study, three psalms have been selected (Pss 35, 63, and 107) and Wendland's Literary Functional Equivalence (LiFE)[2] approach has been chosen for this translation exercise, partly due to its primary assumption that the Bible is literature.

Since a complete Bible translation project[3] is beyond the scope of the present research, some boundaries have to be set. According to Wendland, there are "three essential operations involved in the production of a Bible translation[4] – composition, contextualization,[5] and consultation."[6] The current exercise mainly concentrates on the first critical operation – composition, a process which concerns "the preparation of the actual translated text of Scripture."[7] This step can first be carried out by a single member of

---

2. As noted in chapter 2, Wendland, in his *LiFE-Style Translating*, 126–148, proposes a ten-step exegetical methodology to achieve a poetic LiFE translation. He notes that "various modifications could be made to the ten steps in terms of composition and order of arrangement, and perhaps several steps could be combined into one." In the researcher's exegeses on the three selected psalms, Wendland's exegetical steps have been combined into one as presented in Appendix A except for step 4, 6, 9, which are put in Appendix B, C, D respectively. These appendixes (not included in this book) are available at South African Theological Seminary.

3. In his LiFE project, Wendland recommends the following procedures: project preparation (e.g. the formulation of a translation *Brief*), selection of translators, popular education, supplementary helps, project organization, community interaction, and product evaluation. His special aim is to "encourage a higher level of target audience involvement in the production of a more idiomatically expressed, rhetorically phrased, artistically toned version of the Scriptures in a local vernacular language." See Wendland, *Translating the Literature of Scripture*, 377–379.

4. Wendland, *LiFE-Style Translating*, 406.

5. Contextualization is related to "the various methods of providing the target audience with the conceptual background knowledge needed to correctly understand and apply the translated text." See Wendland, *LiFe-Style Translating*, 406. This process of contextualizing a biblical text through supplementary aids relies extraordinarily on the participation of a target audience (Wendland, 406). Supplementary aids are a variety of paratextual tools such as "book and chapter introductions, sectional headings, cross-references, a glossary or mini-dictionary, maps, diagrams, timelines, illustrations, and footnotes or margin notes" (Wendland, 376).

6. Consultation "involves the translation staff (a team of translators plus their advisers and reviewers), the administrative committee that is overseeing and facilitating the project, and members of the general public for whom the version at hand is being prepared – the TL audience/readership." See Wendland, *LiFe-Style Translating*, 407.

7. Wendland, 406.

a translation team to produce a basic draft, followed by the team assessing the initial trial draft.[8]

Following this method, the present author first composed a basic draft of the three selected psalms according to LiFE.[9] Then, the initial draft was submitted to the present advisers for revision. These constitute the first half of the operation of composition in this translation exercise. The language of this draft is similar to that used in CUV because the present researcher intended to demonstrate that CUV is hard for children to read, and thus that a more accessible version is needed. In the second half of the operation of composition, based on the revised draft, the task of producing a more artistic and readable version for all generations through a LiFE approach[10] was conducted by the intergenerational Bible translation team (IBTT)[11] that was trained by the present researcher. Another main task for the IBTT was to assess the accuracy of the translations of נֶפֶשׁ in the three selected psalms.

In accordance with the preceding arguments, this chapter begins with the summary of the training course for the IBTT, followed by the exercise of intergenerational Bible translation of Psalms 35, 63, and 107.

---

8. Wendland, 148; Wendland, *Translating the Literature of Scripture*, 295, 297.

9. In terms of LiFE, the most appropriate Chinese literary genre for Hebrew psalms is Chinese new poetry (新詩 *xīn shī*) from the present researcher's perspective. New poetry has been developed since May Fourth Movements of 1919 in China. See Guó Róng Féng 馮國榮, 新詩譜: 新詩格式創制研究 [The spectrum of new poetry: A study on the forms of new poetry] (Běi jīng: People's Publishing House, 2010), 1. New poetry has similarities with Hebrew psalms. For example, both of them can be composed with flexibility. Sometimes, they look like prose; sometimes, their structure demonstrates neat parallelism. For an overall exploration on the forms of new poetry, see Féng 馮, 新詩譜 [The spectrum of new poetry].

10. There is a slight modification in the LiFE approach when taking the *Skopos* (purpose) of the present translation exercise into consideration; namely, to produce a more artistic and readable Bible version for both young and adult readers. Thus, in cases where the more literary-poetic phrases cannot be grasped by young readers, even with the help of immediate context or illustrations, etc., the IBTT will replace them with other easier, but still beautiful substitutes.

11. The biblical, theological, theoretical and social-scientific foundations for the IBTT, see chapter 3.

5.2 The Training Course for the Intergenerational Bible Translation Team

Since involving different generations, including children, in the exercise of Bible translation is a pioneering initiative, the participants' experience with intergenerational learning is crucial to make the translation exercise run smoothly. Thus, the researcher herself, a homeschooling mother, found it suitable to convene homeschooling families to participate in this exercise. Thus, all participants are familiar with such a learning atmosphere and environment. The task of recruiting the IBTT was entrusted to Mujen Home Educators Association, the largest homeschooling community in Taiwan. Potential participants had to meet the following requirements:

- Experience with intergenerational learning
- Regular church attendance
- Interest in learning about biblical Hebrew and Bible translation

The IBTT comprised thirteen members including the present researcher (four children, four teenagers, and four adults whose ages range from seven to fifty-one years old). As suggested by Wendland, the IBTT needed to receive a basic training. The curriculum[12] for the team designed by the author is as follows:

- An overview of IIM
- An overview of Chinese Bible translation history
- An overview of the LiFE approach
- An introduction to biblical Hebrew
- An introduction to the book of Psalms
- The possible meanings of the Hebrew word נֶפֶשׁ

After receiving the basic training, the IBTT led by the present researcher was ready to engage in the exercise of the intergenerational Bible translation. Its tasks were to assess the accuracy of the translations of נֶפֶשׁ and to produce a more artistic and readable Bible version for all generations through the application of the LiFE approach.

The process of the translation exercise in each class consisted of:

---

12. Since the IBTT consists of different age groups, including children, some creative teaching methods were used in the training courses, such as language-learning games.

Before class: taking the researcher's draft of each psalm, grade 1 students[13] highlighted words, phrases, or sentences that were beyond their understanding. As noted, young children might have some limitations in their reading comprehension, but their ability to speak is sufficient for most types of discussion. This part of the exercise was done with the help of adults who read the initial draft to children without too much explanation.

During class:[14] The researcher first guided the IBTT to go through the structure of the selected psalms in the hope that the team could see the whole picture of the psalms before delving into the details. Then, the researcher led the team to read the psalms word for word in Hebrew and to do the parsing selectively due to the limitation of time and children's comprehension. Next, critical grammatical or syntactical issues were explained when needed. This was followed by the exploration of the literary devices used in the selected Hebrew psalms.

After the preceding warm-ups, the team's brainstorming time mainly focused on three dimensions: (a) determining the appropriate meaning of נֶפֶשׁ in each occurrence in the selected psalms; (b) suggesting Chinese counterparts corresponding to the literary devices employed in the selected Hebrew psalms; (c) identifying easier alternatives for the words, phrases, or sentences incomprehensible for grade 1 students.

After class: the assignments for the team members were (a) reviewing the translated psalms, and (b) re-thinking or re-examining the translations derived from the discussion in the class and then handing in their further suggestions, if any, to the researcher before the next class.

Wrapping up: the researcher gathered the opinions from the assignments completed by the participants and integrated the most appropriate ones into the IBTT version (IBTTV) produced in class. Then, the revised version was presented and finalized in the next class.

---

13. In order to better grasp as to what extent grade 1 students can understand from the Bible, the researcher invited a grade 1 student (not among the team members) to read the initial draft one-on-one before the actual exercise of the IBTT.

14. The handouts used in the class included: (1) the structure of the selected psalms and (2) the Hebrew-Chinese interlinear with complete Chinese and English translations of the selected psalms produced by the researcher.

After the brief description of the training course, the remainder of this chapter delves into the three selected psalms and reports the results gleaned from the exercise of the intergenerational Bible translation.

5.3 The Exercise in Intergenerational, Literary Bible Translation

For each psalm, after a brief presentation of the overall structure, each sub-section consists of two focal points related to the translation enterprise:

- The appropriate translation of נֶפֶשׁ, which begins with (1) the literature review on the existing translations of נֶפֶשׁ in each occurrence of the three selected psalms, followed by (2) the exploration/discussion/comment of the IBTT on the translation.
- The version readable for all generations by the IBTT through the LiFE approach, which is the section consisting of (1) tables, which compare the initial draft by the present researcher (the language used in the draft is similar to that of CUV)[15] with the revised version by the IBTT, and (2) notes, which focus on prominent issues, such as literary devices, the choice of easier words, phrases, and sentences for children.

Due to the limitation of space, the following exploration or discussion will only concentrate on the sections where נֶפֶשׁ occurs. Space also does not allow the present researcher to include the complete and interesting discussion of the IBTT, which have been recorded during the class. Mostly, only the results of the discussion are reported in this paper. The processes of the discussion are only presented selectively.

5.3.1 Psalm 35

Psalm 35, a psalm of petition, is structured as follows:

- Section 1 (vv. 1–3): The petition for divine help and deliverance (×1)[16]

---

15. As noted above, this is to demonstrate that CUV is not easy for children, which makes it necessary to produce a new version readable for children.

16. The numerals in the parentheses indicate the number of occurrences of נֶפֶשׁ in that section.

- Section 2 (vv. 4–8): The expectations of retribution for the enemies (×2)
- Section 3 (vv. 9–10): The promise to praise Yahweh for deliverance (×1)
- Section 4 (vv. 11–16): The lament over the enemies repaying good for evil (×2)
- Section 5 (v. 17): The lament on the need for divine deliverance (×1)
- Section 6 (v. 18): The promise to praise Yahweh publicly
- Section 7 (vv. 19–21): The petition not to allow the false enemies to triumph
- Section 8 (vv. 22–26): The petition for Yahweh's righteous judgment to humiliate the enemies (×1)
- Section 9 (vv. 27–28): The promise to praise Yahweh continually

Within this song of petition, the Hebrew word נֶפֶשׁ occurs eight times.

5.3.1.1 Section 1 of Psalm 35 (vv. 1–3)

In this section expressing the psalmist's petition for divine help and deliverance, נֶפֶשׁ occurs once (v. 3).

5.3.1.1.1 The appropriate translation of נֶפֶשׁ in Psalm 35:3

5.3.1.1.1.1 The existing translations

In Psalm 35:3, CUV renders נֶפֶשׁ as "靈魂 *líng hún* (spirit-soul)," and NIV 1984[17] as "soul." However, in their revised editions (i.e. RCUV of 2010 and NIV 2011 respectively), נֶפֶשׁ is rendered as "我 *wǒ* (me)," which is the translation used in the prominent Chinese versions,[18] such as CNV, LZZ, TCVRE, CCB, CNET, DCT.

---

17. This chapter mainly uses Chinese versions for comparison. English versions are referred to only when needed.

18. The prominent Chinese versions in this chapter are related to Bible versions produced by Christians (There are several versions produced by Catholics). They are CUV, RCUV, CNV, LZZ, TCVRE, CCB, CNET, DCT. Though there are some other important versions, such as CCV and CSBT, their translations on the Psalms were not available at the time of the researcher's writing.

5.3.1.1.1.2 The exploration/discussion/comment of the IBTT

For the IBTT, נֶפֶשׁ as "我 wǒ (me)" here is an appropriate rendering. In this section, the psalmist pleads for Yahweh's help and deliverance. In the context of the dialogue between the psalmist and Yahweh (though imaginary), the first personal pronoun rendered here can well present the psalmist as an independent individual who is pleading.[19]

5.3.1.1.2 The version readable for all generations by the IBTT through LiFE

The following table demonstrates the differences of Chinese translations between the initial draft by the researcher and IBTTV. The differences are marked in bold.

Section 1 (vv. 1–3): The Petition for Divine Help and Deliverance	
IBTTV	**The Initial Draft**
01a. 耶和華啊，與我相爭的，[求你與他們]相爭！ (Same as the right column)	耶和華啊，與我相爭的，[求你與他們]相爭！ *yē hé huá ā, yǔ wǒ xiàng zhēng de, [qiú nǐ yǔ tā men] xiàng zhēng*! Contend, Yahweh, with those who contend with me;
01b. 與我**戰鬥**的，[求你與他們]**戰鬥**！ *yǔ wǒ zhàn dòu de, [qiú nǐ yǔ tā men] zhàn dòu*! **fight** against those who **fight** against me.	與我**爭戰**的，[求你與他們]**爭戰**！ *yǔ wǒ zhēng zhàn de, [qiú nǐ yǔ tā men] zhēng zhàn*! **fight** against those who **fight** against me.
02a. 握緊大小盾牌， (Same as the right column)	握緊大小盾牌， *wò jǐn dà xiǎo dùn pái*, Take hold of shield and buckler,

---

19. In sections like this, the present author summarizes the more appropriate or accurate comments from the IBTT, including the author's own comments. Sometimes scholars' arguments are quoted if needed. As to the full comments of the team members on the translations of נֶפֶשׁ, see Appendix A.

02b.	起來**幫助我**； *qǐ lái bāng zhù wǒ*; and rise up **to help me**.	起來**成為我的幫助**； *qǐ lái chéng wéi wǒ de bāng zhù*; and rise **as my help**.
03a.	取出長矛戰斧， (Same as the right column)	取出長矛戰斧， *qǔ chū zhǎng máo zhàn fǔ*, Draw out spear and battle-axe
03b.	對付那些追趕我的人； (Same as the right column)	對付那些追趕我的人； *duì fù nà zhuī gǎn wǒ de rén*; against those who pursue me;
03c.	求你對我說， (Same as the right column)	求你對我說： *qiú nǐ duì wǒ shuō*: say to me,
03d.	「**你的拯救就是我**。」 「*nǐ de zhěng jiù jiù shì wǒ*。」 "**It is me who saves you.**"[20]	「**我是你的拯救**。」 「*wǒ shì nǐ de zhěng jiù*。」 "**I am your salvation.**"

Notes:

- As the pattern of typical petition psalms indicates, the first verse of Psalm 35 introduces the divine name and the imperative calling for help. This imperative verse is a neat parallel bicolon (except the divine name) with 3+2 rhythm. The construction of the imperative verbs רִיבָה "contend"[21] and לְחַם "fight" and their respective cognate accusative יְרִיבַי "those who contend with me"[22] and לֹחֲמָי "those who fight against me" is a kind of grammatical paronomasia.[23] This is a rhetorical device used to emphasize the

---

20. Another English translation for the 你的拯救就是我 *nǐ de zhěng jiù jiù shì wǒ* is "Your salvation is me." However, this fails to present the Chinese emphasis on "me."

21. רִיבָה "contend" is the lengthened form of the Qal imperative of the root רִיב, which is commonly employed as a legal disputation; here, the parallelism with לחם "fight" suggests a military sense. Cf. Peter C. Craigie, *Psalms 1–50*, ed. Bruce M. Metzger et al., 2nd ed., Word Biblical Commentary 19 (Nashville, TN: Nelson Reference & Electronic, 2004), 286; Robert Alter, *The Book of Psalms: A Translation with Commentary* (New York: Norton, 2007), 121.

22. יְרִיבַי "those who contend with me" is cognate with the imperative רִיבָה "contend," but the Greek version has ἀδικοῦντάς "who do me injustice." See Allen P. Ross, *A Commentary on the Psalms*, vol. 1 (Grand Rapids, MI: Kregel Academic & Professional, 2011), 759.

23. Lunn denotes that the construction of verb + cognate accusative "is most often, though not exclusively, found in poetry." See Nick Lunn, "Paronomastic Constructions in

psalmist's urgent cry to God for help through the repetition of the identical Hebrew root.[24]

Chinese translations here could reflect the grammatical paronomasia faithfully, but the accusatives (i.e. "與我相爭的 *yǔ wǒ xiàng zhēng de* [those who contend with me]" and "與我爭戰的 *yǔ wǒ zhēng zhàn de* [those who fight against me]"), needed to be put before the imperative verbs (i.e. "相爭 *xiàng zhēng* [contend]" and "爭戰 *zhēng zhàn* [fight]"), when taking Chinese syntax into consideration. Besides, in verse 1b, the Chinese rendering for לְחַם was "爭戰 *zhēng zhàn* (fight)" in the initial draft, which was revised as "戰鬥 *zhàn dòu* (fight)" in IBTTV, a readable phrase for children.

- In verses 2–3, with vivid (anthropomorphic) and militaristic expressions, the psalmist makes a plea for Yahweh to arm himself with shield, buckler, spear, and battle-axe to get ready to fight and thus help and save the petitioner. According to Berlin's multi-aspect and multi-level nature of parallelism,[25] מָגֵן "shield" parallels צִנָּה "buckler"[26] on the level of the word in 2a; חֲנִית "spear" parallels סְגֹר "battle-axe"[27] in 3a. מָגֵן וְצִנָּה with Hiphil imperative הַחֲזֵק "take hold of," in turn, is parallel to חֲנִית וּסְגֹר with Hiphil imperative הָרֵק "draw out" on the level of the line. The neat parallelism between the first part of verse 2 and verse 3 binds the two verses closely even if the remainder of the lines are

---

Biblical Hebrew," *Notes on Translation* 10, no. 4 (1996): §5.2.

24. Robert G. Bratcher and William David Reyburn, *A Translator's Handbook on the Book of Psalms* (New York: United Bible Societies, 1991), 329.

25. Adele Berlin, *The Dynamics of Biblical Parallelism*, revised and expanded (Grand Rapids, MI; Cambridge, UK: Eerdmans, 2008), 25.

26. מָגֵן "shield" is related to a small shield made of thick leather, and צִנָּה "buckler" to a body shield woven from reeds, which is as long as the warrior is tall. With these two carried by an arm-bearer, the warrior would be completely protected. See Ross, *A Commentary on the Psalms*, vol. 1, 766; Ḥakham, *The Bible: Psalms with the Jerusalem Commentary*, vol. 1, 265.

27. The vocalization of the word סְגֹר in the MT seems to indicate an imperative of the verb "close, shut off." However, according to the finding of the Qumran scrolls, it should be understood as a noun, the name of a weapon, a battle-axe. See Bratcher and Reyburn, *A Translator's Handbook*, 329; cf. Ḥakham, *The Bible: Psalms with the Jerusalem Commentary*, vol. 1, 265. Many commenters point it to either סָגַר or סֶגֶר. See Ross, *A Commentary on the Psalms*, vol. 1, 759 n.3.

not identical grammatically. Here, it is possible to maintain this parallelism in the Chinese translation.

- In verse 2a, מָגֵן was rendered as "小盾牌 *xiǎo dùn pái* (small shield)"; צִנָּה as "大盾牌 *dà dùn pái* (big shield)." In Chinese expressions, when the "小 *xiǎo* (small)" and the "大 *dà* (big)" are combined, the former needs to be arranged after the latter, and thus "大小盾牌 *dà xiǎo dùn pái* (big and small shield)," instead of "小大盾牌 *xiǎo dà dùn pái* (small and big shield)."

- The IBTT suggested that children would find it easier to understand the four weapons if they are properly illustrated. The following drawing was done by a thirteen-year-old girl.

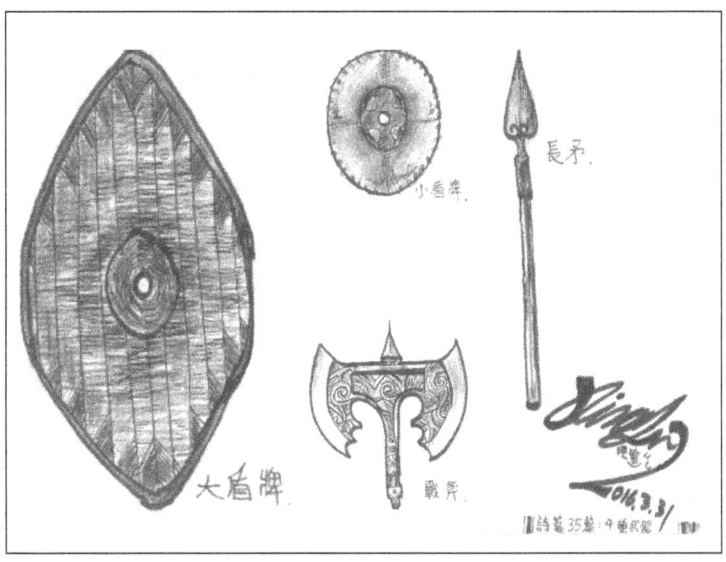

- In verse 2b, the replacement of the noun with the verb was to make the colon more readable for children. That is, "rise to help me" (起來幫助我 *qǐ lái bāng zhù wǒ*) in IBTTV is easier than "rise as my help" (起來成為我的幫助 *qǐ lái chéng wéi wǒ de bāng zhù*) in the initial draft. The same principle might also apply to verse 3d (i.e. replacing "I am your salvation" with "I will save you," as in NIrV, an easy English version comprehensible for children). However, in order to make this colon rhyme[28] with verse 3c in Chinese, "I/me" was put at the end of the colon, and the noun "your salvation" was retained. Thus, "說 *shuō* (say)" in verse 3c rhymes with "我 *wǒ* (me)" in verse 3d. Though the translation of the subject אֲנִי is put at the end of the colon, it is emphasized by the Chinese expression "就是我 *jiù shì wǒ* (It is me [who save you])."

- In the Hebrew text of this section, there are יְ (v. 1a), יְ (vv. 1b, 3b) and יְ (vv. 2b, 3c, 3d) found at the end of the cola, which makes this section rhyme well. With a few variations, the Chinese rhyming words in IBTTV were arranged in verses 1b (鬥 *dòu*), 2b (我 *wǒ*), 3c (說 *shuō*), 3d (我 *wǒ*).[29]

5.3.1.2 Section 2 of Psalm 35 (vv. 4–8)

The psalmist's expectations of retribution for the enemies are delineated in this section, where נֶפֶשׁ occurs in verses 4 and 7.

5.3.1.2.1 The appropriate translation of נֶפֶשׁ in Psalm 35:4

5.3.1.2.1.1 The existing translations

In this verse, נֶפֶשׁ appears to refer to "性命 *xìng mìng* (physical life)"[30] in all prominent Chinese versions with two different expressions for the combination of בקשׁ and נֶפֶשׁ: "尋索我命 *xún suǒ wǒ mìng* (seek my life)" (CUV, RCUV, CNV, LZZ, CNET) and "殺我 *shā wǒ* (to kill me)" (TCVRE, CCB, DCT).

5.3.1.2.1.2 The exploration/discussion/comment of the IBTT

This section describes the psalmist's retributive expectations regarding the enemies who contend with him and fight against him, trying to defeat him and even take his life (v. 1). This is supported by verse 7, where a deadly pit of netting is prepared for the psalmist, and by verse 17, where

---

28. Rhyme is a poetic device used in Chinese new poetry (新詩 *xīn shī*).

29. In Mandarin Phonetic Symbols, the end component of 鬥 *dòu* is "ㄡ *ou*," whose pronunciation is very similar to that of the end component "ㄛ *o*" in 我 *wǒ*, 說 *shuō*. Thus, 鬥 *dòu* could be viewed as one of the rhyming words in this section.

30. In Chinese, 性命 *xìng mìng* refers specifically to physical or bodily life. 生命 *shēng mìng* is related to life in general.

the enemies, like lions, anticipate his destruction. Thus, the very thing that the enemies earnestly seek (בקשׁ) here is the psalmist's physical life (נֶפֶשׁ). Such severe threat without reason (vv. 7, 11, 15, 19) forces the psalmist to expect Yahweh's punishment on the wicked.

The literal translation for מְבַקְשֵׁי נַפְשִׁי is "那尋索我命的 *nà xún suǒ wǒ mìng de* (those who seek my life)." However, the expression "尋索我命 *xún suǒ wǒ mìng* (seek my life)" was generally difficult for grade 1 students. The following rendering is preferable – "那些要取我性命的人 *nà xiē yào qǔ wǒ xìng mìng de rén* (those who want to take my physical life)."

5.3.1.2.2 The appropriate translation of נֶפֶשׁ in Psalm 35:7

5.3.1.2.2.1 The existing translations
Falling within the same section (vv. 4–8), נֶפֶשׁ in verse 7 seems also to refer to "性命 *xìng mìng* (physical life)" in the majority of prominent Chinese versions except for TCVRE, CCB, DCT, which takes the meaning "我 *wǒ* (me)."

5.3.1.2.2.2 The exploration/discussion/comment of the IBTT
At the beginning of this section (v. 4), the enemies are delineated as those who seek the psalmist's life. It is reasonable to infer that the "pit of netting" (שַׁחַת רִשְׁתָּם) the enemies dig and hide (v. 7) is intended for capturing the psalmist. In this trap, his physical life will be in danger. The unusual rhetorical construction of שַׁחַת "pit" and רֶשֶׁת "net" is used to accentuate the danger which the enemies impose on the psalmist.[31] This implies that the "pit of netting" itself is deadly; it may lead to the death of anyone who falls into it.

At first glance, נֶפֶשׁ as "corpse" is another possible translation of this text (i.e. the enemies dig the pit for the psalmist's corpse), which seems to indicate further the enemies' malice and their determination to take the psalmist's life. Nonetheless, this would imply that the psalmist is killed before being put in the pit. In other words, the pit is dug just for placing a dead body, not for causing death. If this is the case, the enemies do not need to hide the pit and maliciously design a "pit of netting," a deadly trap for the psalmist, which contradicts the description of verse 7a: "they *hid the pit of their net* for me."

---

31. John Goldingay, *Psalms*, vol. 1, Baker Commentary on the Old Testament Wisdom and Psalms (Grand Rapids, MI: Baker Academic, 2006), 493.

In brief, נֶפֶשׁ as "性命 *xìng mìng* (physical life)" is the most appropriate rendering in this verse.

5.3.1.2.3 The version readable for all generations by the IBTT through LiFE

Section 2 (vv. 4–8): The Expectations of Retribution for the Enemies	
IBTTV	The initial draft
04b. 讓那**些**要**取我性命**的人， *ràng nà xiē yào qǔ wǒ xìng mìng de rén,* Let those who **want to take my physical life**	讓那**尋索我命**的， *ràng nà xún suǒ wǒ mìng de,* Let those who **seek my life**
04a. **丟臉到抬不起頭**； *diū liǎn dào tái bù qǐ tóu;* **lose their face, that they cannot lift up their head**;	**蒙羞受辱**； *méng xiū shòu rǔ;* **be put to shame and be disgraced**;
04d. 讓那**些**設計害我的人， *ràng nà xiē shè jì hài wǒ de rén,* let those who plan my disaster	讓那設計害我的， *ràng nà shè jì hài wǒ de,* let those who plan my disaster
04c. 慚愧**到想要逃走**。 *cán kuì dào xiǎng yào táo zǒu.* be ashamed, that **they want to run away**.	**退後**慚愧。 *tuì hòu cán kuì.* **be turned back** and be ashamed.
05a. 讓他們像**稻米的殼被風**[吹散]， *ràng tā men xiàng dào mǐ de ké bèi fēng [chuī sàn],* Let them be like **the husks of rice that the wind [drives away]**,	讓他們像**風前的糠秕**， *ràng tā men xiàng fēng qián de kāng bǐ,* Let them be like **chaff before the wind**,
05b. 有耶和華的**天使趕走**[他們]。 *yǒu yē hé huá de tiān shǐ gǎn zǒu [tā men].* with the **angel** of the LORD **driving** [them] away.	有耶和華的**使者趕逐**[他們]。 *yǒu yē hé huá de shǐ zhě gǎn zhú [tā men].* with the **messenger** of the LORD **thrusting** [them] away.

06a. 讓他們的路又暗又滑， (Same as the right column)	讓他們的路又暗又滑， ràng tā men de lù yòu àn yòu huá, Let their path be dark and slippery,
06b. 有耶和華的**天使**追趕他們。 yǒu yē hé huá de tiān shǐ zhuī gǎn tā men。 with the **angel** of the LORD pursuing them.	有耶和華的**使者**追趕他們。 yǒu yē hé huá de shǐ zhě zhuī gǎn tā men。 with the **messenger** of the LORD pursuing them.
07a. 因為**沒有原因**地，他們為我**藏了**網羅的坑， yīn wéi méi yǒu yuán yīn dì, tā men wéi wǒ cáng le wǎng luó de kēng, For **without reason** they **hid** the pit of their net for me;	因**無故**地他們為我**暗藏**網羅的坑， yīn wú gù dì tā men wéi wǒ àn cáng wǎng luó de kēng, For **without reason** they **hid** the pit of their net for me;
07b. **沒有原因**地，他們為我的性命挖[坑]。 méi yǒu yuán yīn dì, tā men wéi wǒ de xìng mìng wā [kēng]。 **without reason** they dug [it] for my physical life.	**無故**地他們為我的性命挖[坑]。 wú gù dì tā men wéi wǒ de xìng mìng wā [kēng]。 **without reason** they dug [it] for my physical life.
08a. 讓**災難**在他還不知道的時候臨到他， ràng zāi nán zài tā hái bù zhī dào de shí hòu lín dào tā, Let **disaster** come upon him when he does not expect it;	讓**災禍**在他還不知道的時候臨到他， ràng zāi huò zài tā hái bù zhī dào de shí hòu lín dào tā, Let **disaster** come upon him when he does not know it;
08b. 讓他所**藏**的網羅纏住他， ràng tā suǒ cáng de wǎng luó chán zhù tā, let the net he **hid** catch him;	讓他所**暗設**的網羅纏住他， ràng tā suǒ àn shè de wǎng luó chán zhù tā, let the net he **hid** catch him;
08c. 讓他陷入**災難**！ ràng tā xiàn rù zāi nán! let him fall into **disaster**!	讓他陷入**災禍**！ ràng tā xiàn rù zāi huò! let him fall into **disaster**!

Notes:

- In Hebrew, the two halves of verse 4 exhibit the same syntactic surface structure.³² Each half comprises a pair of jussives with related meaning, followed by a participial phrase delineating the subject. Moreover, this tetracolon rhymes neatly: verse 4a rhymes with verse 4c (וּ in וְיִכָּלְמוּ and וְיַחְפְּרוּ); verse 4b with verse 4d (יִ in נַפְשִׁי and רָעָתִי). Of the finite verbs, one (סוג) is related to the actual unsuccessful attack: "turn back"; three (חפר, כלם, בוש) are all related to the consequence: shame.³³

The initial draft for the three finite verbs associated with shame was generally difficult for grade 1 students. The first two in verse 4a (i.e. "蒙羞 *meng xiū* [be put to shame]" and "受辱 *shòu rǔ* [be disgraced]") were replaced with easier phrases; the third in verse 4c (i.e. "慚愧 *cán kuì* [be ashamed]") was retained since it could be grasped through the parallelism of vv. 4a and 4c).³⁴ Thus, "丟臉 *diū liǎn* (lose their face)," a common Chinese expression for shame, was substituted for "蒙羞 *méng xiū* (be put to shame)"; "抬不起頭 *tái bù qǐ tóu* ([they] cannot lift up [their] head)," a Chinese saying for disgrace, was substituted for "受辱 *shòu rǔ* (be disgraced)."

In verse 4c, "退後 *tuì hòu* (be turned back)" was replaced with "想要逃走 *xiǎng yào táo zǒu* ([they] want to run away)." This is because the phrase can not only interpret "be turned back" well, but also make this colon rhyme with its parallel colon (v. 4a). Accordingly, IBTTV has rhyming words 頭 *tóu* and 走 *zǒu* in verse 4a and verse 4c respectively. It also has "人 *rén* (people)" at the end of both verse 4b and verse 4d. Thus, the revised translations by the IBTT correspond to the Hebrew text as a rhyming tetracolon.

---

32. Berlin, in *The Dynamics of Biblical Parallelism*, 53, classifies this as syntactic parallelism with no transformation.

33. Goldingay, *Psalms*, vol. 1, 492.

34. The IBTT maintained that in view of translating through the LiFE approach, a difficult but beautiful and poetic word or phrase could be kept if the context can explain it well.

The word order in this tetracolon needs to be rearranged as verse 4b → verse 4a → verse 4d → verse 4c in Chinese translation.

- The "糠秕 *kāng bǐ* (chaff)" in verse 5 is such a difficult phrase that even some adult participants failed to pronounce it correctly. Its explanation might work well (i.e. the husks of grain). However, the "穀物 *gǔ wù* (grain)" is not easy for grade 1 students. Thus, a more specific description is needed, such as the husks of rice or wheat, two staple crops in China. The former "稻米的殼 *dào mǐ de ké* (the husks of rice)" was chosen by the IBTT.

  The simile "like chaff before the wind" was generally difficult for children to perceive as well. Thus, "that the wind drives away" was added to make the simile easier to grasp: "像稻米的殼被風吹散 *xiàng dào mǐ de ké bèi fēng chuī sàn* (like the husks of rice that the wind drives away)."

- After the simile in verse 5a, the metaphor in verse 6a more directly and forcefully[35] describes the fate of the enemies. The metaphors חֹשֶׁךְ "dark" and חֲלַקְלַקּ "slippery"[36] mean that the enemies will be "confused and hindered as they try to flee and do not find an easy way."[37] The Chinese counterparts for the metaphors (i.e. "又暗又滑 *yòu àn yòu huá* [dark and slippery]"), were generally understood by grade 1 students.

- In verse 7, 網子 *wǎng zǐ* is an easier rendering for רֶשֶׁת "net," but it fails to convey the idea that the net here is designed for catching something (i.e. the psalmist). This can be expressed well by the Chinese phrase "網羅 *wǎng luó* (net),"[38] but it is generally difficult for young readers. However, this could be compensated

---

35. Wendland, in *Analyzing the Psalms*, 142, notes that a metaphor "functions in much the same way as a simile, except more directly and thus often more forcefully."

36. In biblical Hebrew, the doubling of the final two root letters, e.g. חֲלַקְלַקּ, indicates intensity. See Ḥakham, *The Bible: Psalms with the Jerusalem Commentary*, vol. 1, 266.

37. Ross, *A Commentary on the Psalms*, vol. 1, 767.

38. The 羅 *luó* in Chinese means "to snare birds with a net." See Dr.eye electronic Chinese dictionary.

by illustrations (top left: by an eight-year-old boy, top right: by an eleven-year-old boy, bottom: by a thirteen-year-old girl).

- Verse 8 abruptly shifts from employing the plural for the enemies to referring to a single individual, who is presumably representative of them all, making the psalm more *vivid*.[39] According to Berlin, this is a kind of morphological parallelism (contrast in number),[40] which might serve as a rhetorical marker of the end of the section.

  To make the psalm more *vivid* as noted above, the IBTT decided to retain the singular collective sense here after the poetic device used was explained.

---

39. Alter, *Book of Psalms*, 122; Goldingay, *Psalms*, vol. 1, 493.
40. Berlin, *Dynamics of Biblical Parallelism*, 44.

- Challenging words or phrases can here be replaced by easier ones in this section: "使者 *shǐ zhě* (messenger)" → "天使 *tiān shǐ* (angel)," "趕逐 *gǎn zhú* (thrusting away)" → "趕走 *gǎn zǒu* (driving away)" (vv. 5–6); "無故 *wú gù* (without reason)" → "沒有原因 *méi yǒu yuán yīn* (without reason)," "暗藏 *àn cáng* (hid)" → "藏了 *cáng le* (hid)" (v. 7); "災禍 *zāi huò* (disaster)" → "災難 *zāi nán* (disaster)," "暗設 *àn shè* (hid)" → "藏 *cáng* (hid)" (v. 8).
- This section (vv. 4–8) demonstrates an envelope structure (*Inclusio*). In verse 4, the enemies are planning the psalmist's "disaster" (רָעָה). In verse 8, the psalmist hopes that the enemies can fall into "disaster" (שׁוֹאָה). Thus, רָעָה "disaster" of verse 4 and שׁוֹאָה "disaster" of verse 8 respectively mark the beginning and the ending of the same discourse unit.[41] The envelope structure is obvious in Hebrew text since both words are arranged in the last colon of their respective verses. In Chinese translation, the colon where רָעָה "disaster" is located needs to be switched to the middle of the verse, but the envelope structure is still discernible.

5.3.1.3 Section 3 of Psalm 35 (vv. 9–10)

This section is related to the psalmist's promise to praise Yahweh for deliverance. The word נֶפֶשׁ occurs once (v. 9).

5.3.1.3.1 The appropriate translation of נֶפֶשׁ in Psalm 35:9

5.3.1.3.1.1 The existing translations

Though well-known English versions, such as NIV 1984 (and its revised edition of 2011), NASB 1995, ESV, NRSV, and KJV, translate נַפְשִׁי as "my soul" here (an unfortunate translation as Brueggemann argues, see §4.2.1), Chinese versions render it as "我的心 *wǒ de xīn* (my heart)" or "我 *wǒ* (I)." The former is found in CUV, RCUV, CNV, LZZ; the latter in TCVRE, CCB, CNET, DCT.

---

41. Gerald H. Wilson, *Psalms Volume 1*, The NIV Application Commentary (Grand Rapids, MI: Zondervan, 2002), 580.

5.3.1.3.1.2 *The exploration/discussion/comment of the IBTT*

This section (vv. 9–10) is an abrupt shift[42] from the preceding retributive expectations to out-loud rejoicing. Such joy and delight result from the psalmist's trust in Yahweh in general (v. 9a), his deliverance in particular (v. 9b). The psalmist's intensity of delightful feelings here can't be expressed faithfully by the renderings of נַפְשִׁי as "我的心 *wǒ de xīn* (my heart)"[43] or "我 *wǒ* (I)" in the existing Chinese versions. נַפְשִׁי as "我整個人 *wǒ zhěng gè rén* (my whole person)" is a more appropriate translation since it indicates that not only the psalmist's heart, but also his body, his whole being feels delightful. It conveys the psalmist's intensity of feelings more strongly. This is further substantiated by the parallel כָּל עַצְמוֹתַי "我所有的骨頭 *wǒ suǒ yǒu de gǔ tóu* (all my bones)" in verse 10. When עֶצֶם "bone," a figure of the seat of emotions as well, is employed parallel to נֶפֶשׁ "the whole person," it may imply the entire person (a synecdoche of part-whole relation).[44]

5.3.1.3.2 The version readable for all generations by the IBTT through LiFE

Section 3 (vv. 9–10): The Promise to Praise Yahweh for Deliverance	
IBTTV	**The initial draft**
09a. 但我整個人在耶和華裡面歡喜， (Same as the right column)	但我整個人在耶和華裡面歡喜， *dàn wǒ zhěng gè rén zài yē hé huá lǐ miàn huān xǐ,* But my whole person will rejoice in Yahweh,

---

42. According to Beth, the abrupt shift here serves several purposes: "First, it contrasts the acts of the one praying [with] the enemies who harm without cause. Second, it serves as an additional reason or motivation for God to save the one who has trust in God's grace and power. Finally, it is the way [believers] under stress react." See Beth LaNeel Tanner, "Psalm 35," in *The Book of Psalms*, by Nancy deClaissé-Walford, R. A. Jacobson, and Beth LaNeel Tanner, NICOT (Grand Rapids, MI: Eerdmans, 2014), 336.

43. As discussed in chapter 4, the semantic fields of נֶפֶשׁ and לֵבָב overlap (i.e. both of them can be employed to express the feeling/will/thought of a person, but the former strongly conveys the *intensity* of such feeling/will/thought). More discussions, see §4.2.4.4 and §4.6.

44. R. B. Allen, "עֶצֶם," in *Theological Wordbook of the Old Testament*, eds. R. L. Harris, G. L. Archer, Jr., and B. K. Waltke (Chicago, IL: Moody, 1999), 690.

09b. 在祂的救恩中快樂。 (Same as the right column)	在祂的救恩中快樂。 zài tā de jiù ēn zhōng kuài lè。 and delight in his salvation.
10a. 我**整個人**都說： wǒ zhěng gè rén dōu shuō： **My whole person** will say,	我**所有的骨頭**說： wǒ suǒ yǒu de gǔ tóu shuō： **All my bones** will say,
10b.「耶和華啊，誰能像你— (Same as the right column)	「耶和華啊，誰能像你— 「yē hé huá ā, shuí néng xiàng nǐ— 'Yahweh, who is like You –
10c. 搭救**弱小**的人脫離那比他**強大**的， dā jiù ruò xiǎo de rén tuō lí nà bǐ tā qiáng dà de, delivering a **weak** person from someone **strong**er than him,	搭救**弱勢**的人脫離那比他**強壯**的， dā jiù ruò shì de rén tuō lí nà bǐ tā qiáng zhuàng de, delivering a **weak** person from someone **strong**er than him,
10d. **弱小**需要的人脫離那**搶**他的?」 ruò xiǎo xū yào de rén tuō lí nà qiǎng tā de?」 a **weak** and needy person from someone who **robs** him?'	**弱勢**需要的人脫離那**搶奪**他的?」 ruò shì xū yào de rén tuō lí nà qiǎng duó tā de?」 a **weak** and needy person from someone who **robs** him?'

Notes:

- Generally speaking, replacing abstract nouns with verbs would make a translation easier for young readers, but this cannot be applied to each occurrence due to, for example, poetic or rhythmic considerations. This is the case here.

The abstract noun יְשׁוּעָה "salvation," a challenging word for children, occurs in both verse 3 and verse 9. In the former case, יְשׁוּעָה as a noun was retained for the sake of rhyme (see §5.3.1.1.2). Here, יְשׁוּעָה as a noun was also kept on account of its parallel יהוה "Yahweh" as a noun. Difficult though it might be, "salvation" here could be understood by children with the help of the specific descriptions of God's deeds of salvation in the following cola (vv. 10c, 10d).

- In verse 10a, the literal translation "我所有的骨頭說 *wǒ suǒ yǒu de gǔ tóu shuō* (all my bones will say)" could hardly be grasped by children because bones cannot speak, said a grade 1 student. A forty-two-year-old adult pointed out that an illustration of dancing bones that praise God next to the verse might help. However, this probably causes some negative associations among children. An eleven-year-old boy stated that God would strike those praising him with lightning (since only bones are seen, rather than a whole person).

  Actually, in line with the Israelites, the Chinese people also regard the "bone" as the seat of feeling or thought,[45] but its usage as a subject that can speak is not a common Chinese expression. Here, Allen's argument on the parallelism of עֶצֶם "bone" and נֶפֶשׁ "the whole being" noted above is helpful: when the former parallels the latter, it denotes "the entire person" (整個人 *zhěng gè rén*) as well. Thus, both נֶפֶשׁ and עֶצֶם here were rendered as "整個人 *zhěng gè rén* (the whole person)," which, nonetheless, fails to reflect the rhetorical beauty in the parallelism of the Hebrew poetry.

- In verse 10c, עָנִי "weak" parallels חָזָק "strong" (contrast in meaning). The Chinese translations in the initial draft (i.e. "弱勢 *ruò shì* [weak]" and "強壯 *qiáng zhuàng* [strong]"), were generally difficult for children. After brainstorming, a grade 1 student suggested easier substitute phrases (i.e. "弱小 *ruò xiǎo* [weak]" and "強大 *qiáng dà* [strong]" respectively). This makes the contrast even more obvious since "弱 *ruò* (weak)" is the opposite of "強 *qiáng* (strong)," and "小 *xiǎo* (small)" the opposite of "大 *dà* (big)."

- עָנִי "the weak" with the מִן expressions (v. 10c) parallels the hendiadys[46] of עָנִי "the weak" and אֶבְיוֹן "the needy" with the

---

45. Such as "恨之入骨 *hèn zhī rù gǔ* (to hate somebody to the bone)," which indicates that the hatred is very extreme; "刻骨銘心 *kè gǔ míng xīn* (engraved in the bones and printed on the heart)," which refers to something unforgettable.

46. Hendiadys is related to "the expression of one idea through two formally coordinate terms." See Ross, *A Commentary on the Psalms*, vol. 1, 105. Thus, the hendiadys of עָנִי "the weak" and אֶבְיוֹן "the needy" is to express a single idea: "the weak person who is therefore

מִן expressions (v. 10d). The מִן "from" expressions identify the stronger ones (v. 10c), even more specifically, the one who robs (v. 10d), from whom the vulnerable people need rescue.[47] There is no difficulty in translating the parallelism here into Chinese.

- In verse 10d, the challenging phrase "搶奪 qiǎng duó (rob)" was replaced by the shorter "搶 qiǎng (rob)."

5.3.1.4 Section 4 of Psalm 35 (vv. 11–16)

The psalmist's lament over the enemies repaying good for evil[48] is the main theme of section four with two appearances of the word נֶפֶשׁ (vv. 12, 13).

5.3.1.4.1 The appropriate translation of נֶפֶשׁ in Psalm 35:12

5.3.1.4.1.1 The existing translations
Similar to the case in Psalm 35:3, נֶפֶשׁ as "靈魂 líng hún (spirit-soul)" and "soul" in CUV and NIV 1984 respectively have been revised as "我 wǒ (me)" in their new editions (i.e. RCUV and NIV 2011). The rest of the prominent Chinese versions regard נֶפֶשׁ as "我 wǒ (me)" except for CNET, where it is rendered as "我身 wǒ shēn (my body)."

5.3.1.4.1.2 The exploration/discussion/comment of the IBTT
This verse is within the section spelling out the psalmist's lament over the enemies repaying evil for good. Of the evil things the enemies impose on the psalmist, one is to leave him like someone who has lost children. נַפְשִׁי as first personal pronoun here can appropriately indicate an independent individual who has lost family members.

5.3.1.4.2 The appropriate translation of נֶפֶשׁ in Psalm 35:13

5.3.1.4.2.1 The existing translations
Here, CUV, RCUV, CNV translate נֶפֶשׁ as "心 xīn (heart)." LZZ renders it as "自己 zì jǐ (self)." No obvious corresponding renderings for נֶפֶשׁ are found in TCVRE, CCB, CNET, DCT. It is worth noting that although

---

needy." See Goldingay, *Psalms*, vol. 1, 494. The word pair is also found in Pss 37:14; 40:17; 70:5, etc.

47. Goldingay, *Psalms*, vol. 1, 494.
48. Ross, *A Commentary on the Psalms*, vol. 1, 769.

CNV translates נֶפֶשׁ as "心 *xīn* (heart)" in this passage, it views נֶפֶשׁ as "身體 *shēn tǐ* (body)" in Isaiah 58:3, where fasting is also associated with the affliction of one's own body (刻苦己身 *kè kǔ jǐ shēn*). Along with CNV, CCB has נֶפֶשׁ as "身體 *shēn tǐ* (body)" in Isaiah 58:3 even if it does not translate נֶפֶשׁ with this meaning here.

5.3.1.4.2.2 The exploration/discussion/comment of the IBTT
Contrary to the enemies' wicked conduct, the psalmist repays good for evil by showing true empathy for the sick enemies: wearing sackcloth (v. 13a), fasting (v. 13b), and praying (v. 13c) to draw "God's attention to their need."[49] In verse 13b, the psalmist afflicts his נֶפֶשׁ by means of fasting.

Since humans are both physical and psychological creatures, it would be strange only to feel sorrow, but not to express it by, for example, abstaining from food which affects the body.[50] Indeed, when fasting to show empathy and praying for others, the body suffers. Therefore, נֶפֶשׁ as "身體 *shēn tǐ* (body)" is a more appropriate translation in this text.

5.3.1.4.3 The version readable for all generations by the IBTT through LiFE

Section 4 (vv. 11–16): The Lament Over the Enemies Repaying Good for Evil	
IBTTV	**The initial draft**
11a. 兇惡的證人起來， (Same as the right column)	兇惡的證人起來， *xiōng è de zhèng rén qǐ lái,* Violent witnesses arise;
11b. **一直問**我所不知道的事。 *yī zhí wèn wǒ suǒ bù zhī dào de shì.* they **continually ask** me about things I do not know.	**盤問**我所不知道的事。 *pán wèn wǒ suǒ bù zhī dào de shì.* they **cross-question** me about things I do not know.
12a. 他們對我以惡報善， (Same as the right column)	他們對我以惡報善， *tā men duì wǒ yǐ è bào shàn,* They repay me evil for good,

---

49. Goldingay, *Psalms*, vol. 1, 496.
50. Cf. Goldingay, 496.

12b. 使我[痛苦得]像失去孩子。 shǐ wǒ tòng kǔ dé xiàng shī qù hái zǐ。 and leave me [in pain] like one who has lost children.	使我像失去孩子。 shǐ wǒ xiàng shī qù hái zǐ。 and leave me like one who has lost children.
13a. 但是我，在他們生病的時候，我穿麻衣[表示傷心]； dàn shì wǒ, zài tā men shēng bìng de shí hòu, wǒ chuān má yī [biǎo shì shāng xīn]； But I, when they were sick, **wore sackcloth [to show my sorrow]**；	但是我，在他們生病的時候，我的穿著是麻衣； dàn shì wǒ, zài tā men shēng bìng de shí hòu, wǒ de chuān zhe shì má yī； But I, when they were sick, **my clothing was sackcloth**；
13b. 我不吃東西來使我的身體受苦； wǒ bù chī dōng xī lái shǐ wǒ de shēn tǐ shòu kǔ； I **stopped eating food to cause pain to my body**；	我以禁食來刻苦己身； wǒ yǐ jìn shí lái kè kǔ jǐ shēn； I **afflicted my body with fasting**；
13c. 我所求的都回到我自己的懷中。 wǒ suǒ qiú de dōu huí dào wǒ zì jǐ de huái zhōng。 **what I plead** kept returning to my bosom.	我的禱告回到我自己的懷中。 wǒ de dǎo gào huí dào wǒ zì jǐ de huái zhōng。 **my prayer** kept returning to my bosom.
14a. 好像[哀悼]我的朋友兄弟，我[傷心地]來回走著； hǎo xiàng āi dào wǒ de péng yǒu xiōng dì, wǒ shāng xīn dì lái huí zǒu zhe； **As if** [mourning] for my friend or brother, **I walked about** [sadly]；	宛如[哀悼]我的朋友兄弟，我來回踱步； wǎn rú [āi dào] wǒ de péng yǒu xiōng dì, wǒ lái huí duó bù； **As if** [mourning] for my friend or brother, **I walked about**；

14b. 好像哀悼[我的]母親，我非常傷心地跪著。 hǎo xiàng āi dào wǒ de mǔ qīn, wǒ fēi cháng shāng xīn dì guì zhe。 **as if** mourning for [my] mother, **I bowed down very sadly.**	宛如哀悼[我的]母親，**我陰鬱地跪下**。 wǎn rú āi dào [wǒ de] mǔ qīn, wǒ yīn yù dì guì xià。 **as if** mourning for [my] mother, **I bowed down, gloomy.**
15a. 我跌倒時，他們卻歡喜，聚在一起； wǒ diē dǎo shí, tā men què huān xǐ, jù zài yī qǐ； But when I stumbled, they rejoiced and **gathered together**;	我跌倒時，他們卻歡喜、**聚集**； wǒ diē dǎo shí, tā men què huān xǐ、jù jí； But when I stumbled, they rejoiced and **gathered together**;
15b. 他們**聚在一起**反對我； tā men jù zài yī qǐ fǎn duì wǒ； they **gathered together** against me;	他們**聚集**反對我； tā men jù jí fǎn duì wǒ； they **gathered together** against me;
15c. 我並不認識那些攻擊我的人； wǒ bìng bù rèn shí nà xiē gōng jī wǒ de rén； **I did not know** those who attacked me;	我所不認識的攻擊者 wǒ suǒ bù rèn shí de gōng jī zhě **assailants I did not know**
15d. 他們撕裂我，並不停止。 tā men sī liè wǒ, bìng bù tíng zhǐ。 **they** tore at me without ceasing.	撕裂我，並不停止。 sī liè wǒ, bìng bù tíng zhǐ。 tore at me without ceasing.
16a. 像那最不敬虔、不正直的嘲笑者， xiàng nà zuì bù jìng qián、bù zhèng zhí de cháo xiào zhě, As the most ungodly **dishonest mockers**,	像那最不敬虔、**彎曲的嘲弄者** xiàng nà zuì bù jìng qián、wān qū de cháo nòng zhě As the most ungodly **twisted mockers**
16b. 他們向我咬牙切齒。 (Same as the right column)	他們向我咬牙切齒。 tā men xiàng wǒ yǎo yá qiē chǐ。 they grind their teeth against me.

Notes:

- In verse 12b, the psalmist's emotion "pain" was added to make the verbless clause more explicit for children: "and leave me [in pain] like one who has lost children."
- In the Hebrew text, verse 11b and verse 12b rhyme (יְ in יִשְׁאָלוּנִי and לְנַפְשִׁי). In IBTTV, the 事 *shì* and the 子 *zǐ* at the end of verse 11b and verse 12b respectively can be viewed as rhyming words since their pronunciations are very close.
- In traditional Chinese custom, when an immediate family member dies, one needs to wear mourning clothes made of flax or hemp. This is so-called "披麻帶孝 *pī má dài xiào*," which is similar to the mourning image portrayed in verse 13a even though no one has died. However, for grade 1 students who have no such experiences, it is hardly easy to grasp the implication of wearing sackcloth,[51] "a piece of clothing worn by people in times of sorrow and mourning."[52] Thus, the IBTT added the phrase "to show my sorrow" (表示傷心 *biǎo shì shāng xīn*) right after the "sackcloth."

  Besides, the verbless clause "my clothing was sackcloth" (שַׂק לְבוּשִׁי) was replaced by "I wore sackcloth" (我穿麻衣 *wǒ chuān má yī*) since the verb clause is more understandable for children.
- In the last colon of verse 13, the expression "my prayer kept returning to my bosom" is ambiguous. It occurs only here.[53] There is considerable disagreement over the meaning of this clause,[54] for example, "his prayer was continual"[55] (the verb is

---

51. Sackcloth (שַׂק) refers to "a large woven cloth, usually woven from goat-hair, and therefore usually black in the East." See L. Koehler, W. Baumgartner, and J. J. Stamm, "שַׂק," in *The Hebrew and Aramaic Lexicon of the Old Testament*, trans. M. E. J. Richardson (Leiden: Brill, 1994–2000), 1350.

52. Koehler et al., "שַׂק," 1350.

53. Goldingay, *Psalms*, vol. 1, 496.

54. Bratcher and Reyburn, *A Translator's Handbook*, 334.

55. A similar interpretation is from Ḥakham, who explains this clause graphically: "Those who engage in earnest prayer often bend their heads and place their hands upon their hearts, so that the prayers that leave their mouths return, as it were, to their bosoms. The psalmist means to say: I would pray at length for their recovery." See Ḥakham, *The Bible: Psalms with the Jerusalem Commentary*, vol. 1, 268.

progressive *yiqtol*); "his prayer was with humility"; "his prayer might redound to his own advantage"; or "the prayer would return either unanswered or as a blessing (cf. Matt 10:33)."[56] No matter how diverse the interpretations are, it is clear that the psalmist prays for his sick enemies.[57]

The ambiguity of this colon also perplexed the IBTT. Since there is no right answer here, the ambiguity was retained with a slight adjustment in wording by replacing "my prayer" with a more explicit expression: "what I plead" (kept returning to my bosom).

- At first glance, verse 14 appears to be somewhat difficult (due to the ellipsis of words in both cola). However, the meaning of this verse is made explicit when the syntactic parallelism is recognized.

For the purpose of stress, the כְּ prepositional phrases in both cola of verse 14 are arranged before the verbs. Thus, the syntactic structure in this bicola works aba'b':[58] prepositional phrase + verb // prepositional phrase + verb. This syntactic parallelism might indicate the ellipsis of אָבֵל "one mourning" in the first colon and the ellipsis of לִי "to me" in the second colon. Thus, "the expression 'one mourning' in the second colon explains the [כְּ] expression in the first (lit., 'like [one mourning] a friend, like [one mourning] a brother')."[59] The second כְּ prepositional phrase "intensifies the first, with its reference not merely to one mourning a friend or brother,"[60] but also to one mourning one's mother.

This Hebrew syntactic parallelism was presented in the initial draft by the researcher, but the diction was generally difficult for young readers, such as "宛如 *wǎn rú* (as if)," "哀悼 *āi dào* (mourning)," "陰鬱的 *yīn yù de* (gloomy)." Therefore, the draft

---

56. Ross, *A Commentary on the Psalms*, vol. 1, 770.
57. Ross, 770.
58. Goldingay, *Psalms*, vol. 1, 497.
59. Goldingay, 497.
60. Goldingay, 497.

needs to be made easier, but the syntactic parallelism should remain. With some adjustments, the IBTT translated this verse as follows:

好像[哀悼]我的朋友兄弟，我[傷心地]來回走著；
hǎo xiàng āi dào wǒ de péng yǒu xiōng dì, wǒ shāng xīn dì lái huí zǒu zhe;
As if [mourning] for my friend or brother, I walked about [sadly];

好像哀悼[我的]母親，我非常傷心地跪著。
hǎo xiàng āi dào wǒ de mǔ qīn, wǒ fēi cháng shāng xīn dì guì zhe.
as if mourning for [my] mother, I bowed down very sadly.

Here, the easier phrase "好像 *hǎo xiàng* (as if)" was substituted for "宛如 *wǎn rú* (as if)." "哀悼 *āi dào* (mourning)," a challenging phrase, was retained with the help of the lexical addition "傷心地 *shāng xīn dì* (sadly)" in the second half of verse 14a. The very difficult phrase "陰鬱的 *yīn yù de* (gloomy)" was employed to intensify the sadness of the psalmist, so the IBTT replaced it with "非常 *fēi cháng* (very)": very sadly (v. 14b).

The Hebrew text has the rhyming י in the end of verses 13b (נַפְשִׁי), 14a (הִתְהַלָּכְתִּי), 14b (שַׁחוֹתִי); IBTTV has the 著 *zhe* at the end of verses 14a, 14b.

- In verse 16b, though the Chinese idiom "咬牙切齒 *yǎo yá qiē chǐ* (grinding one's teeth)" is not easy for grade 1 students, it was preserved with the help of the illustration by a seven-year-old girl.[61] This is, on the one hand, to maintain the rhetorical beauty of the poetry, on the other hand, to make this colon rhyme with verse 15d (齒 *chǐ* and 止 *zhǐ* respectively).[62]

---

61. This girl was the one who helped the researcher perceive more about what is understandable for grade 1 students before the formal translation exercise. She was not included in the IBTT.

62. The pronunciations of 止 *zhǐ* and 齒 *chǐ* are very similar, though the Mandarin Phonetic Symbols of these two words are not identical.

It is noteworthy that no rhyme is found in verses 15–16 in the Hebrew text, but the IBTT grasped any possible opportunity in making the translated poetry rhyme.[63] This makes the Chinese renderings more beautiful and easier for children to chant or memorize.

- Here are some more challenging words or phrases being replaced by easier ones in this section: "盤問 *pán wèn* (cross-question)" → "一直問 *yī zhí wèn* (continually ask)" (v. 11); "禁食 *jìn shí* (fasting)" → "不吃東西 *bù chī dōng xī* (stopped eating food)," "刻苦己身 *kè kǔ jǐ shēn* (afflicted my body)" → "使我的身體受苦 *shǐ wǒ de shēn tǐ shòu kǔ* (to cause pain to my body)" (v. 13); "聚集 *jù jí* (gathered together)" → "聚在一起 *jù zài yī qǐ* (gathered together)," "攻擊者 *gōng jī zhě* (assailants)" → "攻擊我的人 *gōng jī wǒ de rén* (those attacked me)" (v. 15); "彎曲 *wān qǔ* (twisted)" → "不正直 *bù zhèng zhí* (dishonest)," "嘲弄者 *cháo nòng zhě* (mockers)" → "嘲笑者 *cháo xiào zhě* (mockers)" (v. 16).

---

63. The external evaluator of the dissertation noted that this could be regarded as applying the principle of "compensation," where certain TL artistic-rhetorical features are inserted into the translation to supply what may have been lost from the SL elsewhere.

5.3.1.5 Section 5 of Psalm 35 (v. 17)

This section describes the psalmist's lament on the need for divine deliverance.[64] There is one occurrence of נֶפֶשׁ.

5.3.1.5.1 The appropriate translation of נֶפֶשׁ in Psalm 35:17

5.3.1.5.1.1 The existing translations

נֶפֶשׁ as "性命 xìng mìng (physical life)" in RCUV of 2010 is substituted for נֶפֶשׁ as "靈魂 líng hún (spirit-soul)" in CUV. In accordance with RCUV, CNV and CCB render נֶפֶשׁ as "性命 xìng mìng (physical life)." It is translated as "我 wǒ (me)" in LZZ, TCVRE, CNET, DCT.

5.3.1.5.1.2 The exploration/discussion/comment of the IBTT

One possible meaning of נַפְשִׁי here is "我的全人 wǒ de quán rén (my whole being)" in that the psalmist is under attack, both physically (e.g. physical attack in vv. 4, 7) and psychologically (e.g. verbal attack in vv. 15, 20–21). Thus, the psalmist is pleading with God to rescue his "whole being" (every aspect of his life, including reputation) from the enemies' ravages. However, when considering the parallelism of נַפְשִׁי (v. 17b) and יְחִידָתִי "my only life" (v. 17c), the most immediate context, נַפְשִׁי as "我的性命 wǒ de xìng mìng (my physical life)" is more fitting.

5.3.1.5.2 The version readable for all generations by the IBTT through LiFE

Section 5 (v. 17): The Lament on the Need for Divine Deliverance	
IBTTV	**The initial draft**
17a. 主啊！你還要看多久？ (Same as the right column)	主啊！你還要看多久？ *zhǔ ā! nǐ hái yào kàn duō jiǔ?* Lord, how long will you look on?
17b. 救我的性命脫離他們的毀滅， (Same as the right column)	救我的性命脫離他們的毀滅， *jiù wǒ de xìng mìng tuō lí tā men de huì miè,* rescue my physical life from their destruction;

---

64. Ross, *A Commentary on the Psalms*, vol. 1, 772.

17c. [救]我唯一的生命脫離**這獅子**[**般的敵人**]！ *[jiù]wǒ wéi yī de shēng mìng tuō lí zhè shī zǐ bān de dí rén!* [rescue] my only life **from the [enemies who are like] lions**!	[救]我唯一的生命脫離**獅子**！ *[jiù]wǒ wéi yī de shēng mìng tuō lí shī zǐ!* [rescue] my only life **from the lions**!

Notes:

- The second and third colon of verse 17 form a pair: the parallel objects and the parallel מִן expressions in abb'a' order.[65] The chiastic parallelism here does not work well in Chinese. Translating the two cola in aba'b' order is more appropriate.
- The word כְּפִיר "lion" is used to portray different things in the Hebrew OT. For example, Proverbs 19:12 says, "A king's rage is like the roar of a lion [כְּפִיר]." In Hosea 5:14, כְּפִיר "lion" is associated with God's punishment. Therefore, in order to avoid confusion among children, the translation "lion" in verse 17c was combined with the enemies according to the context.

5.3.1.6 Section 8 of Psalm 35 (vv. 22–26)

The psalmist's petition not to allow the false enemies to triumph is the main theme of the last section (vv. 19–21). Here, the psalmist pleads for Yahweh's judgment to humiliate the enemies. The word נֶפֶשׁ occurs once here (v. 25).

5.3.1.6.1 The appropriate translation of נֶפֶשׁ in Psalm 35:25

5.3.1.6.1.1 The existing translations

CUV, RCUV, CNV, LZZ, CNET translate נֶפֶשׁ here as "心願 *xīn yuàn* (wish)." DCT has "心意 *xīn yì* (mind)." CCB translates נַפְשֵׁנוּ idiomatically: "我們如願以償了 *wǒ men rú yuàn yǐ cháng le* (we have our wishes fulfilled)"; TCVRE has "這正是我們所要的 *zhè zhèng shì wǒ men suǒ yào de* (This is exactly what we want)."

---

65. Goldingay, *Psalms*, vol. 1, 498.

5.3.1.6.1.2 *The exploration/discussion/comment of the IBTT*

The last section (vv. 19–21) depicts the verbal attack from the enemies. The purpose of their false accusation is to destroy the psalmist completely. This is implied by the direct speech "we have devoured him" (בִּלַּעֲנוּהוּ) in verse 25c, a parallel of another direct speech in 25b: הֶאָח נַפְשֵׁנוּ. Given these two are closely connected, the appropriate translation of נֶפֶשׁ related to בלע "devour" is "胃口 *wèi kǒu* (appetite)": "阿哈！[這正合]我們的胃口！*ā hā! [zhè zhèng hé] wǒ men de wèi kǒu* (Aha, [this fits] our appetite!)."[66]

In spite of נֶפֶשׁ "appetite" and בלע "devour" differ formally, they utilize the same metaphor[67] to connote what the enemies want: to completely "destroy so there would be no trace of [the psalmist]."[68]

5.3.1.6.2 The version readable for all generations by the IBTT through LiFE

Section 8 (vv. 22–26): The Petition for Yahweh's Righteous Judgment to Humiliate the Enemies

IBTTV	The initial draft
22a. 耶和華啊！你已經看見了， 求你不要沉默； (Same as the right column)	耶和華啊！你已經看見了，求你不要沉默； *yē hé huá ā! nǐ yǐ jīng kàn jiàn le, qiú nǐ bù yào chén mò*； Yahweh! You have seen; do not be silent.
22b. 我的主啊！求你不要遠離我。 (Same as the right column)	我的主啊！求你不要遠離我。 *wǒ de zhǔ ā! qiú nǐ bù yào yuǎn lí wǒ*。 My Lord, do not be far from me.

---

66. In the Chinese language, "合我們的胃口 *hé wǒ men de wèi kǒu* (fit our appetite)" can be considered synonymous with "我們想要 *wǒ men xiǎng yào* (we want)."

67. Goldingay, *Psalms*, vol. 1, 501.

68. Ross, *A Commentary on the Psalms*, vol. 1, 775. Ḥakham, in *The Bible: Psalms with the Jerusalem Commentary*, vol. 1, 272, notes that the use of the metaphor בלע "devour" to connote "destroy" is also found in Lam 2:2, where "Without pity, the Lord has swallowed up all the dwellings of Jacob." (NIV 2011).

23a. 求你**起來**,求你**醒來**,還我清白! *qiú nǐ qǐ lái, qiú nǐ xǐng lái, hái wǒ qīng bái!* **Rouse yourself** and **wake up to prove me right!**	求你**奮起**,求你**醒起**,**為我審判**! *qiú nǐ fèn qǐ, qiú nǐ xǐng qǐ, wéi wǒ shěn pàn!* **Rouse yourself** and **wake up to judge for me;**
23b. 我的神啊,我的主啊,為我**辯白**! *wǒ de shén ā, wǒ de zhǔ ā, wéi wǒ biàn bái!* my God, my Lord, **defend** me!	我的神 – 我的主啊,**為我爭辯**! *wǒ de shén – wǒ de zhǔ ā, wéi wǒ zhēng biàn!* my God, my Lord, **to contend** for me!
24a. 耶和華啊,我的神啊,求你按你的公義**證明我的清白**, *yē hé huá ā, wǒ de shén ā, qiú nǐ àn nǐ de gōng yì zhèng míng wǒ de qīng bái,* Yahweh, my God, **prove me right** according to your righteousness,	求你按你的公義**審判我**,耶和華 – 我的神啊, *qiú nǐ àn nǐ de gōng yì shěn pàn wǒ, yē hé huá – wǒ de shén ā,* **Judge me** according to your righteousness, Yahweh, my God,
24b. **不讓**他們向我**炫耀**! *bù ràng tā men xiàng wǒ xuàn yào!* and **let** them **not gloat** over me!	**不容**他們向我**誇耀**! *bù róng tā men xiàng wǒ kuā yào!* and **let** them **not rejoice** over me!
25a. 別讓他們心裏說: (Same as the right column)	別讓他們心裏說: *bié ràng tā men xīn lǐ shuō:* Do not let them say in their heart,
25b.「**哈**![這正合]我們的胃口!」 「*hā! [zhè zhèng hé] wǒ men de wèi kǒu!*」 "**Ha**, [this fits] our appetite!"	「**阿哈**![這正合]我們的胃口!」 「*ā hā! [zhè zhèng hé] wǒ men de wèi kǒu!*」 "**Aha**, [this fits] our appetite!"
25c. 別讓他們說:「我們把他吞沒!」 (Same as the right column)	別讓他們說:「我們把他吞沒!」 *bié ràng tā men shuō:*「*wǒ men bǎ tā tūn mò!*」 Do not let them say, "We have devoured him."

26b. 讓那喜歡我[**遇到**]災難的人 *ràng nà xǐ huān wǒ [yù dào] zāi nán de rén* Let those who rejoice over my disaster	讓那喜歡我[**遭**]災難的 *ràng nà xǐ huān wǒ [zāo] zāi nán de* Let those who rejoice over my disaster
26a. 一同**丟臉**慚愧！ *yī tóng diū liǎn cán kuì!* **lose their face** and be ashamed altogether;	一同**蒙羞**慚愧！ *yī tóng méng xiū cán kuì!* **be put to shame** and be ashamed altogether;
26d. 讓那**自大的人** *ràng nà zì dà de rén* let those **who are proud**	讓那向我妄自尊大的 *ràng nà xiàng wǒ wàng zì zūn dà de* let those **who magnify themselves over me**
26c. **穿上丟臉**恥辱！ *chuān shàng diū liǎn chǐ rǔ!* **be clothed in losing face** and disgrace.	**披戴羞愧**恥辱！ *pī dài xiū kuì chǐ rǔ!* **be clothed in shame** and disgrace.

Notes:

- Verse 23 consists of two Hiphil imperative verbs, two nouns with preposition לְ and pronominal suffix (1cs), and two invocations, structured as aa′bcc′b′.[69] It is easy to keep this structure in the Chinese translation.

    In the first colon, the verb הָעִירָה, the Hiphil of עור, appears only once as an imperative.[70] The Hiphil of עור "is intransitive and has the same meaning as הִתְעוֹרֵר, 'rouse yourself,'" which is employed here to make it resemble and rhyme with הָקִיצָה, "wake up."[71] Since grade 1 students could hardly comprehend the translated rhyming pairing of "奮起 *fèn qǐ* (rouse yourself)" and "醒起 *xǐng qǐ* (wake up)" in the initial draft, the IBTT replaced it with "起來 *qǐ lái* (rouse yourself)" and "醒來 *xǐng lái* (wake up)."

---

69. Goldingay, *Psalms*, vol. 1, 500.
70. Goldingay, 500.
71. Ḥakham, *The Bible: Psalms with the Jerusalem Commentary*, vol. 1, 271 n. 8.

The judicial language here (i.e. "為我審判 *wéi wǒ shěn pàn* [to judge for me]" and "為我爭辯 *wéi wǒ zhēng biàn* [to contend for me]") is unfamiliar to grade 1 students. The illustration by a thirteen-year-old girl does not help because the scene is not common in young children's daily life. In the former case, "to judge for me" was replaced with the easier phrase "還我清白 *hái wǒ qīng bái* (to prove my right)." This is gleaned from Tanner's argument: "in ancient times God's coming to judge the world was seen as a good thing, and indeed the way to vindication for God's people."[72] In the latter case, "為我辯白 *wéi wǒ biàn bái* (defend me)" was substituted for "to contend for me." This makes the cloa of verse 23 rhyme.

During the IBTT's lengthy discussion of these two phrases, an eight-year-old boy demonstrated his understanding of the word "judge" by the illustrations on the next page.

- In Chinese poetry, invocation usually appears at the beginning of a colon.

In verses 23, and 24, the Hebrew pairing of invocation related to God is put in the middle of the verses. In the former (v. 23), the word order of the invocation can be maintained because it is located at the beginning of the second colon. In the latter (v. 24), however, the Hebrew invocation at the end of the

---

72. Tanner, "Psalm 35," 337.

first colon needs to be switched to the beginning of that colon in the Chinese translation.

- The first half of verse 26 is parallel to the second, each of which comprises the psalmist's wish and the delineation of the enemies, arranged aba'b'.[73] This syntactic surface structure is also found in verse 4. Similar to that in verse 4, the word order in this

---

73. Goldingay, *Psalms*, vol. 1, 501.

tetracolon also needs to be adjusted as verse 26b → verse 26a → verse 26d → verse 26c in the Chinese translation.

The enemies here are described as those who rejoice over the psalmist's disaster (שְׂמֵחֵי רָעָתִי)[74] and magnify themselves over the psalmist (הַמַּגְדִּילִים עָלָי). These force the psalmist to make an urgent request similar to that in verse 4 to let the enemies know shame and disgrace. This forms a strong connection between the beginning and the conclusion of the psalm.[75] Such semantic and structural connections can be displayed in Chinese translation.

- In verse 26c, the psalmist highlights the nouns בֹּשֶׁת וּכְלִמָּה "shame and disgrace" by poetically "picturing the shame as a clothing that covers and clings to the attackers."[76] Such imagery is not difficult for children to grasp if the diction is easy enough. Thus, "披戴 *pī dài* (be clothed)" was replaced with the easier phrase "穿上 *chuān shàng* (be clothed)"; "羞愧恥辱 *xiū kuì chǐ rǔ* (shame and disgrace)" with "丟臉恥辱 *diū liǎn chǐ rǔ* (losing face and disgrace)." Though "恥辱 *chǐ rǔ* (disgrace)" is a challenging phrase, it might be understood by children when it is combined with the easier phrase "丟臉 *diū liǎn* (losing face)." In the same vein, the difficult phrase "慚愧 *cán kuì* (be ashamed)" in verse 26a was kept since it is juxtaposed with the easier phrase "丟臉 *diū liǎn* (lose face)," which is a substitute for "蒙羞 *méng xiū* (put to shame)" in the initial draft.

- The Hebrew text of this section rhymes very well. Verses 22b (מִמֶּנִּי), 23a (לְמִשְׁפָּטִי), 23b (לְרִיבִי), 24a (אֱלֹהָי), 24b (לִי), 26b (רָעָתִי), and 26d (עָלָי) end with ִי or ָי. Verses 25b (נַפְשֵׁנוּ) and 25c (בִּלַּעֲנוּהוּ) end with וּ. In IBTTV, the rhyming lines do not exactly correspond to those in the Hebrew text, but the Chinese translations still demonstrate the rhyme with beauty. In verses 22, and 23, the first colon rhymes with the second: 默 *mò* and 我 *wǒ* in verse 22, 白 *bái* in both of the cola of verse 23. The three cola

---

74. שָׂמֵחַ is the adjective form of שמח in vv. 19, 24, all of which are used to indicate the enemies' rejoicing over the psalmist.

75. Tanner, "Psalm 35," 337.

76. Goldingay, *Psalms*, vol. 1, 501.

of verse 25 also rhyme well: 說 *shuō* (v. 25a), 口 *kǒu* (v. 25b),[77] and 沒 *mò* (v. 25c). The last rhyme of the section is located in verse 26b and verse 26d, both of which have 人 *rén*.

- Here are some more challenging words or phrases being replaced by easier ones in this section: "審判我 *shěn pàn wǒ* (judge me)" → "證明我的清白 *zhèng míng wǒ de qīng bái* (vindicate me)," "不容 *bù róng* (let not)" → "不讓 *bù ràng* (let not)," "誇耀 *kuā yào* (rejoice)" → "炫耀 *xuàn yào* (gloat)" (v. 24); "阿哈 *ā hā* (Aha)" → "哈 *hā* (Ha)" (v. 25); "向我妄自尊大的 *xiàng wǒ wàng zì zūn dà de* (those who magnify themselves over me)" → "那自大的人 *nà zì dà de rén* (those who are proud)" (v. 26).

5.3.2 Psalm 63

Four occurrences of the Hebrew word נֶפֶשׁ are found in Psalm 63, a psalm of praise, whose structure can be viewed as consisting of two parallel portions, each one composed of two strophes:

A (1–2) + A' (6–8) = Psalmist's expression of longing for Yahweh

B (3–5) + B' (9–11) = Psalmist's expression of praise for Yahweh[78]

Based on the structure above, Psalm 63 is divided into four sections:
- Section 1 (vv. 1–2): Longing for God's presence (×1)
- Section 2 (vv. 3–5): Praise for God's provision (×1)
- Section 3 (vv. 6–8): Longing for God's presence (×1)
- Section 4 (vv. 9–11): Praise for God's protection (×1)

5.3.2.1 Section 1 of Psalm 63 (vv. 1–2)

The first section describes the psalmist's longing for God's presence. One occurrence of נֶפֶשׁ is found in verse 1.

5.3.2.1.1 The appropriate translation of נֶפֶשׁ in Psalm 63:1

5.3.2.1.1.1 The existing translations

In Psalm 63:1, נַפְשִׁי is rendered as "我 *wǒ* (I)" in CUV and TCVRE, as "我的心靈 *wǒ de xīn líng* (my heart-spirit)" in RCUV and DCT, as "我的

---

77. In Mandarin Phonetic Symbols, the pronunciation of ㄡ in 口 *kǒu* (v. 25b) is similar to that of ㄛ in 說 *shuō* (v. 25a) and 沒 *mò* (v. 25c).

78. This structure is suggested by the external evaluator of the present dissertation.

心 wǒ de xīn (my heart)" in CNV, LZZ and CCB, and as "我的靈 wǒ de líng (my spirit)" in CNET.

5.3.2.1.1.2 The exploration/discussion/comment of the IBTT

In order to accentuate the intensity of his yearning for God's presence, the psalmist arranges verse 1 as follows: the preformative "I" in the verb אֲשַׁחֲרֶךָ "I seek you earnestly" (v. 1a) is elucidated and amplified by the parallel of נַפְשִׁי (v. 1b) and בְשָׂרִי (v. 1c). Thus, translating נַפְשִׁי as "我 (I)" obviously fails to convey the intensity of the feeling. It is more suitable to translate נַפְשִׁי here as "我全人 wǒ quán rén (my whole being)." This implies that not only the psalmist's heart but also his whole being is thirsty and yearning for God.

One might challenge the translation of נַפְשִׁי as "my whole being" here, suggesting that the "I" as a human being in verse 1a comprises both psychological and physical parts, Thus, נַפְשִׁי and בְשָׂרִי should be rendered as "my heart/spirit" (psychological) and "my body" (physical) respectively. Nevertheless, the language the Bible authors use is not always so clear-cut or systematic. For example, Philippians 4:6 states, "Do not be anxious about anything, but in every situation, by *prayer* and *petition*, with thanksgiving, present your requests to God" (emphasis added). Here, prayer and petition are juxtaposed as if they belong to different categories. In fact, prayer includes petition. In the same vein, נַפְשִׁי and בְשָׂרִי do not need to be classified as two different categories (heart/spirit v.s. body); נַפְשִׁי "my whole being" includes בְשָׂרִי "my body."

Another similar instance is found in Psalm 35:9–10, where נֶפֶשׁ and עֶצֶם "bone" might also be interpreted as indicating psychological and physical dimensions of a person respectively. However, as discussed in §5.3.1.3.1.2, when these two terms are parallel to each other, both of them are related to "the whole/entire being."

5.3.2.1.2 The version readable for all generations by the IBTT through LiFE

Section 1 (vv.1–2): Longing for God's Presence	
IBTTV	**The initial draft**
01a. 神啊，你是我的神，我**從早晨就來**尋求你； *shén ā, nǐ shì wǒ de shén, wǒ cóng zǎo chén jiù lái xún qiú nǐ;* God, you are my God, I seek you **from the morning**;	神啊，你是我的神，我**切切地**尋求你； *shén ā, nǐ shì wǒ de shén, wǒ qiē qiē dì xún qiú nǐ;* God, you are my God, I seek you **earnestly**;
01d. 在乾旱疲乏無水之地， (Same as the right column)	在乾旱疲乏無水之地， *zài qián hàn pí fá wú shuǐ zhī dì,* in a dry and weary land, without water,
01b. 我全人**渴望**你， *wǒ quán rén kě wàng nǐ,* my whole being **thirsts for** you;	我全人**渴慕**你， *wǒ quán rén kě mù nǐ,* my whole being **thirsts for** you;
01c. 我**全身想望**你。 *wǒ quán shēn xiǎng wàng nǐ.* my **whole body yearns for** you.	我**肉身切慕**你。 *wǒ ròu shēn qiē mù nǐ.* my **body yearns for** you.
02a. 如此，我曾在聖所**看見**你， *rú cǐ, wǒ céng zài shèng suǒ kàn jiàn nǐ,* Thus, I have **seen** you in the sanctuary,	如此，我曾在聖所**瞻仰**你， *rú cǐ, wǒ céng zài shèng suǒ zhān yǎng nǐ,* Thus, I have **seen** you in the sanctuary,
02b. 看到你的**榮耀和能力**。 *kàn dào nǐ de róng yào hé néng lì.* beholding your **glory and power**.	看到你的**能力和榮耀**。 *kàn dào nǐ de néng lì hé róng yào.* beholding your **power and glory**.

Notes:

- In verse 1, the connotation of the verb שחר "seek" is complemented by the verbs צמא "thirst" of verse 1b and כמה "yearn" of verse 1c. Then, verse 1d indicates the location where the event of the previous cola takes place. Thus, verse 1 as a whole is arranged "abb'c in its description of the king's recurrent seeking of God."[79]

In Chinese, phrases related to time or location are usually put close to the beginning of sentences. When translating verse 1 into Chinese, the word order sounds better as follows: verse 1a → verse 1d → verse 1b → verse 1c (i.e. acbb', instead of the preceding abb'c).

- The verb שחר "seek" is probably a denominative from the noun שַׁחַר, the word for "dawn," and is often rendered "to seek early."[80] Verse 6 may suggest a more literal interpretation of this verb:[81] to seek God in the morning. This "offers some justification for the Orthodox Church's designating this a morning psalm."[82] A more derived sense of this verb is "to seek earnestly."[83]

  In line with CUV, the initial draft has "切切地尋求 *qiē qiē dì xún qiú* (seek earnestly)," a beautiful phrase in Chinese but generally difficult for grade 1 students to comprehend. Therefore, the IBTT decided to use its literal meaning: to seek God *from* the morning. The preposition "from" is preferred because it signifies that not just *in* the morning, but *from* the morning (to the end of a day), the psalmist seeks God. Thus, IBTTV has "我從早晨就來尋求你 *wǒ cóng zǎo chén jiù lái xún qiú nǐ* (I seek you from the morning)."

- In verse 1b and verse 1c, the selection of the verbs צמא "thirst"[84] and כמה "yearn"[85] makes these two cola rhyme more neatly:

---

79. Goldingay, *Psalms*, vol. 2, 256.

80. Marvin E. Tate, *Psalms 51–100*, ed. Bruce M. Metzger et al., Word Biblical Commentary 20 (Dallas, TX: Word Books, 1998), 127.

81. This recurrence marks the beginning (*anaphora* [a-X, a'-Y], see §2.3.3.7.1.7) of the second portion of the psalm (vv. 6–11).

82. Goldingay, *Psalms*, vol. 2, 256.

83. Allen P. Ross, *A Commentary on the Psalms*, vol. 2 (Grand Rapids, MI: Kregel Academic & Professional, 2013), 382.

84. In the Psalms, "the only other occurrence of the metaphor of thirst for God" is found in 42:2. See Goldingay, *Psalms*, vol. 2, 256.

85. The verb כמה "yearn" occurs only once in the Bible. See Amos Ḥakham, *The Bible: Psalms with the Jerusalem Commentary*, vol. 2, ed. and trans. Israel V. Berman (Jerusalem:

צָמְאָה rhymes with כָּמַהּ;[86] נַפְשִׁי with בְּשָׂרִי; לְךָ is repeated in the middle of both cola.

Again, "渴慕 *kě mù* (thirst)" and "切慕 *qiē mù* (yearn)" are Chinese phrases with beauty but generally beyond grade 1 students' comprehension. They were replaced by "渴望 *kě wàng* (thirst)" and "想望 *xiǎng wàng* (yearn)" respectively. These two Chinese phrases rhyme, corresponding to the rhyming Hebrew verbs צָמְאָה and כָּמַהּ.

נַפְשִׁי "my whole being" and בְּשָׂרִי "my body" have the same ending vowel ִי. It is hard here to find Chinese counterpart for this collocation regarding rhyme. An alternative way is to make the initial words of the Chinese collocation identical. Thus, "我肉身 *wǒ ròu shēn* (my body)" in the draft was replaced with "我全身 *wǒ quán shēn* (my whole body)." The latter makes the first two words of the phrase identical to those in the phrase "我全人 *wǒ quán rén* (my whole being)."

- In metaphorical terms, verse 1d describes the wilderness as "dry and weary land, without water." The word אֶרֶץ "land" (at the beginning of this colon) is modified by both צִיָּה "dry" (the attributive genitive) and עָיֵף "weary"[87] (the adjective), and further clarified by בְּלִי־מָיִם "without water."[88] It is not difficult to translate these metaphorical terms into Chinese, but the word אֶרֶץ "地 *dì* (land)" needs to be switched to the end of this colon: "乾旱疲乏無水之地 *qián hàn pí fá wú shuǐ zhī dì* (a dry, weary,[89] and waterless land)." In the initial draft, there are two difficult Chinese words in this combination (旱 *hàn* and 乏 *fá*), but the

---

Mosad Harav Kook, 2003), 38.

86. Ḥakham, in *The Bible: Psalms*, vol. 2, 38, notes that though צמא "thirst" and כמה "yearn" are written here in the past tense, they are aimed to convey the present. This "may be classified as an instantaneous perfect." See Ross, *A Commentary on the Psalms*, vol. 2, 382–383.

87. The word עָיֵף refers to loss of strength due to thirst. See Ḥakham, *The Bible: Psalms*, vol. 2, 38.

88. Ross, *A Commentary on the Psalms*, vol. 2, 383.

89. "A weary land" in Chinese would suggest figuratively a plot of ground that had been over-farmed.

- IBTT preserved these words since they might be perceived by children through the immediate context (i.e. waterless land).
- In verse 2a, the IBTT replaced "瞻仰 zhān yǎng (see)" with the easy one: "看見 kàn jiàn (see)."

  The hendiadys of עֹז "power" and כָּבוֹד "glory" in verse 2b denotes "God's splendid power."[90] The IBTT suggested switching the word order of the hendiadys, so that verse 2a can rhyme with verse 2b.
- The Hebrew rhyming words in this section are found in verses 1a, 2a, and 2b (ךָ in אֲשַׁחֲרֶךָּ, חֲזִיתִיךָ and וּכְבוֹדֶךָ), and in verses 1b and 1c (י in נַפְשִׁי and בְשָׂרִי). IBTTV's rhyming words are as follows: 你 nǐ (vv. 1a, 1b, 1c, 2a), 地 dì (v. 1d), and 力 lì (v. 2b).

5.3.2.2 Section 2 of Psalm 63 (vv. 3–5)

The main theme of this section is the praise for God's provision. Verse 5 has נֶפֶשׁ appearing once.

5.3.2.2.1 The appropriate translation of נֶפֶשׁ in Psalm 63:5

5.3.2.2.1.1 The existing translations

The word נַפְשִׁי in this verse is rendered as "我的心 wǒ de xīn (my heart)" in all prominent Chinese versions except for TCVRE, which translates נַפְשִׁי as "我的靈 wǒ de líng (my spirit)."

5.3.2.2.1.2 The exploration/discussion/comment of the IBTT

In verse 1, נַפְשִׁי as the subject is translated as "我全人 wǒ quán rén (my whole being)" to accentuate the intensity of the psalmist's thirst for God. Here, the psalmist repeats נַפְשִׁי as the subject to introduce a contrary image: no longer thirsty, the psalmist now feels as if satisfied with the richest food through prayers (v. 4). This causes him to feel the closeness of God. When one enjoys the richest food, not only one's body is satisfied, but also one's heart. Thus, translating נַפְשִׁי as "我整個人 wǒ zhěng gè rén (my whole person)" here can greatly emphasize the psalmist's joyous satisfaction of communion with God.

---

90. Goldingay, *Psalms*, vol. 2, 257.

5.3.2.2.2 The version readable for all generations by the IBTT through LiFE

Section 2 (vv. 3–5): Praise for God's Provision

IBTTV	The initial draft
03a. 因你的慈愛比生命更好， (Same as the right column)	因你的慈愛比生命更好， *yīn nǐ de cí ài bǐ shēng mìng gèng hǎo,* For your lovingkindness is better than life;
03b. 我的嘴唇要頌讚你。 (Same as the right column)	我的嘴唇要頌讚你。 *wǒ de zuǐ chún yào sòng zàn nǐ.* my lips will praise you.
04a. 所以，我要一生稱頌你， (Same as the right column)	所以，我要一生稱頌你， *suǒ yǐ, wǒ yào yī shēng chēng sòng nǐ,* So I will bless you throughout my life;
04b. 我要奉你的名舉手[**禱告**]。 *wǒ yào fèng nǐ de míng jǔ shǒu dǎo gào.* in your name I will lift my hands [**in prayer**].	我要奉你的名舉手。 *wǒ yào fèng nǐ de míng jǔ shǒu.* in your name I will lift my hands.
05a. 我整個人就像**吃飽了最豐盛的美味**， *wǒ zhěng gè rén jiù xiàng chī bǎo le zuì fēng shèng de měi wèi,* As with **the richest delicacies** my whole person **is satisfied**;	我整個人就像**飽足了肥油脂肪**， *wǒ zhěng gè rén jiù xiàng bǎo zú le féi yóu zhī fáng,* As with **suet and fatness** my whole person **is satisfied**;
05b. 我的口要以歡呼的嘴唇讚美。 (Same as the right column)	我的口要以歡呼的嘴唇讚美。 *wǒ de kǒu yào yǐ huān hū de zuǐ chún zàn měi.* with resounding lips my mouth praises (you).[91]

---

91. The round bracket denotes that "you" is added in English expression, but it is not necessary for Chinese.

Notes:
- In verses 3, and 4, the Chinese phrases "頌讚 *sòng zàn* (praise)" and "稱頌 *chēng sòng* (bless)" were generally difficult for grade 1 students, but young children in the IBTT could grasp their meanings well since they are frequently used in the church and put into practice during worship. For example, one grade 1 student said, "頌讚 *sòng zàn* (praise)" is to praise God more deeply; "頌讚 *sòng zàn* (praise)" and "稱頌 *chēng sòng* (bless)" are at the same extent or intensity in terms of praising God.
- The two cola of verse 4 are parallel in both content and phonology. In terms of the former (content), "I will bless you" substantially corresponds to "in your name, I will lift up my hands" (ברך "bless," a denominative verb from בֶּרֶךְ "knee,"[92] is an implicit parallel of "hands").[93] As to the latter (phonology), the first letter of each word in the first colon is reversely repeated in the first letter of each word in the second, arranged abcc'b'a'. It is very hard to find the Chinese counterpart for such stylistic device.

    Moreover, the chiastic parallelism regarding the syntax here cannot be reproduced in Chinese, since the word בְחַיָּי "throughout my life" needs to be put before the verb "bless": "我要一生稱頌你 *wǒ yào yī shēng chēng sòng nǐ* (lit, I will, throughout my life, bless you)." Thus, the Chinese rendering was structured as aba'b', maintaining the beauty of parallelism, though in a reverse way.
- The connotation of verse 4b was not very clear for both young and adult participants because the raising of hands is combined with "in your name." Ḥakham asserts that "lifting hands" is related to "the ancient custom of praying with raised hands pointing toward heaven."[94] Accordingly, the IBTT suggested adding "in prayer" at the end of this colon.

---

92. J. N. Oswalt, "ברך," in *Theological Wordbook of the Old Testament*, eds. R. L. Harris, G. L. Archer, Jr., and B. K. Waltke (Chicago, IL: Moody, 1999), 132.

93. Cf. Goldingay, *Psalms*, vol. 2, 258.

94. Ḥakham, *The Bible: Psalms*, vol. 2, 40.

- In verse 5, the simile כְּמוֹ חֵלֶב וָדֶשֶׁן "as with suet and fatness" is used to compare the satisfaction of the psalmist's whole being with feasting on the richest food.[95] The hendiadys of חֵלֶב "suet" and דֶשֶׁן "fatness"[96] is employed to heighten the sense of how rich the meal is.[97] This is supported by passages such as Leviticus 3:16–17, where worshippers are not allowed to eat suet because "all the fat is the Lord's."[98]

  The literal translation of this hendiadys (i.e. "肥油脂肪 *féi yóu zhī fáng* [suet and fatness]") is not beautiful at all in terms of Chinese poetry. On the other hand, suet and fatness are not the richest food from contemporary Chinese people's perspective. A generic expression, the richest food, works well in Chinese. The IBTT's choice of the Chinese translation "最豐盛的美味 *zuì fēng shèng de měi wèi* (the richest delicacies)," rather than "最豐盛的食物 *zuì fēng shèng de shí wù* (the richest food)," was to make this colon rhyme with the following colon, which ends with "讚美 *zàn měi* (praise)" in IBTTV.

- Each colon of verse 4, and 5 has the ending vowels ִי (בְחַיַּי and כַפַּי) or ִי (נַפְשִׁי and פִּי). Not exactly corresponding to the rhyming pattern in the Hebrew text, IBTTV has verse 3a rhyming with verse 4b (好 *hǎo* and 告 *gào*). Both verse 3b and verse 4a end with 你 *nǐ*. 美味 *měi wèi* in verse 5a rhymes with 讚美 *zàn měi* in verse 5b as noted above.

5.3.2.3 Section 3 of Psalm 63 (vv. 6–8)

This section repeats the main theme of section 1 (i.e. longing for God's presence). Verse 8 has נֶפֶשׁ appearing once.

---

95. Cf. Ross, *A Commentary on the Psalms*, vol. 2, 385.
96. חֵלֶב "suet" and דֶשֶׁן "fatness" are crucial words "in the context of sacrifices." See Ḥakham, *The Bible: Psalms with the Jerusalem Commentary*, vol. 2, 40.
97. Tate, *Psalms 51–100*, 124.
98. Goldingay, *Psalms*, vol. 2, 259.

5.3.2.3.1 The appropriate translation of נַפְשִׁי in Psalm 63:8

5.3.2.3.1.1 The existing translations
Again, נַפְשִׁי as "我的心 *wǒ de xīn* (my heart)" is preferred by the majority of prominent Chinese versions (i.e. CUV, RCUV, CNV, LZZ, CCB). It is rendered as "我 *wǒ* (I)" in TCVRE, DCT, and as "我靈 *wǒ líng* (my spirit)" in CNET.

5.3.2.3.1.2 The exploration/discussion/comment of the IBTT
Serving as the ending of this section, which describes the psalmist's longing for God's presence, this verse perfectly demonstrates the intimacy between the psalmist and God: the psalmist (נַפְשִׁי) clings to God, and God's right hand upholds the psalmist. Given the close relationship, the psalmist's heart definitely clings to God as rendered in the existing Chinese versions. However, when the second colon of this verse is considered, one finds that not only the psalmist's heart clings to God, but also his body. This is supported by the description that God's right hand upholds him (i.e. upholds him physically). Subsequently, the most appropriate translation of נַפְשִׁי here is "我整個人 *wǒ zhěng gè rén* (my whole person)": My whole person clings to you (דָּבְקָה נַפְשִׁי אַחֲרֶיךָ). This could best elaborate the psalmist's extraordinary gladness and complete trust in God.

5.3.2.3.2 The version readable for all generations by the IBTT through LiFE

Section 3 (vv. 6–8): Longing for God's Presence	
IBTTV	**The initial draft**
06a. 甚至，我在**床**上懷念你， *shèn zhì, wǒ zài chuáng shàng huái niàn nǐ,* Indeed, I remember you upon my **bed**;	甚至，我在**鋪蓋**上懷念你， *shèn zhì, wǒ zài pū gài shàng huái niàn nǐ,* Indeed, I remember you upon my **bedclothes**;
06b. 我**整晚**對著你**輕聲細語**。 *wǒ zhěng wǎn duì zhe nǐ qīng shēng xì yǔ.* **all night long** I **speak** to you **softly**.	我**在夜更**對你**喃喃低語**。 *wǒ zài yè gèng duì nǐ nán nán dī yǔ.* **in the night watches** I **talk** to you **quietly**.

07a. 因為你曾**經**是我的幫助， *yīn wéi nǐ céng jīng shì wǒ de bāng zhù,* For you have been my help;	因為你曾是我的幫助， *yīn wéi nǐ céng shì wǒ de bāng zhù,* For you have been my help;
07b. 我在你翅膀**影子**下歡呼。 *wǒ zài nǐ chì bǎng yǐng zǐ xià huān hū.* in the **shadow** of your wings I resound.	我在你翅膀**蔭**下歡呼。 *wǒ zài nǐ chì bǎng yīn xià huān hū.* in the **shadow** of your wings I resound.
08a. 我整個人緊靠著你； (Same as the right column)	我整個人緊靠著你； *wǒ zhěng gè rén jǐn kào zhe nǐ;* My whole person clings to you;
08b. 你的右手扶持著我。 (Same as the right column)	你的右手扶持著我。 *nǐ de yòu shǒu fú chí zhe wǒ.* your right hand upholds me.

- In ancient China, night watchmen (更夫 *gèng fū*) beat gongs to tell people what time it was during the night. This traditional custom is no longer familiar to contemporary children. Therefore, the rendering "夜更 *yè gèng* (the night watches)" in the draft (v. 6b) was replaced with "整晚 *zhěng wǎn* (all night long)" due to the plural form of אַשְׁמוּרָה "night watch."

    The two cola of verse 6 form a syntactic chiasmus: a verb followed by a prepositional phrase in the first colon and the second arranged in reversed order (abb'a'). This does not work in Chinese since phrases related to location (bedclothes[99] or bed in v. 6a) or time (the night watches or all night long in v. 6b) should be put at the beginning of the colon.

- In verse 8b, the challenging but beautiful verb "扶持 *fú chí* (uphold)" in the initial draft was kept since it can be perceived by means of the illustration from an eleven-year-old boy.

---

99. The plural "my bedclothes" is related to "the covers or sheets used when sleeping . . . there are usually at least two: one below, and one above." See Ḥakham, *The Bible: Psalms*, vol. 2, 40.

When God's "right hand" (יְמִין) in verse 8b was discussed, a grade 2 student noted that it indicates God's mighty hand, an interpretation in accordance with Bratcher and Reyburn's argument: the word יְמִינֶךָ "your right hand" is "a symbol of God's might."[100] Therefore, the IBTT did not add any interpretative word before יְמִינֶךָ "your right hand," contrary to NIrV (a version comprehensible for children), which has "your *powerful* right hand" for יְמִינֶךָ (italics added).

In verse 8, the ending of each word is arranged as הָ → יְ → ךָ in the first colon; as יְ → הָ → ךָ in the second colon (abcb'a'c). Such an arrangement is hard to imitate in Chinese. However, it is worthy of preserving the beauty of poetry in Chinese translation through other means.

The pronominal suffix הָ in both the qatal דָּבְקָה "cling to" and the qatal תָּמְכָה "uphold," a wordplay in the Hebrew original,[101] has no Chinese counterpart. But their phonological similarity can be somewhat maintained by means of adding "著 zhe" in both "緊靠著 jǐn kào zhe (cling to)" and "扶持著 fú chí zhe (uphold)." Thus, IBTTV has:

我整個人緊靠著你； *wǒ zhěng gè rén jǐn kào zhe ǐ*；

---

100. Bratcher and Reyburn, *A Translator's Handbook*, 550.

101. Samuel L. Terrien, *The Psalms: Strophic Structure and Theological Commentary* (Grand Rapids, MI: Eerdmans, 2003), 463.

My whole person clings to you;

你的右手扶持著我。*nĭ de yòu shŏu fú chí zhe wŏ*。
your right hand upholds me.

The Chinese words that are repeated in both cola are arranged as 我 *wŏ* → 緊靠著 *jǐn kào zhe* → 你 *nĭ* in the first colon, as 你 *nĭ* → 扶持著 *fú chí zhe* → 我 *wŏ* in the second colon. This makes verse 8 as a whole work abcc'b'a', a chiastic structure in both content and phonology.

- Here are some more challenging words or phrases being replaced by easier ones in this section: "鋪蓋 *pū gài* (bedclothes)" → "床上 *chuáng shàng* (bed)," "喃喃低語 *nán nán dī yǔ* (talk quietly)" → 輕聲細語 *qīng shēng xì yǔ* (speak softly)" (v. 6); "陰 *yīn* (shadow)" → "影子 *yǐng zǐ* (shadow)" (v. 7).

5.3.2.4 Section 4 of Psalm 63 (vv. 9–11)

The final section describes the praise for God's protection through the contrasting fates of the enemies and God's people. The word נֶפֶשׁ occurs once here (v. 9).

5.3.2.4.1 The appropriate translation of נֶפֶשׁ in Psalm 63:9

5.3.2.4.1.1 The existing translations

In Psalm 35:4, the juxtaposition of בקשׁ and נֶפֶשׁ is literally translated as "seek my life" (尋索我命 *xún suǒ wǒ mìng*) in CUV, RCUV, CNV, LZZ, CNET, or simply "kill me" (殺我 *shā wǒ*) in TCVRE, CCB, DCT. Here, the renderings of the same combination seem to be more complicated in all of these versions except for DCT. This is because their translators relate יְבַקְשׁוּ נַפְשִׁי (they seek my life) to לְשׁוֹאָה (destruction), viewing the latter as the psalmist's destruction. On these grounds, CUV, RCUV, CNET have "尋索要滅我命 *xún suǒ yào miè wǒ mìng* (seek to destroy my life)." CNV has "尋索我、要殺我 *xún suǒ wǒ、yào shā wǒ* (seek me and kill me)." LZZ has "尋索我命、要毀滅我命 *xún suǒ wǒ mìng、yào huǐ miè wǒ mìng* (seek my life and destroy my life)." CCB has "圖謀毀滅我 *tú móu huǐ miè wǒ* (plot to destroy me)." TCVRE simply states: "殺害我 *shā hài wǒ* (kill me)."

However, the second colon of this verse signifies that it is the enemies' destruction, instead of the psalmist's, as Ross asserts.[102] Aligned with this thread, DCT has "那些想殺我的人將被剷除 *nà xiē xiǎng shā wǒ de rén jiāng bèi chǎn chú* (those who want to kill me will be eradicated)."

5.3.2.4.1.2 The exploration/discussion/comment of the IBTT
In verse 9, the fronted וְהֵמָּה "but they" introduces new participants (the enemies) who want to seek the psalmist's נֶפֶשׁ. From the miserable fate that the enemies will encounter (vv. 9b–10) (i.e. being destroyed and eaten by jackals), it is reasonable to infer that the enemies who want to kill the psalmist (seek his life) dig their own grave. In line with the preceding Chinese versions, the IBTT, with great unanimity, renders נֶפֶשׁ here as "性命 *xìng mìng* (physical life)."

5.3.2.4.2 The version readable for all generations by the IBTT through LiFE

Section 4 (vv. 9–11): Praise for God's Protection	
IBTTV	**The initial draft**
09a. 但他們，就是那些**想取我性命**的人必滅亡, *dàn tā men, jiù shì nà xiē xiǎng qǔ wǒ xìng mìng de rén bì miè wáng*, But they, to [their own] destruction, want to **take my physical life**;	但他們，就是那些**尋索我命**的人必滅亡, *dàn tā men, jiù shì nà xiē xún suǒ wǒ mìng de rén bì miè wáng*, But they, to [their own] destruction, **seek my life**;
09b. 他們必去到地的最低之處。 (Same as the right column)	他們必去到地的最低之處。 *tā men bì qù dào dì de zuì dī zhī chù*。 they will go to the lowest [place] of the earth.
10a. 他們必被刀劍**打倒**, *tā men bì bèi dāo jiàn dǎ dǎo*, They will **be struck down** by the sword;	他們必被刀劍**擊倒**, *tā men bì bèi dāo jiàn jī dǎo*, They will **be struck down** by the sword;

---

102. Ross, *A Commentary on the Psalms*, vol. 2, 378, 387.

10b. 必成為豺狼的食物。 (Same as the right column)	必成為豺狼的食物。 bì chéng wéi chái láng de shí wù。 they will become the food of jackals.
11a. 但是王必在神裡面歡喜， (Same as the right column)	但是王必在神裡面歡喜， dàn shì wáng bì zài shén lǐ miàn huān xǐ, But the king will rejoice in God;
11b. 每一個指著[神]**發誓保證**的都要**快樂**， měi yī gè xiàng [shén] fā shì bǎo zhèng de dōu yào kuài lè, all who **swear** by [God] **are glad**,	每一個指著[神]**發誓**的都要**歡躍**， měi yī gè zhǐ zhe [shén] fā shì de dōu yào huān yuè, all who **swear** by [God] **exult**,
11c. 因為說謊之人的口必被**止住**。 yīn wéi shuō huǎng zhī rén de kǒu bì bèi zhǐ zhù。 for the mouth of those who speak falsehood will **be stopped up**.	因為說謊之人的口必被**堵住**。 yīn wéi shuō huǎng zhī rén de kǒu bì bèi dǔ zhù。 for the mouth of those who speak falsehood will **be stopped up**.

Notes:

- In order to facilitate understanding by young children, the literal translation "尋索我命 xún suǒ wǒ mìng (seek my life)" in verse 9a needs to be replaced by "取我性命 qǔ wǒ xìng mìng (take my physical life)."

- The word תַּחְתִּי "low, nether" (v. 9b), a derivative from תַּחַת, occurs twenty times in the MT. Most occurrences of the juxtaposition of תַּחְתִּי and אֶרֶץ (six out of eight times in Ezekiel)[103] are used to refer to "the place of those who have died."[104]

---

103. In Ezek 26:20; 31:14, 16, 18; 32:18, 24, the juxtapositions אֶרֶץ תַּחְתִּית and תַּחְתִּיּוֹת denote the "netherworld," which are contrary to the juxtaposition אֶרֶץ חַיִּים, "land of the living" in Ezek 26:20; 32:23–27, 32. See T. Desmond Alexander, "תַּחְתִּי," in *New International Dictionary of Old Testament Theology and Exegesis*, ed. Willem A. VanGemeren (Grand Rapids, MI: Zondervan, 1997), 288.

104. R. F. Youngblood, "תַּחַת," in *Theological Wordbook of the Old Testament*, eds. R. L. Harris, G. L. Archer, Jr., and B. K. Waltke (Chicago, IL: Moody Press, 1999), 968.

Grade 1 students could hardly comprehend the implication of "去到地的最低之處 *qù dào dì de zuì dī zhī chù* (go to the lowest [place] of the earth)." An illustration by a twelve-year-old girl may be helpful.

- שְׁעָלִים "jackals" (v. 10b), rendered as 豺狼 *chái láng* in the initial draft, is unfamiliar to grade 1 students. The substitute "野狗 *yě gǒu* (stray dogs)" is more understandable, but the IBTT decided to keep the rendering "豺狼 *chái láng* (jackals)" with the aid of its real photo. The attached illustration of jackals was made by a six-year-old girl.[105]

- In verse 11b, the Chinese phrase "發誓 *fā shì* (swear)" was generally beyond grade 1 students' understanding.[106] The seven-year-old girl, who read the initial draft with the researcher one-on-one, related it to "保證 *bǎo zhèng* (promise)," such as that she promised her mother to do the cleaning. Since the semantic ranges of "swear" and "promise" are not identical, the IBTT suggested putting these two together. This is because the latter can help children to understand the former and thus learn the hard phrase "發誓 *fā shì* (swear)."

  There is a phonological connection between the Niphal participle of שבע "those who swear" and the Qal imperfect 3fs of שבע "she (נֶפֶשׁ) is satisfied" (v. 5).[107] The phonological connection[108] implies that those satisfied by God are those who swear allegiance to him. It is hard to find the Chinese counterpart for such a phonological connection.

- The Hitpael of הלל [109] (v. 11b) was rendered as "歡躍 *huān yuè* (exult)" in the initial draft, which is difficult. Since its parallel, the Qal of שמח "rejoice"[110] (v. 11a), was rendered as "歡喜 *huān xǐ* (rejoice)," it could be replaced with "快樂 *kuài lè* (be glad)." This is because "歡喜快樂 *huān xǐ kuài lè* (rejoice and be glad)" is a common combination in the Chinese language.

---

105. The girl was not an official member of the IBTT, but she attended each class with her family.

106. The IBTT tried to find easier synonyms of "發誓 *fā shì* (swear)," but they are also difficult, such as "起誓 *qǐ shì* (swear)" and "立誓 *lì shì* (vow)."

107. Cf. Wilson, *Psalms Volume 1*, 892 n. 13.

108. The phonological connection between verse 5 and verse 11 forms an *epiphora* [X-a, Y-a'] (§2.3.3.7.1.7), indicating the ends of the first (vv. 1–5) and the second portion (vv. 6–11) of Ps 63.

109. The verb הלל is an "onomatopoeic word that suggests making a lalalalala sound or ululating." See Goldingay, *Psalms*, vol. 2, 703. Sometimes, its Hitpael takes the meaning "being proud, boast" as in 1 Kgs 20:11. See Ḥakham, *The Bible: Psalms*, vol. 2, 42; L. Koehler, W. Baumgartner, and J. J. Stamm, "הלל," in *The Hebrew and Aramaic Lexicon of the Old Testament*, trans. M. E. J. Richardson (Leiden: Brill, 1994-2000), 249.

110. This collocation is also found in Ps 105:3.

- Although this is not a rhyming section in the Hebrew text, the IBTT made all three verses of the section rhyme. The rhyming words are 處 *chù*, 物 *wù*, and 住 *zhù* in verses 9b, 10b, and 11c respectively.
- Here are some more challenging words or phrases being replaced by easier ones in this section: "被擊倒 *bèi jī dǎo* (be struck down)" → "被打倒 *bèi dǎ dǎo* (be struck down)" (v. 10); "被堵住 *bèi dǔ zhù* (be stopped up)" → "被止住 *bèi zhǐ zhù* (be stopped up)" (v. 11).
- The psalmist utilizes paronomasia to produce "an effective inclusion for the psalm: God's response when the suppliant searches [שחר] is to stop up [סכר]" those speaking falsehood (שֶׁקֶר).[111] Again, such a phonological connection is hard to reproduce in Chinese translation.

5.3.3 Psalm 107

The word נֶפֶשׁ appears five times in Psalm 107, which is a psalm of thanksgiving. It has the following structure:

Prelude (vv. 1–3): A call to the redeemed for thanksgiving

Part 1: The redeemed from the lands need to give thanks

- Section 1 (vv. 4–9): The people who were lost in the wilderness need to give thanks (×3)
- Section 2 (vv. 10–16): The prisoners need to give thanks
- Section 3 (vv. 17–22): The sick need to give thanks (×1)
- Section 4 (vv. 23–32): The people going down to the sea need to give thanks (×1)

Part 2: Yahweh's sovereignty over the whole world

- Section 1 (vv. 33–38): Yahweh's sovereignty over nature
- Section 2 (vv. 39–41): Yahweh's sovereignty over human society

Postlude (vv. 42–43): A closing call for moral reflection[112]

---

111. Goldingay, *Psalms*, vol. 2, 262.

112. Leslie C. Allen, *Psalms 101–150*, eds. Bruce M. Metzger et al., rev. ed., Word Biblical Commentary 21 (Nashville, TN: Nelson, 2002), 91.

5.3.3.1 Part 1: Section 1 of Psalm 107 (vv. 4–9)
This section describes that the first group of people being lost in the wilderness are called to give thanks to Yahweh. Here, נֶפֶשׁ occurs three times (vv. 5, 9).

5.3.3.1.1 The appropriate translation of נֶפֶשׁ in Psalm 107:5

5.3.3.1.1.1 The existing translations

The word נֶפֶשׁ here is rendered as "心 *xīn* (heart)" in CUV and RCUV, as "心靈 *xīn líng* (heart-spirit)" in CNV, as "精神 *jīng shén* (spirit)" in LZZ. There are no corresponding renderings for נֶפֶשׁ in TCVRE, DCT, CCB, and CNET. The first two versions have a similar interpretation of verse 5b: TCVRE has "一切希望都斷絕了 *yī qiē xī wàng dōu duàn jué le* (all hopes were cut off)"; DCT has "[你們] . . . 幾乎把一切的希望都放棄 [*nǐ men*] . . . *jǐ hū bǎ yī qiē de xī wàng dōu fàng qì* ([you] . . . almost gave up all hopes)." CCB translates this colon as "[他們] . . . 陷入絕境 [*tā men*] . . . *xiàn rù jué jìng* ([they] . . . fell into despair)"; CNET as "[他們] . . . 疲倦發昏 [*tā men*] . . . *pí juàn fā hūn* ([they] . . . grew weary and faint)."

5.3.3.1.1.2 The exploration/discussion/comment of the IBTT

This section refers to the people who were lost in the wilderness. They were hungry and thirsty; their נֶפֶשׁ grew faint. When hungry and thirsty, one grows faint not only physically, but also mentally. Thus, נְפָשִׁים here should be rendered as "他們整個人 *tā men zhěng gè rén* (their whole person)" to accentuate the intensity of both physical and mental strain.

5.3.3.1.2 The appropriate translation of נֶפֶשׁ in Psalm 107:9

5.3.3.1.2.1 The existing translations

While CUV and LZZ render נֶפֶשׁ in both cola of verse 9 as "心 *xīn* (heart)," other prominent Chinese versions except for RCUV translate them as "人 *rén* (person)." RCUV retains נֶפֶשׁ as "心 *xīn* (heart)" in the first colon and revises it as "人 *rén* (person)" in the second colon.

5.3.3.1.2.2 The exploration/discussion/comment of the IBTT

Corresponding to verses 4–5, where the people being lost in the wilderness felt hungry and thirsty, נֶפֶשׁ in verse 9a and verse 9b should be rendered as

"人 *rén* (person)," (i.e. "口渴的人 *kǒu kě de rén* [the thirsty person]" and "飢餓的人 *jī è de rén* [the hungry person]" respectively).

5.3.3.1.3 The version readable for all generations by the IBTT through LiFE

Part 1: Section 1 (vv. 4–9): The People Who Were Lost in the Wilderness Need to Give Thanks	
IBTTV	**The initial draft**
04a. 他們迷失在曠野裡、在沙漠中迷路， (Same as the right column)	他們迷失在曠野裡、在沙漠中迷路， *tā men mí shī zài kuàng yě lǐ、zài shā mò zhōng mí lù,* They lost themselves in the wilderness; in the desert [they lost] their way;
04b. 他們找不到可居住的**城市**。 *tā men zhǎo bù dào kě jū zhù de chéng shì.* they did not find a **city** to live.	他們找不到可居住的**城**。 *tā men zhǎo bù dào kě jū zhù de chéng.* they did not find a **city** to live.
05a. 又飢又渴， (Same as the right column)	又飢又渴， *yòu jī yòu kě,* Hungry and also thirsty,
05b. 整個人發昏。 (Same as the right column)	整個人發昏。 *zhěng gè rén fā hūn.* their whole person grew faint.
06a. 於是他們在急難中哀求耶和華**的幫助**， *yú shì tā men zài jí nán zhōng āi qiú yē hé huá de bāng zhù,* Then they, in their distress, cried to Yahweh **for help**;	於是他們在急難中哀求耶和華， *yú shì tā men zài jí nán zhōng āi qiú yē hé huá,* Then they cried to Yahweh in their distress;
06b. 他就**把他們從災難中救出**； *tā jiù bǎ tā men cóng zāi nán zhōng jiù chū;* he, **from their troubles, saved them**.	他就**搭救他們脫離禍患**； *tā jiù dā jiù tā men tuō lí huò huàn;* he **delivered them from their troubles**.

07a. 並使他們走在正確的道路， (Same as the right column)	並使他們走在正確的道路， *bìng shǐ tā men zǒu zài zhèng què de dào lù,* And he caused them to walk on the right way,
07b. 前往可居住的**城市**。 *qián wǎng kě jū zhù de chéng shì.* to go to a **city** to live.	前往可居住的**城**。 *qián wǎng kě jū zhù de chéng.* to go to a **city** to live.
08a. 讓他們向耶和華感謝他的慈愛， (Same as the right column)	讓他們向耶和華感謝他的慈愛， *ràng tā men xiàng yē hé huá gǎn xiè tā de cí ài,* Let them give thanks to Yahweh for his lovingkindness,
08b. 和他對世人所做**神奇之事**； *hé tā duì shì rén suǒ zuò de shén qí zhī shì;* and his **wonderful things** done for humankind.	和他對世人所做的**奇事**； *hé tā duì shì rén suǒ zuò de qí shì;* and his **wonders** for humankind.
09a. 因為他使乾渴的人得到滿足， (Same as the right column)	因為他使乾渴的人得到滿足， *yīn wéi tā shǐ qián kě de rén dé dào mǎn zú,* For he satisfied the thirsty person;
09b. 使飢餓的人得飽美物。 (Same as the right column)	使飢餓的人得飽美物。 *shǐ jī è de rén dé bǎo měi wù.* filled the hungry person with good things.

Notes:

- In verse 4a, the expression בְּישִׁימוֹן דָּרֶךְ is difficult. Some understand it as a construct or an inverted construct; others argue that the word דָּרֶךְ belongs to the second colon. These observations are questioned by Ḥakham who suggests that the first colon demonstrates a chiastic structure: the phrase תָּעוּ בַמִּדְבָּר "They lost themselves in the wildernesses" stands in chiastic parallelism with the phrase בִּישִׁימוֹן דָּרֶךְ "[their] way in the desert." Here, דֶּרֶךְ "way" might be taken with the verb תעה.[113]

Accordingly, a possible translation is as follows: They lost themselves in the wilderness; in the desert [they lost] their way. This chiastic parallelism within a colon can be rendered faithfully in Chinese: 他們迷失在曠野裡、在沙漠中迷路 *tā men mí shī zài kuàng yě lǐ、zài shā mò zhōng mí lù*.

- The statement of verse 6, the first of two recurring refrains in the psalm,[114] is reiterated in verses 13, 19, and 28 with slightly different but synonymous verbs.[115]

  Verse 6 has three difficult phrases: "哀求 *āi qiú* (cried)" in the first colon; "搭救 *dā jiù* (delivered)" and "禍患 *huò huàn* (troubles)" in the second. The first one, "哀求 *āi qiú* (cried)," was retained with the noun "幫助 *bāng zhù* (help)" added at the end of the first colon, as DCT does: they cried to Yahweh for help. There were two adjustments in the second colon. First, the difficult phrases "搭救 *dā jiù* (delivered)" and "禍患 *huò huàn* (troubles)" were replaced with "救出 *jiù chū* (saved)" and "災難 *zāi nán* (troubles)" respectively. Second, the word order of the second colon was rearranged to make the bicola rhyme. That is, "幫助 *bāng zhù* (help)" in verse 6a rhymes with "救出 *jiù chū* (saved)" in verse 6b, as suggested by DCT. Thus, IBTTV corresponds to the rhyme in the Hebrew text, which has the ending ם in verse 6a and ם in verse 6b.

---

113. Amos Ḥakham, *The Bible: Psalms with the Jerusalem Commentary*, vol. 3, ed. and trans. Israel V. Berman (Jerusalem: Mosad Harav Kook, 2003), 100 n. 2. Ḥakham's argument could be supported by the similar wordings in the second half of Isa 43:19: אָשִׂים בַּמִּדְבָּר דֶּרֶךְ בִּישִׁמוֹן נְהָרוֹת "I will make a way in the wilderness and rivers in the desert" (ESV). There בַּמִּדְבָּר דֶּרֶךְ and בִּישִׁמוֹן נְהָרוֹת are not constructs; both דֶּרֶךְ "way" and נָהָר "river" serve as the objects of the verb. The same pairing of בַּמִּדְבָּר and בִּישִׁמוֹן connects these two passages together to convey the message: though people cannot find a way, Yahweh promises to make a way for them. Cf. John Goldingay, *Psalms*, vol. 3, Baker Commentary on the Old Testament Wisdom and Psalms (Grand Rapids, MI: Baker Academic, 2008), 250.

114. Alter, *Book of Psalms*, 384.

115. The psalmist employs each of these four verses to be a transition from the first part of each section to the second. The former delineates the distress of the people; the latter depicts how Yahweh delivers them. See Bratcher and Reyburn, *A Translator's Handbook*, 922.

- Verse 7 parallels verse 4 neatly. וַיַּדְרִיכֵם "and he caused them to walk" parallels תָּעוּ "they lost themselves"; בְּדֶרֶךְ יְשָׁרָה "on the right way" parallels בִּישִׁימוֹן דָּרֶךְ "[their] way in the desert"; לָלֶכֶת אֶל־עִיר מוֹשָׁב "to go to a city to live" parallels עִיר מוֹשָׁב לֹא מָצָאוּ "they did not find a city to live."[116]

  The semantic parallelism between verse 4 and verse 7 works well in IBTTV.

- Verse 8 is the second refrain, which recurs in each section (vv. 15, 21, 31) at the same place, using the same words.[117]

  In verse 8b, grade 1 students could hardly understand the Chinese combination of "奇 qí (wonderful)" and "事 shì (things)." An eleven-year-old boy noted that "奇蹟 qí jì (miracles)" might work since it appears in the Bible frequently. However, God did not perform miracles in this section. Next, "神奇的事 shén qí de shì (wonderful things)" was proposed by a twelve-year-old girl and then supported by a forty-five-year-old adult, but there was another "的 de" just next to the phrase in question. This caused the construction to become awkward in Chinese. At this point, a sixteen-year-old boy solved the problem by replacing the 的 de with its synonym 之 zhī. Thus, IBTTV has "他對世人所做的神奇之事 tā duì shì rén suǒ zuò de shén qí zhī shì (his wonderful things done for humankind)" for this colon.

- Verse 9, a verse resuming the theme of verse 5, is arranged chiastically (verb + object // object +verb).[118] In this case, the Hebrew syntactic chiasmus works in Chinese, but there is another way to translate this verse into Chinese more poetically (i.e. placing the object in the first colon before the

---

116. Ḥakham, *The Bible: Psalms*, vol. 3, 101; see also Guó Dìng Zhāng 張國定, 詩篇 [Psalms (IV)], 天道聖經註釋 [Tiān Dào Bible Commentary] (Hong Kong: Tiān Dào Publishing House, 2004), 11.

117. Alter, *The Book of Psalms*, 384; Charles A. Briggs and Emilie Grace Briggs, *A Critical and Exegetical Commentary on the Book of Psalms*, vol. 2, International Critical Commentary on the Holy Scriptures of the Old and New Testaments (Edinburgh: T & T Clark, 1909), 359.

118. Mitchell J. Dahood, *Psalms III: 101–150*, The Anchor Bible (Garden City, NY: Doubleday, 1970), 83.

verb). This makes the Chinese renderings of the bicola parallel neatly (aba'b'):

因為他使乾渴的人得到滿足,
yīn wéi tā shǐ qián kě de rén dé dào mǎn zú,
For he satisfied the thirsty person;

使飢餓的人得飽美物。
shǐ jī è de rén dé bǎo měi wù.
filled the hungry person with good things.

Such Chinese renderings make the bicola rhyme as well.

- The "城市 *chéng shì* (city)" is substituted for the "城 *chéng* (city)" in verse 4b and verse 7b. This makes these two cola rhyme with verse 8b, which has the aforementioned "神奇之事 *shén qí zhī shì* (wonderful things)." Another group of rhyming words in this section is found in verses 4a (路 *lù*), 6a (助 *zhù*), 6b (出 *chū*), 7a (路 *lù*), 9a (足 *zú*), and 9b (物 *wù*).

5.3.3.2 Part 1: Section 3 of Psalm 107 (vv. 17–22)

In this section, the sick are called to give thanks to Yahweh. The word נֶפֶשׁ occurs once here (v. 18).

5.3.3.2.1 The appropriate translation of נֶפֶשׁ in Psalm 107:18

5.3.3.2.1.1 The existing translations

Only CUV and RCUV translate נֶפֶשׁ here as "心 *xīn* (heart)." CNV views נַפְשָׁם as a personal pronoun "他們 *tā men* (they)." This understanding is also found in DCT, but the latter replaces the "they" with "你們 *nǐ men* (you)." All other prominent Chinese versions relate the term to the appetite. TCVRE, CCB, CNET render the first colon as "they lost their appetite" with slight differences in Chinese expressions. Finally, LZZ has "他們的胃口厭惡各樣食物 *tā men de wèi kǒu yàn è gè yàng shí wù* (their appetite loathed all food)."

5.3.3.2.1.2 The exploration/discussion/comment of the IBTT

Following the "fools" in verse 17, it is appropriate to understand נַפְשָׁם here as the personal pronoun of the "fools": "他們 *tā men* (they)." On the other hand, it seems to be reasonable to render נֶפֶשׁ as "appetite" (胃口 *wèi kǒu* or

食慾 *shí yù*) since the word "food" is found at the beginning of the colon. However, it appears to be redundant and not fluent in Chinese expressions when נַפְשָׁם as the subject of verse 18a is rendered as "their appetite": "他們的胃口厭惡各樣食物 *tā men de wèi kǒu yàn è gè yàng shí wù* (their appetite loathed all food)," as LZZ suggests.

Briefly, an appropriate translation for נַפְשָׁם as the subject here is "他們 *tā men* (they)" who loathed all food because of their foolishness.

5.3.3.2.2 The version readable for all generations by the IBTT through LiFE

Part 1: Section 3 (vv. 17–22): The Sick Need to Give Thanks	
IBTTV	**The initial draft**
17a. 愚笨人，因自己不順服的行為 *yú bèn rén, yīn zì jǐ bù shùn fú de háng wéi* **Fools**, because of their **disobedient behavior**,	愚妄人，因自己悖逆的行徑 *yú wàng rén, yīn zì jǐ bèi nì de háng jìng* **Fools**, because of their **rebellious way**,
17b. 和自己的罪過吃了苦頭。 *hé zì jǐ de zuì guò chī le kǔ tóu.* and because of their iniquities, **had a rough time**.	和自己的罪惡受苦楚。 *hé zì jǐ de zuì è shòu kǔ chǔ.* and because of their iniquities, **were afflicted**.
18a. 他們**討厭所有的**食物， *tā men tǎo yàn suǒ yǒu de shí wù,* They **hated all** food,	他們**厭惡各樣**食物， *tā men yàn è gè yàng shí wù,* They **loathed all** food,
18b. 就**走近**死亡的**門口**。 *jiù zǒu jìn sǐ wáng de mén kǒu.* and **drew near the doors** of death.	就**臨近**死亡之**門**。 *jiù jiē jìn sǐ wáng zhī mén.* and **drew near the gates** of death.
19a. 於是他們在急難中哭求耶和華**的幫助**， *yú shì tā men zài jí nán zhōng kū qiú yē hé huá de bāng zhù,* Then they cried to Yahweh **for help** in their distress;	於是他們在急難中哭求耶和華， *yú shì tā men zài jí nán zhōng kū qiú yē hé huá,* Then they cried to Yahweh in their distress;

19b. 他就**把他們從災難中救出**。 tā jiù bǎ tā men cóng zāi nán zhōng jiù chū。 he, **from their troubles, saved them**.	他就**拯救他們脫離禍患**。 tā jiù zhěng jiù tā men tuō lí huò huàn。 he **saved them from their troubles**.
20a. 他發出話語醫治他們， (Same as the right column)	他發出話語醫治他們， tā fā chū huà yǔ yī zhì tā men， He sent his word and healed them;
20b. 救[他們]脫離**死亡的坑**。 jiù [tā men] tuō lí sǐ wáng de kēng。 he rescued [them] from **their pits of death**.	救[他們]脫離**他們的[冥]坑**。 jiù [tā men] tuō lí tā men de míng kēng。 he rescued [them] from **their pits [of death]**.
21a. 讓他們向耶和華感謝他的慈愛， (Same as the right column)	讓他們向耶和華感謝他的慈愛， ràng tā men xiàng yē hé huá gǎn xiè tā de cí ài， Let them give thanks to Yahweh for his lovingkindness,
21b. 和他對世人所做的**神奇之事**； hé tā duì shì rén suǒ zuò de shén qí zhī shì； and his **wonderful things** done for humankind.	和他對世人所做的**奇事**； hé tā duì shì rén suǒ zuò de qí shì； and his **wonders** for humankind.
22a. 讓他們獻上感恩祭， (Same as the right column)	讓他們獻上感恩祭， ràng tā men xiàn shàng gǎn ēn jì， Let them sacrifice thanksgiving sacrifices,
22b. 歡呼地**說出他所做的事**。 huān hū dì shuō chū tā suǒ zuò de shì。 and **tell of what he has done** with acclamation.	歡呼地**述說他的作為**。 huān hū dì shù shuō tā de zuò wéi。 and **declare his works** with acclamation.

Notes:

- In verse 17, the psalmist uses the Hitpael יִתְעַנּוּ "they are afflicted" (occurring only here with this meaning) to establish a paronomasia with וּמֵעֲוֺנֺתֵיהֶם "and because of their iniquities."[119] Though the psalm acknowledges "that not all trouble comes from sin, in the exile [עָוֺן leads to ענה], as is appropriate."[120] In the initial draft, the former is rendered as "罪惡 *zuì è* (iniquities)," and the latter as "受苦楚 *shòu kǔ chǔ* (were afflicted)." This signifies that it is not easy to find the Chinese counterpart for the wordplay here. However, the more dynamic translations aimed at facilitating better understanding by young readers move closer to the wordplay. IBTTV replaces the former with "罪過 *zuì guò* (iniquities)," and the latter is replaced with "吃了苦頭 *chī le kǔ tóu* (had a rough time)," which makes the two words in the combination rhyme.[121]
- In verse 18b, the IBTT replaced "死亡之門 *sǐ wáng zhī mén* (the gates of death)" with "死亡的門口 *sǐ wáng de mén kǒu* (the doors of death)," which makes this colon rhyme with verse 17b (i.e. 頭 *tóu* in v. 17b and 口 *kǒu* in v. 18b).
- As mentioned above, verse 19 is one of the four first refrains in the psalm. Thus, the translation of this verse should correspond to that in the previous ones (i.e. vv. 6, 13).[122]

  Even if grade 1 students had no difficulty with verse 19a, the IBTT still kept the phrase "幫助 *bāng zhù* (help)" used in verse 6a, a phrase added to facilitate better understanding by young readers. This was to maintain the consistency of the first refrains. Similarly, the difficult verb "拯救 *zhěng jiù* (saved)" in the second colon was replaced with the easy one "救出 *jiù chū* (saved)," as done in verse 6b.

---

119. Ḥakham, *The Bible: Psalms with the Jerusalem Commentary*, vol. 3, 104.

120. Goldingay, *Psalms*, vol. 3, 253.

121. In Mandarin Phonetic Symbols, the pronunciation of ㄛ in 過 *guò* is similar to that of ㄨ in 頭 *tóu*.

122. Verse 13, the second of the first refrain, is not discussed in this chapter because there is no נֶפֶשׁ occurring in that corresponding section.

- The word שְׁחִיתוֹתָם (their pits)[123] in verse 20b corresponds to the combination שַׁעֲרֵי מָוֶת "the gates of death" in verse 18: the fools draw near the gate of death, but God rescues them from their pits. Comparing the verses here with Job 33:20, 22, one finds that both the fools and Job are reported as loathing food, which causes the former to draw near the gates of death, and the latter to draw near the pit.[124] Thus, the context implies that the pit is the pit into which one goes when one dies. Thus, the initial draft had "冥坑 *míng kēng* (their pits of death)" for the word שְׁחִיתוֹ־תָם, which was replaced by an easier phrase "死亡的坑 *sǐ wáng de kēng* (their pits of death)" in IBTTV.

- In this section, the first set of the Hebrew rhyming words is found in verses 17a (פִּשְׁעָם), 18a (נַפְשָׁם), 19a (לָהֶם), 19b (יוֹשִׁיעֵם), 20a (וְיִרְפָּאֵם), 20b (מִשְּׁחִיתוֹתָם), 21b (אָדָם). The second set is found in 22a (תּוֹדָה), 22b (בְּרִנָּה). Because it is hard to follow the Hebrew rhyming pattern, IBTTV has verse 17b (頭 *tóu*) rhyming with verse 18b (口 *kǒu*); verse 19a (助 *zhù*) with verse 19b (出 *chū*); verse 21b (事 *shì*) with verse 22b (事 *shì*).

- Here are some more challenging words or phrases being replaced by easier ones in this section: "愚妄人 *yú wàng rén* (the fool)" → "愚笨人 *yú bèn rén* (the fool)," "悖逆的行徑 *bèi nì de háng jìng* (rebellious way)" → "不順服的行為 *bù shùn fú de háng wéi* (disobedient behavior)" (v. 17); "厭惡 *yàn è* (loathed)" → "討厭 *tǎo yàn* (hated)," "各樣食物 *gè yàng shí wù* (all food)" → "所有的食物 *suǒ yǒu de shí wù* (all food)," "臨近 *lín jìn* (drew near)" → "走近 *zǒu jìn* (drew near)" (v. 18); "禍患 *huò huàn* (troubles)" → "災難 *zāi nán* (troubles)" (v. 19); "奇事 *qí shì* (wonders)" → "神奇之事 *shén qí zhī shì* (wonderful things)" (v. 21); "述說 *shù shuō* (declare)" → "說出 *shuō chū* (tell of)," "

---

123. There is no consensus on the form and meaning of the word שְׁחִיתוֹתָם; cf., for example, Ḥakham, *The Bible: Psalms*, vol. 3, 105; Bratcher and Reyburn, *A Translator's Handbook*, 926; Dahood, *Psalms III*, 86; A. A. Anderson, *The Book of Psalms: Volume 2 Psalms 73-150*, New Century Bible Commentary (London: Marshall, Morgan & Scott, 1972), 754.

124. Michael D. Goulder, *The Psalms of the Return (Book V, Psalms 107-150): Studies in the Psalter, IV*, Journal for the Study of the Old Testament Supplement Series 258 (Sheffield: Sheffield Academic, 1998), 122.

他的作為 *tā de zuò wéi* (his works)" → "他所做的事 *tā suǒ zuò de shì* (what he has done)" (v. 22).

5.3.3.3 Part 1: Section 4 of Psalm 107 (vv. 23–32)

Here the main theme is that the people going down to the sea need to give thanks. The word נֶפֶשׁ is found only once in verse 26.

5.3.3.3.1 The appropriate translation of נֶפֶשׁ in Psalm 107:26

5.3.3.3.1.1 The existing translations

Again, in this verse, CUV and RCUV render נֶפֶשׁ as "心 *xīn* (heart)." CNV follows this rendering in this case. TCVRE and CNET translate it as "勇氣 *yǒng qì* (courage)" and "力量 *lì liàng* (strength)" respectively. LZZ regards it as "神魂 *shén hún* (mind-soul)." CCB and DCT render this colon very dynamically. CCB has "他們嚇得面無人色 *tā men xià dé miàn wú rén sè* (they were scared, looking ghastly pale)." DCT has "在驚險之中你們都嚇得魂不附體 *zài jīng xiǎn zhī zhōng nǐ men dōu xià dé hún bù fù tǐ* (in danger, you all were scared out of your wits)."

5.3.3.3.1.2 The exploration/discussion/comment of the IBTT

This section depicts the redeemed who were at sea and encountered a severe storm. In fear, those on the ship had not only a trembling body, but also a trembling heart. This means that both physiological and psychological reactions were triggered by this great danger. Therefore, נַפְשָׁם as "他們整個人 *tā men zhěng gè rén* (their whole person)" is an appropriate rendering to emphasize the intensity of their fear: "他們整個人因為災難而顫抖 *tā men zhěng gè rén yīn wéi zāi nán ér chàn dǒu* (their whole person trembled because of the trouble)."

5.3.3.3.2 The version readable for all generations by the IBTT through LiFE

Part 1: Section 4 (vv.23–32): The People Going Down to the Sea Need to Give Thanks

IBTTV	The initial draft
23a. 那些搭船下海， (Same as the right column)	那些搭船下海， *nà dā chuán xià hǎi*, Those who went down to the sea in ships,

23b. 在大水中工作的， (Same as the right column)	在大水中工作的， *zài dà shuǐ zhōng gōng zuò de,* who did work on great waters,
24a. 那些人 – 他們看見**耶和華所做的事**， *nà xiē rén – tā men kàn jiàn yē hé huá suǒ zuò de shì,* those – they saw **the things Yahweh had done**,	那些人 – spo 他們看見**耶和華的作為**， *nà xiē rén – tā men kàn jiàn yē hé huá de zuò wéi,* those – they saw **Yahweh's deeds**,
24b. 和他在深海中的**神奇之事**。 *hé tā zài shēn hǎi zhōng de shén qí zhī shì.* and his **wonderful things** in the deep sea.	和他在深海中的**奇事**。 *hé tā zài shēn hǎi zhōng de qí shì.* and his **wonders** in the deep sea.
25a. 因他發出命令**掀起**狂風， *yīn tā fā chū mìng lìng xiān qǐ kuáng fēng,* For he commanded and **raised** a stormy wind,	因他發出命令**興起**狂風， *yīn tā fā chū mìng lìng xìng qǐ kuáng fēng,* For he commanded and **raised** a stormy wind,
25b. 狂風捲起波浪。 (Same as the right column)	狂風捲起波浪。 *kuáng fēng juǎn qǐ bō làng.* and it lifted up its waves.
26a. 他們上到天空， (Same as the right column)	他們上到天空， *tā men shàng dào tiān kōng,* They went up to the heavens;
26b. 下到**深海中**； *xià dào shēn hǎi zhōng;* (they) went down to **the midst of the depths**;	下到**深海**； *xià dào shēn hǎi;* (the)y went down to **the depths**;
26c. 他們整個人因為災難而**發抖**。 *tā men zhěng gè rén yīn wéi zāi nán ér fā dǒu.* their whole person **trembled** because of the trouble.	他們整個人因為災難而**顫抖**。 *tā men zhěng gè rén yīn wéi zāi nán ér chàn dǒu.* their whole person **trembled** because of the trouble.

27a. 他們搖搖晃晃，東倒西歪，好像**喝醉了酒**， tā men yáo yáo huǎng huǎng, dōng dǎo xī wāi, hǎo xiàng hē zuì le jiǔ, They reeled and staggered, as if they **were drunk**;	他們搖搖晃晃，東倒西歪，好像**醉酒的人**， tā men yáo yáo huǎng huǎng, dōng dǎo xī wāi, hǎo xiàng zuì jiǔ de rén, They reeled and staggered like **the drunk**;
27b. 他們**一點辦法也沒有**。 tā men yī diǎn bàn fǎ yě méi yǒu。 they **did not have any solution at all**.	他們**全部的智慧都混亂了**。 tā men quán bù de zhì huì dōu hún luàn le。 all their **wisdom was confused**.
28a. 於是他們在急難中哀求耶和華**的幫助**， yú shì tā men zài jí nán zhōng āi qiú yē hé huá de bāng zhù, Then they cried to Yahweh **for help** in their distress;	於是他們在急難中哀求耶和華， yú shì tā men zài jí nán zhōng āi qiú yē hé huá, Then they cried to Yahweh in their distress;
28b. 他就**把他們從災難中領出**。 tā jiù bǎ tā men cóng zāi nán zhōng lǐng chū。 he **brought them out from their disaster**.	他就**帶領他們脫離禍患**。 tā jiù dài lǐng tā men tuō lí huò huàn。 he **brought them out from their troubles**.
29a. 他使狂風暴雨止息， (Same as the right column)	他使狂風暴雨止息， tā shǐ kuáng fēng bào yǔ zhǐ xī, He made the storm into a calm,
29b. 波浪平靜， (Same as the right column)	波浪平靜， bō làng píng jìng, and their waves became still.
30a. 因為安靜了，他們就歡喜， (Same as the right column)	因為安靜了，他們就歡喜， yīn wéi ān jìng le, tā men jiù huān xǐ, They rejoiced because they grew silent,
30b. 他就領他們到想要去的海港。 (Same as the right column)	他就領他們到想要去的海港。 tā jiù lǐng tā men dào xiǎng yào qù de hǎi gǎng。 and he led them to their desired harbor.

31a. 讓他們向耶和華感謝他的慈愛， (Same as the right column)	讓他們向耶和華感謝他的慈愛， ràng tā men xiàng yē hé huá gǎn xiè tā de cí ài, Let them give thanks to Yahweh for his lovingkindness,
31b. 和他對世人所做的**神奇之事**； hé tā duì shì rén suǒ zuò de shén qí zhī shì; and his **wonderful things** done for humankind.	和他對世人所做的**奇事**； hé tā duì shì rén suǒ zuò de qí shì; and his **wonders** for humankind.
32a. 讓他們在百姓的會眾中尊崇他， (Same as the right column)	讓他們在百姓的會眾中尊崇他， ràng tā men zài bǎi xìng de huì zhòng zhōng zūn chóng tā, And let them exalt him in the congregation of the people,
32b. 在長老的聚會中讚美他！ (Same as the right column)	在長老的聚會中讚美他！ zài zhǎng lǎo de jù huì zhōng zàn měi tā! and let them praise him in the assembly of the elders.

Notes:

- The first two cola of verse 26 form a neat parallel: verb + noun // verb + noun. The word שָׁמַיִם "the heavens" parallels תְהוֹמוֹת "the depths," manifesting that the waves (v. 25) are so raging that they lift the ships very high, causing the people aboard to feel like that they are "reaching the sky"; so raging that "the troughs between the waves then plunge the ships so low," causing the people aboard to feel like that they "are descending to the ocean's deepest depths."[125] This is rhetorical hyperbole.

---

125. Goldingay, *Psalms*, vol. 3, 255.

It is easy to translate the parallel into Chinese:

他們上到天空，

tā men shàng dào tiān kōng,

They went up to the heavens;

下到深海；

xià dào shēn hǎi;

(they) went down to the depths;

Though the preceding translations in the initial draft presented a neat parallel, the IBTT suggested replacing "深海 *shēn hǎi* (the depths)" with "深海中 *shēn hǎi zhōng* (the midst of the depths)." The latter not only makes the cola rhyme (空 *kōng* and 中 *zhōng*), but also manifests the hyperbole used here.

- In verse 27a, the simile כַּשִּׁכּוֹר "like the drunk" implies that the seafarers are "losing their sanity and [do] not know what to do. This fits well with what is stated in the parallel clause."[126]

The word חָכְמָה "wisdom" in the second colon refers to "the navigational skill of the sailors."[127] The Hitpael of the verb בלע [128] means "to show oneself confused."[129] Thus, this colon reads: "all their wisdom was confused" (他們全部的智慧都混亂了 *tā men quán bù de zhì huì dōu hún luàn le*). This was generally ambiguous for grade 1 students.

During the brainstorming session, the aforementioned interpretation of the simile כַּשִּׁכּוֹר "like the drunk" in the first colon was referred to: the seafarers are losing their sanity and do not know what to do. An eight-year-old boy suggested translating the implicit second colon as follows: "他們完全想不出辦法 *tā men wán quán xiǎng bù chū bàn fǎ* (they could not figure out a solution)." This inspired a fifty-year-old adult to propose a rendering that makes this colon rhyme with the first colon: "他

---

126. Ḥakham, *The Bible: Psalms*, vol. 3, 107.

127. Anderson, *Book of Psalms*, 755.

128. The verb בלע is also used in Isa 28:7 to report that the priest and the prophet are confused (נִבְלְעוּ) by wine. See Ḥakham, *The Bible: Psalms*, vol. 3, 107.

129. L. Koehler, W. Baumgartner, and J. J. Stamm, "בלע," in *The Hebrew and Aramaic Lexicon of the Old Testament*, trans. M. E. J. Richardson (Leiden: Brill, 1994–2000), 135.

們一點辦法也沒有 *tā men yī diǎn bàn fǎ yě méi yǒu* (they did not have any solution at all)" (i.e. 酒 *jiǔ* in v. 27a rhymes with 有 *yǒu* in v. 27b).

- Verse 28a reprises verse 6a verbatim. Verse 13a is repeated in verse 19a verbatim. Thus, in each of the first part of the first refrain, the respective verb used is צעק, זעק, זעק, and צעק, which works abb'a'. Following the Hebrew arrangement, IBTTV renders the verbs as "哀求 *āi qiú* (cried)," "哭求 *kū qiú* (cried)," "哭求 *kū qiú* (cried)," and "哀求 *āi qiú* (cried)" respectively.

  The psalmist adds more variations in the use of the verbs in the second colon of the first refrain: נצל "to deliver (Hiphil)" in verse 6b, ישע "to save (Hiphil)" in verse 13b and verse 19b, and יצא "to bring out (Hiphil)"[130] in verse 28b. The future forms with 3mp suffix in the psalm are rhymed. Aligned with the Hebrew text, the IBTT made these four cola rhyme as well: "救出 *jiù chū* (saved)" in verses 6b, 13b, 19b,[131] and "領出 *lǐng chū* (brought out)" in verse 28b.

- The psalmist arranges verse 32 chiastically: verb + בְּ expression // בְּ expression + verb. This syntactic chiasmus cannot be imitated in the Chinese translation because both of the בְּ expressions denote places, which need to be put at the beginning of the cola in Chinese.

- In this section, the rhyming Hebrew words are found in verses 28a (לָהֶם), 28b (יוֹצִיאֵם), 29b (גַּלֵּיהֶם), 30b (חֶפְצָם), 31b (אָדָם), and 32a (עָם). Again, for the sake of being easy to chant and memorize, the IBTT made efforts to make the psalm rhyme to a greater extent. Both verse 24a and 24b have the word 事 *shì* at the end of the cola. Verse 25a (風 *fēng*) rhymes with verse 26a (空 *kōng*) and verse 26b (中 *zhōng*); verse 26c (抖 *dǒu*) with verse 27a (酒 *jiǔ*) and verse 27b (有 *yǒu*); verse 28a (助 *zhù*) with verse

---

130. The verb יצא "to bring out" is "the standard expression for Yahweh's bringing the people out of Egypt . . . [Here] Yahweh's deliverance brings about a new exodus." See Goldingay, *Psalms*, vol. 3, 255.

131. The verb נצל and the verb ישע are rendered with the same phrase "救出 *jiù chū* (to save)" since it is hard to find another easy Chinese phrase to signify the differences between these two Hebrew verbs.

- 28b (出 *chū*); verse 29a (息 *xī*) with verse 30a (喜 *xǐ*). Both verse 32a and verse 32b end with 他 *tā*.
- Some more difficult words or phrases being replaced by easier ones (hard → easy) in this section: "耶和華的作為 *yē hé huá de zuò wéi* (Yahweh's deeds) " → "耶和華所做的事 *yē hé huá suǒ zuò de shì* (the things Yahweh had done)," "奇事 *qí shì* (wonders)" → "神奇之事 *shén qí zhī shì* (wonderful things)" (v. 24); "興起 *xìng qǐ* (raised)" → "掀起 *xiān qǐ* (raised)" (v. 25); "顫抖 *chàn dǒu* (trembled)" → "發抖 *fā dǒu* (trembled)" (v. 26); "禍患 *huò huàn* (troubles)" → "災難 *zāi nán* (disaster)" (v. 28); "奇事 *qí shì* (wonders)" → "神奇之事 *shén qí zhī shì* (wonderful things)" (v. 31).

5.4 Further Discussions/Observations

According to the purposes of the study, the tasks of the IBTT focus on (1) assessing the accuracy of the translations of נֶפֶשׁ in each occurrence of the three selected psalms, and (2) producing a readable Bible version for all generations through the LiFE approach. What follows are further discussions/observations arising from these two aspects. Besides, the critical issue caused by the translations of נֶפֶשׁ (see chapter 4) will also be further discussed.

5.4.1 The Appropriate Translation of נֶפֶשׁ in the Three Selected Psalms

The word נֶפֶשׁ occurs seventeen times in the three selected psalms. Their appropriate renderings are listed as follows:

5.4.1.1 נֶפֶשׁ as Personal Pronoun

- Psalm 35:3 – נֶפֶשׁ with a personal suffix (1cs) is employed to present the psalmist as an individual who talks to God (imaginary though).
- Psalm 35:12 – נֶפֶשׁ with a personal suffix (1cs) is used to denote the psalmist as an individual who feels like as if he has lost his children.
- Psalm 107:18 – Since the term "food" is mentioned at the beginning of the verse, נֶפֶשׁ with a personal suffix (3mp) as the

subject of the first colon should be better understood as "their appetite" (their appetite loathed all food). Nonetheless, such a translation is redundant and not natural in Chinese expressions. In this case, נַפְשָׁם as "他們 *tā men* (they)" works better: they loathed all food.

Notes: The first two cases demonstrate that if נֶפֶשׁ is used to represent individuals, its rendering as personal pronoun is appropriate. The third case manifests a complicated translation issue. Although an appropriate rendering is determined according to the context, a natural and/or poetic expression of the TL might influence the final decision.

5.4.1.2 נֶפֶשׁ as *"the Whole Being/Person"*

- Psalm 35:9 – נֶפֶשׁ with a personal suffix (1cs) as the subject of the bicola is associated with the psalmist's rejoicing in Yahweh and delight in his salvation. As discussed in §4.2.4.4, when constructed with words and phrases regarding feelings, the appropriate translation for נֶפֶשׁ is "the whole being/person" since נֶפֶשׁ as personal pronoun,[132] or "heart,"[133] or "soul" in English versions[134] fails to convey the intensity of such feelings in Chinese. Here, the psalmist's entire person feels joyful and delighted. The rendering "my whole person" is further substantiated by the parallel "all my bones" (v. 10) (see §5.3.1.3.1.2), a figure of the seat of emotions as well.[135]

- Psalm 63:1 – In poetry, נֶפֶשׁ with a personal suffix is usually used to parallel a simple pronoun[136] or to be involved in the inflection of the verb, etc.[137] Here, it as the subject parallels the preformative "I" in the verb אֲשַׁחֲרֶךָּ "I seek you earnestly" (v. 1a). It also parallels בְשָׂרִי in verse 1c. Since this verse is to convey the psalmist's yearning for God, it is suitable to translate נַפְשִׁי here as "my whole being" to express the intensity of such feelings. As

---

132. For example, TCVRE, CCB, CNET, DCT.
133. For example, RCUV, CUV, CNV, LZZ.
134. For example, NIV 2011, NIV 1984, NASB 1995, ESV, NRSV, KJV 1900.
135. Allen, "עֶצֶם," 690.
136. Brotzman, "Man and the Meaning of נפשׁ," 403.
137. Johnson, *Vitality of the Individual*, 16.

discussed earlier, the collocation of נֶפֶשׁ and בָּשָׂר[138] in verses 1b, 1c is not related to the psychological aspect over the physical aspect. They are collocated to parallel the "I" in the first colon, and thus put an emphasis on the psalmist's yearning for God.

- Psalm 63:5 – In verse 1, נַפְשִׁי "my whole being" as the subject is used to introduce the intensity of the psalmist's thirst for God. Here, the same usage is to introduce a contrary image: the psalmist's joyous satisfaction of communing with God through prayers (v. 4). Such satisfaction makes the psalmist feel like one who enjoys the richest food. Thus, the appropriate rendering of נַפְשִׁי in Chinese here is "my whole person," which conveys the intensity and completeness of this joyous satisfaction.

- Psalm 63:8 – Rather than "my soul" (NIV 1984) or "my heart" (RCUV), נַפְשִׁי as the subject of verse 8a should be rendered as "my whole person" (i.e. the psalmist's whole person clings to God). Such a rendering accentuates the intensity of the psalmist's complete trust in God. The second colon supports this rendering since it implies the physical being (i.e. the psalmist's body which is upheld by God).

- Psalm 107:5 – The psalmist uses נַפְשָׁם as the subject of verse 5b to express the intensity of growing faint in mind and body because of hunger and thirst. Thus, the translation "their whole person" is appropriate.

- Psalm 107:26 – While facing trouble resulting from a severe storm, both the heart and the body of those on the ship trembled. Accordingly, נַפְשָׁם as the subject can be translated as "their whole person," which is an appropriate rendering to emphasize the intensity of their fear in Chinese.

Notes: The preceding cases indicate that when נֶפֶשׁ as the subject in Hebrew is structured with words or phrases regarding feelings, its appropriate rendering in Chinese is "the whole being/person." This accentuates the intensity of such feelings.

---

[138]. In the Psalms, the same collocation only occurs in 16:9–10 and 84:2. See Goldingay, *Psalms*, vol. 2, 257.

5.4.1.3 נֶפֶשׁ as "Physical Life"

- Psalm 35:4 – Psalm 35:1 introduces the threat from the enemies, which is identified as a threat to physical life in verse 7 and verse 17. In verse 7, the enemies dig and hide a deadly pit of netting for the psalmist. Verse 17 describes the enemies as lions intending to destroy the psalmist. Thus, what the enemies seek (בקשׁ) earnestly here is the psalmist's physical life (נֶפֶשׁ). This is in accordance with the observation of Seebass, Westermann, and Brotzman: when נֶפֶשׁ as the object is juxtaposed with the verb בקשׁ, the appropriate rendering of the combination is "seek someone's life."[139]

- Psalm 35:7 – The danger the psalmist faces is emphasized by the unusual expression "pit of netting," which seems to emphasize the fact that the enemies are seeking to destroy the psalmist's "physical life" (לְנַפְשִׁי "for my physical life"). Here, נַפְשִׁי serves as the object of the preposition לְ.

- Psalm 35:17 – The appropriate rendering of נֶפֶשׁ with personal suffix (1cs) as the object here is "my physical life." This is substantiated by the reference to the destruction of the psalmist and the parallelism of נַפְשִׁי (v. 17b) and יְחִידָתִי "my only life" (v. 17c).

- Psalm 63:9 – The enemies' miserable fate (i.e. being destroyed and eaten by jackals [vv. 9b–10]) implies that the enemies who want to kill the psalmist are in fact digging their own grave. Thus, the juxtaposition of בקשׁ and נַפְשִׁי is again better rendered as "seek my physical life."

Notes: The foregoing discussions show that when נֶפֶשׁ as the object follows the verb בקשׁ, its appropriate rendering is "physical life." This is also the case when נֶפֶשׁ as the object is put within the context related to risks (Ps 35:7, 17), as suggested by Brotzman.[140]

When comparing §5.4.1.2 with §5.4.1.3, one finds that the critical distinction between נֶפֶשׁ as "the whole being/person" and נֶפֶשׁ as "physical

---

139. Seebass, "נפש," 513; Westermann, "נפש," 753; Brotzman, "Plurality of 'Soul,'" 45.
140. Brotzman, "Plurality of 'Soul,'" 61; see also Seebass, "נפש," 512.

life" consists in the fact that נֶפֶשׁ is usually employed as the subject in the former, and as the object in the latter. This is also observed by Seebass and Westermann.[141]

5.4.1.4 נֶפֶשׁ *as "Person"*

- Psalm 107:9 – In Psalm 107:4–5, the psalmist describes that the people in the wilderness felt hungry and thirsty. This closely connects to verse 9, where the similar language is used. Accordingly, it is suitable to view נֶפֶשׁ in both verse 9a and verse 9b as "人 *rén* (person)": "the thirsty person" and "the hungry person" respectively.

Notes: If נֶפֶשׁ as the object is juxtaposed with an attributive adjective as in 9b or attributive participle as in 9a, it could be rendered as "person."

5.4.1.5 נֶפֶשׁ *as "Appetite"*

- Psalm 35:25 – The word נַפְשֵׁנוּ in the first direct speech, "Aha, [this fits] our appetite!" (v. 25b) is parallel to the word בִּלַּעֲנוּהוּ "We have devoured him" in the second direct speech (v. 25c) even though they differ formally. Thus, נֶפֶשׁ as "appetite" best corresponds to the verb "devour."

Notes: When structured with words or phrases related to food or eating, נֶפֶשׁ as "appetite" is an appropriate rendering. However, natural and/or poetic Chinese expressions might influence the rendering in this category, as the case in Psalm 107:18 (§5.4.1.1).

5.4.1.6 נֶפֶשׁ *as "Body"*

- Psalm 35:13 – When fasting, one's body suffers. Thus, an appropriate rendering of נֶפֶשׁ here is "body."

Notes: When the combination of ענה (Piel) and נֶפֶשׁ and the term "fasting" are closely connected, נֶפֶשׁ could be rendered as "body." This also appears in Isaiah 58:3, where fasting is associated with the affliction of one's own body (刻苦己身 *kè kǔ jǐ shēn*), as CNV and CCB suggest.

Briefly, the appropriate renderings of נֶפֶשׁ in Psalms 35, 63, and 107 are personal pronoun (Pss 35:3, 12; 107:18), "the whole being/person" (Pss

---

141. Seebass, "נפש," 512; Westermann, "נפש," 752.

35:9; 63:1, 5, 8; 107:5, 26), "physical life" (Pss 35:4, 7, 17; 63:9), "person" (Ps 107:9a, 9b), "appetite" (Ps 35:25), and "body" (Ps 35:13). The results denote that the translations of נֶפֶשׁ in the three selected psalms fall within the semantic range proposed by the present author (see §4.2.6).

The preceding are the general findings that are derived from the Bible translation exercise. In what follows, the critical issue caused by the translations of נֶפֶשׁ will be further discussed.

5.4.2 The Critical Issue Regarding the Chinese Translations of נֶפֶשׁ

As noted in chapter 4, Watchman Nee's misinterpretation of נֶפֶשׁ is one of the reasons that led him to develop a tripartite anthropology with theological implications, leading to great controversy among contemporary Chinese scholars and uncertainty among ordinary Christians. The translations of נֶפֶשׁ as "靈魂 *líng hún* (spirit-soul)"/ "靈 *líng* (spirit)" or "心 *xīn* (heart)" in the most popular and authoritative Bible version (i.e. CUV), play a crucial role in reinforcing Chinese Christians' acceptance of Nee's trichotomy. The results of reconsidering the translation of נֶפֶשׁ in this chapter make explicit that it is not appropriate to take its meaning as "靈魂 *líng hún* (spirit-soul)"/ "靈 *líng* (spirit)" or "心 *xīn* (heart)." The preceding exploration indicates that such inappropriate translations of נֶפֶשׁ are found in CUV, RCUV and other prominent Chinese versions as well (see the table below). If the problematic renderings of נֶפֶשׁ in the prominent Chinese versions can be revised as IBTTV suggests, the controversy among Chinese theologians resulting from Nee's tripartite anthropology and confusion among Chinese Christians concerning this theological implication may be better addressed.

The discussion in the process of Bible translation in this chapter also makes clear that there are obvious differences in the translations of נֶפֶשׁ among prominent Chinese versions. This again necessitates reconsidering its translation in every occurrence in the OT.

The Renderings of נֶפֶשׁ		
Verse	The Prominent Chinese Versions	IBTTV
Ps 35:3	my spirit-soul (CUV)	I

Ps 35:9	my heart (CUV, RCUV, CNV, LZZ)	my whole being/person
Ps 35:12	my spirit-soul (CUV)	I
Ps 35:13	my heart (CUV, RCUV, CNV)	my body
Ps 35:17	my spirit-soul (CUV)	my physical life
Ps 63:1	my heart-spirit (RCUV, DCT) my heart (CNV, LZZ, CCB) my spirit (CNET)	my whole being/person
Ps 63:5	my heart (CUV, RCUV, CNV, LZZ, CCB, CNET, DCT) my spirit (TCVRE)	my whole being/person
Ps 63:8	my heart (CUV, RCUV, CNV, LZZ, CCB) my spirit (CNET)	my whole being/person
Ps 107:5	their heart (CUV, RCUV) their heart-spirit (CNV)	their whole being/person
Ps 107:9a	heart (CUV, RCUV, LZZ)	person
Ps 107:9b	heart (CUV, LZZ)	person
Ps 107:18	their heart (CUV, RCUV)	they
Ps 107:26	their heart (CUV, RCUV, CNV) their mind-soul (LZZ)	their whole being/person

5.4.3 The Version Readable for All Generations by the IBTT through LiFE

As stated, CUV, published in 1919, is the most popular and influential Chinese Bible version. However, its language is generally difficult for children to understand. In order to determine its difficulty for grade 1 students,[142] the present researcher proposed a translation close to that of CUV. Examining the tables in §5.3, it can be seen that about three-fifths of the cola in question contain at least one difficult word(s) or phrase(s). These findings point to the need for a new more child-friendly Bible for Chinese readers.

---

142. As it is well known, grade 1 students' reading abilities are limited. The difficulty here indicates what is not understandable for them when someone reads the Bible to them.

This exercise has also clearly shown that it is possible to compose an easier but more meaningful Bible version that retains the beauty of Hebrew poetry in Chinese. Following Wendland's LiFE approach, the IBTT paid more attention to the literary devices used in the Hebrew text and made efforts to find their Chinese counterparts. What follows are instances of comparing the translations of IBTTV through LiFE with those of CUV.[143]

5.4.3.1 Parallelism and Chiasm

It has been shown that parallelism and Chiasm can be imitated and appreciated in Chinese.

In Psalm 107:4a, the Hebrew text demonstrates syntactic chiasmus (see §5.3.3.1.3). This is presented in IBTTV, which has "他們迷失在曠野裡、在沙漠中迷路 *tā men mí shī zài kuàng yě lǐ、zài shā mò zhōng mí lù* (They lost themselves in the wilderness; in the desert [they lost] their way)." Whereas, there is no such a chiastic parallelism in CUV, which has "他們在曠野荒地漂流 *tā men zài kuàng yě huāng dì piāo liú* (They wandered in desert wastes)."

Another example is found in the first colon of the first refrain in Psalm 107 (i.e. vv. 6a, 13a, 19a, and 28a), where the verbs are arranged as abb'a' (צעק, זעק, זעק, and צעק). Again, the Hebrew arrangement of the verbs is followed by IBTTV, which has "哀求 *āi qiú* (cried)," "哭求 *kū qiú* (cried)," "哭求 *kū qiú* (cried)," and "哀求 *āi qiú* (cried)" respectively. On the contrary, CUV and its revised version RCUV of 2010 translate all the verbs as "哀求 *āi qiú* (cried)," failing to convey the beauty of the Hebrew poetry.

5.4.3.2 Rhyme

Rhyme is one of the poetic devices used in Chinese new poetry (新詩 *xīn shī*).[144] Rhyming poems are easier for children to chant and memorize, so the IBTT grasped every opportunity to make the Chinese translation rhyme. What follows are examples of comparing the rhyme in IBTTV and that in RCUV:

---

143. An exhaustive comparison between these two versions regarding their usage of literary devices is beyond the scope of the study.

144. As noted in footnote 9 of chapter 5, Chinese new poetry is the most appropriate Chinese literary genre for Hebrew psalms.

Psalm 63:5–7		
line	RCUV	IBTTV
1	我在床上記念你 *nǐ*,	我整個人就像吃飽了最豐盛的美味 *wèi*,
2	在夜更的時候思念你 *nǐ*;	我的口要以歡呼的嘴唇讚美 *měi*。
3	我的心像吃飽了骨髓肥油 *yóu*,	甚至，我在床上懷念你 *nǐ*,
4	我也要以歡樂的嘴唇讚美你 *nǐ*。	我整晚對著你輕聲細語 *yǔ*。
5	因為你曾幫助了我 *wǒ*,	因為你曾經是我的幫助 *zhù*,
6	我要在你翅膀的蔭下歡呼 *hū*。	我在你翅膀陰影下歡呼 *hū*。

Notes: In RCUV, lines 1, 2, and 4 end with the same word 你 *nǐ*, which makes the rhyme more monotonous. In IBTTV, with different words, line 1 rhymes with line 2; line 5 with 6.

Psalm 63:9–11		
line	RCUV	IBTTV
1	但那些尋索要滅我命的人 *rén*	但他們，就是那些想取我性命的人必滅亡 *wáng*,
2	必往地底下去 *qù*;	他們必去到地的最低之處 *chù*。
3	他們必被刀劍所殺 *shā*,	他們必被刀劍打倒 *dǎo*,
4	成為野狗的食物 *wù*。	必成為豺狼的食物 *wù*。
5	但是王必因神歡喜 *xǐ*,	但是王必在神裡面歡喜 *xǐ*,
6	凡指著他發誓的都要誇耀 *yào*,	每一個指著神發誓保證的都要快樂 *lè*,
7	因為說謊之人的口必被塞住 *zhù*。	因為說謊之人的口必被止住 *zhù*。

Notes: In RCUV, the rhyming words are found in lines 4 and 7. In IBTTV, the rhyming words are found in lines 2, 4, and 7, which are located at the end of v 9, 10, and 11 respectively.

5.5 Conclusion

The preceding discussion has demonstrated that IBTTV, an easy-to-understand Bible version for readers of all ages, including children, maintains the poetic beauty of the psalms as much as possible. This was fully demonstrated and carried out by translating the Bible through Wendland's LiFE methodology. Moreover, its translations of the word נֶפֶשׁ in the three selected psalms may contribute to a reduction in the controversy caused by Watchman Nee's trichotomy. All of these results were achieved by the IBTT, ranging from young children to middle-aged adults, which can serve as an example of IIM.

CHAPTER 6

Conclusion – Findings and Implications

6.1 Introduction

The goals of this study as defined in chapter 1 are numerous. Sensing that past and current translations in Chinese have not been adequate on some levels, this study has attempted to apply a new approach to Bible translation: Wendland's LiFE approach with a focus on intergenerational participation. As an object of study, three psalms were selected with a focus on a specific translation issue: the interpretation and rendering of the word נֶפֶשׁ in Chinese.

This final chapter first provides a summary of what has been found while reconsidering the translations of נֶפֶשׁ in the three selected psalms with special reference to Chinese, followed by the application of the findings to the use of נֶפֶשׁ in the Psalter and in the OT as a whole. Second, a summary of the foundations for intergenerational participation in Bible translation is offered. Third, this chapter reports the feedback from the participants, the comments from professionals, and the researcher's reflections concerning the intergenerational Bible translation through the LiFE approach. Fourth, some suggestions for further research are presented along with the researcher's final comments.

6.2 Summary of Research Findings Regarding נֶפֶשׁ

The Hebrew term נֶפֶשׁ is "as hard to define as it is to translate," writes Jacob.[1] This is demonstrated by its erroneous translations in both Chinese and English versions, resulting in the misinterpretation and misunderstanding of God's Word (§4.1). The issue becomes more complicated due to the influence of etymological studies, adding some meanings to the polysemous word נֶפֶשׁ (§4.2.2). Unfortunately, the divergence in the various senses given for נֶפֶשׁ in prominent English lexicons also complicates the issue (§§4.1, 4.6). These make it necessary to reconsider its semantic range and its translations in the Bible.

After examining the literature (§4.2), the researcher identifies the following possible meanings of נֶפֶשׁ in the OT: (1) breath, (2) living creature, person, (3) vital self (pronominal use, the whole being/person), (4) life (especially physical life in Chinese), (5) desire, appetite, (6) corpse, body. The translation exercise in chapter 5 is an attempt to apply these senses to its translation into Chinese (Mandarin) in the three selected psalms.

The Hebrew word נֶפֶשׁ occurs seventeen times in Psalm 35, 63, and 107. Drawing upon the results in chapter 5, the appropriate renderings of נֶפֶשׁ in the three selected psalms are: נֶפֶשׁ as personal pronoun, "the whole being/person," "physical life," "person," "appetite," and "body." All the preceding renderings are included in the semantic range of נֶפֶשׁ that the researcher proposes (see above).

What follows are findings derived from translating נֶפֶשׁ in the three selected psalms:

- When נֶפֶשׁ is employed to represent individuals, it is appropriate to render it as a personal pronoun (Pss 35:3, 12; 107:18).
- When נֶפֶשׁ as the subject is combined with words or phrases regarding feelings, its appropriate rendering is "the whole being/person" (全人/整個人 *quán rén /zhěng gè rén*). Thus, the intensity of such feelings is conveyed faithfully (Pss 35:9; 63:1, 5, 8; 107:5, 26).
- When נֶפֶשׁ as the object occurs in the text with reference to risks, or more specifically, is juxtaposed with the verb בקשׁ, the

---
1. Jacob, "Anthropology of the Old Testament," 617.

rendering "physical life" (性命 *xìng mìng*) is preferred (Pss 35:4, 7, 17; 63:9).
- When נֶפֶשׁ as the object is combined with an attributive adjective or attributive participle, it could be rendered as "person" (人 *rén*) (Ps 107:9a, 9b).
- When נֶפֶשׁ is combined with words or phrases related to food or eating, it is appropriate to translate it as "appetite" (胃口 *wèi kǒu*) (Ps 35:25). Psalm 107:18 is an exception in this regard. There, "appetite" in נַפְשָׁם is omitted (נַפְשָׁם "they" loathed all food) since it is redundant and not natural in common Chinese expressions.
- When נֶפֶשׁ is structured with the Piel form of the verb ענה and with the word "fasting," one can take its meaning as "body" (身體 *shēn tǐ*) (Ps 35:13).

The results above indicate that the possible meanings of נֶפֶשׁ proposed by the researcher work well in the three selected psalms. This shows that the current renderings of נֶפֶשׁ in most Chinese versions as "靈魂 *líng hún* (spirit-soul)"/ "靈 *líng* (spirit)"/ "魂 *hún* (soul)" or "心 *xīn* (heart)"[2] are not the most appropriate renderings (§5.4.2). As noted in §4.6, such renderings reinforce the acceptance of Watchman Nee's tripartite theological anthropology among Chinese Christians and have led to much controversy among contemporary Chinese theologians. Revising these translations and using more appropriate renderings may not only contribute to reducing the controversy and correcting certain theological and anthropological misunderstandings, but also lead to a more understandable Bible translation.

If the majority of the renderings of נֶפֶשׁ in the three selected psalms are not appropriate as substantiated by the arguments in chapter 5, all its translations in the Psalms need to be reconsidered.

The following are findings gleaned from the researcher's reconsidering all the translations of נֶפֶשׁ in the Psalms (occurring 144 times):[3]

---

2. See §4.6 for the reason why the Chinese "heart" is involved in the controversy caused by Nee's trichotomy.

3. See Appendix I in the researcher's dissertation at South African Theological Seminary.

- נֶפֶשׁ as vital self, which is divided into three sub-categories:

    נֶפֶשׁ **as "the whole being/person"** (51 out of 144 occurrences in the Psalms). As the findings from the three selected psalms indicate, when נֶפֶשׁ serves as the subject within the context with reference to feelings, it is appropriate to render it as "the whole being/person." In some cases in the subcategory, נֶפֶשׁ serves as object, vocative, or the second nominative of the sentence. All these usages are also found in texts related to feelings. The translation of נֶפֶשׁ as "the whole being/person" can express the intensity of feelings faithfully.

    נֶפֶשׁ **as personal pronoun** (26 out of 144 occurrences in the Psalms). In this subcategory, נֶפֶשׁ in most cases serves as the object of the verb (eleven times) or preposition (ten times). It is employed as the subject only five times. In these occurrences, individuals are accentuated. Therefore, translating נֶפֶשׁ as a personal pronoun is appropriate.

    נֶפֶשׁ **as reflexive pronoun** (6 out of 144 occurrences in the Psalms). When the subject and object are the same, or the subject is accentuated, נֶפֶשׁ can be rendered as a reflexive pronoun. The usage of נֶפֶשׁ in this subcategory is to serve as the object of the verb (three times), or preposition (two times), or as the subject (once).

- נֶפֶשׁ as "physical life" (49 out of 144 occurrences in the Psalms). This translation is appropriate when the text is related to risks or touches on the issues of God's salvation, protection, life or death, or punishment, etc. In most cases, נֶפֶשׁ in this category serves as the object of the verb (thirty-eight times) or preposition (six times). Only in four occurrences is it used as the subject. In one occurrence (Ps 57:4), נֶפֶשׁ is fronted to "establish a specific frame of reference for the theme of the clause that follows."[4]

- נֶפֶשׁ as "person" (2 out of 144 occurrences in the Psalms). In the whole book of the Psalms, the translation of נֶפֶשׁ as "person" only occurs twice in Psalm 107:9, where it is used as part of the

---

4. Steven E. Runge and Joshua R. Westbury, eds., *The Lexham Discourse Hebrew Bible: Glossary* (Bellingham, WA: Lexham Press, 2012), §Topical frame.

object of the verb and is combined with an attributive adjective or participle.
- נֶפֶשׁ as "desire/appetite" (5 out of 144 occurrences in the Psalms). When the text refers to strong craving, the appropriate rendering of נֶפֶשׁ is "desire." If the context is also associated with food or eating, its appropriate translation is "appetite." As discussed above, an exception of the latter is found in Psalm 107:18, where the "appetite" in נַפְשָׁם is left out when the common Chinese expression is considered. In all appearances in this category, נֶפֶשׁ serves as the object of the preposition except for Psalm 35:25, where נַפְשֵׁנוּ occurs in a verbless clause.
- נֶפֶשׁ as "body" (5 out of 144 occurrences in the Psalms). נֶפֶשׁ could be rendered as "body" when the text refers to physical torment or action. It is used as the object of the verb (two times) or preposition (once), or as the subject of the verb (two times).

In line with the results derived from the three selected psalms, all the preceding appropriate translations of נֶפֶשׁ in the Psalms again fall within the semantic range proposed by the researcher. Thus, it is unnecessary and inappropriate to translate it as "spirit-soul/spirit/soul" or "heart" in the Psalms. Apart from this issue, there are also inappropriate translations resulting from etymological considerations (see §4.6). An apparent example is the rendering of נֶפֶשׁ as "neck/throat," which is found in Psalm 69:1 (LZZ, TCVRE, CNET) and Psalm 105:18 (CNV, LZZ, CNET, DCT). In both cases, CUV and RCUV render נֶפֶשׁ as personal pronoun. The present author translates the former as a personal pronoun; the latter as "body."

The findings from the translation of נֶפֶשׁ in the three selected psalms and the entire book of Psalms show that it is inappropriate to translate it as "spirit-soul/spirit/soul" or "heart." Moreover, it is necessary to reconsider its renderings influenced by etymological considerations, such as neck/throat and perfume (e.g. Isa 3:20). Since the possible meanings of נֶפֶשׁ that the author gleans from a literature review also work well in the book of the Psalms, it is advantageous to apply all the possible senses to the entire OT. The meanings of "breath" and "corpse," which do not appear in the Psalms, could be included.

After dealing with the issue regarding the translations of the word נֶפֶשׁ, this study now turns to a discussion of the translation itself. As mentioned in §4.5.2, Watchman Nee's misinterpretation of נֶפֶשׁ is caused by his misunderstanding of the so-called literal translation. This signifies not only the importance of the task of Bible translation, but also that of translators' understanding of translation theory. However, there is a critical issue in contemporary Chinese Bible translation (i.e. conducting the practice of Bible translation without a systematic, rigorous translation theory drawing upon contemporary translation studies [§2.2.4]). Although translation studies developed into a separate or specialized academic discipline during the 1970s (§2.3.2.2.3.1), this had little impact on Chinese Bible translation. Thus, Péng points out the significance of informing the audience of the approach employed in Bible translation.[5]

Though this study does not undertake a complete translation project, the use of translation theory and method is still needed in order to determine the most appropriate translations of נֶפֶשׁ in the three selected psalms. The understanding of translation theory and method can prevent the present translation task from the similar mistake made by Watchman Nee. Since the Bible is literature, Wendland's Literary Functional Equivalence (LiFE) was used for the translation task of the present research.

This study also shows that Wendland's LiFE methodology is a viable model which, if properly applied, can yield fruitful results. In this approach, there are "three essential operations involved in the production of a Bible translation – composition, contextualization, and consultation."[6] In order to "encourage a higher level of target audience involvement in the production" of a Bible version, Wendland accentuates the importance of the target audience's participation in the processes of contextualization and consultation.[7] Wendland's proposition stimulated the researcher to involve children as Bible readers in producing a translation for all generations. Furthermore, following Cheung, the author also tried to integrate theories from different

---

5. Péng 彭, "Contemplating the Future of Chinese Bible Translation," 15.
6. Wendland, *LiFE-Style Translating*, 406.
7. Wendland, 406–407.

disciplines into the translation experiment.[8] This has led to what could be considered a successful intergenerational translation project.

6.3 Summary of the Foundations for Intergenerational Participation in Bible Translation

Children are an integral part of the church (§3.3.2). Intentional intergenerational ministry (IIM) (§3.4) is a promising approach to involve them in the church. One of the crucial components for churches to effectively develop IIM is to produce a Bible version readable for all generations. Thus, the target audience in the present study is those of different generations in the church, including children who need the whole Bible (§3.3.3). For that reason, children as readers should be crucial participants of a Bible translation project intended for various generations. They can take part in the operations of contextualization and consultation (§5.1).

Since children are social agents (§3.2.2.1), sources of revelation of insights (§3.3.2.6), etc., their voices need to be heard and respected. Besides, research on children's language development indicates that children are competent to participate in the discussion of Bible translation and offer suggestions (§3.3.4). Thus, the present author suggests that in producing an easier Bible version for all generations, children as readers can contribute to the enterprise of Bible translation, not only in the processes of contextualization and consultation, but also in that of composition.[9] One of the reasons is that they can suggest words and phrases readily understandable for young readers. Such translations could be more appropriate than those composed by middle-aged professionals whose speech is more conservative (§3.3.4). Accordingly, in this study, children and persons from other age groups were crucial members of the translation team to produce an easier Bible version for all generations. The team was designated as the intergenerational Bible translation team (IBTT).

---

8. Cheung, "Twentieth Century Translation," 13.

9. After the sample exercise, the researcher found that composition and contextualization cannot be strictly distinguished when involving children in the translation team. The reason is that in the process of composition, the team already partially contextualized the Bible as they made the difficult parts of the initial draft easier for young children by introducing illustrations or explicit interpretation.

Due to the constraints of space, only the exercise of composition was included in this research. Composition refers to "the preparation of the actual translated text of Scripture."[10] A single member of a translation team first produces an initial draft, which is then assessed by the team.[11] Drawing upon Wendland, the researcher first produced an initial draft of the three selected psalms according to LiFE, which was then revised by the present advisers. Next, on the basis of the draft, the enterprise of composing a more artistic and readable version for all generations through LiFE approach was conducted by the IBTT. Another task for the IBTT was to assess the translations of נֶפֶשׁ, which is the primary focus of the research. The team members were competent with these two areas after receiving the training courses, including an overview of the LiFE approach and the possible meanings of the Hebrew word נֶפֶשׁ (§5.2).

Having been a homeschooling mother of two sons for a decade, the researcher witnessed the blessings and potential of various generations' learning God's Word together. Such a learning atmosphere and environment is unfamiliar to the majority of Chinese people in contemporary society, defined by isolation and age segregation (§3.4.1). Since involving children and teenagers in the exercise of Bible translation is a pioneering task, it was ideal to recruit the team from homeschooling communities[12] as they are used to learning in an intergenerational environment or setting. Accordingly, the requirements for the IBTT members were that they should:

- Have experience with intergenerational learning
- Attend church regularly
- Be interested in learning biblical Hebrew and Bible translation

After providing the IBTT with the basic training (§5.2), the researcher led the team to launch the exercise in intergenerational, literary Bible translation on Psalms 35, 63, and 107.

---

10. Wendland, *LiFE-Style Translating*, 406.

11. Wendland, *Translating the Literature of Scripture*, 295, 297.

12. The researcher is very grateful for the support of Mujen Home Educators Association in convening the IBTT.

6.4 Feedback, Comments, and Reflections Regarding Intergenerational, Literary Bible Translation

This exercise in intergenerational, literary Bible translation was an interesting and exciting journey for both the team members and the researcher. What follows are the feedback from the participants, the researcher's reflections on Wendland's LiFE, and the researcher's general observations regarding Bible translation. Since this was a pioneering exercise concerning Bible translation, it was decided to invite some OT scholars to review the newly translated psalms. Their general comments are quoted right after the feedback of the participants.

6.4.1 The Feedback from the Participants

The IBTT, comprising twelve members whose age ranged from seven to fifty-one years old, was recruited by Mujen Home Educators Association, the largest homeschooling community in Taiwan. After the translation exercise, an open-ended questionnaire was prepared to collect the feedback from the IBTT members, which is summarized and divided into the following major categories (for the complete individual feedback, see Appendix B).

6.4.1.1 The Motivation of Participation

Over half of the participants, being children and teenagers, were encouraged by parents or friends (×five) to participate in this study. Others wanted to experience the translation exercise because they thought that it is an interesting, different, and helpful task (×three). For some, their love of learning was their motivation (×two). Parents treasured this opportunity since they could engage in activities or study the Bible with their own children (×two). Adults wanted to understand the meaning of God's Word in Hebrew (×two). One stated her love of biblical languages as her major motivation. Another noted that the reason why he joined the translation exercise is to let more people understand God's Word in other kinds of languages.

Already it can be seen that parents and friends play a critical role in influencing children's and teenagers' willingness to participate in such a project. This implies that relationship is an important part of the life of children and teenagers. For these two age groups, interesting and different activities also motivated them to participate. Adults were driven by the more specific want to learn biblical Hebrew in order to help them further understand God's Word.

As the feedback indicated, the parents who participated wanted to involve themselves in their children's lives, including studying the Bible together. Having been a children's worker in the church over fifteen years, the researcher has observed that the majority of contemporary Chinese Christian parents take it for granted that teaching children God's Word is the responsibility of teachers at church. However, God gives parents the priority and responsibility to teach their children his word and apply it to every aspect of life (Deut 6:5–9). This has been put into practice by Christian homeschooling families who are good examples of IIM. The results of this experiment show that such intergenerational activities need to be encouraged at church, meaning the church will be inclusive for all and meet its full potential.

6.4.1.2 The Study of Biblical Hebrew

Learning biblical Hebrew was a new experience for all of the participants except two, a mother and her eight-year-old son who felt that Hebrew was not so difficult and really liked the time when all participants got together to read God's Word in Hebrew (the boy was the first one to recite a paragraph in Hebrew during the exercise). Among the new learners, some noted that they felt a sense of accomplishment when they read the Hebrew texts aloud (×two). Others mentioned that the language-learning games encouraged them to study Hebrew harder (×four). A seven-year-old boy stated that the Hebrew letters are very pretty. A thirteen-year-old girl said that learning biblical Hebrew was an excellent experience, helping her understand more about the Bible. Some pointed out that the more challenging parts of biblical Hebrew include verb conjugation, and vowels, etc. (×three).

Since learning biblical Hebrew was not the main focus of the translation exercise, none of the questions in the questionnaire focused specifically on this aspect, but all participants referred to this from different perspectives. Though some pointed out the difficult parts of biblical Hebrew, none disliked it. This was probably because the researcher guided the participants to focus more on the semantic aspect of the Hebrew text. Once there was a need to deal with grammatical issues, more interactive teaching methods would be used.

6.4.1.3 Game as an Effective Way to Produce Happy Learners

Two-thirds of the participants referred to the games employed in the class. This was because the games were fun or exciting (×three), and they encouraged the participants to study harder (×four) even though some of them felt nervous during the games (×five). An eleven-year-old boy stated that through games, the participants bonded and grew to know more about each other, which in turn, helped the process of translation. An adult aged fifty wrote that the use of games created a happy and caring atmosphere, which reinforced the participation of different age groups.

Again, no specific question in the questionnaire was related to games, but the participants of different age groups provided their positive feedback regarding the use of games in the process of the translation exercise. The feedback demonstrated that the use of games not only helped improve the team chemistry, but also helped increase the participants' impetus to learn. This is consistent with the famous quote by Landreth in his *Play Therapy: The Art of the Relationship* – "Toys are children's words and play is their language."[13]

In conclusion, learning through games is an effective way to produce happy learners of all ages.

6.4.1.4 The Experience of the Bible Translation Exercise

All participants enjoyed the process of the Bible translation exercise except two who noted that it was not easy for them to absorb it or to keep up. One of the two felt that Bible translation was a very tiring process, but very valuable (however, she liked learning biblical Hebrew). Those who enjoyed it felt that it was wonderful, interesting, exciting, refreshing, and was a great, happy, valuable experience (×ten). What follows are their reasons:

- The Bible translation exercise provided the opportunity to learn biblical Hebrew, the history of Bible translation, translation methods, etc., to hear different opinions, and funny and interesting ideas. This exercise enabled them to help translators in producing a readable Bible version for all generations, to see how younger children can understand God's Word. They

---

13. Garry L. Landreth, *Play Therapy: The Art of the Relationship*, 3rd ed. (New York: Routledge, 2012), 156.

gained a better understanding of God's Word through more accessible translations.
- Participants felt a great sense of achievement.
- The exercise helped participants better understand the process of Bible translation and the challenge that confronts translators.
- It helped them recognize the significance of sharing the gospel with children.
- It helped the participants experience God's love.
- It stimulated the participants' interest in delving into God's Word and cultivated critical thinking.
- It reinforced the participants' confidence either in reading the Bible or in trying new things.

It is clear that the Bible translation exercise had a very positive impact on the participants. It could serve as an in-depth Bible study for ordinary believers in the church. Therefore, if a Bible translation project could involve as many readers as possible in some parts of the processes of translation, not only could the new version be widely accepted, but also the participants' life, thought, and knowledge of God's Word, etc., could be enhanced.

6.4.1.5 *Understanding the Task of Bible Translation*

Before the Bible translation exercise, about half of the participants did not know, or had never heard of Bible translation. Some had heard of it but had never come into contact with it or put any thought into it (×three). Others thought that Bible translation is something out of reach, and that only professionals can do (×three). Three participants noted that they knew about Bible translation, but only one explicitly stated that Bible translation is a task of rendering Hebrew and Greek texts in other languages.

After the Bible translation exercise, the participants demonstrated apparent improvement in their understanding of Bible translation:
- Bible translation involves translating the Bible in its original language into a language that I can understand (this was understood by four participants, including a seven-year-old boy).
- It is a hard task that enables one to read the Bible and understand the truth.
- It is translating the Hebrew Bible into different Bibles that fit various cultural groups.

- It allows more people to understand the word of God.
- It is a sophisticated process that requires a deep understanding of the Bible.
- It is hard because of the need for constant editing. Translators bear enormous pressure.

As to the question of who can do Bible translation, two-thirds of the participants stated that those with passion, enthusiasm, or a willing heart could do it. A sixteen-year-old boy noted that Bible translation must be led by an experienced leader who is competent in theology and biblical languages. What follows are two more detailed responses to this question:

- An adult aged fifty years responded, "This intergenerational Bible translation exercise is to make the challenging parts of the Bible easier, that all the readers, including children, can understand. Those who are guided by experienced translators can do it."
- An adult aged forty-two years pointed out, "I used to think people involved in Bible translation require extensive knowledge of the Bible and language skills. But now I think it is more appropriate to involve a group of people in the task of Bible translation. After all, the purpose of Bible translation is to make God's Word more understandable. Thus, the more input, the better."

The feedback indicated that participants developed a new understanding concerning the task of Bible translation. For example, before the translation exercise, the majority of the participants had no idea or only knew a little bit about Bible translation. After the exercise, a seven-year-old boy understood what Bible translation was although he did not express it with professional language. Before, the participants thought that Bible translation should only be conducted by professionals. After the exercise, they acknowledged that to make God's Word more understandable for ordinary readers, especially for children, readers' participation is needed and beneficial.

6.4.1.6 The Importance of Bible Translation
All participants recognized the importance of Bible translation. Three prominent reasons are listed:
- Bible translation helps spread God's Word

A seven-year-old boy noted that if translation did not exist, he would not be able to read the Chinese Bible. Some stated that Bible translation is an essential part of spreading God's Word so that people all over the world can hear and understand it (×eight). A thirteen-year-old girl pointed out that Bible translation makes it possible for younger children to read the Bible and understand God's Word.

- Bible translation makes God's Word more understandable

    An eleven-year-old boy said, "Many people still do not understand the message of the Bible. So there is a need for a Bible that is easy to understand and retains the original meaning at the same time." For the participants, the Bible translation exercise itself helped them better understand God's Word (×seven).

- Bible translation influences the interpretation of God's Word

    A twelve-year-old girl noted that Bible translation is a serious endeavor since any translation mistake can cause the reader to misunderstand the true message. This was echoed by a sixteen-year-old boy and a forty-two-year-old adult. The former stated that using the correct words is of importance because it can change a person's view of theology. The latter pointed out that every mistake can potentially change the content of the Bible. According to her, erroneous translations are dangerous since Christians live according to the teachings of the Bible.

Though each had a different perspective, all participants acknowledged the importance of Bible translation. The feedback also revealed the positive influence that the Bible translation project had on the participants. The exercise proved beyond a shadow of a doubt that it is worthwhile to involve readers in a Bible translation project.

6.4.1.7 Generations Together in Bible Translation

All participants valued the experience of intergenerational Bible translation. They not only got the opportunity to hear different opinions and innovative ideas of different age groups, but also had the chance to know more about each other and to learn how to communicate and compromise.

In the intergenerational team, the opinions of different age groups were all respected. A mother wrote that the special translation experience "breaks the traditional view of Bible translation by collecting the opinion of different people. Even [my seven-year-old son] can participate in it" by sharing his contribution to the discussion with older people. Her son said: "I liked it when everyone asked me for my opinion because everyone would listen to me and ask me whether or not I can understand the translation."

Other significant comments regarding the intergenerational Bible translation were made:
- I believe this is a very good method for Bible translation since both adults and children have their own contribution to the translation task (a twelve-year-old girl).
- I think working with people of different age groups on Bible translation is something that Christians should do. This is a special kind of fellowship. In order to obtain the goal, we learned how to compromise, communicate, and listen to each other (a forty-two-year-old adult).
- Involving different generations is important because the Bible is meant for all various age groups to read (a forty-year-old adult).

In brief, for the participants, the intergenerational Bible translation approach was not only feasible, but also valuable, especially for a Bible version comprehensible for readers of all ages, including children.

In the past, it has been assumed that only professionals could conduct the task of Bible translation. However, this exercise shows that to produce a Bible version readable for the target audience, it is necessary to involve them in certain parts of the operations of translation as Wendland suggests. This not only makes the new version more acceptable, but also expands the horizon of the participants, such as knowing more about God's Word, recognizing the importance of Bible translation, and then further supporting the task of Bible translation. The exercise in this study even allowed participants to obtain or improve their knowledge of biblical Hebrew. Finally, the intergenerational Bible translation team itself served to show that IIM is an effective means of accomplishing an important church-related task.

6.4.2 The Comments of OT Scholars

Since the intergenerational Bible translation is a pioneering approach, it seems important to invite OT scholars[14] to review the newly translated psalms.

Kyungrae Kim, PhD

Kyungrae Kim is the professor, academic dean, and vice president of Faith Bible Seminary, which belongs to the Faith Bible Association. He received his PhD in Textual Criticism from Hebrew University of Jerusalem. Dr Kim revised the researcher's initial draft, and later that of the IBTTV, paying particular attention to renderings of נֶפֶשׁ. He notes:

> Translating an ancient and sacred text needs godliness of translators as well as linguistic skills. I have no doubt of the godliness of the present translator. She has been well trained in biblical languages for about ten years. She is also well versed in Chinese which is her mother tongue and the target language of this translation.
>
> Her translation is quite close to the original meanings in every detail, with some considerations of the readers (i.e. children). I was also able to notice her consideration of rhyme in the Chinese language, too. Her choice of vocabularies for rhyme is to be praised.
>
> For some dubious vocabularies or forms, she did good research and followed very balanced opinions. It is also quite lovely to see the illustrations which may be used for better understanding. I believe children will like it.
>
> Finally, her translation of the Hebrew noun "*nefesh*" is quite interesting, and generally speaking, well done. See the following table.

---

14. The order of the OT scholars is according to the receiving date of the reviews. They wrote their comments here in English.

Reference		Translation	Comment
35:3	נַפְשִׁי	我 (me)	Good
35:4	נַפְשִׁי	我性命 (my physical life)	Well fits the context
35:7	נַפְשִׁי	我的性命 (my physical life)	Well fits the context
35:9	נַפְשִׁי	我整個人 (my whole person)	Well fits the context
35:12	נַפְשִׁי	我 (I)	Good
35:13	נַפְשִׁי	我的身體 (My body)	Good
35:17	נַפְשִׁי	我的性命 (my physical life)	Good
35:25	נַפְשֵׁנוּ	這正合我們的胃口 ([this fits] our appetite)	Very interesting
63:1[2]	נַפְשִׁי	全人 (my whole being)	Well fits the context
63:5[6]	נַפְשִׁי	我整個人 (my whole person)	Well fits the context
63:8[9]	נַפְשִׁי	我整個人 (my whole person)	Well fits the context
63:9[10]	נַפְשִׁי	我性命 (my physical life)	Well fits the context
107:5	נַפְשָׁם	整個人 (their whole person)	Well fits the context
107:9a,	נֶפֶשׁ	人 (person)	Good
107:18	נַפְשָׁם	他們 (they)	No other choice
107:26	נַפְשָׁם	他們整個人 (their whole person)	Good

Paul Theophilus, PhD

Paul Theophilus is the president of the Alliance Bible School of Central and South America (Panama), and the president of Grace to Chinese International Inc. He received his PhD from Southern Baptist Theological Seminary, USA. He notes:

> Beside some minor corrections, over all [the researcher has] done a good job. [She has] obviously used modern Chinese language and punctuation in [her] translation. Furthermore, the fresh style [she] adopted is to be commended. All these will certainly attract modern-day readers – child, young men and average people – to enjoy reading the Scripture. [She has] achieved the purpose of her effort.

Grace Ko, PhD

Grace Ko is the assistant professor of biblical studies at Canadian Chinese School of Theology. She received her PhD from University of St Michael's College, Toronto. Concerning the translation of the three psalms, she notes:

> Overall, [the translation] does retain the beauty of parallelism of the original Hebrew text and is very readable in Chinese . . . It is never easy to retain all the poetic features in translation, but [the researcher does] what [she] can, and I think it is a fine piece of work.

Daisy Yulin Tsai, PhD

Daisy Yulin Tsai is the associate professor of Old Testament at Logos Evangelical Seminary. She received her PhD from Trinity International University. Here she makes the following comments:

> According to Yu, her translation, instead of emphasizing accuracy of "word for word," adopts "thought for thought" method and intends to present a Chinese translation with modern poetic style. Generally speaking, her translation is faithful, except for an unusual translation in Psalm 35:3b and a few places that I believe revision is needed to be more faithful to the original Hebrew Bible. In Psalm 35:3b, the independent pronoun אֲנִי is the subject, but she translated it into a complement and the complement יְשֻׁעָתֵךְ to be the subject. Overall, it is an impressive project. She has put in a lot of hard work, evident in the presentation of her translation, and deserves praise for that.
>
> I have two reminders for her future study or anyone who is interested in doing Hebrew Bible translation. The following paragraphs discuss the translation of Hebrew poetic parallelism and figurative language, with this dissertation as an example. They are by no mean to undermine her exceptional work and its contribution to Bible translation.
>
> First, as *NIDOTTE* indicates, נֶפֶשׁ usually refers to the inner person, it rarely denotes "a soul" in any full sense. Most likely, it is a synecdoche, representing both one's physical and non-physical composition: the whole person. Thus Yu

insistently translates most נַפְשִׁי into "my whole person" in Chinese. However, considering the feature of Hebrew poetic parallelism, one needs to think about other possible alternatives in translation, not rigidly conform to only one translation of "my whole person" in her version of Psalm 35:9–10. In Psalm 35:9–10, נַפְשִׁי (v. 9) is a semantic parallel with עַצְמוֹתַי (v. 10). Therefore, many translations (i.e. Chinese, English, French, and German, etc.) translate them into "my soul" and "my bones" respectively to represent the artistic effect and sense of poetic parallelism. For instance, in Psalm 63:1 נַפְשִׁי and בְשָׂרִי are another pair of contrast synonyms. Here, Yu displays her awareness of the parallelism and translates them into "my whole person" and "my whole body." "Person" and "body" in Chinese, unfortunately, cannot connote the contrasting concepts of inner and outer as the original Hebrew text (נַפְשִׁי: and בְשָׂרִי) and its context intends. In order to present the contrast parallelism, instead of sticking to the single definition of נֶפֶשׁ (the whole person), most translations choose to treat the text with two separate connotations with "my soul" and "my flesh." Understanding the text and translating it into another language often requires going beyond the lexicon meaning of a single word. Most importantly, one has to consider the genre, the context, and the sensibility of linguistics. Yu has done a tremendous job with most of the text, treating it for the audience of children and young readers. This also requests even more scrutiny in reviewing her translation. I would suggest that נֶפֶשׁ can be translated in a broader way.

In addition to the previous concern about Yu's consistent translation of "the whole person," the second reservation is that this translation seems to forgo the figurative language that is prominent for the poetic genre. The instances in Psalm 35:9–10 and 63:1 could be represented with "my soul" with "my bones," and "my soul" with "my flesh." This not only pays homage to the Hebrew poetic parallelism, but faithfully presents the figurative language of allusions. Figurative language is the substance and beauty of poetry. It is used abundantly in Hebrew poetry, and the Psalmists often employed allusions to bring their poems to life. For example, Psalm 35:17b, "Rescue . . ., my only life from 'the lions'" is plainly understandable. Yu translates "the lions" into "lion-like enemy." Such translation would assume that modern Chinese readers, or children, can't understand allusion or that modern Chinese poetry doesn't tolerate allusions. To translate figurative language in this way, as well as rewriting in vernacular instead of poetic language, has lessened the exquisiteness, implication, and the fun of reading poetry. Readers, especially children, have vivid imagination. They can read between the lines, to form pictures in their minds. The aesthetic of modern Chinese poetry has many aspects, which includes using allusions still. Too many colloquial explanations would take away from the poetic essence. She's done more work than she needs to with her translations. I'd suggest keeping the figurative language as it is in the original text.

The suggestions from the preceding OT scholars indicate which aspects may need attention in further research, e.g. in the operation of consultation, where negotiation or a mutual "exchange of views" is necessary.[15]

After the feedback from the participants and the comments from OT scholars, the following sections are dedicated to the researcher's reflections on the exercise in the intergenerational Bible translation through LiFE approach.

6.4.3 The Reflection on Wendland's LiFE

In the exercise of Bible translation, the researcher experienced the importance of translating the Bible through a literary approach since the Bible itself is literature. In this regard, Wendland's *LiFE-Style Translating* offers unambiguous instructions to translators. What follows are the most relevant and valuable parts for the purpose of the translation exercise – to produce a more artistic, readable Bible version for readers of all ages, including children.

---

15. Wendland, *LiFE-Style Translating*, 407.

Conclusion – Findings and Implications

First of all, Wendland's LiFE provides translators with "the opportunity to be both individually and collectively resourceful and innovative in the use of language, whether to a greater or lesser degree."[16] This allows for creativity and makes the translation task far more interesting. The dynamic, rather than literal, approach is beneficial for producing an easier Bible version. For instance, in Psalm 35:4, "蒙羞 *méng xiū* (be put to shame)," "受辱 *shòu rǔ* (be disgraced)," and "慚愧 *cán kuì* (be ashamed)" were generally difficult for grade 1 students. The IBTT replaced the first two with a common Chinese expression "丟臉 *diū liǎn* (lose [their] face)" and a Chinese saying "抬不起頭 *tái bù qǐ tóu* ([they] cannot lift up [their] head)" respectively, and then made verse 4a and verse 4c rhyme (no rhyme in CUV). This was achieved by paraphrasing "退後 *tuì hòu* (be turned back)" in verse 4c as "想要逃走 *xiǎng yào táo zǒu* (want to run away)." The rhyming words are marked in bold.

Verse 4a 丟臉到抬不起**頭** *tóu*;
(lose their face, that they cannot lift up their **head**;)

Verse 4c 慚愧到想要逃**走** *zǒu*。
(be ashamed, that they want to run **away**.)

Being encouraged by the freedom provided by Wendland's LiFE approach, the IBTT grasped every possible opportunity to make the Chinese translations rhyme, a poetic device used in Chinese new poetry (新詩 *xīn shī*), which is good for children to chant and memorize.

Second, Wendland proposes a ten-step exegetical methodology to achieve a poetic LiFE translation.[17] The steps helped the researcher do a thorough exegesis that paved the way for the translation exercise. Some examples are listed below:

Step 5 (discover and evaluate the artistic and rhetorical features) guided the researcher to focus on the poetic devices used in the psalms, which helped while dealing with some difficult texts. For example, discerning the poetic device of ellipsis for emphasis in parallelism helped the researcher better grasp what the psalmist was trying to express. At first glance, the expression in Psalm 35:14 is not clear. But when the ellipsis of "mourning" (אָבֵל) in verse 14a and "my" (לִי) in verse 14b is identified, it is not difficult to

---

16. Wendland, 110.
17. Wendland, 126–148.

understand the whole verse: "As if [mourning] for my friend or brother . . . ; as if mourning for [my] mother." Another example is found in Psalm 107:4, where the chiastic parallelism in verse 4a implies that the verb "they lost" (תָּעוּ) at the beginning of the colon should be applied to the latter half of the colon (i.e the verb תעה might be taken with the noun "way" [דֶּרֶךְ]: "They lost themselves in the wilderness; in the desert [they lost] their way").[18]

It is worth noting that in most cases in the three selected psalms, Hebrew chiastic parallelism cannot be rendered in Chinese.[19] For instance, if translating Psalm 35:17b and c into Chinese according to the chiastic structure in Hebrew, the Chinese translation would be as follows, which does not reflect the beautiful parallelism in Chinese poetry (the translation here is based on the initial draft by the researcher):

救我的性命脫離他們的毀滅，

(rescue my physical life from their destruction;)

從獅子[那裏救回]我唯一的生命！

(from the lions [rescue] my only life!)

The following is preferable in terms of Chinese poetry:

救我的性命脫離他們的毀滅，

(rescue my physical life from their destruction;)

[救]我唯一的生命脫離獅子！

([rescue] my only life from the lions!)

Though challenging, the chiastic parallelism should be maintained in Chinese translation if the situation permits, as suggested in Wendland's step 10 (coordinate form-functional matches).[20] The case of Psalm 107:4 discussed above is a good example. Another good example is found in Psalm 63:8, where with some adjustments, the structure (abb'a' in Hebrew text) is arranged as abcc'b'a' in Chinese: 我 "I" → 緊靠著 "cling" → 你 "you" in the first colon; 你 "you" → 扶持著 "uphold" → 我 "me" in the second colon:

---

18. Ḥakham, *The Bible: Psalms*, vol. 3, 100 n. 2.

19. For example, Pss 35:17, 18; 63:6; 107:9, 11, 16, 32.

20. Wendland, in *LiFE-Style Translating*, 148, points out that "the function of a particular SL device [may] have to be reproduced by a different TL form," but the goal is "to keep the divergence in such cases as small as possible, even though at times only a complete reformation will do."

我整個人緊靠著你；(My whole person clings to you;)
你的右手扶持著我。(your right hand upholds me.)

Another area where Wendland's model was helpful was the advice concerning word studies (step 6). Grade 1 students could hardly understand the meaning of "切切地尋求 *qiē qiē dì xún qiú* (seek earnestly)" in Psalm 63:1, but a word study[21] of the verb שחר helped solve the issue. According to Tate and Goldingay, the literal meaning of שחר could be "to seek early" or "to seek in the morning."[22] IBTTV has the latter with a little adjustment, which makes this colon explicit for young children: "God, you are my God, I seek you from the morning." This signifies that careful examination of the meanings of words or phrases provides more options for translators in terms of diction, especially when producing a comprehensible Bible version for readers of all ages, including children.

The analysis of step 6 (do a complete discourse analysis) was helpful in composing the title for each section, which enabled the reader to grasp the theme of each section easily.

Similarly, going beyond step 6 in Wendland's methodology and applying step 9 (determining the functional and emotive dynamics of a text) led to an improved translation. For example, the primary speech act in Psalm 35:12 is lament; the accompanying attitudes and emotions include pain and upset. Thus, the IBTT made explicit the expression of this emotion, by adding the words "in pain" to make the verse more understandable for young readers: "使我痛苦得像失去孩子" (and leave me [in pain] like one who has lost children).

Third, Wendland's LiFE approach allows the involvement of as many readers as possible in the operations of contextualization and consultation, so that the new version can be widely accepted. This was one of the reasons that spurred the researcher to go further to involve children and teenagers in making the initial draft by the researcher readable for young readers (the latter part of the operation of composition). The exercise in the intergenerational, literary Bible translation proved that they were very competent

---

21. The phrase "word study" does not appear in the ten-step exegetical methodology, but it is included in step 6 (do a complete discourse analysis), where "the basic lexical, syntactic, and semantic shape of the discourse" is examined. See Wendland, *LiFE-Style Translating*, 142.

22. Tate, *Psalms 51–100*, 127; Goldingay, *Psalms*, vol. 2, 256.

at this task. They contributed to the assessment of the translations of נֶפֶשׁ (see Appendix A). They also made very creative suggestions throughout this translation exercise, confirming Holmes' observation that vernacular speech is "high in childhood and adolescence, and then steadily reduce[s] as people approach middle age when societal pressures to conform are greatest."[23] What follows are some examples of their creative suggestions (the words in bold):

- Psalm 35
  verse 4a 丟臉到抬不起頭；
  (lose their face, that they cannot lift up their head;)
  verse 4c 慚愧到**想要逃走**。
  (be ashamed, that they **want to run away**.)
  verse 10c 搭救**弱**小的人脫離那比他**強**大的
  (delivering a **weak** person from someone **stronger** than him; a suggestion by a seven-year-old boy)
- Psalm 63:6b 我整晚對著你**輕聲細語**。
  (all night I **speak to you softly**.)

Time efficiency is another good reason to involve children and teenagers in producing an easier Bible version. When creative ideas are provided, younger children can give immediate feedback with regard to their understanding of the ideas. This allows the discussions to be more time efficient and brings out the most critical reason to involve them: IBTTV is really understandable for young readers even if some revisions might be needed after assessment.

On the contrary, if there are only middle-aged biblical scholars with a conservative speech in the translation team, no matter how hard they try to produce a readable version for young readers, the translation will never reach its objective of speaking to young readers. In this exercise, the researcher found that young children knew much more than adults assumed. They understood God's Word directly translated from original biblical languages with easier wording, and sometimes with lexical additions, etc.

This exercise shows how crucial it is to work according to an adopted methodology, confirming Peng's call for transparency (i.e. informing the audience of the translation approach used). Through this exercise, Wendland's

---

23. Holmes, *An Introduction to Sociolinguistics*, 168.

LiFE proved very effective, especially for the translation of Psalms, The Bible is literature, and this approach enables translators to compose a more rhetorically phrased, artistically toned Bible translation.

6.4.4 Some General Observations Regarding Bible Translation

Besides confirming other's approaches, this exercise allowed the researcher to make some general observations about the Bible translation task.

As noted above, before beginning a project, it is essential to identify both the translation theory and method to be adopted and for translators to be trained in both. Thus, translators will be more focused, and no longer bothered by the issue of literal or free translation. The theory and methodology itself will guide them. For example, Wendland's LiFE approach is inclined to be more dynamic. With a translation theory and method in mind, translators will have criteria to follow, such as the choice and use of words and phrases in translating. For example, when Wendland's LiFE was used in this translation exercise, the IBTT was encouraged to choose words or phrases that not only are natural and easy to understand, but also help lines rhyme.

Once a specific translation theory and method has been decided upon, it is good to inform the audience of the approach employed so that they can discern whether the Bible version will meet their needs or not.

Besides, the *Skopos* (purpose) of a translation project must be explicitly described. Since this study did not intend to conduct a complete translation project, the details concerning a project *Skopos*[24] is not covered here. Nonetheless, it was still necessary to inform the IBTT of the purpose before the translation exercise (i.e. to produce a more artistic, readable Bible version for readers of all ages, including children). For example, the explicitness of the purpose helped reduce translators' struggle in choosing appropriate words and phrases. In Psalm 63:1c, the translation "切慕 *qiē mù* (yearning)" is such a beautiful phrase in Chinese that the majority of the IBTT members were reluctant to replace it with any other substitute. However, when reminded of the purpose of the translation exercise, the IBTT chose another less beautiful, but easier phrase for young children.

---

24. For more details, see Wendland, *Translating the Literature of Scripture*, 25–27.

Except for DCT, CNLT, and CNET, etc., which are translations based on English versions, more and more Chinese biblical scholars understand the importance of translating the Bible from the original biblical languages. During this exercise, it became evident that it is even more important to translate the Bible from the original biblical languages when producing a readable version for young readers. This is mainly because the language used in such a version is relatively new to Chinese translators who have no other corresponding versions for reference. Thus, referring to the original biblical languages is an important step in understanding the meaning and identifying appropriate and easy expressions for young readers.

The significance of translator-training lessons, translation theory and method, translation project *Skopos*, and the importance of translating the Bible from the original biblical languages are not new, as they are emphasized in Wendland's[25] and others' works regarding Bible translation.

6.5 Future Perspectives

The researcher recommends that prominent Chinese Bible societies can cooperate with churches to involve children and teenagers in modifying their translations in such a way that God's Word becomes easier for young readers to understand. As this research demonstrates, children and teenagers are creative and competent at making the Bible easier.[26] This is one of the possible ways to develop IIM in the church. What follows are some preliminary suggestions for making this happen.[27]

6.5.1 Expanding the Horizon

After this research, the author hopes that at least one prominent local Bible society or organization will recognize the significance of producing a Bible suitable for children since they need to hear God's Word, meaning the *whole*

---

25. For example, *Translating the Literature of Scripture* of 2004, and *LiFE-Style Translating* of 2011.

26. Children and teenagers also demonstrate the potential of contributing to hermeneutics and Scripture communication generally. For issues regarding children and hermeneutics, see Wall's article of 2006 "Childhood Studies, Hermeneutics, and Theological Ethics."

27. For an outline of a complete translation project, see Wendland, *LiFE-Style Translating*, ch. 3, 7; Wendland, *Translating the Literature of Scripture*, ch. 11.

Bible. This exercise has shown that it is advantageous to involve as many children, teenagers, and adults as possible in making Bible versions easier for all generations, including children. This, in turns, affects how such versions are received and used.

This study shows that IIM is an approach that can bear fruit, and that can certainly be developed in various domains within the church ministry.

Though only serving as an example, the study carried out on נֶפֶשׁ in the OT shows how important it is to understand the semantic range of a term. In the case of נֶפֶשׁ, combining IIM and LiFE has opened up broader biblical and theological perspectives for both adults and children.

Along with future perspectives, certainly, several steps can be taken.

6.5.2 Training Church Leaders

After making church leaders aware of the need of a more artistic and comprehensive Bible for people of all ages, the local Bible society could organize intergenerational Bible translation workshops,[28] involving as many leaders from different churches as possible. The training course would include biblical languages, translation theory and method, IIM, and the value of children and childhood from biblical and theological perspectives.

6.5.3 Training Congregations

Leaders from different churches (with the assistance of the Bible society) could then establish their intergenerational Bible translation team (IBTT) at their local churches, made up of adults (both younger and older), teenagers, and children. The IBTT is provided with easier training courses.[29]

6.5.4 Launching the Intergenerational Bible Translation

At this point, each church leader would be responsible for a certain part of the Bible. The Bible society would prepare the necessary materials for the leader, e.g. exegetical analyses (including the artistic and rhetorical features), the interlinear Bible, and the provisional translation.

---

28. Cf. Wendland, *Analyzing the Psalms*, 237–251.

29. For example, translation methodology is too hard for children. What the IBTT really needs is the example that can illustrate the method. For example, if Wendland's LiFE is used, sample translations through the approach need to be presented and explained.

Then, the teams would follow the process as outlined in §5.2. Once a draft of a section is accepted by the team, that text could be submitted to the Bible society for reviewing. The consultants of a given Bible society could then give their immediate feedback as to which part calls for reconsideration. This could be carried out through the internet. Once the composition by IBTT (the second half of the operation of composition, see §5.1) is done, the operations of contextualization[30] and consultation will follow.[31]

As the feedback from the IBTT members of this research indicates, the exercise in Bible translation helps believers gain more in-depth understanding of God's Word, increase the knowledge of biblical Hebrew, recognize the importance of Bible translation, and support the task of Bible translation. It is hoped that this exercise can inspire various Bible societies also to attempt to produce Bibles *for* and *by* people of all different generations, including children and teenagers, permitting a renewed unity within the church and a deeper understanding of God's Word.

6.6 Final Comments

Children are an integral part of the church who need to hear God's Word. It is worthwhile for the Christian community to invest time, energy, money, etc., in producing an artistic and readable Bible version accessible to them, allowing them to contribute wholeheartedly to the enterprise of Bible translation. In this study, children and older people contributed to the process of reconsidering the translations of the word נֶפֶשׁ and the production of a more understandable translation of Psalms 35, 63, and 107. If the challenging task of Bible translation could be accomplished by a team of different age groups, including children, then most church ministries can be done in the same way. Today's churches need to be revived through the power of

---

30. As noted in footnote 9 of this chapter, the second half of the operation of composition and contextualization cannot be strictly distinguished when involving children in the translation team. This is because some components of contextualization are already introduced in the process of the second half of the composition, such as illustrations by children or teenagers. Thus, the researcher suggests that the second half of the composition conducted by the IBTT should be combined with the operation of contextualization, in which some interesting theories are employed, such as mental-space theory suggested by Wendland, *LiFE-Style Translating*, 367–375.

31. Wendland, ch. 7.

the reconnection of all generations, including children, to "bring Christ's intergenerational message of unconditional love to an aging society suffering from generational isolation, separation and neglect."[32] This study provides a practical example of how this can be done.

---

32. Gambone, *All Are Welcome*, vii.

APPENDIX A

The IBTT's Suggestions on the Translation of נֶפֶשׁ

What is the most appropriate translation of נֶפֶשׁ in each occurrence? Please provide your reason.

Psalm 35:3c

- I think the translation "me" is fine. This is because the previous two verses are both about "Lord and I"; thus using "me" in this context is fine (Chén, Yì、Lóng, Shū Rén).
- The previous verse is written in first person, so there is nothing more suitable other than "me" (Gāo, Zǐ Xīn、Huáng, Huì Rú).
- I don't think there is a need for a change because this passage is written in first person (Huáng, Bǐng Jūn).
- "Me." It is because objects that are able to talk should be living ones. Thus it should be translated as "me" (Lǚ, Nǎi Wǎi、Lǚ, Yìng Xuān、Lǚ, Nǎi Yuán、Gān, Xiàn Píng).
- "Me" is the most suitable and reasonable translation because only by using "me" can truly express the feelings (Chén, Wén Qí).

Psalm 35:4b

- "Physical life." Reasoning: the foregoing text mentions that those seeking נֶפֶשׁ are the author's enemies who want to defeat the author. According to the context, it is the enemies who are seeking נֶפֶשׁ. Thus, the very thing the enemies are seeking is "physical life" (Lǚ, Nǎi Wǎi、Lǚ, Yìng Xuān、Lǚ, Nǎi Yuán、Gān, Xiàn Píng).

- Because the "seek" seems to express the intent of putting someone to death; thus using "physical life" is the most suitable (Gāo, Zǐ Xīn、Huáng, Huì Rú).
- My life. Because according to the context, the enemies are searching the author to take away his life; thus translating it to "my life" is suitable (Chén, Yì、Lóng, Shū Rén).
- From the context, the main purpose of the enemies is to either injure or murder him, thus I think we should use "life" (Huáng, Bǐng Jūn).

Psalm 35:7b

- "Physical Life." Because the passage above says "those who seek my life," thus they dig the pit for my "physical life" is more reasonable (Lǚ, Nǎi Wǎi、Lǚ, Yìng Xuān、Lǚ, Nǎi Yuán、Gān, Xiàn Píng).
- I think the translation can be changed to "dead body." This is because the enemies are trying to take the author's physical life, but by changing it to "dead body" will further show the enemy's evil intentions (Chén, Yì、Lóng, Shū Rén).
- "Physical life," because the previous text mentions "digging a pit," which is similar to that prepared by Joseph's brothers as they plot against Joseph by trying to take away his "physical life" (Gāo, Zǐ Xīn、Huáng, Huì Rú).
- Because the main purpose of digging the pit is to hurt him, and "life" is the most specific word to describe it (Huáng, Bǐng Jūn).

Psalm 35:9a

- "The whole being." Because "I" cannot express fully how joyful the person is; thus using "the whole being" is better here (Gāo, Zǐ Xīn、Huáng, Huì Rú).
- Using "the whole person" can express his integrity and the intensity of his emotions the best (Huáng, Bǐng Jūn).
- "The whole being," because the ability to be "joyful" indicates that it is a living being. In this case, it is the author. And the preceding text corresponds to this (joy in God's salvation) by

saying how the author wants the Lord to save him (Lǚ, Nǎi Wǎi、Lǚ, Yìng Xuān、Lǚ, Nǎi Yuán、Gān, Xiàn Píng).
- "The whole person." The ability to become joyful is appeared at multiple levels, including spiritual and bodily (Chén, Yì、Lóng, Shū Rén).

Psalm 35:12b
- Because only "I" can feel forlorn (Huáng, Bǐng Jūn).
- "I," because "forlorn" is a feeling, and the subject is the author, thus using "I" is the most suitable (Lǚ, Nǎi Wǎi、Lǚ, Yìng Xuān、Lǚ, Nǎi Yuán、Gān, Xiàn Píng).
- "I," because it makes the passage flow better (Chén, Yì、Lóng, Shū Rén).
- "I," because "forlorn" is a human emotion (Gāo, Zǐ Xīn、Huáng, Huì Rú).

Psalm 35:13b
- "My body," because fasting is directly related to the body (Lǚ, Nǎi Wǎi、Lǚ, Yìng Xuān、Lǚ, Nǎi Yuán、Gān, Xiàn Píng).
- "Body," because fasting is a training on the body (Chén, Yì、Lóng, Shū Rén).
- "Body," because it is the body afflicted the most while fasting (Gāo, Zǐ Xīn、Huáng, Huì Rú).
- Because fasting has a direct impact on the human body, so only using "my body" can describe it properly (Huáng, Bǐng Jūn).

Psalm 35:17b
- "Physical life," because what the enemies want to hurt is the author's physical life according to the previous passage (Lǚ, Nǎi Wǎi、Lǚ, Yìng Xuān、Lǚ, Nǎi Yuán、Gān, Xiàn Píng).
- "Physical life," because it fits the context (Chén, Yì、Lóng, Shū Rén).
- "Physical life"; the use of the "physical life" can express the thought of rescuing someone (Gāo, Zǐ Xīn、Huáng, Huì Rú).

- The passage describes the author's enemies who want to attack every part of his whole being, so "the whole being" is the better term here (Huáng, Bǐng Jūn).

Psalm 35:25b

- I think "appetite" is suitable here because the next colon mentions "devour." So the use of "appetite" makes the meaning of the sentence more complete (Chén, Yì、Lóng, Shū Rén).
- "Appetite," because "appetite" fits well with the next colon which says "We have devoured him" (Huáng, Bǐng Jūn).
- "Appetite," which can convey the desire of the enemies (Gāo, Zǐ Xīn、Huáng, Huì Rú).
- "Desire, appetite." The previous verses denote that the enemies are saying that God did not help the author. So the best translation is "this is our desire (this fits our appetite)" (Lǚ, Nǎi Wǎi、Lǚ, Yìng Xuān、Lǚ, Nǎi Yuán、Gān, Xiàn Píng).

Psalm 63:1b

- "The whole being," because it is followed by the verb "thirst," it has to be related to living being/human. It also parallels "the whole body" in the next colon. Thus, it should be translated as "the whole being" (Lǚ, Nǎi Wǎi、Lǚ, Yìng Xuān、Lǚ, Nǎi Yuán、Gān, Xiàn Píng).
- "The whole being." Because in the possible meanings of נֶפֶשׁ, only "the whole being" and "the life" can thirst for things, but only the use of "the whole being" can express the intensity (Huáng, Bǐng Jūn).
- Because 1a says "I" earnestly seek you, thus using "my whole being" can further accentuate the subject who seeks earnestly (Chén, Yì、Lóng, Shū Rén).

Psalm 63:5a

- The whole being, which can emphasize the feeling of fullness (Gāo, Zǐ Xīn、Huáng, Huì Rú).

- It is used to accentuate the meaning of the passage, so it should be translated as "the whole being" (Lǚ, Nǎi Wǎi、Lǚ, Yìng Xuān、Lǚ, Nǎi Yuán、Gān, Xiàn Píng).
- The whole being. From the context, the fullness here is not just on a physical level, thus using "the whole being" is better (Huáng, Bǐng Jūn).
- Because only using "the whole being" can accentuate the feeling of fullness (Chén, Yì、Lóng, Shū Rén).

Psalm 63:8a

- The whole being, because it can display his complete trust (Gāo, Zǐ Xīn、Huáng, Huì Rú).
- Because of extreme joyfulness, the author wants to cling to God. Thus, the translation as "the whole being" is suitable (Lǚ, Nǎi Wǎi、Lǚ, Yìng Xuān、Lǚ, Nǎi Yuán、Gān, Xiàn Píng).
- "The whole being." From the context, the psalmist is putting in all his trust (Huáng, Bǐng Jūn).
- Because only "body" and "the whole being" can express such a physical contact. Also, the next colon mentions "uphold," which is an action that needs to be imposed on a physical entity (Chén, Yì、Lóng, Shū Rén).

Psalm 63:9

- My life. It can accentuate the thought of killing the opponent (Gāo, Zǐ Xīn、Huáng, Huì Rú).
- The enemies are those who want to harm the psalmist; they want to take his life away. Thus translating it as physical life is the most suitable (Lǚ, Nǎi Wǎi、Lǚ, Yìng Xuān、Lǚ, Nǎi Yuán、Gān, Xiàn Píng).
- My life, which corresponds to 10a: the enemies must be struck down by the sword (Huáng, Bǐng Jūn).
- Only "my physical life" is what the enemies want to seek and then destroy (Chén, Yì、Lóng, Shū Rén).

Psalm 107:5b
- "The whole person." Because being faint applies to both physical and mental dimensions (Chén, Yì Lóng, Shū Rén).
- "The whole person." Only the whole being can be faint (Huáng, Bǐng Jūn).
- The whole person, which puts on more emphasis (Gāo, Zǐ Xīn、Huáng, Huì Rú).
- Only living being can experience the feeling of being faint, which in this case is the psalmist. Here, the translation as "the whole person" puts on more emphasis than that as "person" (Lǚ, Nǎi Wǎi、Lǚ, Yìng Xuān、Lǚ, Nǎi Yuán、Gān, Xiàn Píng).

Psalm 107:9a and 9b
- "Person." It corresponds to the previous verses, which obviously denote the person who is both hungry and thirsty (Chén, Yì、Lóng, Shū Rén).
- "Person," because the last verse mentions humankind, it does not indicate specific objects (Gāo, Zǐ Xīn、Huáng, Huì Rú).
- Being able to become satisfied and be filled with good things should be the abilities of living creatures, which are human beings here. Also in this case, it does not represent a particular human (e.g. the psalmist in Ps 63), so it should be translated as "person" (Lǚ, Nǎi Wǎi、Lǚ, Yìng Xuān、Lǚ, Nǎi Yuán、Gān, Xiàn Píng).
- "Person." Only using person can include the physical and non-physical parts of the person. And using "the whole person" here makes the expression too redundant (Huáng, Bǐng Jūn).

Psalm 107:18a
- "They." Because it is in third person, masculine, plural. And translating it as "their appetite" makes the expression redundant (Huáng, Bǐng Jūn).
- Continuing from the previous verse (also because in Hebrew it is plural), it should mean "they" (Lǚ, Nǎi Wǎi、Lǚ, Yìng Xuān、Lǚ, Nǎi Yuán、Gān, Xiàn Píng).

- "They." "They" is a pronoun for "the fools" (Chén, Yì、Lóng, Shū Rén).

Psalm 107:26c

- I think in verse 26c the translation "the whole being" is appropriate because the disaster causes not only the body to tremble, but also "the whole person" (Chén, Wén Qí).
- "The whole being," because it puts more emphasis (Gāo, Zǐ Xīn、Huáng, Huì Rú).
- "The whole being," because it can express better that both the physical and the non-physical parts of the person are trembling (Huáng, Bǐng Jūn).
- Trembling mainly occurs in human body. And the context is about physical things, thus using "the whole being" here is the most suitable (Lǚ, Nǎi Wǎi、Lǚ, Yìng Xuān、Lǚ, Nǎi Yuán、Gān, Xiàn Píng).

APPENDIX B

The Feedback from the Participants of the IBTT

The Feedback from 呂乃崴 Lǔ, Nǎi Wǎi (seven years old)

1. Please describe your experience of the Bible translation exercise.
Very happy, as I never had this experience

2. What did you enjoy most about the exercise?
I liked the review games. For example, the review game "Hit the fly" was very fun and exciting, but I was too scared to play it.

I liked it when everyone asked me for my opinion, because everyone would listen to me and ask me whether or not I can understand the translation.

3. Did you find some parts of the translation project difficult or less enjoyable? If so, please describe those parts and explain why you found this difficult.
Nothing.

4. What do you think, why you were doing this exercise?
I never thought about it, because I did not know about it. My mother told me to join.

I really enjoyed it after I joined, and I also look forward to the next opportunity. I think the Hebrew letters are very pretty.

5. What will you do with the translations? How do you feel about that?
I cannot think of anything.

6. What did you know about Bible translation before you participated in this exercise?
I do not know.

7. Now that you have participated in a Bible translations exercise, (1) how do you feel about it, (2) What is it, (3) who does it and (4) how important is it? (The questions here are more challenging for 乃葳 Nǎi Wǎi.)

(1) If translation does not exist, I would not be able to read the Chinese Bible.

(2) Taking a language I do not understand into something I can understand.

(3) Anyone willing to learn.

(4) Very important, so that everyone can understand what God wants us to know.

8. How do you feel about the participation of people of different ages in a Bible translation exercise? How did it work in this project?
(1) Nothing really, but I liked it when everyone had to come to the same conclusion. It is good to learn to hear different opinions.

(2) He did not know how to answer.

The Feedback from 楊俊晴 Yáng, Jùn Qíng (eight years old)

1. Please describe your experience of the Bible translation exercise.
I feel very good about the translation exercise because it's very good for mind and soul.

2. What did you enjoy most about the exercise?
I really liked the time when we got together to read God's Word in the original language.

3. Did you find some parts of the translation project difficult or less enjoyable? If so, please describe those parts and explain why you found this difficult.
I think it is not so difficult for me because I already knew how to read God's Word in the original language.

4. What do you think, why you were doing this exercise?
The reason why I'm doing the translation exercise is to let more people understand God's Word in other kind of languages.

5. What will you do with the translations? How do you feel about that?
I will teach.

I feel that it's great because we can read in the original language and we can help the translators.

6. What did you know about Bible translation before you participated in this exercise?
I knew about bible translation because I read God's Word in the original language and it's very exciting for me to know more about the original language.

7. Now that you have participated in a Bible translations exercise, (1) how do you feel about it, (2) what is it, (3) who does it and (4) how important is it?
(1) I feel great to do this for God because he wants us to help him with his kingdom.

(3) God does it for us.

(4) It's important for us because it's spiritual bread for our mind and soul.

8. How do you feel about the participation of people of different ages in a Bible translation exercise? How did it work in this project?
It was exciting to work with a group of people no matter what language they speak or how old they are.

The Feedback from 陳文祈 Chén, Wén Qí (eleven years old)

1. Please describe your experience of the Bible translation exercise.
I felt a great sense of achievement while translating the Hebrew Bible, which made me feel that I was part of it. Also I learned Hebrew through the process of translation. It was a nice experience.

2. What did you enjoy most about the exercise?
My favorite part was to read the Hebrew Bible, although I was following the teacher, but I still felt accomplished.

3. Did you find some parts of the translation project difficult or less enjoyable? If so, please describe those parts and explain why you found this difficult.
The spelling of Hebrew – adding/removing "dots" will cause the sound to be different. I felt that this was my weakest part. I think I need to study harder in this regard.

4. What do you think, why you were doing this exercise?
I always wanted to learn a new language, and I was provided this opportunity. Also because people I know were also registering for it, so I also joined.

5. What will you do with the translations? How do you feel about that?
Because of the experience of discussion in this exercise, I want to discuss and translate with friends and families later on.

6. What did you know about Bible translation before you participated in this exercise?
Never heard of Bible translation; also not sure what we would be translating.

7. Now that you have participated in a Bible translations exercise, (1) how do you feel about it, (2) what is it, (3) who does it and (4) how important is it?
(1) Through the process of translation, I was able to learn more about God's Word

(3) I think everyone can do it as long as they have the heart and the passion to do it.

(4) I think it is very important as I believe that many people still do not understand the message of the Bible. So there is a need for a Bible that is easy to understand and retains the original meaning at the same time.

8. How do you feel about the participation of people of different ages in a Bible?
I had class with people of different age groups I found that everyone had different opinions. Because of the participation of different age groups, I experienced the parent-child interactive relationship. Also due to the age difference, team chemistry was very important. Through games and socializing, we bonded and grew to know more about each other, which in turn, helped the process of translation.

The Feedback from 黃炳君 Huáng, Bǐng Jūn (eleven years old)

1. Please describe your experience of the Bible translation exercise.
To further my understanding on the process of translation, also to learn a new language in Hebrew.

2. What did you enjoy most about the exercise?
I enjoyed working on Bible translation with everyone as we would often have funny and interesting ideas.

3. Did you find some parts of the translation project difficult or less enjoyable? If so, please describe those parts and explain why you found this difficult.
None.

4. What do you think, why you were doing this exercise?
It was very interesting in a sense that it was different.

5. What will you do with the translations? How do you feel about that?
N/A

6. What did you know about Bible translation before you participated in this exercise?
I understood.

7. Now that you have participated in a Bible translations exercise, (1) how do you feel about it, (2) what is it, (3) who does it and (4) how important is it?
(1) Interesting.

(2) Translating Hebrew Bible into different Bibles that fit different cultural groups

(3) Someone who is willing and competent, and has enough time.

(4) Very important.

8. How do you feel about the participation of people of different ages in a Bible translation exercise? How did it work in this project?
(1) Interesting.

(2) After discussing, we figured out phrases or sentences that are suitable for younger children.

The Feedback from 陳逸 Chén, Yì (twelve years old)

1. Please describe your experience of the Bible translation exercise.
This is my first time learning Hebrew, and also my first time translating the Bible. The exercise was not only interesting, but it also helped me to understand more about the Bible.

2. What did you enjoy most about the exercise?
I liked studying through the games. It encouraged me to memorize vocabularies more diligently. The games were fun and exciting.

3. Did you find some parts of the translation project difficult or less enjoyable? If so, please describe those parts and explain why you found this difficult.
Nothing really, everything was interesting to me.

4. What do you think, why you were doing this exercise?
My mother asked me whether I was interested. I thought it would help me so I joined.

5. What will you do with the translations? How do you feel about that?
I could compare the Bible with the new translation during my daily devotions. I have never tried it before, so I do not know how it will turn out.

6. What did you know about Bible translation before you participated in this exercise?
Taking Greek and Hebrew into other languages.

7. Now that you have participated in a Bible translations exercise, (1) how do you feel about it, (2) what is it, (3) who does it and (4) how important is it?
(1) I think it is a wonderful thing to translate one language into another language. It is even more wonderful when translating the Bible myself. This is very interesting.

(2) I think Bible translation is taking Bible of other languages into a language that a person needs.

(3) I believe anyone can be involved in translation as long as they have the language skills and the heart for it.

(4) The important aspect in Bible translation is that any mistake can cause the reader to misunderstand it, so this is a very vital task.

8. How do you feel about the participation of people of different ages in a Bible translation exercise? How did it work in this project?
(1) It was a very special experience for me, because everyone was of different age groups with different experiences, thus having different opinions on

things. I believe this is a very good method for Bible translation since both adults and children have their own contribution to the translation task.

(2) We were led by the teacher who taught us Hebrew and then guided us to translate the Bible together.

The Feedback from 高子馨 Gāo, Zǐ Xīn (twelve years old)

1. Please describe your experience of the Bible translation exercise.
It is my first time to learn a language that I have never experienced.

2. What did you enjoy most about the exercise?
Games, because they were fun.

3. Did you find some parts of the translation project difficult or less enjoyable? If so, please describe those parts and explain why you found this difficult.
Strong verb conjugation, because I did not really understand.

4. What do you think, why you were doing this exercise?
I wanted to experience it.

5. What will you do with the translations? How do you feel about that?
I did not know I could also be involved in Bible translation. I used to think only professionals can do it.

6. What did you know about Bible translation before you participated in this exercise?
I did not know.

7. Now that you have participated in a Bible translations exercise, (1) how do you feel about it, (2) what is it, (3) who does it and (4) how important is it?
(1) It is not easy for me to absorb.

(2) I think Bible translation is taking something of a different language into something that is legible.

(3) Anyone with passion and enthusiasm can be involved in the process of Bible translation.

(4) Bible translation is very important, so that people of all countries may understand the word of God.

8. How do you feel about the participation of people of different ages in a Bible translation exercise? How did it work in this project?
(1) Having different and innovative ideas.

(2) Before the exercise in Bible translation, teacher taught us the basics of biblical Hebrew, including pronunciation and letters, noun, personal pronoun, verb, etc.

The Feedback from 呂映萱 Lǚ, Yìng Xuān (thirteen years old)

1. Please describe your experience of the Bible translation exercise.
I felt that it was an excellent experience because I not only learned Hebrew, but also understood more about the Bible.

2. What did you enjoy most about the exercise?
I enjoyed playing games the most. Because I thought I would not be able to follow along. However, through games, I realized that I can catch on some part of the lesson. This made me feel accomplished. Whenever I lost, I examined where I did not understand and needed improvement.

3. Did you find some parts of the translation project difficult or less enjoyable? If so please describe those parts and explain why you found this difficult.
I felt that Bible translation was harder; also I did not enjoy it as much. Probably because I did not participate as much, or maybe I was not able to keep up.

4. What do you think, why you were doing this exercise?
Because I felt that this was a very special experience, also I participated with friends I knew.

5. What will you do with the translations? How do you feel about that?
I understood more about the Bible after the translation experience.

6. What did you know about Bible translation before you participated in this exercise?
Only knew about Bible translation, but never came in contact with it. I used to think that only scholars can do it.

7. Now that you have participated in a Bible translations exercise, (1) how do you feel about it, (2) what is it, (3) who does it and (4) how important is it?
(1) I felt that Bible translation is a very tiring process, but very valuable.

(2) I think Bible translation is a mission that let everyone be able to read the Bible and understand the truth.

(3) Anyone, as long as you have the heart to do it.

(4) Very important, super important! So that younger children can also read the Bible and understand Jesus.

8. How do you feel about the participation of people of different ages in a Bible translation exercise? How did it work in this project?
(1) I felt that it was pretty good, because we all have different opinions. Adults sometimes would use terms that children do not think about, and vice versa.

(2) We always started the class with a game to recall what we have learned. Then the teacher would use PowerPoint to teach us Hebrew. Lastly we would do the translation. The translation process was done verse by verse, and we would not move on to the next verse until the younger children understood the translation.

The Feedback from 呂乃源 Lǚ, Nǎi Yuán (sixteen years old)

1. Please describe your experience of the Bible translation exercise.
Very refreshing as I have never tried reading the Hebrew Bible. I never thought that Bible translation would be this difficult.

2. What did you enjoy most about the exercise?
Learning Hebrew pronunciation, because I found it the easiest so I often felt accomplished.

3. Did you find some parts of the translation project difficult or less enjoyable? If so, please describe those parts and explain why you found this difficult.
Luckily, not really.

4. What do you think, why you were doing this exercise?
Joined with my mother.

5. What will you do with the translations? How do you feel about that?
I do not know.

6. What did you know about Bible translation before you participated in this exercise?
I do not understand it fully. I do not understand the difference between word-for-word translation and sense-for-sense translation.

7. Now that you have participated in a Bible translations exercise, (1) how do you feel about it, (2) what is it, (3) who does it and (4) how important is it?
(1) Bible translation is hard, needing constant editing. Translators are supposed to bear enormous pressure.

(2) Bible translation is an important part of spreading God's Word.

(3) Bible translation must be led by an experienced leader who is competent with theology and biblical languages.

(4) Bible translation can change a person's view on theology, so using the correct word is very important.

8. How do you feel about the participation of people of different ages in a Bible translation exercise? How did it work in this project?
Everyone had their own speaking/writing style; knowing how to balance them was what we had to learn.

The Feedback from 黃滿貞 Huáng Mǎn Zhēn (forty years old)

1. Please describe your experience of the Bible translation exercise.
It was a privilege to have this experience. My children and I were always excited when I took them to the Bible translation group every Wednesday.

2. What did you enjoy most about the exercise?
Being able to translate the Bible with other people using a language that I understand was very interesting.

3. Did you find some parts of the translation project difficult or less enjoyable? If so, please describe those parts and explain why you found this difficult.
I found out that my Chinese vocabulary is very limited. But the 2.5 hours passed by really quickly as we all worked together to translate the Bible (it was also a challenge taking care of my youngest child at the same time!)

4. What do you think, why you were doing this exercise?
Being able to participate, it was like a gift from heaven, like winning the lottery.

5. What will you do with the translations? How do you feel about that?
Because of this experience, we think of the Hebrew word whenever we encounter a word that we recognize. I would be happy to share it to other people in the future when the situation presents itself.

6. What did you know about Bible translation before you participated in this exercise?
I understood what translation is but I did not know what Bible translation is and how important and fun it can be.

7. Now that you have participated in a Bible translations exercise, (1) how do you feel about it, (2) what is it, (3) who does it and (4) how important is it?
(1) Bible translation was fun but not easy, needed to put in a lot of effort.

(2) Bible translation is a sophisticated process that requires a deep understanding of the Bible.

(3) Anyone with the passion can join as Bible is written for everyone to read.

(4) Very important, to spread the correct meaning of the word of God.

8. How do you feel about the participation of people of different ages in a Bible translation exercise? How did it work in this project?
Very important, through the activities, we got to know each other more. Also, involving different generations was important because the Bible is meant for all different age groups to read.

The Feedback from 龍淑仁 Lóng, Shū Rén (forty-two years old)

1. Please describe your experience of the Bible translation exercise.
Previous I would almost exclusively read CUV, unless there is something I do not understand. Once this is the case, I will take a look at different versions to help me understand.

I had no idea about Bible translation method. So naturally I would not know that the translation approaches used in Bible versions are different and play an important role for understanding God's Word. However, through the Bible translation exercise, I not only understood the history of Bible translation, different translation methods, but also learned God's Word through biblical Hebrew. It was such a valuable experience.

2. What did you enjoy most about the exercise?
I enjoyed the part where we tried to figure out the most suitable translation so that younger children can understand it while not losing the original meaning.

There were times of argument. But this created the opportunity to hear different opinions and considerations when everyone provided their reasoning to their translation. This was very interesting.

3. Did you find some parts of the translation project difficult or less enjoyable? If so, please describe those parts and explain why you found this difficult.
Nothing in particular, but I felt stressed while playing the "mini games." It was not that I disliked it, but I always tried my hardest which caused me stress. Even so, I still enjoyed participating in the games.

4. What do you think, why you were doing this exercise?
Before this translation exercise, I already tried doing Hebrew exegesis through internet resources. But it was hard without a teacher's step-by-step guidance.

Besides, one of the reasons why I decided to do homeschooling was that my child's life can be built on God's Word deeper. Therefore, I really treasured this exercise that my daughter and I could have on studying the Bible.

5. What will you do with the translations? How do you feel about that?
In this exercise, I myself had the opportunity to understand God's Word through easier translations. I also had the opportunity to think how to let younger children understand God's Word, i.e., translating the Bible for children. Reading the Bible is not only for myself anymore, but also for delivering the gospel. As Hebrew 8:11 says "because they will all know me, from the least of them to the greatest."

God's salvation is for everyone; he does not take favor. His care about children really touches my heart.

6. What did you know about Bible translation before you participated in this exercise?
I knew a little bit, but never really put my thoughts into it.

7. Now that you have participated in a Bible translations exercise, (1) how do you feel about it, (2) what is it, (3) who does it and (4) how important is it?
(1) I think Bible translation is very important, because every mistake can potentially change the context of the Bible. It would be dangerous if we live according to the teachings of the Bible, yet the translation of the Bible is incorrect. I firmly believe that Bible translation is a serious, important task.

(2) I think the purpose of Bible translation is that people of different nations, languages, ages in the whole world can hear and understand God's Word, so that "the earth will be filled with the knowledge of the glory of the Lord, as the waters cover the sea" (Hab 2:14).

(3) I used to think people involved in Bible translation requires extensive knowledge of the Bible and language skills. But now I think it is more appropriate to involve a group of people in the task of Bible translation. After all, the purpose of Bible translation is to make God's Word more understandable. Thus, the more the input the better.

8. How do you feel about the participation of people of different ages in a Bible translation exercise? How did it work in this project?
I think it is very interesting. I think working with people of different age groups on Bible translation is something that Christians should do. This is a special kind of fellowship. In order to obtain the goal, we learned how to compromise, communicate, and listen to each other. For me, it was much more work and less efficient than working by myself. But Jesus himself is a good example of this. He allows humble human beings to work with him and to participate in his plan.

We always make mistakes, but his love and truth always guide us and lead us on the correct path.

The Feedback from 甘憲平 Gān, Xiàn Píng (forty-three years old)

1. Please describe your experience of the Bible translation exercise.
I was very thankful for the experience. I realized how little I know about God's miraculous wonders. 乃源 nǎi yuán, my eldest son at his age of 16, is very conservative, and would not consider baptism unless he is very sure of his faith. He got baptized recently. I believe the Bible translation exercise provided him with the opportunity to build close relationship with God.

I always wanted to do things with the family as a whole. Although my ability was not comparable to the kids, but I wanted to participate in the translation process, so I encouraged my children to join me as well (they initially did not have much courage and confidence in themselves). In the end, my three children learned more than me, which made me really happy.

Through the sharing with the teacher and other students, I learned more about the history of Bible. My Bible study with my children seems to proceed smoother than before because of my increase in knowledge. Also, I am eager to set apart more time to read the Bible. Although sometimes I do not understand it right away, I do not feel discouraged as much anymore. I think it is because through this experience, my attitude towards reading the Bible have changed dramatically. My English is not good, and I did not understand much of Hebrew, but I experienced God's love throughout the translation process. God changed me and now I love to read his words and spend time with him. Also I love to share with my friends all the wonderful things he has done for my family. I do not know if there will be another opportunity, but I definitely found this experience to be more than what I could ever ask for.

2. What did you enjoy most about the exercise?
I was inspired by teacher's explanation as well as the excellent PowerPoint resources. Those really helped me to think critically during my meditation and discussion with other students.

There is a huge difference in age and personality in the translation team. But through discussion and critique, I was able to understand and learn many things that I would never have thought of myself. Such critical thinking learned in the exercise was not just used in the class. I also applied it to my everyday life and my studies. It really helped dramatically.

3. Did you find some parts of the translation project difficult or less enjoyable? If so, please describe those parts and explain why you found this difficult.
Games, because I was not able to learn as fast. This made me nervous and unable to respond well during the games. But my teacher always allowed me to learn and observe from the side, which enhanced my confidence to review afterwards.

4. What do you think, why you were doing this exercise?
I love to learn, and I hope to gain something out of it (my ability is not very good, I am grateful that I and my children were accepted as students).

5. What will you do with the translations? How do you feel about that?
Ever since this experience, I am able to sense and understand passage of the Bible better.

Not only the three translated psalms, but my son 乃崴 nǎi wǎi (grade 1) and I also took an extra step to start reading the Bible from its beginning.

I am not sure what the reason is, but the Bible is more understandable to me now.

As for 乃崴 nǎi wǎi, he loves reading the Bible ever since he joined the exercise. Although he does not understand much of it, but he encourages his siblings and I to read as well. This is a great blessing to my family. We only know a bit of Hebrew, but I firmly believe that God has brought the passion of reading the Bible into my family through 乃崴 nǎi wǎi.

6. What did you know about Bible translation before you participated in this exercise?
Not sure, I thought it was something out of reach. But this experience not only enhances my confidence, but also enhances my children's confidence. We believe that we will be able to gain something out of it if we are willing to try it. We should not belittle ourselves, because God will provide everything that we need.

7. Now that you have participated in a Bible translations exercise, (1) how do you feel about it, (2) what is it, (3) who does it and (4) how important is it?
(1) I like it very much; I could picture what was happening during the time when the passage was written.

(2) Allow more people to understand the word of God.

(3) Have language skill. But more importantly, have a willing heart.

(4) Bible translation is very important so that the word of God can be spread. throughout the world without being affected by environmental and language barrier. Also taking the words into audio or braille so that illiterate or blind people can also hear the word of God.

8. How do you feel about the participation of people of different ages in a Bible translation exercise? How did it work in this project?
(1) Very special, as this experience breaks the traditional view of Bible translation by collecting the opinion of different people. Even 乃崴 nǎi wǎi can participate in it by providing his idea for older people to do discussion. The fact that 乃崴 nǎi wǎi can participate in the wonderful course made both 乃崴 nǎi wǎi and I surprised and happy.

(2) The process of the translation exercise: Using games for review → teacher provided material as well as PowerPoint for new information → practice speaking Hebrew → Bible translation by asking whether the younger children can understand the translation or not. If not, more discussion will be made to find words that everyone can understand. Also pictures were used to help the younger children to understand the Bible easier.

The Feedback from 黃慧如 Huáng, Huì Rú (fifty-one years old)

1. Please describe your experience of the Bible translation exercise.
I learned that some of the names of the books in the Old Testament implies God's promise and will. Amazing!

2. What did you enjoy most about the exercise?
The words of God became clearer as the discussion went on.

3. Did you find some parts of the translation project difficult or less enjoyable? If so, please describe those parts and explain why you found this difficult.
Personally, Hebrew letters, inflection, personal pronoun were hard for me to absorb, but I did not dislike it. Probably because as a housewife, my thoughts were distracted.

4. What do you think, why you were doing this exercise?
Wanted to understand the meaning of God's Word in Hebrew.

5. What will you do with the translations? How do you feel about that?
I could feel God's will as the names of the books in Hebrew were explained. For example, Nahum means "comfort" in Hebrew.

6. What did you know about Bible translation before you participated in this exercise?
Not sure.

7. Now that you have participated in a Bible translations exercise, (1) how do you feel about it, (2) what is it, (3) who does it and (4) how important is it?
(1) The word of God is worth pondering, meditating. Very enjoyable and good experience.

(2) Taking a foreign language into a language that I can understand.

(3) This intergenerational Bible translation exercise is to make the challenging parts of the Bible easier, that all the readers, including children, can understand. Those who are guided by experienced translators can do it.

(4) Very important, because more people will understand the creator's will to all of us.

8. How do you feel about the participation of people of different ages in a Bible translation exercise? How did it work in this project?
Very exciting, and I was looking forward to it.

All individuals had their own understanding of the Bible. This helped me to understand God's mighty power and realized how small I am when compared to him. Thus, human beings must be humble and fear him.

During the process, I could feel our teacher's humble and gentle guidance, attempting to help all participants understand. Every word was considered carefully.

The teacher used games in the process as she tried to create a happy and caring atmosphere, so that every one of different age groups could join.

I appreciate every individual that has taken the role of Bible translation, as I am encouraged, for which I am full of thankfulness. I hope we all can be touched by God's Words.

Bibliography

Ackroyd, P. R., and C. F. Evans, eds. *The Cambridge History of the Bible*. Vol 1. New York: Cambridge University Press, 2004.

Alanen, Leena. "Women's Studies/Childhood Studies: Parallels, Links and Perspectives." In *Children Taken Seriously: In Theory, Policy and Practice*, edited by Jan Mason and Toby Fattore, 31–45. London; Philadelphia: Jessica Kingsley, 2006.

Alderson, Priscilla. *Children's Consent to Surgery*. Milton Keynes: Open University Press, 1993.

Alexander, Philip S. "Jewish Aramaic Translations of Hebrew Scriptures." In *Mikra: Text, Translation, Reading and Interpretation of the Hebrew Bible in Ancient Judaism and Early Christianity*, edited by Martin Jan Mulder and Harry Sysling, 217–254. Peabody, MA: Hendrickson, 2004 [1988].

Alexander, T. Desmond. "תַּחְתִּי." In *New International Dictionary of Old Testament Theology and Exegesis*, vol. 4, edited by Willem A. VanGemeren, 288. Grand Rapids, MI: Zondervan, 1997.

Allen, A. L. "Children as Disciples, Not Simply Discipled: Reconsidering the Role of Children in the Christian Church," 2014. Accessed 15 May 2014. http://www.inter-disciplinary.net/probing-the-boundaries/wp-content/uploads/2014/05/allenchildpaper.pdf.

Allen, Holly Catterton. "Bringing the Generations Back Together: Introduction to Intergenerationality." *Christian Education Journal* 9, no. 1 (2012): 101–104.

———. "Bringing the Generations Together: Support from Learning Theory." *Christian Education Journal*, Series 3, Vol. 2, no. 2 (2005): 319–333.

———. "Nurturing Children's Spirituality in Intergenerational Christian Settings." In *Children's Spirituality: Christian Perspectives, Research, and Applications*, edited by Donald Ratcliff, Marcia McQuitty, Margaret Lawson, and Holly Catterton Allen, 266–283. Eugene, OR: Cascade, 2004.

Allen, Holly Catterton, and Christine Lawton Ross. *Intergenerational Christian Formation: Bringing the Whole Church Together in Ministry, Community and Worship*. Downers Grove, IL: IVP Academic, 2012.

Allen, Leslie C. *Psalms 101–150*. Edited by Bruce M. Metzger, David A. Hubbard, Glenn W. Barker, John D. W. Watts, and Ralph P. Martin. Rev. ed. Word Biblical Commentary 21. Nashville, TN: Nelson, 2002.

Allen, R. B. "עָצַם." In *Theological Wordbook of the Old Testament*, edited by R. L. Harris, G. L. Archer, Jr., and B. K. Waltke. Chicago, IL: Moody, 1999.

Alter, Robert. *The Book of Psalms: A Translation with Commentary*. New York: W. W. Norton & Co., 2007.

Anderson, A. A. *The Book of Psalms: Volume 2 Psalms 73–150*. New Century Bible Commentary. London: Marshall, Morgan & Scott, 1972.

Anderson, Herbert, and Susan B. W. Johnson. *Regarding Children: A New Respect for Childhood and Families*. Louisville, KY: Westminster John Knox, 1994.

Aquinas, Thomas. *New English Translation of St Thomas Aquinas's Summa Theologiae*. Translated by Alfred J. Freddoso. Accessed 25 October 2014. http://www3.nd.edu/~afreddos/summa-translation/Part%201/st1-ques37.pdf.

Archard, David. *Children: Rights and Childhood*. London: Taylor & Francis e-Library, 2005. Accessed 25 June 2014. http://books.scholarsportal.info/viewdoc.html?id=10684.

Arichea, Daniel C. "Theology and Translation: The Implications of Certain Theological Issues to the Translation Task." In *Bible Translation and the Spread of the Church: The Last 200 Years*, edited by Philip C. Stine, 40–67. Leiden; New York: Brill, 1990.

Ariès, Philippe. *Centuries of Childhood: A Social History of Family Life*. Translated by Robert Baldick. New York: Vintage Books, 1962.

Asbridge, Nigel. "What Is a Child?" In *Through the Eyes of a Child: New Insights in Theology from a Child's Perspective*, edited by Anne Richards and Peter Privett, 1–20. London: Church House, 2009.

Augustine of Hippo. *Confessions*. Translated by, with an introduction by, R. S. Pine-Coffin. Harmondsworth: Penguin Books, 1961.

———. "On Christian Doctrine." In *Nicene and Post-Nicene Fathers: St Augustin's City of God and Christian Doctrine*, vol. 2, edited by P. Schaff. Translated by J. F. Shaw, 513–597. Buffalo, NY: Christian Literature Co., 1887.

Bailey, James L. "Experiencing the Kingdom as a Little Child: A Rereading of Mark 10:13–16." *Word & World* 15, no. 1 (1995): 58–67.

Bakke, O. M. *When Children Became People: The Birth of Childhood in Early Christianity*. Translated by Brian McNeil. Minneapolis, MN: Fortress Press, 2005.

Baldwin, C. C. "Notes on the Revision of the Mandarin New Testament." *The Chinese Recorder and Missionary Journal* 38 (1907): 22–31, 91–101.

Balswick, Jack O., Pamela Ebstyne King, and Kevin S. Reimer. *The Reciprocating Self: Human Development in Theological Perspective*. Downers Grove, IL: InterVarsity Press, 2005.

Bandura, Albert. "On the Psychosocial Impact and Mechanisms of Spiritual Modeling." *International Journal for the Psychology of Religion* 13, no. 3 (2003): 167–173.

Banks, Robert J. "The Biblical Approach to Community." *Christian Education Journal* 13, no. 3 (1993): 18–28.

———. *Paul's Idea of Community: The Early House Churches in Their Cultural Setting*. Revised edition. Grand Rapids, MI: Baker Academic, 1995.

Barnabas. "The Epistle of Barnabas." In *The Ante-Nicene Fathers (Vol. 1): The Apostolic Fathers with Justin Martyr and Irenaeus*, edited by A. Roberts, J. Donaldson, and A. C. Coxe, 137–150. Buffalo, NY: Christian Literature Co., 1885.

Barnwell, Katharine. *Bible Translation: An Introductory Course in Translation Principles*. 3rd revised edition. Dallas, TX: Summer Institute of Linguistics, 1986.

———. *Teacher's Manual to Accompany Bible Translation: An Introductory Course in Translation Principles*. 3rd edition. Dallas, TX: Summer Institute of Linguistics, 1987.

Barr, James. *The Semantics of Biblical Language*. Eugene, OR: Wipf & Stock, 1961.

Barrera, Julio Trebolle. *The Jewish Bible and the Christian Bible: An Introduction to the History of the Bible*. Translated by Wilfred G. E. Watson. Grand Rapids, MI: Eerdmans, 1998.

Barth, Karl. *Church Dogmatics: The Doctrine of the Word of God* (Vol. I.1 § 8–12). Edited by Geoffrey W. Bromiley and Thomas Forsyth Torrance. London; New York: T & T Clark, 2009.

Barton, Stephen C. *Discipleship and Family Ties in Mark and Matthew*. Cambridge; New York: Cambridge University Press, 1994.

———. "Living as Families in the Light of the New Testament." *Interpretation* 52, no. 2 (1998): 130–144.

Bassnett, Susan. *Translation*. London: Routledge, 2014.

———. *Translation Studies*. London; New York: Routledge, 2005.

Bassnett, Susan, and Andre Lefevere, eds. *Translation, History and Culture*. London: Pinter, 1990.

Bays, Daniel H. *A New History of Christianity in China*. Blackwell Guides to Global Christianity. Chichester; Malden, MA: Wiley-Blackwell, 2012.

Beckwith, R. T. *The Old Testament Canon of the New Testament Church and Its Background in Early Judaism*. Grand Rapids, MI: Eerdmans, 1985.

Beekman, John, and J. Callow. *Translating the Word of God: With Scripture and Topical Indexes*. Grand Rapids, MI: Zondervan, 1974.

Berlin, Adele. *The Dynamics of Biblical Parallelism*. Revised and expanded. Grand Rapids, MI; Cambridge, UK: Eerdmans, 2008.

Bernard, Henry. 天主教十六世紀在華傳教誌 [The Catholic mission records of 16th century in China]. Translated by Xùn Huá Xiāo 蕭濬華. Taipei: Taiwan shāng wù yìn shū guǎn, 1964.

Berryman, Jerome W. *Children and the Theologians: Clearing the Way for Grace*. Harrisburg, PA: Morehouse, 2009.

———. *Godly Play: An Imaginative Approach to Religious Education*. Minneapolis, MN: Augsburg Press, 1991.

Betts, R. G. "Wycliffe Associates EasyEnglish: Challenges in Cross-Cultural Communication," 2003. Accessed 6 January 2014. http://www.mt-archive.info/CLT-2003-Betts.pdf.

Bickerman, Elias J. *The Jews in the Greek Age*. Cambridge, MA: Harvard University Press, 1988.

Black, Janet K. "Assessing Kindergarten Children's Communicative Competence." In *Language, Children and Society: The Effect of Social Factors on Children Learning to Communicate*, edited by Olga K. Garnica and Martha L. King, 37–51. International Series in Psychobiology and Learning. Oxford, UK: Pergamon Press, 1979.

Black, Jeremy, Andrew George, and Nicholas Postgate, eds. "*Napištu(m).*" In *A Concise Dictionary of Akkadian*, 239. Wiesbaden, Germany: Otto Harrassowitz, 2000.

Bloesch, Donald G. *God, the Almighty: Power, Wisdom, Holiness, Love*. Downers Grove, IL: InterVarsity Press, 1995.

Bluebond-Langner, Myra, and Jill E. Korbin. "Challenges and Opportunities in the Anthropology of Childhoods: An Introduction to 'Children, Childhoods, and Childhood Studies.'" *American Anthropologist* 109, no. 2 (2007): 241–246.

Bohr, P. Richard. "Jesus, Christianity, and Rebellion in China: The Evangelical Roots of the Taiping Heavenly Kingdom." In *The Chinese Face of Jesus Christ*, edited by Roman Malek, 613–661. Monumenta Serica Monograph Series 50. Sankt Augustin: Institut Monumenta Serica; Sankt Augustin: China-Zentrum, 2002.

Bottigheimer, Ruth B. *The Bible for Children: From the Age of Gutenberg to the Present*. New Haven, CT: Yale University Press, 1996.

———. "Bible Reading, 'Bibles' and the Bible for Children in Early Modern Germany." *Past and Present* 139 (1993): 66–89.

Bratcher, Robert G., and William David Reyburn. *A Translator's Handbook on the Book of Psalms*. New York: United Bible Societies, 1991.

Briggs, Charles A. "The Use of נפש in the Old Testament." *Journal of Biblical Literature* 16, no. 1/2 (1897): 17–30.
Briggs, Charles A., and Emilie Grace Briggs. *A Critical and Exegetical Commentary on the Book of Psalms*. Vol. 2. International Critical Commentary on the Holy Scriptures of the Old and New Testaments. Edinburgh: T & T Clark, 1909.
Bromiley, G. W. "Filioque." In *Evangelical Dictionary of Theology*, edited by Walter A. Elwell. Grand Rapids, MI: Baker Academic, 2001.
Broomhall, Marshall. *The Bible in China*. London; Toronto: China Inland Mission, 1934.
———. *Robert Morrison: A Master-Builder*. Modern Series of Missionary Biographies. New York: George H. Doran Co., 1924.
Brotzman, Ellis R. "Man and the Meaning of נפש." *Bibliotheca Sacra* 145 (1988): 400–409.
———. *Old Testament Textual Criticism: A Practical Introduction*. Grand Rapids, MI: Baker Books, 1994.
———. "The Plurality of 'Soul' in the Old Testament with Special Attention Given to the Use of *Nepeš*." Doctoral dissertation, New York University, 1987.
Brown, F., S. R. Driver, and C. A. Briggs. "נפש." Enhanced Brown-Driver-Briggs Hebrew and English Lexicon. Oak Harbor, WA: Logos Research Systems, 2000.
Brown, Michelle P. "Spreading the Word." In *In the Beginning: Bibles before the Year 1000*, edited by Michelle P. Brown, 45–76. Washington, DC: Freer Gallery of Art & Arthur M. Sackler Gallery, Smithsonian Institution, 2006.
Bruckner, James K. "A Theological Description of Human Wholeness in Deuteronomy 6." *Ex Auditu* 21 (2005): 1–19.
Brueggemann, Walter. *Theology of the Testimony, Dispute, Advocacy*. Minneapolis, MN: Fortress Press, 1997.
———. "Vulnerable Children, Divine Passion, and Human Obligation." In *The Child in the Bible*, edited by, Marcia J. Bunge, Terence E. Fretheim, and Beverly Roberts Gaventa, 399–422. Grand Rapids, MI: Eerdmans, 2008.
Bultmann, Rudolf. *Theology of the New Testament: With a New Introduction by Robert Morgan*. Translated by Kendrick Grobel. Waco, TX: Baylor University Press, 2007.
Bunge, Marcia J. "Beyond Children as Agents or Victims: Reexamining Children's Paradoxical Strengths and Vulnerabilities with Resources from Christian Theologies of Childhood and Child Theologies." In *The Given Child: The Religions' Contribution to Children's Citizenship*, edited by Trygve Wyller and Usha S. Nayar, 27–50. Göttingen: Vandenhoeck & Ruprecht, 2007.

———. "Biblical and Theological Perspectives and Best Practices for Faith Formation." In *Understanding Children's Spirituality: Theology, Research, and Practice*, edited by Kevin E. Lawson, Kindle edition, 3–25. Eugene, OR: Cascade, 2012.

———. "Biblical and Theological Perspectives on Children, Parents, and 'Best Practices' for Faith Formation: Resources for Child, Youth, and Family Ministry Today." *Dialog* 47, no. 4 (2008): 348–360.

———. "The Child, Religion, and the Academy: Developing Robust Theological and Religious Understandings of Children and Childhood." *The Journal of Religion* 86, no. 4 (2006): 549–579.

———. "Christian Understandings of Children: Central Biblical Themes and Resources." In *Children, Adults, and Shared Responsibilities: Jewish, Christian, and Muslim Perspectives*, edited by Marcia J. Bunge, 59–78. Cambridge, UK: Cambridge University Press, 2012.

———. "The Dignity and Complexity of Children: Constructing Christian Theologies of Childhood." In *Nurturing Child and Adolescent Spirituality: Perspectives from the World's Religious Traditions*, edited by Karen Marie Yust, A. N. Johnson, S. E. Sasso, and Eugene C. Roehlkepartain, 53–68. Lanham, MD; Toronto: Rowman & Littlefield, 2006.

———. "Historical Perspectives on Children in the Church." In *Toddling to the Kingdom: Child Theology at Work in the Church*, edited by John Collier, 98–113. London, UK: Child Theology Movement Ltd., 2009.

———. "Historical Perspectives on Children in the Church: Resources for Spiritual Formation and a Theology of Childhood Today." In *Children's Spirituality: Christian Perspectives, Research, and Applications*, edited by, Donald Ratcliff, Marcia McQuitty, Margaret Lawson, and Holly Catterton Allen, 42–53. Eugene, OR: Cascade, 2004.

———. "A More Vibrant Theology of Children." *Christian Reflection: A Series in Faith and Ethics* (2003): 11–19.

———. "Rediscovering the Dignity and Complexity of Children: Resources from the Christian Tradition." *Sewanee Theological Review* 48, no. 1 (2004): 51–63.

Bunge, Marcia J., and Haddon Willmer. "How Does History Help Us?" In *Toddling to the Kingdom: Child Theology at Work in the Church*, edited by John Collier, 114–120. London, UK: Child Theology Movement, 2009.

Burke, David G. "The First Versions: The Septuagint, the Targums, and the Latin." In *A History of Bible Translation*, edited by Philip A. Noss, 59–89. Roma: Edizioni di storia e letteratura, 2007.

Burns, Stephen. *Worship in Context: Liturgical Theology, Children and the City*. Peterborough, UK: Epworth, 2006.

Cain, Andrew, and Josef Lössl. "Introduction." In *Jerome of Stridon: His Life, Writings and Legacy*, edited by Andrew Cain and Josef Lössl, 1–9. Farnham, UK; Burlington, VT: Ashgate, 2009.

Calvin, John. *Commentaries on the Book of Moses Called Genesis*. Vol. 2. Translated by John King. Grand Rapids, MI: Eerdmans, 1948.

———. *Commentary on the Book of Psalms*. Vol. 1. Translated by James Anderson. Grand Rapids, MI: Eerdmans, 1949.

———. *Commentaries*. Vol. 6. Grand Rapids, MI: Eerdmans, 1984.

Cameron, John. "The Rabbinic Vulgate?" In *Jerome of Stridon: His Life, Writings and Legacy*, edited by Andrew Cain and Josef Lössl, 117–129. Farnhams; Burlington, VT: Ashgate, 2009.

Camps, Arnulf. "Father Gabriele M. Allegra, O.F.M. (1907–1976) and the Studium Biblicum Franciscanum: The First Complete Chinese Catholic Translation of the Bible." In *Bible in Modern China: The Literary and Intellectual Impact*, edited by Irene Eber, Sze-kar Wan, and Knut Walf, 55–76. Sankt Augustin: Institut Monumenta Serica, 1999.

Carroll, John T. "Children in the Bible." *Interpretation* 55, no. 2 (2001): 121–134.

———. "'What Then Will This Child Become?': Perspectives on Children in the Gospel of Luke." In *The Child in the Bible*, edited by, Marcia J. Bunge, Terence E. Fretheim, and Beverly Roberts Gaventa, 177–194. Grand Rapids, MI: Eerdmans, 2008.

Carson, D. A. *Exegetical Fallacies*. 2nd ed. Grand Rapids, MI: Baker, 1996.

———. "The Limits of Dynamic Equivalence in Bible Translation." *Evangelical Review of Theology* 9, no. 3 (1985): 200–213.

Cavalletti, Sofia. *The Religious Potential of the Child: Experiencing Scripture and Liturgy with Young Children*. Translated by Patricia M. Coulter and Julie M. Coulter. Chicago, IL: Liturgy Training Publications, 1992.

Chan, Elsie. "Translation Principles and the Translator's Agenda: A Systemic Approach to Yan, Fu." In *Crosscultural Transgressions: Research Models in Translation Studies II: Historical and Ideological Issues*, edited by Theo Hermans, 61–75. Manchester, UK: St Jerome, 2002.

Charles, R. H., ed. *The Letter of Aristeas*. Oxford: Clarendon, 1913. Accessed 7 January 2014. http://www.ccel.org/c/charles/otpseudepig/aristeas.htm.

Chechowich, Faye E. "Intergenerational Ministry: A Review of Selected Publications since 2001." *Christian Education Journal*, Series 3, Vol. 9, no. 1 (2012): 182–193.

Chén, Dé Hóng Leo 陳德鴻. 世紀中國翻譯理論: 風氣、問題與爭辯 [Twentieth-century Chinese translation theory: Modes, issues and debates]. Amsterdam; Philadelphia: J. Benjamins, 2004.

Chén, Shàng Yǔ 陳上宇. "《大秦景教流行中國碑》 – 碑文：譯文、原文、英文," [The Nestorian Stele-Inscription: Modern Chinese translation, original text, English translation], 2011. Accessed 14 April 2014. http://blog.sina.com.cn/s/blog_621e6d160102dukl.html.

Chén, Shù Yú 陳漱渝. "五四新文化運動和五四文學革命" [The May 4th New Cultural Movement and the May 4th Literary Revolution]. *Journal of Jiāngsū Administration Institute* 50, no. 2 (2010): 130–136.

Chéng, Zhì Yí 誠質怡. "聖經之中文譯本" [The Chinese translation of the Bible]. In 聖經漢譯論文集 [Essays on Chinese Bible translation], edited by Bǎo Luó Jiǎ 賈保羅, 1–28. Hong Kong: Christian Fǔ qiáo Publishing, 1965.

Cheung, Andy. "A History of Twentieth Century Translation Theory and Its Application for Bible Translation." *Journal of Translation* 9, no. 1 (2013): 1–15.

Chow, Alexander. *Theosis, Sino-Christian Theology and the Second Chinese Enlightenment: Heaven and Humanity in Unity*. New York, NY: Palgrave Macmillan, 2013.

Chrysostom, John. *Baptismal Instructions*. Translated by and annotated by Paul W. Harkins. Ancient Christian Writers: The Works of the Fathers in Translation 31. Westminster, MD: Newman, 1963.

———. *Homily on Matthew*, 2014. Accessed 1 July 2014. http://www.newadvent.org/fathers/200162.htm.

Chukovsky, Kornei. *From Two to Five*. Edited and translated by Miriam Morton. 2nd edition. Berkeley; Los Angeles; London: University of California Press, 1971.

Clark-Soles, Jaime. *Death and the Afterlife in the New Testament*. New York: T & T Clark, 2006.

Clement of Alexandria. "Paedagogus." In *The Ante-Nicene Fathers, Vol. 2: Fathers of the Second Century: Hermas, Tatian, Athenagoras, Theophilus, and Clement of Alexandria* (Entire), edited by A. Roberts, J. Donaldson, and A. C. Coxe, 207–298. Buffalo, NY: Christian Literature Co., 1885.

———. *Stromateis, Book 2 Ch. 23: On Marriage*, 2014. Accessed 10 September 2014. http://www.earlychristianwritings.com/text/clement-stromata-book2.html.

Clines, David J. A., ed. "נפש." In *The Dictionary of Classical Hebrew*, vol. 5, 724–734. Sheffield: Sheffield Academic Press, 2001.

Cockerill, Gareth Lee. *The Epistle to the Hebrews*. The New International Commentary on the New Testament. Grand Rapids, MI; Cambridge, UK: Eerdmans, 2012.

Collins, Billie Jean, Bob Buller, John F. Kutsko, and Society of Biblical Literature, eds. *The SBL Handbook of Style: For Biblical Studies and Related Disciplines*. 2nd edition. Atlanta, GA: SBL, 2014.

Comenius, Johannes Amos. *The School of Infancy*, 1631. Accessed 14 July 2016. http://www.christianitytoday.com/history/issues/issue-13/from-archives-school-of-infancy.html.

Couture, Pamela D. *Seeing Children, Seeing God: A Practical Theology of Children and Poverty*. Nashville, TN: Abingdon, 2000.

Craigie, Peter C. *Psalms 1–50*. Edited by Bruce M. Metzger, David A. Hubbard, Glenn W. Barker, Glenn W. Barker, and Ralph P. Martin. 2nd edition. Word Biblical Commentary 19. Nashville, TN: Nelson Reference & Electronic, 2004.

———. "Wisdom, Wisdom Literature." In *Baker Encyclopedia of the Bible*, edited by W. A. Elwell, B. J. Beitzel, H. Douglas Buckwalter, and Walter R. Hearn, 2149–2150. Grand Rapids, MI: Baker, 1988.

Cunningham, Hugh. *Children and Childhood in Western Society since 1500*. 2nd edition. Harlow, UK; New York: Pearson Longman, 2005.

Cyprian of Carthage. "The Epistles of Cyprian: Epistle 58: To Fidus, on the Baptism of Infants." In *The Ante-Nicene Fathers, Vol. 5: Fathers of the Third Century: Hippolytus, Cyprian, Novatian*, edited by A. Roberts, J. Donaldson, and A. C. Coxe, 353–354. Buffalo, NY: Christian Literature Co., 1886.

Dahood, Mitchell J. *Psalms III: 101–150*. The Anchor Bible. Garden City, NY: Doubleday, 1970.

Davids, Peter H. *The Epistle of James: A Commentary on the Greek Text*. The New International Greek Testament Commentary. Grand Rapids, MI: Eerdmans, 1982.

———. *The First Epistle of Peter*. The New International Commentary on the New Testament. Grand Rapids, MI: Eerdmans, 1990.

Deeks, David, and Angela Shier-Jones. "Moulding and Shaping: Education." In *Children of God: Towards a Theology of Childhood*, edited by Angela Shier-Jones, 63–84. Peterborough: Epworth, 2007.

de Saussure, Ferdinand. *Course in General Linguistics*. Translated and annotated by Roy Harris. Chicago, IL: Open Court, 1986.

de Troyer, Kristin. "'And God Was Created...': on Translating Hebrew into Greek." In *The Bible through Metaphor and Translation: A Cognitive Semantic Perspective*, edited by Kurt Feyaerts, 205–218. Religions and Discourse 15. Oxford; New York: Lang, 2003.

DeVries, Dawn. "'Be Converted and Become as Little Children': Friedrich Schleiermacher on the Religious Significance of Childhood." In *The Child in Christian Thought*, edited by Marcia J. Bunge, 329–349. Grand Rapids, MI: Eerdmans, 2001.

———. "Toward a Theology of Childhood." *Interpretation* 55, no. 2 (2001): 161–173.

de Waard, Jan, and Eugene A. Nida. *From One Language to Another: Functional Equivalence in Bible Translating*. Nashville, TN: Nelson, 1986.

Dines, Jennifer M. *The Septuagint*. London: T & T Clark, 2004.

Dirksen, Peter B. "The Old Testament Peshiṭta." In *Mikra: Text, Translation, Reading, and Interpretation of the Hebrew Bible in Ancient Judaism and Early Christianity*, edited by M. J. Mulder and H. Sysling, 255–297. Peabody, MA: Hendrickson, 2004.

Di Vito, Robert A. "Old Testament Anthropology and the Construction of Personal Identity." *The Catholic Biblical Quarterly* 61 (1999): 217–238.

Dogniez, Cécile. "Some Similarities between the Septugint and the Targum of Zechariah." In *Translating a Translation: The LXX and Its Modern Translations in the Context of Early Judaism*, edited by H. Ausloos et al., 89–102. Bibliotheca Ephemeridum Theologicarum Lovaniensium 213. Leuven; Dudley, MA: Peeters, 2008.

Duàn, Qí 段琦. 中國基督教本色化史稿 [The history of enculturation of Chinese Christianity]. Taipei: Christian Cosmic Light Holistic Care Organization, 2005.

Eckert, Penelope. "Age as a Sociolinguistic Variable." In *The Handbook of Sociolinguistics*, edited by Florian Coulmas, 151–167. Oxford, UK: Blackwell, 1997.

Elkind, David, and John H. Flavell, eds. *Studies in Cognitive Development: Essays in Honor of Jean Piaget*. London; New York: Oxford University Press, 1969.

Ellington, John. "Schleiermacher Was Wrong: The False Dilemma of Foreignization and Domestication." *The Bible Translator* 54, no. 3 (2003): 301–317.

Ellingworth, Paul. *The Epistle to the Hebrews: A Commentary on the Greek Text*. The New International Greek Testament Commentary. Grand Rapids, MI: Eerdmans; Carlisle: Paternoster Press, 1993.

Eng, Milton. *The Days of Our Years: A Lexical Semantic Study of the Life Cycle in Biblical Israel*. New York: T & T Clark, 2011.

Erikson, Erik H. *Childhood and Society*. 2nd edition. New York: Norton, 1963.

Estep Jr., James Riley. "Spiritual Formation as Social: Toward a Vygotskyan Developmental Perspective." *Religious Education* 97, no. 2 (2002): 141–164.

Féng, Guó Róng 馮國榮. 新詩譜: 新詩格式創制研究 [The spectrum of new poetry: A study on the forms of new poetry]. Běi jīng: People's Publishing House, 2010.

Fiedler, Margie. "Across the Generations in Retreat and Camping Ministry." In *Across the Generations: Incorporating All Ages in Ministry: The Why and How*,

edited by Vicky Goplin, Jeffrey Nelson, Mark Gardner, and Eileen K Zahn, 96–103. Minneapolis: Augsburg Fortress, 2001.
Filson, Floyd V. "The Significance of the Early House Churches." *Journal of Biblical Literature* 58, no. 2 (1939): 105–112.
Flesher, Paul V. M., and Bruce D. Chilton. *The Targums: A Critical Introduction*. Waco, TX: Baylor University Press, 2011.
Foley, Toshikazu S. *Biblical Translation in Chinese and Greek: Verbal Aspect in Theory and Practice*. Leiden; Boston: Brill, 2009.
Fontana, Michela. *Matteo Ricci: A Jesuit in the Ming Court*. Lanham; Boulder; New York; Toronto; Plymouth, UK: Rowman & Littlefield, 2011.
Fowler, James W. *Faith Development Theory and the Aims of Religious Socialization*. Paper read at a special meeting of the Religious Education Association, Oct 24–26 1975 in Milwaukee, WI.
———. *Faithful Change: The Personal and Public Challenges of Postmodern Life*. Nashville, TN: Abingdon, 1996.
———. *Stages of Faith: The Psychology of Human Development and the Quest for Meaning*. San Francisco, CA: Harper & Row, 1981.
———. *Weaving the New Creation: Stages of Faith and the Public Church*. San Francisco, CA: HarperSanFrancisco, 1991.
Francis, James M. M. *Adults as Children: Images of Childhood in the Ancient World and the New Testament*. Bern: Lang, 2006.
Frazier, James. "All Generations of Saints at Worship." In *Across the Generations: Incorporating All Ages in Ministry: The Why and How*, edited by Vicky Goplin, Jeffrey Nelson, Mark Gardner, and Eileen K Zahn, 56–63. Minneapolis, MN: Augsburg Fortress, 2001.
Fredericks, D. C. "נפשׁ." In *New International Dictionary of Old Testament Theology & Exegesis*, vol. 3, edited by W. VanGemeren, 133–134. Grand Rapids, MI: Zondervan, 1997.
Fretheim, Terence E. "'God Was with the Boy' (Genesis 21:20): Children in the Book of Genesis." In *The Child in the Bible*, edited by Marcia J. Bunge, Terence E. Fretheim, and Beverly Roberts Gaventa, 3–23. Grand Rapids, MI: Eerdmans, 2008.
———. "יָדַע (Yādaʿ)." In *New International Dictionary of Old Testament Theology and Exegesis*, vol. 2, edited by Willem A. VanGemeren, 409–414. Grand Rapids, MI: Zondervan, 1997.
Fù, Jìng Mín 傅敬民. 聖經漢譯的文化資本解讀 [The cultural and capital interpretation of translating the Bible into Chinese]. Shàng Hǎi: Fù Dàn University Publisher, 2009.
Galbraith, Mary. "Hear My Cry: A Manifesto for an Emancipatory Childhood Studies Approach to Children's Literature." *The Lion and the Unicorn* 25, no. 2 (2001): 187–205.

Gálik, Marián. *Influence, Translation, and Parallels: Selected Studies on the Bible in China*. Sankt Augustin, Germany: Monumenta Serica Institute, 2004.

Gambone, James V. *All Are Welcome: A Primer for Intentional Intergenerational Ministry and Dialogue*. Crystal Bay, MN: Elder Eye, 1998.

———. *Together for Tomorrow: Building Community through Intergenerational Dialogue*. Crystal Bay, MN: Elder Eye Press, 1997.

Gardner, Howard. *Multiple Intelligences: New Horizons in Theory and Practice*. Completely revised and updated. New York: Basic Books, 2006.

Gardner, J. *Mend the Gap: Can the Church Reconnect the Generations?* Nottingham: InterVarsity Press, 2008.

Garnier, A. J. 賈立言. "漢文聖經本小史" [Chinese versions of the Bible]. In 新約聖經流傳史略 – 附漢文聖經本小史(賈立言 著) [The New Testament and its transmission: With an essay on the Chinese versions of the Bible by Garnier], edited by George Milligan, 87–146. Hong Kong: Shí zhēn Publishing, 1999 [1934].

Gentzler, Edwin. *Contemporary Translation Theories*. London: Routledge, 1993.

———. "A Global View of Translation Studies: Towards an Interdisciplinary Field." In *Translation, Globalisation, and Localisation: A Chinese Perspective*, edited by Wang Ning and Sun Yifeng, 111–126. Clevedon, UK; Buffalo, NY: Multilingual Matters, 2008.

Gernet, Jacques. 中國與基督教 [China and Christianity]. Shanghai: Shanghai Classics Publishing, 2003.

Ginsburg, Herbert P., and Sylvia Opper. *Piaget's Theory of Intellectual Development*. Englewood Cliffs, NJ: Prentice-Hall, 1988.

Glassford, Darwin. "Fostering an Intergenerational Culture." In *The Church of All Ages: Generations Worshiping Together*, edited by Howard Vanderwell, 71–93. Herndon, VA: Alban Institute, 2008.

Gobbel, A. Roger, and Gertrude G. Gobbel. *The Bible: A Child's Playground*. Philadelphia, PA: Fortress, 1986.

Gold, Penny Schine. *Making the Bible Modern: Children's Bibles and Jewish Education in Twentieth-Century America*. Ithaca: Cornell University Press, 2004.

Goldingay, John. *Psalms*. Vol. 1. Baker Commentary on the Old Testament Wisdom and Psalms. Grand Rapids, MI: Baker Academic, 2006.

———. *Psalms*. Vol. 2. Baker Commentary on the Old Testament Wisdom and Psalms. Grand Rapids, MI: Baker Academic, 2007.

———. *Psalms*. Vol. 3. Baker Commentary on the Old Testament Wisdom and Psalms. Grand Rapids, MI: Baker Academic, 2008.

Gordon, Cyrus H. "*Npš*." *Ugaritic Textbook*. Roma: Editrice Pontificio Istituto Biblico, 1998.

Gottlieb, Wolf. "The Term '*Nepeš*' in the Bible: A Re-Appraisal." *Glasgow University Oriental Society Transactions* 25 (1976): 71–84.

Goulder, Michael D. *The Psalms of the Return (Book V, Psalms 107–150): Studies in the Psalter, IV*. Journal for the Study of the Old Testament Supplement Series 258. Sheffield: Sheffield Academic Press, 1998.

Grant, Frederick C. *Translating the Bible*. Greenwich, CT: Seabury, 1961.

Green, Joel B. *Body, Soul, and Human Life: The Nature of Humanity in the Bible*. Grand Rapids, MI: Baker Academic, 2008.

———. "Soul." In *The New Interpreter's Dictionary of the Bible*, vol. 5, edited by Katharine D. Sakenfeld, 359. Nashville, TN: Abingdon, 2009.

Greenspoon, Leonard. "Septuagint." In *The New Interpreter's Dictionary of the Bible*, vol. 5, edited by Katharine D. Sakenfeld, 171–176. Nashville, TN: Abingdon, 2009.

Gregory of Nyssa. "On Infants' Early Deaths." In *The Nicene and Post-Nicene Fathers, Vol. 5: Gregory of Nyssa*, edited by P. Schaff and H. Wace, 372–381. New York: Christian Literature Co., 1893.

Grenz, Stanley J. *Theology for the Community of God*. Grand Rapids, MI: Eerdmans, 2000.

Gresham, John L. "The Social Model of the Trinity and Its Critics." *Scottish Journal of Theology* 46 (1993): 325–343.

Gruenler, Royce G. "John 17:20-26." *Interpretation* 43, no. 2 (1989): 178–183.

Gundry-Volf, Judith M. "The Least and the Greatest: Children in the New Testament." In *The Child in Christian Thought*, edited by Marcia J. Bunge, 29–60. Grand Rapids, MI: Eerdmans, 2001.

———. "'To Such as These Belongs the Reign of God': Jesus and the Children." *Theology Today* 56, no. 4 (2000): 469–480.

Gunkel, Hermann. *The Psalms: A Form-Critical Introduction*. Translated by Thomas M. Horner. Biblical Series 19. Philadelphia: Fortress, 1967.

Gutt, Ernst-August. *Relevance Theory: A Guide to Successful Communication in Translation*. Dallas, TX: Summer Institute of Linguistics, 1992.

Ḥakham, Amos. *The Bible: Psalms with the Jerusalem Commentary*. Vol. 1. Edited and translated by Israel V. Berman. Jerusalem: Mosad Harav Kook, 2003.

———. *The Bible: Psalms with the Jerusalem Commentary*. Vol. 2. Edited and translated by Israel V. Berman. Jerusalem: Mosad Harav Kook, 2003.

———. *The Bible: Psalms with the Jerusalem Commentary*. Vol. 3. Edited and translated by Israel V. Berman. Jerusalem: Mosad Harav Kook, 2003.

Hamilton, Victor P. *The Book of Genesis: Chapters 1–17*. NICOT. Grand Rapids, MI: Eerdmans, 1990.

Harkness, Allan G. "Intergenerational and Homogeneous-Age Education: Mutually Exclusive Strategies for Faith Communities." *Religious Education* 95, no. 1 (2000): 51–63.

———. "Intergenerational Education for an Intergenerational Church?" *Religious Education* 93, no. 4 (1998): 431–447.

———. "Intergenerationality: Biblical and Theological Foundations." *Christian Education Journal*, Series 3, Vol. 9, no. 1 (2012): 121–134.

Harvey, Julien. "Is Biblical Man Still Alive?" *Biblical Theology Bulletin: A Journal of Bible and Theology* 3, no. 2 (1973): 167–193.

Hé, Yà Fú 何亞福. "'一胎化'政策的由來及影響" [The origin and influence of the 'one-child policy'], 2014. Accessed 6 January 2014. http://blog.boxun.com/hero/wiyouzhiguang/73_1.shtml.

Heckel, Theo K. "Body and Soul in Saint Paul." In *Psyche and Soma: Physicians and Metaphysicians on the Mind-Body Problem from Antiquity to Enlightenment*, edited by John P. Wright and Paul Potter, repr., 117–131. Oxford: Clarendon Press, 2006.

Hellerman, Joseph H. *When the Church Was a Family: Recapturing Jesus' Vision for Authentic Christian Community*. Nashville, TN: B & H Academic, 2009.

Hengel, Martin. *The Septuagint as Christian Scripture: Its Prehistory and the Problem of Its Canon*. Translated by Mark E. Biddle. Grand Rapids, MI: Baker Academic, 2004.

Hermans, T. "Norms and the Determination of Translation. A Theoretical Framework." In *Translation, Power, Subversion*, edited by Román Álvarez and M. Carmen-África Vidal, 25–51. Clevedon; Philadelphia: Multilingual Matters, 1996.

Herzog, Kristin. *Children and Our Global Future: Theological and Social Challenges*. Cleveland, OH: Pilgrim Press, 2005.

Hicks, Peter. *The Journey So Far: Philosophy Through the Ages*. Grand Rapids, MI: Zondervan, 2003.

Hill, Harriet, Ernst-August Gutt, Margaret Hill, Christoph Unger, and Rick Floyd. *Bible Translation Basics: Communicating Scripture in a Relevant Way*. Dallas, TX: SIL International, 2011.

Hill, Jonathan. *The History of Christian Thought*. Oxford: Lion, 2003.

Hinsdale, Mary Ann. "'Infinite Openness to the Infinite': Karl Rahner's Contribution to Modern Catholic Thought on the Child." In *The Child in Christian Thought*, edited by Marcia J. Bunge, 406–445. Grand Rapids, MI: Eerdmans, 2001.

Holmes, James. "The Name and Nature of Translation Studies." In *The Translation Studies Reader*, edited by Lawrence Venuti, 180–192. New York; London: Routledge, 2004 [1972].

Holmes, Janet. *An Introduction to Sociolinguistics*. 2nd edition. Harlow, UK: Person, 2001.

Horn, Cornelia B., and John W. Martens. *"Let the Little Children Come to Me:" Childhood and Children in Early Christianity*. Washington, DC: Catholic University of America Press, 2009.

Houtman, Alberdina, and Harry Sysling. *Alternative Targum Traditions: The Use of Variant Readings for the Study in Origin and History of Targum Jonathan*. Studies in the Aramaic Interpretation of Scripture 9. Leiden; Boston: Brill, 2009.

Hung, Eva. "Translation in China: An Analytical Survey." In *Asian Translation Traditions*, edited by Eva Hung and Judy Wakabayashi, 67–99. Manchester; Northampton, MA: St Jerome, 2005.

Hurowitz, Victor A. "A Forgotten Meaning of *Nepeš* in Isaiah LVIII 10." *Vetus Testamentum* 47, no. 1 (1997): 43–52.

Ibita, Ma. Marilou, and Reimund Bieringer. "(Stifled) Voices of the Future: Learning about Children in the Bible." In *Children's Voices: Children's Perspectives in Ethics, Theology and Religious Education*, edited by Annemie Dillen and Didier Pollefeyt, 73–115. Leuven: Peeters, 2010.

"Introduction." In *Records of the General Conference of the Protestant Missionaries of China*, Held at Shanghai, May 7–20. Shàng hǎi, China: American Presbyterian Mission Press, 1890.

Irenaeus. *Proof of the Apostolic Preaching*. Translated and annotated by Joseph P. Smith. Ancient Christian Writers: The Works of the Fathers in Translation 16. Westminster, MD: Newman Press, 1952.

Jacob, Edmund. "The Anthropology of the Old Testament." In *Theological Dictionary of the New Testament*, vol. 9, edited by Gerhard Kittel and Gerhard Friedrich, translated by Geoffrey W. Bromiley, 617–631. Grand Rapids, MI: Eerdmans, 1974.

Jakobson, Roman. "On Linguistic Aspects of Translation." In *The Translation Studies Reader*, edited by Lawrence Venuti, 113–118. London: Routledge, 2000 [1959].

James, Allison. "Understanding Childhood from an Interdisciplinary Perspective: Problems and Potentials." In *Rethinking Childhood*, edited by Peter B. Pufall and Richard P. Unsworth, 25–37. New Brunswick, NJ: Rutgers University Press, 2004.

Jeeves, Malcolm. *Human Nature: Reflections on the Integration of Psychology and Christianity*. West Conshohocken, PA: Templeton Foundation, 2006.

Jellicoe, Sidney. *The Septuagint and Modern Study*. Oxford: Clarendon, 1968.

Jensen, David H. *Graced Vulnerability: A Theology of Childhood*. Cleveland: Pilgrim Press, 2005.

Jewett, Robert. *Paul's Anthropological Terms: A Study of Their Use in Conflict Settings*. Leiden: Brill, 1971.

Jewish Publication Society. "A Short History of Bible Translations." In *The Jewish Bible*, 33–50. JPS Guide. Philadelphia, PA: Jewish Publication Society, 2008.

Jinbachian, Manuel. "Introduction: The Septuagint to the Vernaculars." In *A History of Bible Translation*, edited by Philip A. Noss, 29–57. Rome: Edizioni de storia e letteratura, 2007.

Jobes, Karen H., and Moisés Silva. *Invitation to the Septuagint*. Grand Rapids, MI: Baker Academic, 2000.

John, Griffith. "Leading Rules for Translation." *The Chinese Recorder and Missionary Journal* 16 (1885): 381–386.

Johnson, Aubrey R. *The Vitality of the Individual in the Thought of Ancient Israel*. 2nd edition. Cardiff, UK: University of Wales Press, 1964.

Johnstone, Patrick, and Jason Mandryk. *Operation World*. 6th edition. Carlisle, UK: Paternoster, 2001.

Joosten, Jan. "The Old Testament in the New: The Syriac Versions of the New Testament as a Witness to the Text of the OT Peshitta." In *The Peshitta: Its Uses in Literature and Liturgy: Papers Read at the Third Peshitta Symposium*, edited by B. ter Haar Romeny, 99–106. Leiden; Boston: Brill, 2006.

———. "The Old Testament Quotations in the Old Syriac and Peshitta Gospels: A Contribution to the Study of the Diatessaron." *Textus*, no. 15 (1990): 55–76.

———. "Tatian's Diatessaron and the OT Peshitta." *Journal of Biblical Literature* 120, no. 3 (2001): 501–523.

Juckel, Andreas. "Research on the Old Syriac Heritage of the Peshitta Gospels. A Collation of MS Bibl. Nationale Syr. 30 (Paris)." *Hugoye: Journal of Syriac Studies* 12, no. 1 (2009): 41–115.

Justin Martyr. "Dialogue of Justin, Philosopher and Martyr with Trypho, a Jew." In *The Ante-Nicene Fathers: The Apostolic Fathers with Justin Martyr and Irenaeus*, vol. 1, edited by A. Roberts, J. Donaldson, and A. C. Coxe, 194–270. Buffalo, NY: Christian Literature Co., 1885.

Kaufman, Stephen A. "Targums." In *The New Interpreter's Dictionary of the Bible*, vol. 5, edited by Katharine D. Sakenfeld, 471–473. Nashville, TN: Abingdon, 2009.

Kedar, Benjamin. "The Latin Translations." In *Mikra: Text, Translation, Reading and Interpretation of the Hebrew Bible in Ancient Judaism and Early Christianity*, edited by Martin J. Mulder and Harry Sysling, 299–338. Peabody, MA: Hendrickson, 2004 [1988].

Kehily, Mary Jane. "Understanding Childhood: An Introduction to Some Key Themes and Issues." In *An Introduction to Childhood Studies*, edited by Mary Jane Kehily, 1–16. Maidenhead; New York: Open University Press, 2009.

Kim, Hayeon. "Multiple Authorship of the Septuagint Pentateuch." *Bulletin of Judaeo-Greek Studies* 40 (2007): 2–3.

Kirk, Daphne. *Reconnecting the Generations: Empowering God's People, Young and Old, to Live, Worship and Serve Together*. Suffolk: Kevin Mayhew, 2001.

Kirk, P. "Holy Communicative? Current Approaches to Bible Translation." In *Translation and Religion: Holy Untranslatable?*, edited by Lynne Long, 89–104. Clevedon, UK: Multilingual Matters, 2005.

Klein, Michael L. "Converse Translation: A Targumic Technique." *Biblica* 57, no. 4 (1976): 515–537.

Koehler, George E. *Learning Together: A Guide for Intergenerational Education in the Church*. Nashville, TN: Discipleship Resources, 1977.

Koehler, L., W. Baumgartner, and J. J. Stamm. "בלע." In *The Hebrew and Aramaic Lexicon of the Old Testament*, translated by M. E. J. Richardson, 135. Leiden: Brill, 1994–2000.

———. "הלל." In *The Hebrew and Aramaic Lexicon of the Old Testament*, translated by M. E. J. Richardson, 249. Leiden: Brill, 1994–2000.

———. "נפש." In *The Hebrew and Aramaic Lexicon of the Old Testament*, translated by M. E. J. Richardson, 712–713. Leiden: Brill, 1994–2000.

———. "שָׁקַ." In *The Hebrew and Aramaic Lexicon of the Old Testament*, translated by M. E. J. Richardson, 1349–1350. Leiden: Brill, 1994–2000.

Kohlberg, Lawrence. *Collected Papers on Moral Development and Moral Education*. Cambridge, MA: Harvard University Laboratory for Human Development, 1973.

———. "Development as the Aim of Education." *Harvard Educational Review* 42, no. 4 (1972): 449–496.

———. *Essays on Moral Development, Vol. 2: The Psychology of Moral Development*. San Francisco, CA: Harper & Row, 1984.

Köhler, Ludwig. *Old Testament Theology*. Translated by A. S. Todd. Philadelphia, PA: Westminster Press, 1957.

Komonchak, Joseph A., Mary Collins, and Dermot A. Lane, eds. "*Koinōnia*." In *The New Dictionary of Theology*, edited by Joseph A. Komonchak, Mary Collins, and Dermot A. Lane, 557. Wilmington, DE: Michael Glazier, 1987.

Laidlaw, John. *The Bible Doctrine of Man: Or, The Anthropology and Psychology of Scripture*. Edinburgh: R. Clark, 1895.

Lamsa, George M. *The Holy Bible from Ancient Eastern Manuscripts: Containing the Old and New Testaments Translated from the Peshitta, the Authorized Bible of the Church of the East*. Philadelphia: A. J. Holman, 1957.

Landreth, Garry L. *Play Therapy: The Art of the Relationship*. 3rd edition. New York: Routledge, 2012.

Larson, Mildred L. *Meaning-Based Translation: A Guide to Cross-Language Equivalence*. Lanham, MD: University Press of America, 1984.
Laurin, Robert. "The Concept of Man as a Soul." *The Expository Times* 72, no. 5 (1961): 131–134.
Lausanne Theology Working Group. "The Whole Church Taking the Whole Gospel to the Whole World," 2010. Accessed 17 July 2016. https://www.lausanne.org/content/twg-three-wholes.
Lave, Jean, and Etienne Wenger. *Situated Learning: Legitimate Peripheral Participation*. Cambridge; New York: Cambridge University Press, 1991.
Lees, J. "Letter to a Friend on Wen-Li v. Vernacular." *The Chinese Recorder and Missionary Journal* 23 (1892): 178–181.
Lefevere, André. *Translating Literature: The German Tradition from Luther to Rosenzweig*. Assen: Van Gorcum, 1977.
Lefevere, André, and Susan Bassnett. "Introduction: Where Are We in Translation Studies?" In *Constructing Cultures: Essays on Literary Translation*, edited by Susan Bassnett and André Lefevere, 1–11. Clevedon; Philadelphia: Multilingual Matters, 1998.
LeFever, Marlene D. *Creative Teaching Methods*. Elgin, IL: D. C. Cook, 1996.
LeVine, Robert A. "Child: Historical and Cultural Perspectives." In *The Child: An Encyclopedic Companion*, edited by Richard A. Shweder, 143–147. Chicago; London: University of Chicago Press, 2009.
Levý, Jiří. "Translation as a Decision Process." In *The Translation Studies Reader*, edited by Lawrence Venuti, 148–171. London: Routledge, 2000 [1967].
Lewis, Gordon R., and Bruce A. Demarest. *Integrative Theology*. Vol. 3. Grand Rapids, MI: Zondervan, 1994.
Lǐ, Jǐn Lún 李錦綸. "聖經研究對於整全人觀的提示" [Implications of current biblical research on a holistic view of man]. *China and the Gospel Journal* 3, no. 1 (2003): 109–126.
———. "對中國教會人觀的系統性反省" [Reflection on the anthropology of the China church]. *China and the Gospel Journal* 3, no. 1 (2003): 141–153.
———. *永活上帝生命主: 獻給中國的教會神學* [The living God as the master of life: Devoted to Chinese church theology]. Taipei: Zhōng-Fú Publishing Ltd. Co., 2004.
Lǐ, Zhì Gāng 李志剛. *基督教早期在華傳教史* [A history of early Christian missions in China]. Taipei: Taiwan shāng wù yìn shū guǎn, 1985.
Liáng, Jiā Lín 梁家麟. "華人諾斯底主義的屬靈觀: 倪拓聲 '人的破碎與靈的出來' 研讀" [The spiritual perspective of a Chinese gnosticism: Studies on Watchman Nee's 'The breaking of the outer man and the release of the Spirit']. In *倪拓聲的榮辱升黜* [Watchman Nee: His glory and dishonor], 185–275. Hong Kong: Graceful House, 2004.

Liào, Yuán Wēi 廖元威. "倪柝聲三元論人觀" [Watchman Nee's tripartite anthropology]. *China and the Gospel Journal* 3, no. 1 (2003): 53–69.

Lín, Róng Hóng 林榮洪. 屬靈神學: 倪柝聲思想的研究 [The spiritual theology of Watchman Nee]. 3rd edition. Hong Kong: Chinese Alliance Press, 2003.

Linton, Calvin D. "The Importance of Literary Style in Bible Translation Today." In *The NIV: The Making of a Contemporary Translation*, edited by Kenneth L Barker, 15–33. Grand Rapids, MI: Academie Books, 1986.

Lunn, Nick. "Paronomastic Constructions in Biblical Hebrew." *Notes on Translation* 10, no. 4 (1996): 31–52.

Luó, G 羅光. 利瑪竇傳 [The biography of Matteo Ricci]. Tái zhōng: Guāng qǐ Publishing, 1960.

Luther, Martin. "On Translation: An Open Letter." In *Word and Sacrament I*, edited by E. T. Bachmann and H. T. Lehmann, 181–202. Luther's Works 35. Philadelphia, PA: Fortress, 1960 [1530].

Lys, Daniel. "The Israelite Soul According to the LXX." *Vetus Testamentum* 16, no. 2 (1966): 181–228.

Maas, Robin. "Christ as the Logos of Childhood: Reflections on the Meaning and Mission of the Child." *Theology Today* 56, no. 4 (2000): 456–468.

Mägi, Gunnar. "Intergenerational Church: A Philosophy of Ministry and an Educational Curriculum for a Cross-Generational Community of Faith." Master's thesis, University of Tartu, 2004.

Magiera, Janet M. *Aramaic Peshitta New Testament Translation: With Explanatory Footnotes Marking Variant Readings, Customs, and Figures of Speech*. San Diego: Light of the Word Ministry, 2006.

Mài, Jīn Huá 麥金華. 大英聖書公會與官話《和合本》聖經翻譯 [The British and Foreign Bible Society and the translation of the Mandarin Chinese Union Version]. Hong Kong: Christian Study Center on Chinese Religion and Culture, 2010.

Malherbe, Johannes S. "Big Words and Little Ears: Bible Translation and Children in Africa." The Bible Interpretation and Translation in Africa Conference. Pietermaritzburg, SA: University of KwaZulu-Natal, 2005.

Marshall, Kathleen, and Paul Parvis. *Honouring Children: The Human Rights of the Child in Christian Perspective*. Edinburgh: Saint Andrew Press, 2004.

Marter, E. W. "The Hebrew Concept of 'Soul' in Pre-Exilic Writings." *Andrews University Seminary Studies* 2 (1964): 97–108.

Martineau, Mariette, Joan Weber, and Leif Kehrwald. *Intergenerational Faith Formation: All Ages Learning Together*. New London, CT: Twenty-Third Publications, 2008.

Martinson, Roland D., and Diane E. Shallue. "Foundations for Cross-Generational Ministry." In *Across the Generations: Incorporating All Ages in Ministry: The Why and How*, edited by Vicky Goplin, Jeffrey Nelson, Mark Gardner, and Eileen K. Zahn, 4–10. Minneapolis, MN: Augsburg Fortress, 2001.

May, Scottie, Beth Posterski, Catherine Stonehouse, and Linda Cannell. *Children Matter: Celebrating Their Place in the Church, Family, and Community*. Grand Rapids, MI: Eerdmans, 2005.

Mazor, Yair. *Who Wrought the Bible?: Unveiling the Bible's Aesthetic Secrets*. Madison, WI: University of Wisconsin Press, 2009.

McIntosh, Gary L. *One Church, Four Generations: Understanding and Reaching All Ages in Your Church*. Grand Rapids, MI: Baker Books, 2002.

McNaughton, William. "Introduction." In *Literary Translation: Quest for Artistic Integrity*, by Di Jin, xiii–xix. Manchester, UK; Northampton, MA: St Jerome, 2003.

McRay, J. R. "*Koinōnia*." In *Evangelical Dictionary of Theology*, edited by Walter A. Elwell, 445. Grand Rapids, MI: Baker Academic, 2001.

Mead, Margaret. *Culture and Commitment: The New Relationships Between the Generations in the 1970s*. Revised and updated. New York: Columbia University Press, 1978.

Menconi, Peter. *The Intergenerational Church: Understanding Congregations from WWII to WWW.com*. Littleton, CO: Sage, 2010.

Mercer, Joyce Ann. *Welcoming Children: A Practical Theology of Childhood*. St Louis, MO: Chalice, 2005.

Merhaut, Jim. "Outcomes and Practices of Intergenerational Faith Formation." In *Generations Together: Caring, Praying, Learning, Celebrating, & Serving Faithfully*, edited by Kathie Amidei, Jim Merhaut, and John Roberto, Kindle edition, ch. 4. Naugatuck, CT: Lifelong Faith Publications, 2014.

Merhaut, Jim, and John Roberto. "A Congregational Toolkit for Becoming Intentionally Intergenerational." In *Generations Together: Caring, Praying, Learning, Celebrating, & Serving Faithfully*, edited by Kathie Amidei, Jim Merhaut, and John Roberto, Kindle edition, ch. 5. Naugatuck, CT: Lifelong Faith Publications, 2014.

Metzger, Bruce M. *The Bible in Translation: Ancient and English Versions*. Grand Rapids, MI: Baker Academic, 2001.

———. *The Early Versions of the New Testament: Their Origin, Transmission, and Limitations*. Oxford: Clarendon, 1977.

Meyers, Patty. *Live, Learn, Pass It On: The Practical Benefits Of Generations Growing Together In Faith*. Nashville, TN: Discipleship Resources, 2006.

Michaels, J. Ramsey. *The Gospel of John*. The New International Commentary on the New Testament. Grand Rapids, MI; Cambridge, UK: Eerdmans, 2010.

Miller-McLemore, Bonnie J. "Childhood Studies and Pastoral Counseling." *Sacred Spaces: The E-Journal of the American Association of Pastoral Counselors* 6 (2014): 7–52.

———. *Let the Children Come: Reimagining Childhood from a Christian Perspective*. San Francisco, CA: Jossey-Bass, 2003.

Milne, William. 新教在華傳教前十年回顧 [A retrospect of the first ten years of the Protestant mission to China]. Zhèng zhōu, China: Elephant Publishing, 2008 [1820].

"Modern Standard Chinese," 2014. Accessed 24 April 2014. http://zh.wikipedia.org/wiki/現代標準漢語.

Mojola, Aloo Osotsi, and Ernst Wendland. "Scripture Translation in the Era of Translation Studies." In *Bible Translation: Frames of Reference*, edited by Timothy Wilt, 1–25. Manchester, UK: St Jerome, 2003.

Moltmann, Jürgen. "Child and Childhood as Metaphors of Hope." *Theology Today* 56, no. 4 (2000): 592–603.

Montgomery, Heather. *An Introduction to Childhood: An Anthropological Perspective of Children's Lives*. Malden, MA: Wiley-Blackwell, 2009.

Moran, Gabriel. *Interplay: A Theory of Religion and Education*. Winona, MN: Saint Mary's Press, 1981.

Morris, Leon. *The Gospel according to John*. The New International Commentary on the New Testament. Grand Rapids, MI: Eerdmans, 1995.

Morrison, Eliza Armstrong. 馬禮遜回憶錄(全集): 他的生平與事工 [Memoirs of the life and labors of Robert Morrison, D. D.] Translated by Zhào Míng Dèng 鄧肇明. Hong Kong: Chinese Christian Literature Council, 2008 [1839].

Moule, A. C. "A Manuscript Chinese Version of the NT (British Museum, Sloane 3599)." *Journal of the Royal Asiatic Society* 85, no. 1 (1949): 23–33.

Moule, G. E. "Mr. John's Version: Or Another?" *The Chinese Recorder and Missionary Journal* 16 (1885): 378–380.

Mounstephen, Philip, and Kelly Martin. *Body Beautiful?: Recapturing a Vision for All-Age Church*. Cambridge, UK: Grove Books, 2004.

Mountain, Vivienne. "Four Links between Child Theology and Children's Spirituality." *International Journal of Children's Spirituality* 16, no. 3 (2011): 261–269.

Munday, Jeremy. *Introducing Translation Studies: Theories and Applications*. New York: Routledge, 2012.

Murphy, Nancey. *Bodies and Souls, or Spirited Bodies?* Cambridge; New York: Cambridge University Press, 2006.

Murtonen, A. "The Living Soul: A Study of the Meaning of the Word *Nephesh* in the Old Testament Hebrew Language." *Studia Orientalia* 23, no. 1 (1958): 3–101.

Nee, Watchman. *The Release of the Spirit*. Richmond, VA: Christian Fellowship Publishers, 2000 [1955].

———. *The Spiritual Man*. Vol. 1. Anaheim, CA: Living Stream Ministry, 1998.

———. *The Spiritual Man*. Vol. 3. Anaheim, CA: Living Stream Ministry, 1998.

———. 屬靈人 [The spiritual man]. Hong Kong: Christian Press, 2006 [1928].

Nelson, C Ellis. *Where Faith Begins*. Atlanta: John Knox, 1967.

Neufeldt, Victoria, ed. "Literature." *Webster's New World College Dictionary*. New York: Macmillan, 1996.

Neuwirth, Rav Yehoshua Y. *The Halachoth of Educating Children*. Jerusalem: Feldheim, 1999.

Ngien, Dennis. *Apologetic for Filioque in Medieval Theology*. Milton Keynes: Paternoster, 2005.

Nida, Eugene A. *God's Word in Man's Language*. New York: Harper & Brothers, 1952.

———. *Toward a Science of Translating: With Special Reference to Principles and Procedures Involved in Bible Translating*. Leiden: Brill, 1964.

Nida, Eugene A., and Charles Taber. *The Theory and Practice of Translation*. Leiden: Brill, 1969.

Nolland, John. *The Gospel of Matthew*. The New International Greek Testament Commentary. Grand Rapids, MI: Eerdmans; Milton Keynes, UK: Paternoster, 2005.

Nord, Christiane. *Translating as a Purposeful Activity: Functionalist Approaches Explained*. Manchester: St Jerome, 1997.

Norman, Jerry. "The Beginnings of Chinese Writing." In *Classical Chinese Literature: An Anthology of Translations*, edited by John Minford and Joseph S. M. Lau, 6–9. New York: Columbia University Press; Hong Kong: Chinese University Press, 2000.

Norton, Gerard J. "Jews, Greeks and the Hexapla of Origen." In *The Aramaic Bible: Targums in Their Historical Context*, edited by D. R. G. Beattie and M. J. McNamara, 400–419. Journal for the Study of the Old Testament Supplement Series 166. Sheffield: JSOT Press, 1994.

Noss, Philip A. "A History of Bible Translation: Introduction and Overview." In *A History of Bible Translation*, edited by Philip A. Noss, 1–25. Rome: Edizioni di storia e letteratura, 2007.

Nye, Rebecca. *Children's Spirituality: What It Is and Why It Matters*. 3rd impression. London: Church House, 2013.

Olofsson, Staffan. *The LXX Version: A Guide to the Translation Technique of the Septuagint*. Coniectanea Biblica, Old Testament Series 30. Stockholm: Almquist & Wiksell, 1990.

Origen. "Commentary on the Gospel of Matthew." In *The Ante-Nicene Fathers*, vol. 9, edited by A. Menzies, translated by J. Patrick, 409–512. New York: Christian Literature Company, 1897.

Orsi, Robert A. "A Crisis about the Theology of Children." *Harvard Divinity School Bulletin* 30, no. 4 (2002): 27–29.

Osborne, Grant R. *The Hermeneutical Spiral: A Comprehensive Introduction to Biblical Interpretation*. Downers Grove, IL: InterVarsity Press, 2006.

Oswalt, J. N. "ברך." In *Theological Wordbook of the Old Testament*, edited by R. L. Harris, G. L. Archer, Jr., and B. K. Waltke, 132–133. Chicago, IL: Moody, 1999.

Owen, D. R. G. *Body and Soul: A Study of the Christian View of Man*. Philadelphia, PA: Westminister, 1956.

Palumbo, Giuseppe. *Key Terms in Translation Studies*. London; New York: Continuum, 2009.

Pamudji, P. "Little Flock Trilogy: A Critique of Watchman Nee's Principal Thought on Christ, Man, and the Church." Doctoral dissertation, Drew University, 1985.

Parkhurst, John. "נפש." *A Hebrew and English Lexicon, without Points*. London: printed for B. Law, No. 13, Ave-Maria-Lane, in Ludgate-Street; and W. Faden, the Corner of St Martin's Lane, Charing-Cross, 1778.

Parunak, H. Van Dyke, Richard Whitaker, and Emanuel Tov, eds. *Biblia Hebraica Stuttgartensia: With Westminster Hebrew Morphology*. Revised electronic edition. Stuttgart; Glenside, PA: Deutsche Bibelgesellschaft; Westminster Theological Seminary, 2004.

Pattemore, Stephen. "Framing Nida: The Relevance of Translation Theory in the United Bible Societies." In *A History of Bible Translation*, edited by Philip A. Noss, 217–263. Roma: Edizioni di storia e letteratura, 2007.

Peacock, Heber. "Translating the Word for 'Soul' in the OT." *The Bible Translator* 27, no. 2 (1976): 216–219.

Pedersen, Johannes. *Israel, Its Life and Culture*. Vol. 1. London: Oxford University Press, 1926.

Péng, Guó Wěi 彭國瑋. "Contemplating the Future of Chinese Bible Translation: A Functionalist Approach." *The Bible Translator* 63, no. 1 (2012): 1–16.

Philo, Judaeus. *The Works of Philo: Complete and Unabridged*. Translated and updated by C. D. Yonge. Peabody, MA: Hendrickson, 1995.

Piaget, Jean. *Six Psychological Studies*. Translated by Anita Tenzer. New York: Random House, 1967.

Piaget, Jean, and Bärbel Inhelder. *The Psychology of the Child*. Translated by Helen Weaver. New York: Basic Books, 1969.

Pinnock, Clark H. *Flame of Love: A Theology of the Holy Spirit*. Downers Grove, IL: InterVarsity Press, 1996.

Pitkin, Barbara. "Psalm 8:1–2." *Interpretation* 55, no. 2 (2001): 177–180.

Plantinga, Jr., Cornelius. "Gregory of Nyssa and the Social Analogy of the Trinity." *The Thomist* 50 (1986): 325–352.

Porter, F. C. "The Pre-Existence of the Soul in the Book of Wisdom and in the Rabbinical Writings." In *Old Testament and Semitic Studies in Memory of William Rainey Harper*, edited by Robert Francis Harper, Francis Brown, and George Foot Moore, 205–270. Chicago, IL: University of Chicago Press, 1908.

Powell, Tabitha Michelle. "The Negative Impact of the One Child Policy on the Chinese Society as It Relates to the Parental Support of the Aging Population." Master's thesis, Georgetown University, 2012.

Prest, Eddie. *From One Generation to Another*. Capetown: Training for Leadership, 1993.

Pridmore, John S. *The New Testament Theology of Childhood*. Hobart, Australia: Ron Buckland, 1977.

Pritchard, Gretchen Wolff. *Offering the Gospel to Children*. Cambridge, MA: Cowley, 1992.

Prunč, Erich. *Einführung in Die Translationswissenschaft* [Introduction to translation science]. Graz: Institut für Translationswissenschaft, 2001.

Pufall, Peter B., and Richard P. Unsworth. "Introduction: The Imperative and the Process for Rethinking Childhood." In *Rethinking Childhood*, edited by Peter B. Pufall and Richard P. Unsworth, 1–21. New Brunswick, NJ: Rutgers University Press, 2004.

———. "Preface." In *Rethinking Childhood*, edited by Peter B. Pufall and Richard P. Unsworth, ix–xi. New Brunswick, NJ: Rutgers University Press, 2004.

Rahner, Karl. *Further Theology of the Spiritual Life 2*. Translated by David Bourke. Theological Investigations 8. New York: Seabury, 1977.

Ráo, Xiào Bǎi 饒孝柏. 屬靈人的再思 [Rethinking on "the spiritual person"]. Taipei: Campus Evangelical Fellowship, 2010.

Ratcliff, Donald. "The Spirit of Children Past: A Century of Children's Spirituality Research." *Christian Education Journal* 4, no. 2 (2007): 218–237.

Reis, David M. "Thinking with Soul: *Psychē* and *Psychikos* in the Construction of Early Christian Identities." *Journal of Early Christian Studies* 17, no. 4 (2009): 563–603.

Rèn, Dōng Shēng 任東升. 聖經漢譯文化研究 [Study on the translation of Bible translation into Chinese]. Hú běi: Hú běi Education Press, 2007.

Ricci, Matteo. 天主實義 (下卷) [The true meaning of the Lord of heaven (vol. 2)]. Taipei: Institute for National Defense and Security Research and Zhōng huá dà diǎn biān yìn huì, 1967 [1603].

Richards, Lawrence O. *A Theology of Christian Education*. Grand Rapids, MI: Zondervan, 1975.

Rieber, Robert W., and Aaron S. Carton, eds. *The Collected Works of L. S. Vygotsky, Vol. 1: Problems of General Psychology*. Translated by and with an introduction by Norris Minick. New York: Plenum, 1987.

Roberto, John. *Becoming a Church of Lifelong Learners: The Generations of Faith Sourcebook*. New London, CT: Twenty-Third Publications, 2006.

———. "Our Future Is Intergenerational." *Christian Education Journal*, Series 3, Vol. 9, no. 1 (2012): 105–120.

Roberts, A., J. Donaldson, and A. C. Coxe, eds. "The Pastor of Hermas." In *The Ante-Nicene Fathers, Vol. 2: Fathers of the Second Century: Hermas, Tatian, Athenagoras, Theophilus, and Clement of Alexandria* (Entire), 20–30. Buffalo, NY: Christian Literature Co., 1885.

Roberts, Bleddyn J. "The Manuscripts, Text and Versions." In *The Cambridge History of the Bible, Vol. 2: The West from the Fathers to the Reformation*, edited by G. W. H. Lampe, Electronic edition, 1–26. New York: Cambridge University Press, 2004 [1969].

Roberts, Dana. *Secrets of Watchman Nee: His Life, His Teachings, His Influence*. Orlando, FL: Bridge-Logos, 2005.

———. *Understanding Watchman Nee: The Newest Book on Watchman Nee*. Plainfield, NJ: Logos-Haven Books, 1980.

Robinson, Douglas. *Western Translation Theory: From Herodotus to Nietzsche*. Manchester, UK: St Jerome, 1997.

Robinson, H. Wheeler. *The Christian Doctrine of Man*. Edinburgh: T & T Clark, 1926.

———. *The Religious Ideas of the Old Testament*. New York: Charles Scribner's Sons, 1921.

Ross, Allen P. *A Commentary on the Psalms*. Vol. 1. Grand Rapids, MI: Kregel, 2011.

———. *A Commentary on the Psalms*. Vol. 2. Grand Rapids, MI: Kregel, 2013.

Ross, Christine M. "Four Congregations That Practice Intergenerationality." *Christian Education Journal* 9, no. 1 (2012): 135–147.

———. "A Qualitative Study Exploring Characteristics of Churches Committed to Intergenerational Ministry." PhD dissertation, Saint Louis University, 2006.

Runge, Steven E., and Joshua R. Westbury, eds. *The Lexham Discourse Hebrew Bible: Glossary*. Bellingham, WA: Lexham Press, 2012.

Runge, Steven E., Joshua R. Westbury, and Kristopher Lyle, eds. *The Lexham Discourse Hebrew Bible*. Bellingham, WA: Lexham Press, 2014.

Sadler, Judith. "Learning Together: All-Age Learning in the Church." In *Learning in the Way: Research and Reflection on Adult Christian Education*, edited by Jeff Astley, 113–123. Herefordshire, UK: Gracewing, 2000.

Sand, A. "ψυχή." In *Exegetical Dictionary of the New Testament*, vol. 3, edited by Horst R. Balz and Gerhard Schneider, 500–503. Grand Rapids, MI: Eerdmans, 1990.

Sanneh, Lamin. "Gospel and Culture: Ramifying Effects of Scriptural Translation." In *Bible Translation and the Spread of the Church: The Last 200 Years*, edited by Philip C. Stine, 1–23. Leiden; New York: Brill, 1990.

Schleiermacher, Friedrich. *The Christian Household: A Sermonic Treatise*. Translated by Dietrich Seidel and Terrence N. Tice. Schleiermacher Studies and Translations 3. Lewiston, NY: Edwin Mellen, 1991.

Schwartz, Theodore. "The Acquisition of Culture." *Ethos* 9 (1981): 10–16.

Schweizer, Eduard. "ψυχή: The New Testament." In *Theological Dictionary of the New Testament*, vol. 9, edited by Gerhard Kittel, Geoffrey W. Bromiley, and G. Friedrich, 637–657. Grand Rapids, MI: Eerdmans, 1974.

Scorgie, Glen G. "Introduction and Overview." In *The Challenge of Bible Translation: Communicating God's Word to the World*, edited by Glen G. Scorgie, Mark L. Strauss, and Steven M. Voth, 19–36. Grand Rapids, MI: Zondervan, 2003.

Seebass, H. "נפש." In *Theological Dictionary of the Old Testament*, vol. 9, edited by G. Johannes Botterweck, Helmer Ringgren, and Heinz-Josef Fabry. Translated by John T. Willis, David E. Green, and Douglas W. Stott, 497–519. Sheffield: Sheffield Academic, 1998.

Seeligmann, Isaac L. "Problems and Perspectives in Modern Septuagint Research." *Textus* 15 (1990): 169–232.

Seligson, Miriam. *The Meaning of נפש מת in the Old Testament*. Helsinki, Finland: Societas Orientalis Fennica, 1951.

Shedinger, Robert F. "Did Tatian Use the Old Testament Peshitta? A Response to Jan Joosten." *Novum Testamentum* 41, no. 3 (1999): 265–279.

Shier-Jones, Angela. "The Never-Land of Religion and the Lost Childhood of the Children of God." In *Children of God: Towards a Theology of Childhood*, edited by Angela Shier-Jones, 181–205. Peterborough: Epworth, 2007.

Shweder, Richard A. "Introduction." In *The Child: An Encyclopedic Companion*, edited by Richard A. Shweder, xxvii–xxxvii. Chicago; London: University of Chicago Press, 2009.

Silva, Moisés. *Biblical Words and Their Meaning: An Introduction to Lexical Semantics*. Revised and expanded edition. Grand Rapids, MI: Zondervan, 1994.

Sī-Mǎ, Guāng 司馬光. 資治通鑑 [History as a mirror (Vol. 248)], 1071–1086. Accessed 8 July 2016. http://www.angelibrary.com/oldies/zztj/248.htm.
Simpson, J., ed. "Childhood." *Oxford Dictionary*. Accessed 22 July 2016. http://www.oed.com.myaccess.library.utoronto.ca/view/Entry/31631?redirectedFrom=childhood#eid.
Sisemore, Timothy A. "Theological Perspectives on Children in the Church: Reformed and Presbyterian." In *Nurturing Children's Spirituality: Christian Perspectives and Best Practices*, edited by Holly Catterton Allen, 93–109. Eugene, OR: Cascade, 2008.
Siu, Paul. "The Doctrine of Man in the Theology of Watchman Nee." Master's thesis, Bethel Theological Seminary, 1979.
Slavkov, Nikolay. "What Is Your 'First' Language in Bilingual Canada? A Study of Language Background Profiling at Publicly Funded Elementary Schools across Three Provinces." *International Journal of Bilingual Education and Bilingualism*, 2015: 1–18.
Smith, C. Ryder. *The Bible Doctrine of Man*. London: Epworth Press, 1951.
Smith, Kevin. *Academic Writing and Theological Research: A Guide for Students*. Johannesburg, SA: South African Theological Seminary Press, 2008.
Smith, S. M. "Perichoresis." In *Evangelical Dictionary of Theology*, edited by Walter A. Elwell, 906–907. Grand Rapids, MI: Baker Academic, 2001.
Snailum, Brenda. "Implementing Intergenerational Youth Ministry Within Existing Evangelical Church Congregations." *Christian Education Journal* 9, no. 1 (2012): 165–181.
Snell-Hornby, Mary. *Turns of Translation Studies: New Paradigms or Shifting Viewpoints?* Amsterdam; Philadelphia: John Benjamins, 2006.
Soffer, Arthur. "The Treatment of Anthropomorhisms and Anthropopathisms in the Septuagint." In *Studies in the Septuagint: Origins, Recensions, and Interpretations: Selected Essays, with a Prolegomenon by Sidney Jellicoe*, edited by Harry M. Orlinsky, 85–107. New York: KTAV, 1974.
Solberg, A. *Negotiating Childhood: Empirical Investigations and Textual Representations of Children's Work and Everyday Lives*. Stockholm: Nordic Institute for Studies in Urban and Regional Planning, 1994.
Spillett, Hubert W. *A Catalogue of Scriptures in the Languages of China and the Republic of China*. London: British and Foreign Bible Society, 1975.
Spurgeon, Charles H. *The Treasury of David: An Expository and Devotional Commentary on the Psalms*. Grand Rapids, MI: Baker Books, 1983.
Stacey, David. *The Pauline View of Man: In Relation to Its Judaic and Hellenistic Background*. London: Macmillan; New York: St Martin's Press, 1956.
———. "St Paul and the 'Soul.'" *The Expository Times* 66 (1955): 274–277.
Stafford, Wess. *Too Small to Ignore: Why the Least of These Matters Most*. Colorado Springs, CO: WaterBrook, 2007.

Stein, Robert H. *Luke*. The New American Commentary 24. Nashville, TN: Broadman & Holman, 1992.

Steinberg, Naomi. *The World of the Child in the Hebrew Bible*. Sheffield, UK: Sheffield Phoenix, 2013.

Stine, Philip C. *Let the Words Be Written: The Lasting Influence of Eugene A. Nida*. Atlanta: SBL, 2004.

Stinger, Charles L. *Humanism and the Church Fathers: Ambrogio Traversari (1386–1439) and Christian Antiquity in the Italian Renaissance*. Albany: State University of New York Press, 1977.

Stockwell, Peter. *Cognitive Poetics: An Introduction*. London: Routledge, 2002.

Stonehouse, Catherine. *Joining Children on the Spiritual Journey: Nurturing a Life of Faith*. Grand Rapids, MI: Baker Books, 1998.

Strandenaes, Thor. *Principles of Chinese Bible Translation: As Expressed in Five Selected Versions of the New Testament and Exemplified by Mt 5: 1–12 and Col 1*. Uppsala Universitet, Sweden: Almqvist & Wiksell International, 1987.

Strange, W. A. *Children in the Early Church: Children in the Ancient World, the New Testament and the Early Church*. Carlisle, UK: Paternoster, 1996.

Stuart, Douglas K. *Exodus*. Vol. 2. The New American Commentary. Nashville: Broadman & Holman, 2006.

Swete, H. B. *An Introduction to the Old Testament in Greek*. Cambridge: Cambridge University Press, 1914.

Sysling, Harry. "Translation Techniques in the Ancient Bible Translations: Septuagint and Targum." In *A History of Bible Translation*, edited by Philip A. Noss, 279–305. Roma: Edizioni di storia e letteratura, 2007.

Talay-Ongan, Ayshe. *Typical and Atypical Development in Early Childhood: The Fundamentals*. New York: Teachers College Press, 1998.

Tán, Shù Lín 譚樹林. *馬禮遜與中西文化交流* [Robert Morrison and Sino-Western cultural communication]. Hangzhou: Chinese Academy of Fine Arts Press, 2003.

Táng, Chóng Róng 唐崇榮. *聖靈的引導: 動力的生活* [The guidance of the Holy Spirit: A life full of impetus]. Taipei: Zhōng fú Publishing Co., 2004.

Tanner, Beth LaNeel. "Psalm 35." In *The Book of Psalms*, by Nancy deClaissé-Walford, R. A. Jacobson, and Beth LaNeel Tanner, 331–337. NICOT. Grand Rapids, MI: Eerdmans, 2014.

———. "Psalm 63." In *The Book of Psalms*, by Nancy deClaissé-Walford, R. A. Jacobson, and Beth LaNeel Tanner, 519–521. NICOT. Grand Rapids, MI: Eerdmans, 2014.

Tate, Marvin E. *Psalms 51–100*. Word Biblical Commentary 20, edited by Bruce M. Metzger, David A. Hubbard, Glenn W. Barker, John D. W. Watts, and Ralph P. Martin. Dallas, TX: Word Books, 1998.

Tawil, Hayim. "נפש." In *An Akkadian Lexical Companion for Biblical Hebrew: Etymological-Semantic and Idiomatic Equivalents with Supplement on Biblical Aramaic*, 244–246. Jersey City, NJ: KTAV, 2009.
"Teleology." Accessed 10 July 2016. https://en.wikipedia.org/wiki/Teleology#Etymology.
Terrien, Samuel L. *The Psalms: Strophic Structure and Theological Commentary*. Grand Rapids, MI: Eerdmans, 2003.
Tertullian. "On Baptism." In *The Ante-Nicene Fathers, Vol. 3: Latin Christianity: Its Founder, Tertullian*, edited by A. Roberts, J. Donaldson, and A. C. Coxe, 669–680. Buffalo, NY: Christian Literature Co., 1885.
———. "On Monogamy." In *The Ante-Nicene Fathers, Vol. 4: Fathers of the Third Century: Tertullian, Part Fourth; Minucius Felix; Commodian; Origen, Parts First and Second*, edited by A. Roberts, J. Donaldson, and A. C. Coxe, 59–73. Buffalo, NY: Christian Literature Co., 1885.
The Commission on Children at Risk. "Hardwired to Connect: The New Scientific Case for Authoritative Communities." In *Authoritative Communities: The Scientific Case for Nurturing the Whole Child*, edited by Kathleen Kovner Kline, 3–68. New York: Springer Verlag, 2008.
"The Official Spoken Language in Ancient China," 2017. Accessed 28 February 2017. http://mypage.direct.ca/w/wfung/heshantongyi/Chinese%20Antiquity%20Language/Chinese%20Antiquity%20Language.html.
Tkacz, C. Brown. "Labor Tam Utilis: The Creation of the Vulgate." *Vigiliae Christianae* 50, no. 1 (1996): 42–72.
Tomas, Stuart. "נפש and the Doctrine of Men in the OT." Master's thesis, Trinity Evangelical Divinity School, 1986.
Toury, Gideon. *Descriptive Translation Studies – And Beyond*. Amsterdam; Philadelphia: John Benjamins, 1995.
Tov, Emanuel. "The Septuagint." In *Mikra: Text, Translation, Reading and Interpretation of the Hebrew Bible in Ancient Judaism and Early Christianity*, edited by Marti Jan Mulder and Harry Sysling, 161–188. Peabody, MA: Hendrickson, 2004 [1988].
———. *Textual Criticism of the Hebrew Bible*. 3rd revised and expanded edition. Minneapolis: Fortress, 2012.
Towner, W. Sibley. "Children and the Image of God." In *The Child in the Bible*, edited by Marcia J. Bunge, Terence E. Fretheim, and Beverly Roberts Gaventa, 307–323. Grand Rapids, MI: Eerdmans, 2008.
Uchida, Keiichi 內田慶市. "馬禮遜參照的漢譯聖書: 新發現的白日昇譯新約聖經稿本" [The Chinese Bible used by Robert Morrison: A newly discovered manuscript of the New Testament translated by Jean Basset]. In 自上帝說漢語以來：《和合本》聖經九十年 [Ever since God speaks Chinese: The 90th anniversary of the Chinese Union Version Bible],

edited by Pǐn Rán Xiè 謝品然 and Qìng Bào Zéng 曾慶豹, 53–68. Bible Translation and Hermeneutics Series. Hong Kong: Center for Advanced Biblical Studies and Application, 2010.

Vanderwell, Howard. "Biblical Values to Shape the Congregation." In *The Church of All Ages: Generations Worshiping Together*, edited by Howard Vanderwell, 17–33. Herndon, VA: Alban Institute, 2008.

Vendryes, J. *Language: A Linguistic Introduction to History*. London; New York: Routledge, 2013 [1925].

Vermeer, H. J. "Skopos and Commission in Translational Action." In *The Translation Studies Reader*, edited by L. Venuti, 227–238. New York; London: Routledge, 2004 [1989].

Volf, Miroslav. *After Our Likeness: The Church as the Image of the Trinity*. Grand Rapids, MI: Eerdmans, 1998.

von Rad, Gerhard. *Old Testament Theology*. Vol. 1. Louisville, KY: Westminster John Knox, 2001.

Wall, John. *Ethics in Light of Childhood*. Washington, DC: Georgetown University Press, 2010.

———. "Childhood Studies, Hermeneutics, and Theological Ethics." *The Journal of Religion* 86, no. 4 (2006): 523–548.

———. "Child: Religious and Philosophical Perspectives." In *The Child: An Encyclopedic Companion*, edited by Richard A. Shweder, 143–147. Chicago; London: University of Chicago Press, 2009.

Waltke, Bruce K. "נפשׁ." In *Theological Wordbook of the Old Testament*, edited by R. L. Harris, G. L. Archer, Jr., and B. K. Waltke, 587–591. Chicago, IL: Moody, 1999.

Waltke, Bruce K., and Charles Yu. *An Old Testament Theology: An Exegetical, Canonical, and Thematic Approach*. Grand Rapids, MI: Zondervan, 2007.

Wáng, Níng, and Yi Feng Sūn. "Introduction." In *Translation, Globalisation and Localisation: A Chinese Perspective*, edited by Níng Wáng and Yi Feng Sūn, 1–12. Clevedon, UK; Buffalo, NY: Multilingual Matters, 2008.

Wāng, Wéi Fán 汪維藩. "聖經譯本在中國" [The Chinese versions of the Bible]. *Studies in World Religions* 49, no. 1 (1992): 71–84.

Ward, Carrie. *Together: Growing Appetites for God*. Chicago, IL: Moody, 2012.

Warne, Graham J. *Hebrew Perspectives on the Human Person in the Hellenistic Era: Philo and Paul*. Lewiston, NY: Mellen Biblical Press, 1995.

Wasserstein, Abraham, and David Wasserstein. *The Legend of the Septuagint: From Classical Antiquity to Today*. Cambridge: Cambridge University Press, 2006.

Weber, Hans-Ruedi. *Jesus and the Children: Biblical Resources for Study and Preaching*. Atlanta: John Knox, 1979.

Wegner, Paul D. *The Journey from Texts to Translations: The Origin and Development of the Bible*. Grand Rapids, MI: Baker Books, 1999.

Weitzman, M. P. *The Syriac Version of the Old Testament: An Introduction.* Cambridge, UK; New York: Cambridge University Press, 1999.

Welter, Paul. *Learning from Children.* Wheaton, IL: Tyndale House, 1984.

Wendland, Ernst R. *Analyzing the Psalms: with Exercises for Bible Students and Translators.* 2nd edition. Dallas, TX: SIL International, 2002.

———. *Contextual Frames of Reference in Translation: A Coursebook for Bible Translators and Teachers.* Manchester, UK; Kinderhook, NY: St Jerome, 2008.

———. *LiFE-Style Translating.* 2nd edition. Dallas, TX: SIL International, 2011.

———. "A Literary Approach to Biblical Text Analysis and Translation." In *Bible Translation: Frames of Reference*, edited by Timothy Wilt, 179–230. Manchester, UK; Northampton, MA: St Jerome, 2003.

———. *Translating the Literature of Scripture: A Literary-Rhetorical Approach to Bible Translation.* Dallas, TX: SIL International, 2004.

Wēng, Shào Jūn 翁绍軍. 漢語景教文典詮釋 [Sino-Nestorian document: Commentary and exegesis]. 歷代基督教思想學術文庫 [Chinese academic library of Christian thought in history 102]. Hong Kong: Institute of Sino-Christian Studies, 1995.

Wenger, Etienne. "Communities of Practice." 2016. Accessed 10 October 2016. https://www.learning-theories.com/communities-of-practice-lave-and-wenger.html.

Werner, Eberhard. "The Mandate for Bible Translation: Models of Communication and Translation in Theory and Practice in Regard to the Science of Bible Translation," 2013. Accessed 25 January 2014. http://www.sil.org/resources/archives/51438.

Wertsch, James V., and Barbara Rogoff. "Editors' Notes." In *Children's Learning in the "Zone of Proximal Development,"* edited by Barbara Rogoff and James V. Wertsch, 1–6. San Francisco, CA: Jossey-Bass, 1984.

Westerhoff, John H. *Will Our Children Have Faith?* Revised and expanded edition. Harrisburg, PA: Morehouse, 2000.

Westermann, Claus. "נפשׁ." In *Theological Lexicon of the Old Testament*, edited by Ernst Jenni and Claus Westermann. Translated by Mark E. Biddle, 743–759. Peabody, MA: Hendrickson, 1997.

White, James. "Erasmus of Rotterdam: His New Testament and Its Importance." Accessed 17 July 2016. http://vintage.aomin.org/erasmus.html#1-20.

White, James W. *Intergenerational Religious Education: Models, Theory and Prescription for Interage Life and Learning in the Faith Community.* Birmingham: Religious Education Press, 1988.

White, Keith J. "The Child in the Midst of the Biblical Witeness." In *Toddling to the Kingdom: Child Theology at Work in the Church*, edited by John Collier, 154–160. London, UK: Child Theology Movement, 2009.

———. "'He Placed a Little Child in the Midst': Jesus, the Kingdom, and Children." In *The Child in the Bible*, edited by, Marcia J. Bunge, Terence E. Fretheim, and Beverly Roberts Gaventa, 353–374. Grand Rapids, MI: Eerdmans, 2008.

———. "Insights into Child Theology through the Life and Work of Pandita Ramabai," 1–11, 2006. Accessed 1 June 2014. http://www.childtheology.org/wp-content/uploads/2013/02/OCMS-31.10.06.pdf.

Williams, C. S. C. "The History of the Text and Canon of the New Testament to Jerome." In *The Cambridge History of the Bible, Vol. 2: The West from the Fathers to the Reformation*, edited by G. W. H. Lampe, 27–53. New York: Cambridge University Press, 2004.

Williams, P. J. "Versions, Ancient." In *The New Interpreter's Dictionary of the Bible*, vol. 5, edited by Katharine D. Sakenfeld, 733-738. Nashville, TN: Abingdon, 2007.

Willmer, Haddon, and Keith J. White. *Entry Point: Towards Child Theology with Matthew 18*. London, UK: WTL, 2013.

Wilson, Gerald H. *Psalms Volume 1*. The NIV Application Commentary. Grand Rapids, MI: Zondervan, 2002.

Windle, Kevin, and Anthony Pym. "European Thinking on Secular Translation." In *The Oxford Handbook of Translation Studies*, edited by Kirsten Malmkjaer and Kevin Windle, Electronic edition, §1. Oxford; New York: Oxford University Press, 2012.

Wolff, Hans Walter. *Anthropology of the Old Testament*. Translated by Margaret Kohl. London: SCM, 1974.

Wonderly, William L. *Bible Translations for Popular Use*. London: United Bible Societies, 1968.

Woodhead, Martin. "Childhood Studies: Past, Present and Future." In *An Introduction to Childhood Studies*, edited by Mary Jane Kehily, 2nd edition, 17–31. Maidenhead, UK; New York: Open University Press, 2009.

Wordnik. "*Neanis*," 2014. Accessed 9 January 2014. http://www.wordnik.com/words/neanis.

Wright, David F. "How Controversial Was the Development of Infant Baptism in the Early Church?" In *Church, Word, and Spirit: Historical and Theological Essays in Honor of Geoffrey W. Bromiley*, edited by James E. Bradley and Richard A. Muller, 45–63. Grand Rapids, MI: Eerdmans, 1987.

Wright III, Benjamin G. "The Jewish Scriptures in Greek: The Septuagint in the Context of Ancient Translation Activity." In *Biblical Translation in Context*, edited by Frederick W. Knobloch, 3–18. Bethesda, MD: University Press of Maryland, 2002.

Wú, Dongsheng John. *Understanding Watchman Nee: Spirituality, Knowledge, and Formation*. Kindle Edition. Eugene, OR: Wipf & Stock, 2012.

———. "Watchman Nee on Revelation: Gnosticism or Divine Illumination Tradition?," 2013. Accessed 12 November 2014. http://www.christiansquare.org:8081/criasia/research/paper/2013-03.pdf.

Würthwein, Ernst. *The Text of the An Introduction to the Biblia Hebraica*. Translated by Erroll F. Rhodes. 2nd revised edition. Grand Rapids, MI: Eerdmans, 1995.

Xiào, Cái Wàng 肖才望. "呂振中《新譯新約全書》譯本考察" [An exploration of the literal translation of the New Testament by Lǚ Zhèn-Zhōng]. *Journal of Shānxī Agriculture University (Social Science Edition)* 12, no. 2 (2013): 109–112.

Xǔ, Mù Shì 許牧世. "中文聖經翻譯簡史" [A brief history of Chinese Bible translation]. *Jǐng Fēng* 69 (1982): 28–36.

———. 經與釋經 [The Bible and hermeneutics]. Hong Kong: Chinese Christian Literature Council, 1983.

Xú, Tāo 徐弢. "倪柝聲的三元論思想探究" [An inquiry on the trichotomy theory of Watchman Nee]. *China Graduate School of Theology Journal* 54 (2013): 39–52.

Xú, Zōng Zé 徐宗澤. 明清間耶穌會士譯者提要 [The abstract from the translators of the Jesuits during Míng and Qīng Dynasty]. Shàng hǎi, China: Shàng hǎi Century, 2010.

Yán, Fù 嚴復. 天演論 [Evolution and ethics]. Hú běi, China: Miǎn yáng lú shì shèn shǐ jī zhāi mù kē Publish, 1898.

Yáng, Fù Xué 楊富學. "回鶻景教研究百年顧" [Century in retrospect of researching Huí Gǔ Nestorians]. *Dūn Huáng Research* 68 (2001): 167–173.

Yáng, Qìng Qiú 楊慶球. 會遇系統神學 [Encountering systematic theology]. Hong Kong: China Graduate School of Theology, 2001.

Yáng, Sēn Fù 楊森富. 中國基督教史 [History of Christianity in China]. 4th edition. Taipei: Taiwan shāng wù yìn shū guǎn, 1984.

Youngblood, R. F. "תַּחַת." In *Theological Wordbook of the Old Testament*, edited by R. L. Harris, G. L. Archer, Jr., and B. K. Waltke, 968–969. Chicago, IL: Moody, 1999.

Yu, Ning. *The Chinese HEART in a Cognitive Perspective: Culture, Body, and Language*. Berlin; New York: Mouton de Gruyter, 2009.

Zēng, Qìng Bào 曾慶豹. "無所憑依、無因而起: 倪柝聲的神學人類學及其文化底蘊" [The theological anthropology of Watchman Nee: In the context of Taoist tradition]. *Sino-Christian Studies* 12 (2011): 159–187.

Zerbe, Gordon. "Paul on the Human Being as a 'Psychic Body': Neither Dualist nor Monist." *Direction Journal* 37, no. 2 (2008): 168–184.

Zetzsche, Jost Oliver. *The Bible in China: The History of the Union Version or the Culmination of Protestant Missionary Bible Translation in China*. Monumenta

Serica Monograph Series 45. Sankt Augustin, Germany: Monumenta Serica Institute, 1999.

Zhān, En Shèng 詹恩勝. "評介夏著 – 天國的隕落: 太平天國宗教再研究" [The review of a book 'Heaven's Fall: the further study of Taiping Heavenly Kingdom's Religion' by Xia Chun Tao]. *Zhōng Zhèng History Journal* 13 (2010): 165–184.

Zhāng, Guó Dìng 張國定. 詩篇 [Psalms (IV)]. 天道聖經註釋 [Tiān Dào Bible Commentary]. Hong Kong: Tiān Dào Publishing House, 2004.

Zhāng, Yàn Qín 張艷琴. "析漢語景教經典的改寫譯經思想" [Analyzing the thought of rewriting and translation of Chinese Nestorian classics]. *Journal of Ji-Nan University (Philosophy and Social Sciences)* 28, no. 6 (2006): 141–145.

Zhào, Bì Chǔ 趙壁礎. 重譯景教碑 [Re-translating the Nestorian Stele]. 中華民族探源叢書: 景教歷史系列 [The history of the Luminous Religion 1]. Austin, TX: Bì Chǔ Bookstore, 2006.

Zhào, Wéi Běn 趙維本. 譯經溯源: 現代五大中文聖經翻譯史 [Tracing Bible translation: A history of the translation of five modern Chinese versions of the Bible]. Hong Kong: China Graduate School of Theology, 1993.

———. 佳蹤重尋:譯經先鋒列傳 [A beautiful legacy: The pioneers of Chinese Bible translation]. Singapore: Singapore Bible college, 2007.

Zhū, Bǎo Huì 朱寶惠. 重譯新約全書 [The New Testament translated from the original]. Nán Jīng, China: xīn yì shèng jīng liú tōng chù, 1936.

Zhū, Qiān Zhī 朱謙之. 中國景教 [The Luminous Religion in China]. Běi Jīng, China: Dōng-fāng Publishing House, 1993.

Zhuāng, Róu Yù 莊柔玉. 基督教聖經中文譯本權威現象研究 [A study of the phenomenon of authoritativeness in the Chinese translations of the Protestant Bible]. 譯經叢書 [Monograph Series on Bible Translation 1]. Hong Kong: International Bible Society, 2000.

———. "《和合本》在中文聖經多元系統中的位置—前景與挑戰" [The position of the Chinese Union Version in the Chinese Bible polysystem: Prospective and challenge]. *China Graduate School of Theology Journal* 49 (2010): 27–43.

Zimmerli, Walther. *Ezekiel 1: A Commentary on the Book of the Prophet Ezekiel*. Edited by Frank Moore Cross, Klaus Baltzer, and Leonard Jay Greenspoon. Translated by Ronald E. Clements. Hermeneia. Philadelphia, PA: Fortress, 1979.

Zlotowitz, Bernard M. *The Septuagint Translation of the Hebrew Terms in Relation to God in the Book of Jeremiah*. New York: KTAV, 1981.

Zuck, Roy B. *Precious in His Sight: Childhood and Children in the Bible*. Grand Rapids, MI: Baker Books, 1996.

List of Chinese Dictionaries Used

現代漢語詞典 [Modern Chinese Dictionary]
漢語大詞典 [Chinese Dictionary]
譯典通電子字典9.0 旗艦版 [Dr.eye electronic dictionary (9.0 ultimate ed.)]

Subject Index

A

age segregation 143, 166, 167, 320
anaphora 93–95, 272
anthropological term 1, 176, 197, 205
anthropomorphic 26
anthropomorphism 30, 91, 190
anti-anthropomorphic 26
Apocrypha 34
apocryphal 26
Aramaic dialect 29, 31
artistic text analysis 87
authoritative community 165

B

Bible as literature 78, 79
Bibles for children 136
Bibles in Easy English 136
Bible translation history 9, 20, 37
biblical poetry 81, 88
body of Christ 120, 145, 150, 162

C

chiasmus 96, 279, 291, 310
chiastic 262, 276, 281, 289, 290, 310, 334
child 101–106, 118, 120
childhood 101–105, 107, 113, 114
childhood studies 6, 100–108, 110–113, 140, 143

children 101, 103–106, 115, 119, 122, 125, 128
children as social agents 101
children's Bibles 99, 133, 136, 137, 139, 140
child theologies 110
Child Theology Movement 121
Chinese Bible translation 5, 9, 10, 14, 15, 20, 39, 44, 52, 55, 57–60, 98, 142, 234, 318
Chinese Bible translation history 9, 20, 234
Chinese new poetry 233, 310, 333
church as body 164
classical Chinese 40, 42, 45, 46, 50, 52
cognitive poetics 81, 84
common language 12, 13, 141
community of God 159
composition 15, 16, 32, 85, 88, 89, 97, 142, 232, 233, 318–320, 330, 340
condensed expression 88, 91
conservative Bible translators 16
consultation 8, 9, 15, 142, 232, 318, 319, 332, 335, 340
content 66, 73, 80, 88, 91, 92, 94
contextualization 8, 9, 15, 142, 232, 318, 319, 335, 340
contextualized 41, 319

407

covenant community 145, 149, 150
culture of intergenerationality 166, 167

D
deuterocanonical 25, 36
developmental theory 151, 159
diachrony 180
dichotomy 1, 19, 67, 97, 197, 205
domesticating translations 64
domestication 16, 66, 79
dualism 1, 176–178, 195, 197, 198, 201, 204, 205, 221
dynamic equivalence 70, 73, 77, 81

E
Easy wén lǐ 50–53
ellipsis 258, 333
emotive meaning 72
emphatic devices 88
enculturation 42, 59, 144
epiphora 93, 95, 285
etymological 3, 179–182, 205, 212, 216, 218, 227, 314, 317
etymology 3, 4, 179, 180–182, 205, 212

F
figurative language 88, 94, 330, 331, 332
first language 12
foreignization 16, 66, 79
form 80, 88
formal equivalence 16, 73
function 80, 88, 96
functional equivalence 16, 77–79, 81, 82, 86

G
general Bibles 136

H
hapax legomena 179, 180
hardwired to connect 165
Hebrew poetry 88–91, 93, 95, 96, 252, 310, 332
hendiadys 252, 274, 277
Hexapla 24, 25, 31, 33
highly literate country 12
High wén lǐ 45, 50–53
hyperbole 95

I
IBTTV 235, 238, 241, 242, 244, 246, 250, 254, 257, 259, 261, 263, 268, 271, 272, 274, 275, 277, 278, 280, 282, 288, 290, 291, 293, 295–297, 308, 310, 311, 328, 335, 336
IIM 6, 7, 10, 17, 140, 143–145, 150, 151, 156, 158, 159, 166–169, 171, 172, 231, 234, 319, 322, 327, 338, 339
Inclusio 249
intentional intergenerational ministry 145, 319
intercultural 19, 76, 84
inter-dependencies 121
interdisciplinary 19, 61, 76, 100, 102, 106
interdiscipline 76
intergenerational Bible translation team 6, 9, 10, 12, 17, 100, 144, 230, 233, 234, 319, 339
intergenerational culture 167
intergenerational learning 166, 169–172, 234, 320
intergenerational ministry 6, 12, 100, 113, 133, 140, 143, 144, 168, 231
Interlingual translation 69
Intersemiotic translation 69

Subject Index

Intralingual translation 68

K
koinōnia 164

L
Latin Vulgate 32, 35–38
LiFE 11, 77, 83, 86–88, 97, 98, 142, 232–234, 236, 238, 244, 246, 250, 254, 261, 263, 271, 275, 278, 282, 288, 293, 297, 309, 310, 312, 313, 318, 320, 321, 332, 333, 335, 337, 339
linguistic meaning 72
literalism 30, 67
literal translation 2, 29, 33, 44, 58, 62, 176, 211, 219, 220, 228, 231, 243, 252, 277, 283, 318
literal-versus-free translation 19
literary functional-equivalence 79, 86
Literary Functional Equivalence 10, 77, 232, 318
literary genres 13, 81
literary translation 67, 69

M
Mandarin 39, 50–56, 59, 314
Mandarin Phonetic Symbols 242, 259, 269, 295
Masoretic Text 15, 27
meaning-based approach 26
metaphor 90, 102, 117, 139, 150, 160, 163, 202, 247, 263, 272
metaphorical 162, 273
metaphors 65, 90, 117, 247
Modern Standard Chinese 39
mother tongue 12, 55, 57–59, 140, 142, 328

N
Nestorian Stele 40

O
oral 20, 28, 66, 85
oral Bible translation 20

P
parallel 24, 88, 91, 96, 170, 187, 208, 246, 250, 251, 262, 263, 267, 269, 270, 276, 285, 292, 331
parallelism 91, 233, 239, 246, 248, 252, 253, 258, 259, 261, 262, 276, 290, 291, 310, 330, 331, 333, 334
parallel phrasing 88
parallels 226, 252, 291
paronomasia 286, 295
pathetic periphrasis 187
perichoresis 160
Peshiṭta 31–34
poetic device 248, 333
poetic structures 88
popular language 12, 13
primary translations 21, 31
rabbinic literature 27

R
receptor language 19, 72, 73
re-composition 84, 86
re-conceptualization 84
referential meaning 72
relevance theory 79, 81, 83
rhetorical 37, 77, 81, 83, 87, 91, 94, 97, 199, 243, 248, 252, 259, 260, 333, 339
rhetorical construction 243
rhetorical text analysis 87
rhyme 242, 246, 251, 257, 259, 260, 265, 266, 268, 269, 272–274, 277, 286, 290, 292, 295, 310, 311, 328, 333, 337

rhymes 242, 246, 268, 273, 277, 290, 311
rhyming 242, 246, 257, 259, 265, 268, 273, 274, 277, 286, 292, 296, 310, 311, 333
rhythm 92

S

secondary translations 31
Semitic languages 181–183, 194, 212
sense-for-sense 62, 63
Septuagint 21–28, 30, 31, 33, 34, 37, 176, 179, 183, 195–197, 204, 205, 218, 227
shifting patterns 88, 92
simile 90, 247, 277
situated learning theory 151, 158, 159
Skopos 16, 63, 81, 82, 85, 86, 98, 233, 337, 338
social learning theory 151, 156, 159
social trinity 160
socio-cultural learning theory 151, 154, 159
sound effects 88, 89
source language (SL) 19, 48, 73, 77, 81, 82, 84, 86, 88, 97, 260, 334
stylistic device 276
synchrony 180
synecdoche 90, 193, 250, 330
syntactic 8, 71, 92, 142, 246, 258, 259, 267, 279, 291, 335
Syriac Peshiṭta 31, 33, 34

T

target language (TL) 48, 62–64, 68, 77, 82, 85, 86, 88, 97, 227, 232, 260, 328, 334
Targumim 21, 27–30, 227
teleological 69

ten-step exegetical methodology 97, 232, 333, 335
tertiary translations 31
the family of God 146, 162, 163
theology of childhood 110, 114, 118, 120
translation 84–86
translation principles 5, 19, 49, 54, 56, 59, 60, 68
translation studies 4–6, 10, 19, 20, 60–62, 64, 66, 69, 73–78, 97, 172, 231, 318
translation techniques 26, 28, 30, 33, 37
translation theory 4, 5, 9, 14, 35, 56, 59–63, 66, 68, 77, 81, 231, 318, 337–339
trichotomy 2, 3, 197, 199, 203–205, 218, 224–226, 228, 229, 231, 312, 315
tripartite anthropology 2, 176, 225, 228, 231

V

vernacular speech 7, 141, 336
vernacular translations 38

W

whole gospel 138–140
word-for-word 62, 63
wordplay 280, 295

Author Index

A

Alderson, Priscilla 106
Allen, A. L. 100, 120, 121
Allen, Holly Catterton 148, 156, 158, 159, 161, 164–168, 170, 171
Allen, R. B. 252
Anderson, Herbert 118, 125
Archard, David 104, 111
Arichea, Daniel C. 16
Ariès, Philippe 107
Asbridge, Nigel 102
Augustine of Hippo 23, 36, 80, 135

B

Balswick, Jack O. 163
Bandura, Albert 156–158
Banks, Robert J. 147, 162
Barth, Karl 161
Barton, Stephen C. 163
Bassnett, Susan 10, 62, 63, 66
Berlin, Adele 248
Berryman, Jerome W. 110, 117, 138
Bluebond-Langner, Myra 103
Bottigheimer, Ruth B. 137
Bratcher, Robert G. 280
Briggs, Charles A. 1, 179
Broke, Sebastian 22
Broomhall, Marshall 54
Brotzman, Ellis R. 184

Brueggemann, Walter 1, 148, 178, 179, 215, 249
Bultmann, Rudolf 199
Bunge, Marcia J. 109–111, 118

C

Calvin, John 116, 125, 126
Carroll, John T. 111
Carson, D. A. 180
Cavalletti, Sofia 129
Chechowich, Faye E. 143
Chén, Dé Hóng Leo 60
Cheung, Andy 77, 318
Chow, Alexander 222
Chrysostom, John 131
Chukovsky, Kornei 8
Clement, Alexander 130
Clement, of Alexandria 117, 129
Cockerill, Gareth Lee 204
Comenius, Johannes Amos 117
Couture, Pamela D. 113, 124, 127
Cyprian of Carthage 119, 131

D

Demarest, Bruce A. 150
de Saussure, Ferdinand 180
DeVries, Dawn 151
de Waard, Jan 77, 81, 82

E
Eckert, Penelope 141
Ellington, John 16
Ellingworth, Paul 203
Erikson, Erik H. 151–154

F
Fiedler, Margie 166
Foley, Toshikazu S. 41
Fowler, James W. 151, 153, 154

G
Galbraith, Mary 103, 104
Gambone, James V. 6, 145, 169
Gentzler, Edwin 60
Gobbel, A. Roger 137
Gobbel, Gertrude G. 137
Goldingay, John 188, 212, 335
Green, Joel B. 177
Greenspoon, Leonard 25
Gregory of Nyssa 120, 160
Grenz, Stanley J. 160
Gruenler, Royce G. 160
Gundry-Volf, Judith M. 127
Gunkel, Hermann 13
Gutt, Ernst-August 83
Gvozdev, A. N. 8, 141

H
Ḥakham, Amos 178, 247, 257, 276, 289
Heckel, Theo K. 198
Hellerman, Joseph H. 163
Hermans, T. 76
Herzog, Kristin 118
Hicks, Peter 197
Hinsdale, Mary Ann 132
Holmes, James 74
Holmes, Janet 336

I
Irenaeus 23, 130

J
Jacob, Edmund 3, 4, 185, 193, 213, 218, 314
Jakobson, Roman 68, 69
James, Allison 104–106
Jeeves, Malcom 200
Jensen, David H. 123–125
Jerome 35–38, 62, 63, 80
Jewett, Robert 198, 199
Jinbachian, Manuel 20
Johnson, Aubrey R. 187–189, 192, 194
Johnson, Susan B. W. 118, 125
Joosten, Jan 32
Justin 24

K
Kedar, Benjamin 38
Kehily, Mary Jane 101
Kehrwald, Leif 169
Koehler, George E. 170
Kohlberg, Lawrence 151, 153
Korbin, Jill E. 103

L
Laidlaw, John 177
Landreth, Gary L. 323
Laurin, Robert 193
Lave, Jean 158
Lee, Witness 220
Lefevere, André 10, 62, 63, 66
LeVine, Robert A. 103
Levý, Jiří 69, 70
Lewis, Gordon R. 150
Liáng, Jiā Lín 225
Liào, Yuán Wēi 225
Lǐ, Jǐn Lún 224
Lín, Róng Hóng 224, 225

Linton, Calvin D. 79
Lunn, Nick 239
Luther, Martin 55, 64, 80, 123, 136, 140, 141
Lys, Daniel 196

M

Malherbe, Johannes 136, 140
Marter, E. W. 189, 190
Martineau, Mariette 169, 170
Martin, Kelly 149
May, Scottie 138
Mazor, Yair 79
McIntosh, Gary L. 148
Mead, Margaret 156, 157
Menconi, Peter 166
Mercer, Joyce Ann 114, 118, 120, 127
Metzger, Bruce M. 35
Meyers, Patty 166
Michaels, J. Ramsey 201, 202
Miller-McLemore, Bonnie J. 109, 110, 117, 127
Mojola, Aloo Osotsi 78
Moltmann, Jürgen 117, 118, 127
Montgomery, Heather 103, 111
Morrison, Robert 44–48, 59
Mounstephen, Philip 149
Munday, Jeremy 71
Murphy, Nancey 1, 176

N

Nee, Watchman 2, 4, 11, 176–178, 205, 218–229, 231, 312, 315, 318
Neuwirth, Rav Yehoshua Y. 135
Nida, Eugene A. 2, 68, 70–73, 77, 78, 81, 82, 177
Nord, Christiane 81

O

Origen 24, 25, 33, 130
Owen, D. R. G. 178

P

Pamudji, P. 222
Parkhurst, John 1, 179
Pedersen, Johannes 192
Péng, Guó Wěi 5
Penn-Lewis, Jessie 221, 222
Philo 23, 26
Piaget, Jean 151, 152, 153
Prest, Eddie 160
Pritchard, Gretchen Wolff 137, 139
Pufall, Peter B. 111

R

Rahner, Karl 114, 115, 120, 132, 151
Ráo, Xiào Bǎi 220
Reyburn, William David 280
Ricci, Matteo 43
Roberto, John 166, 169, 170
Roberts, Dana 221, 222
Robinson, H. Wheeler 177, 188, 199
Ross, Allen P. 247, 282
Ross, Christine Lawton 148, 156, 158, 159, 161, 164, 165, 167, 168, 170, 171
Rudolph, Wilhelm 126

S

Sand, A. 199
Sanneh, Lamin 16
Schleiermacher, Friedrich 63–67, 118, 132
Schwartz, Theodore 107
Schweizer, Eduard 200, 202–204
Seebass, H. 186–188, 190
Seligson, Miriam 192
Shier-Jones, Angela 115
Shweder, Richard A. 103

Silva, Moisés 180, 181
Smith, C. Ryder 177
Snailum, Brenda 167, 168
Snell-Hornby, Mary 10, 62, 64, 73, 75
Spurgeon, Charles H. 126
Stacey, David 199
Stockwell, Peter 84
Sully, James 107
Sūn, Yi Feng 61

T
Taber, Charles 71
Talay-Ongan, Ayshe 141
Táng, Chóng Róng 225
Tanner, Beth LaNeel 266
Tate, Marvin E. 335
Tertullian 130
Toury, Gideon 74
Tov, Emanuel 26
Trypho 24

U
Unsworth, Richard P. 111

V
Vendryes, J. 179
Volf, Miroslav 160
Vygotsky, Lev 155

W
Wall, John 101, 108–111, 338
Waltke, Bruce K. 13
Wáng, Níng 61
Ward, Carrie 135
Weber, Hans-Ruedi 135
Weber, Joan 169
Weitzman, M. P. 32, 33
Wendland, Ernst 10, 11, 13–15, 77–89, 92, 97, 98, 142, 232, 234, 247, 310, 312, 318, 320, 321, 327, 332–338, 340
Wenger, Etienne 158
Werner, Eberhard 81
Westermann, Claus 190, 194
White, James 140
White, James W. 149, 166
White, Keith J. 121, 128
Willmer, Haddon 119, 128
Wolff, Hans Walter 183, 186, 194, 195
Wonderly, William L. 12
Woodhead, Martin 102
Wright, David F. 119
Wú, Dongsheng John 225, 226

X
Xú, Tāo 218

Y
Yáng, Qìng Qiú 226
Yu, Charles 13
Yu, Ning 207

Z
Zēng, Qìng Bào 224, 225
Zhū, Bǎo Huì 56, 57
Zimmerli, Walther 182

Scripture Index

Old Testament

Genesis
1:1–2 160
1:20 213
1:21 .... 209, 213
1:24 213
1:26 160
1:27 119
1:28 115
1:30 213
2:7 .... 178, 184,
   185, 209, 213, 214,
   217, 222, 226, 228
2:19 213
3:19 184
9:4 192
9:10 213
9:12 213
9:15 213
9:16 213
11 20
12 116
12:2 116
12:5 186
12:13 .... 187, 207
13:16 116
15:5 116
17 116

17:7 149
18:19 133
23:8 208
24:60 115
27:4 187
27:19 187
27:25 187
27:31 187
30:20 116
33:5 115
35:18 .... 183, 210,
   214, 217
42:21 188
46:15 186
48:15–16 116
49 116

Exodus
2 117
3:15 145
4:19 191
10:2 133
12:4 186
13:8, 14 133
15:9 208
20:6 145
21:23 191

22:22–24 123
23:9 207

Leviticus
3:16–17 277
7:18 211
11:10 .... 209, 213
11:43–44 188
11:46 213
17:10 186
17:11 192
17:14 192
19:28 209
20:25 208
21:1 209
23:30 186
24:18 .... 191, 209
26:11 188

Numbers
5:2 195
6:6 194
6:11 195
12:8 27
21:5 188
31:35 209
31:40 209

35:31 191	**2 Samuel**	**Psalms**
	1:9 210	4:7 27
Deuteronomy	17:8 188	6:3 188
4:9 133	23:17 191	6:5 192
6:5 200		8 125
6:6–9 148	**1 Kings**	8:2 .... 125, 126
6:7 133	17:21 .... 215, 217	16:10 .... 201, 209,
6:20 133	17:21–22 184	215, 217
6:20–22 138	18:12 128	17:12 90
10:17–18 123	19:2 191	23:3 .... 175, 209
11:19 133	19:4 .... 191, 211	25:13 208
12:23 192		31:7 188
14:28–29 123	**2 Kings**	33:11 145
19:21 191	4:27 188	34 134
23:24 193	23:3 207	35:9–10 270
31:9–12 134		35:1 242
31:12–13 146	**1 Chronicles**	35:2 241
	11:19 .... 191, 211	35:3 .... 237, 241,
Joshua	28:9 208	251, 253, 308
2:13 192		35:4 .... 242, 243,
8:35 134	**2 Chronicles**	246, 249, 261, 267,
11:11 208	20 147	268, 281, 333, 336
		35:5 247
Judges	**Nehemiah**	35:6 247
5:18 192	8:2 134	35:7 .... 242, 243,
5:21 210	8:2–3 147	247, 261
9:17 191	8:7–8 .... 20, 28	35:8 249
12:3 206	12:27–43 147	35:9 .... 249, 251,
16:30 187		309, 314
18:25 188	**Job**	35:10 .... 250, 251,
	6:11 208	252, 253
1 Samuel	10:1 188	35:11 .... 243, 257
1:10 188	11:20 210	35:12 .... 253, 257,
3 125	23:13 190	309, 335
3:1 125	27:3 184	35:13 .... 253, 254,
3:1–14 128	30:25 187	257, 309, 315
3:20 117	32: 213	35:14 .... 258, 259,
18:1 .... 214, 217	33:4 184	333
19:11 192	33:20 296	35:15 .... 260, 261
	33:22 296	35:16 259
	41:21 210	

35:17............ 242, 261, 262, 309, 334	78:18.................... 193	12:10.................... 193
35:19..................... 243	89:1...................... 148	17:6..................... 116
35:20–21................ 261	102:12.................... 145	19:12.................... 262
35:22..................... 268	105:18.................... 317	23:2..................... 193
35:23............ 265, 266, 268	107:17.................... 296	24:14.................... 207
35:24..................... 266	107:4............ 289, 291, 292, 310, 334	**Ecclesiastes**
35:25............ 262, 263, 315, 317	107:4–5................ 287	6:7..................... 193
35:26............ 267, 268, 269	107:5............ 287, 291, 309, 314	**Song of Songs**
42:5..................... 188	107:6............ 290, 292, 295, 310	1:7..................... 188
43:5..................... 188	107:7............ 291, 292	5:6..................... 210
49:9..................... 206	107:8............ 291, 292	**Isaiah**
49:15..................... 192	107:9............ 287, 291, 292, 309, 315, 316	3:20.................... 317
57:4..................... 316	107:13........... 290, 295, 310	3:25..................... 91
63:1............ 188, 269, 271, 272, 274, 309, 314, 335, 337	107:15.................... 291	5:14..................... 183
63:2............ 207, 274	107:17............ 292, 295	7:7..................... 91
63:3............ 276, 277	107:18............ 292, 293, 295, 296, 309, 315, 317	7:14..................... 24
63:4............ 274, 276, 277	107:19........... 290, 295, 296, 310	9:6..................... 117
63:5............ 188, 274, 277, 285, 309, 314	107:20.................... 296	10:18.................... 210
63:5–7..................... 311	107:21............ 291, 296	29:8..................... 210
63:6............ 272, 279, 336	107:22.................... 296	41:4..................... 145
63:8............ 188, 278, 280, 281, 309, 314, 334	107:26........... 297, 309, 314	42:1..................... 190
63:9............ 281, 282, 283, 286	107:28............ 290, 310	44:20.................... 192
63:9–11................... 311	107:31.................... 291	51:8..................... 146
63:10............ 282, 286	119...................... 134	53:11............ 188, 216, 217
63:11............ 285, 286	119:90.................... 146	56:11............ 193, 210
69:1............ 3, 183, 216, 217	127:3.................... 116	58:3..................... 254
72:13.................... 192	128:1, 3–4.............. 116	58:10............ 181, 216, 217
78:1–8.................... 138	145:4.................... 148	61:10.................... 188
	Proverbs	**Jeremiah**
	2:10................ 215, 217	1:6..................... 128
	6:30.................... 210	2:24............... 193, 210
		4:10.................... 210
		4:31.................... 188
		5:9..................... 190
		5:29.................... 190

6:8 .... 190, 207	13:20 183	**Amos**
9:8 190	27:13 209	5:17 95
9:11 27	33:6 191	6:8 190
12:7 190	47:9 213	
51:14 190		**Jonah**
52:29 186	**Daniel**	2:5–7 183
	4:3 145	2:7 188
Lamentations		4:3 191
5:19 145	**Hosea**	
	5:14 262	**Habakkuk**
Ezekiel	11:11 95	2:5 210
7:19 217		
13:18 208	**Joel**	
13:18–20 186	1:3 134	
13:19 194	2:28 149	

New Testament

Matthew	9:37 127	**Acts**
5:18 138	10:13–16 .... 129, 131	2:27 215
10:28 200	10:14 117	2:42 150
10:33 258		2:46–47 149
10:34–38 163	**Luke**	4:32–35 149
11:25 127	1:48 145	12:12 149
18:1–5 .... 128, 129	1:66 128	16:15 149
18:1–6 149	2:41–47 147	16:33 149
18:3 .... 117, 128	2:46–47 134	22:3 134
18:4 129	9:48 127	
18:5 .... 117, 127, 128	14:25–27 163	**Romans**
	16:22 201	16:1 162
19:13–14 149	18:13–16 129	16:13 163
21:14–16 126	18:15–17 120	
28:19 148	23:43 201	**1 Corinthians**
		12:21–23 163
Mark	**John**	12:27 150
3:31–35 163	4:46–54 123	15:44 198
5:35–43 123	10:24 202	15:45 .... 213, 214
7:24–30 123	10:24a 201	15:46 198
8:35 200	12:27 201	
9:14–29 123		

2 Corinthians
4:4 51

Galatians
4:6 162
6:10 163

Ephesians
4:11–16 118
4:15–16 150
5:21 150
6:1–3 147

Colossians
3:20 147
4:9 162

1 Thessalonians
5:23 .... 199, 200,
221, 222, 227

2 Timothy
3:15 .... 128, 134,
138
3:16 138
3:17 138

Philemon
2 162
4:6 270
4:10 162

Hebrews
4:12 .... 203, 221,
222, 227

James
1:21 204
5:20 204

1 Peter
4:7–11 118
5:1–5 147

3 John
2 202

Revelation
6:9 .... 202, 203
18:13 201
18:14 201
20:4 .... 202, 203

Langham Literature and its imprints are a ministry of Langham Partnership.

Langham Partnership is a global fellowship working in pursuit of the vision God entrusted to its founder John Stott –

> *to facilitate the growth of the church in maturity and Christ-likeness through raising the standards of biblical preaching and teaching.*

Our vision is to see churches in the majority world equipped for mission and growing to maturity in Christ through the ministry of pastors and leaders who believe, teach and live by the Word of God.

Our mission is to strengthen the ministry of the Word of God through:
- nurturing national movements for biblical preaching
- fostering the creation and distribution of evangelical literature
- enhancing evangelical theological education

especially in countries where churches are under-resourced.

Our ministry

Langham Preaching partners with national leaders to nurture indigenous biblical preaching movements for pastors and lay preachers all around the world. With the support of a team of trainers from many countries, a multi-level programme of seminars provides practical training, and is followed by a programme for training local facilitators. Local preachers' groups and national and regional networks ensure continuity and ongoing development, seeking to build vigorous movements committed to Bible exposition.

Langham Literature provides majority world preachers, scholars and seminary libraries with evangelical books and electronic resources through publishing and distribution, grants and discounts. The programme also fosters the creation of indigenous evangelical books in many languages, through writer's grants, strengthening local evangelical publishing houses, and investment in major regional literature projects, such as one volume Bible commentaries like *The Africa Bible Commentary* and *The South Asia Bible Commentary*.

Langham Scholars provides financial support for evangelical doctoral students from the majority world so that, when they return home, they may train pastors and other Christian leaders with sound, biblical and theological teaching. This programme equips those who equip others. Langham Scholars also works in partnership with majority world seminaries in strengthening evangelical theological education. A growing number of Langham Scholars study in high quality doctoral programmes in the majority world itself. As well as teaching the next generation of pastors, graduated Langham Scholars exercise significant influence through their writing and leadership.

To learn more about Langham Partnership and the work we do visit **langham.org**

Lightning Source UK Ltd.
Milton Keynes UK
UKHW02f0758060918
328419UK00011B/848/P